THE OXFORD BIBLE COMMENTARY

T0346705

THE OXFORD BIBLE COMMENTARY

THE APOCRYPHA

EDITED BY
MARTIN GOODMAN

SERIES EDITORS
John Barton
John Muddiman

OXFORD
UNIVERSITY PRESS

OXFORD

UNIVERSITY PRESS

Great Clarendon Street, Oxford OX2 6DP
United Kingdom

Oxford University Press is a department of the University of Oxford.
It furthers the University's objective of excellence in research, scholarship,
and education by publishing worldwide. Oxford is a registered trade mark of
Oxford University Press in the UK and in certain other countries

© Oxford University Press 2001

The moral rights of the author have been asserted

First published in this updated selection 2012
Reprinted 2013

All rights reserved. No part of this publication may be reproduced, stored in
a retrieval system, or transmitted, in any form or by any means, without the
prior permission in writing of Oxford University Press, or as expressly permitted
by law, by licence or under terms agreed with the appropriate reprographics
rights organization. Enquiries concerning reproduction outside the scope of the
above should be sent to the Rights Department, Oxford University Press, at the
address above

You must not circulate this work in any other form
and you must impose this same condition on any acquirer

British Library Cataloguing in Publication Data
Data available

Library of Congress Cataloging in Publication Data
Data available

ISBN 978-0-19-965081-1

LIST OF CONTENTS

LIST OF CONTRIBUTORS

John Barton, Oriel and Laing Professor of the Interpretation of Holy Scripture, University of Oxford.

George J. Brooke, Rylands Professor of Biblical Criticism and Exegesis, University of Manchester.

John J. Collins, Holmes Professor of Old Testament, Yale Divinity School.

Robert Doran, Samuel Williston Professor of Greek and Hebrew, Amherst College, Massachusetts.

David J. Elliott, The Oratory School, Reading.

Joseph A. Fitzmyer, SJ, Professor Emeritus, Catholic University of America, Washington DC.

Martin Goodman, Professor of Jewish Studies; Fellow of Wolfson College, University of Oxford.

Peter Hayman, formerly University of Edinburgh.

William Horbury, Emeritus Professor of Jewish and Early Christian Studies, University of Cambridge.

Sara Japhet, Professor Emeritus, Department of Bible, the Hebrew University of Jerusalem.

Amy-Jill Levine, E. Rhodes and Leona B. Carpenter Professor of New Testament Studies and Professor of Jewish Studies, Vanderbilt Divinity School, Nashville.

George W. E. Nickelsburg, Professor Emeritus, University of Iowa.

Sarah Pearce, Ian Karten Professor of Ancient Jewish Studies, University of Southampton.

Uriel Rappaport, Professor Emeritus, University of Haifa.

Adele Reinhartz, Professor, Department of Classics and Religious Studies, University of Ottawa.

Alison Salvesen, University Research Lecturer; Supernumerary Fellow in Oriental Studies, Mansfield College, University of Oxford.

ABBREVIATIONS

GENERAL

AB	Anchor Bible
ABD	D. N. Freedman (ed.), *Anchor Bible Dictionary* (6 vols.; New York: Doubleday, 1992)
AJS Review	*Review of Association for Jewish Studies*
AnBib	Analecta biblica
ANET	James B. Pritchard (ed.), *Ancient Near Eastern Texts Relating to the Old Testament* (Princeton: Princeton University Press, 3rd edn, 1969)
AOAT	Alter Orient und Altes Testament
APOT	R. H. Charles (ed.), *Apocrypha and Pseudepigrapha of the Old Testament* (2 vols.; Oxford: Clarendon, 1913)
ARW	*Archiv für Religionswissenschaft*
b.	Babylonian Talmud
B	4th-cent. MS of part of NT, in the Vatican Library
BCE	Before Common Era
Bib.	*Biblica*
BN	*Beiträge zur Namenforschung*
BZAW	Beihefte zur ZAW
CBC	Cambridge Bible Commentary
CBQ	*Catholic Biblical Quarterly*
CD	Cairo Geniza, Damascus Document
CE	Common Era
CII	*Corpus inscriptionum iudaicarum*
CP	*Classical Philology*
CQ	*Church Quarterly*
CRINT	Compendia rerum iudaicarum ad novum testamentum
CSCO	Corpus scriptorum christianorum orientalium
D	Deuteronomist source in the Pentateuch
DJD	Discoveries in the Judaean Desert
E	Elohist source in the Pentateuch
ET	English Translation
FCB	Feminist Companion to the Bible
FGrH	F. Jacoby, Die Fragmente der griechischen Historiker (Berlin: Weidmann, 1923–58)

frag.	Fragment
FRLANT	Forschungen zur Religion und Literatur des Alten und Neuen Testaments
GCS	Greichische christliche Schriftsteller
Gk.	Greek
H	Holiness Code
HB	Hebrew Bible
HDR	Harvard Dissertations in Religion
Heb.	Hebrew
HSCP	*Harvard Studies in Classical Philology*
HSM	Harvard Semitic Monographs
HTR	*Harvard Theological Review*
ICC	International Critical Commentary
IEJ	*Israel Exploration Journal*
INJ	*Israel Numismatic Journal*
JBL	*Journal of Biblical Literature*
JJGL	*Jahrbuch für jüdische Geschichte und Literatur*
JJS	*Journal of Jewish Studies*
JQR	*Jewish Quarterly Review*
JSHRZ	Jüdische Schriften aus hellenistisch-römischer Zeit
JSJ	*Journal for the Study of Judaism in the Persian, Hellenistic and Roman Period*
JSNT	*Journal for the Study of the New Testament*
JSNTSup	Journal for the Study of the New Testament—Supplement Series
JSOT	*Journal for the Study of the Old Testament*
JSOTSup	Journal for the Study of the Old Testament—Supplement Series
JSP	*Journal for the Study of the Pseudepigrapha*
JSS	*Journal of Semitic Studies*
JTS	*Journal of Theological Studies*
Lat.	Latin
LCL	Loeb Classical Library
LXX	Septuagint
m.	*Mishnah*
marg.	margin
Midr.	*Midrash*
MLB	Modern Language Bible
MNTC	Moffatt New Testament Commentary
MS	Monograph Series; manuscript
MSU	Mitteilungen des Septuaginta-Unternehmens
Mt.	Mount
MT	Masoretic Text

NJBC	R. E. Brown, J. A. Fitzmyer, and R. E. Murphy (eds.), *The New Jerome Biblical Commentary* (London: Geoffrey Chapman, 1989)
OBO	Orbis biblicus et orientalis
OBT	Overtures to Biblical Theology
OCB	*Oxford Companion to the Bible*
OG	Old Greek
OL	Old Latin
OTL	Old Testament Library
OTP	J. H. Charlesworth (ed.), *The Old Testament Pseudepigrapha* (2 vols.; Garden City, N.Y.: Doubleday, 1983–5)
PAAJR	*Proceedings of the American Academy of Jewish Research*
PG	J. Migne, *Patrologia graeca*
pl.	Plural
PSBA	*Proceedings of the Society of Biblical Archaeology*
RB	*Revue biblique*
REJ	*Revue des études juives*
RSN (= SNR)	*Revue Suisse de Numismatique = Schweizerische Numismatische Rundschau*
RSR	*Recherches de science religieuse*
RTR	*Reformed Theological Review*
SANT	Studien zum Alten und Neuen Testament
SB	Sources bibliques
SBL	Society of Biblical Literature
SBLDS	SBL Dissertation Series
SBLEJL	SBL Early Judaism and its Literature
SBLMS	SBL Monograph Series
SBLTT	SBL Texts and Translations
SC	Sources chrétiennes
SCI	*Scripte Classica Israelica*
SCM	Student Christian Movement
SEG	*Supplementum Epigraphicum Graecum*
SJLA	Studies in Judaism in Late Antiquity
SJT	*Scottish Journal of Theology*
SPCK	Society for Promoting Christian Knowledge
s.v.	sub vide
SVTP	Studia in Veteris Testamenti pseudepigrapha
t.	Tosefta
TDNT	G. W. Bromiley (ed. and trans.), *Theological Dictionary of the New Testament* (10 vols.; Grand Rapids, Mich.: Eerdmans, 1964–78).
tr.	translation(s), translated (by)
v.	Versus
Vg	Vulgate

VL	Vetus Latina
VT	*Vetus Testamentum*
VTSup	Vetus Testamentum, Supplements
y.	Jerusalem Talmud
ZAW	*Zeitschrift für die alttestamentliche Wissenschaft*
ZPE	*Zeitschrift für Papyrologie und Epigraphik*
ZTK	*Zeitschrift für Theologie und Kirche*

ANCIENT SOURCES

'Abot R. Nat	*'Abot de Rabbi Nathan*
Aesch.	Aeschylus
Ag.	*Agamemnon*
Pers.	*Persae*
Ap. Met.	Apuleius, *Metamorphoses*
Ap. Con.	*Apostolic Constitutions*
Apoc. Abr.	*Apocalypse of Abraham*
Apoc. Bar.	*Apocalypse of Baruch*
Arist. Eth. Nic.	Aristotle, *Ethica Nicomachea*
Arr. Anab.	Arrian, *Anabasis*
As. Mos.	*Assumption of Moses*
Athenagoras	
Apol.	*Apologia*
Leg. pro Christ.	*Legatio pro Christianis*
Aug.	Augustine
Conf.	*Confessions*
De civ. Dei	*De civitate dei*
De Gen. c. Manich.	*De Genesi contra Manichaeos*
En.	*Enarrationes in Psalmos*
Barn.	*Epistle of Barnabas*
B. Bat.	*Baba Batra*
B. Qam.	*Baba Qamma*
B. Mes.	*Baba Mesi'a*
Ber.	*Berakot*
Cic. Tusc.	Cicero, *Tusculanae Disputationes*
Clem. Al. Strom.	Clement of Alexandria, *Stromateis*
Coptic Apoc. Zeph.	*Coptic Apocalypse of Zephaniah*
Cyp. Test.	Cyprian, *Testimoniorum libritres*
Did.	*Didache*
Diod. Sic.	Diodorus Siculus
Diog. Laert.	Diogenes Laertius

Ep. Arist.	*Epistle of Aristeas*
Epicurus	
Ep. Men.	*Epistula ad Menoeceum*
Eur.	Euripides
Bacch.	*Bacchae*
Phoen.	*Phoenissae*
Eusebius	
Hist. eccl.	*Historia Ecclesiastica*
Praep. evang.	*Praeparatio evangelica*
Flacc.	Flaccus
Frg. Tg.	*Fragmentary Targum*
Gen. Rab.	*Genesis Rabbah*
Git.	*Giṭṭim*
Gos. Pet.	*Gospel of Thomas*
Hdt.	Herodotus
Herm. Sim.	*Hermas, Similitudes*
Hes.	Hesiod
Op.	*Opera et Dies*
Theog.	*Theogonia*
Ignatius	
Eph.	*Ephesians*
Smyrn.	*Letter to the Smyrnaeans*
Irenaeus	
Adv. haer.	*Adversus haereses*
Jos.	Josephus
Ag. Ap.	*Against Apion*
Ant.	*Antiquities of the Jews*
J.W.	*Jewish War*
Jub.	*Jubilees*
Justin	Justin Martyr
Apol.	*Apologia*
Lev. Rab.	*Leviticus Rabbah*
Lucr.	Lucretius
Mak.	*Makkot*
Mart. Isa.	*Martyrdom of Isaiah*
Meg.	*Megilla*
Origen	
C. Cels.	*Contra Celsum*
De princ.	*De principiis*

Paus.	Pausanius
Pesiq. R.	*Pesiqta Rabbati*
Philo	Philo Judaeus
Abr.	*De Abrahamo*
Dec.	*De Decalogo*
Det.	*Quod deterius potiori insidiari soleat*
Fug.	*De fuga et inventione*
Gig.	*De gigantibus*
Leg. ad Gaium	*Legatio ad Gaium*
Migr. Abr.	*De migratione Abrahami*
Opif.	*De opificio mundi*
Somn.	*De somniis*
Spec. Leg.	*De specialibus legibus*
Virt.	*De virtutibus*
Vit. Cont.	*De vita contemplativa*
Vit. Mos.	*De vita Mosis*
Plato	
Phd.	*Phaedo*
Phdr.	*Phaedrus*
Rep.	*Respublica*
Symp.	*Symposium*
Tim.	*Timaeus*
Pliny	
Nat. Hist.	*Natural History*
Plut.	Plutarch
Art.	*Artaxerxes*
Cic.	*Cicero*
Cleom.	*Cleomenes*
De Is. et Os.	*De Iside et Osiride*
Luc.	*Lucullus*
Thes.	*Theseus*
Polyb.	Polybius Polycarp
Ps.-Philo	Pseudo-Philo
Bib. Ant.	*Biblical Antiquities*
LAB	*Liber Antiquitatum Biblicarum*
Ps.-Phoc.	Pseudo-Phocylldes
Pss. Sol.	*Psalms of Solomon*
1QapGen20	Qumran Cave I, *Genesis Apocryphon*
1QH	Qumran Cave I, *Hôdayôt (Thanksgiving Hymns)*
1QM	Qumran Cave I, *War Scroll*
1QpHab	Qumran Cave I, *Pesher on Habakkuk*
1QS	Qumran Cave I, *Serek hayyahad (Rule of the Community, Manual of Discipline)*
2Q18	Qumran Cave 2, frags. of Slrach
4QDibHam	Qumran Cave 4, Words of the Luminaries

4QpJer	Qumran Cave 4, *Pesher on Jeremiah*
4QSapA	Qumran Cave 4, Sapiential Work A
11QPss	Qumran Cave 11, *Psalms Scroll*
11QTemple	Qumran Cave 11, *Temple Scroll*
Rab.	*Rabbah*
Sanh.	*Sanhedrin*
Sib.Or.	*Sibylline Oracles*
Soph.	Sophocles
El.	*Electra*
Oed.Rex	*Oedipus Rex*
Strabo, *Geog.*	*Geographical Sketches*
T. 12 *Patr.*	*Testaments of the Twelve Patriarchs*
T. Abr.	*Testament of Abraham*
Tac. *Ann.*	Tacitus, *Annales*
Tert.	Tertullian
Adv. Marc.	*Adversus Marcionem*
Apol.	*Apologeticus*
T. Gad	*Testament of Gad*
Tg. Ps.-J.	*Targum Pseudo-Jonathan*
T. Job	*Testament of Job*
T. Levi	*Testament of Levi*
T. Napht.	*Testament of Naphtali*
Xen. An.	Xenophon, *Anabasis*
y.	Jerusalem Talmud
Yebam.	*Yebamot*

1. Introduction to the Apocrypha

MARTIN GOODMAN

A. Definition. 1. The term 'apocrypha' was never used in antiquity to denote the separate corpus of disparate books which are printed under this heading in some modern Bibles. The current use of the term was popularized through the practice of Protestant scholars during the Reformation in distinguishing these books, which were standard in Catholic Bibles, from canonical biblical writings. This use reflected more general uses of the term in late antiquity.

2. The Greek word 'apocrypha' means books that have been hidden away in some sense. The term was sometimes used in antiquity to refer to books that contained mysterious or secret teachings, but although many such esoteric writings were known and highly regarded by both Jews and Christians (cf. 2 Esd 14:45–6), the description of them as apocryphal was rare. Other Christian writers described as 'apocrypha' those books which were reckoned to be spurious or heretical and thus unfit for Christian use (e.g. Athanasius and Rufinus, both in the 4th cent. CE). The use of the term to refer to the corpus of books that now forms an appendix to the OT began with Jerome in the early fifth century. Jerome was concerned to define the limits of the OT canon and elected to exclude those books found in the Greek and Latin versions but not in the Hebrew. He did not condemn these books as unworthy but only as non-canonical and hence useful for general edification rather than to define church dogma.

3. Since the MSS of Greek and Latin Bibles do not all contain precisely the same works, but all contain the writings included in the OT as defined by Protestants, the extent of the Apocrypha is not entirely fixed. Some biblical MSS include 3 and 4 Maccabees and Ps 151 which, since they are not part of the HB, have therefore sometimes been treated as part of the Apocrypha. Conversely, during disputes in the Reformation about the religious importance of the Apocrypha, some theologians declared unfitting for the corpus those writings that seemed to them to lack value; thus Luther excluded from his version of the Apocrypha both 1 and 2 Esdras. The books discussed in this Commentary are those commonly found in those Protestant English Bibles in which the Apocrypha is printed.

B. History. 1. Septuagint. The creation of the Apocrypha is part of the history of the translation of the HB into Greek. The Septuagint, so-called because of the foundation legend that it was the work of seventy (or seventy-two) translators, was produced gradually during the third and second centuries BCE. According to the *Letter of Aristeas*, the translation of the Pentateuch was produced by translators sent to Alexandria from Jerusalem by the high priest Eleazar at the behest of King Ptolemy II Philadelphus (283–246 BCE) and, although the detailed historicity of this legend is dubious, and it is more likely that the work was commissioned by Greek-speaking Jews, the Alexandrian origin of the work is plausible since a festival to celebrate the translation was held there regularly in the first century CE (Philo, *vit. Mos.* 2.7 (41)). But the other books were translated piecemeal and quite possibly in other parts of the Greek-speaking diaspora. All that is certain is that the main body of the Writings and the Prophets were available by the late second century BCE, when the grandson of the author of Ecclesiasticus, Jesus son of Sira, referred, in the prologue to his translation of his grandfather's work, to the existence of Greek versions of 'the Law, the prophecies and the rest of the books'. In the same passage the grandson of Jesus son of Sira referred to the impossibility of precise translation: 'What was originally expressed in Hebrew does not have exactly the same sense when translated into another language.' In this he was quite correct, and the translators of different books in the Septuagint varied between those who aimed at a very literal rendering and those who apparently aimed more at reproducing the mood of the original. In the latter case the Greek version often necessarily included a great deal of interpretation and (to a lesser extent) elaboration; the authors both inspired and were part of a much wider movement of translating Jewish texts into Greek in this period, often producing work so distinctly Hellenic that they should be treated as compositions in their own right. It is in this context that the material now found in the Apocrypha was composed.

2. The transmission of the Septuagint in antiquity was almost entirely through Christian rather than Jewish copyists. Some fragments of the Pentateuch, the minor prophets, and indeed some of the apocrypha survive in Jewish MSS from pre-Christian times, and further papyrus fragments including parts of Wisdom and Sirach from the second to third centuries CE were found at Antinoopolis in Egypt, but the main witnesses to the text are the Christian MSS of the fourth century, the Codex Vaticanus and the Codex Sinaiticus, and the rather later (between the late fourth and early sixth centuries) Codex Alexandrinus. Christians from the beginning treated the Septuagint as a sacred text in its own right and not simply as a translation of the Hebrew.

3. At the time when the Septuagint translations and the apocrypha were composed, books were written on papyrus or leather scrolls and each book would normally have been written on a separate scroll. Thus the issue of what was to be included together with the other books of the Greek Bible only really arose with the Christian adoption of the Codex. Most of the books of the apocrypha are to be found in each of the great codices of the Septuagint from late antiquity without any indication that they are not part of the canon of Scripture, but they are found in different places within the text and not all are consistently included. Thus, for example, the Prayer of Manasseh is not in any of our ancient copies of the Septuagint, but some Septuagint MSS include 3 and 4 Maccabees and Ps 151, which were not to be treated as part of the Apocrypha when the corpus was defined in the Reformation, and by contrast 2 Esdras is not found in any Greek codex of the Septuagint. From all this it is clear that Christians in late antiquity on the whole treated the Apocrypha as part of the canon of sacred Scripture, but since the limits of the canon were still disputed, some books were more consistently treated in this way than others.

4. Confirmation of this view can be found in the lists of canonical works of the OT compiled by Christian authors in late antiquity, in which the books of the apocrypha are found in varying numbers and order. Many Greek Christian writers of the second and third centuries regularly cited apocryphal books, using the same formulas to introduce quotations that they used to cite texts from the OT. However, a few Christian authors, such as Melito of Sardis in the second century and Origen in the third, were aware that although the apocryphal books were

to be found in the Septuagint and were therefore 'Scripture' they were not in use among Jews as part of the HB, and in the fourth century Cyril of Jerusalem, Gregory of Nazianzus, and Amphilochius did not include any of the apocrypha in the lists of canonical books that they drew up.

C. Use of the Apocrypha in the Early Church. 1. There is no direct quotation from the apocrypha in the NT, and it is difficult to be certain whether parallel expression and allusions, of which many can be identified, show use of the apocrypha by the authors of the NT or the influence of a common tradition. Thus, for instance, many expressions in the letters of Paul and in Hebrews use imagery close to that in Wisdom of Solomon (e.g. Heb 1:1–3 = Wis 7:25–7), and Heb 11:35–7 alludes to the martyrdom story found in 2 Macc 6–7. Direct borrowing is not, of course, impossible, but these themes may have had much wider currency than just the surviving literature.

2. In contrast numerous quotations from the apocrypha can be found in patristic writings. Among Greek-speaking Christians, Wisdom of Solomon was quoted by 1 *Clement* at the end of the first century and in the *Epistle of Barnabas* from the early second; Ecclesiasticus and 2 Esdras were also quoted by Barnabas; Tobit was quoted by Polycarp in the mid-second century; the stories of Susanna and the other apocryphal Additions to Daniel were included by Hippolytus of Rome in his commentary on Daniel. These citations generally treated the text of the apocrypha as inspired like the rest of Scripture. In the fragmentary Muratorian Canon, to be dated probably to *c*.200, the Wisdom of Solomon actually appears as part of the NT, albeit with an indication that this is not certain. Among Latin Christians, such as Tertullian and Cyprian, the apocryphal books were accorded even higher esteem, doubtless encouraged in the view by their inclusion in the Old Latin version of the OT, which was translated from the Septuagint. The main dissenting voice was that of Jerome, who made much use of the HB in creating his new Latin translation, the Vulgate, in the early fifth century. Jerome was persuaded to include some of the apocrypha in the Vulgate on the grounds that these were popular books, but in the margins he marked as missing in the Hebrew the Additions to Daniel and Esther, and, although he translated Tobit and Judith, later MSS of the Vulgate imported into Jerome's corpus the Old Latin versions of the other books. This ambivalent attitude was best summed up by Jerome himself in the Prologues to a number of these books: in his view the apocryphal books might be read by Christians and contained much of value, but they were not canonical and thus should not be used to establish the doctrines of the church. This view coexisted unhappily among Latin Christians with the powerful advocacy of the canonical status of these books urged by Jerome's contemporary Augustine. Among Greek Christians canonical status was generally taken for granted, but early Syriac patristic authors used an OT even more restricted than the Hebrew—of the apocrypha they knew only Ecclesiasticus, which they treated as canonical.

D. Identification of the Apocrypha as a Distinct Corpus. **1.** Treatment of the apocryphal books as quasi-Scripture precluded recognition by patristic authors of these books as constituting a distinct literary corpus. Even Jerome, who applied the term 'apocrypha' to these writings (above, A.2), treated them only negatively: the apocrypha were defined as the books found in Greek and Latin Bibles but not in the Hebrew. The insights of Jerome were for the most part ignored during the Middle Ages. Most Christians treated all the books found in the Septuagint and the Vulgate as of equal value, and many of the books of the apocrypha were widely read and popular. None the less some scholars continued to distinguish the apocrypha from the distinctive authority of the books found in the Hebrew OT, from Nicholas of Lyra and Wycliffe in the fourteenth century to Cardinal Ximenes, editor of the Complutensian Polyglot edition of the Bible in 1514–17.

2. The attitude of Protestant scholars in the Reformation was thus not entirely a break with recent Christian practice. In 1520 Andreas Bodenstein of Karlstadt published a tractate distinguishing the apocryphal books from those in the Hebrew OT and dividing the apocrypha itself into two groups of non-canonical but holy books (e.g. Tobit, Wisdom, and Sirach) and foolish writings 'worthy of the Censor's ban' (i.e. 1 and 2 Esdras, Baruch, the Prayer of Manasseh, and the Additions to Daniel). Following this lead, many Protestant Bibles in the vernacular, most influentially Luther's German translation completed in 1534, placed the books of the Apocrypha in a separate appendix after the books of the OT, with a preface stating that these books 'are not held equal to the sacred scriptures, and yet are useful and good for reading'. The treatment of the Apocrypha as a separate corpus became standard in Protestant Bibles, although there continued to be rare exceptions, such as the place of the Prayer of Manasseh in the Geneva Bible published in English in 1560, between 2 Chronicles and Ezra, with a note about its apocryphal status.

3. This attitude in Protestant churches provoked a vigorous response by the Catholic church, with the declaration in the Council of Trent in 1546 of an anathema on anyone who did not recognize as sacred and canonical all the books found in the Vulgate, although the same Council rather inconsistently denied the canonical status of the Prayer of Manasseh and 1 and 2 Esdras; as a result, these books were after 1593 regularly printed as a separate appendix, while the rest of the books treated by Protestants as the apocrypha continued to be printed as part of the biblical text as in older editions of the Vulgate. None the less it remained useful for Catholics to distinguish the Apocrypha as a separate corpus and these books were thus often termed by Catholics 'deutero-canonical'.

4. The books of the Apocrypha do not play a major role in contemporary Christianity even among Roman Catholics. Among Protestants the lower status given to these books early led to their omission altogether in many printed Bibles. Among Calvinists the Apocrypha was rejected altogether as wholly without authority, and arguments about the value of these books continued among Protestants in many countries through the nineteenth century. Among the Protestant churches, the most positive attitude towards the apocrypha is found in the Anglican church, in which extensive use is made of these books in the liturgy.

E. Jewish Attitudes to the Books of the Apocrypha. **1.** The late Second Temple period, when the apocrypha were written, was a time of intense literary activity among Jews (see below, G.16). The basis of that activity was the books now found in the HB, but it is unclear when and how precisely Jews came to agree on the limits of a canon of inspired Scripture. Thus it is entirely possible that soon after their composition the writings now found in the Apocrypha were treated by Jews as similar in nature and authority to the books in their Bible. On the other hand the statement by Josephus (*Ag. Ap.* 1.43) that 'there are not with us myriads of books, discordant and discrepant, but only twenty-two, comprising the history of all time, which are justly accredited' almost certainly refers to the biblical books and shows that, even if a fixed canon was not yet generally agreed, the idea that there might be such a canon was familiar. The discovery among the Dead Sea scrolls of fragments of Ecclesiasticus (also found at Masada), the Letter of Jeremiah (in Greek), and Tobit shows that these books were read by some Palestinian Jews before 70 CE, and the lack of the other apocryphal books among the finds may be accidental, although it is worth noting in contrast the discovery at Qumran of parts of every book of the HB except Esther. Josephus used 1 Esdras, 1 Maccabees, and the additions to Esther, but his failure to refer to the other books of the Apocrypha may in some cases be only because they were not sufficiently historical to be of use to him. It should be noted that, if Josephus really meant to insist that Jews used a fixed number of historical texts (see above) but himself follows the version of Jewish history in 1 Esdras, either he did not possess the biblical books of Ezra and Nehemiah or he believed 1 Esdras to be canonical and the biblical books to be lacking in authority.

2. Early rabbinic literature shows no awareness of any of the books of the Apocrypha apart from Sirach. This is unsurprising for those books that existed only in Greek, but more surprising for Tobit and Judith, which certainly existed in Aramaic and perhaps in Hebrew, and 1 Maccabees, which was probably originally composed in Hebrew; at any rate a Hebrew version was known to Origen and to Jerome (see below, F.6). Citations of Sirach (under the name 'Ben Sirah') in early rabbinic texts are quite frequent and are sometimes preceded by the same introductory formula ('as it is written') which was used to introduce passages from the Writings, the third part of the OT (cf. b. B. Qam. 92b). It is clear from this that Sirach was highly regarded, but not that the rabbis treated this text as equal in status to those in the biblical corpus; the rabbinic discussions over which texts 'render the hands unclean' reveal doubts about the status of a number of books that are included in the biblical corpus (e.g. Song of Songs and Ecclesiastes), but not about Sirach. The rabbis may not have used most of the apocryphal texts but they were aware of some of the traditions referred to in those texts. Most important was the festival of Hanukkah, which celebrated the events described in 1 and 2 Maccabees, but there are also occasional rabbinic references to the martyrdom story of Hannah and her sons found in 2 Maccabees (cf. b. Git. 57b) and to the stories found in the Additions to Daniel.

3. The contents of some of the books of the Apocrypha came back to the attention of Jews in the Middle Ages through the wide dissemination of Hebrew versions of some of the stories. The narratives of Tobit and Judith were popular, as was *Megillat Antiochus*, which repeated in outline some of the material found in the books of Maccabees. Ecclesiasticus, known to the rabbis as Ben Sira, was presumably still known to some Jews in the original Hebrew even in the high Middle Ages, since large portions of the text were found in the Cairo Genizah in 1896, but the uniqueness of this manuscript find, and the scarcity of references to the work in rabbinic literature after antiquity, suggest that the book was not widely read, although the composition in the medieval period of a new work, the *Alfabet of Ben Sira*, demonstrates the continuing prestige thought to attach to the work of Ben Sira himself. The real revival of Jewish interest in the apocrypha came in the Renaissance, when scholarly Jews became aware of the existence of a large Jewish literature in Greek, and a translation of the apocrypha into Hebrew was published in the early sixteenth century. Since then Jewish scholars have made much use of these books in the study of Jewish literature and history, but these writings have never reverted to their original status as sources of religious edification.

F. Description of the Books of the Apocrypha.

1. Size. The corpus of the Apocrypha is about one-fifth of the length of the OT and over two-thirds that of the NT. The books are of very unequal length. Sirach is the longest, almost as long as Exodus. The Prayer of Manasseh consists of one brief chapter.

2. Genres. The books included in the Apocrypha show no generic uniformity. 1 Esdras, 1 Maccabees, and 2 Maccabees are, or purport to be, historical works. Tobit, Judith, and the Additions to Daniel are essentially moralizing romances. Sirach is a work of wisdom literature similar to Proverbs; Wisdom of Solomon is a more high-flown and high instance of the same genre. 2 Esdras is apocalyptic. The Prayer of Manasseh is an example of devotional literature.

3. Dates of Composition. The only book in the Apocrypha whose date of composition can be ascertained fairly precisely is Sirach, since the grandson of the author, who translated the book into Greek, stated in the prologue to the translation that he had arrived in Egypt 'in the thirty-eighth year of the reign of

Euergetes', i.e. in 132 BCE; his grandfather must therefore have composed the original Hebrew in the first half of the second century BCE. For some of the other writings (1 Esdras, the Additions to Esther, 1 Maccabees) a final *terminus ante quem* is the end of the first century CE because Josephus knew and used them; the date of the translation of the Hebrew book of Esther into Greek is given by a colophon which probably fixes it to 114 BCE, but it is possible that the Additions that are found only in the Greek text (and hence are now found in the Apocrypha) were composed separately after the completion of the main translation and were only later inserted into the narrative. Composition before *c.*100 CE is also likely for the bulk of 2 Esdras since the book was early cited by Christians. It is in any case unlikely that any Jewish writing would have been adopted by Christians with the enthusiasm accorded to the Apocrypha if it had been composed much after that date.

4. The earliest date that most of these books could have been written is in most cases less easy to state. 1 and 2 Maccabees cannot have been composed before the events they describe; the author of 1 Maccabees thus wrote after 134 BCE, the author of 2 Maccabees after 163 BCE. In theory all the other books may have originated much earlier, in the Persian period; this is entirely possible, for instance, of Tobit. Arguments for a later date, after *c.*300 BCE, are commonly advanced, but they rely upon the general nature of these writings, and especially alleged reflections of political events, rather than any specific temporal indication in the texts, and they are thus only hypothetical.

5. Places of Composition. There is no reason to assume that all these books were either written or (in some cases) translated in the same place; only the translation of Sirach can be confidently located in Alexandria in the Egyptian delta. Those writings originally composed in Hebrew or Aramaic (see C.5) may have been written either in the Land of Israel or in Babylonia or Syria or even in Egypt (e.g. Tobit). Those written in or translated into Greek may originate from any part of the Eastern Mediterranean world, including quite possibly Judea, since some knowledge of Greek can be presumed among educated circles in Jerusalem from at least the third century BCE (see below, G.15).

6. Original Languages. Because of the process of transmission of this corpus of texts (see B.1, 3–4), all of them have been preserved in

Greek, but this does not mean that all were therefore originally composed in Greek. The Hebrew or Aramaic origin of the book of Tobit is now certain because of the discovery of five Tobit MSS, four in Aramaic and one in Hebrew, among the Dead Sea scrolls. In contrast the original Semitic version of Judith and of 1 Maccabees can only be hypothesized from the nature of the Greek text, although an Aramaic version of Judith was known to Jerome in the early fifth century and a Hebrew text of 1 Maccabees was known to Origen in the third century. There is no reason to doubt that both 2 Maccabees and the Wisdom of Solomon were originally written in Greek, but for the rest of the Apocrypha the original language is uncertain. In the third century CE Julius Africanus argued that the play on words in the Greek text of Susanna shows that this narrative was originally composed in Greek, but it is also possible that this was the work of an ingenious translator.

7. Authors. Most of the authors of the apocryphal books are anonymous or pseudonymous and their identities can only be surmised from the contents of their writings. The exceptions are Jesus ben Sira, author of Ecclesiasticus, who identified himself in the text (50:27) as a Jerusalemite, and his grandson, who translated his work and, according to his statement in the prologue, wrote in Egypt. 2 Maccabees is an abridgement of a larger work in five volumes by a certain Jason of Cyrene (2 Macc 2:23), but beyond the facts that his name indicates that he came from Cyrenaica (modern Libya) and that the details in the narrative suggest (if they derive from Jason) that he had spent some time in Judea, nothing else can be said about him. Despite the preservation of the Apocrypha eventually through Christian rather than Jewish copyists since the end of the first century CE (see B.2), there is no reason to doubt that most of what is found in these books was written by Jews except for 2 Esd 1–2; 15–16; these passages, which are found in the Latin Vulgate, are missing in the oriental translations and appear to be additions by a Christian author. Christian interpolations into the texts of other books of the Apocrypha are possible but seem to have been rare, presumably because these texts were from early on treated as Scripture.

8. Readership. So far as is known, everything in the Apocrypha, apart from the Christian interpolations (see C.6), was written originally primarily for a Jewish readership. Only in the case of the Wisdom of Solomon is it reasonable to speculate that the author may in part have had in mind also Gentile readers: the address to the 'judges and kings of the earth' (Wis 1:1; 6:1) is a literary fiction, but the attack on the foolishness of idolatry (chs. 13–15) may have been genuinely aimed at Gentile pagans, although its prime intention may more plausibly have been to guide Jews away from any temptation to indulge in such worship, and the book as a whole contains so many veiled allusions to biblical history that only Jewish readers could have appreciated it fully. In any case, and whatever the aims of the authors, there is no evidence that any ancient pagan in fact read any of these works.

G. Historical Background. 1. Political Events In the Hellenistic World. The political event of most significance in the shaping of the Apocrypha was the conquest of the Levant by Alexander the Great of Macedon in 331 BCE. For nearly two centuries before the arrival of Alexander, the Land of Israel lay under Persian rule. The Persian state was on the whole content to interfere little with the lives of its subjects, and the small province of Judah was allowed to develop its own distinctive culture around the temple city of Jerusalem. This quiet, parochial existence was shattered by Alexander, who brought Greek culture in all its forms to the Jews.

2. Alexander inherited the throne of Macedon from his father Philip at the age of 20 in 336 BCE and almost immediately embarked on an ambitious campaign to conquer the Persian empire. Astonishing success in a series of battles brought him by the time of his death in 323 BCE control of the whole of the Near East up to the borders of India. Within his new empire lay not just the Jewish homeland and temple but also the great centre of Jewish exile in Mesopotamia. For the next 200 years Jewish history was continually affected by the intrigues and ambitions of Alexander's Macedonian successors. After a period of turmoil following Alexander's death, his generals eventually parcelled out his huge conquests among themselves. Of the great dynastic empires that thus came into existence by 301 BCE, the two most to affect the Jews were the dynasty founded by Ptolemy I Soter, with its base in Egypt, and the rival dynasty of Seleucus I Nicator, which had essentially two main bases, one in Mesopotamia and the other in northern Syria.

3. From 301 to 198 BCE Jerusalem lay under the rule of the Ptolemies, lying at the northern fringes of the Ptolemaic state, but the territory of the Land of Israel was disputed by the Seleucids in six wars in the course of the third century, and eventually the Seleucid king Antiochus III in 198 BCE wrested control of the southern Levant into his own hands as part of a general expansion of his kingdom. The result was a change in the method of state control of Judea. In essence the Ptolemaic dynasty ruled through a large bureaucracy, in part a necessity because of the reliance of Egyptian agriculture on irrigation which depended on state regulation; in contrast the much more diffuse empire of the Seleucids relied heavily on co-operation by local élites, who were given incentives to administer their regions on behalf of the state. Hence in the Seleucid empire there were more (or more openly recognized) routes to advancement for non-Greeks than in the Ptolemaic state, but with the proviso that non-Greek élites were expected to behave in Greek fashion if they were to be granted such control over their own communities. In Jerusalem the Jewish ruling élite was essentially the high priest and his associates. During the course of the first quarter of the second century BCE some members of this élite proved sufficiently attracted to the prospect of power to adopt Greek names and some Greek customs. It is possible (although it is hard to tell whether this was actually their intention) that the gradual adoption of this alien culture would have led in time to the end of a distinctively Jewish culture and religion. In any case the process was abruptly halted by the Maccabean revolt.

4. The Maccabean Revolt. In 168 BCE the Seleucid king Antiochus IV Epiphanes ordered the abolition of the ancient cult in the temple in Jerusalem and the conversion of the shrine to pagan worship. Neither the new divinity to whom the temple was dedicated nor the precise causes of this highly unusual attack by a Hellenistic king on an ancestral religion can be stated with certainty; the main sources of evidence are the books of Maccabees in the Apocrypha, which provide as explanation the internal divisions within the Jewish ruling class, and in particular the desire of some high priests to embrace Hellenism as a route to political power, but the wider policy of Antiochus, who first expanded his power through a dramatic campaign south into Egypt and was then compelled to withdraw by the threat of Roman intervention, may have been equally or even more responsible. At any rate this attack provoked an uprising led by Mattathias, a priest from Modiin, north-west of Jerusalem, and his five sons, of whom Judas Maccabee emerged in the course of the struggle as supreme leader. By 164 BCE guerrilla warfare had succeeded and the temple was purified and rededicated.

5. Hasmonean Rule. Control of the temple did not automatically bring political independence. There continued to be a Seleucid garrison in Jerusalem until probably 129 BCE. Nor did the family of Mattathias and Judas immediately reap in full the fruits of their victory: when the temple cult was restarted by Judas, the new high priest was a certain Alcimus, an associate of the high priest from before the war; Mattathias died during the war and Judas himself was killed in battle in 161 BCE. On the death of Alcimus in 159 BCE there was a hiatus in the high priesthood until 152 BCE, when Judas's brother Jonathan had himself appointed to the post. From that date to 37 BCE all the high priests came from this family. The dynasty was called by the name 'Hasmonean', a reference back to an ancestor of Mattathias. At first the Hasmoneans ruled Judea as vassals, in effect, of the Seleucid kings, but they took advantage of the disintegration of the Seleucid state through internal dissension and the machinations of the Romans, whose interest in the eastern Mediterranean increased during the second century BCE. By the 120s BCE the Hasmonean high priest John Hyrcanus was sufficiently independent to commence campaigns to expand the region of Jewish rule outside Judea, and by 112 BCE the whole region of Idumea, to the south of Judea, had been forced by him to convert to Judaism. A similar policy of expansion and incorporation was followed by his son Aristobulus, who in 104–103 BCE compelled the Itureans who lived in Galilee to become Jews.

6. The brief rule of Aristobulus (104–103 BCE) marked something of a shift in the nature of Hasmonean rule. Aristobulus was still high priest, and his right to power was still justified by the dynasty's role as the leaders of the revolt in the 160s, but he liked to be known as 'philhellene' (a lover of Greek culture) and he had himself declared king. In his rule, and that of his successor Alexander Jannaeus (103–76 BCE), the Hasmonean dynasty behaved much like other Hellenistic rulers, using mercenary soldiers to establish themselves as a regional superpower. When Jannaeus died, his widow Alexandra Jannaea Salome became queen (76–67 BCE), in a fashion found elsewhere in the Hellenistic world but not previously among Jews. In the process the relationship of the Hasmoneans with their Jewish subjects at times became stormy.

7. The decline of the Hasmonean dynasty was a direct product of the ambitions of Rome. During the 70s BCE the remnants of the Seleucid state fell into Roman hands and in 63 BCE the Roman general Pompey the Great took advantage of quarrels between Hyrcanus and Aristobulus, the two sons of Alexandra Jannaea Salome, to intervene ostensibly on the side of Hyrcanus. Thus Pompey besieged Jerusalem and inaugurated the ensuing history of misunderstandings between Jews and Romans by desecrating the Holy of Holies in the temple simply out of curiosity to know whether it was true that there was no cult image in the shrine. From that date Judea lay in effect within the Roman empire, although for much of the next century Rome preferred to exercise control through proxy Jewish rulers, a procedure common in Rome's administration of her empire elsewhere.

8. Herodian Rule. The transfer of Roman patronage from the Hasmonean dynasty to Herod the Great in 40 BCE was not a result of standard Roman policy, for Rome usually sought client kings from within the ranks of existing native dynasties. Nor was it remotely to be expected on the Jewish side, since Herod was an Idumean, descended on his father's side from the people converted to Judaism less than a century before by John Hyrcanus and on his mother's side from a Nabatean Arab, and thus ineligible for the high priesthood. Herod was proclaimed king of Judea by the Roman senate and consuls out of desperation caused by the internal disintegration of the Roman state.

9. The period of civil war that had first engulfed the Mediterranean world in 49 BCE with the struggle of Pompey and Julius Caesar did not abate until the victory of Octavian, the future emperor Augustus, in the battle of Actium in 31 BCE. In the meantime the Roman state was in turmoil and in 40 BCE the Parthians, whose empire in this period was based in Mesopotamia, took advantage of Roman disarray to invade the southern Levant. The Hasmonean ruler and high priest Hyrcanus (67–40 BCE) was carried off into exile in Babylonia and replaced by his nephew, the pro-Parthian Antigonus. The Romans, who had no Hasmonean adult male to put forward in opposition, chose Herod instead simply because he had already proved himself an energetic aide to Hyrcanus and a loyal friend to Rome.

10. Herod's first act once proclaimed king was to join his Roman patrons in a sacrifice to Jupiter on the Capitol, and when he eventually captured his capital in 37 BCE it was through the efforts of Roman legionaries commanded by a Roman general. It is not surprising that, after this inauspicious start, Herod's relationship with his subjects was never easy. He ruled until 4 BCE through repression, constantly fearful of plots, not least by members of his own family. His grandiose building plans, which included the massive reconstruction of the Jerusalem Temple, did not succeed in endearing him to his people. His success in ruling through fear was demonstrated by the eruption of widespread revolts when he died. His son Archelaus, appointed ethnarch of Judea by the Roman emperor Augustus, proved incapable of imposing control in the same way, and in 6 CE he was sent by Augustus into exile in the south of France. Judea came under the direct rule of a Roman governor.

11. Roman Rule. Judea was controlled directly by Rome for many centuries from 6 CE, with the exception of the glorious three-year rule from 41 to 44 CE of Agrippa I, Herod's grandson, who owed his throne to his machinations in Roman politics and his role in bringing to power the new emperor Claudius, and the periods of Jewish revolt in 66–70 and 132–5 CE.

12. There was a revolt in 6 CE when a census was imposed as part of the organization of the new province, but this phenomenon can also be observed in other provinces in this period. Despite a mass protest in 40 CE when the emperor Gaius Caligula attempted to have a statue of himself erected in the temple, and occasional disturbances in Jerusalem at the times of mass pilgrimage on the festivals, the Romans left Judea lightly garrisoned down to 66 CE and evidently did not consider the Jews a particular threat. The revolt in 66–70 CE may thus have come as something of a surprise. At any rate it appears that Roman war aims changed during its course: a war which began as an attempt to make the Jews give sacrifices in their temple on behalf of the emperor ended with the total destruction of the temple. It is probable that the exceptional ferocity of the final Roman assault on the temple owed much to the need of the Roman commander Titus to win rapid prestige in Rome for himself and his father Vespasian, since Vespasian had seized power in a bloody civil war the previous year and, lacking any other qualifications for supreme office, used the victory over the Jews

as evidence of his beneficence to the empire. Hence the superfluity of monuments in Rome to commemorate the defeat of the Jews, and the impossibility of an immediate rebuilding of the temple.

13. The destruction in 70 CE was a terrible disaster for all Jews, but the temple had been destroyed before and eventually rebuilt, so it is wrong to imagine universal Jewish despair. The institution of national Jewish leadership, the high priesthood, was now gone, and the Roman state probably saw no need for any new Jewish spokesman. Most Jews probably continued in their old beliefs and hoped for the temple to be restored. Eventually the rabbis evolved a new type of Judaism which could flourish without a temple, and the Roman state formally recognized the rabbinic patriarch as the political leader of the Jews, but, so far as is known, neither of these processes took place until long after the temple's destruction.

14. Jewish Settlement. Judea was the homeland of the Jews throughout this period, and by its end Jerusalem was one of the greatest cities of the eastern Mediterranean, but there was also a large Jewish population in the diaspora. Some of these Jews had been carried into captivity in Babylonia at the time of the destruction of the First Temple and the Babylonian community remained considerable throughout the Second Temple period, although little is known of its history. The diaspora in the eastern Mediterranean world outside Israel grew rapidly from the third century BCE to the first century CE, partly because of the settlement of descendants of slaves taken captive in the numerous wars which affected the region, partly because of the use of Jews by Hellenistic monarchs as mercenaries settled in Asia Minor and in Egypt, partly through economic migration in the face of overpopulation in the homeland, and partly (but to an unknown degree) through the accretion to Jewish communities of Gentile proselytes. By the early first century CE Jewish communities were to be found in all the coastal areas in the eastern Mediterranean from Greece round to Cyrene in Libya as well as in the city of Rome, in the interior of western Asia Minor on the Anatolian plateau, and in large numbers in the countryside in Syria and in Egypt, while the largest diaspora communities were in the great Hellenistic capital cities of Alexandria and Antioch. After the defeat of 70 CE Jews were even more dispersed, but the emergence of a diaspora in the western

Mediterranean cannot be attested until late-Roman times.

15. Cultural Developments. Jews in this period were profoundly affected both in the Land of Israel and in the Mediterranean diaspora by the Greek culture spread and promoted by Alexander the Great and his successors. In this respect Jews were part of a much wider phenomenon in which native cultures throughout the Near East fused to a greater or lesser extent with the culture of the Graeco-Macedonian dynasties which ruled over them; the amalgamated cultures which resulted have been termed 'Hellenistic' by scholars since the nineteenth century. Thus the use of the Greek language was widespread in the Land of Israel by the first century CE, although it was probably in more common use in towns and in cities. Jews also adopted Greek architecture, political forms, literary genres, and, to a limited extent, philosophical ideas. Much of this adoption was apparently both gradual and unselfconscious: Hellenistic culture was simply the milieu in which Jews from the time of Alexander found themselves living. Only with regard to the events preceding and during the Maccabean revolt did the adoption of Greek culture and opposition to it acquire wider significance because of the preference of the Seleucids to give greater political power to natives who Hellenized (see above G.4). It is thus only in the books of the Maccabees that Judaism is explicitly contrasted to Hellenism. The Hasmonean rulers themselves, despite their dynasty's founding myth based on their opposition to Hellenism, adopted much of Greek culture. It is probable that the degree of Hellenization varied among Jews of different places of origin and different classes of society. Richer Jews, and those from big cities, especially Jerusalem, were more likely to speak Greek and operate easily within Greek cultures. In most diaspora communities, apart from Babylonia, Greek was probably the main language of religious as well as secular discourse, and there was little knowledge of Hebrew or Aramaic. In the Land of Israel, both Hebrew and Aramaic were in general use down to the end of the Second Temple period, but the native Jerusalemite Josephus proved capable at the end of the first century CE of writing complex literary works in Greek, albeit in a style for which he felt it necessary to apologize (Jos. *Ant.* 20. 263–4).

16. Religious Developments. By the time the books of the Apocrypha were composed there had emerged many different varieties of Judaism, but Jews did have a common core to their religion. All pious Jews had in common their devotion to the one God who was worshipped in Jerusalem, and the belief that God had both chosen his people for care and (all too often) chastisement, and that God's instructions for the correct way for a Jew to live were contained within the Torah, which was itself encapsulated within the Pentateuch. Judaism had become a religion of the book, and there was a general (but not universal) consensus that real prophetic inspiration was no longer possible. The main grounds for disagreement lay in differing interpretations of what precisely the Pentateuch requires, and religious leaders, whether priestly or lay, tended to gain their authority from their expertise in such interpretation.

17. Many of the disputes attested in writings of this period concerned the conduct of the temple cult in Jerusalem. Since Jews held that there should be only one such temple (although in fact a second temple existed in Leontopolis in Egypt down to 72 CE), the correct performance by the priests of the sacrifices and other offerings made in the temple was of immense importance to all. There was widespread interest in, and disagreement about, the notion of physical purity both as a requirement for worship in the temple and as a metaphor for spiritual purity. Among some Jews this led to high value being placed on an ascetic lifestyle. Jews debated also more philosophical and theological questions such as whether there is life after death (a tenet in which most but not all Jews came to believe from around the mid-second century BCE); the nature of the events to precede the end of the world towards which history was generally agreed to be heading; the nature and role of a messianic figure in those events; the relationship between human free will and divine intervention; the role of angels as intermediaries between man and God; the extent to which customary interpretation of the Pentateuchal laws could itself be taken to reflect the divine will. These debates were sometimes acrimonious but by no means always so, since the areas of agreement among Jews far outweighed the areas in dispute: thus Josephus (*Ag. Ap.* 2.179–81) could state that, in contrast to Greeks, a characteristic of Jews was their 'admirable harmony ... Unity and identity of religious belief, perfect uniformity in habits and customs, produce a very beautiful concord in human character. Among us alone will be heard no contradictory statements about God ... Among us alone will be seen no difference in the conduct of our lives.'

18. The Emergence of Sects. It is all the more surprising that this same author, Josephus, provides the best evidence that a characteristic of Judaism in this period which distinguished it from the biblical age was the emergence within the religion of groups or parties that defined themselves by their distinctive theologies. In many passages he referred to the three, or sometimes four, haireseis (lit. choices) among the Jews, which he defined as the Pharisees, the Sadducees, the Essenes, and the Fourth Philosophy (about which Josephus is the sole witness). These groups were not strictly sectarian, since they all appear to have participated in mainstream Jewish life, but they all had special doctrines of their own; at least in the case of the Essenes they had a strong communal organization; and in each case they defined themselves as different from other Jews. More clearly sectarian in the sense that they viewed themselves as legitimate in contrast to the rest of Israel were the group (or groups) which produced the communal writings among the Dead Sea scrolls found at Qumran. It is possible that these Dead Sea sectarians are to be identified with one or other of the groups known from the classical sources, but it is no less possible that this group was a separate sect unknown until the chance discovery of the scrolls in 1947. These groups are first attested in the Hasmonean period. This may be through chance, and the groups may have existed before this time since the narrative in Josephus' histories becomes so much more detailed from precisely this period, but it is also possible that the development of sectarianism was a product of the complexities of Jewish life in the land of Israel during the second century BCE.

19. Literary Developments. The new kinds of literature produced by Jews in this period were, like the religious innovations of the time, mostly the product of an intense attachment to the biblical text on the one hand, and the influence of the wider Hellenistic world on the other. The books contained within the Apocrypha comprise only a very small portion of the total literary output of Jews in this period. Many other Jewish writings were preserved by Christians for religious edification and instruction independently from the biblical corpus; such texts included the writings of Josephus and Philo as well as the heterogeneous collection of other works known to modern scholars

(rather misleadingly, since not all are pseudepigraphic) as the 'Pseudepigrapha'. A quite different body of writings in Hebrew and Aramaic were handed down through the Jewish rabbinic tradition; although none of the extant rabbinic texts, including the Mishnah, the foundation document of rabbinic Judaism, existed in its present form before c.200 CE, they incorporate much earlier literary material. Since the writings preserved by Christians and those preserved by Jews overlap to such a small extent, it is a reasonable assumption that both traditions selected the material they found valuable from a much larger pool. That this is so was confirmed by the discovery at Qumran of the Dead Sea scrolls which included many religious texts about whose existence there had previously been no trace. This highly fluid literary tradition provides the background for understanding the literary and religious aims of the authors of the Apocrypha.

20. Some at least of the works composed in the late Second Temple period continued within the genres to be found in the HB; thus there was religious poetry in the style of the Psalms, wisdom literature comparable to Proverbs, and so on. But there were also new kinds of writing. The main literary innovations in the post-biblical period were the development of different types of commentary on the Bible, including rewritten versions such as the book of *Jubilees*, systematic expansions of biblical lemmata, as in some rabbinic midrashim, and many other forms of biblical interpretation; the genre of apocalyptic, in which a story is told of the revelation of a divine message to a sage; philosophical treatises, most notably in the writings of Philo of Alexandria; the composition of tragedies in the Greek style but on Jewish themes, of which only one, a play on the Exodus by a certain Ezekiel, is partially extant; the development of communal rules, as at Qumran; and, perhaps most importantly, the adoption of Greek genres of historiography to describe the past. In all these cases it is probable that the literary form had some connection to the ideas expressed in the text—so, for instance, it is not accidental that eschatological speculation is to be found quite frequently, although by no means always, in apocalyptic writings. Similarly, the transmission of many quasi-prophetic texts in this period either under a pseudonym ('pseudepigrapha') or anonymously must be connected to the belief that genuine prophecy belonged to an earlier age.

H. The Apocryphal Books and History. 1. Our lack of precise knowledge about the date and place of composition of many of the books of the Apocrypha (F.3–5) precludes any certain deduction about the relationship between most of these writings and the historical background outlined in G. It is thus possible that the Additions to Daniel, Tobit, and the Letter of Jeremiah should be understood against the background of the Babylonian Diaspora, and that Wisdom of Solomon and the additions incorporated in the Greek Esther were products of the Jewish community in Egypt in the late Hellenistic age (so e.g. Nickelsburg 1981), but since the circumstances in which these writings were produced can only be deduced from their contents, any argument that the contents reveal the impact of the circumstances in which they were composed is dangerously circular.

2. However, some books in the Apocrypha can be more precisely located. Thus Sirach was composed in the Land of Israel in the first quarter of the second century BCE when the country lay under Seleucid control and Greek culture was being enthusiastically adopted by the upper class of Jerusalem for whom Jesus ben Sira wrote. It is thus significant that, although his thought contains elements apparently derived from Hellenistic philosophy, and especially Stoicism, ben Sira wrote in Hebrew and within the traditional Jewish genre of wisdom literature. On the other hand the book contains no explicit polemic against Greek culture, so if he wrote in opposition to Hellenism he did so only indirectly. From the period following the Maccabean revolt originate of course both 1 and 2 Maccabees. 1 Maccabees appears to be an attempt by a Judean Jew to justify the assumption of power by the Hasmonean dynasty by referring back to their great deeds at the time of the rebellion. 2 Maccabees contains an edifying reminiscence for diaspora readers of the heroic deeds of the rebels, putting these comparatively recent events into the same category of the revelation of divine care for Israel to be found in biblical stories about the distant past. The book of Judith, with its interest in political as well as religious freedom, may also belong to this period, but the evidence is uncertain. The only other work in the Apocrypha for which a moderately sure origin can be postulated is 4 Ezra, the Jewish apocalypse incorporated into 2 Esd 3–14, which appears to have constituted a reaction by a Judean Jew to the destruction of the temple in 70 CE.

I. The Apocrypha and the Bible. 1. Some of the works in the Apocrypha derive their literary form primarily from their relationship to biblical texts. In no case is this relationship in the form of a phrase-by-phrase commentary, unlike some rabbinic midrashim (see above, G.19), but the types of association are different in each case.

2. **Rewritten Bible.** 1 Esdras is a Greek translation of a version of the biblical book of Ezra incorporating material from Chronicles and Nehemiah. It is uncertain whether it is best to explain the book by suggesting that the author possessed something like the Masoretic Hebrew text of Chronicles, Ezra, and Nehemiah before he wrote and then adapted it for his own purposes, or that he translated an independently preserved Hebrew text of the biblical books, but if the former is the case, 1 Esdras constitutes a free reworking of the biblical account similar to the relationship of the book of Jubilees to Genesis and relationship of the *Temple Scroll* found at Qumran to Deuteronomy.

3. **Additions to Biblical Books.** The passages inserted into the Hebrew book of Esther and now found in Greek Esther serve to enhance the dramatic and religious appeal of the original version and to bolster its historicity through the citation of verbatim copies of royal edicts. The author of these additions has made no attempt to alter or comment on the biblical story, but only to increase its impact in the spirit of the original. The Prayer of Manasseh, in which the king admits his sins and begs forgiveness from God, was similarly intended to supplement the biblical account in 2 Chronicles because 2 Chr 33:18–19 mentions that such a prayer is recorded elsewhere. The difference in this case is that the prayer was not preserved in the text of Chronicles in the Septuagint but only as a separate text.

4. **Imitation of Biblical Books.** Baruch is a hortatory prophecy so similar in tone and content to the Hebrew book of Jeremiah that it was treated by some Christians from the second century CE as a supplement to the biblical book. This notion was doubtless aided by references in the book of Jeremiah to Baruch as the prophet's secretary and references to the Babylonian exile in Baruch itself. The book of Baruch contains rather disparate material (narrative, prayer, instruction in the form of a poem about Wisdom, and comfort for the people in a poem about Zion), but all the elements are familiar from the prophetic books of the Bible.

J. The Apocrypha as Independent Compositions. 1. Most of the books in the Apocrypha are self-standing compositions and can be appreciated without reference to the Bible; this includes even those stories, like that of Susanna, which survive only through incorporation into a Greek translation of a biblical book. These works thus reflect many of the literary developments attested in Jewish society in the late Second Temple period (see G.19–20), although it is worth noting that many of the religious concerns expressed in other Jewish texts of this time (an interest in purity, temple ritual, asceticism, life after death, and so on, see G.16–18) are not as prominent in the Apocrypha as might be expected.

2. Wisdom Literature. Sirach can be assigned to the same wider genre of wisdom literature to which the biblical book of Proverbs belongs, but although it is close both in form and in content to the biblical model, it includes also much that is novel. Like other Jewish wisdom texts, Sirach deals with practical advice and religious problems, but this work is the earliest extant writing of its kind explicitly to identify divine wisdom with the Torah (24:8–29) and to provide a historical perspective by alluding to the laudable deeds of previous generations in Israel (chs. 44–9).

3. Philosophy. On the surface, the Wisdom of Solomon appears to be another offshoot of the biblical genre of wisdom literature, but it often diverges from that genre into philosophical rhetoric, using sophisticated Hellenistic rhetorical devices in order to present both a general attack on godlessness and a novel picture of Wisdom as an independent hypostasis alongside God. In the process of describing the nature of this hypostasis and in his picture of the nature of mankind the author makes use of concepts borrowed from Stoicism and perhaps Middle Platonism. The result is a work of philosophy, albeit on a level rather unsophisticated in comparison to, for example, the writings of Philo.

4. Historical Works. 1 Maccabees is a straightforward narrative history, and in that sense it is similar to and undoubtedly deliberately imitates biblical historiography, but in contrast to the biblical books the author of this work emphasizes the competence and wisdom of the human figures in the study, especially those of the Maccabean dynasty, rather than the effects of divine intervention. 2 Maccabees is a work firmly within the Greek tradition of 'pathetic' history in which dramatic events

were written up in an attempt to induce the reader to empathize with the characters, although this work too is specifically Jewish in the moral and religious lessons explicitly derived by the author from his story; how many of these characteristics were the work of Jason of Cyrene and how much the work of the epitomator who produced the current text of 2 Maccabees is unknown.

5. Didactic Stories. The Apocrypha includes a number of stories which, despite their historical setting, seem to have been intended not for instruction about the past so much as to give ethical and religious guidance, and to instil in readers an awareness of the power of divine providence, despite the problems faced by even the most pious. Among such stories are the book of Judith (which deals with the delivery of Jerusalem from the Assyrian Holophernes through the intrigues of the beautiful and good eponymous heroine) and the book of Tobit, which deals with the trials and tribulations of the charitable and pious hero and his son Tobias.

6. Of the Additions to Daniel, the story of Susanna and the story of Bel and the Dragon have similar qualities as edifying fictions. Neither tale is particularly well integrated into the biblical text of Daniel, and these writings thus served a very different purpose to the additions found in the Greek Esther (see 1.3.). The story of Susanna illustrates the wisdom of Daniel, who saves her from the wicked lechery of the elders who accused her of adultery, and the correctness of her decision to trust God even when she appeared doomed. The narrative of Bel and the Dragon reveals the foolishness of idolatry; in this case the story may have originated not just in the imagination of its pious author but also in midrashic extrapolation from verses in Jeremiah or Isaiah. The third Addition to Daniel, the Prayer of Azariah and the Song of the Three Jews, is a rather different writing from the other two. It consists of two poetic compositions, both of which probably existed as separate works before their insertion into the Daniel corpus.

7. Apocalyptic. 2 Esdras is the sole example in the Apocrypha of a literary genre whose popularity in this period has been confirmed by the discovery of fragments of apocalyptic texts among the Dead Sea scrolls (see G.19–20). The original Jewish part of the extant text (2 Esd 3–14) is divided into three dialogues and four visions, all described by Ezra himself. Ezra is taught by an angel a divine theodicy for the

---

---

world which makes sense of the disaster of the destruction of the temple by reassuring him of the coming judgement and the beginning of a new age.

K. The Impact of the Apocrypha. The books of the Apocrypha have been little read in any tradition over recent centuries, particularly because they are no longer printed in most translations of the Bible, but their influence is pervasive (Metzger 1957: 205–38). In particular, European art, literature, and music contain numerous allusions to the stories of Tobit, Judith, Susanna, Judas Maccabee, and the Maccabean martyrs, and sententious sayings culled from Sirach have become clichés in many languages. Among Jews the most obvious impact of the Apocrypha, apart from the festival of Hanukkah which celebrates the events described in 1 and 2 Maccabees (but without most Jews knowing the original books), has been in the popularity among Jews from medieval to modern times of the names Judah, Susanna, Judith, and Raphael.

REFERENCES

Metzger, B. M. (1957), *An Introduction to the Apocrypha* (New York: Oxford University Press).

Nickelsburg, G. W. (1981), *Jewish Literature between the Bible and the Mishnah* (London: SCM).

2. Tobit

JOSEPH A. FITZMYER, SJ

INTRODUCTION

A. Text and Language. 1. The book of Tobit is preserved in four fragmentary Aramaic texts (pap4QTob[a] ar, 4QTob[b] ar, 4QTob[c] ar, 4QTob[d] ar) and in one fragmentary Hebrew text (4QTob[e]), which together preserve about one-fifth of the book. These copies date roughly from mid-first century BCE to mid-first century CE. The full form of the book is preserved mainly in Greek and Latin versions, but also in various derivative versions (Arabic, Armenian, Coptic (Sahidic), Ethiopic, and Syriac). Derivative forms are also found in medieval Aramaic and Hebrew versions of the book.

2. The Qumran fragmentary Aramaic and Hebrew texts have been published in DJD 19. In general, these Semitic forms of the book are related to the long recension of the Greek and Latin versions.

3. The Greek version of Tobit is known in three forms: (*a*) The Long Recension (G[II]), preserved in the fourth-century Codex Sinaiticus (discovered in 1844), and part of it in both the eleventh-century MS 319 (Vatopedi 513), and sixth-century MS 910 (Oxyrhynchus Papyrus 1076). Sinaiticus has two major lacunae, 4:7–19*b* and 13:6*i*–10*b*, the first of which is covered by MS 319; also a number of minor omissions of phrases or clauses, which sometimes make the comprehension of its context difficult, but which can be supplied from other Greek forms or the Old Latin version. This recension is used in the NRSV; the numbering of verses here follows that of this recension in the critical text of Hanhart (1983). (*b*) The Short Recension (G[I]), preserved mainly in the fourth-century Codex Vaticanus, the fifth-century Codex Alexandrinus, and he eighth-century Codex Venetus, and also in a host of minuscule MSS. This form of the Greek text was used before the discovery of Sinaiticus. (*c*) The Intermediate Recension (G[III]), preserved in MSS 44, 106, 107. It may have some pertinence for Tob 6:9–13:8; for the rest it reproduces the text of Vaticanus.

4. The Latin version is likewise known in two forms: (*a*) The Long Recension, preserved in the Vetus Latina (VL), for which there is no modern critical text. One must use the eighteenth-century text of P. Sabatier and supplement it with readings from MSS that have subsequently been published or come to light. This long recension is related to G[II], but sometimes it is closer to the Qumran Aramaic and Hebrew texts than that Greek recension. (*b*) The Short Recension, preserved in the Vulgate (Vg) and found in the critical edition of the Monks of San Girolamo (1950). The relation of this form of the book, long used in the Roman Catholic tradition, to a Greek version is problematic; at times it differs considerably from the VL and Greek recensions. Jerome admitted that he dashed off the translation of it in one day (*unius diei laborem arripui*), having found a Jewish interpreter who could read Aramaic and translate it for him into Hebrew, which he then rendered into Latin (*Ep. ad Chromatium et Heliodorum; PL* 29. 23–6). As a result it differs notably from the Qumran Aramaic form known today and from G^{11}.

5. Other versions of Tobit and the medieval Aramaic and Hebrew forms are considered secondary because they seem to be derived from G^1.

6. The book was probably composed originally in Aramaic, because the Qumran Hebrew form now known has peculiarities relating it to a late post-exilic form of the language and contains words and syntagmemes that argue for an Aramaic substratum. This issue is debated, and some have been trying to maintain that the original was Hebrew. The matter is still unresolved.

B. Subject-Matter and Literary Genre. 1. The book is named after its principal character, Tobit, a model of Jewish piety. He was a law-abiding Israelite, who had been captured and deported with his wife Hannah and his son Tobias from the northern kingdom of Israel to Nineveh. There he suffered in various ways and was finally blinded. Praying to die, but recalling in his old age that he had deposited a considerable sum of money in far-off Rages in Media, he decided to send Tobias to get the money. At the same time at Ecbatana in Media, a young relative, Sarah, was also praying to die, because she suffered from the vituperation of maidservants, since all seven men to whom she had been given in marriage were slain by an evil demon Asmodeus, as they sought to approach her. In answer to the prayers of the two of them, Tobit and Sarah, God sent the angel Raphael to Nineveh. Raphael accompanied Tobias on his journey to Media to get his father's money. *En route,* when Tobias bathed in the Tigris, a large fish tried to swallow his foot. Raphael told Tobias to catch the fish and extract its gall, heart, and liver for use as medicine. At Ecbatana in Media Tobias married his kinswoman Sarah and used the fish's heart and liver to smoke the demon away on his wedding night. Tobias then sent Raphael on to Rages to fetch the money. When Raphael returned, Tobias took the money and Sarah his wife and came back to Nineveh, to his father's house, where he used the fish's gall as a medicament to remove white films from Tobit's eyes. Then, when Tobit and Tobias wanted to pay Raphael for his aid, the angel revealed who he was and disappeared, having instructed Tobit to offer thanks to God. Tobit composed a hymn of praise, instructed Tobias to leave the wicked city of Nineveh, once his mother had died, and then passed away. After Tobias buried his mother beside his father, he departed with Sarah for Media, where he continued to dwell with his parents-in-law. There he learned of the destruction of Nineveh.

2. Though some modern scholars (Miller 1940) have argued for a historical kernel in the story, most commentators regard the Book of Tobit as a Semitic novel composed for an edifying and didactic religious purpose. Its fictional character is seen in various historical and geographical improbabilities (see comments on 1:2, 4, 15, 21; 6:2; 9:2; 11:1; 14:15) and in its use of folkloric motifs ('The Grateful Dead' and 'The Monster in the Bridal Chamber').

C. The Religious Teaching. The purpose of the book is clearly didactic edification. Jews faithful to God, to obligations imposed by the Mosaic law, and to their ancestral customs, even in the time of persecution and deportation, are rewarded for their loyalty and fidelity. God is thus seen not to have abandoned his faithful servants. The book inculcates the teaching of Deuteronomic retribution (see Deut 28), mutual respect for tribal relations, support for family life, monogamous marriage, and the giving of alms. It incorporates numerous maxims characteristic of wisdom literature.

D. Date and Place of Composition. The Aramaic of the Qumran form of Tobit relates it to other second/first-century Aramaic compositions known from the Dead Sea scrolls. The Qumran copies thus support the generally recognized date of composition of the book in the early second century BCE. Although the Tobit story recounts events of the eighth-century deportation of Jews from Israel, the post-exilic customs of tithing, the recognition of prophetic writings as sacred, and the absence of any awareness of the Maccabean revolt support that dating of the composition of the book. Whether it was composed in the Mesopotamian diaspora or in Judah itself, or even elsewhere, cannot be determined.

E. Canonicity. Tobit is not part of the canon of the Hebrew Scriptures or of the Protestant OT canon. It is found in the collection of Alexandrian Jewish writings (LXX), and is regarded as a deuterocanonical book in the Roman Catholic church; it is also used as canonical in Eastern Orthodox churches. Jerome did not regard it as canonical and dashed off his Latin version of it only at the insistence of two bishops (who apparently did consider it canonical).

F. Outline.

COMMENTARY

The Double Situation in Nineveh and Ecbatana (1:1–3:17)

(1:1–2) Tobit *Tōb(e)it* is the Greek form of Aramaic *Ṭôbî*, the father's name, which is a shortening of *Ṭôbīyāh*, the son's name, meaning, 'YHWH is my good'. The name characterizes what God does for both in the book. *Tobiel*, the name of Tobit's father, means, 'El (God) is my good'. The tribe of Naphtali was named after its eponymous ancestor, son of Jacob and second son of Bilhah, the maidservant of Rachel (Gen 30:8). The tribe resided in northern Galilee, near Beth-shemesh and Beth-anath (Judg 1:33). 'Shalmaneser' (Gk. *Enemessaros*): the Assyrian king Shalmaneser V (727–722 BCE) began the siege of Samaria, capital of the northern kingdom (2 Kings 17:5), but it capitulated only after his death (721), to his successor, the usurper Sargon II (722–705), who eventually deported Israelites to captivity in Assyria (2 Kings 17:6; cf. 18:9–13). Thisbe was a Galilean town otherwise unknown. Kedesh Naphtali was a town in Upper Galilee, mentioned in Josh 20:7. From it Tiglath-pileser III (745–727) had earlier (733–732) deported Jews to Assyria (2 Kings 15:29). Asher was probably Hazor (Josh 11:1; 2 Kings 15:29). Phogor was another Galilean town otherwise unknown.

(1:3–22) Tobit's Background Until 3:6 the story is recounted in the first person singular. Tobit tells of his piety and struggle to lead an upright Jewish life both in Israel and in exile. v. 3, the ancient city of Nineveh became the capital of Assyria under Sennacherib (705–681) and functioned as such during the last decades of the Assyrian empire. It was located on the east bank of the Tigris River, a site today opposite part of the town of Mosul in northern Iraq. See Jon 1:2; 3:2–7; 4:11; Nah 2:7–8; 3:1–19; Zeph 2:13. v. 4, 'deserted the house of David and Jerusalem', according to 1 Kings 12:19–20 the revolt of the northern tribes occurred in the days of Jeroboam in 922 BCE, but Tobit speaks of it taking place in his youth. 'Chosen from … all the tribes', see Deut 12:1–14; 2 Sam 6:1–19; 1 Kings 5:5; 2 Kings 23:23. v. 5, 'on all the mountains', high places are mentioned in Hos 10:5, 8; Ezek 6:1–14. 'Calf', see 1 Kings 12:26–33, where Jeroboam setup shrines in Dan and Bethel so that people would not have to go to Jerusalem to celebrate feast-days. The calf was probably intended as a base for YHWH's throne, but soon it came to be an object of worship itself. Jeroboam also encouraged the offering of sacrifice on high places (1 Kings 14:9). v. 6, 'everlasting decree', see Deut 12:11, 13–14; 2 Chr 11:16. To such a decree Tobit affirms his fidelity, whence arises his loneliness in the face of the apostasy of the rest of Israel; 'first fruits of the crops', see Ex 23:16; 34:22; Num 18:21–30; Deut 14:22–3; 18:4; 'firstlings of the flock', see Ex 13:2; 34:19; Lev 27:26; Deut 14:23. The first and best part of crops and flocks were to be dedicated to God and his service. v. 7, 'the tenth', or 'the tithe', mentioned in Num 18:21–30; Deut 18:1–5; 26:12; Lev 27:30–1; 'second tenth', this tithe could be converted to money and brought to Jerusalem every seventh year and spent there (Deut 14:24–6). v. 8, 'third year' tithe, see Deut 26:12; 14:28–9; cf. Josephus, *Ant.* 4.8.22 §240. Tobit is depicted as religiously carrying out the tithe-regulations as they were interpreted in post-exilic Israel; 'Deborah', Tobit credits his grandmother with his religious training. v. 9, 'Anna', called *Ḥannāh* ('grace') in Qumran Aramaic texts; 'Tobias' is the Greek form of the son's name, *Ṭôbīyāh*, see TOB 1:1. v. 10, 'food of Gentiles', Mosaic law prescribed what foods were clean and unclean for Jewish people (Lev 11:1–47; Deut 14:3–20). Unclean food, eaten by Gentiles, caused ritual impurity for Jews. So Tobit is depicted faithfully observing dietary regulations even in captivity. v. 12, 'mindful of God', Tobit is motivated in his fidelity by the Deuteronomic ideas of divine retribution (Deut 28:1–68); whence his prosperity and prominent status in Assyria. v. 13, 'Shalmaneser', see TOB 1:2. v. 14, Media was a realm south-east of Nineveh, situated today in northern Iran. It was under Assyrian domination 750–614 BCE; 'ten talents', this great sum of money becomes an important motif in the story, providing the background for Tobias's journey to Media, his catching of the fish, and his marriage to Sarah, who along with Tobit is eventually cured by the fish's innards. Rages was a town in Media; it is not mentioned in Sinaiticus, but read in G¹. Its ruins are found today about 5 miles south-east of Teheran in Iran. v. 15, 'his son Sennacherib', Sennacherib (705–681 BCE) was actually the son of Sargon II, who succeeded Shalmaneser V. v. 16, 'many acts of charity', lit. 'I made many alms'. v. 17 makes it clear that eleēmosynai has to be understood in a broad sense, including food, clothing, and even burial. Tobit's generosity is extolled, for he practised it even when it was dangerous for him, in his status as a captive. His activity in burying the dead reflects the Jewish horror of corpses left unburied, especially those of fellow Jews. v. 18, 'when he came fleeing from Judea', i.e. Sennacherib, who had unsuccessfully attacked Jerusalem (2 Kings 18:13–19:37; cf. Isa 36:1–37:38). Sennacherib's fate is duly ascribed to a decree of heaven; 'put to death many Israelites'. This was done in retaliation for the king's failure to take Jerusalem. 'Looked for them'. Perhaps to expose them to further ridicule and disgrace. v. 21, 'forty days', or 'forty-five days' (VL), or 'fifty days' (G¹, Peshitta); 'killed him', see 2 Kings 19:37, where his sons are named as Adrammelech and Sharezer; 'Ararat', also mentioned in 19:37, the traditional spot where Noah's ark landed (Gen 8:4) is today in modern Armenia; 'Esar-haddon', another son of Sennacherib (2 Kings 19:37), he reigned 681–669 BCE. Rightly named in 4QTobᵃsrḥdwn, he is called Sacherdonos in Greek versions and Archedonassar or Archedonosor in VL; 'Ahikar', in Aramaic Aḥîqar; a well-known counsellor of Assyrian kings. See Story and Wisdom of Ahiqar, partly preserved in fifth-century Aramaic papyri from Elephantine (ANET 427–30); and in later legends of many languages (APOT ii. 715–84). Tobit here makes him a 'son of my brother [kinsman] Hanael', thus giving him a Jewish background, v. 22, 'appointed him as Second to himself' (my tr.). The Greek ek deuteras is unclear; NRSV renders

it, 'reappointed him'. However, 4QTobᵃ reads tnyn lh, 'second to him(self)', i.e. made him an Assyrian turtānu/tartānu, an official mentioned in 2 Kings 18:17; Isa 20:1.

(2:1–316) Tobit's Troubles and Prayer 2:1, 'Pentecost', the Greek name for the wheat-harvest feast that followed 'fifty days' or 'seven weeks' after Passover (Ex 23:16; 34:22; Lev 23:15–21; Deut 16:9–11). 2:2, 'poor person', Tobit shows his concern to carry out the injunction of Deut 16:11 about strangers, widows, and orphans on the feast. 2:3, 'lies there strangled', another Israelite executed, see 1:18. 2:4, burial after sunset would be less likely to be detected. 2:5, 'washed myself', to remove the ritual defilement from contact with a corpse (Num 19:11–13). 2:6, see Am 8:10. 2:10, 'white films', a primitive description of a cause of blindness; 'four years', see 14:2; Elymais, the Greek name for ancient Elam, a district north-east of the head of the Persian Gulf; see 1 Macc 6:1. 2:12, 'Dystrus', the Macedonian month Dystros corresponded to the Jewish winter month of Shebat, roughly Jan.–Feb. of the modern calendar. 2:14, 'flushed with anger against her', Tobit, otherwise so righteous, could get angry with his wife, even over a supposed theft, in which she might have been only indirectly involved; 'your righteous deeds', Anna's rebuke of Tobit and his righteousness reminds one of the taunt of Job's wife (Job 2:9). Her vituperation finds a parallel in that of the maid in 3:8. 3:1–6, Tobit's prayer: in this first formal prayer of the book, Tobit begs God for pardon from offences unwittingly committed and for release from this life, which he finds so greatly burdened with affliction, distress, and insult. 3:6, 'eternal home', i.e. Sheol, described in Job 7:9–10; 10:21–2; 14:12 as an abode from which no one returns; 'it is better for me to die', cf. Jon 4:3, 8; also Num 11:15 (Moses); 1 Kings 19:4 (Elijah); Job 7:15 (Job).

(3:7–15) Sarah's Troubles and Prayer The narrative shifts to the third person. v. 7, 'on the same day', this temporal note will dramatically join various parts of the story together (see 3:16; 17; 4:1). Ecbatana was the capital of ancient Media, on the site of modern Hamadan in northern Iran. 'Sarah', her name means 'princess'. Her plight parallels that of Tobit in Nineveh. Ragouēl is the Greek form of Aramaic 'Rĕ'û'ēl, 'friend of El (God)', the name of Moses' father-in-law (Ex 2:18); 'reproached', in this case the vituperation comes from a maid, who blames Sarah for the death of seven husbands-to-be. v. 8, 'wicked demon Asmodeus', probably a Persian name (*Aešma daeva*, 'demon of wrath') used for the spirit that afflicts Sarah; cf. the folktale, 'The Monster in the Bridal Chamber'. See Tob 6:14–15. v. 10, 'intended to hang herself', Gen 9:5–6 was usually understood as a prohibition of suicide. Sarah thinks better of it, realizing the reproaches that would come upon her father; 'in sorrow to Hades', Sarah echoes a biblical refrain; see Gen 37:35; 42:38; 44:29, 31; 'pray the Lord that I may die', her prayer parallels that of (Tobit 3:6). v. 11, 'With hands outstretched towards the window', Sarah prays facing Jerusalem, as does Daniel (Dan 6:11); cf. 1 Kings 8:44, 48; Isa 28:2; 'Blessed are you', she uses the traditional beginning of Jewish prayer, as will Tobias (8:5) and Raguel (8:15); cf. Ps 119:12; 1 Chr 29:10; Jdt 13:17. In this second formal prayer, Sarah protests her innocence, her purity, and her lack of responsibility for the death of the seven husbands, begging God to deliver her from continued life and vituperation. v. 15, 'I should keep myself as a wife', Sarah apparently does not know of Tobias, but recognizes the duty, emphasized in this book (1:9; 4:12–13; 6:12; 7:10) to marry within her ancestral family; cf. Gen 24:4, 38, 40; Num 36:6–8.

(3:16–17) God's Commission of Raphael to Go to Their Aid v. 16, 'At that very moment', see 3:7. The prayers of Tobit and of Sarah are heard simultaneously by God. v. 17, the angel's name, *Rāpā'ēl*, means 'God has healed', a name indicating the source of the cures to come to Tobit and Sarah; 'At the same time', again the note of simultaneity.

Preparations for Tobias's Journey (4:1–6:1)

(4:1–21) Tobit's Speech v. 1, 'That same day', the simultaneity is joined with the motif of the money (1:14). v. 2, 'I have asked for death', see 3:6. vv. 3–19, to Tobias Tobit delivers a speech, which is a cross between a farewell discourse (so DiLella 1979) and a sapiential exhortation, with a group of maxims inculcating the virtues of the life that Tobit has himself been leading. These maxims recommend filial duty to parents (4:3–4), pursuit of uprightness (4:5–6), giving of alms (4:7–11, 16–17), avoidance of fornication (4:12), marriage within the ancestral family (4:12), love of kindred (4:13), avoidance of pride, sloth, and drunkenness (4:13, 15), prompt payment of wages (4:14), the Golden Rule (4:15), and the praise, reverence, and trust of God (4:5, 19). Many of these counsels can also be found in Proverbs, Sirach, and other collections of ancient Near Eastern wisdom. v. 3, 'Honour your mother', cf. Ex 20:12. v. 6 'will prosper in all', the Deuteronomic doctrine of virtue rewarded by earthly prosperity and of sin recompensed by disaster (Deut 28:1–68; cf. Ps 1:1–3; Prov 10:27–30). v. 7, a lacuna in Sinaiticus begins here and lasts until v. 19; 'give alms', this counsel constitutes a major teaching of this book (see 12:8–9; 14:10–11), as also of Sirach (4:3–5; 7:10b; 29:9–13; 35:9–10; 40:17, 24); 'your face', cf. Sir 4:4–6; Prov 19:17; Deut 15:7–8. v. 9, 'treasure', cf. Sir 29:11–12. v. 10, 'darkness', Sheol; see TOB 3:6. v. 12, 'marry a woman', see comment on 3:15; 'Noah, Abraham, Isaac, and Jacob', Noah's wife is not named in the OT, but in Jub. 4:33: 'Her name was Emzara, daughter of Rakeel, his father's brother.' Abram married Sarai/Sarah (Gen 11:29); Isaac married Rebekah (Gen 24:67; 25:20); and Jacob married Rachel (Gen 29:28). v. 13, 'pride', see Prov 16:18; 'idleness', see Prov 19:15; Sir 22:1–2. v. 14, 'pay them at once', see Lev 19:13c; Deut 24:15. v. 15, 'what you hate', a negative form of the Golden Rule; 'Do not drink wine to excess', see Prov 23:29–35; Sir 31:25–31. v. 17, 'bread on the grave of the righteous', the meaning of this counsel is disputed. It seems to recommend what is otherwise prohibited: the pagan practice of putting food on graves (Deut 26:14c; cf. Sir 30:18). Yet it may be an echo of *Wisdom of Aḥiqar*, Syriac A 2.10 (*APOT* ii.730): 'Myson, pour out your wine on the graves of the righteous rather than drink it with evil people.' Hence it is sometimes understood to refer to meals brought to mourners (the 'cup of consolation', Jer 16:7) as a sign of sharing in their grief at the death of a good person (cf. Ezek 24:17, 22). Others think that it recommends the giving of alms in honour of the deceased. v. 19, 'bless the Lord God', Tobit commends prayer to his son as the basis of a good and upright life, realizing that God freely disposes of his creatures. v. 20, 'ten talents', the speech ends with the money motif, see comment on 1:14.

(5:1–6:1) Raphael Engaged to Accompany Tobias to Media v. 3, 'bond', Greek *cheirographon* denoted a 'handwritten document', often composed in duplicate, which could be torn in two so that it might guarantee the obligation to repay and later be matched on payment. v. 4, 'found the angel Raphael', as the reader realizes, Tobias does not recognize him as an angel; this folkloric technique is used also in Gen 18:2–22 (cf. Heb 13:2). v. 6, 'two days', from Ecbatana to Rages was actually about 185 miles. Arrian tells that Alexander took eleven days of forced march to go from one to the other (Anab. 3.19.83.20.2). The storyteller uses 'two days' to imply a far-away place. v. 12, 'Why do you need to know', heavenly messengers were reluctant to reveal their identity; cf. Gen 32:29. v. 13, 'Azariah', his name means, 'YHWH has helped', a covert identification of his role, which will be played out in the story; 'son of . . . Hananiah', the patronymic means, 'YHWH has been gracious'. v. 14, 'Nathan', a shortened form of Nathaniah, 'YHWH has given', a form found in some MSS; 'Shemeliah', probably a corrupted form of She-lemiah, Šelemyāh(û), 'YHWH has recompensed'; other texts read Shemaiah, Šěma'yāh(û), 'YHWH has heard'; 'Jerusalem', see 1:6. v. 15, 'drachma', a craftsman's normal daily wage. v. 18, 'his mother', again Anna does not approve of Tobit's decision to send Tobias to Media. Her disapproval will play itself out in the rest of the story. v. 19, the meaning of this verse is disputed. Peripsēma may mean, not 'ransom' (NRSV), but 'refuse'. VL: 'Nunquam esset pecunia illa, sed purgamento sit', to which MS G adds 'filio meo'. v. 21, 'my sister', a term of affection, used even by husbands of their wives; see 7:11, 15; 8:4, 7, 21; 10:6. v. 22, 'a good angel', i.e. a guardian angel. Tobit does not recognize what Raphael is.

Tobias's Journey to Media (6:2–18)

v. 2, 'The dog', the dog appears again in the story only when Tobias begins to come home (11:4), probably acting there as a herald of the return of the travellers. The Tigris was actually west of Nineveh (see comment on 1:3) and would not have been crossed en route to Media. v. 3, 'large fish', Tobias's wrestling with the fish is part of the romantic thrust of the story; the fish is subdued, and its heart, liver, and gall become vital elements in the narra-tive, which uses folklore about the curative qualities offish organs. v. 6, 'ate', in the Qum-ran texts and G[11] the verb is singular. In many of the other forms of the story it is plural, meaning that the angel also ate; see 12:19. v. 9, 'the gall', Pliny notes that fish gall 'heals scars and removes superfluous flesh about the eyes' (Nat. Hist. 32.24.69). v. 11, 'Sarah', Tobias now first learns of Sarah as his kinswoman; see TOB 3:15. v. 12, 'who loves her dearly', this clause is omitted in G[1], G[11], and the Peshitta, but is found in 4QTob[b] and VL instead of the last clause in NRSV, v. 12. v. 13, 'book of Moses', see Num 36:6–8, which does not men-tion a death penalty. v. 14, 'demon . . . killed

them', see 3:8. v. 15, 'to bury them', a major concern of this book (1:17; 4:3–4; 14:2, 10). v. 16, 'your father's house', see 4:12–13. v. 18, 'pray', prayer too may be needed to get rid of the demon, but the author is more concerned to set marital intercourse in a proper perspective; 'she was set apart for you', i.e. in God's provi-dence; cf. Gen 24:14, 44; 'You will save her', i.e. from a lonely and unmarried future.

Marriage of Tobias and Sarah (7:1–10:14)

(7:1–16) Tobias Arrives at Raguel's House and Marries Sarah The arrival scene may be modelled on that of Jacob at Haran (Gen 29:4–6). v. 2, 'Edna', she is called Anna in VL, a confusion with Tobit's wife's name. v. 5, 'in good health', no mention is made of Tobit's blindness, even though Raguel later speaks about it in 7:7. To get around this discrepancy, vv. 4–5 are omitted in the Peshitta and Vg; G[1] adds in v. 7: 'Hearing that Tobit had lost his sight, he was grief-stricken and wept.' v. 11, 'seven . . . kinsmen', see 3:15; 'she is your sister', see comment on 5:21. v. 12, 'gave her to Tobias', in marriage. v. 13, 'marriage contract', this ancient Jewish custom is not mentioned in the OT. For an example, see the Elephantine con-tract of Mibtahiah's marriage (Cowley 1923: 44 §15; ANET 222): 'She is my wife, and I am her husband from this day forever'; 'to which he affixed his seal', this clause is omitted in G[1], abridged in G[11], but read in VL at the end of the verse; 4QTob[a] has preserved one word of it, wḥtm, 'and he sealed [it]'. v. 16, 'the Lord of heaven', God, in whose providence Sarah has been kept for Tobias, will assure the joy of their marital life; 'Take courage', lit. 'be brave', an encouragement used in the book in contexts mentioning healing (5:10; 11:11).

(8:1–21) Sarah is Cured of the Demon v. 2, 'incense', used domestically to fumigate or per-fume a house. In obedience to Raphael's instruction (6:17), Tobias burns the fish's heart and liver on its embers to create a smoke that will drive Asmodeus away. v. 3, 'Egypt', the demon flees to Egypt, traditionally considered the home of magic (see Ex 7:11; 1QapGen 20:20), where Raphael, having pursued Asmodeus, binds and renders him ineffective. vv. 5–7, To-bias's prayer, the third formal prayer, is uttered in obedience to Raphael's instruction (6:18): he praises God, the creator and author of human marriage (Gen 2:24), and begs the grace of a long life together with Sarah. v. 5, 'Blessed', cf. Song of Thr 3. v. 9, 'went to sleep', the presumption is that they consummated the marriage. The Vg of 8:4 speaks of three nights of continence before consummation: 'Sarra, exsurge; deprecemur Deum hodie et cras et secundum cras, quia istis tribus noctibus Deo iungimur; tertia autem transacta nocte in nostro erimus coniugio.' That addition is not found in the Qumran texts, Greek versions, Peshitta, or VL but corresponds to another addition in the Vg of 6:18. 'Dug a grave', for Tobias, in fear that he too might have succumbed to Asmodeus, for Raguel knows nothing of the flight of the demon. vv. 15–17, Raguel's prayer, the fourth formal prayer, on learning of Tobias's safety, begins as Sarah's did; see TOB 3:11. Raguel thanks God for his mercy and compassion. v. 20, 'fourteen days', Raguel doubles the usual time of a wedding celebration; see 11:18; cf. Judg 14:12. In Gen 24:54–5 Rebekah's brother and mother insist on her staying for ten days after the marriage; from it probably comes the 'ten days' in some MSS of the Peshitta here.

(9:1–6) Raphael is Sent to Get Tobit's Money v. 2, 'Travel to Rages', this was a lengthy journey (see TOB 5:6), but Tobias trusts Azariah. v. 3, 'oath', see 8:20. In the NRSV and some other Bibles v. 3 follows v. 4. v. 5, 'counted out . . . the money bags', so Gabael is depicted as another trustworthy and dependable person in the story. v. 6, 'wedding celebration', the author gives the impression that it was but a short distance to the wedding in Ecbatana; 'blessed him', Gabael repeats the blessing of Raguel; see 7:7.

(10:1–14) Tobias Prepares to Return to Nineveh v. 1, 'kept counting', Tobit knows nothing of Tobias's marriage and the two-week wedding celebration but speculates about the delayed return of Tobias. v. 4, 'My child has perished', Anna gives the most pessimistic interpretation of the delay. Again, she rebukes Tobit; cf. 2:14; 5:18. v. 7, 'Tobias', he understands his parents' fears, even as Raguel tries to dissuade him from departing so soon. v. 10, 'half of all his property', Tobias, as the husband of Sarah, Raguel's only child, has become his heir. Thus the story has joined the two families, of Tobit and Raguel. v. 11, Raguel's farewell includes a prayer, invoking 'the Lord of heaven', a title often used of God in the post-exilic period (see 10:13–14; Ezra 1:2; Jdt 5:8). The farewell prayers of Raguel and Edna sound yet again the religious chords of the entire story, as Tobias undertakes his return journey with joy and happiness.

Homecoming of Tobias and Cure of Tobit's Eyes (11:1–18)
v. 1, 'Kaserin . . . opposite Nineveh', G^{11} omits a preceding sentence that VL has: 'They set out and travelled until they came to Haran', a place half-way between Ecbatana and Nineveh. G^1 gives Nineveh itself as the place they have reached and the scene where Raphael, not mentioned in ch. 10, reappears. The diversity of location is probably owing to the problematic 'Kaserin opposite Nineveh'. No such place is known. Torrey (1922) argued that Kaserin and Nineveh were respectively Ctesiphon and Seleucia, towns farther south on the Tigris on the caravan-route from Mesopotamia to Media. If he were right, Tobias and Raphael would have travelled from a town on the west bank and would have had to cross the Tigris; see TOB 6:2. v. 4, 'the gall', Tobias is to use it on the eyes of Tobit; 'the dog', see TOB 6:2. Sinaiticus reads rather *ho kyrios*, 'the Lord'. The Peshitta of 11:6 depicts Anna seeing the dog coming, and the Vg of 11:9 reads: 'Then the dog that was with them on the road ran ahead and coming on as a herald took delight in the charms of its tail.' So Anna was apprised of the coming of her son. v. 5, 'the road', see 10:7. Despite her belief that Tobias has perished (10:4), Anna continued her vigil. v. 7, 'Raphael', again the angel's instructions are important, and Tobias obediently does what he has been told: he uses the fish's gall to restore Tobit's sight. v. 9, 'Anna ran up to her son', reading *Hanna edramen* instead of *anedramen*. v. 11, 'blew into his eyes', so Tobias cures his father's blindness, and the peak of the story is reached; 'Take courage', see TOB 7:16; 'made them smart', G^{11} reads *epedōken* (corrupt); read rather *epedakē*, which would agree with *momordit* (VL). v. 14, 'light of my eyes', said of Tobias, it sums up the sense of the entire story, in which the contrast of darkness and light has played a significant role; recall 2:10; 3:17; 5:10; 10:5; 11:8; 14:10. vv. 14b–15, Tobit's prayer of praise, the fifth formal prayer of the book, ascribes both affliction and cure to God, and ends, 'Now I see my son Tobias!' v. 15, 'reported to his father', Tobias's report sums up the success of his trip: he has brought the money, he has married Sarah, and she is on her way here. v. 17, 'Tobit acknowledged that God', this expresses the expected reaction of the upright Tobit, who now understands that the affliction of blindness has led only to good for him and his whole family. v. 18, 'Ahikar', see TOB 1:21; 'his nephew Nadab', $4QTob^d$ bears the correct form of Ahiqar's

nephew's name, *Nadin*. It so appears also in the Elephantine version of the Ahiqar story. G¹, however, reads Nasbas; G¹¹, *Nadab*; the VL, *Nadab* or *Nabal*; the Peshitta omits the name; 'seven days', see TOB 8:20.

Revelation of Raphael's Identity (12:1–20)

v. 1, 'see to paying the wages', Tobit had advised prompt payment of wages (4:14); now he summons Tobias to carry out that counsel, and with a bonus (recall 5:15–16). v. 4, 'half of all that he brought back', this is usually regarded as a folkloric motif derived from 'The Grateful Dead', in which a guide is rewarded with half of all the hero acquires. vv. 6–10, Raphael's answer begins with a didactic, sapiential discourse, in which he urges Tobit and Tobias to praise God (cf. Isa 38:16–20), to pursue good and not evil, to pray, fast, and give alms, and practise righteousness. v. 8, 'Prayer with fasting', so G¹ and VL; but G¹¹ reads, 'Prayer with fidelity'. v. 9, 'almsgiving saves from death', see 4:7–10, 16 and comment there. v. 10, 'their own worst enemies', Raphael's closing verdict on sinners. vv. 11–15, Raphael reveals his identity as one of the seven Angels of the Presence; so he appears in 1 Enoch (Gk.) 9:1; 20:3. The other six are Michael (Dan 10:13, 21; 12:1), Gabriel (Dan 8:16; 9:21), Uriel (2 Esdr 4:1), Sariel, Raguel, and Remiel. The seven names appear together in 1 Enoch (Gk.) 20:2–8, where they are called 'archangels'. v. 12, 'I who brought', Raphael functions as the intercessor for praying mortals and as one who tests them. vv. 16–18, Raphael seeks to dispel fear of himself by ascribing all to God, whose messenger he has been. v. 19, 'a vision', the text of this verse is garbled in the versions. G¹¹ has: 'You saw me that I ate nothing'; G¹: 'I was seen by you all the days as neither eating nor drinking anything'; VL: 'You saw that I was eating, but you saw with your sight.' Fragmentary 4QTob^b preserves only, 'I did not drink'. v. 20, 'acknowledge God', i.e. give God the praise that is due.

Tobit's Song of Praise (13:1–18)

The sixth formal prayer in the book imitates Ex 15:1–18. Tobit obeys the angel's instruction to praise and thank God for his deliverance. He expresses concern for deported Israelites still in Assyria and prays for the restoration of Jerusalem. All of this is done with words and phrases echoing Psalms and Deutero- and Trito-Isaiah (esp. 54:11–12; 60:1–4; 66:10–14). The song has two parts: vv. 1–8 laud God's mercy and sovereignty; vv. 9–18 proclaim the rebuilding of

Jerusalem. Some commentators have thought that chs. 13–14 were a later addition to the book, but they appear in both the Aramaic and Hebrew copies from Qumran; so they must be an original part of the composition. v. 2, 'Afflicts, and … shows mercy', God is recognized to be in control of all. v. 3, 'before the nations', Israel is called on in its exile to acknowledge God even there. v. 6, Sinaiticus lacks vv. 6i–10b, for which one must follow G¹. vv. 5–6, the theme of Deuteronomic retribution reappears; see comments on 1:12; 4:6. v. 9, 'Jerusalem, the holy city', cf. Isa 52:1; 48:2; Neh 11:1; 'deeds of your hands', idols. v. 10, 'tent', God's tabernacle, the temple, vv. 12–14, Tobit utters a curse and a blessing on people as they will react to the future of Jerusalem. vv 16–17, 'Jerusalem will be built', Tobit's song echoes the vision of the new Jerusalem in Isa 54:11–12.

Epilogue (14:1–15)

The conclusion recounts the last advice given by Tobit before he dies. v. 2, 'Fifty-eight years old', so his age is given in 4QTob^a, 4QTob^b, VL, and G¹, whereas G¹¹ reads 'sixty-two years old'; 'after regaining it', G¹¹ gives no length of time that Tobit lived, but VL reads 'fifty-four years', which seems to be what 4QTob^e once read; 'giving alms', again Tobit's life is so summed up. v. 3, 'seven sons', so the VL, which may be supported by 4QTob^a and 4QTob^c; but this is not clear, because the final t could also be the ending of 'six', which would then agree with G¹, 'six sons'. G¹¹ omits the number. v. 4, 'Nahum', see Nah 1:1; 2:8–10,13; 3:18–19; cf. Zeph 2:13. Tobit is made to speak from the eighth-century perspective about the coming destruction of Nineveh and the exile of 'all the inhabitants of the land of Israel' (after 587 BCE). G¹ substitutes 'Jonah' for 'Nahum'. 'Samaria and Jerusalem', the capitals of Israel and Judah are mentioned in 4QTob^c and G¹¹, whereas G¹ omits Samaria, and VL omits both. The theme of desolation and rebuilding emphasizes what has happened in Tobit's own life. v. 5, 'the temple', its rebuilding is foretold in Isa 66:7–16; Ezek 40:1–48:35; Zech 14:11–17. v. 6, 'will all be converted', Tobit reflects a widespread post-exilic Jewish conviction (see Isa 45:14–15; Zech 8:20–3). v. 9, 'leave Nineveh', Tobit repeats his advice (14:3); v. 10 explains why. v. 10, 'Nadab', or Nadin; see TOB 11:18; 1:21. As the villain of the Ahiqar story, Nadin epitomizes what is wrong with Nineveh. Ahiqar had educated his nephew Nadin to succeed him as counsellor of Assyrian kings, but he treacherously plotted to have his uncle put to death. Ahiqar hid and was finally vindicated (came into the light), whereas Nadin died in a dungeon (in darkness). Again the motif of light/darkness is used to characterize the relation of good Ahiqar and evil Nadin; see comment on 11:14; 'gave alms', this sums up Ahiqar's life, as it did Tobit's (14:11); see TOB 4:7–10; 12:9; 14:2. v. 12, 'Buried her', Tobias obeys Tobit's last instructions. v. 14, 'One hundred and seventeen', some VL MSS read 118. v. 15, 'destruction of Nineveh', in 612 BCE Nineveh fell after a three-month siege to the combined forces of Babylonians and Medes, under kings Nabopolassar and Cyaxares. The fall of Nineveh likewise exemplifies Deuteronomic retribution: the wicked are punished. See TOB 1:12; 4:6. 'Cyaxares', Sinaiticus and G^1 strangely read *Nabouchodonosor kai Asouēros*; Hanhart (1983) reads *Achiacharos*, reflecting the VL Achicar, which seems to be a confusion of the name with Ahiqar.

REFERENCES

Cowley, A. (1923), *Aramaic Papyri of the Fifth Century B.C. Edited with Translation and Notes* (Oxford: Clarendon; repr. Osnabrück: Zeller, 1967).

DiLella, A. A. (1979), 'The Deuteronomic Background of the Farewell Discourse in Tob 14:3–11', *CBQ* 41: 380–9.

Hanhart, R. (1983), *Tobit*, Septuaginta: Vetus Testamentum graecum, 8/5 (Göttingen: Vandenhoeck & Ruprecht).

Miller, A. (1940), *Das Buch Tobias übersetzt und erklärt*, Die Heilige Schrift des Alten Testaments, 4/3 (Bonn: Hanstein), 1–116.

Monks of San Girolamo (1950), *Biblia Sacra iuxta latinam Vulgatam versionem ad codicum fidem ... cura et studio monachorum Sancti Benedicti ... edita* (Rome: Vatican Polyglot), viii.

Torrey, C. C. (1922), '"Nineveh" in the Book of Tobit', *JBL* 41: 237–45.

3. Judith

AMY-JILL LEVINE

INTRODUCTION

By combining theological convictions and narrative motifs familiar from the HB with Hellenistic literature's increasing attention to character development, pathos, and personal piety, the book of Judith epitomizes Second Temple Judaism's attempt to define itself in the light of Greek culture. Along with other Jewish narratives in the OT Apocrypha such as Bel and the Dragon, Susanna, and Tobit, the book of Judith provides instruction on Jewish identity even as it inspires and entertains.

A. Genre. 1. Whether labelled novella, novel, historical fiction, or romance (see details in Wills 1995), the book of Judith should be regarded as fiction, as the opening lines clearly signal. The more blatant errors include the identification of Nebuchadnezzar as ruler of Assyria rather than Babylon, and of his capital as Nineveh (1:1), which had been destroyed by the Babylonians in 612 BCE, before Nebuchadnezzar ascended the throne. The same chapter claims that Ecbatana was captured by Nebuchadnezzar; it fell instead to Cyrus of Persia in 550 BCE. Disrupting even the internal attempts at verisimilitude, the Ammonite Achior's recitation of Jewish history includes reference to both the destruction of the Jerusalem Temple by Nebuchadnezzar and its rebuilding, following Persia's defeat of Babylon.

2. Consistent with the fictional genre is the absence from any other ancient sources of several major figures, of whom Arphaxad the ruler of the Medes (1:1–6) is the most conspicuous example, as well as of several nations, such as the Cheleoudites (1:6) and the Rassites (2:23). Although the book of Judith includes several specific dates and times, such as the year of a king's reign (1:1, 13) and the number of days of a particular siege (7:20; 15:11), the enumerations function more to convey a sense of verisimilitude—this is what ancient historiography looks like—than they do to demonstrate historicity.

B. Date. 1. The date by which the book of Judith must have been written is the late first century CE; its first external reference is not, as might be expected, the Jewish historian Josephus nor any of the Dead Sea scrolls. Rather, it is in the Christian text, *1 Clement* 55:4–5, which lists Judith as among several women empowered by divine grace to accomplish 'many manly deeds' and who 'asked from the elders of the city permission' to enter the enemy camp. **2.** Establishing the date of composition is more difficult, in part because of the book's genre. The first three chapters may show knowledge of the Achaemenid king Artaxerxes III Ochus (358–338 BCE), who did mount western campaigns (in 350 and 343), did attack Sidon (cf. Jdt 2:28), and had both a general named Holofernes and a courtier named Bagoas. Yet knowledge of such events does not preclude the author's adapting this information for a fictional retelling.

3. The majority of today's scholars who regard the volume as fiction offer much later datings than the fourth century. While Volkmar argued that the book reflects the events of 70 CE, with Nebuchadnezzar representing Trajan and Judith the faithful Jewish population, and Gaster associated Nebuchadnezzar with Pompey's entry into Jerusalem in 63 BCE, Ball's association of Judith with Judah Maccabee and Nebuchadnezzar with Antiochus IV Epiphanes is probably correct (details in Moore 1985).

4. The Maccabean connection is supported by several plot motifs. First, whereas Antiochus Epiphanes and his supporters banned circumcision, Achior, Holofernes' erstwhile general, submits to the operation in his conversion to Judaism. Second, and more suggestive, the death of Holofernes resembles Judah Maccabee's defeat of the Syrian general Nicanor; 1 Macc 7:47 states, 'Then the Jews seized the spoils and the plunder; they cut off Nicanor's head and the right hand that he had so arrogantly stretched out, and brought them and displayed them just outside Jerusalem' (for additional connections, see Moore 1985).

5. The geographical centre of the book of Judith, the town of Bethulia, is another possible clue to the book's Hasmonean date. Bethulia appears to be located in Samaritan territory, which was annexed by the Hasmonean ruler, John Hyrcanus, in 107 BCE. By this time, Hyrcanus had destroyed the capital, Shechem, and torched the Samaritan Temple on Mt. Gerizim. Given the positive attitude the book of Judith displays towards Samaritan territory, the book's date may well be several generations after the conquest.

6. By invoking the outrages of Antiochus and his minions and the successful insurrection against his forces, Judith celebrates Jewish independence, praxis, and theology. As a new Judah (whose name means 'Jewish man'), Judith ('Jewish woman') corrects the priestly leaders' weak theology, defeats the Syrian king, and preserves the Temple for Jewish worship. Unlike Judah's successors, the Hasmonean dynasty that eventually assumed the roles of both king and high priest, however, Judith serves more in the model

of the biblical judges than she does either as monarch or cleric. Dying childless, she passes on no dynastic legacy. Perhaps then the volume praises Judah even as it subtly critiques his heirs. That Judith's age at her death, 105 years (16:23), is the number of years of independent Jewish rule may be a clue to a first-century BCE dating for the volume.

7. As a fictional study rather than a historical report, the book of Judith can be read by people of various times and settings as depicting the problems faced by the covenant community when threatened with external enemies and internal doubts. The almost supernatural evil of Holofernes, a general who marched his army from Nineveh to Cilicia, a 300-mile journey, in three days, permits him to become the model of any villain. Moreover, detached from history, the volume serves various allegorical purposes; Martin Luther, for example, regarded the book of Judith as an allegory of Jesus' Passion (for multiple other appropriations, see Brine et al., 2010; Stocker 1998).

C. Language and Culture. 1. Best preserved in two of the three major uncial Greek codices, Vaticanus and Alexandrinus, as well as in the uncial Basiliano-Vaticanus (the third major codex, Sinaiticus, shows signs of later editing), the book of Judith may have an Aramaic or Hebrew original (Moore 1985); scholars have argued that in preparing his translation of the book into Latin for his Vulgate, the Christian author Jerome utilized an Aramaic source: he speaks of translating only the texts found in 'Chaldean'. However, one could equally argue that the author of Judith wrote in an elegant, Hebraicized Greek (Craven 1983).

2. Other ancient versions rely either upon the Septuagint (e.g. the Old Latin) or upon the Vulgate (e.g. various Hebrew versions as well as, from the Middle Ages, midrashic iterations).

3. Whether Second-Temple Aramaic or Greek, the book of Judith is permeated by Hellenistic motifs. In the wake of Alexander the Great (d. 323), Jewish communities in both Israel and the Diaspora developed new forms of self-definition under pressures to assimilate and acculturate. Such struggles are noticeable in the OT Apocrypha; the volumes reflect intense concerns for Jewish practices (e.g. dietary observances, circumcision, conversion), relationship to the Gentile world, and personal piety. Yet the books are also preserved in the Greek language and reflect Greek culture. For example, in the book of Judith, Greek culture underlies the wearing of olive wreaths (15:13) and the custom of reclining to dine (12:15). The *thyrsus* Judith carries recollects Bacchantes, who, like Judith, confound gender roles, take heads from unwitting men, and celebrate their god, despite threats against their practice, through dancing and prayer. Scholars have even found allusions in the book to Herodotus' account of the Persian invasions of Greece in the fifth century BCE (Camponigro 1992).

4. The location of composition is, like the date, debated. Most scholars argue for a Judean provenance; if the original version were in Aramaic rather than Greek, this argument would be strengthened. However, just as the fictional nature of the tale foils any secure attempt at dating, so its fictional depictions of geography undermine any secure attempt at establishing provenance.

D. Religious Beliefs and Practices. 1. Although the book of Judith has few references to divine intervention (4:13), theological concerns are paramount. Sounding somewhat like Rahab (Josh 2), Achior the Ammonite gives a relatively complete summary of God's relationship to Israel and concludes with the warning, 'their Lord and God will defend them' (5:21).

2. Notable are the volume's depiction of personal piety and struggle for a faithful approach to the problem of theodicy. Concerning the former: Judith, like her sisters in the OT Apocrypha (Susanna, Esther of the Greek Additions, Sarah of the book of Tobit) prays; like them as well, she is pious, well schooled in the traditions of her community, and chaste even in the presence of lecherous threat.

3. The innocence of these women leads directly to the question of theodicy. Esther, Susanna, and Sarah are all tested and are all found worthy; so too, Judith argues against the Deuteronomic theology mouthed by Uzziah, the Bethulian leader, which insists that the onslaught of the enemy general Holofernes is punishment for the people's sins. Judith responds that the Assyrian campaign is not a punishment but the means by which God proves the people's fidelity. More, she condemns Uzziah's willingness to put God to the test by stating that, if divine help does not come within five days, he will surrender.

4. Like Greek Esther and, especially, the book of Daniel (a work probably composed during or immediately after the Maccabean revolt), the book of Judith emphasizes Jewish self-definition by accentuating dietary concerns: Greek Esther speaks of avoiding the Persian king's libations; Daniel refuses to dine at Nebuchadnezzar's table (Dan 1:8) and so, along with his friends, resorts to a vegetarian regime; Judith eats only kosher food (10:5; 11:13; 12:2). Finally, like the story of Tobit, the book of Judith emphasizes the Jerusalem Temple (4:2–3, 12; 8:21, 24; 9:8, 13; 16:20) as a place to be protected, to be entered undefiled, and to serve as the location for votive offerings, celebrations, and worship.

5. Such concerns for piety have been regarded both as indicative of Pharisaic piety and as in contravention of it. The former suggestion can also be supported by Judith's calendrical observances and ritual washings; the latter suggestion is premised upon the conversion of the Ammonite Achior, despite Deuteronomy's prohibition of Ammonites (and Moabites) entering the covenant community (Deut 23:3). However, lack of secure information on Pharisaic thought of the Hasmonean period makes any suggestion tentative.

6. Similar problems apply to explanations for Judith's absence from the canon of the synagogue. Justifications ranged from the conversion of the Ammonite, to his conversion apart from ritual immersion, to the volume's universalism seen as incompatible with (hypothetical) Pharisaic exclusiveness, to the (more likely) arguments that the book was known to be late (Daniel gained entry because of its back-dating to the Babylonian Exile), fictional, and/or composed originally in Greek. Again, any argument on the absence of Judith from the canon of Judaism must remain tentative.

E. Aesthetics and Ethics. 1. Because the titular heroine does not appear until midway through her story, the volume has been regarded as unbalanced. However, closer reading indicates substantial connections and correctives between the first and last seven chapters (Craven 1983). Paragraphs 2–4 below are examples of the balance:

2. Chs. 1–7 emphasize military campaigns, fear engendered by overt show of strength, and success based on armaments, numbers of soldiers, and male dominance; at the end of this section, Achior appears condemned, Nebuchadnezzar triumphant, and the Bethulians doomed. Chs. 8–16 provide the corrective by emphasizing Judith's personal history (e.g. her genealogy), clever strategizing, deception, and the power of the individual. For these reasons and others, commentators typically divide the book between the first and second eight chapters (Craven 1983). One notable exception is the theory of Ernst Haag (1963), which suggests the book of Judith forms a tripartite structure (1–3; 4–8; 9–16).

3. Characterization serves to yoke the two parts. In the first seven chapters, Achior provides the transition. His speech relates Assyrian plans and Jewish abilities, and his forced removal from the military camp to the outskirts of Bethulia shows the division between the two areas both geographically and ideologically. This most unlikely of heroes will enter Israel not only as an involuntary exile, but also as a willing convert, as his circumcision attests. Judith is Achior's opposite: the second section of the book depicts her traversing from Bethulia to the enemy camp, but through her own will rather than as an outcast. Whereas Achior truthfully summarizes Jewish history and is not believed, Judith dissembles about plans for the Temple sacrifices and is believed. While Achior undergoes circumcision and therefore changes both identity and appearance, Judith only feigns change: her make-up can be washed off and her festive clothes replaced by sackcloth.

4. Judith is also the opposite of Holofernes. The Assyrian general insists that everyone worship Nebuchadnezzar as divine, although the king had not actually given this order (Craven 1983). That is, Holofernes interprets his task theologically. Judith does the same: she invokes God through prayer, but her actions are of her own devising. Furthermore, unlike Greek Esther, Susanna, or Tobit's Sarah, who receive divine aid, Judith's prayers are answered by her own machinations rather than by explicitly miraculous interventions.

5. Just as the book of Judith is frequently regarded as aesthetically uneven, so it is often condemned as ethically untenable. Interpreters have excoriated the heroine, who lies, who lulls her victim into a false sense of security, who kills. Such a focus misses the narrative's irony the single woman dispatches a ruthless butcher intent on raping her. Judith decapitates the general, with his own sword no less, by the 'hand of a woman' (the phrase appears several times). Nothing could be more ignominious (see Judg 9:53). Enhancing the irony are the numerous *double entendres* along with the fainting of the seasoned soldier Achior at the sight of Holofernes' head, and the name of the theologically weak Bethulian leader, Uzziah, which means 'God is my defence'.

6. Yet irony and self-defence do not preclude the fact that the book, and its heroine, can be regarded as dangerous. More cunning than Jael (Judg 4–5), who dispatches the enemy general Sisera by tucking him into bed, giving him milk, and then pounding a tent peg into his temple, Judith seeks out her victim, takes the head as a trophy, and then facilitates the slaughter of the Assyrian army and the looting of their camp (White 1992). More dangerous than Jael, the 'wife of Heber the Kenite' and therefore distanced from the covenant community, Judith is 'one of us'. More threatening to traditional gender roles than Deborah, who is aided by Barak and is called a 'mother in Israel', Judith as book and as character subverts the social expectations for men and women. Judith remains independent, her female slave runs her estate, she refuses all sexual advances, the men she encounters are at best inept, even her donkey is female (Craven 1983). Perhaps then it is not surprising that the book insists upon its fictional status, that Judith finally retires to her house, and that she does not produce children.

7. The connection of the books of Judith and Judges is, however, a helpful corrective to those who find her story unethical or unladylike. Judith is, in terms of characterization, in the model of the charismatic, successful early judges and their associates: she is resourceful and brave like Jael; she is a mother figure in her protection of the community like Deborah; she is sly (and even conveys a possible hint of sexual scandal) like Ehud. As with the judges, the land remains at peace until her death.

8. The book of Judith evokes more than the stories of the judges, and herein lies a major part of its aesthetic import. Throughout, by drawing upon other texts, it adds to its own literary richness as well as contributes to the tradition-history of its literary predecessors. Most apparent is the book's connection to Gen 34, the rape of Dinah. From the (probably) Samaritan setting of Bethulia, to Judith's descent from Simeon, to her promise to protect the 'virgin' (Heb. *bĕtûlâ*), to the deceitful conquest, and even to the suggestions in each story of the unmanning of the enemy, the Apocryphal narrative recapitulates the earlier story. Indeed, the character of Judith redeems that of Simeon (as do two other Second-Temple texts, *Jubilees* 30, and the *Testament of Levi*), condemned for his violence by Jacob (Gen 49:5–7).

9. Like Jacob, Judith travels from her home, cleverly defeats an enemy who has been feigning friendship, and escapes hostile territory unnoticed. Judith may also be compared to Moses: both faced lack of water and a suffering people with weakening theologies (Ex 17; Num 20; Deut 33); both, seeking divine help, preserve and strengthen the covenant community (Van Henten 1995). Like Abigail, Judith descends a mountain, takes her own food, humbles herself before a military leader (David), and is involved with a drunk man who dies (Nabal); see 1 Sam 25 (Van Henten 1995). Like Esther, with whom she is typically paired in both ancient manuscript collections and modern interpretation, Judith uses her physical charms along with her clever words and loyalty to her people to defeat a genocidal enemy. Like the Maccabees, she rescues her people from false worship as well as military conquest.

10. Given Judith's composition during the Hellenistic era, it is not inappropriate to compare her also with Greek figures. Like Medusa, her looks prove deadly (see Bal 1994 for art-historical and literary connections); like Euripides' Bacchae, she carries a *thyrsus* and produces the decapitated head of a ruler. For more on connections between Judith and Greek fiction, see Wills 1995.

COMMENTARY

Nebuchadnezzar's Threat (1:1–16)

The book of Judith opens with an overtly fictional conceit: Nebuchadnezzar, the infamous king of Babylon who destroyed the Jerusalem Temple in 587 BCE, is named the ruler of Assyria, the empire which in 722 destroyed the northern kingdom of Israel. He is depicted as ruling from Nineveh, the Assyrian capital which his father had sacked in 612 BCE. This mythic setting makes the story always relevant: Nebuchadnezzar represents any who seek to obliterate the Jewish community. The conceit also allows the horror of the scene to be contained; from the opening sentence, readers also know that at least this threat to the community will not come to fruition.

The chapter continues to mitigate the ominous references to Nebuchadnezzar, first by fiction and then by means of exaggeration. Arphaxad, identified as the king of Media but unknown to history, prepares to defend his lands against Nebuchadnezzar by constructing major fortifications around his capital, Ecbatana: the towers are 150 ft. high, with foundations 90 ft. thick; the gates, 60 ft. wide, permitted entire armies to parade through.

Contributing to the exaggeration of the fortifications is the language: the opening sentence in Greek is several lines long, which English translations typically break up.

Nebuchadnezzar also seeks strength in numbers: he rallies much of what is now southern Turkey. However, the populations from Persia to Jerusalem to Egypt to Ethiopia refuse to join him, for they regarded him as 'ordinary' or, literally, 'as an equal' (v. 11). The irony continues: Nebuchadnezzar is more than the average king, as recognition of his name even today demonstrates. Increasing the irony, Holofernes will insist that Nebuchadnezzar be worshipped as a god.

Prompted by Arphaxad's insult to his military strength, Nebuchadnezzar seeks revenge; among his targets are Judea, Egypt, Moab, Ammon; thus Judea is now threatened together with, rather than by, its traditional enemies.

The battle begins with the despoliation of Ecbatana. The Greek literally states that the city's beauty was 'turned to shame' (v. 14). The motif of shame, recurring at e.g. 4:12; 5:21; 8:22; 9:2, anticipates Judith: by placing herself in a situation of seduction that would traditionally be considered shameful for a woman, she will succeed in humiliating the Assyrian men and saving her people.

Nebuchadnezzar's army returns to Nineveh for four months of recuperation. With the fall of Ecbatana, the fate of the rest of the Mediterranean and Asia Minor is, apparently, sealed.

Nebuchadnezzar's Plan (2:1–13)

Irony continues as Nebuchadnezzar broadcasts his 'secret strategy' (v. 2) to his ministers, nobles, his general Holofernes, and the readers. His self-appellation, 'Great King, lord of the whole earth', continues the hyperbole of ch. 1, and it establishes the theological challenge of the book. Holofernes is ordered to take 'experienced soldiers' (v. 5; lit. men confident in their own strength; the inference is that one should be confident in God's strength (Moore 1985)) to occupy all the territories, slaughter the rebellious, and capture the rest for Nebuchadnezzar to kill later. The general, ordered to follow his 'lord's' commands (v. 13) is thus a parallel to Judith, who will follow her 'lord's' commands. That the number of infantry soldiers Holofernes takes, 120,000, matches the number of Antiochus' troops (1 Macc 15:13) appears more than coincidental.

Nebuchadnezzar orders Holofernes to have 'all the land to the west' prepare for him 'earth and water' (v. 7), traditional Persian tokens of submission. Should they fail, he promises, again hyperbolically, the destruction of their peoples until the rivers overflow with corpses. The repetition of terms concerning water anticipates again the second half of the book, where Holofernes attempts to enforce Bethulia's submission by severing its water supply. The king concludes his orders first by taking the oath, 'as I live, and by the power of my kingdom', and then by promising that he will accomplish his plans 'by [his] own hand' (v. 12). The oath is reminiscent of the divine proclamation of Deut 32:39–41; Nebuchadnezzar is again seen to be setting himself up as a false god. The promise augurs Judith's repeated point that vengeance will be taken 'by my hand'—that of a woman (8:33; 12:4).

Holofernes' Campaign (2:14–3:10)

Holofernes begins his campaign by mustering an army comparable in its exaggerated description to the fortifications of Ecbatana (1:2–4). Contributing to the numbers, and the threat, of his army, are its multifarious followers; like a locust plague (2:20) they demolish all in their path: Put and Lud, the Rassisites and Ishmaelites, Cilicia and Arabia, Midian and Damascus. Their amazing feats are matched by their miraculous, or at least humorously exaggerated, feet: the army traverses 300 miles, from Nineveh to Cilicia, in three days (2:21). Hearing of Holofernes' victories, the coastal cities, including Tyre and Sidon, Jamnia and Ascalon, petition for peace. The reference to Jamnia (2:28) may recall Judah Maccabee, who burned the city in 164 BCE. The local populations offer everything: land, livestock, even the people as slaves. They greet Holofernes with garlands (Gk. 'crowns'), dancing, and tambourines. He, however, mercilessly demolishes their sanctuaries and 'woods' (groves dedicated to a goddess?) so that all nations *will* worship Nebuchadnezzar alone, 'that all their dialects and tribes should call upon him as a god' (3:8). This scene will be reversed in ch. 12, when Judith, with garlands, dancing, and tambourines, brings Holofernes' head to Jerusalem and her God. Holofernes next advances towards the Esdraelon plain, near Dothan. Camping for a month between Geba and Scythopolis, he readies his army to attack Judea.

Israel Threatened (4:1–15)

Hearing of Holofernes' attacks, including his sacking of sanctuaries, the Israelites in Judea are terrified; in particular they are 'alarmed both for Jerusalem and for the Temple of the Lord their God' (v. 2). The concern is, moreover, poignant: the people had recently returned from exile and recently rededicated the Temple (v. 3). Although some scholars look on this verse as a gloss, its date is consistent with the purification of the Temple by Judah Maccabee and his supporters (I Macc 4:36–61; 2 Macc 10:3–5).

That the Israelites warn their neighbours, including 'every district of Samaria' (v. 4), poses another historical quandary. Samaria, the former northern kingdom of Israel, was in the post-exilic period commonly Judea's enemy (Neh 4, 13; Ezra 4). The Hasmonean John Hyrcanus conquered Samaria in 107 BCE; it remained in Judean hands until 63 BCE, when Roman hegemony began.

The Israelites together with the neighbouring peoples fortify their villages and stock food, but given Arphaxad's unsuccessful preparations their efforts appear hopeless. Joakim the high priest, together with the Jerusalem council (Gk. gērousia) orders the populations of Bethulia and its environs to guard the hill-country passes and thereby protect Judea. This Joakim is otherwise unknown. Neh 12:26 mentions a high priest Joiakim, but he did not have the military authority that this figure does. The first leader of the post-exilic period with both Temple and military control was the Hasmonean Jonathan (see 1 Macc 10:18–21). The indication that the high priest was in Jerusalem 'at the time' (v. 6) would be gratuitous except during Hasmonean times, when priest-kings involved with military manœuvres did leave Jerusalem. That the gērousia (see also 11:14; 15:8) is replaced by the Sanhedrin (synedrion) under John Hyrcanus II in about 67 BCE may narrow the date of composition.

The Israelites comply with Joakim's request. The men, women, and children of Jerusalem and the resident aliens and servants also fast, don sackcloth, prostrate themselves before the Temple, and drape the cattle (see Jon 3:8) and even the altar (v. 10) with sackcloth. This public expression of religiosity, especially fasting, becomes increasingly common in the post- exilic period, as Esth 4:1–3 and 1 Macc 3:44–8 attest. The people's prayers are both personal and communal: they seek protection lest children be carried off, women raped (lit. for booty), towns destroyed, and the Temple profaned.

The Lord hears their prayers, but it will take several chapters before the people recognize this response. Meanwhile, they continue to fast and wear sackcloth while the priests make burnt as well as votive and voluntary offerings for the house of Israel.

Achior Recounts the History of Israel (5:1–24)

Holofernes is furious upon learning of the Israelite fortifications, including the closing of mountain passes, the garrisoning of hilltops, and the laying of traps in the plains. Summoning the rulers of Israel's traditional enemies, Moab and Ammon, he seeks information from these 'Canaanites' concerning the resistance: their identity, numbers, the size and resources of their army, the source of their power, and their king (v. 3). Achior the Ammonite leader responds with a recitation of Israel's history. However, aside from identifying the people, he answers none of the other questions. The omission is pregnant: their numbers are irrelevant given what one woman can accomplish; their king and the source of their power is, as readers well know, God.

Locating Israel internationally, Achior begins by recounting its Chaldean origins, its rejection of local gods in favour of the 'God of heaven' (v. 8), and its consequent expulsion. He explains that, fleeing to Mesopotamia the people, upon divine command, settle in Canaan where they prosper. Next, moving to Egypt because of a famine, they again prosper until their numbers prompt the king to enslave them. Their God, answering their prayers, afflicts Egypt with plagues. Israel's divine protection will continue as a theme through the speech: it is again confirmed when, as the Israelites flee Egypt, God dries up the Red Sea and leads the people through the Sinai. Driving out the desert peoples, the Israelites inhabit Amorite land. They then cross the Jordan, take the hill country, and expel the Canaanites, Perizzites, Jebusites, Shechemites, and Gergesites (v. 16). With the exception of the Shechemites, the list matches the summary statements of Gen 15:20; Ex 3:8, 17; Deut 7:1; Josh 9:1; 11:3; Ezra 9:1; and Neh 9:8. Perhaps the inclusion of the Shechemites is meant to anticipate Judith's reference (9:2) to Simeon's conquests in Gen 34. Ironically, the existence of Achior, the Ammonite narrator, along with his Canaanite allies, belies any total conquest.

Achior observes that the Israelites are protected as long as they remain faithful to their God. When they sin, they are defeated and taken into exile; their Temple is destroyed, and their towns occupied by enemies. Having repented, the people are returned to their land. Thus Achior advises that, if the Israelites are faithful, Holofernes should change his plans

lest he be defeated and his army become a laughingstock. Although Achior spoke truthfully, Holofernes' officers reject his advice: viewing Israel as weak they assert to 'Lord Holofernes' that his army 'will swallow them up' (v. 24). Ironies abound. First, the people do lack military strength; the officers are correct. Second, it is an Ammonite general, rather than the Israelite high priest, who recognizes the connection between faithfulness and security and so Israel's divine protection. Third, Achior proves prophetic: his comments foreshadow the plot. Fourth, the image of the rapacious army plays upon the trope of food common throughout the book: the people in Bethulia fear starvation, but Judith will avoid Holofernes' table and her servant will transport Holofernes' head in a food bag. Finally, whereas Achior's truthful statements are not believed, Holofernes and his troops will trust the deceiving Judith.

Achior's Fate (6:1–21)

Holofernes' reaction recalls biblical traditions. First, he questions not only Achior's advice, but also his association with Ephraimite mercenaries (v. 2). Ephraim is another name for the northern kingdom of Israel, destroyed in the eighth century by Assyria. Rhetorically, Holofernes thus begins reconstituting the covenant community. Second, he accuses Achior of playing the prophet; whereas biblical prophets typically encourage the repentance of Israel, Achior seeks the protection of the Assyrian general; yet both speak the truth and are usually not believed by rulers. Finally, Holofernes asks, 'What god is there except Nebuchadnezzar?' (v. 2). This god, Holofernes insists, will erase the memory of Israel. Thus Holofernes threatens even more than Nebuchadnezzar commanded.

For his words, Achior is banished from the Assyrian camp and delivered (v. 7, lit. 'they will bring you back') to the hill country of Israel; perhaps the expression indicates that Holofernes thought Achior was already on the Israelites' side. Holofernes then vows to kill him during the siege. The conversation ends with the general's snide observation that if Achior believed his own words he would not be depressed. The Greek is literally 'do not let your face fall' (v. 9); Holofernes unknowingly prophesies his own fate. Achior's presence in Bethulia will in turn prove fortuitous: he will be able to identify the severed head (14:6–8).

Under a rain of stones from the Israelites, Holofernes' slaves bind Achior and leave him near the springs below Bethulia. Achior is then taken by the Israelites to their rulers, Uzziah the Simeonite, Chabris, and Charmis. The rulers summon the elders, and all the young men and women assemble as well. Questioned by Uzziah, Achior relates Holofernes' plans and his own recitation of Israelite history. The Bethulians respond by praying that the enemy's arrogance be punished and the people's plight be pitied. They also commend Achior; Uzziah takes him home and gives a banquet (v. 21, lit. drinking party; one that will stand in contrast to Judith's encounters with Holofernes) where, together with the elders, he prays for help.

Bethulia under Siege (7:1–32)

Holofernes' forces, 170,000 infantry and 12,000 cavalry, as well as soldiers with the baggage train, begin the siege; the Israelites stand guard in fear. On the second day, Holofernes secures the city's water source. Returning to his main forces, he is then visited by the rulers of Israel's traditional enemies, the 'children of Esau' (v. 8), the Moabites, and others who urge him to forgo a battle. (The reference to Esau may refer to the Idumaeans, who were defeated by Judah Maccabee in 164 BCE (see 1 Macc 5:1–5) and then converted to Judaism under John Hyrcanus around 120 BCE.) They advise that he wait until thirst and starvation leave the Bethulian men, women, and children dying in the streets. Prolonged death will be, in the enemy's view, appropriate punishment for the city's rebellion. Agreeing, Holofernes places the area surrounding Bethulia under guard by thousands of Assyrians, Ammonites, and the children of Esau. The plan was to prevent any man (Gk. andros) from leaving (v. 13); keeping the gender-specific Greek permits irony, for no man will leave Bethulia, but only Judith and her female slave.

As Holofernes' generals predicted, the children grow listless, and young men and women faint in the streets. Their courage depleted, and convinced that God has abandoned them for their (unnamed) sins and the sins of their ancestors, the population condemns Uzziah and the elders for not making a treaty with the Assyrians. Better to be slaves, the men insist, than to watch their wives and children die from thirst. The choice of slavery or death evokes the Exodus generation (Ex 14:10–12; 16:3) as well as that of the Jews facing the campaign of Antiochus Epiphanes (1 Macc 1:52–3). The cry that 'God has sold us into their hands' (v. 25; see Esth 7:4) will be corrected by the saving ability of Judith's hand. As the people cry to heaven, Uzziah

exhorts courage. He promises that if there is no rescue after five days, he will accede to their wishes. Dejected, the men return to their posts, the women and children to their homes. For the moment kept apart from men and military concerns, the women will later join Judith as well as their male relatives in the celebration of victory (15:12–13).

Judith's Introduction (8:1–36)

News of the siege finally reaches the widow Judith; separate from the community, she has not been affected by the lack of water nor involved in the political discussions. The narrative keeps her even more detached by inserting a very long genealogy, the longest of any biblical woman, immediately after her introduction: interest shifts from the dying population, who believe they suffer for the sins of their ancestors, to Judith's (righteous) forefathers. With names among the sixteen generations such as Merari, who was a son of Levi (Gen 46:11); Shelumiel, a Simeonite leader who aided Moses (Num 1:6; 2:12; 7:36, 41; 10:19); Gideon, a judge; Elijah, a prophet; Hilkiah, a prophet; Nathaniel, a prophet; and Israel, Judith appears destined for greatness. However, the majority of these names do not represent the well-known figures; at best they are evocative. It is Judith herself who brings the glory to her line.

Even Judith's name, meaning 'Jewish woman', is portentous: this only named woman in the story will both protect and embody the covenant community (Levine 1992). A widow, Judith recalls the God known as the protector of widows (Ps 68:5; Sir 35:15); the covenant community is also depicted as a widow (Isa 54:4; Lam 1:1; 5:3–4). However, Judith's mourning, unlike that of the Judeans in Babylon, is not caused by sin; rather, her husband Manasseh, also from the tribe of Simeon, had died from sunstroke while supervising his servants as they bound barley sheaves. His inglorious death will be repeated by Holofernes, who is also wounded in the head, takes to his bed, and dies (cf. 8:3; 13:2). Manasseh's disgrace may be exacerbated by his name, which he shares with the king to whom is attributed Jerusalem's destruction (see 2 Kings 21:12–15; 23:26–7; 24:3–4).

By marrying endogamously, Judith conformed to recommended practice (Num 36; Tob 1:9). She does not, however, submit to levirate marriage, even though she is childless and the Bethulian leader, Uzziah, is a fellow Simeonite. Yet Uzziah is weak, and Judith neither needs nor desires a spouse. Given her actions, perhaps her widowhood is fortunate; the shame her actions might cause a husband would be enormous. Judith's mourning epitomizes extreme piety. She lives in a rooftop shelter, wears sackcloth around her waist, and dresses in widow's clothes. Every day save sabbaths, new moons, and Jewish festivals, she fasts. Nevertheless, she remains 'shapely and beautiful' (v. 7; see Gen 29:17 concerning Rachel) as well as rich in gold and silver, male and female servants, livestock and fields, all inherited from her husband. Finally, so well known is her piety that 'no one spoke ill of her' (v. 8). This too is ironic; few maintain such spotless reputations. The specified length of her mourning, three years and four months (v. 4) or forty months, may suggest the number of years Israel spent in the wilderness; it also parallels the thirty-four days of the siege of Bethulia (7:20); Judith's sackcloth recollects that of the townspeople (and cattle).

Upon hearing of the people's protest and Uzziah's response, Judith sends her slave, the one in charge of all her property, to summon the town elders. Gender roles are reversed: a female slave commands a major estate; a widow demands obedience from city officials. The Bethulian elders receive from Judith strong rebuke: how do they dare test, place conditions upon, or presume to know the thoughts of God? Rather, the people should continue to pray and await deliverance. Then, like Achior, Judith recites the history of Israel: their ancestors had been punished for worshipping idols, but the present generation has remained faithful. Consequently they must have hope. Judith next observes that, given Bethulia's strategic location, its fall would entail the sack of Jerusalem and the destruction of the Temple. Were the people then taken captive, they would become a disgrace in the eyes of all. Therefore, she concludes, Bethulia must be an example for the rest of Judea: the people should thank God for putting them to the test, just as Abraham was tested at Isaac's near-sacrifice (Gen 22) and Jacob at Laban's house (Gen 28).

Uzziah acknowledges Judith's wisdom yet fails to recognize the import of her words: he first makes the excuse that he was 'compelled' (v. 30) to acquiesce by the people, and then he urges her, perhaps condescendingly, to pray; since she is a 'God-fearing woman' (v. 31) God will send rain at her request. Judith does not deign to respond to these comments. Instead, she announces she will do something memorable 'through all generations' (v. 32). But she

refuses to divulge her plans. Again, the leaders acquiesce; whether out of desperation, because they are cowed by her resolve, because they trust her judgement, or because, as some more cynical commentators suggest, they are happy to be rid of her, is unclear; saying, 'may the Lord God go before you, to take vengeance on our enemies', they depart for their posts. That Judith acts while the ostensible leaders react reverses gender roles; psychoanalytically oriented readers would even suggest that the leaders are symbolically castrated. They will, of course, find a better example for this insight a few chapters later.

Judith's Prayer (9:1–14)

Extended prayers, particularly by women, feature prominently in Hellenistic-Jewish literature; examples include Susanna, Esther (in the Greek Additions), Sarah of the book of Tobit, and the martyr mother of 2 and 4 Maccabees; comparable models include the prayers of Daniel, his friends, and Tobit.

Judith prays at the time of the incense offering in the Jerusalem Temple; the note anticipates her pilgrimage there following Holofernes' defeat. The prayer begins by invoking the God of her ancestor Simeon, omitted from her genealogy. Just as Simeon took revenge on the 'strangers who had...polluted [a virgin's] womb' (v. 2)—the reference is to the sacking of Shechem following the rape of Dinah (Gen 34)—so Judith seeks to protect Bethulia: the city's name evokes the Hebrew word *bĕtûlâ*, meaning 'virgin', and it sounds like *bêt-'ēl* ('house of God') and *bêt-ᶜăliyā* ('house of ascents'). Dinah's name goes unmentioned, and this omission highlights the connection to Bethulia even as it places increasing emphasis on Simeon. Finally, in a reversal of the episode of Dinah, who 'went out' (Gen 34:1) to visit the women of the land but instead was attacked by Shechem, the local prince, Judith will go out to the Gentile camp, where she will 'unman' the general who had planned her seduction. The mention of deception in v. 3 (the prayer utilizes forms of the term 'deceit' four times) hints at Judith's yet unnamed plan.

Her unabashed celebration of the rape (see 4:12) of the Shechemite women, the selling of their daughters into slavery, and the distribution of their property among the Israelites recollects the fear of the Bethulians. That such militaristic ideology appears in the context of theological egalitarianism (Judith notes that God 'strikes slaves as well as princes', v. 3) is typical in ancient narrative. That a woman would praise the victimization of other women is also not atypical (e.g. Judges 5).

Following the recitation of Simeon's victory, Judith prays that God now help her, not a warrior but a widow (v. 4), since God is the ally of the weak (v. 11). Then, typical in Hellenistic-Jewish prayers, she celebrates God's omnipotence, omniscience, and creative powers. Against these attributes, the boasts of the Assyrians are empty and insulting. Because, Judith says, the Assyrians plan to desecrate the Temple, to knock off the horns of its altars with a sword, so God should strike them down. Like Esther, who asks for 'eloquent speech' (Add Esth 14:13), Judith asks for a beguiling tongue ('deceitful words', v. 13). Deceit will be her weapon, so that Holofernes will be killed 'by the hand of a woman' (v. 10; the 'hand' motif appears 9 times more: 2:12; 8:33; 9:2, 9; 12:4; 13:14,15; 15:10; 16:5), as was Sisera by the deceitful Jael (Judg 4–5, see 9). To emphasize the insult, in the Greek Judith speaks not of a 'woman' but uses the generic 'female' (see also Judg 9:54 on Abimelech's fear of the shame of being killed by a woman).

Judith's Plan (10:1–17)

As Esther transforms from mourning to magnificence (Add Esth 15:1), so Judith removes her sackcloth, bathes (how she obtained water given the siege is unexplained), applies perfume, dons a tiara, and puts on the clothes she wore when she celebrated with her deceased husband. Among her accessories are chains, typically translated as 'anklets' (v. 4); Judith may be wearing a step-chain, designed to shorten her stride and make her appear more 'feminine' (Moore 1985; see Isa 3:16). The connection to Isaiah may also suggest that 'earrings' should be translated 'nose-ring' (Moore 1985). Thus she presents a picture of pampered helplessness. On the other hand, perhaps she should be seen as arming herself for battle. Bedecked with jewellery and dressed to kill, she intends to draw the attention of any man who sees her. Then, accompanied by her maid, who carries a skin of wine, jug of oil, and bag with roasted grain, fig cakes, and bread, she ventures to the city gate. Seeing her, Uzziah and the elders are struck by her beauty. Judith orders the gates open, and as she and her maid journey to the enemy camp, the leaders stare after her.

Caught by an Assyrian patrol, Judith is questioned about her nationality. Honestly she replies she is a Hebrew; by using that term rather than 'Israelite', perhaps Judith sought to evoke the time when the people were enslaved in Egypt. Dishonestly she adds that she is fleeing from the Assyrian onslaught and to Holofernes, to whom she will tell the way (v. 13; the term could refer either to the means or to the path) by which he can conquer the hill country. The soldiers, struck by her beauty, promise her protection and flounder in attempts to find the lucky one-hundred to escort her to the general (v. 17).

Judith's Promises to Holofernes (10:18–11:23)

Judith's arrival stirs the enemy camp; the soldiers, judging by her, speculate that they had best destroy all the Israelite men; with 'women like this among them . . . they will be able to beguile the whole world!' (10:19). Holofernes rises from his ornate bed to greet Judith. He and his attendants are also struck by her beauty. After accepting her obeisance, Holofernes exhorts her to courage (11:1), for he has never hurt anyone who chooses to follow Nebuchadnezzar. The comment is disingenuous, given his earlier massacres (2:10; 3:78). He apparently assumes, mistakenly, that she would be afraid of him. As for the siege, he asserts that the Israelites, refusing such loyalty, have brought about their own situation.

Judith's response is a masterpiece of *double entendre*. She states she will speak nothing false to '[her] lord'; she claims that if he follows her advice, 'my lord will not fail to achieve his purposes' (11:6). She then moves to mocking, in stating that because of Holofernes, not only people, but also beasts, cattle, and birds, serve Nebuchadnezzar (11:7). Mentioning Achior in the one verse of this dialogue in which she does not in some degree dissemble, Judith acknowledges the truth of his statements; however, she lies in stating that the people have resolved to sin by eating the first fruits and tithes consecrated to the priests, which the people are forbidden even to touch; they are but waiting for permission from the Jerusalem council (11:12–13). No law forbids such touching, but Holofernes would not know that.

Finally, Judith states that God sent her to accomplish with Holofernes 'things that will astonish the whole world' (11:16). Claiming loyalty to the God of heaven who has given her foreknowledge, she tells Holofernes that she will withdraw to the valley every night to pray, and that God will tell her when the Israelites have transgressed. At that time, she will guide Holofernes to victory. The general along with his attendants is so delighted by Judith's words, and beauty, that he promises her, upon the completion of her prediction, that her God will be his God (see Ruth 1:16), she shall dwell in Nebuchadnezzar's palace (hardly something Judith desires), and her fame shall encompass the world.

Judith in the Assyrian Camp (12:1–9)

Holofernes invites Judith to dine on his 'delicacies' (v. 1, a term not found elsewhere in the LXX, and perhaps suggestive of self-indulgence (Moore 1985)), but he insists on eating her simple meal of kosher food. The general is concerned for her well-being, since there are no other Israelites in his camp who might replenish her supply, but Judith, echoing her prayer (9:10), assures him that the Lord will accomplish by her 'hand' what is planned before her supplies are exhausted. Judith's comments reinforce Holofernes' trust: surely someone so faithful to diet would not lie regarding the Bethulians' transgressions.

Escorted by Holofernes' attendants to her tent, Judith begins the first of a three-day pattern. She sleeps until midnight and at the morning watch, leaves for the valley of Bethulia to bathe herself and pray; ritually pure, and giving the Assyrians no reason to distrust her, she returns to her tent (v. 8).

Judith Serves her Lord (12:10–13:10)

The fourth night, Holofernes holds a drinking party (see 6:21). He asks Bagoas, the eunuch in charge of his personal affairs, to persuade the 'Hebrew woman' (12:11) to join the party; were she not to do so, he and his associates will be disgraced. Were Judith able to refuse his advances (the term refers to sexual intercourse; see Sus 54), she would make him a laughingstock. Bagoas' request conveys a double meaning. Addressing Judith as *paidiskē* (12:13), he could be complimenting her as 'maiden' or insulting her as 'serving girl' or even 'prostitute'. With his invitation that she become as the women who serve Nebuchadnezzar in the palace (11:4) the sexual undertone continues. Unlike Vashti's response to the eunuchs who invite her to the king's banquet (Esth 1), Judith affirms that she will do whatever is pleasing in the eyes of '[her] Lord' and that will be something to boast of until the day of her death.

Seeing Judith reclining on lambskins, Holofernes' appetite becomes uncontrolled: having planned to have intercourse with her from the moment he saw her, he can almost taste conquest. He encourages her to enjoy herself (12:17) and to 'be with us' (see Gen 39:10; Tob 3:8; Sus 20–1); the sexual implications become increasingly overt. Judith feeds his fantasy by accepting his invitation to drink, for 'today is the greatest day of my whole life' (12:18). So delighted is Holofernes that he drinks more than he had ever before consumed. As it is growing late, his retinue leaves, and Bagoas closes the tent from the outside. Dead drunk, Holofernes lies sprawled on his bed. Judith, alone with him (for the full ten verses of 13:1–10), offers one final prayer for strength (she always prays before her major undertakings), yanks the general's sword from the bedpost, grabs his hair, and with two strokes beheads him. This new Jael, who struck the temple of Sisera after giving him something to drink and lulling him into a false sense of safety (Judg 5:26), or new David, who felled Goliath and then decapitated him (1 Sam 17:51), Judith has rescued her people by striking the head of the enemy force. Holofernes' death is, as Judith had prayed, by the hand of a female.

The decapitation has been interpreted both as a perverse sacrifice and as a scene of castration. Regarding the former, Judith does appear to function in a priestly manner: she wears special clothes, bathes for ritual purity, is sexually abstinent, painlessly slits the throat of the victim, receives the aid of a helper in disposing of the victim's parts, and retains a portion for communal (visual) consumption (see 16:18–20). Regarding the latter, the connection of the story of Judith to Gen 34 already provides a reference to genital wounding, and modern commentators read the symbolic value of Judith's action by connecting decapitation to castration (Dundes 1974; Levine 1992).

Quickly leaving the tent, Judith hands Holofernes' head to her waiting servant, who puts it in the food sack. Then the women leave, as they had done the previous nights, 'to pray'. The female donkey, laden excessively with the spoils from Holofernes' tent, will later prove just as doughty as her mistress (Craven 1983).

Return to Bethulia (13:11–20)

Returning to Bethulia, Judith calls the sentries to open the gate, for 'God is with us' (13:11). The entire town, surprised that she has returned and thus, apparently, not as secure in their faith as she, welcomes her. Then Judith publicly praises God, and in testimony to divine protection displays Holofernes' head and the canopy from his bed. Celebrating her action, she repeats her prayer now as thanksgiving, 'The Lord has struck him down by the hand of a woman' (v. 15). Preserving her reputation, she also avers that nothing sinful, defiling, or disgraceful occurred. The people, in response, bless God.

Uzziah then praises Judith as most blessed of all women (see Judg 5:24 and Lk 1:48); his prayer is that her story redound to everlasting honour, for she risked her life to avert disaster. His calling her 'daughter' (v. 18) may be a continuation of his paternalism, his recognition of Judith as a member of Israel's family, a distinguishing of her from Deborah the 'mother' in Israel, or even an indication of her relatively young age. Saying 'Amen', the people assent.

Judith's Military Instructions (14:1–10)

Judith, taking control of military strategy, instructs Bethulia's leaders to hang Holofernes' head from the battlements of the town wall; the heads of Goliath (1 Sam 17:54), Saul (1 Sam 31:9–10); Ahab's family (2 Kings 10:7–8); Nicanor (1 Macc 7:47; 2 Macc 15:35); and John the Baptist (Mt 14:8) were similarly displayed. Then, at dawn, they are to prepare for battle but not descend to the plain. When the Assyrians see the attack forming, they will rush to Holofernes, only to find a decapitated corpse. While they panic, Israel will strike.

Summoned by Judith, Achior faints (lit. falls on his face; see 6:9) at the sight of the head. Revived, he prostrates himself before Judith, blesses her 'in every tent of Judah' (v. 7; see Judg 5:24), and asks her to relate her experiences in the Assyrian camp. When she finishes, the entire town cheers. Seeing what the God of Israel had accomplished, Achior submits to circumcision; his descendants, although Ammonites (see Deut 23:3), remain among Israel 'to this day' (v. 10; see Josh 6:25). Achior is reminiscent of Ruth who, as a Moabite, should also have been prevented from joining Israel. Both leave their people, their gods, and their land, and both affiliate with the covenant community through a female, maternal representative (in Ruth's case, Naomi). Achior has also been seen as an expression of the ideology of proselytism and a type of Abraham (Roitman 1992) and as a type of Barak (White 1992).

Assyrian Defeat (14:11–15:7)

The Israelites, bolstered by Judith's deed, set out to the mountain passes; the Assyrian generals, so convinced of their opponents' weakness that they view the incursion as suicidal (14:13), go to wake Holofernes. Bagoas, expecting to find Holofernes sleeping next to Judith, begins the panic: seeing the headless corpse and then finding Judith's tent empty, he rushes out crying

that the Hebrew woman has shamed the house of Nebuchadnezzar. Headless, the Assyrian soldiers flee to the hills; there the waiting Israelites kill many and pursue the rest to the Damascus borders. Other Israelites, those who had not directly engaged the Assyrian army (the women? the weak?) loot the camp; there being so much booty, every village prospers.

Israel Celebrates Victory (15:8–14)

Joakim the high priest, with the council, arrives to bless Judith, the 'great boast of Israel' who by her own hand (v. 9) rescued her people. Having looted the Assyrian camp, the Israelites present Judith with Holofernes' tent, silver dinnerware, and equipment. Judith loads the spoils on carts and hitches them to her mules. As the women of Israel come to praise her and perform a dance in her honour (see 3 Macc 6:32, 35; 7:16), she distributes branches (thyrsus; see 2 Macc 10:7) to them. These branches were also carried by the Bacchantes, the worshippers of Dionysus. The book of Judith may even be read as a parody of the worship of the wine god: here the decapitated head is of Holofernes, not Pentheus, yet gender roles are still muddled and drunkenness leads to downfall.

Then all the women crown themselves with olive leaves and, with Judith at their head, dance; the men, armed and with garlands, follow her to Jerusalem.

Judith's Hymn (16:1–18)

Judith's hymn, sung also by all the people, is an amalgam of Hebrew and Greek ideas. For the Hebrew tradition, women's celebration of victory in song is a common motif (Ex 15:20–1); Craven (1983) proposes that Jdt 16 parallels Miriam's Song at the Sea (Judg 11:34; 1 Sam 18:6–7). Like the Song of Deborah (Judg 5), Judith's hymn invokes the God who crushes wars and delivers Israel, personalizes the enemy in terms of its threats, and celebrates the heroine's role. Reflecting its Hellenistic context as well as heightening Israel's supremacy, the hymn compares the captivating and successful Judith with the inability of the Titans as well as the Medes and the Persians to defeat Holofernes.

Judith then sings a 'new song' to the invincible God, who can move mountains and melt rocks, whom no one can resist. Emphasizing her maternal role in contrast to her designation of 'daughter' (13:18), she speaks of the threats to her infants, children, young men and women (v. 4). Highlighting again the Hellenistic setting, she exalts herself even over the Titans (v. 6).

Celebrating the Israelites' miraculous victory, she contrasts the Assyrian might with their defeat by 'sons of slave girls' (or young women, v. 12). She ends with the wisdom motif that fear of the Lord is more precious than sacrifice and the apocalyptic motif of the eternal vengeance taken by God against those who rise against Israel.

The image of consigning flesh to fire and worms (see Sir 7:17; 2 Macc 9:9 on the fate of Antiochus Epiphanes; Mk9:48) may suggest a belief in life after death and so be another indication of a relatively late date.

Celebration at the Temple (16:18–20)

In Jerusalem, the victorious people worship; once purified, they sacrifice their burnt offerings, votive offerings, and gifts. While entry into the Temple would require worshippers to be in a state of ritual purity, the explicit mention of this concern underscores two motifs of the book: the interest in Jewish piety and the defeat of the Gentile forces. Judith dedicates Holofernes' property: the bed canopy becomes a votive offering, much like Goliath's sword (1 Sam 21:9) and Saul's armour (31:10). For three months, the celebration in Jerusalem continues.

Epilogue (16:21–3)

Judith returns to Bethulia but not to her rooftop. Many men seek to wed her, but she remains celibate until her death at the age of 105. At this time, she frees her slave (thereby belying artistic renditions which typically depict the slave as much older than Judith) and distributes her property to her near relatives and to those of her husband. Judith is interred in the same burial cave as Manasseh. The people mourn for her seven days (see Sir 22:12), a Second-Temple innovation.

The last line recollects the stories of the Judges: no one threatens Israel again during Judith's lifetime, or for a long time after her death.

REFERENCES

Bal, M. (1994), 'Head Hunting: "Judith on the Cutting Edge of Knowledge"', *Journal for the Study of the Old Testament* 63: 3–34.

Brine, K. R., E. Ciletti, and H. Lähnemann (eds.), *The Sword of Judith: Judith Studies across the Disciplines* (Cambridge: Open Book, 2010).

Camponigro, M. S. (1992), 'Judith, Holding the Tale of Herodotus', in VanderKam (1992), 47–59.

Craven, T. (1983), *Artistry and Faith in the Book of Judith*, SBLDS 70 (Chico, Calif.: Scholars Press).

Dundes, A. (1974), 'Comment on "Narrative Structures in the Book of Judith"', in W. Wuellner (ed.), *Protocol Series of the Colloquies of the Center for Hermeneutical Studies in Hellenistic and Modern Culture*, 11: 28–9.

Haag, E. (1963), *Studien zum Buche Judith: Seine theologische Bedeutung und literarische Eigenart*, Trierer Theologische Studien, 16 (Trier: Paulinus-Verlag).

Levine, A.-J. (1992), 'Sacrifice and Salvation: Otherness and Domestication in the Book of Judith', in VanderKam (1992), 17–30.

Moore, C. A. (1985), *Judith. A New Translation with Introduction and Commentary*, AB 40 (Garden City, N.Y.: Doubleday).

Roitman, A. D. (1992), 'Achior in the Book of Judith: His Role and Significance', in VanderKam (1992), 31–45.

Stocker, M. (1998), *Judith: Sexual Warrior, Women and Power in Western Culture* (New Haven: Yale University Press).

VanderKam, J. (1992) (ed.), *'No One Spoke Ill of Her': Essays on Judith*, Early Judaism and its Literature, 2 (Atlanta: SBL).

Van Henten, J. W. (1995), 'Judith as Alternative Leader: A Rereading of Judith 7–13', in Athalya Brenner (ed.), *A Feminist Companion to Esther, Judith and Susanna* (Sheffield: Academic Press), 224–52.

White, S. (1992), 'In the Steps of Jael and Deborah: Judith as Heroine', in VanderKam (1992), 5–16.

Wills, L. (1995), *The Jewish Novel in the Ancient World* (Ithaca, N.Y. and London: Cornell University Press).

4. Esther (Greek)

ADELE REINHARTZ

INTRODUCTION

A. Background. Vivid testimony to the popularity of the story of Esther in the Hellenistic Jewish milieu is the presence of a lengthy Greek version in the Septuagint (LXX Esther). This is generally considered to be a free translation of a Hebrew text similar to, or perhaps even identical with, the later Masoretic version (MT Esther) included among the Writings of the Tanak. Greek Esther shares with its Hebrew counterpart the engaging characters of Vashti, Ahasuerus, Mordecai, Esther, and Haman, its basic story-line concerning Haman's anti-Jewish plot and the means by which it is thwarted, as well as many of the details of setting, dialogue, and description. Yet the presence of six major sections (the Additions) not attested in the MT (or presumably, its Heb. *Vorlage*), the many smaller additions and omissions, and, most strikingly, the presence of over fifty references to God, transform LXX Esther into a different story. This story contrasts with MT Esther not only in portraying the inner spiritual struggles of its main characters but also in attributing the outcome of the plot to the divine hand.

B. Textual History. 1. In addition to LXX Esther, the story of Esther exists in another Greek version, often referred to as the Alpha Text (AT). The AT is similar though not identical to LXX Esther in the content and wording of the six Additions, but differs substantially from it in those sections that are paralleled in MT Esther. AT Esther is shorter than LXX Esther, due in part to the absence of many personal names, numbers, dates, and repetitious elements. Differences in content also abound. For example, AT omits the theme of the unalterability of Persian law, as well as the aetiology of the Purim festival and the lengthy instructions for Purim observance (cf. AT Esth 8:30, 47). Equally striking is its ending. In contrast to the LXX, in which Addition F concludes the book with a colophon, and the MT, which ends with a testimonial to the greatness and popularity of Mordecai, AT's version of F ends with Mordecai's interpretation of his initial dream (cf. A).

2. How does one account for the similarities and differences among the Hebrew and Greek versions of Esther? The body of LXX Esther is similar to MT Esther (and therefore presumably to the Heb. version available to the Gk. translator) in the content and structure of its story. These similarities support much of LXX Esther being based on a Hebrew original similar to the MT. Significant differences in wording, however, suggest that LXX Esther was a rather free translation of the Hebrew original. Some of the differences reflect stylistic or theological changes, as in 2:20, in which Mordecai's words to the newly chosen queen include not only the instruction to keep her Jewish identity a secret but also to maintain the fear of God and keep God's laws. A number of substantive differences also exist. For example, MT Esth 2:19 refers to the king's 'gate'. Assuming that the translator found 'gate' in his Hebrew version, the Greek

should have read *pulē*. The fact that *aulē* (court) appears instead, however, suggests copyist error (Moore 1977: 175). A similar conclusion emerges from discrepancies within AT and Greek Esther concerning the date of the anti-Jewish pogrom: the thirteenth of Adar, reflecting the Hebrew original (3:12; 8:12; 9:1; E 16:20), or the fourteenth (B 13:6; Moore 1977: 192–3). To the free rendition of Hebrew Esther were added six sections, four of which appear to have been translated from a Hebrew source or sources independent of the Hebrew *Vorlage* of the MT (Additions A, C, D, F) and two of which were probably composed in Greek (Additions B, E).

3. More complex is the relationship between the AT and LXX. Paton (1908: 38) considered AT to be a recension of some form of the LXX, arguing that there were too many parallels between them to view the latter as an independent translation of the Hebrew. Bickerman (1950) suggested that the AT was a recension of an abbreviated Greek Esther, as was Josephus' paraphrase, *Ant.* 11 ∬183–96, which lacks the first and sixth of the Additions which are present in both AT and LXX. More recently Emanuel Tov (1982: 25) has contended that the AT is a translation or more accurately, perhaps, 'a midrash-type of rewriting of the biblical story' which corrects the LXX towards a Hebrew or Aramaic text which differed from the later MT. Fox (1992: 209–10) suggests a similarly complex theory. He posits the existence of a proto-AT, as the Greek translation of an original Hebrew text that differed from the Hebrew text used by the translator of LXX Esther. Proto-AT was then redacted by someone who had access to LXX Esther. Comparing proto-AT and LXX, this redactor drew on the latter to supplement the former. Hence the redactor did not set out to borrow the deutero-canonical Additions but rather moved sequentially through the two texts, transferring material from the LXX to fill the gaps perceived in proto-AT. Most scholars, however, hold to the view that AT is a separate Greek translation based upon a Hebrew or Aramaic text quite different from the MT (Clines 1984: xxv). The Additions in AT were borrowed directly from the LXX, as indicated by the strong verbal agreement between their respective forms of these sections. Hence the AT has become an important factor not only in the textual history of the Greek versions but also in the composition history of the Hebrew Esther (Fox 1991b; Clines 1984; Wills 1990; 1995).

C. The Additions: Introductory Issues. 1. The six major Additions are as follows:

A. Mordecai's dream and the plot of the two eunuchs against the king.
B. The text of the king's edict authorizing the destruction of Persian Jewry.
C. The prayers of Mordecai and Esther.
D. Esther's approach to the king.
E. The edict reversing the decree of destruction.
F. The interpretation of Mordecai's dream, followed by the colophon.

2. There is little doubt that the Additions are secondary to the body of the text, that is, not present in any Hebrew *Vorlage*. The Additions are not found in any of the standard versions of Esther, except those that are recognized as having been based on the LXX, such as Old Latin, Coptic, and Ethiopic as well as *Sefer Jossipon*, a tenth-century work in which Hebrew translations of Josephus' versions of the Additions are present (Moore 1977: 154). Origen (185?–254), in his *Epistle to Africanus*, 3, testifies that several Additions, namely the prayers of Esther and Mordecai (C) and the royal letters (B, E), did not appear in the Hebrew texts current in his own day. Because of their absence from the Hebrew, Jerome (340?–420) placed the Additions at the end of the canonical portion of his own Latin translation rather than in the locations in which they are found in LXX Esther. Finally, Additions A and F (Mordecai's dream and its interpretation) are not present in Josephus' paraphrase of Esther, though this is not evidence that they were not yet in existence at this time.

3. Four of the Additions (A, C, D, F) give clear internal evidence of having been translated from Hebrew (though no Heb. source is extant) while Additions B and E, the royal edicts, are Greek compositions (Moore 1977: 155; 1982: lxx). All six Additions, however, probably had a Jewish origin (Moore 1977: 160), betraying the concerns and perspectives of diaspora Jewry. Their presence in the LXX and the Vulgate led the Christian church to regard them as canonical, and they were sanctioned by the Council of Carthage in 397 CE and by several later councils, including Trent in 1546. Luther and later Protestants, however, considered the Additions to be apocryphal rather than canonical.

D. Date and Provenance. 1. The earliest possible date is that of the final form of the Hebrew version, probably the early Hellenistic period, though earlier versions may have gone back to the late Persian period. The latest possible date is *c.*93–4 CE, when Josephus used Additions B, C, D, and E in his paraphrase. LXX Esther, however, ends with a colophon, which, if authentic, provides the basis for a more precise dating. The colophon attributes the translation to one Lysimachus son of Ptolemy, in Jerusalem, and claims that it was brought to Egypt by a priest and Levite named Dositheus in the fourth year of the reign of Ptolemy and Cleopatra. Questions have been raised about the authenticity of the colophon, based on its content. How can Dositheus be both priest and Levite? Why would the translation have been done in Jerusalem and for whom (Enslin 1972: 19)? Many scholars, however, accept the colophon as authentic. Moore (ibid. 161), for example, argues that the body of the story as well as all the Additions were translated by Lysimachus except B and E, whose original language is Greek. Because Greek was present in Graeco-Roman Palestine, notes Bickerman (1944: 357), LXX Esther is a remarkable and unusual example of Palestinian Greek.

2. If the colophon is authentic, then identifying the reigning Ptolemy provides a date for the Greek translation as a whole. Several Ptolemies had a reign of at least four years and wives named Cleopatra, including Ptolemy XII (77 BCE), favoured by Bickerman (1944), Ptolemy XIV (around 48 BCE), and Ptolemy VIII Soter II, who lived in around 114 BCE, favoured by Moore (1977: 250). In general terms, therefore, LXX Esther may be dated to the late second or early first century BCE.

3. Provenance is difficult to determine, and is directly related to the assessment of the text's purpose. Moore (ibid. 167) suggests that the royal edicts, Additions B and E, may have originated in some sophisticated non-Palestinian centre such as Alexandria, whereas the others may have originated in Palestine, since their theological content is compatible with that of other Palestinian texts of this period such as Daniel, Judith, and some of the Qumran material. Linda Day (1995: 231–2) suggests that the AT, which does not emphasize the Purim festival, may be the product of a Hellenized Jewish community in a diaspora setting, facing the challenge of living Jewishly among a Gentile (i.e. non-Jewish, polytheistic) majority. In contrast, LXX Esther, which retains the MT's emphasis on the aetiology and celebration of Purim, may have been shaped by a Jewish community in Palestine itself or, alternatively, a traditionally observant diaspora Jewish community experiencing increased tension or discrimination at the hands of non-Jews. Such tension would account for the anti-Gentile sentiments expressed in Additions A, C, and F. If so, the story's intent may have been to underscore the necessity of, and dangers inherent in, working with the Gentile power structure while maintaining a primary allegiance to the Jewish people (Wills 1995: 120).

E. Purpose and Genre of LXX Esther. 1. Why did the translator include the six Additions and make the numerous other changes that distinguish LXX Esther from its Hebrew prototype? Most answers to this question reflect upon LXX Esther's inclusion of over fifty references to God, in contrast to MT Esther in which direct divine references are absent. Divine titles and other references to God are found primarily in the Additions. Addition C, which conveys the prayers of Esther and Mordecai, mentions God in virtually every verse, as does Addition F, the interpretation of Mordecai's dream. But the LXX translator has added a number of references to God in the canonical material as well. For example, 2:20, which describes Esther's obedience to Mordecai in her decision not to divulge her ethnic identity, also indicates that she is to fear God and keep his laws even as she commences a new life in the harem of a Gentile king. In 4:8 Mordecai calls upon Esther not only to go to the king but also to call upon the Lord in her effort to avert the evil decree instigated by Haman. Artaxerxes' insomnia is attributed to the Lord in 6:1, while the premonition of Haman's wife concerning Haman's downfall is ascribed to the fact that the living God is with Mordecai (6:13). The Greek word used most frequently in reference to the divine is *theos* (God), with *kyrios* (Lord) as the next most frequent term. Other descriptive terms are 'king' (*basileus*, C 13:9, 15; 14:3, 12), and 'saviour' (*soter*, 15:2). Phrases, such as 'the living God, most high and mighty' (E 16:16), 'the God of Abraham' (C 13:15; 14:18) and 'the all-seeing God' (D 15:2; 16:4) are also employed.

2. The effect of these references, both in their variety and quantity, is to insert God very securely into the story as the one through whom the salvation from danger occurred. God's prominence in the plot is in contrast to the MT's emphasis on the human agents, Mordecai and Esther (Fox 1991a: 273). Moore comments, however, that LXX Esther's religious concerns are reflected

not only in the addition of references to God but also in the emphasis on particular themes, such as God's providential care of Israel (A, F), God's miraculous intervention in history (D 15:8), the efficacy of prayer and fasting (C), and the importance of cult and temple (C 14:9).

3. Clines, however, argues that the function of the Additions is not wholly or even primarily to introduce the explicit language of divine causation into a deficient Hebrew original, but to recreate the book in the mould of post-exilic Jewish history, as exemplified by the books of Ezra, Nehemiah, and Daniel. Just as God stirs up the spirit of Cyrus in Ezra 1:1 and of returnees in 1:5, so does he change the spirit of the king to gentleness in LXX Esther D 15:8 and keep him from sleeping in 6:1. In Dan 2, as in Additions A and F, the meaning of history is conveyed through dreams and their interpretations, while Ezra 9, Neh 1, and Dan 9 contain exemplary prayers of supplication similar to the prayers of Mordecai and Esther in Addition C (Clines 1984: 169–70).

4. In addition to religious motivations and concerns, the Greek translation may have been intended to increase the story's dramatic appeal (Moore 1977: 153). The aura of authenticity is strengthened by Additions B and E which in florid Greek purport to be the texts of royal edicts authorizing (B) and repealing (E) the mass destruction of Persian Jewry. Moore (ibid. 220–2) suggests that Esther's prayer (C) and the detailed description of her emotions and behaviour upon approaching the king (D) combine to make Esther a more realistic character and to suggest a similarity to Judith, a link frequently made by the Church Fathers as well as by contemporary scholars (Day 1995: 222–5). Certainly LXX Esther differs from its Hebrew *Vorlage* in describing the inner thoughts and feelings of its principal characters.

5. Such observations have led some scholars to conclude that LXX Esther is a Hellenistic Jewish novel, influenced by the Graeco-Roman novel genre (Wills 1990; 1995). This suggestion does not rule out a didactic purpose or a historical kernel, but does emphasize the imaginative and entertaining aspects of the book, including its fanciful setting, adventurous tone, and detailed portrayal of its central figures (Wills 1995: 1). Day's (1995: 215–22) study, which focuses on the characterization of Esther in MT, LXX, and AT, argues that there is not enough direct correspondence between these Esthers and the heroines of Greek novels to conclude that LXX and AT were intended as explicit reworkings of their Hebrew prototypes towards the Greek novel genre.

F. Procedure in the Commentary. I. This commentary will focus on LXX Esther, which is the basis of the NRSV translation. The attempt will be made to see it in its own terms, as a text which is coherent in and of itself. Some comparative comments will be made throughout, however, both with respect to the AT and, more frequently, with respect to the MT. Relatively greater attention will be paid to the Additions, but the material which parallels the MT will also receive comment. In keeping with the judgement that LXX Esther is a novel, the primary emphases in the commentary will be upon the development of plot and character. The Additions will be referred to by letter (Additions A to F), but the chapter and verse designations of the NRSV, which are based on Jerome's placement of the Additions at the end of his translation, are also included.

G. Outline.
Addition A: Mordecai's Dream (11:2–12); *The Eunuchs' Plan* (12:1–6)
Setting the Stage (1:1–3:13)
Addition B: The King's Edict against the Jews (13:1–7)
The Plot is Revealed (3:14–4:17)
Addition C: The Prayers of Mordecai and Esther: (13:8–14:19)
Addition D: Esther's Approach to the King: (15:1–16)
The Villain is Unmasked (5:3–8:12)
Addition E: The Official Repeal of the First Edict: (16:1–24)
Events of Adar (8:13–10:3)
Addition F: Interpretation of Mordecai's Dream (10:4–13); *Colophon* (11:1)

COMMENTARY

Addition A (11:2–12; 12:1–6)

(11:2–12) Mordecai's Dream LXX Esther begins with an introduction to Mordecai and a description of his dream. Mordecai is described in terms of his lineage (son of Shimei, son of Kish, of the tribe of Benjamin), ethnic identity (a Jew), home (Susa), status (a great man), occupation (serving in the court of the king), and, perhaps most important, his personal history. This history, repeated in 2:6, links him strongly with the national history of Israel: he was a captive of King Nebuchadnezzar after the Babylonian conquest of Judea in 597–6 BCE. It also, however, poses a chronological difficulty. Even

if Mordecai were only a year old at the time of the Conquest, he would still have been about 115 years old in the third year of Xerxes (1:3) and about 119 years old at Esther's ascension to the throne, when Esther herself would have been approximately 60 years old (1:6). The problem may be resolved in several ways. Perhaps the one exiled was not Mordecai but Kish, his great-grandfather (cf. NRSV translation of MT Esth 2:6). Alternatively, the text may have disregarded historical accuracy in order to connect this story to the larger biblical framework of exile and redemption. Similar 'errors' occur in other Jewish novels from this period, as in Jdt 1:1, in which Nebuchadnezzar is described as the ruler of Assyria based in Nineveh.

This lengthy and detailed introduction to Mordecai serves two purposes. First, it impresses upon the reader his importance, both as a character in the story and as a player in the king's court. Here is a Jew who spends much time in contact with Gentile royalty and officialdom. Second, it indicates that he had previously experienced suffering at the hands of Gentile kings, having been exiled from the land of Israel to Babylonia. The story therefore immediately raises the question of Gentile-Jewish relations and evokes the historical tensions in that relationship.

It is this information, then, that we carry into our reading of Mordecai's dream. In images similar to the prophecies against the Gentiles in Joel 3:2, Zeph 1:15, and Zech 14:2 (Moore 1977: 180), this dream describes a battle between two dragons, and the persecution of 'the righteous nation' at the hands of 'the nations'. When the righteous nation calls for help, however, God intervenes. A great river springs forth, there is light, sun, and the exaltation of the lowly who devour those held in honour. Mordecai realizes that this dream is a foretelling of God's plan, and he continues to ponder it after he awakes.

The dream provides an interpretative framework for the book which it introduces, encouraging us to see it as an apocalyptic battle in which the Gentiles' attempt to destroy the Jews will be thwarted by God, resulting in salvation and the reversal of the status quo in which the Jewish nation is in a subordinate position to others. The broad context of danger and salvation is provided not only by the reference to the Babylonian Exile, but also by the date of Mordecai's dream, namely, the first of Nisan. The main event of this month in the

Jewish calendar is the festival of Passover, which celebrates God's incursion into history to redeem the Israelites from slavery in Egypt. The Exodus is traditionally seen both as the finest example of God's providential care for Israel and as the prototype of future salvation. The allusion to the Exodus is strengthened by the reference to Israel's outcry (11:10), which calls God into action in Mordecai's dream as it does in Ex 3:7 (cf. also Jdt 4:9). Finally, the dream, which is similar to other late biblical dreams such as Dan 2:19, readjusts the focus of the story from that of conflict between Haman and Mordecai, or between Haman and the Jews, or between the Jews and their enemies, to a wider focus, namely, a cosmic conflict between Israel, which is God's righteous nation, and the rest of humankind (Clines 1984: 171–2).

(12:1–6) The Eunuchs' Plan The transition to the second episode is abrupt. Mordecai overhears two of Artaxerxes' eunuchs plotting to lay hands on the king; they confirm their plan to him, and he informs the king, who cross-examines the eunuchs, extracts a confession, and then executes them. Mordecai is rewarded by the king and given a position in the royal court. The entire event is then portrayed as the cause of Haman's grudge against Mordecai. The episode therefore introduces Haman as Mordecai's adversary and provides a rationale for his hatred as well as for Mordecai's position as a courtier, essential for the rest of the story.

In doing so, however, the episode also differs from MT Esther as well as from the LXX story itself as it develops in subsequent chapters. Puzzling is the designation of Haman as *bougaios* (Bougean), a term repeated in 3:1 but completely distinct from the MT identification of Haman as an Agagite. Also unclear is the precise nature of Mordecai's position in the royal court. Is he a courtier before the story begins, as the first episode (11:3) might imply, or does he become so only in this episode (12:5)? Furthermore, the incident contradicts 3:3–6, which attributes Haman's hatred to Mordecai's refusal to bow down. Finally, what is the connection between this episode and the dream? Though the AT 1:11 claims that the eunuchs' plot makes plain to Mordecai the significance of his dream, its full meaning will become clear only as the book proceeds, to be confirmed in Addition F with which the narrative concludes. Nevertheless, the AT 1:18 version of this episode may foreshadow the plot structure of the story

as a whole, by referring to the hatred of Haman and his desire to take revenge on Mordecai and his people (cf. 12:6). Similarly, the otherwise curious comment in AT 11:17 that the king 'gave' (*edoken*) Haman to Mordecai as part of his reward for revealing the plot may intimate Mordecai's later replacement of Haman as the king's right-hand man (AT 8:52; cf. NRSV 8:15; 10:3).

Setting the Stage (1:1–3:13) After these prefatory incidents, LXX Esther begins with the story proper, paralleling the opening episodes of MT Esther. The setting is Susa, the capital of the Persian empire, in the third year of Artaxerxes' reign, that is, one year after the dream recounted in Addition A. The king's lengthy and decadent drinking party is described in lavish detail (1:1–8), with brief mention of the drinking party that Queen Vashti holds in the king's palace for her friends (1:9). Vashti's refusal to answer the king's call to display her beauty before his guests leads in this version, as in the MT, to a lengthy and farcical flurry concerning the potential threat that her insolence poses to family harmony and male authority throughout the kingdom (1:16–22). Only by banishing Vashti and issuing a solemn declaration ordering women to obey their husbands can the king alleviate this threat.

But whereas the Ahasuerus of the MT later remembered, and perhaps regretted, Vashti's fate (2:1; for the rabbis' views on the king's remorse see *Esther Rab.* 5:2), the Artaxerxes of the LXX forgets about her, and, as in MT, proceeds to choose her successor by means of a contest among the eligible young women in the kingdom (2:2–5). Mordecai is reintroduced by his lineage and personal history as a captive of Nebuchadnezzar, but the narrative focus shifts quickly to Esther, Mordecai's beautiful niece and foster-child. Esther immediately begins the elaborate and lengthy preparations which will result in her selection as the new queen. Throughout this process Esther remains silent about her Jewish identity, as instructed by Mordecai (2:10). Her selection as queen is celebrated by the remission of taxes, and predictably, by a lengthy banquet reminiscent of the feast which had led to the banishment of Esther's predecessor.

Three discrepancies between MT and LXX Esther may be mentioned briefly. According to Moore (1977: 186), the translator failed to see the three phrases in MT 2:1 ('he remembered Vashti', 'what she had done', and 'what had been decreed against her') as parallel to one another, and instead thought the latter two to be explanations of the first, concluding therefore that the king remembered Vashti herself no longer. A second difficulty occurs in 2:7. According to the MT, Mordecai took Esther to be his daughter, a more reasonable statement in light of the narrative context than the LXX's assertion that he took her as a wife. In this case too Moore (ibid.) posits the LXX translator's misreading of the Hebrew consonants (bt), which are the same for 'daughter' as for 'house'. A third discrepancy, concerning the length and timing of each candidate's 'audience' (or audition) with the king, does not permit a similar solution. Whereas both the MT and the AT describe the young woman as spending the night with the king, that is, from the evening (MT: 'ereb; AT: hespera) of one day to the morning (MT: bōqer; AT: prōi) of the next, the LXX uses less specific temporal designations that may imply that she spent from the afternoon (deilē) of one day to some unspecified time the following day (hēmera) (2:14). From this language Day (1995: 42–3) concludes that the choice of queen was made on more than sexual ability, since the longer time together would have included meals, conversation, evening's entertainment, possibly a palace tour in addition to a sexual encounter at night. This suggestion seems highly speculative, however, given the indeterminate meaning of the Greek terms and the questionable assumption that the king's sexual activity was limited to the nocturnal hours.

Whether or not other activities took place, it is clear from the processes of preparation and selection that the main criteria for the king's choice were beauty and sexual satisfaction. Hence Esther's success emphasizes not only her beauty but also the fact that she had sexual relations with a Gentile king. Both of these points will be addressed later on in the story (Addition C).

This section also introduces a narrative thread concerning the relationship between Mordecai and Esther. From the beginning of Addition A, it is clear that Mordecai, as Esther's elder and a man, dominates this relationship, a position that is reinforced by his role as her guardian, her obedience to his command not to reveal her people or her country (2:10), and his monitoring of her welfare in the courtyard of the harem (2:11). Her ascension to the throne, however, is a potential threat to Mordecai's dominant position in their relationship. The threat is defused, for the moment, by the narrator who goes beyond the MT in emphasizing that Esther continued to obey Mordecai's word not only in this matter but in all matters pertaining to faith and lifestyle: she was to fear God and keep his laws, 'just as she had done when she was with him' (2:20). Though her wordly status may now surpass Mordecai's, the essential structure of their relationship remains unchanged. At the same time, however, her royal role, along with his own still-vague status as a courtier, provides occasion and justification for Mordecai's continued presence in the king's courtyard.

Mordecai's presence in the royal precincts sets the stage for his discovery of the plot by two of Artaxerxes' eunuchs to kill their master, a fact which Mordecai divulges to Esther who in turn informs the king. The king investigates and hangs the two, and writes a memorandum praising Mordecai, to be put in the royal library. This episode, which parallels closely MT Esther 2:19–23, points to the secondary nature of the similar plot recounted in the second part of Addition A. In this section, however, as in the MT, the intrigue is conveyed to the king by Esther and not by Mordecai directly as in Addition A. This point may be further indication of the adjustment in their relationship wrought by Esther's new role. The reward for Mordecai is, as yet, no more than appreciative recognition.

At this point Haman is again introduced, this time as the newly appointed chief Friend (MT: minister) of the king. His plot against the Jews has its roots in the enmity between Mordecai and Haman. Although this enmity had been attributed in Addition A to Mordecai's action vis-à-vis the two eunuchs, in 3:2–6 it is portrayed as a consequence of Mordecai's refusal to do obeisance to Haman once the latter has been elevated to chief Friend of the king (3:1). Because Mordecai's refusal is apparently related to the fact that he is a Jew (3:4), Haman's (rather exaggerated) response is to plot to destroy all the Jews under Artaxerxes' rule. The fourteenth day of Adar is chosen by lots as the date for the pogrom, and the king is persuaded that the destruction of these people, who observe different laws and 'do not keep the laws of the king', would be to his benefit. Of even greater benefit, perhaps, are the ten thousand talents of silver which Haman offers to the king's treasury. Although the king's comment: 'Keep the money' might be taken to imply altruism, it is not in fact a refusal of the money but rather has the force of 'if you really want to spend your money that way, be my guest' (Moore 1977: 189). The king takes the bait and gives his signet ring to Haman, authorizing him to do whatever he wished with 'that nation' (3:10–11).

Addition B (13:1–7): The King's Edict against the Jews

Addition B purports to be the letter sent throughout the kingdom to put Haman's plan into place. Though broadcast in the king's name, the context, particularly 3:12, makes it clear that the letter has been written by the king's secretaries in accordance with Haman's instructions. The letter features three main themes: first, the ostensible desire of the king to restore peace and tranquility to the land (v. 2), second, the aggrandizement of Haman, the king's second in command who through his superior judgement, goodwill, and fidelity has determined the course of action to assure this result (v. 3), and finally, the vilification of the Jews, that alien and disobedient people wilfully preventing the kingdom from attaining stability (vv 4–5).

Florid and bombastic in style, Addition B has been compared to various other purported edicts recorded in biblical and apocryphal works. Clines (1984: 173) sees B's closest parallel in the letter to King Artaxerxes written by the Samaritans against the inhabitants of Judah and Jerusalem in Ezra 4:11–16. Moore (1977: 199) points out similarities between B and Ezra 4:17–22, the reply of Artaxerxes to the Samaritans (cf. also Ezra 1:2–4; 6:3–12; 7:11–38). He argues, however, that B is closest to, and may have been modelled after, Ptolemy Philopator's letter in 3 Macc 12–29, though LXX Esther as a whole predates 3 Maccabees. Whether or not B drew directly from any of these sources, its effect is to deepen the impression of historicity and strengthen the royal Persian setting of the story (ibid. 159).

The tone, style, and content emphasize Haman's hand in the matter. To a diaspora Jewish reader, however, the accusations against the Jews may have sounded quite familiar, echoing views expressed by various Graeco-Roman writers (e.g. Diodorus; cf. Stern 1974: 180–4). The edict permits the (Graeco-Roman Jewish) audience to compare their experience with that of the Jews in Esther's story, and therefore implicitly encourages a belief that divine deliverance will come to them as it does to the Jews of Artaxerxes' Persia by the end of the story.

The Plot is Revealed (3:14–4:17) The posting of the document throws Mordecai and the Jews of Susa into mourning. Mordecai is not permitted to enter the court in mourning garb, and refuses Esther's offer of other clothing. Under these conditions, the two protagonists must formulate and communicate a plan of action through the good offices of Esther's eunuch Hachratheus. In MT Esther, Mordecai's initial message to Esther is not conveyed in direct speech but is summarized briefly by the narrator who focuses on the courtier's charge that Esther entreat the king on behalf of her people. In LXX Esther, however, the words of Mordecai are given.

While the substance is the same as the summary in MT, in the LXX Mordecai takes this opportunity to remind Esther of 'the days when you were an ordinary person, being brought up under my care', an admonition intended to give greater force to his command to 'Call upon the Lord; then speak to the king on our behalf, and save us from death' (4:8). This speech serves both to maintain the 'proper' hierarchy of relationship between Mordecai and Esther and to emphasize that an appeal to God through prayer is essential if tragedy is to be averted.

The exchanges that follow are similar to those in the MT. Esther expresses her fears of entering the king's presence unbidden, fears that are countered by Mordecai's warning that she herself will not escape; if she does not cooperate, he threatens, help will come to the Jews 'from another [no doubt divine] quarter', but she will perish. Furthermore, Mordecai notes, Esther's ascension to royalty may have been intended for this express purpose. Esther agrees to go, asking only that the Jews of Susa gather and fast for three days and nights, as will Esther and her maids.

Addition C: The Prayers of Mordecai (13:8–18) and Esther (14:1–19)

These prayers were presumably uttered during the three days of fasting stipulated by Esther. Mordecai's prayer, in 13:8–18, praises God as Lord and Creator of the universe and saviour of Israel, and clarifies—perhaps more for the reader's sake than for God's—that his refusal to bow down to Haman was not due to insolence or desire for personal aggrandizement but to a conviction that humans are not to be honoured above God. Mordecai begs God to save Israel, and invokes the memory of the Exodus as the time-honoured paradigm of salvation. After the prayer the narrator notes that all Israel cried out mightily, 'for their death was before their eyes'. This final remark, and indeed the prayer as a whole, are reminiscent of Mordecai's dream in Addition A. The fact that the outcry of 'the righteous nation' inspired God's intervention in the prophetic dream assures the readers that Israel's outcry in Artaxerxes' Persia will also be followed by divine salvation.

These themes are repeated, though in a different context and at greater length, in Esther's prayer (14:1–19). Before praying, Esther changes her royal apparel for 'the garments of distress and mourning', anoints herself with ashes and dung instead of her usual perfumes, and thoroughly debases her physical body (v. 2). More than a sign of mourning, the change in clothing is consistent with her profound feelings of fear and despair as well as with her identity as a daughter of Israel. In contrast to Mordecai's prayer, which focused upon the past and God's love for and redemption of Israel, Esther's prayer is much more personal even when it refers to the same saving events of Israel's history. Esther places her fate directly in God's hands, speaking of what she has heard from infancy concerning God's election of Israel and God's fulfilment of the divine promises to Israel. Attributing Israel's dispersion to sin, she describes the impending destruction as an intensification of Israel's 'bitter slavery' under Persian rule.

The nations, declares Esther, magnify a mortal king. She pleads with God not to surrender the divine sceptre to that which has no being, apparently in oblique reference to Artaxerxes, although no direct claims for the king's divinity are made in LXX Esther. Hence the current crisis is portrayed as a conflict between God, the true king, and Artaxerxes, who claims to be God. Finally, Esther prays for eloquent speech, in what may be an allusion to Ex 3 and Moses, who similarly desired eloquent speech in order to speak to a foreign king (Ex 4:10).

The justification of her behaviour that Esther includes in her prayer seems, like Mordecai's, to be directed more towards the reader (or listener, as during Purim) than to God. An audience dismayed and puzzled by the marriage of a pious Jewish maiden to a decadent Persian king may have been heartened by Esther's declaration of abhorrence of the 'splendour of the wicked', 'the bed of the uncircumcised and of any alien' (v. 15), and the royal crown, which she

likens to a 'filthy rag' (lit. menstrual rag) not to be worn on days of leisure. Esther's royal life is a masquerade. Though she has slept with the Persian king, however reluctantly, she has not violated the dietary laws by eating at the royal table or by drinking the wine of libations to the gods. In this manner readers are reassured that she has maintained her resolve to fear God and keep the divine commandments, as she had been instructed by Mordecai (2:20).

These prayers not only speak of Israel's cry for help, but actually constitute the means by which Israel's representatives, Mordecai and Esther, do so. For this reason Addition C functions as a turning point in the story, just as in Mordecai's dream the nation's outcry is followed by salvation. Secondly, the prayers constitute a blueprint for Jewish behaviour in the Diaspora: Jews should refrain from bowing down to human dignitaries, and should continue to maintain dietary laws, but may compromise even basic principles when necessary for survival, as Esther did in sleeping with an uncircumcised man. Third, the prayers provide a point of comparison with other texts. Clines (1984: 173) compares them to the exemplary prayers of supplication in Ezra 9, Neh 1, and Dan 9, but perhaps more telling are the prayers in Jdt 9 and Tob 3:11–15 in which faith in God's saving acts is a central theme. Judith, like Esther, is a woman of prominence, the only person capable of saving her people from annihilation. Her act too is preceded by a prayer, and involves mortal danger, as well as a (potential) erotic connection to the Gentile leader, Holofernes, whom she must confront and deceive. There are differences, of course. Judith's act is more dramatic; Esther's enemy is not the king whose anger she fears but his viceroy, who engineered the plot to kill the Jews. Nevertheless, these two women protagonists are cut from similar cloth (cf. Day 1995: 222–6; Moore 1977: 167; Enslin 1972: 15–21).

Addition D (15.1–16): Esther's Approach to the King

This Addition is an expansion of the brief description of Esther's approach to the king in MT Esth 5:1–2. After three days of fasting and prayer, Esther prepares herself by changing her clothing. In this act Esther is similar to the Tamar of Genesis (34:14, 19), as well as to Judith (Jdt 10:3–4) and Asenath (*Joseph and Asenath*, 14:14–15) who change their clothing as deliberate strategies in their encounters with the men who figure prominently in their plans. Just as she had to wear humble clothes when approaching God, her true King, so must Esther wear resplendent clothing to approach the earthly king whom she feared more, despite her own royal status.

After invoking God's aid, Esther, supported by two maids, approaches the king, who, seated on a royal throne, clothed in the full array of majesty, and covered with gold and jewels, appears 'most terrifying' to her (v. 6). Initially, her fears about approaching him unsummoned seem to be justified: he responds to her approach with fierce anger. Esther saves her skin by behaving like the genteel woman she has dressed herself to be: she faints and collapses. God then changes the king's spirit to gentleness. Artaxerxes takes her in his arms till she comes to, comforts her with gentle words, and reassures her that she will not die 'for our law applies only to our subjects' (v. 10). Perhaps in explanation of her collapse, Esther describes the king as an angel of God who inspires fear at his glory, wonderful, and with a countenance full of grace, and promptly faints a second time, inspiring further attempts to revive and comfort her.

The king's reference to himself as Esther's 'brother' (LXX; NRSV marg.) in this exchange is taken by most interpreters as a general term of warmth, though Brownlee (1966: 168) argues that in Egypt married couples referred to each other as brother and sister. In addition, there may be some irony in this form of address, given their ethnic differences and her extreme fear in approaching him.

A more pressing question, however, is why indeed did Esther faint, not once but twice? Moore (1977: 218; cf. Day 1995: 102), reasonably, comments that three days of fasting may indeed have weakened Esther, rendering her inadequate to the challenge of overcoming her fear, the challenge for which she had begged for divine assistance. Noting the parallels between Esther's description of the king and biblical portrayals of kingship, including Gentile monarchs (1 Sam 29:9; 2 Sam 14:7, 20; 19:27; Ezek 28:2), Brownlee (1966: 164–70) suggests that despite the disclaimers in her prayer, Esther may have felt herself to have been in the presence of the angelic or divine, in which case fainting was not an inappropriate response. A final suggestion, plausible in light of the book's soteriology, is that Esther's fainting may be attributed to God, who may have required some human act as a catalyst for

overcoming the king's anger and gaining her the sympathetic hearing necessary for turning the plot of the story.

(5:3–8:12) The Villain is Unmasked The conflict between Haman and Mordecai comes to a head in this section. Just at the moment that Haman is ready to ask the king for permission to hang Mordecai on the giant gallows that he has prepared, the king, during a bout of insomnia, comes across the memorandum concerning the assassination plot which Mordecai had foiled and seeks Haman's advice on how to honour his saviour. Instead of executing Mordecai as planned, Haman must honour him as he himself would have wished to be honoured (6:1–13). Recognizing that Mordecai has the living God with him, Haman's friends and wife see this act prophetically, as a sign of Haman's future downfall. Shortly thereafter Esther unmasks Haman as villain at the second of two dinners at which the king and Haman are her only guests. Like her prayer in Addition C, Esther's plea to Artaxerxes is phrased in terms which emphasize that Haman's wicked plot threatens not only the Jewish people, but also Esther herself, as a Jew. Both plot lines are neatly resolved when Haman is hanged on the gallows which he had prepared for Mordecai and the king authorizes Esther to write a decree replacing the one dictated by Haman (7:7–10, 8:1–12).

In a reprise of 3:12–13, the secretaries are summoned to write an edict, to be broadcast throughout the empire. The date, the twenty-third of Nisan, recalls both the month of the Exodus and that of Mordecai's dream in Addition A, and hence is associated with the theme of divine salvation. The edict is written with the king's authority, sealed with his ring, and conveys his command that the Jews observe their own laws and give themselves free rein in defending themselves against attack. The context makes it clear, however, that the letter was initiated by Esther (8:5), and written by her and Mordecai in the king's name (8:8), a point which seems to have been overlooked by scholars (such as Moore 1977: 234; Wills 1995: 126) who attribute the letter directly to the king.

In this section, as in its parallel in MT Esther, the king gives Mordecai Haman's ring and his position as the king's righthand man, and Esther gives him authority over Haman's estate (8:2). Although the king's command to write a new edict and seal it with his ring is addressed only to Esther (8:7; in contrast to the MT in which both Esther and Mordecai are named), the fact that the verbs 'write' and 'seal' in 8:8 are in the plural indicates that both Esther and Mordecai are intended. In this section, therefore, Mordecai not only replaces Haman in relationship to the king, but also achieves parity with Esther, thereby eliminating the discrepancy between their relative status in the social realm and their father-child relationship in the private and religious spheres. The portrayal of Esther also changes, however. No longer fearful and coy, Esther is given a measure of royal power, which she exercises along with Mordecai in the composition of the edict.

Addition E (16:1–24): The Official Repeal of the First Edict

Similar in style to Addition B, Addition E undoes the substance of the earlier edict and carries forward the divine plan for the rescue of the Jews. Most of the Addition is devoted to the discrediting of Haman, beginning with a lengthy reflection on the fact that some people who receive great honours respond by plotting evil against their benefactors and the innocent (vv. 2–6). The real threat to the peace and stability of the kingdom comes not from the Jews but from Haman. Haman was not a Persian by birth but an alien devoid of Persian kindliness, whose real goal was to use his position of power to transfer the kingdom of the Persians to the Macedonians (v. 14). The second theme, the role of the Jews, is dealt with rather quickly, by dismissing Haman's earlier charges and emphasizing the righteousness of the Jews' laws and their status as 'children of the living God, most high, most mighty', who also directs the affairs of the Persian kingdom (vv. 15–16). Finally, the edict orders the populace not to put the earlier letters into execution, since their author himself has been executed. This new edict, which must be circulated and displayed, allows for the Jews to live under their own laws, and to be given reinforcements so that they may defend themselves from attack. The thirteenth day of Adar is to become a day of joy rather than destruction. The edict concludes by specifying this day as a festival day not only for the Jews but for the entire empire, as 'a reminder of destruction for those who

plot against us' (v. 23) and promises swift punishment for those who transgress its stipulations (v. 24).

Though ostensibly addressed to the Persian empire by Artaxerxes, the edict, like the prayers of Mordecai and Esther, is more plausible as a message from the implied author to the diaspora Jewish audience of Greek Esther itself. As such it sanctions the celebration of Purim, celebrates the reversal of fortunes and the fulfilment of Mordecai's dream, and, perhaps most important, stresses that Jews should live by their own excellent laws even in the Diaspora. This focus on the reader may also explain the edict's references to Haman as a Macedonian, which contrast with the earlier, obscure descriptions of Haman as a *bougaios* (A, 12:6; 3:1). Moore suggests that this variation is an updated term of reproach, meant not to provide historical accuracy but to identify Haman as a despised person from the point of view of the reader. The label can be used to support a Hasmonean date for the book, since the term 'Macedonian' would have been a term of disparagement familiar to readers in this period (Moore 1977:178, 236).

(8:13–10:3) **Events of Adar** This section describes the posting of the letter, the elevation of Mordecai, and the conversion of many Gentiles, albeit out of fear. The narrator apparently delights in the Persians' fear of the Jews, and of Mordecai in particular, whose name was to be held in honour throughout the kingdom (9:3). Esther continues to exercise a role as royal counsel, advising the king to let the Jews continue their killing on the morrow, and to hand the bodies of Haman's sons over to the Jews for hanging. These two points are responsible for Esther's post-biblical reputation as a bloodthirsty woman on a par with Jael of Judg 4–5 (ibid. 242). The narrator notes that on the next day 300 people were killed but no looting occurred, while in the countryside 15,000 Gentiles were killed (compared to 75,000 according to the MT), without plundering. The description, institution, and validation of the annual festival, whose main features are merrymaking and the giving of gifts to friends and to the poor, are associated with both Mordecai and Esther, implying their parity not only *vis-à-vis* the Persian kingdom but also as leaders of Persian Jewry.

Addition F: Interpretation of Mordecai's Dream (10:4–13); Colophon (11:1)

The explanation of Mordecai's dream in its general outlines is no doubt superfluous to the reader/listener who has been led to recognize the Purim story itself as the fulfilment of that dream. Nevertheless the interpretation of its details provides a satisfying closure to the narrative. The river in the dream is Esther, while the two dragons are Haman and Mordecai. These identifications lead Moore (ibid. 181) to conclude that Esther is the human hero of the piece, rather than Mordecai, whom he sees as the hero of the MT Esther. The righteous nation is Israel; the surrounding nations—the Gentiles—are her enemies. The Lord rescued Israel, an event which led to joyous celebration on the thirteenth and fourteenth days of Adar. The dream and its interpretation, as introduction and conclusion, therefore provide a soteriological framework for the story as a whole, placing the events in the context of God's love for Israel and the divine propensity to come to Israel's rescue from persecution and destruction at the hands of idolatrous enemies.

Addition F concludes with a colophon that purports to provide the details of the text, its date, and its translation. Whether or not the colophon is authentic, and can therefore be used for dating the text, it, like Additions B and E, creates an aura of authenticity as well as providing explicit acknowledgement of the status of this storyas a translation of a Hebrew original. The colophon is absent from AT, which follows the interpretation of Mordecai's dream with a concluding statement concerning the j oyous celebration on the fourteenth and fifteenth days of Adar.

Conclusion

LXX Esther, like any translation, is also an interpretation of its sources. The six Additions as well as numerous smaller changes redraw the main characters, amplify some of the details, and, most noticeably, explicitly situate the story-line in the context of the covenantal relationship between God and Israel. While comparisons of LXX Esther with the versions of the Esther story in the MT and the AT are fruitful (cf. Day 1995; Moore 1977), LXX Esther repays consideration in its own right, clearly reflecting the Hellenistic Diaspora situation and commonality of genre and concerns with other narrative works from the last two centuries BCE. The social dilemmas faced by Jews in the Diaspora, the importance of family, group identity, religious practice, the theological conviction that God continues to care for God's people in exile, and the necessity of compromise all figure in this story, contributing to its ancient popularity and its continuing relevance.

REFERENCES

Bickerman, E. J. (1944), 'The Colophon of the Greek Book of Esther', *JBL* 63: 339–62.

—— (1950), 'Notes on the Greek Book of Esther', *PAAJR* 20: 101–33.

Brownlee, W. H. (1966), 'Le Livre Grec d'Esther et la Royauté Divine', *RB* 73: 161–85.

Clines, D. J. A. (1984), *The Esther Scroll: The Story of the Story* (Sheffield: JSOT).

Day, L. (1995), *Three Faces of a Queen: Characterization in the Books of Esther* JSOTSup 186 (Sheffield: Sheffield Academic Press).

Enslin, M. S. (1972), *The Book of Judith* (Brill: Leiden).

Fox, M. V. (1991a), *Character and Ideology in the Book of Esther* (Columbia, S.C.: University of South Carolina Press).

—— (1991b), *The Redaction of the Books of the Esther: On Reading Composite Texts*, SBLMS 40 (Atlanta: Scholars Press).

—— (1992), 'The Redaction of the Greek Alpha-Text of Esther', in Michael Fishbane et al. (eds.), *Sha'arei Talmon: Studies in the Bible, Qumran, and the Ancient Near East presented to Shemaryahu Talmon* (Winona Lake, Ind.: Eisenbrauns), 207–20.

Moore, C. A. (1977), *Daniel, Esther and Jeremiah: The Additions*, AB 44 (New York: Doubleday).

—— (1982) (ed.), *Studies in the Book of Esther* (New York: Ktav).

Paton, L. B. (1908), *The Book of Esther*, ICC (Edinburgh: T. & T. Clark).

Stern, M. (1974) (ed.), *Greek and Latin Authors on Jews and Judaism*, 1: *From Herodotus to Plutarch* (Jerusalem: Israel Academy of Sciences and Humanities).

Tov, E. (1982), 'The "Lucianic" Text of the Canonical and the Apocryphal Sections of Esther: A Rewritten Biblical Book', in Shemaryahu Talmon (ed.), *Textus: Annual of the Hebrew University Bible Project*, 10 (Jerusalem: Magnes), 1–25.

Wills, L. (1990), *The Jew in the Court of the Foreign King: Ancient Jewish Court Legends*, HDR 26 (Minneapolis: Fortress).

—— (1995), *The Jewish Novel in the Ancient World* (Ithaca, N.Y.: Cornell University Press).

5. The Wisdom of Solomon

WILLIAM HORBURY

INTRODUCTION

A. Teaching. 1. This book, preserved in Greek and in versions made from the Greek, forms a high point not only in ancient Jewish literature but also in Greek literature as a whole; yet it belongs above all to the sapiential stream of Jewish biblical tradition, and crowns the series of earlier biblical wisdom-books: Proverbs, Job, Ecclesiastes, Ecclesiasticus (Sirach). In the early church it was one of the books linked with Solomon, together with Proverbs, Ecclesiastes, the Song of Songs, and the non-canonical *Psalms, Odes,* and *Testament of Solomon* (ET in Sparks 1984: 649–751); but Solomonic authorship was often questioned, and some ascribed Wisdom to the author of Ecclesiasticus (Jesus son of Sirach of Jerusalem, early 2nd cent. BCE), or to the Jewish philosopher-exegete Philo of Alexandria (*c.*25 BCE–*c.*50 CE) (Horbury 1994a; 1995).

2. The Wisdom of Solomon begins with instruction to kings on wisdom, as regards the suffering and vindication of the righteous (see chs. 1–5); the doctrine of immortality is presented as the confirmation of the righteousness of God. From these chapters, which are close to the judgement scenes in 1 Enoch and the *Psalms of Solomon,* and opposed to the this-wordly emphasis of Ecclesiastes and Sirach, the church drew a theology of martyrdom and an interpretation of the passion of Christ. Then in chs. 6–10 King Solomon emerges by implication as the speaker, telling the Gentile kings how he prayed when young for the heavenly gift of wisdom, as is related in 1 Kings 3 and 2 Chr 1. Recollections of his ardent love for wisdom are mingled with praise for her in terms that appropriately suggest 'the spirit of wisdom and understanding' promised to the Davidic king (Isa 11:2); she is an all-pervasive loving spirit issuing from God, the fashioner and guardian and renewer of all things as well as the giver of knowledge and the guide of life. Wisdom is set in the divine realm, following Prov 8 with the young Solomon; these chapters differ markedly from Eccl 1–2, in which the old king views wisdom as an ultimately pointless human acquisition. Lastly, chs. 11–19 praise God through a meditation on the Exodus that inculcates repentance and faith and defends providence (14:3; 17:2) and the election of God's 'people' (12:19, etc.); a digression (chs. 13–15) on the origins of Gentile idolatry has affinities with the beginning of Romans. Throughout chs. 11–19 the writer continues to address to God, rather than the kings of the earth, which was begun in ch. 9, and wisdom is named only in one passage (14:2, 5); these chapters recall Sirach in their theodicy (Crenshaw 1975) and in their dependence on the biblical histories, but otherwise they show less kinship with the sapiential books than with Jewish exegesis of Exodus and Christian paschal homily (17:1).

3. Four great characteristics of Wisdom's teaching can be discerned throughout. First, it has an element of mysticism, in the sense of the soul's quest for the divine (Wis 2:13; 13:6), especially divine wisdom (7:10; 8:2); conversely, the immanent deity is the lover of souls (1:4; 7:27; 11:26–12:1; 16:21). Secondly, to some extent by contrast, it is also focused on the people of God (9:7; 12:19, etc.), although Israel is not named— much as in 1 Peter the church is central, but the word *ekklēsia* is lacking. A link with the mystical element is formed by verses on inspired or ecstatic communal praise (10:21; 19:9). Thirdly, it is permeated by zeal for righteousness (Wis 1:1) in collective and individual morality; God helps the righteous, divine punishments are just (5:20; 12:15; 16:24), and God's people and their heroes are exemplars of virtue. Lastly, in accord with its emphasis on the nation (Barclay 1996: 181–91), Wisdom shows deep familiarity with Scripture and interpretative tradition; artistic allusion is pervasive (Chester 1988). Many biblical characters are portrayed, but, like Israel, they are all unnamed (Wis 4:10).

4. In biblical style, but with a tinge of philosophical language, Wisdom welcomes a number of Greek philosophical conceptions. Broadly speaking, the book sounds both Platonic and Stoic. Its mystical strand has affinities with Plato; 'understanding [*phronēsis,* cf. 7:7] would arouse terrible love [cf. 7:10; 8:2], if such a clear image of it were granted [cf. 7:22–8:1] as would come through sight' (Plato, *Phdr.* 250D). Wisdom is more particularly indebted to Plato, perhaps through intermediaries, on the virtues, pre-existence, primal matter, and beauty (8:7, 19; 11:17; 13:3), and in the treatment of the soul (Wis A.3; 8:20; 9:15–17; 15:8); but Plato's theory of archetypal ideas (Stead 1994: 18–21), which is central in Philo's theology, here stays in the background (9:8; 13:7). Wisdom's own central conception of a beautifully ordered world guided by immanent spirit (Wis 1:7; 8:1; 19:18) has antecedents in the biblical sapiential tradition (Wis A.1; A.3), but comes mainly from Plato as interpreted by the Stoics.

5. The book defends providence, afterlife, and the reward of virtue. These Platonic themes became central in the Stoic and Epicurean philosophies of the second and first centuries BCE (Acts 17:18; Stead 1994: 40–53). Philosophers then nurtured by the Greek cities of Syria and Palestine include the Stoics Poseidonius of Apamea and Antiochus of Ascalon, and the Epicurean Philodemus of Gadara; all drew upon the classical philosophers, and were influential among educated Romans as well as Greeks (Hengel 1974: 86–7). Wisdom takes, broadly speaking, the Stoic side; Stoics argued for a universe pervaded and directed by a vital force (Wis 1:7), and the survival of righteous souls, but Epicureans envisaged non-intervening deities and souls which perished with the body. In the first century CE Josephus (*Vita*, 12) compares the Pharisees to the Stoics, and his outline of Sadducaic opinion recalls Epicureanism.

6. 'Wisdom' itself (Gk. *sophia*, Lat. *sapientia*, 1:4, etc.) was a weighty term in philosophical vocabulary. In Plato it included morality and the art of government (*Rep*. 4.6, 428B–429A), in Aristotle it was identified with abstract philosophy and knowledge of principles as opposed to practice (*Eth. Nic.* 6.7, 1141^b), but its practical moral association was strong among the Stoics. They linked *sophia* and *sapientia* with their ideal figure of the imperturbably virtuous Wise, the true king among mortals, who goes 'where heavenly wisdom leads' (Horace, *Epistles*, 1.3.27).

7. Platonic and Stoic *sophia* therefore readily converged with the moral as well as intellectual portrayal of *sophia* in the biblical wisdom-books (Wis A.3; A.9). Educated Jews were aware of possible associations between Judaism and the Greek schools of thought, as can be inferred from Josephus. Thus Aristobulus, in the Egyptian Jewish community of the second century BCE, mentions Pythagoras, Plato, and the Aristotelians in his fragmentarily preserved Pentateuchal comments, and urges that the philosophers drew on Moses (Hengel 1974: 163–9; Collins 1985; Barclay 1996: 150–8; Wis 6:12). Wisdom does not give names, but shows similar awareness, especially with regard to Stoicism. Like Aristobulus, but implicitly, it urges that the wisdom of biblical tradition anticipates

and includes the philosophical truths and virtues (7:17–27; 8:7); at the same time it implicitly modifies biblical tradition, and integrates it fully into Hellenic culture (Chester 1988: 164). In the church this aspect of the book led to assertions (in line with the earlier Jewish argument seen in Aristobulus) that Wisdom itself was the original source of Platonic and Stoic doctrines (Wis 7:24; 11:17).

8. The philosophy of Wisdom leads it also to differ, on points debated by early Christians, from what in the end became the most approved church teaching. The soul is preexistent and not originated in connection with conception (Wis 8:19); the world is made from pre-existent matter rather than *ex nihilo* (Wis 11:17); and the soul's future life is described (A.9) without reference to the body (Stead 1994: 29–30).

9. Within the Apocrypha the philosophical theology of Wisdom recalls 2 Maccabees, which is likewise concerned with martyrdom and afterlife, but speaks of resurrection (*anastasis*) rather than immortality (*athanasia*); Wisdom expresses future hope just as vividly, but seems to expect a spiritual rather than carnal revival of the righteous (Wis 3:7). The personified wisdom of Wis 7–10, linked with the wise king of Israel, compares and contrasts (Wis 7:22) with that of Sir 24 and Bar 3:9–4:2, linked with the Jerusalem temple and identified with the Pentateuchal law; all three passages are patriotic Israelite developments of the goddess-like figure of cosmic wisdom in Prov 8–9 and Job 28, could have been associated by Greekspeaking readers with the philosophical and moral overtones of *sophia* noted above, and owe something to contemporary portrayals of Isis (Knox 1939: 69–81; Wis 7:22). The cosmos in Wisdom is a world of spirits, good and bad, including 'the spirit of the Lord' (1:7), 'angels' (16:20), and 'the devil' (2:24), as is already the case in the LXX, and wisdom herself is spiritual, as already noted (7:22–7); correspondingly, human beings are envisaged above all as 'souls' (2:22, etc.; Wis A.3), which are probably held to be pre-existent, as in Plato and Philo (Wis 8:19). In assessment of this spiritual aspect of Wisdom it is noteworthy that, for Stoics, the world-soul and individual souls were material, even if superfine (7:22–4; Hengel 1974: 199–200). Philosophy had links with widespread conceptions of energetic good and evil spirits (P. Merlan in Armstrong 1970: 32–7), and spiritual immortality (Wis 3:7) need not have seemed insubstantial by contrast with resurrection, which could itself be envisaged spiritually (Mk 12:25).

10. Among the NT books Wisdom has affinity not only with Romans (Wis A.2) but also with the speeches in Acts on repentance and faith, with the sapiential morality of James, and with the vindication of righteous suffering in 1 Peter. In the treatment of wisdom and *logos* as intermediaries (Wis 7:22; 9:1) Wisdom also shows kinship with the Christology of word, spirit, radiance, and image in John, Paul, and Hebrews. From a wider range of ancient Jewish literature, Philo's philosophical exegesis of Scripture, Josephus's presentation of the Jewish schools of thought as philosophies, and 4 Maccabees on Jewish martyrdom as adherence to true philosophy, all broadly resemble Wisdom as Jewish expositions of Judaism using Greek philosophical terms. It should be stressed, however, that all these NT and other works are written in Greek prose, and are far removed from Wisdom's adherence to biblical poetic style (Wis B.1). The portrayal of Christianity as a philosophical school by the Apologists, such as Justin Martyr (later 2nd cent.) and Tertullian (early 3rd cent.), adapts the philosophical interpretation of Judaism attested in Wisdom (Wis A.4–8). Similarly, rabbinic biblical exposition current in third-fifth-century Galilee and embodied in the Talmud and Midrash, although it is handed down in Hebrew and Aramaic rather than Greek, evinces a debt to philosophical vocabulary and Greek conceptions of a spiritual cosmos which once again recalls Wisdom.

11. Affinities between Wisdom and Christian books later than the NT emerge in 1 *Clement* (Wis 4:10) and in the mythopoeic treatment of wisdom's love for the Father (cf.8:4; 9:9) by Valentinus and his school, as recounted in the later second century by Irenaeus (*Haer.* 1.2). Signs of Wisdom's direct influence on the church are evident from this time onwards (Wis C.1). Wisdom helped to mould not only dogmatic and moral theology, but also baptismal instruction, hymnody, and prayer. The philosophic and exegetical treatment of wisdom as intermediary in Wisdom 7–10 was joined with the Pauline view of Christ as the wisdom of God (Wis 10:1); Christological indebtedness to Wisdom is especially striking in the early third-century Origen (Wis 1:4; 7:22). Wisdom also formed the clearest biblical source for the notion of pure universal love permeating and ordering the cosmos (Wis 7:22–8:1; 11:20–12:1; 14:3; 16:7,12).

12. In the fourth century Athanasius (*Festal Letter,* 39) put Wisdom first among those books which (he says) are not canonical, but were approved by the fathers for reading to newcomers (catechumens). Jerome (Wis B.1) likewise stressed that Wisdom was outside the canon, but endorsed the reading of this and other approved extra-canonical books for edification, as is recalled in the sixth of the Thirty-Nine Articles (1562). Augustine, by contrast, worked for church recognition of these approved books as canonical, and noted Wisdom's prophetic witness to Christ (*De civ. dei,* 17.20). The later Christian West found Wisdom congenial, as medieval commentaries show (Smalley 1986); the book's influence on forms of prayer (Wis 1:7; 3:7; 8:1; 9:1; 11:24; 16:6, 20) appears at its most famous in the antiphon O *Sapientia* (8.1). The old acclamation of Christ as the wisdom of the Father's heart, echoed in the poems of Prudentius (end of 4th cent.), was reunited with mystical passages of Wisdom in the warm Christ-mysticism of the Swabian Henry Suso (Seuse) (*c.*1295–1366); in the language of courtship as well as piety he called himself 'servant of the eternal wisdom' (Wis 7:10; 10:9).

B. Form. 1. 'The very style has a scent of Greek eloquence', as Jerome noted in the letter introducing his Latin translation of the books of Solomon from the Hebrew (Weber et al. 1975: ii. 957, lines 17–18). The scent arises mainly from literary and philosophical vocabulary (Wis A.4), occasional patches of rhetorical style, and thematic contacts with such typically Greek concerns as consolation (3:13–4:19). Nevertheless, the form of Wisdom belongs chiefly to Hebrew literature. It recalls the third- to first-century BCE Judean continuation of Hebrew wisdom poetry attested in the Dead Sea scrolls, including the apocryphal Ps 154 (Vermes 1997: 302–3, 393–425; van der Woude 1995), and it is comparable with the form of the Greek *Psalms of Solomon* (*c.*60–40 BCE), for it resembles the translations of Psalms, Proverbs, and Sirach preserved in the LXX, and replicates in Greek the stressed parallelistic verse of the HB. This would not necessarily be expected of a Jewish poetical book current in Greek. Jews loved Greek verse in the quantitative metres of classical poetry, as literature and inscriptions composed or sponsored by Jews attest (Horbury and Noy 1992: pp. xx–xxiv); the moral hexameter *Sentences* of Ps.-Phocylides (van der Horst 1985; Barclay 1996: 336–46) form a metrical Jewish work broadly comparable with Wisdom. The classical metres are set aside in Wisdom, however, for a form redolent of ancestral Jewish Scripture, in line with the book's strong national feeling (Wis A.3).

Indeed, it is not impossible that Wisdom 1–10 is a version of a text also issued in Hebrew or Aramaic. On the other hand, Wisdom's occasional transitions from biblical parallelism to hymn-like prose, such as the list of epithets in 7:22–3, sometimes give it a mixed Hebraic and rhetorical style like that seen on a small scale in the hymn of Rev 15:3–4.

2. A formal feature visible throughout the book is correspondence between speeches or descriptions. Within sections, units of text have been arranged to show parallels of sense and to return to an opening theme (as with the two speeches of the ungodly, 1:16–2:24; 5:1–23, and perhaps also with the four distinct passages that can be discerned between them). Suggested divisions naturally differ, but there is a good case for some intentional correspondence. The prevalence of this structural care (Grabbe 1997: 18–23) then recalls the prevalent consistency of style, but it does not cancel the marked thematic variation between chs. 1–10 and 11–19 (Wis A.2). These sections probably represent at least two separate compositions (Wis 9 introduction; 11:2), following the same conventions but not necessarily written by the same author.

3. It is correspondingly difficult to name a Greek literary genre to which the book in its present state belongs, although Jewish wisdom literature in general has some kinship with the proverbial and moralistic literature of the Greeks (Wis A.4–8). If lack of Greek metre is overlooked, Wisdom broadly recalls the didactic poetry on philosophical and moral subjects which flourished in Hellenistic authors such as Aratus (3rd cent. BCE), found a Jewish echo in Ps.-Phoc, and was later imitated by Roman poets such as Lucretius, Virgil, and Horace (Wis A.4). The biblical allusions of Wisdom roughly correspond to classical dependence on Homer and the mythical tradition. Didactic compositions in prose or verse could inculcate virtue and knowledge through exhortation (protreptic, cf. Wis 1–6) and praise (encomium, cf. Wis 7–10). In the twentieth century Wisdom was identified with protreptic and encomium in turn. The book can be loosely classified in Greek terms as a protreptic work, but it differs as a whole from the kind of Greek prose or verse composition which this classification evokes. Aspects of the book recalling Greek and Roman didactic poetry, including moral exhortation, are perhaps less important as indications of genre than as clues to the popularity of Wisdom in antiquity and the Middle Ages

(A.12), when classical didactic literature was also relished.

4. The genre seems better classified in biblical terms as 'sapiential'; the book furthers the literary tradition followed in the wisdom-books of Proverbs, Job, and Ecclesiastes, but it does so in a more consciously Israelite and biblically oriented manner, in this respect resembling Sirach (Wis D). Unlike the Hebrew and Greek Sirach, however, Wisdom presents itself as wisdom of the inspired Solomon (7:7). Might it therefore be classed as pseudepigraphic prophecy, and be called an apocalypse, like 1 Enoch which it seems to echo? No, even though Wisdom declares the future and interprets Scripture in prophetic fashion, and exemplifies the thematic overlap between wisdom-books and apocalypses (2 Esd); for the centrality of wisdom in chs. 1–10 makes the book as a whole more sapiential than apocalyptic.

C. Setting. 1. Wisdom echoes the eptuagint of the Prophets as well as the Pentateuch, and probably draws on 1 Enoch 1–36 and 91–108 (Wis A.2). It is therefore unlikely to be earlier than the second century BCE. It was valued in the early church, but its lack of Christian allusion suggests that it is not a Christian work. In the second century BCE it was known to Irenaeus, as Eusebius notes (*Hist. eccl.* 5.8.8), and was named with comment in the Muratorian Canon (Horbury 1994a); it also received a Latin translation, later incorporated by Jerome into the Vulgate, which forms the earliest surviving interpretation of Wisdom. Wisdom was explicitly quoted by Christian writers from Clement of Alexandria (c.150–215) onwards. Earlier allusions in Paul, 1 Clement, and Justin Martyr are probable but not certain. Wisdom is therefore likely to have been current by the early years of the first century CE, at latest. The vocabulary includes Greek words not otherwise attested before the first century CE, but the body of extant Greek literature from the previous century is not large.

2. A date in or near Caligula's principate (37–41 CE) has often been suggested, in line with the old ascription to Philo (Wis A.1) that Jerome notes (in his comment cited in Wis B.1). This date is one of those which might suit address to the kings of the earth (6:1) and opposition to ruler-cult and idolatry (chs. 13–15), with the depiction of persecution (chs. 1–6), for these are themes of Philo's defence of the Alexandrian Jews under Caligula; but the academic tone of the remarks on ruler-cult is less urgent than would be natural under Caligula, and this date allows less time than would be expected for the book to gain the high esteem implied by its Christian usage. The first-century BCE date which has also often been suggested for Wisdom seems preferable. Address to kings and a theory of pagan cult would suit the Greek as well as the Roman period of Jewish history. In chs. 1–6, on persecution, the argument seems to be directed against internal foes, as in 1 Enoch and the Psalms of Solomon. These chapters can then be tentatively associated with Sadducaic-Pharisaic strife, in which afterlife was a prominent topic (Wis 3:1); persecution of those who defended it figured in the bloody repression of the Pharisees under Alexander Jannaeus in the early first century BCE. The Egyptian Jewish community, in close touch with Judea and probably including Judean refugees, seems the likeliest cradle for the Greek text of the whole book, perhaps between 100 and 50 BCE; these dates are speculative, but they would suit the points of contact with both Sirach and the Psalms of Solomon noted above. Sirach was put into Greek probably in 132 BCE, with what seems (especially but not only in the longer form of the Greek text) a fresh recognition of reward and punishment hereafter, specifically for circulation among Egyptian Jews. Their Greek epitaphs attest a difference of opinion on afterlife like that evinced between the Sadducee-like Ecclesiastes and the Hebrew Sirach on the one side, and the Pharisee-like Wisdom and Psalms of Solomon on the other (Horbury 1994b). The young and still righteous Solomon of Wisdom endorses the Pharisaic-Stoic preaching of 'justice, self-control, and the coming judgement' (Acts 24:25). Sirach was translated to aid Jewish education (Prologue), and Wisdom will have been valued for this reason as well as for its special doctrine. Its Christian educational use (Wis A.11–12) probably had Jewish antecedents.

D. Character. The special contribution of Wisdom to Jewish sapiential literature and the Christian sacred library is highlighted by its contrasts with the often comparable book of Sirach. Sirach is scribal wisdom in mainly proverbial form, but its author gives his name in accord with Greek convention; Wisdom is hortatory and expository rather than proverbial, but is anonymously presented as royal wisdom from the mouth of Solomon, in the manner of post-biblical prophecy like Enoch (Wis B.4). Sirach is not unaffected by the Greek world,

but sticks to ancestral Jewish modes of expression; Wisdom shows equal pride in Jewish tradition, but manifestly incorporates Greek terminology and thought (Wis A.4–9). Sirach is a Judean book translated for Egypt, Wisdom probably arose in Egypt but in contact with Judea (Wis C.2). Sirach depicts the social round of a wise scribe, but Wisdom looks with royal and prophetic eye on scenes of martyrdom, divine judgement, and biblical story (Wis A.2). Sirach in Hebrew sounds mainly sceptical of afterlife, Wisdom preaches immortality (Wis A.9; C.2). In Sirach biblical knowledge subserves proverbs and poems, in Wisdom expanded biblical narrative shapes the structure of the book (Wis A.2). In Sirach wisdom takes root in the people and is identified with the law (ch. 24), in Wisdom she is known to the king, and not identified with the law (Wis A.9); she is seen above all as a world-soul bringing individual souls to God. In Sirach wisdom herself speaks (ch. 24), in Wisdom her ardent disciple (chs. 6–9). Both books present her as loving and beloved, but only Wisdom clearly links this mystical theme with afterlife and the divine and human spirit.

COMMENTARY

Love Righteousness, for Unrighteousness Cannot be Hidden and Leads to Death (1:1–16).

(1:1–5) Righteousness, the Great Virtue Needed by Kings, Must be Sought in a Whole-Hearted Quest for the Divine Spirit of Wisdom With the exhortations characteristic of wisdom herself (Prov 2:20; 8:1; 9:3) and her prophetic 'children' (Lk 7:35; 11:49; Wis 7:27), the writer addresses those 'who judge the earth' (1:1, my tr.); they are 'rulers' (NRSV), being 'kings' as well as 'judges' (6:1–2), but their judicial office is in view, as with Solomon (1 Kings 3:3–28). 'Love righteousness' echoes psalms of kingship (Ps. 2:10–11; 45:7; 72:1–4). This hint at the form of a manual for kings commended Wisdom to an intellectual Jewish public, given the keen current interest in political and moral philosophy (Wis A.4–7). The significance gained by the first line in Christian political thought emerges when Dante sees its letters displayed by heavenly spirits (Paradiso, 18.70–117).

Righteousness, the characteristic virtue of the Israelites and their martyrs and heroes in Wisdom (as at 2:12; 3:1; 5:1; 10:4; 18:7), was exalted in Greek tradition as the principle of civic life and a cardinal virtue (Wis 8:7), indeed as 'the entirety of virtue' (Arist. *Eth. Nic.* 5.1.19, 1130ᵃ8); these views converged with the prominence of righteousness in the OT, there too as a civic principle, but with emphasis on conformity to the will of a righteous deity (Isa 11:4–5; Ps 11:7; 45:7; Wis 15:3). Here this emphasis marks the quick transition in 1:1 to advice on seeking the God of Israel, who is named, as often in Wisdom, by the royal title 'lord' (*kyrios*) used in the LXX. He must be sought wholeheartedly (Deut 4:29), by inward 'goodness', a term used for the unqualified zeal of Phinehas (Sir 45:23) and the generosity of Solomon (Wis 8:15, 19), and by sincerity (*haplotes*, REB 'singleness') of heart, a phrase linked with the kingly large-heartedness of David (1 Chr 29:17 LXX). Singleness of heart ranked high as a virtue (1 Macc 2:60; Col 3:22; 1 *Clem.* 60:2); the 'double-minded' must 'purify the heart' (Jas 1:8; 4:8).

The great example of divine 'manifestation' to those who do not tempt or distrust (v. 2) was Moses (Ex 33: 13, 18–19), by contrast with the rebellious children of Israel in the wilderness (1: 10–11). 'Thoughts' (*logismoi*, v. 3) are also the main obstacle in Prov 15:23 LXX ('an unrighteous thought is an abomination to the Lord'), 2 Cor 10:4–5. 'The power' (RV; NRSV adds 'his') is the divine manifestation itself (Mk 14:62), the spirit identified with wisdom (Wis 1:4–6) and probably also with the angelic spirit of the divine presence who led the Exodus and met rebellion (Ex 3:2; 32:34; Isa 63:9–14; Wis 10, introduction). v. 3 also takes up Isa 59, where perverse ways separate sinners from God (Isa 59:2, 8, quoted at Rom 3:15), and he appears as a warrior to punish them (Isa 59:16–21, also echoed in Wis 5:18).

Wisdom (Wis A.6–7) is named with reverent emphasis at the end of v. 4*a* in Greek (Wis 6:12). If not excluded by sin (cf. 4:10–12) it can 'enter' the soul (v. 4; 7:27) as a 'spirit' (vv. 5–6); the soul likewise enters a body (8:19; Wis A.4; 8). Origen (Wis A. 11), thinking on these lines, held that the Logos entered the pre-existent soul of Christ (Origen, *On First Principles*, 2.63–7; 4–6.4–5). For the body in bond to sin (v. 4) cf. Rom. 6:12–14; 7:14; 8:23.

'Disciplined spirit' (v. 5) seems to imply the human spirit, but the more exact rendering 'spirit of discipline' (RV, REB) is preferable, for divine wisdom ('holy', cf.7:22) is probably the subject, as in vv. 3–4 and 6. For its flight from iniquity cf. Ps 51:10–11. 'Discipline' (*paideia*)—training with instruction—was constantly linked with wisdom (so Prov 1:2; Wis 3:11); here too Jewish and Greek thinking converged.

(1:6–11) The Universal Spirit of Wisdom Conveys All Unrighteous Speech to the Lord The spirit of wisdom is *philanthrōpos* (v. 6; 7:23), 'kindly' to humanity in particular, for she delights in human company (Prov 8:31; Bar 3:37); but this epithet unexpectedly subserves the ruling theme of vv. 6–11, the omnipresence of a *judicial* spirit aware of all thought and speech (Ps 139:1–12, 23–4; Wis 9:11; divine omniscience linked with wisdom, 1 *Enoch*, 84:3). Likewise, v. 7 recalls the Stoic conception (Wis A.2) of a universe in which 'one common soul Inspires and feeds and animates the whole' (Virg., *Aen.* 6.725–6, tr. Dryden); but the spirit is pictured as a world- soul in order to show that it has 'knowledge of the voice' (*phōnē*, see RV), hears all, and knows all languages (1 Cor 14:10–11*a* REB). In the medieval and later Christian West v. 7 was therefore aptly recited at Pentecost (see Acts 2:4), but throughout vv. 7–11 the spirit's linguistic and other knowledge is judicial; the ungodly are detected (v. 8), heard (vv. 9–11) by divine jealousy or zeal (v. 10; 5:17; Isa 59:17 RV, REB), and punished (vv. 8, 9, 11) by unfaltering justice (*dikē*, 8; 2 Macc 8: 11; Acts 28:4). As the Greek deities were *epopsioi*, 'watchers' (Callimachus fr. 85), so the eyes of the Lord run to and fro everywhere (2 Chr 16:9; Prov 15:3; Zech 4: 10). 'Know what is above thee: a seeing eye, and a hearing ear, and all thy doings written in a book' (*m.'Abot*, 2.1). The famous 'grumbling' (vv. 10, 11) of the wilderness generation was strictly punished (Num 14:27–35; 1 Cor 10: 10); the soul's destruction (v. 11) is then probably seen as the penalty as well as the consequence of untruth.

(1:12–16) Do not Court Death by Going Astray, for the World is Made for Life through Righteousness vv. 12–16 expand Prov 8:35–6, the end of the speech by wisdom already echoed in v. 6. In v. 12 'error' (*plane*, 'straying'; Wis 12:24) has overtones of idolatry, the root of all vice. 'Death' (v. 12), coupled with 'destruction' (vv. 12, 14), is personified according to an old biblical tradition probably influenced at various stages by Syrian and Greek myths of a god of death, and exemplified at Job 28:22; Isa 28:15 (taken up in v. 16, below); Hos 13: 14. In v. 13, accordingly, death was not divinely created, but came in 'through the devil's envy' (2:24); all created things, by contrast, were made for life and health (v. 14; Wis 2:23). Because of this contrast between the created and the intruded, 'creatures' (v. 14, NRSV marg.) is preferable to 'generative forces' as a rendering of *geneseis*;

created things have the sap of life in them, not the 'poison of destruction' (RV), the principle of death. 'Hades' (v. 14) usually represents Hebrew *šĕ'ōl* in the LXX, and can therefore be personal (Isa 5:14) as well as topographical; here, where death is personified, Hades is probably imagined as a godlike figure whose 'dominion' is underground, on the lines of Greek myth, as in the Egyptian Jewish epitaph CIJ 1508 (Horbury and Noy 1992: pp. xxiii–xxiv, 63). The single-line v. 15 can be viewed together with the last two lines of v. 14 as forming a triad, on the pattern of vv. 1, 5, 9; in the OL it is followed by the line 'but unrighteousness is the obtaining of death', but this is probably an early expansion. The characteristically Greek term 'immortal' (Wis 3:4) here adorns a maxim found in other words in the Psalms (111:3; 112:3, 9; 119: 142, 144). The 'ungodly' are pictured (v. 16) as in Isa 28: 15 LXX (also echoed at Sir 14: 12) 'we made a covenant with Hades, and a bond with death'; 'him' (NRSV marg.) is perhaps more likely to be Hades, just mentioned, than 'death' (text), but the diabolical power of death (2:24; Heb 2: 14) is in view in either case. This Isaianic 'covenant' became in medieval thought the pact with the devil in witchcraft, as when Dr Faustus made Lucifer 'a deed of gift of body and of soul', conditionally on 'all covenants and articles between us both' (Marlowe, *Doctor Faustus*, ll. 89–91). The covenanters deservedly belong to the 'portion' (*meris*) of Hades, death, or the devil (v. 16; 2:24 RV; NRSV 'company'), implicitly opposed here to 'the Lord's portion' (Deut 32:9, 2 Macc 1:26), (righteous) Israel, wisdom's home (Sir 24:12); an explicit contrast is drawn in Qumran rule literature between those who belong to 'the lot of Belial' and 'the lot of God' (1QS ii 2–5). For the movement of thought from the infernal covenant to the two portions compare 2 Cor 6: 15, where Christ has no concord with Belial, and a believer no *meris* with an unbeliever.

The Ungodly Declare their Falsely Argued Philosophy, and their Resolve to Use their Time in Revelry and Oppression (2:1–20)

This speech, 'full of a kind of evil grandeur rhythmically expressed' (Deane 1881), follows the expressions of doubt or lawlessness imagined by biblical writers (as at Isa 22: 13; Ps 10:4–11; 14: 1; Prov 1: 10–14). These were later developed, with hints at Epicureanism as popularly represented (1 Cor 15:32; 1 Enoch 102:6, 'they [the pious] like us have died'; *Ps. Sol.* 4: 11 (14) 'There is none that sees and judges'). Similarly,

Cain was pictured as saying to Abel, in a dispute before he killed him, 'Did nature create pleasures for the dead?' (Philo, *Det.* 33), or 'There is no judgment, no Judge, and no other world' (*Tg. Ps.-J. Gen.* 4:8). The evocation of both sides of the argument in Wis 2–5 sounds like an echo of the judgement scene in 1 Enoch 102–3.

In vv. 1–5, as in Job 14:1, we have 'but a short time to live, and are full of misery', for there is no 'remedy' (RV 'healing') for death (v. 1, line 3); OL 'refreshment' (*refrigerium*, also at 4:7; often used of afterlife) prematurely introduces the denial of happy immortality implied in the following line, but well displays the link of 'healing' with new life (Deut 32:39; Ps 30:3–4; Hos 6: 1–2) which leads to the coming denial (v. 1, line 4). None was known to 'return' from Hades or, transitively, to 'give release' (RV); the latter seems preferable for its sharper polemic. It implicitly negates the myths of Orpheus and Heracles, the miracles of Elijah and Elisha (Sir 48:5, 14), and the hope of rescue by the supreme deity himself (Hos 13:14); its feeling is both biblical (Ps 89:48) and classical: 'Nor virtue, birth, nor eloquence divine Shall bid the grave its destin'd prey resign: Nor chaste Diana from infernal night Could bring her modest favourite back to light' (Horace, *Odes*, 4.7.21–8, tr. P. Francis).

The materialism of v. 2–4 comparably blends biblical and Hellenic reminiscence, following the more sceptical and mocking the more hopeful side of both traditions. Our birth is haphazard, as Epicureans held cosmic origins to be: 'not by design did the first beginnings of things station themselves' (Lucretius, 5.419, tr. H. A. J. Munro); on the other side, like a refutal of the ungodly, 'Not to blind hazard or accident is our birth and our creation due' (Cic. *Tusc.* 1.118, tr. J. E. King). The philosophers' 'spark' of reason is as temporary as the associated heart-beat (v. 2); Heraclitus' view that the soul was a 'spark' of ethereal fire (Macrobius, *In Somnium Scipionis*, 1.14) is cited as well known by Tertullian, *De Anima* 5.2. When the body dies, the spirit is dispersed (v. 3; Eccl 3:21), and (as in Horace, *Odes*, 4.7.16) 'our best remains are ashes and a shade'. Lastly, the sealed end without 'return' (*anapodismos*, v. 5) for the passing of our shadow seems implicitly to negate Isaiah's miracle of the shadow on the dial, when the sun 'went back' (*anepodisen*, Sir 48:23 REB) and life was regained.

The call to enjoy life (vv. 6–9) was often underlined in poetry by a reminder of death: 'Live, says he, for I'm coming' (Virg. App. *Copa*, 38, tr. H. Waddell); but here death has been the

first consideration (vv. 1–5), and 'Gather ye rosebuds while ye may' (v. 8) leads not simply to
wine or love but to robbery, torment, and murder (vv. 10–20). Heartless sensuality, 'making
use of the creation' (v. 6), is vividly evoked
through concentration (vv. 7–9) on the spring
flowers grabbed for the soon-discarded crowns
of the drunkards (contrast the decorous
bestowal of a wreath at a well-conducted symposium, Sir 32:2); Isa 28 (1–4) is echoed again, as
in 1:16 above. In accord with this floral theme, in
v. 9 probably read *leimon* (meadow) for *hemon*
(of us), as suggested by an additional line in the
OL which otherwise corresponds to v. 9, line 1
NRSV (Kilpatrick 1981: 216; Scarpat 1989–99; see
Gregg 1909), and render 'Let no meadow fail to
share in our revelry'.

In vv. 10–20 the series of hedonistic group
exhortations starting with 'let us enjoy' turns,
with a sinister unveiling of purpose, into the
tyrannical 'let us oppress...lie in wait...test...
condemn'; for this sequence compare Jas 5:5–6,
perhaps an echo of Wisdom. Now the speech
recalls Prov 1:10–14, cited above, an enticement
by the 'ungodly' (LXX) to rob and murder the
'righteous' (LXX). In Wisdom also the victim is
the 'righteous' (*dikaios*, Lat. *iustus*, vv. 10,12,16,18;
3:1), taken by early Christians (Wis A.11–12) to be
Christ amid his enemies prophetically foreseen
(so among others, with reference to v. 12
onwards, Cyp. *Test.* 2.14; Aug. *De civ. dei*, 17.20);
the scene recalls Plato on the inevitable torture
and judicial murder of the *dikaios* (*Rep.* 2.5, 362A,
also referred to Christ by Clem. Al. *Strom.* 5.14),
and biblical accounts of the suffering righteous
(Ps 37:12–13; Isa 53:11; *Ps. Sol.* 13:6–12), from 'righteous Abel' onwards (Mt 23:25; 1 Jn 3:12; Philo
and Targum as cited above; in 1 *Enoch* 22:5–7
Abel leads the spirits' cry for vengeance). The
whole of 2:1–3:11 recalls Isa 57:1–3 LXX: 'See
how the righteous perishes, and none takes it
to heart...from the face of unrighteousness
the righteous was taken away; his grave shall
be in peace, he was taken from the midst. But
draw near, you lawless children...in what did
you take delight, and against whom did you
open your mouth?' In the much-quoted verse
12, for 'lie in wait' see Prov 1:11 and Ps 10:8–9;
'inconvenient' echoes Isa 3:10 LXX, a verse
which Christians also applied to the passion
(*Barn.* 3:7, etc.).

Israel collectively are usually the 'child of
God' (18: 13; Ex 4:22), but suffering individuals
apply this to themselves (Deut 8:5, using the
second person singular; compare *Ps. Sol.* 13:8
'he will admonish the righteous as a child of

love'; Heb 12:57); here then (Wis 2:13,16,18; 14:3 is
collective) the *individual* righteous is the child
claiming God as Father, probably with satirical
reflection of the near-mystical piety (cf.7:27; 8:2;
Wis A.3) which became characteristic of wisdom and martyrology (5:5); see Sir 23:1, 4, 'O
Lord, Father...'; 4Q417 (Sapiential work) fr. 1 ii,
'you will be His first-born son' (tr. Vermes 1997:
405); 'These wounds caused me to be beloved of
my Father in heaven', *Mekilta, Yithro, Bahodesh* 6,
on Ex 20:6 (tr. Lauterbach 1933: ii. 247).

The righteous 'will be protected' (v. 20), for
(rendering more closely with RV margin) 'there
will be a visitation of him' with immortality, as
at Wis 3:7.

The Ungodly, Reasoning Thus, were Blinded to God's Gift of Life (2:21–4)

God's purposes (v. 22, *mystēria*, RV 'mysteries'),
hidden (Mk 4:11) from the impious by a judicial
blinding (Isa 6:9–10) brought on by their wickedness (v. 21; cf. 2 Cor 4:4) are indeed to give the
worthy their 'wages' (*misthos*, as 5:15 and Mt 5:12,
where NRSV has 'reward'); so at 1 Cor 3:7–9 it is
similarly said that the rulers responsible for the
crucifixion would have refrained if only they
had known what God prepares for them that
love him. 'Incorruption' (v. 23; 6:18–19) hints, as
its Pauline usage suggests (Rom 2:7; 1 Cor 15:42,
etc.), at the hope for immortality expounded in
the sequel and expressed here in the bold view
of human creation as the image (7:26; Gen 1:26)
of divine 'eternity' so in the Parables of Enoch,
from near the end of the Second Temple period,
human beings were created like angels, and
'death would not have touched them' (1 *Enoch*,
69:0). The technical term 'devil' in English ren-
derings of v. 24 is in origin a transliteration,
perhaps derived through Latin *diabolus*, of
Greek *diabolos*, 'slanderer', found here; the
English technical term is apt because by the
time of Wisdom '(the) Slanderer' was already
used in Septua- gintal Greek, in a comparably
special sense, to interpret Hebrew *sātān*,
'Accuser' (1 Chr 21:1; Job 1:6; Zech 3:1; cf. Rev
12:9). The serpent in Paradise (Gen 3:1) is here
probably identified with Satan, as in Rev 12:9
(RV 'that old serpent, he who is called the Devil
and Satan'); comparably, a fallen angel tempts
Eve in the passage of the Parables of Enoch just
quoted (1 *Enoch*, 69:6). 'Death entered the world',
echoed in Rom 5:12, recalls not only Gen 3:3, 19,
22, but also Gen 4:3–8 (Abel's murder), quoted
after a citation of Wis 2:24 in 1 *Clem.* 3:4–4:6; yet
the allusion in v. 24 should not be restricted to

Cain. The devil's 'company' is none other than death's company (see Wis 1:16).

The Suffering of the Righteous is Rewarded by Immortality (3:1–9)

The consolation now offered evokes such biblical judgement scenes as Deut 32:39–43; 33:26–9; Isa 66:10–24. The doubts addressed (vv. 2–4) are also specified in other literary development of these scenes, for example Mal 3:13–21 (4:3) 'it is vain to serve God'; 1 Enoch, 102–3, Ps. Sol. 4:11 (14), quoted on Wis 2:1. 'The Sadducees said: It is a tradition among the Pharisees to afflict themselves in this world; yet in the world to come they will have nothing' ('Abot R. Nat. A, 5; tr. Goldin 1955: 39). Here, however, 'the souls of the righteous' are safe (4:17, 5:16) 'in the hand of God' (verse 1), as in Deut 33:3 LXX, 'all the sanctified are under his hands' (applied to Jewish martyrs in 4 Macc 17:19); Wisdom is closer to MT 'in thy hand' (RV). The righteous souls or spirits are kept in hollow places (1 Enoch, 22:9; cf. 2 Esd 4:35, 'in their chambers'; 1 Pet 3:19, in 'prison' or safeguard; Rev 6:9, 'under the altar') until their 'visitation' (vv. 7, 9,13), but can also be pictured in Jerusalem above (3:14; Heb 12:23), blessing the Lord (Song of Thr 64). The 'torment' (basanos) that they are spared will not just be that already inflicted (2:19–20), to which OL torment of death' or 'torment of malice' (3:1) and 'suffered torments among men' (3:4) probably allude, perhaps with martyrdom in view; but the judgement-scene context suggests that 3:1 also envisages punishment after death, like the basanos of the rich man in the parable (Lk 16:23–8; cf. Isa 66:24; Sir 7:17).

The strikingly Hellenic 'seemed to have died' (v. 2; contrast Cor 15:3) recalls Socrates in Plato: 'when death comes to a man, his mortal part, it appears, dies, but the immortal part goes away unharmed . . . the hope is great [cf.v. 4] . . . after I drink the poison I shall no longer be with you, but shall go away to the joys of the blessed' (Phd. 106E, 114C, 115D). With 'in peace' (v. 3 RV) cf. Isa 57:2 LXX (Wis 2:10–20). The apparent punishment of the righteous (v. 4) is not only their suffering (Wis 3:1), but the divine 'sentence' of death itself (Sir 38:22; 41:2–4); cf. Hos 13:14 LXX, 'O Death, where is your judgment?', and the Egyptian Jewish epitaph CIJ 1513 (Horbury and Noy 1992: no. 36), 'If it was decreed that I should live but a short time, yet I have a good hope of mercy.' 'Hope' has the link with afterlife found in Plato as quoted

above on v. 2 and suggested by LXX (Ps 16:9–10, quoted in Acts 2:26; Sir 2:9).

The Hellenic term 'immortality' (v. 4, athanasia, 5 times in Wisdom) could be used together with the more typically biblical language of 'resurrection' (anastasis), as shown by 1 Cor 15:52–4 and Ps.-Phocylides 102–15. Wisdom's vivid sketch of the righteous departed shining in eschatological war and judgement (3:7–8; 5:16) was applied in medieval exegesis to the agility of the glorified risen body (so Aquinas, Summa contra Gentiles, 4.86); and together with the term 'visitation' (Wis 3:7) it has been held to suggest that resurrection was not alien to the outlook reflected here (Puéch 1993: 92–8, 306). Yet Wisdom and 4 Macc speak of immortality without mentioning resurrection, whereas Paul and Ps.-Phocylides both combine the two, and 2 Macc uses equally Hellenic vocabulary but speaks solely of resurrection (Wis A.9); and Wisdom also avoids the imagery of waking (Dan 12:2–3, echoed in other respects). Wisdom then probably reflects preference for the notion of spiritual immortality—no insubstantial form of life (Wis A.9). Contrast the common epitaph-formula 'no one is immortal' (attested at the first-century BCE tomb of Jason in Jerusalem, SEG 33.1276).

To interpret martyr-like suffering as probative or sacrificial (vv. 5–6) was traditional (Job 23:10; Song of Thr 17), to cite afterlife in support (v. 7) rather less so. 'Visitation' (v. 7, taking up 2:20) renders episkopē, Old Latin respectus, a 'looking upon' or 'inspection'; in LXX episkopē and the cognate verb (echoed in old prayers, for instance on Good Friday, for the deity to 'look upon' or 'behold' the church) answer to Hebrew commonly rendered 'visit, visitation' (Gen 50:24–5, etc.). Divine 'visitation' could bring good or ill (19:15) here and hereafter (1QS iv 6–14, tr. Vermes 1997: 102; Ps. Sol. 9:4–5), but the term was used, with echoes as here of its biblical links with 'day' and 'time' (Isa 10:3; Jer 6:15), particularly for final judgement (As. Mos. 1:18; 1 Pet 2:12). Linked too with the human spirit (Job 10:12 RV), it was readily seen as a 'visitation of souls' (Wis 3:13 RV; cf. 1 Pet 2:25 'episkopos of souls'), with special reference to afterlife as in 3:7 and (on resurrection, Wis 3:4) in Ps. Sol. 3:11–12 'when he visits the righteous . . . they that fear the Lord shall rise to life eternal'. Here (vv. 7–8) the righteous, agile in glory (5:16–17; Dan. 12:3), burn sinners like stubble (Ob 18) and judge the world (Dan 7:22; 1 Cor 6:2; Wis 5:16) under the Lord. The 'truth' (v. 9) hidden by false reasoning (1:3; 2:1; 3:10) is now clear; 'at the time of visitation he will destroy it (iniquity) forever and truth will go forth' (1QS iv 1819). Wisdom's reticence perhaps sharpens the hint at vengeance (3:7), but vv. 1–9 are justly prized for explicit attention to peace, hope, brightness, and the kingdom of God.

The Wicked and their Children are Punished, but the Virtuous, though Childless, are Happy (3:10–4:20)

Reassurance that the wicked will be punished is prominent in judgement-scenes (Wis 3:1; 1 Enoch, 102–3). Here the advice 'Do not despair of retribution' (m. 'Abot, 1.8) is entwined with the biblical and classical theme of consolation for childlessness (Wis B.1). The wicked and their seemingly hopeful offspring are doomed (3:10–13, 16–19, following wisdom-texts such as Ps 37:28), and their unlawful issue will not thrive (4:3–6, which has exerted a not always salutary influence as the main biblical comment on illegitimacy); whereas the chaste woman or man without children (3:13–14) can look for fruit at 'the visitation of souls' (3:13 RV; Wis. 3:7) and a place in the heavenly temple (3:14; Wis 9:8)— and for present honour, an immortal memory and the propagation of virtue here below (3:15; 4:1–2). The man's consolation develops that given to the righteous eunuch in Isa 56:3–5, and the train of thought is anticipated in Ps 17:14–15 LXX 'They were satisfied with children ... I shall be satisfied when thy glory is seen'; but the emphasis in Wisdom is on the day of judgement (3:13,18; 4:6).

(4:7–20) The Righteous who Die Young are Happy, but the Wicked End Miserably Comfort for childlessness now leads to another great theme of classical consolation (Wis B.1), the untimely death (cf.43; 14:15) of 'boys and unmarried maids ... and youths entombed before their fathers' eyes' (Virg. Aen. 6.307–8, tr. Dryden). The universality of this theme, touched in epitaphs throughout the centuries but not so explicitly addressed elsewhere in the Bible, has helped to win special esteem for Wisdom. The premature decease of the righteous is viewed (4:7–16) as the rest (v. 7; OL refrigerium, as Wis 2:1) or translation to heaven of those who, like Enoch, soon reached perfection (v. 13; Wis 6:15), being beloved of God, and receive the 'visitation' (Wis 3:7) accorded to the 'holy' or pious (v. 15, hosios (3:9), frequent in Ps. Sol.); the despisers will themselves be dishonoured and forgotten

(vv. 17–20). Allusion to Enoch becomes plain in v. io, echoing gen 5:24 (in vv. 10, 13–14 the Gk. has the singular, despite NRSV 'they'); 1 Clem. 9:3 'having been found righteous he was translated' is probably indebted to Wisdom, but in any case sums up the view of Enoch set out here. This is the first in a series of unnamed biblical portraits (Wis A.3); didactic as well as artistic, they stimulate biblical knowledge, and present the characters as exemplars of virtue. Similarly nameless allusions characterize the Hebrew liturgical poetry (piyyut) of Byzantine Palestine. The lapidary v. 8–9,13, recall Greek grave-epigrams, and have found many later applications; 'that which the wise man hath said concerning Enoch [v. 13] ... the same to that admirable child [king Edward VI] most worthily may be applied' (R. Hooker, Ecclesiastical Polity, 4.14.7). Virtuous youth condemning age (v. 16) is a commonplace (Ps 119: 99–100; Jub. 23:16; Sus 45,52), relevant later on (8:19–21). Even the dead scorn the ungodly (vv. 18–20; Isa 14:16–19).

The Judgement of the Righteous and the Unrighteous (5:1–23)

(5:1–14) The Righteous have Assurance in the Unexpected Judgement but the Unrighteous Lament their Folly With 'boldness in the day of judgement' (1 Jn 4:17, perhaps echoing Wisdom), the righteous (Wis 1:1) will 'stand', as later envisaged for the vindicated Christ (Acts 7:55–6) and his followers (Lk 21:36; Eph 6:13); the unrighteous cannot (Ps 1:5).

The unrighteous repent (v. 3) 'too late and without fruit' (Aug. En. 2 on Ps 48 (49), s. 4, one of his many quotations of 5:3); any earlier chances (12:19–20) were lost. Repentance after death is also viewed as impossible in Lk 16:19–31 and in much rabbinic teaching (so Ruth Rab. 3.3, on 1:17, Montefiore and Loewe 1974: no. 864). The importance of repentance in Wisdom (Wis A.2), as in the Synoptic Gospels and rabbinic teaching, reflects its general prominence in ancient Jewish piety (Philo, Virt. 175–86; the Fifth Benediction of the Amidah).

vv. 3–5 recall earlier mockery of the 'child of God' (Wis 2:13, 16, 18) and the 'lot' (Wis 1:16; Acts 20:32; Col 1:12) of the 'saints'—hagioi, 'holy ones', sometimes angels (Dan 4:17, etc.), but here probably true members of the holy nation (18:9, cf.17:2), ultimately triumphant over sinners (Ps 149:5–9); Christians are entitled hagioi in this sense by Paul (2 Cor 1:1, etc.). Light fails (v. 6) those who leave 'the way of truth' (Ps 119:30 AV;

Prov 4:18–19). After 'sun' (v. 6) probably supply 'of understanding', with some Latin witnesses; cf. 7:26, and 11QPs[a] xxvii 2–4 'David son of Jesse was wise, and a light like the light of the sun … and the Lord gave him the spirit of understanding and illumination' (my tr.; Vermes 1997: 307). 'Arrogance' (v. 8) typified Sodom (Ezek 16:49–50), and tyrannical Jews or Gentiles (*Ps. Sol.* 17:26, 46).

Nine largely biblically inspired short and long similes of transitoriness (vv. 9–12, 14; Job 9:25–6; Prov 30:19; Ps 1:4; Jer 14:8) evoke the fleeting world of the unrighteous and their desires (cf. 1 Jn 2:17); in 9b REB 'messenger galloping by' gives the sense better than NRSV. Archery (v. 12, cf.v. 21) was practised by Jews (Hecataeus in Jos. *Ag. Ap.* 1.201–4). These verses, like those on repentance, will have helped to commend Wisdom for use in baptismal instruction (Wis A.11–12; c.2).

(15–23) The Righteous Receive their Kingdom, and Divine Vengeance on the Unwise Overtakes the Nations The 'reward' (*misthos,* Wis 2:22) sketched in 3:7–9 now appears as a truly royal benefit (3:5) 'in (*en*) the Lord' (v. 1RV; cf. Gen 15:1), that is, in his power to give, but perhaps with the overtone that it is constituted by communion with him; cf. Phil 3:14, 'the prize of the upward call of God in Christ Jesus'. 'Crown' for *basileion* (v. 16a) matches 'diadem' (v. 16b), but 'kingdom' (OL, AV) seems a better translation in 16a, for *basileion* as 'kingdom' is linked with Israel and the saints (Ex 19:6 LXX; cf. Rev 1:6; Dan 7:22 LXX). The whole phrase 'the kingdom of fair majesty (*euprepeia*) and the diadem of beauty' (v. 16, mytr.) then perhaps hints at enthronement (Dan 7:9; Mt 19:28) followed by crowning, at the same time suggesting the indescribability of God's gift. 'In the world to come there is neither eating nor drinking … but the righteous sit enthroned, their crowns upon their heads, and enjoy the lustre of the Shekhinah' (Rab [early 3rd cent. CE] in *Ber.* 17a; Montefiore and Loewe 1974: no. 1658). Hope for a 'kingdom' of the saints (Dan 7:18, 22, 27) in the 'holy land' (12:3) is unmentioned here, but was indicated in 3:8 on their international dominion, and is not precluded by the leaning in Wisdom towards the spiritual (Wis 3:4; A.9); later Christian chiliasm could keep a spiritual emphasis by stressing the descent of a *heavenly* Jerusalem (Rev 21:2; Tert. *Adv. Marc.* 3.24.6 'changed into angelic substance … we shall be translated into that heavenly kingdom').

In this final conflict the righteous are safe (v. 16; Wis 3:1; cf. 1:8; 2 Thess 1:7). Their part in it

(3:7) is here neglected in favour of the marshalling of the elements for divine vengeance (vv. 17, 20–3), a familiar thought (Sir 39:28–9) developed in Wis 16:17, 24; 19:6–22; this ethical interpretation of OT storm-theophanies helps theodicy (Wis A.2), and fits Wisdom's Stoic-like conception of an ordered 'cosmos' (*kosmos,* v. 20, better rendered 'world' (REB) than 'creation' (NRSV), Wis A.4). vv. 17–23 (like Eph 6:13–17; 1 Thess 4:8) take up Isa 59:16–19 on the avenging deity and his panoply of judicial virtue; in the background are the influential hymns to the Divine Warrior put in the mouth of Moses, Ex 15:1–18; Deut 32:1–43 (22–5, 35–43). The unwise, *aphrones,* already denounced for perversity of thought (Wis 1:3) are now (5:20), since they resist divine power, *paraphrones,* the 'frenzied'. AV 5:20 'against the unwise' keeps the link with 1:3; later versions add 'his' and 'foes' in amplification.

Kings are Exhorted to Learn Wisdom (6:1–25)
The exhortation to kings takes up the similar speech in 1:1–16, already echoed (5:20), and introduces the great expansion of Solomon's prayer for wisdom (chs. 7–10) which can be viewed as the second main section of the book (Wis A.2).

(6:1–11) Kings Must Give Heed, for Their Power is from God Kings are reminded (vv. 1–2; cf. Ps 2:10; *Ps. Sol.* 2:32) that they rule by the grace of God as ministers of his 'kingdom' (vv. 3–4) under his scrutiny (vv. 3–n; Wis 1:6–11; 3:7); so Solomon sat 'on the throne of the kingdom of the Lord over Israel' (1 Chr 28:5), or, later, God gave Ptolemy Philadelphus the hegemony in Egypt (*Ep. Arist.* 219). Near vv. 3–4 in wording are Rom 13:1–7; 1 *Clem.* 61:1; and Jos. *J.W.* 2.140 on the Essene oath 'to keep faith with all, especially those in power, since no ruler attains office apart from God'. The OT view took classic form in the Danielic scheme of four successive God-given world-empires (Dan 2:38–40); with and through Paul it influenced the church (Caesar 'was appointed by our God', Tert. *Apol.* 33.1), and it was not far from Greek and Roman thought. 'Monarchs on earth their power extend, Monarchs to Jove submissive bend, And own the sovereign God' (Horace, *Odes* 3.1.1–3, tr. P. Francis). Many Jews served the Seleucids and Ptolemies professionally (Williams 1998: 88–91), but the sentiment led (vv. 3–11; cf. Dante's use of Wis 1:1) to assessment as well as confirmation of human rule. 'Behold, great ones of the earth, the judgment of the Lord, for he is a great king' (*Ps. Sol.* 2:32). God 'takes thought' (v. 7, *pronoei*) providentially (Wis 14:3). 'Holy' (v. 10, *hosiōs*; Wis 4:15) here verges on 'righteous' or 'blameless', as at Lk 1:75; 1 Thess 2:10.

(6:12–25) Wisdom is Soon Found, Kings should Honour her, and her Nature shall be Declared In chs. 1–10 any attempt at describing Wisdom herself is reserved until now, when hearers or readers have been purified by stern narratives of judgement; 1:4–6 stressed that she flees from sin. In 6:12a (Gk.) the place of *sophia* at the end (as in 1:4, 6) is natural, but conveys emphasis and awe: 'Bright and unfading is Wisdom' (12a, tr. Goodrick). With the recurrent light-imagery (5:6; 7:22–6), here placed first, compare Aristobulus (Wis A.7), frag. 5: all light has its origin in wisdom (Collins 1983–5: 841; Hengel 1974: 167). The praise of wisdom (vv. 12–20) first takes up (vv. 12–16) Prov 1:20–1; 8:1–17 (she utters her voice in the streets, loves those who love her, and is found by those who seek early); v. 21 takes up her guidance to kings (Prov 8:15–16).

In vv. 12–16 the themes from Proverbs are reordered into an emotional and intellectual mysticism (Wis A.1; A.11; D): wisdom is first of all to be loved and desired (vv. 12b–13; cf. 21 OL; 7:10; 8:2; Sir 4:12; 24:19, 24), and reflection upon her (vv. 15–16; cf. Sir 14:20–1) is the perfection of understanding.

vv. 17–20, rising to this intellectual challenge with an argument in Greek style (Wis B.1), form a chain-syllogism with six links, in the widely admired manner (cf. Rom 5:3–5; 2 Pet 1:57) termed 'heap-like' (sorites, from *soros*, 'heap'). It is urged that desire for instruction in wisdom (vv. 17, 20) ultimately leads to the kingdom constituted by nearness to God (vv. 19–20; cf. 5:16). This conclusion associates the general Stoic view that wisdom brings a kingdom (Wis A.6) with Wisdom's special emphasis on immortality (vv. 18–19, more exactly 'incorruption', RV; Wis 2:23) as the consequence of virtue.

Kings then should 'honour wisdom' (v. 21; cf. Prov 8:15–16); the advice sums up all they have been told since 1:1–4. OL here 'love wisdom', and then (in a continuation not in the Gk.) 'love the light of wisdom', re-emphasize vv. 12b–13. The royal preacher will now (v. 22) declare her nature and origin from the very beginning (NRSV 'creation' represents *genesis*, 'beginning') without hiding secrets, or rather 'mysteries' (*mystēria*); OL adds 'of God' in explanation, following 2:23 and evoking the sacred aura of this word and wisdom herself (1 Cor 2:7).

Here this combines with the sense of the mysteries of a guild, imparted without envy or grudge (v. 23; Wis 7:13), lest salutary wisdom and wise kingship be lacking (vv. 24–5).

The Wise King Starts to Recount his Prayer and Quest for Wisdom, and Speaks in Her Praise (7:1–8:1)

In the genre termed 'rewritten Bible', exemplified at length in *Jubilees* or Josephus's *Antiquities* (Alexander 1988), a far-reaching expansion of the narratives of Solomon's prayer for wisdom (1 Kings 3:4–15; 2 Chr 1:1–13) begins now (Wis 6:1) from the verses on his tender years.

(7:1–7) Since I Shared the Beginning and End which Come to All, I Prayed The young Solomon (1 Chr 29:1) called himself 'a little child' (1 Kings 3:7), and now speaks memorably of his share in the plight of each crying (v. 3) newborn descendant of the 'first-formed', i.e. Adam (v. 1; Wis 4:10); so at birth the baby 'lies naked on the ground' with 'rueful wauling' (Lucretius 5.224–7, tr. H. A. J. Munro). Gestation lasts ten months (v. 2), as in many sources including 4 Macc 16:7, but not 2 Macc 7:27 (nine); NRSV 'pleasure of marriage' reworks the less restricted euphemism of the Greek, 'pleasure that came with sleep' (RV, similarly REB). Despite the detail, the soul is not mentioned separately (Wis 8:19). Kings have the same entrance and exit as the rest (vv. 5–6). 'Know whence thou camest: from a fetid drop; and whither thou art going: to worm and maggot . . .' (*m. 'Abot*, 3.1). The king therefore prayed (v. 7a), and received understanding (*phronēsis*); he called (NRSV adds 'to God', but perhaps wisdom is invoked, cf. Song of Thr 37, 64) and a spirit of wisdom came (1 Kings 3:12 LXX, 'an understanding and wise heart'; Isa 11:2 'spirit of wisdom and understanding'; Wis A.2); he was like the young disciple who prays for wisdom in Sir 51:13–22; cf. 39:5–6 ('spirit of understanding' given in answer).

(7:8–14) I Preferred Wisdom to Everything Else For the sake of his deep love (8:2) he preferred wisdom to the enjoyment of wealth (vv. 8–9, with 1 Kings 3:11; 2 Chr 1:11; cf. Prov 8:10–11), and also to health, beauty, and light (v. 10); perhaps arduous study (6:14,17; Sir 39:1) away from broad daylight made him like a pale sickly disciple of the wise, but in any case he looked like a disconsolate lover. The unsought good things in fact came together with wisdom (1 Kings 3:13; 2 Chr 1:12) but, loving her for herself (contrast Wis 8:17–18), he did not think of her as producing them (vv. 11–12). He simply learned without guile and taught 'without envy', in generous abundance (v. 13; 6:23); compare Plato's abundant 'philosophy without envy' arising from contemplation of the beautiful (*Symp.* 219D). She opens (v. 14) the possibility of 'friendship with God' (Wis 7:27).

The mystical aspect of 7:8–8:18 appears in Henry Suso's *Life* (14th cent.; Wis A.12); when he longed to see wisdom, as far as he could see her with the inner eye through Scripture, she showed herself to him. 'She shone like the morning star, and burnt like the glowing sun (7:29)...she spread out herself powerfully from end to end of the earth, and gently ordered all things (8:1)...His face became so happy, his eyes so kind, his heart so jubilant, and all his inner senses sang: Above all happiness, above all beauty, I have loved thee, my heart's joy and beauty...' (7:10) (Clark 1952: 23–4).

(7:15–22a) God, the Guide of Wisdom and Corrector of the Wise, Grant me to Speak Aright; he Gave me All my Universal Knowledge, for Wisdom Taught me Once more (Wis 6:12) an attempt to describe wisdom is reverently deferred, here (v. 15) for prayer to wisdom's own guide (cf. Prov 8:22–3, 30). God 'gave' the king's encyclopedic knowledge of the natural world (vv. 17–20; 1 Kings 4:33), but wisdom the fashioner (8:5; Prov 8:30) was in fact the teacher (vv. 21–2), as implied in 1 Kings 4:29–30, 34; God acted through her (9:1–2) as through an intermediary angelic spirit (9:17). The 'powers' (v. 20), better 'violences' (RV), of demonic 'spirits' (alternatively, 'winds'; OL attests both) were quelled by the king (T. Sol.), sometimes through 'roots' (v. 20). Josephus, in his own retelling of 1 Kings 4, relates how Solomon's name and a root and charm prescribed by him were effectually used in the presence of Vespasian for an exorcism; Solomon's wisdom was thus made plain (*Ant.* 8.44–9).

(7:22b–26) Wisdom's Attributes and Essence Now at last Wisdom is portrayed, in a hymn-like philosophic enumeration of her glories. Twenty-one (3 × 7, a felicitous number) epithets of her spirit (vv. 22–3) show her understanding, subtlety (Wis A.9), goodness and might and lead to a series of clauses on her name and titles: *sophia*, breath, emanation, brightness, mirror, image (vv. 24–6).

This passage extends the biblical line of sketches of personified Wisdom (Wis A.9); an intellectually-focused portrait by the loving disciple, it is the counterpart of Sir 24:1–22, a mainly sense-oriented self-portrait by wisdom herself (Wis D). It also recalls verses on a divine spirit (1:7) as inspiring or pervasive (Ex 31:3; Isa 11:2; 63:10–11; Ps 139:7); but its distinctively Hellenic vocabulary underlines its extrabiblical connection with the Stoic world-soul (Wis A.4; Wis 1:7; Knox 1939: 71–7). Clement of Alexandria (Wis C.1) indeed held that the Stoics, identifying the Deity too closely with nature, 'were misled by what is said in Wisdom, Pervades and passes through all...' (v. 24), not understanding that this refers to wisdom rather than God himself (*Strom.* 5.14; cf. 2.19; WIS A. 7). vv. 22b–26 heap up epithets and titles like a hymn, and praise a goddess-like cosmic figure; hence with 7:27–8:16 the passage is compared (Knox 1939: 77–9; Kloppenborg 1982; Wis A.9) with Greek hymns to Isis from the Ptolemaic period, known mainly from inscriptions and forming examples of aretalogy (*aretalogia*), recital of the virtues and wonders of a deity. These include statements in the third person, as here, as well as first-person statements by her (cf. 8:3, and wisdom's self-praise, Sir 24:1–22; Knox 1937) and second-person addresses to her (perhaps cf. 7:7b, but contrast prayer to God for wisdom, 9:4). In philosophical interpretation Isis was the female principle of nature (Plut. *De Is. et Os* 53. 372E) and the mother of the universe (Ap. *Met.* 11.5), and so, like wisdom, came to resemble the world-soul (Hengel 1974: 163).

Wisdom's derived qualities (vv. 25–6) excel just because they flow from 'the Almighty' (v. 25). Her five great titles use current ancient metaphors of outflow or 'emanation' (*aporrhoia*, v. 25); so the order in the universe is 'the emanation (*aporrhoē*) and image of Osiris' (Plut. *De Is. et Os.* 49.371B). Christians at first applied the titles to the Holy Spirit as well as to Christ as spirit (Athenagoras, *Leg.pro Christ.* 10.3; Malherbe 1969), but they are discussed christologically by Origen, *De princ.* 1.2.9–12 (Wis 1:4), and in Latin became part of medieval Christ-devotion. 'Breath', RV marg. 'vapour' (v. 25), recalls Sir 24:3 (from the mouth, like mist); 'reflection' (v. 26, *apaugasma*), better 'radiance' (REB), recurs in Heb 1:3, probably not an echo. OL 'majesty' for 'working' (v. 26, *energeia*, Jn 5:17) reflects noble but less pointed, probably secondary, variant Greek. 'Mirror' (v. 26), later viewed together with 1 Cor 13:12; 2 Cor 3:18; Jas 1:23, held special fascination: 'the Lord is our mirror' (*Odes of Solomon* 13:1); 'through Solomon the saviour is called the spotless mirror of the father, for the holy spirit, the son of God, sees himself redoubled, father in son and son in father, and both see themselves in each other' (Ps.-Cyprian (3rd cent.), *Sinai and Zion*, 13).

(7:27–8:1) Wisdom's Energy and Scope One yet universal (v. 27; 8:1), like the world-soul (Wis 1:7) and the omnipresent Isis (Ap. *Met.* 11.5), she renews all, and mediates between God and the soul by continually 'entering' (Wis 1:4) 'holy souls' (6:10; Wis A.3). 'Friends of God' (6:14) recalls the Hellenistic concept of royal 'Friends' (1 Macc 2:18), and became the title of medieval mystical and prophetic groups (*Gottesfreunde*). Wisdom can do this since (it is implied) her beauty, surpassing light (5:6; 6:12), is dear to God (vv. 28–9; cf.8:3*b*). She conquers vice (v. 30) and everywhere (8:1), again like a world-soul 'stretched through the whole' and 'enveloping the heaven in a circle from without' (Plato, *Tim.* 34B, 36s), orders (more exactly 'manages'; Wis 11:20) all things 'well'; OL 'sweetly' (AV) forms a link with 16:20–1; Sir 24:15. The Advent antiphon O *Sapientia* (Wis A.12), in use by the eighth century, chiefly consists of 8:1 prefaced by Sir 24:3 (close to Wis 7:25*a*).

From Youth I was in Love with Wisdom, through Whom All Good Things Come; Pondering this I Sought her, and Perceiving that God Alone could Give her, I Prayed (8:2–21) Turning back from wisdom's portrait to his own youth, the king again recalls his ardent love (7:10); he sought a mystical marriage (v. 2*b* Wis A.2–4). 'Enamoured' (v. 2*c* renders the strong word *erastēs*, AV 'lover'. vv. 3–4 echo wisdom's self-praise (Prov 8:22–30; Sir 24:2–4); she is near and dear to God (v. 3), initiated into his mind and promoting his work (v. 4), like the most noble Friend (v. 3; 7:27) in a king's privy council (v. 4). The king then justifies his youthful passion by recalling with mature worldly wisdom that she is also (vv. 5–16), as again she herself says (Prov 8:10–21, 34–5), the giver of wealth, righteousness, knowledge, kingship, happiness, and honour; this is why he sought her when young (vv. 9, 17–18). The young king, however, fell in love simply with her beauty (7:12; 8:2), but was then also able to rationalize his choice. The differing attitudes of youth and middle age are tactfully sketched; his first love recalls the Aristotelian exaltation of pure over applied science (Wis A.6).

Righteousness (v. 7; Wis 1:1) here takes the philosophic form of the Greek cardinal virtues (Wis A.7); 'there are four aspects of perfect

virtue; prudence, justice, fortitude, and temperance' (Diogenes Laertius, 3.90, summarizing Plato; cf. Plato, *Phd.* 69*c*). The Mosaic law was held to teach these virtues (e.g. 4 Macc 1:18), and is here perhaps implicitly viewed as the sum of the 'righteousness' taught by wisdom (with whom the law is identified in Sir 24:23, Bar 4:1; Wis A.9). By 'foreknowledge' (v. 8) 'signs and wonders' like the Egyptian night (18:6) are both expected and rightly interpreted in advance. 'Immortality' (vv. 13, 17) is the immortal memory rather than (Wis 3:4) life; 4:1 includes both senses, but in this section the latter is conveyed by 'incorruption' (Wis 6:18–19 RV). Rest with her (v. 16; Sir 6:28) in the palace of Israel's king matches wisdom's own expressed desire for rest, fulfilled in Jerusalem (Sir 24:7–12); this 'friendship' (v. 18) leads to friendship with God (7:27–8), but now the stress falls on earthly benefits; contrast Sir 24:24, part of the longer Greek text (Wis C.2; NRSV marg.), beginning similarly from 'beautiful love', but going on spiritually to fear, knowledge, and holy hope (Wis 3:4).

A youth of parts and purity (vv. 19–20), the king was a 'holy soul' with whom wisdom might live (7:27–8); but even so he had, as he discerningly saw (v. 21), to ask the bride's father, vv. 19–20 are best understood as self-identification with a noble pre-existent soul (Wis A.4), as envisaged by Plato (immortal souls fall from the heavenly regions into mortal bodies, those who have seen the most being embodied as lovers of wisdom or beauty, *Phdr.* 248C–E); compare Philo, *Gig.* 6–16 (the air is full of unseen souls, some descend into bodies, and soul, demon, and angel are different names for one thing) and Essene belief according to Josephus, *J.W.* 2.154 (souls from the subtlest ether become entangled in prison-like bodies; Wis 9:15). v. 21 uses the adjective *encratēs*, OL *continens*, 'in possession of', or alternatively 'continent'. This sense suits v. 20*b*, and v. 21 was often held to speak of prayer for 'the gift of continency' (preface to the marriage service in the English Prayerbooks of 1552 and 1662); 'give what thou commandest' (Aug. *Conf.* 10.29, quoting v. 21).

Give me Wisdom, without which Even the Perfect are of No Account, and Let her Teach me the Mind of God (9:1–189) This prayer up to v. 12 has formed a model (Wis A.12), for example in the primers of private prayer issued under Elizabeth I (Clay 1851: 96,

195, 310). It can be taken to end at v. 12, where the petition closes, or with the chapter (so NRSV); but the whole of chs. 10–19, throughout which the Deity is still being addressed (10:20; 11:4, etc.), can also be taken as its continuation in meditative praise. Chs. 9–19 would then be an extended instance of prayer and praise alluding to a series of deliverances in the Exodus and conquest, like Neh 9:5–32 (prayer) or Ps 136 (praise). It seems possible that 10:1–11:1 has been added to ch. 9, and that 11:2–19:18 has then been added to form a more discursive continuation of this Pentateuchally based praise (Wis A.2; B.2).

The prayer in ch. 9 (divisible into vv. 1–6, 7–12, but thematically continuous) is focused on two petitions for wisdom (vv. 4,10), echoed in v. 17; reasons for asking are given in vv. 5–9, 11–12, and in the semi-detached vv. 13–18 (matching vv. 1–6, 7–12 in length, but in essence meditation, not petition). The address (v. 1a) echoes David's recent prayer (1 Chr 29:18) and adds an anticipation of Solomon's later claim on promised 'mercy' (2 Chr 6:14, 42 RV). Following a familiar prayer-pattern the request begins (vv. 1b–3) from the making of all things (Neh 9:6; Ps 136:5), including viceregal humanity (vv. 2–3; Gen 1:26), by intermediary 'word' (logos; Ps 33:6) and 'wisdom' (Ps 136:5 'understanding', Prov 8.30 'I was beside him', Gen. 1:26 'let us make'). Logos (v. 1b; 16:12; 18:15) seems to function separately beside wisdom, contrary to Christian identification of both with Christ, but as later seen in part of the Targumic tradition: 'By wisdom the Lord created ... and the word of the Lord said, Let there be light' (Frg. Tg. Gen. 1:1–3); the Logos is an angel-like spirit (18:16) in and probably before Philo (Conf. 146; H. Chadwick in Armstrong 1970: 143–5), as Jn 1:1 also suggests.

Wisdom (v. 4) has one of the divine 'thrones' (RV marg., pl., as 18:15; Dan, 7:9; cf. David's 'thrones', v. 12 NRSV marg.; Ps 122:5), like an assessor beside the judge, as befits her uniquely close association with the Deity (vv. 9–11; Prov 8:22–30); the young king asks for her in his insufficiency (cf. 7:1–5; 1 Kings 3:7–8; 2 Chr 1:10), also recalling 1 Kings 3:7–8 with 'servants' (v. 4), alternatively 'children' (RV marg.). He dares to ask, for (v. 7) God himself made him king (1 Kings 3:7; 2 Chr 1:8–9) of the chosen people (1 Kings 3:8–9; 2 Chr 1:9; Wis 10: 15; A.3), God's 'sons and daughters'. The latter come to the fore in 1 Kings 3: 16, just after the prayer; the phrase therefore suits Solomon, but its general familiarity is suggested by

Pentateuchal and prophetic attestation (Deut 32:19; cf. Ex 15: 1, 20–1; Isa 43:6), and confirmed by 2 Cor. 6: 18. God also (v. 8) commanded the building of a temple (by Solomon, 1 Chr 28:6) on the holy hill (Mount Moriah, 2 Chr 3: 1; Wis 12:3), a copy of the heavenly tabernacle (1 Chr 28: 11–19). The return to the underlying biblical narrative in vv. 7–8 is typical of the 'rewritten Bible' genre (Alexander 1988: H7). The notion of a pre-existent divinely prepared heavenly temple met in 8c (see also Ex 15: 17 (LXX 'ready dwelling'); 25:9; Heb 8:5; cf. Wis 16:20 'ready') pervades the LXX versions of Solomon's temple-prayer (1 Kings 8:39, 43, 49 LXX; 2 Chr 6:30, 33, 39 LXX), and also suits a general awareness of Plato's doctrine of ideas (Wis 13:3; A.4).

vv. 13–18 (cf. 1 Cor 2: 11–16; 2 Cor 5:4–9) combine the biblical conviction that we need God-given wisdom (v. 17) because we cannot know God's mind (vv. 13–14; Isa 40:13; 1 Cor 2: 16) with Plato's view (Wis A.4) that the soul is weighed down (v. 15) by the body (Phdr. 81c; 2 Cor 5:4), 'entombed in the body ... in which we are imprisoned like an oyster in its shell' (Plato, Phdr. 250c); cf. Plato and Josephus, quoted on Wis 8: 19. v. 18 leads easily to examples of those 'saved' (10: 1–11: 1); OL 'healed' exemplifies a widespread OL rendering of Greek so(i)zein which strengthened the conception of salvation as cure (Wis 2: 1), and links wisdom here with logos (Wis 9: 1) in 16: 12. The Latin continuation 'whoever pleased thee, O Lord, from the beginning' (cf. 4: 10) is close to clauses in the Greek liturgies (Deane 1881) but is probably an addition; it echoes v. 18b, forms a link with 10: 1, and stresses that wisdom helps the saints (7:27).

Wisdom Saved Adam, Noah, Abraham, Lot, Jacob, Joseph, Moses and the Israelites (10:1–11:1)

This series of Pentateuchal examples, of course unnamed (Wis 4: 10), still follows biblical conventions (Wis 9, introduction) of prayer (Neh 9:5–32) or praise (Ps 136). It can also be read (Knox 1939: 80–1) as a sketch, in the manner of a philosophic Greek historian, of the growth of civilization from world catastrophe (the Fall, the Deluge, and the destruction of the cities of the plain; vv. 1–8) to a righteous monarchy (Jacob, Joseph, vv. 9–E4), preserved by the Exodus (10: 15–11:1). This meditation addressed to God (v. 20) is therefore still suitable as instruction to kings (1:1; 6:1).

Wisdom's guidance (10: 1–2,4, etc.) forms an interpretation and development of the biblical

portrayal of an angelic spirit who guided patriarchs and people, especially in the Exodus and
conquest (Gen 18:2; 19:1; 31:11; 48:16; Ex 3:1; 14:19;
23:23; 33:2; Num 20: 16; Josh 5: 13–14; Neh 9:20;
Isa 63:9–14; Bar 6:7; cf. Wis 1:3). Identification of
this spirit with wisdom was already known; in
Sir 24:4 the angel's pillar of cloud (Ex 14: 19) is
wisdom's throne (10: 17). Yet wisdom was present, and hence active as mediator, from the
beginning (9:9; Prov 8:22–30). Hence in 10:
1–11: 1 the guidance of the patriarchs by the
angelic spirit of wisdom simply continues
wisdom's earliest guidance. Christians, uniting
pre-existent wisdom with the angelic spirit in
the same way, understood both wisdom and
spirit as the pre-existent Christ; so (later 2nd
cent.) Justin Martyr, *Dialogus*, 61.1, on a power
begotten as a beginning (Prov 8:22) and called
Glory, Son, Wisdom, Angel, Lord, Word, and
Commander-in-Chief (Josh 5:13). Jn 12:41; 1 Cor
10:4, 9 already attest this line of thought.

(10:1–3) Adam's deliverance (1–2) from his
'transgression' (*paraptōma*, as Rom 5:15) reflects
contemporary emphasis on his glory (2:23; Sir
49:16) and salvation; in the *Life of Adam and Eve*
(Sparks 1984: 141–67) they find mercy after penitence, cf. v. 1*b*. Cain (v. 3), thought to favour
views like those of the ungodly in Wis 2:1–20,
perished not precisely 'because . . . he killed' but
rather 'in fratricidal passions' (my tr.); he is seen
as a soul, lost in irrational anger (Wis A.9; 1 Jn
3:15). Concern with individual morality and the
career of the soul marks the whole series of
examples (vv. 1, 5, 7, 9, 11, 13, 17, 21), and is
promoted by their labelling with epithets of
virtue.

(10:4–11:1) From Noah (cf. 14:6) to Joseph (vv.
4–14) the unnamed heroes are 'righteous' (Wis
4:10). Wisdom's inward voice is probably credited with Noah's shipbuilding, Abraham's steadfastness, and Joseph's kingship (vv. 4, 5, 13–14;
cf. 7: 16; 9: 11; 8: 10–15, respectively); but she
came as an angel to Lot (v. 6; Gen 19: 15, 17),
Jacob (vv. 10–12; in dreams, vv. 10– 11; cf. Gen
28: 12; 31:11), and the Israelites (v. 17; Ex 14: 19).
She entered into Moses' soul (v. 16; cf. Ex 4: 12),
having first appeared to him (Ex 3: 1), and made
him a 'holy prophet' (11: 1; cf. Deut 18: 15); cf.7:27.
   A high doctrine of Israel (vv. 15, 17, 20; Wis A.
1) is reinforced, first when the kingdom of God
(v. 10) kept in heaven (Mt 3:2; 6:9–10; 1 Pet 1:4) is
revealed (Gen 28: 12) to Jacob/Israel (v. 12*c–d*;
Gen 32:28); and secondly when (v. 21) wisdom
inspires the congregational song at the sea (Ex

15: 1–21). Allusions to the wilderness song of the
dumb (v. 21*a*; Isa 35:6) and the praise offered by
babes (v. 21*b*; Ps 8:2 LXX) suggest the miraculous
and hint at ecstatic hymnody (Wis A. 1; 19:9);
men and women alike, 'filled with ecstasy' (*en-
thousiontes*), formed one choir to sing hymns of
thanksgiving (Philo, *Vit. Cont.* 87). Similarly in
rabbinic exegesis 'the holy spirit rested upon
Israel and they uttered the song'; babes and
sucklings (Ps 8:2) and embryos in the womb
all sang with the angels (*Mekilta, Beshallah, Shirata*
1, on Ex 15: 1; Lauterbach 1933: ii. 7, 11–12).

*The Israelites were Saved, and the Egyptians
Punished, by Water; the Egyptians were
Punished Also through the Same Irrational
Creatures which they had Revered in Idolatry;
God could have Acted More Terribly, but His
Justice is Measured, and He Loves All that Is*
(11:2–12:1)

11:2–19:22 continue the Exodus theme of 10:
15–11: 1, and the address to God begun in 9: 1
(Wis 9, introduction), but contrast as a whole
with 6: 1–11: 1, and can be regarded as forming
the third main section of the book (Wis A. 1).
The structure is no longer governed by the
biblical narratives of Solomon's prayer for wisdom, its antecedents and sequel; instead, the
narratives of the Exodus are determinative. The
figure of Wisdom ceases to be central, and
the hints at a manual for kings, sustained ever
since 1:1 (Wis io, introduction), are given up;
instead, a discursive and homiletic exegetical
meditation is addressed to the deity. Elaborate
and sometimes laboured, it ranges from the
sweet and noble to the grim and grotesque;
but it lacks as a whole the depth of the sections
focused on the suffering righteous and the wise
king. It seems likely to be a separate composition, perhaps by another author, added to
io: 1–11: 1 (Wis 9, introduction; io, introduction;
A. 1, B. 1).
   11:2–12:1 forms a coherent passage, but comprises the beginnings of two separate sequences
within 11: 1–19:22 as a whole. First, vv. 1–14 open
a series of seven contrasts between Egyptians
and Israelites; the remaining six constitute chs.
16–19. The first six contrasts begin from the
Egyptian plagues, the seventh from the Egyptian pursuit of Israel to the Red Sea. The series
echoes the contrasts between Egypt and Israel
which were drawn in the biblical accounts of
the ten plagues and the Exodus (see Ex 8:21–3;
9:4–7, 25–6; 10:22–3; 0:4–7; 12:27; Ps 78:50–3;
Neh 9:11), and received additions later on (Wis

11:6–10); contacts with Philo's account suggest that some of the developed material may already have been traditional at the time of Wisdom. In form, however, the series is primarily indebted to the currency of antithetic comparison as a Greek literary device. Secondly, 11:15–16 discerns the principle that as we sin, so are we punished; this, added to the principle already noted (vv. 5, 13), that the ungodly in the form of Gentile foes are punished by the very things that benefit the holy people, leads to praise of God's love and tempered judgement (11:17–12:27) on idolatrous sinners and then to concentrated examination of the root sin of idolatry, its causes and consequences (chs. 13–15). After this bipartite digression (11:15–12:27; 13:1–15:19), linked with its context especially by the theme of Gentile sin (*Jub* 23:23–4; Gal 2:15) and united throughout its two parts by the theme of idolatry in particular, the series of contrasts between Egypt and Israel begun in 11:1–14 is resumed (16:1–19:22).

11:2–14, taking up the Exodus narrative from 10:20–11:1 (cf. Ex 14:31–15:21) recalls (11:2–3) the wilderness march and battle (Ex 17), focusing like Ps 114:8; 1 Cor 10:4 on the gift of water from the rock (Ex 17:6); this suggests the insight that the people benefit from the very things that punish their foes (11:5), who themselves feel extra chagrin and awestruck terror at the thought (11:13). 11:5 thus brings in the first of the seven contrasts, between (11:6–7; Ex 7: 17–18) the never-failing Nile turned into blood (itself a fitting penalty for the 'infanticidal decree' (11:7, 14; 18:5; Ex 1:22) against the Israelite male children) and (11:7–10) the unlooked-for abundance of fresh water from hard stone after thirst (itself a fitting paternal chastening (Wis 2: 13) which also showed the righteous the torments of their foes, the ungodly. This contrast was later current in the form that the Nile water was bloodied for the Egyptians, but sweet and drinkable for the Hebrews (Philo, *Vit. Mos.* L1.44; Jos. *Ant.* 2.294–5; 3:17).

11:15–16 could start a second contrast, but that is deferred to 16: 1. Instead, the plagues of frogs, lice, and flies (Ex 8:6, 17, 24) are taken with some freedom to have been educational punishments (11:16) by the very things with which the Egyptians sinned when, astray through insensate 'thoughts' (*logismoi*, Wis 1:3), they revered worthless 'animals' (*knodala*, 11:15b; 16:1; the word covers the range of size from AV 'vile beasts' to RV 'wretched vermin'). Cats or crocodiles, with which deities were indeed associated, would have led more naturally than frogs and

unpopular insects to this interpretation; but Wisdom gives out standard anti-Egyptian polemic: 'they have put their trust in…creeping things and vermin' (*knodala*) (*Ep. Arist.* 138); 'be ashamed of deifying polecats and brute beasts (*knodala*)' (*Sib. Or.* frag. 3, 22, tr. J. J. Collins; Charlesworth 1983–5: 1. 471).

11:17–20: the strikingly measured character of divine retribution, on the principle set out in 11:16, is now brought out by a flight of fancy found also in Philo (*Vit. Mos.* 1.19). The almighty hand that shaped the cosmos (11:17) could have sent truly fearsome beasts (11:18–19). 'Formless matter' (11:17), from the philosophical vocabulary, will have been held by the author to agree with Genesis (Wis A.2); 'it was from our teachers that Plato [cf. Tim. 30A, 51A, (69BC)] borrowed his statement that God, having altered formless matter, made the world…the prophetic spirit…said [Gen 1:1–2 LXX]: In the beginning God made the heaven and the earth, but the earth was invisible and unwrought' (Justin (Wis A. 10), 1 *Apol.* 59.1, approving Plato and perhaps echoing Wisdom). The pre-existence of matter is probably allowed in 17 (Wis A.8), for divine power is being asserted, yet words like 'did not make them out of things that existed' (2 Macc 7:28) are not used; these words too could be reconciled with pre-existence, for in Greek thought non-existence tended to signify lack of definite character rather than utter nullity (Stead 1994: 66–8, 107–8), but with fair probability they can be taken as an intended protest against any challenge to divine power implied by preexistence. Growth of objection to the notion of pre-existent matter among Jews in the first two centuries CE is implied by the revised Greek versions of Gen 1:2: the LXX as quoted through Justin Martyr above is replaced by 'nothing and nothing' (Theodotion) or 'emptiness and nothing' (Aquila) (Salve- sen1991: 1–2). 11:17, treated by Origen as a seeming witness to views of pre-existence matter that he opposed (De *princ.* 4.6), was reconciled with creation from nullity by the suggestion that prior creation of matter is assumed; 'we read "…from formless matter"…but that matter itself is made from what is altogether nothing' (Aug. *De Gen. c. Manich.* 1.5).

11:20 passes from uncanny creatures to wind or spirit (7:20) of divine power (5:23); this was indeed reserved for the Egyptians' ultimate punishment (Ex 15:10). Such tempered and proportionate justice marks (11:20c) the divine ordering (*diatassein*; to dispose or ordain, cf. 1 Cor 7:17); the similar 8:1 uses *dioikein*, 'manage', but OL *disponere* and AV, RV, REB 'order' unite 11:20c with 8:1. The triad 'measure and number and weight' would suit Solomon as builder (1 Kings 7:9–12), but 11:20c, with Philo, *Somn.* 2.192–4, on the Deity as the weighing, measure, and number of all things, and 2 Esd 4:36–7, on weighing the world and measuring and numbering the times, primarily echoes a current formula derived from Plato, 'an equality which is equal in measure, weight and number' (laws, 757B). Plato here goes on to speak of the best equality, which is the judgement of Zeus, and the phrase is applied to divine judgement in Wisdom; but it also resembles biblical verses on creation (Job 28:25; Isa 40:12), and *T. Napht.* 2 praises the beautiful order of creation and the human constitution, made 'by weight, measure and rule' (v. 3). Origen correspondingly applied 11:20c to divine creation of the right number of creatures and the right amount of matter; 'he made all things by number and measure; for to God there is nothing either without end or without measure' (*De princ.* 2.9, 4.4). Links with creation and providence (strengthened by association with 8:1) as well as judgement gave 11:20c broad influence as a summary of divine action; it is cited over 30 times by Augustine, for example on the importance of number in Scripture and in the work of creation (*De civ. dei*, 11.30, 12.19).

(11:21–12:2) 11:20, on power and moderation, expands into an equally influential hymn on God's power and love (11:21–12:2; comparably hymn-like are 12:12–18; 15:1–6; 16:13–14). At its heart it claims (11:23) not simply that 'as his majesty is, so also is his mercy' (Sir 2:17 RV), but rather that he is merciful just because he is almighty, cf. 12:16. 11:23a is echoed in the old collect (before 8th cent.) beginning 'O God, who declarestthy almighty power most chiefly in showing mercy and pity' (Gelasian Sacramentary; English Prayerbook (1662), Trinity XI; Tridentine Roman Missal, Pentecost X). As in Acts 17:30; Rom 2:4, his overlooking of sins appeals for repentance (12:10, 19; Wis 5:3).

11:24–12:1 is governed by the remarkable declaration that he loves all things that are, hating nothing that he has made, sparing all things, and immanent in all things. The emphasis lies on all created things, rather than (as in Jon 4:11) on all human beings or living creatures; compare the divine love for 'the world' (*kosmos*) in John (3:16, soon passing to humanity in particular), perhaps also hinted at in Paul on 'the creation' (Rom 8:20–1). Platonic and Stoic views of

the cosmos as a living organism (Wis A.4) will have assisted this way of thinking. Plato stressed the benevolence of the maker who shaped the world and its soul; 'he was good...and desired that all things should be as far as possible like himself' (*Tim.* 29E). In Ps 145:9, *Ps. Sol.* 18:1, not dissimilarly, the Lord's mercy is upon all his works, yet thought is immediately focused on his people in particular. Within the biblical tradition, therefore, 11:24–12:1 forms a landmark in the history of the notion of a God of love, combining Greek universality of scope with the strength of the OT imagery of divine love. They are summed up in the epithet 'lover of souls' (11:26 AV; *philopsychos*), taken up in Charles Wesley's hymn 'Jesu, lover of my soul'; cf. wisdom's entrance into souls (7:27), and the divine 'visitation of souls' (Wis 3:13). NRSV, REB 'who love the living' (similarly RV) does less than justice to the importance of the soul (*psyche*) in Wisdom (A.9). Although souls in human bodies are primarily in view, the thought need not be restricted to them (Wis 8:19). 12:1 finally praises the Deity's omnipresence through his incorruptible (RV, cf. 2:23) spirit; perhaps wisdom (Wis 1:4–6) but, strikingly, wisdom is not named (Wis 11:2). In view of the fresh emphases of 11:2–19:18 it seems unlikely that the identification is assumed.

12:2 spells out the moral of gradual reformative correction that was suggested by 11:15–20, and is now to be further illustrated.

God did not Destroy the Canaanites at Once, as he Might have Done; in Sparing them he Taught his Own Children, but he Scourged the Unrighteous Egyptians with a Terrible Judgement (12:3–27)

(12:2–18) The national consciousness (Wis A.3) of the 'children of God' (v. 7, NRSV marg.), the righteous who worthily inherit his dear and holy land (vv. 3, 7), is at its fiercest here. Destruction at their hand (v. 6) was ordained for the Canaanites, cannibals whose murderous superstition deserved it (vv. 3–5; cf. Lev 18:21; Ps 106:28, 37–8, respectively forbidding and condemning adoption of these customs); but judgement came little by little (vv. 6–10; Ex 23:30), allowing time for repentance (v. 10; Wis 11:23; 5:3) even though they were an accursed race, and divine power fears no enemy (vv. 10–11). The curse of Canaan (v. 10; Gen 9:25–7, predicting servitude; destruction is added in *Jub.* 22:20–1) is reinforced by the list of capital crimes (vv. 3–6) to justify (cf. v. 13) the divine judgement (and implicitly also the conquest, v. 7), and to show the great clemency (v. 10) of gradual retribution—even if it took the form of hornets (v. 8; Ex 23:28). In v. 5c NRSV, with REB v. 6a, follows a probable division of Greek letters which in many MSS have suffered confusion. 'Opportunity to repent' (v. 10), more exactly 'place of repentance' (RV), recurs towards the end of the first century CE in the apocalypses of Ezra and Baruch (2 Esd 9:11; Syriac Apoc. Bar. 85:12, ET in Sparks 1984: 895); Heb 12:17; 1 Clem. 7:5. It is attested in Latin from Livy 44.10 (late 1st cent. BCE) onwards, and Acts 25:16 'opportunity to make a defence', literally 'place of defence', suggests similar Greek use outside the Jewish and Christian communities. Wisdom probably therefore uses a current non-Jewish phrase which gained wide Jewish and Christian circulation through the prominence of repentance.

vv. 12–18 form another hymnlike address to God (Wis 11:21); his absolute sovereignty sets his sentence of destruction above question, but is in any case manifested in righteousness and forbearance; by contrast yet similarly, his seeming forbearance raises questions in Romans, but still no one is qualified to ask (Rom 3:25–6; 9:20–2). 'Those who know' (v. 17) know God, but do not honour him (Rom 1:21).

vv. 19–22 teach repentance and Godlike forbearance. His suffering 'people' (v. 19; 15:14; 16:2, 20; 18:7, 13; 19:5) are being prepared for mercy; their prosperous foes are being given time to repent before a scourging far harsher than God's discipline of his children. The imitation of God (v. 19) was also taught in Plato, the Stoics, and Philo, cf. Lev 11:44; Deut 13:4; Mt 5:45; Eph 5:1; 1 Pet 1:15–16; 1 Clem. 30:1; Abrahams (1924). 'A man highly esteemed says in the Theaetetus [176AB] ... Flight [to heaven] is to become like God, as far as this is possible; and to become like him is to become righteous and holy (hosios), with understanding' (Philo, Fug. 63, quoting Plato).

vv. 22–7, revert to the Egyptians, who ignored the relatively mild rebukes of the earlier plagues (11:15–16; 12:2), but under sterner judgements were angry with their idols and recognized the true God, even as they received his final condemnation. This conclusion balances 11:15–16; in unrighteousness (11:15; 12:23) they were led astray (11:15; 12:24), worshipping ignoble creatures (11:15; 12:24), and punished through the things in which they sinned, holding them to be gods (11:16; 12:24). A weighty term in 11:15–15:19 which gains fresh force through this resumption is 'error' (plane, v. 24; cf.Rom 1:27), with the cognate verb 'go astray' (v. 24; 2:21; 5:6; 13:6; 14:22; 15:4; 17:1). Through the LXX it is specially linked with idolatry; images of the heavenly host are forbidden lest 'being led astray, you should worship them' (Deut 4:19 LXX), the false prophet spoke 'to lead you astray from the Lord' (Deut 13:5 LXX), and the holy people dally with but reject error and idolatry (Isa 30:10, 19–20, 22 LXX).

Those who Worshipped God's Works were not Excused; but Yet More Miserable are Those who Worship what Human Hands have Made (13.1–19)

Idolatry has been the sin underlying the various crimes detailed since 11:15. Now its nature as the root sin is examined (13:1–15:19). Gentile observances posed practical problems for adherents of the God of Israel living near or among non-Jews (see 1 Cor 8, the Mishnah tractate cAboda Zara, and Tertullian On Idolatry; inscriptions and documents in Williams 1998: ii. 46–8, v. 47–55); but chs. 13–15, true in their fashion to the philosophic bent of Wisdom, include not wholly unsympathetic speculation on the origins of idolatry (13:1–9; 14:12–31; Wis c.2), and deal with practical problems only implicitly, by polemic and ridicule (13:10–14:11; 15:1–19; Wis 11:16). The continuation of biblical idol-satire in the Letter of Jeremy (Bar 6) and Bel and the Dragon had been adapted in Greek with a philosophical tinge like that of Wisdom in Epistle of Aristeas 134–8 (2nd cent. BCE) and Sib. Or. 3 (mainly 2nd and 1st cents. BCE).

vv. 1–9, to which Rom 1:18–23 are close, hail and mournfully condemn as mataioi 'foolish', that is 'vain' (RV) or 'empty' (v. 1; Isa 44:9 LXX; cf. Rom 1:21) all who seek (v. 6; Acts 17:27; Wis A.10), yet fail to pass from things seen (v. 8) to 'him who is' (v. 1)—a title (from Ex 3:14 LXX 'I am he that is') 'implying that others lesser than he have not being, as being indeed is'(Philo, Det. 160)—and fail to rise from the power and beauty of creation to 'the author ofbeauty' (v. 3). Plato's doctrine ofideas is in view, as at Wis 9:8 (A.4), with particular reference (vv. 3, 5, 7) to the ascent from 'what has the name of beauty here' to 'beauty itself' (Phdr. 250E; cf.Symp. 211c); LXX shows thatthe thought of divine beauty implied in the Hebrew OT found increasingly explicit expression among Jews (Ps 50:2,11 LXX; 96:6 LXX; Isa 63:1 LXX; Wis 7:28–9; 8:2, on wisdom's beauty).

vv. 10–19, with contrasting sarcasm, follow Isa 44:9–20 and kindred texts in drawing a cartoon of the wretched heathen (v. 10; cf.v. 1; 3:11), whose hope is on or (OL) among 'dead things' (vv. 10, 18; Bar 6:32, 71). He whittles an image out of waste wood, not even wanted for the fire (Isa 44:15–17), to fill up his spare moments (vv. 12–13), fixing it safely in a niche (Isa 41:7), and then petitioning it for health and wealth (vv. 17–19). The piquant contrast between helpless image and divine power was equally familiar to non-Jews, who could likewise treat it satirically; 'the carpenter, in two minds whether to make me into a stool or a Priapus, decided that I should be a god' (Horace, *Satires*, 1.8.1–3). Greek dedications can indeed mention the material and the making of an image with humorous pride before formulating a prayer, precisely in the sequence mocked in vv. 10–19; but they also show an ability to differentiate between image and deity which is ignored in satire like that of Wisdom: 'pray that the herald of the gods may be kind to Timonax, who set me up ... in honour of Hermes the lord' (*Palatine Anthology*, 6. 143, 5th–3rd cent. BCE; the image of Hermes addresses the passer-by).

Wooden Ships, not Wooden Images, Save Seafarers, and Idols are Accursed like their Makers; How Idolatry Began, and How it Brings in Sin and Judgement (14:1–31)

vv. 1–11, still on wood, move to ships and the yet frailer wood of the images of their patron deities (v. 1; Acts 28:11). The sea between Judea and Egypt is the scene of *T. Zeb.* 6:1–3 (Egypt reached in a fishing-boat), *T. Napht.* 6 (storm off Jamnia). Wisdom, named (vv. 2, 5) here uniquely in 11:2–19:22 (Wis A. 1; b.i; 11:2), is the divinely inspired art of the shipwright and navigator; no clear link is made between v. 2 and 7:16 on wisdom as 'fashioner', or vv. 5–6 and 10:4 on the wood of the ark.

Divine 'providence' (*pronoia*; v. 3; 17:2, cf.6:7) is first mentioned in the biblical books here and in 3 Macc (4:21; 5:30). *Pronoia* was a quality of rulers (2 Macc 4:6; 14:9; Acts 24:3) discerned by Plato in the divinity who brought cosmic order out of disorder (*Tim.* 30BC), denied by Epicurus to his tranquil deities, but ascribed by Stoics to the world-soul (Wis A.2; Stead 1994: 42–51, 146–7); divine providence becomes prominent in Philo, Josephus, and 4 Macc (9:24; 13:19; 17:22). Later Jewish references to *pronoia* in synagogue inscriptions from Sardis (3rd–4th cent.; Rajak 1998) are contemporary with Christian defence

and praise of divine providence in Origen (*C. Cels.* 6.71; 7.68) and Eusebius (*Hist. eccl.* 2.14.6). 'Father' (v. 3) is said on behalf of the righteous people of God collectively (contrast the individual, Wis 2:13), as suggested by vv. 6–7 on Noah, who set sail when God 'changed the dry land into sea' (Jos. *Ant.* 1.75) and the giants died (Gen 6:4,17; Sir 16:17; 3 Macc 2:4); he is perhaps the unskilled navigator of v. 4b. 'World' in v. 6b renders *kosmos*, but in 6c *aion*, a future age (Wis 18:4). Blessing (v. 7) on the wood 'by which righteousness comes', applied in the church to the cross (as by Ambrose, *Sermones* 8.23; *PL* 15.130) and in modern study sometimes (improbably) ascribed to Christian authorship, well fits the ark (v. 6) and sharpens the ensuing curse on idols (vv. 8–11); they shall have their prophesied 'visitation' (v. 11; Jer 10:11, 15 (RV 'visitation'); Wis 3:7).

(**14:12–31**) The causes (vv. 12–21) and consequences (vv. 2231) of idolatry are sketched in the conviction that it is the root of sin (vv. 12, 21, 27); 'fornication' (v. 12) has the biblical overtone of disloyalty in religion (Ex 34:15; Ps 73:27 RV). The devising of idols (vv. 12–14) was an innovation (perhaps in the time of Serug, Abraham's great-grandfather, as in *Jub.* 11:4–6, cf. Ps.-Philo, *LAB* 4.16); it will not last for ever (cf. v. 11). vv. 15–21 gain force through touches of sympathy (vv. 15, 17–20; cf. 13:6–7) and echoes (vv. 15, 20) of the Greek Euhemerus (end of 4th cent. BCE; followed in *Sib. Or.* 3:105–61; translated into Latin by Ennius, 2nd cent. BCE), who held that the gods had once been honoured mortals. The link suggested in v. 15 between this view and the cult of the departed child was consciously made by Cicero after the loss of his daughter (45 BCE): 'We see that many former human beings of either sex are among the gods ... Best and most accomplished of women, with the blessing of the immortal gods themselves I shall set you in your consecrated place among them' (*Consolation*, quoted by Lactantius, *Divinae Institutiones* 1.14). Ruler-cult (vv. 6b–21), flourishing throughout the Greek world from the fourth century BCE onwards (Walbank 1984: 84–100), could be seen as evidence on the side of Euhemerus; the composed brevity of Wisdom here contrasts with Philo's vehemence on Caligula's cult (*Legatio* 75–118; Wis C.2).

This error (v. 22) brings, under the name of the 'peace' sought from gods and rulers, what is really internecine war arising from ignorance; for idolatry causes not just the crimes clearly related to it (v. 23; cf. 12:5–6), but the whole range of social evils (vv. 24–6; Rom 1:28–31; *Barn.* 20, where the catalogue starts with idolatry). What appears in idolaters to be ecstatic joy (Wis 10:21; 19:9) is madness, and prophecy falsehood; they live by unrighteousness and false oaths, which will not go unpunished.

The True God is Hailed. The Ambitious Maker of Clay Idols Hopes in Vain, but the Enemies of God's People yet more Childishly Take all the Heathen Idols for Gods, Even Beasts without Sense or Beauty (15:1–19)

(15:1–6) These hymn-like verses (Wis 11:21), used as an Elizabethan model prayer (Clay 1851: 363), begin by varying the formula 'pitiful and merciful, long-suffering and plenteous in mercy, gracious to all' (Ps 145:8–9 LXX) with the significant designations 'true' (*alethes*), over against idols (cf. 1 Thess 1:9; 1 Jn 5:20, *alethinos*) and 'mercifully ruling' (more exactly 'managing' or ordering, as 8:2) 'all things'; cf. Ex 34:6 LXX; Num 14:8 LXX; Ps 86:15 LXX 'long-suffering, plenteous in mercy, and true (*alethinos*)' Ps 86:5 LXX 'gracious, gentle, and plenteous in mercy'; 2 Macc 1:24 'only king and gracious one, only supplier of our needs' (mytr.). 'Gracious' (*chrestos*), notin the LXX Pentateuch, became a solemn and valued description (Ps 25:8 LXX; 34:8 LXX, etc.; 'gracious and merciful', *Ps Sol.* 5:2; io:8); it is the most frequent epithet for the departed in second-century BCE to first-century CE Egyptian Jewish epitaphs (Horbury and Noy 1992: 272).

v. 2 can perhaps be paraphrased 'Ifwe sin we will not give up our loyalty to our God, for we fear his power [*kratos*, probably punitive, as at 2 Macc 3:34; 7:17]; but knowing that our repute reflects on our God, out of love we will not sin.' 'Immortality' (v. 3) is again future life (contrast Wis 8:13), for (Ps 115:4, 8 are echoed) we are not deceived by 'art or man's device' (Acts 17:29, close to v. 4) into Pygmalion-like desire for an image (v. 5); those who make or desire or revere them are worthy of them.

(15:7–13) in a variation on the amateur woodcarver (13:11–19) and the famous sculptor (14:18–20), depicts the maker of clay figures, whose own borrowed soul (v. 8; Wis A.4; 8:19; Ps.- Phoc. 106) must be returned (Lk 12:20; Jos *J.W.* 3.374: do not commit suicide, but return the loan (*chreos*, as here) when it is claimed); and who thinks only of gain (v. 12; Jas 4:13) despite awareness of guilt (v. 13). Jewish potters are attested in second- to first-century BCE Egypt (Williams 1998: 1. 71), and perhaps v. 13 implies criticism of some who sold images.

(15:14–19) turns to Gentile oppressors who adopt all heathen gods without discrimination (Ps 115:5–7 is echoed). The gibe suits Ptolemaic government in Egypt; returning to Milton's 'brutish gods of Nile' (11:15), it prepares for resumption of the series of contrasts between Egypt and Israel which was broken off at 11:14 (Wis 11:2).

Egyptian Animal-Worshippers were Punished by Vermin, but Creatures of Rare Taste were a Benefit to God's People; Egyptians were Slain by Insects, but God's People were Healed after Chastisement by Serpents, the Brazen Serpent Betokening Divine Salvation; Heat and Cold Changed their Nature to Punish and Starve the Ungodly, but to Delight God's People with Angels' Food (16:1–29)

(16:1–4) The second contrast (Wis 11:2, 15–16) sets the fitting torment of *knodala* (v. 1; Wis 11:15) over against the toothsome quails (19:11–12; Ex 16:13); Egyptians lost their appetite, Israelites relished exotic food like epicures. The wonder is recalled with the happiness of Ps 106:40 rather than the shame of Ps 78:26–31.

(16:5–14) The third contrast adds (v. 9) the locusts (Ex 10:1419), which constituted a 'death' (Ex 10:17 RV; LXX *thanatos*), to the flies, by which Egypt was 'destroyed' (Ex 8:24 (RV marg., LXX), used in the second contrast). These tiny insects sufficed to kill the oppressors (vv. 4, 8–9); but when (Num 21:6–9) God's children (vv. 10–11) were bitten by writhing serpents (vv. 5, io), like the dread 'writhing serpent' to be slain by God's own sword (Isa 27:1; RV, REB retain the full echo), it was just a 'warning' (v. 6) wherein they were saved (v. 11) 'sharply' (*oxeos*). NRSV (v. 11) adds 'then' to 'and', without express warrant in the Greek, but perhaps affliction itself is viewed as salvific, and *oxeos* means 'cuttingly' as well as (NRSV) 'quickly'; cf.i Cor 3:15; 5:5; 11:32.

The brazen serpent (vv. 6–8; Num 21:8–9) showed the enemy God's power (v. 4a; Deut 32:24k, 26–7); it was a symbol of salvation (OL *signum salutis*, through Jn 3:14 a designation of the cross; in the medieval and later Western divine office vv. 6, 7, and 8 formed antiphons for Holy Cross Day, 14 September). Not effectual in itself, it recalled the commandment (v. 6b, cf. Mal 4:4; including Deut 6: 16 'Ye shall not tempt', cf.i Cor 10:9) and the healing divine word (vv. 11–12; Ex 15:26; Ps 107:20); in later Jewish teaching, as here, they looked and were saved *if* their hearts were fixed on God's name (*Tg. Ps.-Jn.* Num 21:8, adding this condition).

'Saviour' (v. 7, *sotor*, here only in Wisdom) is a Hellenistic royal title applied to God in LXX (Deut 32:15; Ps 95:1, etc.); 'of all' (probably all *things*, as v. 12, not, as i tim 4:10, people only) gives v. 7 universalist potential (Wis 11:24; A.11), despite particularist stress (v. 10).

(16:13–29) The hymn-like vv. 13–14 (Wis 11:21), developing Deut 32:39, bring in the fourth contrast (see vv. 1, 5; on 16: 15–17: 1a, Dumoulin 1994). In the plague of hail and thunderbolts (v. 16; Ex 9:22–34; Ps 78:48) fire and water seemed to change their nature; fire in the midst of water spared the pestilential frogs, lice, and flies, yet scorched the crops (vv. 17–19), whereas God's people received 'ready' (preexistent, Wis 9:8) heavenly manna, food of angels (Wis A.9) which, snowlike though it was (19:21) remained and took on any taste desired (vv. 20–1). This interpretation, not in Philo, first occurs in Wisdom, perhaps from comparison of Ex 16:31 (honey) with Num 11:8 (fresh oil); so later, in the name of Eleazar of Modin (early 2nd cent. CE), 'anyone who liked what is baked could find in it the taste of anything baked in the world; anyone who preferred cooked food could find in it the taste of any cooked dish' (*Mekilta, Beshallah, Wayassa,* 5; Lauterbach 1933: ii. 118). In the church v. 21 was applied both to word and sacrament (especially through Mt 4:4; Jn 6:57–8); 'the manna is the word of God, and whatever taste is rightly desired when it is taken is immediately there in the mouth when it is eaten' (Gregory the Great, *Moralia in Job,* 31.15); 'O may my mind for ever live from thee, And thou, O Christ, its sweetness ever be' (Aquinas, *Rhythm on the Blessed Sacrament*).

vv. 24–5 (with vv. 17, 23; 19:6, 18–21) allow for miracles in the providential order by envisaging a transmutation of the elements, in accord with Stoic teaching ('the four elements are changed and transmuted up and down', Epictetus frag. 8; Sweet 1965). Harmony wherein even apparently destructive forces work together for good (Judg 5:20; Wis 5:20; 16:17; Rom 8:28) is depicted in Sir 39:16–35 (Crenshaw 1975; Wis 5:17). In Wisdom the harmony can embrace a change of notes (v. 24; 19:18).

v. 28 earnestly commends thanksgiving before dawn and petition 'towards the sunrise' (*pros anatolen*, perhaps hinting at orientation as well as time). The Essenes comparably prayed 'as though beseeching [the sun] to rise' (Jos. *J. W.* 2.128). Thanksgiving each day 'when it is beginning' was generally viewed as a Mosaic ordinance (Jos. Ant. 4.212); the morning Shema is said when it is light yet before sunrise, according to a Mishnaic teaching resembling Wisdom (in the name of Eliezer b. Hyrcanus, end of 1st cent. CE), but later recitation was also acceptable (*m. Ber.* 1:2).

Darkness and Terror Shrouded the Lawless, but Light Guided the Holy (17:1–18:4)

The fifth contrast (Mazzinghi 1995; cf. 16:13) expands Ex 10:22–3, under the heading of 'error' (17:1; Wis 12:24) punished by 'providence' (17:2; Wis 14:3), into a heightened depiction of the haunted darkness that fell upon Egypt (17:2–21), although light shone from the fiery pillar and a temperate sun on God's holy children (18:1–4). Its style is followed in an eerie passage of Melito, *On Pascha* (16–33; late 2nd cent. CE; Wis A.2). The spectres (17:3–6, 18) perhaps are or come from the 'evil angels' who afflicted Egypt (Ps 78:49). 'Inner chamber' (17:4) is a bland rendering of *mychos*, OL here 'cave', used also of hellish 'recesses' (17:14). Lurid flashes of fire, which themselves could not be properly seen, made what *could* be seen by their light seem still worse (17:6, following OL; cf. Goodrick 1913). The wizards of Egypt were humbled (17:7–8, 14–15; Ex 9:11; 2 tim 3:8–9); their night (v. 14), like Hades (Wis 1:14) whence it came, was *adynaton*, perhaps in the less well-attested sense 'intolerable' (AV) rather than 'powerless'. Light shone (18:1–3) on those through whom the light of the law (Prov 6:23) would shortly dawn on the 'world' (*aion*, 18:4; a future age, as in 14:6); in the time of Moses 'the lamp of the eternal law shone on all those in darkness' (*2 Apoc. Bar.* 59:2; Sparks 1984: 877).

The Enemies' Firstborn were Utterly Destroyed, but the Plague on the Righteous was Stayed (18:5–25)

The sixth contrast (cf. 17:1) juxtaposes the death of the firstborn (vv. 5–19; Ex 12:12–14, 21–31) not with the sparing of the righteous (vv. 7–9) 'that night' (v. 6), as in Ex 12:12–13, 27, but with Israel's later plague, when after experiencing death (v. 20) they were spared through the person and office of the high priest (Num 16:41–50); compare the third contrast, between the Egyptian plagues of 'vermin' and the later Israelite plague of serpents (16:5–14). Pharaoh's 'infanticidal decree' is here (v. 5, differing from 11:6) requited by the slaying of the firstborn and then of the Egyptian host. The saints (vv. 6–9) were aware beforehand (v. 6; Wis 8:8); v. 9, with *Jub.* 49:6 and Philo, *Spec. Leg.* 2.148, anticipates the Mishnah's emphasis on passover hymnody:

'therefore are we bound to give thanks, to praise, to glorify, to honour, to exalt, and to bless...so let us say the Hallelujah' (Ps 113–18) (*m. Pesah.* 9.5). The destroyer (Ex 12:23) is in vv. 14–15 the divine word (*logos*), pictured (v. 16) as a great angel (Wis 9:1); this electric description (a Christ- mastide antiphon in medieval and later service-books, cf. Jn 1:14) helped to form the concept of Christmas as 'silent night'.

The 'blameless' Aaron (vv. 21–5) stood between dead and living with his censer (Num 16:46–8); Wisdom adds to Numbers an explicit mention of 'prayer', associated with incense (Ps 141:2; Rev 5:8), and Aaron's 'word' recalling the ancestral covenants, an insertion perhaps modelled on Ex 32:13. His vestment, breastplate, and mitre (v. 24; Ex 28:2–39; 39:1–26) display respectively the cosmos, the glories of the patriarchs, and the divine name itself. This interpretation is spelt out later in Philo (*Vit. Mos.* 2.117–35; *Spec. Leg.* 1.84–97) and Josephus (*J. W* 5.232–5; *Ant.* 3.184–7).

Sinners Justly Met a Strange End in the Sea, but the Righteous were Saved there, for the Elements are Governed in Favour of God's People (19:1–22)
The seventh and last contrast (19:5), from Ex 14:1–15:19, is between the doom that justly filled up the torments of the ungodly by a strange death in the Red Sea (vv. 1,4–5), and the safe passage of God's people amidst a series of wonders (vv. 6–12). The same interchange of elements (vv. 6, 18–21; Wis 16:24) punished the sinners (vv. 13–17) and saved God's servants (vv. 5–12, 22). 'Fate' (v. 4) represents *anankē*, 'necessity', a word here as in Paul (e.g. 1 Cor 9:16) thought compatible with divine predestination. The 'grassy plain' (v. 7), seemingly peculiar to Wisdom, suits the ecstatic gambols of v. 9 (Wis 10:20–1); vv. 7–9 draw not only on Ps 114:3–4 but also on Isa 63:13–14, where the people at the sea are led like a horse in the wilderness or like cattle in a valley (LXX 'plain').

(19:10–21) brings in hitherto unmentioned points from narratives already considered. vv. 10–13 recall 16:1–2 (lice, frogs, quails), then (v. 13) probably 16:16–19, on the plague of hail and lightning which also brought the 'violence of thunder' (v. 13; Ex 9:23, 28–9, 33–4); the thunders that were prominent in this relatively early plague can more naturally be viewed as a 'prior sign' (v. 13) of warning than the thunder just before the Egyptians were drowned (Ps 77:18–19; Jos. *Ant.* 2.343). Worse than the inhospitable Sodomites (vv. 14–17; Wis 10:6; Ezek

16:49) awaiting punishment (v. 15; *episkopē*, Wis 3:7), they too were struck with blindness (17:2, 17; 18:4; Ex 10:23). vv. 20–1 recall 16:17–18, 22–3, but more clearly depict the solidity of the snow-like manna (v. 21; Artapanus 3.37, 3rd- 2nd cent. BCE, tr. J. J. Collins, in Charlesworth 1983–5: ii. 903; Jos. *Ant.* 3.27). 'Heavenly' (v. 21; *amhrōsios*, RV 'ambrosial') underlines 'angels' food' (16:20) with an allusion to the food of the Olympian gods.

v. 22 concludes the address to the Lord taken up in Wis 11:2; as shown by the seven contrasts discerned in the Exodus, his 'people' (Wis A.3; 12:19) have been 'exalted' (Ps 20:6, 8 LXX) and 'glorified' (18:8; Isa 43:4; 44:23 LXX; Sir 24:12; Rom 8:30) by his observant assistance 'at all times' (*Ps. Sol.* 16:4) and 'in all places' (Prov 15:3). Just so (perhaps it is remembered) his 'people' pray 'at all times' (Ps 34:1, 1 Macc 12:11) and 'in all places', at home and abroad (Mal 1:11).

REFERENCES

Abrahams, I. (1924), 'The Imitation of God', in I. Abrahams, *Studies in Pharisaism and the Gospels*, 2nd ser. (Cambridge: Cambridge University Press), 138–82.

Alexander, P. S. (1988), 'Retelling the Old Testament', in Carson and Williamson (1988), 99–121.

Armstrong, A. H. (1970) (ed.), *The Cambridge History of Later Greek and Early Medieval Philosophy* (corr. repr.; Cambridge: Cambridge University Press).

Barclay, J. M. G. (1996), *Jews in the Mediterranean Diaspora* (Edinburgh: T. & T. Clark).

Carson, D. A. and Williamson, H. G. M. (1988) (eds.), *It is Written: Scripture Citing Scripture: Essays in Honour of Barnabas Lindars, SSF* (Cambridge: Cambridge University Press).

Charlesworth, J. H. (1983–5) (ed.), *The Old Testament Pseudepigrapha* (2 vols.; London: Darton, Langman, & Todd).

Chester, A. (1988), 'Citing the Old Testament', in Carson and Williamson (1988), 141–69.

Clark, J. M. (1952), *The Life of the Servant, by Henry Suso* (London: James Clarke).

Clay, W. K. (1851), *Private Prayers put forth by Authority during the Reign of Queen Elizabeth* (Cambridge: Cambridge University Press).

Collins, A. Yarbro (1985), 'Aristobulus', in Charlesworth (1983–5), II. 831–6.

Crenshaw, J. L. (1975), 'The Problem of Theodicy in Sirach', *JBL* 94: 47–64.

Day, J., Gordon, R. P., and Williamson, H. G. M. (1995) (eds.), *Wisdom in Ancient Israel* (Cambridge: Cambridge University Press).

Deane, W. J. (1881), *The Book of Wisdom* (Oxford: Clarendon).

Dumoulin, P. (1994), *Entre la manne et l'eucharistie: Ètude de Sg16, 15–17, 1a,* AnBib 132 (Rome: Pontificio Instituto Biblico).

Goldin, J. (1955), *The Fathers According to Rabbi Nathan,* Yale Judaica Series 10, (New Haven, Conn.: Yale University Press).

Goodrick, A. T. S. (1913), *The Book of Wisdom* (London: Rivingtons).

Grabbe, L. L. (1997), *Wisdom of Solomon,* Guides to Apocrypha and Pseudepigrapha (Sheffield: Sheffield Academic Press).

Gregg, J. A. F. (1909), *The Wisdom of Solomon* (Cambridge: Cambridge University Press).

Hengel, M. (1974), *Judaism and Hellenism,* ET (London: SCM).

Horbury, W. (1994a), 'The Wisdom of Solomon in the Muratorian Fragment', *JTS* n.s. 45: 149–59.

——(1994b), 'Jewish Inscriptions and Jewish Literature in Egypt, with Special Reference to Ecclesiasticus', in J. W. van Henten and P. W. van der Horst (eds.), *Studies in Early Jewish Epigraphy* (Leiden: Brill), 9–43.

—— (1995), 'The Christian Use and the Jewish Origins of the Wisdom of Solomon', in Day, Gordon, and Williamson (1995), 182–96.

Horbury, W., and Noy, D. (1992), *Jewish Inscriptions of Greco-Roman Egypt* (Cambridge: Cambridge University Press).

Horst, P. W. van der (1985), 'Pseudo-Phocylides', in Charlesworth (1983–5), II. 565–82.

Kilpatrick, G. D. (1981), review of Thiele, *Sapientia,* Fascicles i–iv, *JTS* n.s. 32: 214–16.

Kloppenborg, J. S. (1982), 'Isis and Sophia in the Book of Wisdom', *HTR* 75: 57–84.

Knox, W. L. (1937), 'The Divine Wisdom', *JTS* 38: 231–7.

—— (1939), *St Paul and the Church of the Gentiles* (Cambridge: Cambridge University Press).

Lauterbach, J. Z. (1933), *Mekilta de-Rabbi Ishmael* (3 vols.; Philadelphia: Jewish Publication Society of America).

Malherbe, A. J. (1969), 'The Holy Spirit in Athenagoras', *JTS* n.s. 20: 538–42.

Mazzinghi, L. (1995), *Notte di paura e di luce: esegesi di Sap 17, 1–18, 4,* AnBib 134 (Rome: Pontificio Istituto Biblico).

Montefiore, C. G. and Loewe, H. (1974), *A Rabbinic Anthology,* repr. with Prolegomenon by R. Loewe (New York: Schocken).

Puech, E. (1993), *La Croyance des esséniens en la vie future: Immortalité, resurrection, vie éternelle?* (2 vols; Paris: Gabalda).

Rajak, T. (1998), 'The Gifts of God at Sardis', in M. Goodman (ed.), *Jews in a Graeco-Roman World* (Oxford: Clarendon), 229–39.

Scarpat, G. (1989–99), *Libro della Sapienza* (3 vols.; Brescia: Paideia).

Smalley, B. (1986), *Medieval Exegesis of Wisdom Literature,* ed. R. E. Murphy (Atlanta: SBL).

Sparks, H. F. D. (1984) (ed.), *The Apocryphal Old Testament* (Oxford: Clarendon).

Stead, C. (1994), *Philosophy in Christian Antiquity* (Cambridge: Cambridge University Press).

Sweet, J. P. M. (1965), 'The Theory of Miracles in the Wisdom of Solomon', in C. F. D. Moule (ed.), *Miracles* (London: Mowbray), 115–26.

Vermes, G. (1997), *The Complete Dead Sea Scrolls in English* (London: Allen Lane).

Walbank, F. W. (1984), 'Monarchies and Monarchic Ideas', in F. W. Walbank, A. E. Astin, M. W. Frederiksen, and R. M. Ogilvie (eds.), *The Cambridge Ancient History,* VII.1: *The Hellenistic World* (Cambridge: Cambridge University Press), 62–100.

Weber, R. et al. (1975), *Biblia Sacra iuxta Vulgatam Versionem,* 2nd edn (2 vols.; Stuttgart: Württembergische Bibelanstalt).

Williams, M. H. (1998), *The Jews among the Greeks and Romans: A Diasporan Sourcebook* (London: Duckworth).

Woude, A. S. van der (1995), 'Wisdom at Qumran', in Day, Gordon, and Williamson (1995), 244–56.

6. Ecclesiasticus, or The Wisdom of Jesus Son of Sirach

JOHN J. COLLINS

INTRODUCTION

A. Title and Author. 1. The book of Ben Sira is known by various names in Jewish and Christian tradition. The Greek MSS usually provide a title at the beginning and again at the end: The Wisdom of Jesus, son of Sirach. The Latin is similar: The Book of Jesus son of Sirach. The beginning of the book is not extant in Hebrew,

but MSB from the Cairo Geniza refers to the book as The Wisdom of Simon son of Jeshua son of Eleazar son of Sira (51:30; cf. 50:27). The name Simon is probably introduced by mistake, because of the praise of the high priest Simon in ch. 50. The author's grandson, who translated the book into Greek, refers to his illustrious ancestor as 'my grandfather Jesus'. The full name was presumably Jeshua ben Eleazar ben

Sira. The 'ch'in the form Sirach derives from the Greek Sirachides, son or grandson of Sira, and so the Greek and Latin 'son of Sirach' is redundant; here we will use Ben Sira or Sirach. In many MSS of the Latin Vulgate the book is called simply 'Ecclesiasticus', or 'church book'. The medieval Jewish commentator Saadia calls it The Book of Instruction.

2. Ben Sira was evidently a scribe, and he provides a eulogistic account of his way of life in 39:1–11. In his view, the ideal scribe is a man of piety, devoted to the study of the law and to prayer, but also concerned with the wisdom of all the ancients. He also appears before rulers and travels in foreign lands. The book concludes with a quasi-autobiographical poem (51:13–30), in which the author refers to travels in his youth and invites the uneducated to 'lodge in the house of instruction'. The first part (vv. 13–20) of this poem, however, is found independently in 11QPs[a] and its authenticity as a composition of Ben Sira is disputed (J. A. Sanders 1965: 79–85; but see Skehan and DiLella 1987: 576–80, who take it as autobiographical). Regardless of the authenticity of this passage, however, it is likely that the author of the book was a teacher and that it preserves a sample of one kind of instruction offered to the youth of Jerusalem in the period before the Maccabean revolt.

B. Date. The book is exceptional among the wisdom books of the Bible and Apocrypha in disclosing the name of the actual author. The approximate date of composition is also disclosed by the grandson's preface to the Greek translation. The grandson, we are told, arrived in Egypt in the thirty-eighth year of King Euergetes. The reference can only be to Ptolemy VIII (VII) Euergetes II (Physcon), and the date of arrival is 132 BCE. The translation was completed some years later, probably after the death of Euergetes in 117 BCE. If we assume that the grandson was an adult when he moved to Egypt, and that the grandfather's prime was about half a century earlier, we may infer that Ben Sira's book was compiled somewhere in the first quarter of the second century BCE. Since it claims to present accumulated wisdom, it can scarcely be the work of a young man. Consequently, a date towards the end of that period is likely. The glowing praise of the high priest Simon in ch. 50 suggests that he was a contemporary of Ben Sira, although the eulogy was probably written after his death. Simon II was high priest from 219 to 196 BCE. The book shows

no awareness of the upheavals of the time of Antiochus IV Epiphanes (175–164). The prayer in ch. 36 is so alien to the thought world of Ben Sira that it must be regarded as a secondary addition, possibly from the Maccabean period.

C. Genre. Ben Sira's book stands in the tradition of Proverbs, which in turn stood in a tradition of wisdom instruction that is best represented in Egyptian literature. The basic genre of wisdom instruction includes a blend of observational sentences and commands and prohibitions. Sir 3:1–16 is a typical example: 'Those who respect their father will have long life…Honour your father by word and deed.' Traditional wisdom forms of speech in Sirach include comparisons (Sir 20:31: 'Better are those who hide their folly than those who hide their wisdom'), beatitudes (26:1: 'Happy is the husband of a good wife'), numerical sayings (50:25–6: 'Two nations my soul detests and the third is not even a people…'), and hymns in praise of wisdom (1:1–10; 24:1–34). But Sirach also incorporates literary forms that are not part of the repertoire of Proverbs. These include hymns of praise to God (39:12–35; 42:15–43:33) and at least one prayer of petition (22:27–23:6; 36:1–22 is probably a later addition). Some departures from Proverbs have precedents in Egyptian wisdom literature, notably the use of autobiographical narrative (33:16–18; 51:13–30) and the critique of the trades (38:24–34). The most striking formal departure from biblical wisdom, however, is found in the Praise of the Fathers (chs. 44–50) which uses the history of Israel as a source of instructional examples.

D. Ben Sira and Biblical Tradition. 1. One of the hallmarks of the biblical wisdom tradition, as found in Proverbs, Ecclesiastes, and Job, is the lack of reference to the distinctive traditions of Israel. The concern is with humanity as such, not with the special status of one people. Sirach, in contrast, pays considerable attention to Israel and its Scriptures. The grandson, in the preface, says that Sirach 'devoted himself especially to the reading of the Law and the Prophets and the other books of our ancestors', and implies that he envisaged his own book as comparable to the ancestral writings. This interest in the Scriptures cannot be explained simply by the spirit of the times. Ecclesiastes may be close to Sirach in date, but makes no mention of the law and the prophets. Sirach, however, says that all wisdom is 'the book of the covenant of the Most High God, the law that Moses commanded us' (24:23) and he describes the sage as 'one who devotes himself to the study of the law of the Most High...and is concerned with prophecies' (39:1–2). It has been claimed that he cites or alludes to all the books of the HB except Ruth, Ezra, Esther, and Daniel (Skehan and DiLella 1987: 41). This claim is misleading, however. Most of the allusions occur in the Praise of the Fathers. Elsewhere there are frequent allusions to Proverbs and to Genesis, and several to Deuteronomy. But many of the alleged allusions are loose, and may be coincidental. For example, when Sirach writes 'The rich speaks and all are silent, his wisdom they extol to the clouds' (13:23), an allusion to Job 29:21 is often suggested: 'They listened to me, and waited, and kept silence for my counsel.' But the saying is a truism, and the allusion is accordingly doubtful. Despite Sirach's reverence for the law, his teaching remains in the form of wisdom instruction. It is neither legal proclamation nor legal interpretation. He subsumes the law under the rubric of wisdom, as its supreme example. He does not subsume wisdom under the law. Moreover, he ignores certain sections of the law, particularly the cultic and dietary laws of Leviticus. Not all biblical laws are equally useful as illustrations of wisdom, and there remain other avenues to wisdom besides the law of Moses.

2. The extent to which Sirach drew on non-biblical, non-Jewish sources is also controversial. The maximal view (Middendorp 1973) finds over 100 passages where Ben Sira betrays dependence on Greek sources, but here again there is difficulty in distinguishing between imprecise allusion and coincidental commonplace. Many commentators grant an allusion to Homer's *Iliad* 6. 146–9 at Sir 14:18: both passages use the figure of leaves on a tree to express the transience of human life. Even if the allusion be granted, however, we can no more conclude that Sirach had read Homer than that someone who ponders 'to be or not to be' has read Shakespeare. The strongest evidence for Sirach's use of non-Jewish sources concerns the sayings of Theognis and the late Egyptian wisdom book of *Phibis*, preserved in Papyrus Insinger (J. T. Sanders 1983). In both cases, the material bears a strong resemblance to traditional Jewish wisdom. There is also evidence of Stoic influence in the notions of complementary opposites (33:14–15), teleology (39:21), and in the striking affirmation about God that 'He is the all' (43:27). There may be an echo of Epicurean teaching in 41:1–4. Sirach certainly shows no aversion to foreign wisdom, but he seems to have favoured Hellenistic material that resembled Jewish traditions and conversely pays little attention to the most distinctive aspects of Judaism such as the levitical laws.

E. The Text. 1. The textual history of Ben Sira's book is exceptionally complicated. We know from the grandson's prologue that the book was composed in Hebrew, but it has not survived intact in the original language. For many centuries the Hebrew text was known only from rabbinic citations (Schechter 1890–1). At the end of the nineteenth century, however, several fragments were found at Cambridge University, in the collection of MSS recovered from the Cairo Geniza (Schechter and Taylor 1899). These fragments represented four distinct MSS, A, B, C, and D. More leaves of MSS B and C were discovered later. Fragments of another manuscript (MS E) were discovered in the Adler Geniza collection at the Jewish Theological Seminary in New York and yet another (MS F) at Cambridge (see Skehan and DiLella 1987: 51–3). All these Geniza fragments are of medieval origin. They include most of chs. 3–16 and fragments of chs. 18–36. The Dead Sea scrolls yielded further, much older, fragments, from around the turn of the era. Two fragments from Cave 2 (2Q18) contain only four complete words and some letters from ch. 6 (Baillet, Milik, and de Vaux 1962) but 11QPs^a contains Sir 51:13–20, and the last two words of verse 30b (J. A. Sanders 1965). Then 26 leather fragments were found at Masada (Yadin 1965). These dated to the first century CE and contained portions of chs. 39–44. In all, about 68 per cent of the book is now extant in Hebrew (Beentjes 1997). For a time, some scholars expressed doubts about the Hebrew text preserved in the medieval Geniza fragments, and entertained the possibility that it might have been retranslated from Syriac. The Masada fragments, however, confirmed the antiquity of Geniza MSB, and indirectly enhanced the credibility of the other fragments. The present consensus is that the Geniza fragments faithfully preserve a text from antiquity (DiLella 1966; Skehan and DiLella 1987: 54).

2. The Hebrew fragments bear witness to two textual recensions. The second recension is distinguished from the first primarily by additions (e.g. 15:14b, 15c). These passages can be recognized as secondary because they are not found in the primary MSS of the Greek translation, and in some cases they are reflected in overlapping Hebrew fragments. There is also a second Greek recension, which expands the text in

a way similar to the second Hebrew recension. The second Greek recension is also reflected in the OL. One of the distinctive features of this recension is the belief in eternal life and judgement after death. The textual situation is further complicated by the fact that the Greek text is poorly preserved. The edition of the Greek text by J. Ziegler contains more emendations and corrections than any other book of the Septuagint (Ziegler 1965).

3. In all extant Greek manuscripts 30:25–33:13a and 33:13b–36:16a have exchanged places, probably due to the transposition of leaves. The Greek order of these chapters is often given in parentheses. Only the Hebrew order is given here.

F. Structure and Composition. 1. Attempts to discern a literary structure in Ben Sira have met with only limited success. In the judgement of A. A. DiLella 'the book manifests no particular order of subject matter or obvious coherence' (Skehan and DiLella, 1987: 4). In contrast, an elaborate structure has been proposed by M. H. Segal (1972) and W. Roth (1980). These authors distinguish an original book in 1:1–23:27 and 51:1–30. This book was made up of four sections: 1:1–4:10; 4:11–6:17; 6:18–14:19; and 14:20–23:27 + 51:1–30. Each section was introduced by a prologue: 1:1–2:18; 4:11–19; 6:18–37, and 14:20–15:10. Three additional sections were subsequently added: 24:1–32:13; 32:14–38:23; 38:24–50:29. (So Roth 1980. Segal 1972 distinguishes the Praise of the Fathers as an additional section.) Each of these also has a prologue: 24:1–29; 32:14–33:15, and 38:24–39:11. The key to this structure is provided by five passages on wisdom (1:1–10; 4:11–19; 6:18–37; 14:20–15:10, and 24:1–34). These passages seem to mark stresses in the first part of the book, but they have no discernible effect on the passages that precede or follow them (Gilbert 1984: 292–3). There are some indications that the book grew by a series of additions. The personal reflection in 24:30–4 appears to be the conclusion of a section rather than the beginning of the second half of the book. A similar autobiographical note is found in 33:16–18. First-person statements at 39:12 and 42:15 may also mark new beginnings, and the Praise of the Fathers in chs. 44–9 is formally distinct. There is a concentration of hymnic material in chs. 39–43. These observations render plausible the hypothesis that the book grew gradually, but they do not amount to proof.

2. In this commentary the structure proposed by Segal and Roth is modified to yield the following division: Prologue; Part I: 1:1–4:10; 4:11–6:17; 6:18–14:19; 14:20–23:27; 24:1–34. Part II: 25:1–33:18; 33:19–39:11; 39:12–43:33; 44:1–50:29; 51:1–30.

3. Sirach differs from Proverbs in so far as its material is not a collection of individual sayings, but consists of several short treatises. Some of these are devoted to traditional practical wisdom (e.g. relations with women, behaviour at banquets). Others are theological reflections on wisdom and on the problem of theodicy. Even when the material is largely traditional, Sirach often concludes his reflections by commending the fear of the Lord or observance of the law (e.g. 9:15–16; 37:15).

4. The prayer for the deliverance and restoration of Israel in 36:1–22 contrasts sharply in tone and style with the remainder of the book. It may have been added during the upheavals of Maccabean times. Another prayer, in 51:13–30, is attested independently in 11QPs[a] and evidently circulated separately in antiquity. Whether it was composed by Ben Sira remains in dispute.

G. Major Themes. 1. The major theme of the book is the pursuit of wisdom. In accordance with Proverbs (1:7) and Job (28:28), wisdom is identified as 'fear of the Lord': 'The whole of wisdom is fear of the Lord, and in all wisdom there is the fulfilment of the law' (19:20). Wisdom finds its objective expression in 'the book of the covenant of the Most High God, the law that Moses commanded us' (24:23). Yet Ben Sira's emphasis is not on the fulfilment of the specific commandments of the Torah. It is rather on wisdom as a discipline: 'My child, from your youth choose discipline, and when you have grey hair you will still find wisdom' (6:18). The discipline involves meditating on the commandments of the Lord (6:37) but also requires that one 'Stand in the company of the elders. Who is wise? Attach yourself to such a one. Be ready to listen to every godly discourse, and let no wise proverbs escape you' (6:35). The hymn in ch. 51 informs us that wisdom is to be found in 'the house of instruction', but it can also be sought by travel and requested in prayer. Fear of the Lord, then, is an attitude which requires obedience to the commandments but reaches beyond this. It entails reverence towards received tradition, and towards the elders who transmit it. It is a conservative attitude to life. It is often said to be opposed to the Hellenistic wisdom that attracted many in Jerusalem in the pre-Maccabean period (Hengel 1974: 1. 13153). Ben Sira does not polemicize against Hellenism, and is not averse to borrowing Hellenistic notions on occasion. He has little sympathy, however, for the spirit of adventure and innovation and does not appear to advocate new ideas consciously. In so far as Hellenization led some people to reject established Jewish traditions, as eventually happened in the reign of Antiochus IV Epiphanes (cf. 2 Macc 4), Ben Sira would surely have opposed it.

2. The Lord revered by Ben Sira is all-powerful and little short of overwhelming. The hymnic passages in chs. 39 and 42–3 affirm that 'all the works of the Lord are very good, and whatever he commands will be done at the appointed time'. He is closely identified with the power of nature. The climactic declaration 'He is the all' sounds close to pantheism, but Sirach quickly adds that 'he is greater than all his works' (43:28). In these passages Sirach seems to affirm that all that is, is good. God has made everything for a purpose. The world is constituted by complementary pairs, so that evil is necessarily the opposite of the good, and as such contributes to the harmony of the cosmos. All humanity can do is submit to the will of God. Sirach would seem to be influenced by Stoic philosophy here, if only unconsciously. In other passages, however, Sirach affirms a more traditional, Deuteronomic theology of free will: 'Do not say "It was the Lord's doing that I fell away"; for he does not do what he hates. Do not say, "It was he who led me astray"; for he has no need of the sinful' (15:11–12). When Sirach is praising God's creation, even evil has a purposeful role, but when the focus is on human behaviour it is an abomination to be rejected.

3. The problem of theodicy, or the justice of God, recurs intermittently throughout the book. It is made more acute for Sirach by his steadfast rejection of any belief in reward or punishment after death, beliefs which appear in apocalyptic literature around the time that Sirach wrote. 'Whether life lasts for ten years or a hundred or a thousand, there are no questions asked in Hades' (41:4). Having ruled out the possibility of retribution after death, Sirach offers a range of considerations, from simple submission to the divine will to the unconvincing claim that death and bloodshed fall 'seven times more' heavily on sinners than on others (40:8–9; see Crenshaw 1975). There is, of course, an inevitable tension between the affirmation of the omnipotent goodness of God and the reality of evil in the world. While he is less than consistent, Sirach generally insists on human

responsibility. When God created humanity, 'he left them in the power of their own inclination [NRSV: free choice]. If you choose, you can keep the commandments, and to act faithfully is a matter of your own choice' (15:14–15). Sirach does not pause to ponder the origin of the human inclination, a subject that fascinated later writers such as 4 Ezra (cf. 2 Esd 3:20–6).

4. Ben Sira breaks with the tradition of biblical wisdom by devoting extensive attention to the history of Israel. This history is not presented, however, as the history of the acts of God, or even as a sequential narrative. Instead it is cast as the praise of famous men, who stand as examples for future generations. The examples are chosen primarily because of leadership in their exercise of the offices of priest, king, judge, or prophet (Mack 1985: 11–65). Aaron is praised at greater length than Moses, and Phinehas is singled out for his role in securing the covenant of the priesthood. The whole series ends with a eulogy of Simon the Just, who was high priest at the beginning of the second century BCE. It seems fair to conclude that Sirach was an admirer and ally, and perhaps a *protégé*, of the high priest Simon. History for Sirach is not a process leading to a goal but a storehouse of examples from which the scribe may draw lessons that are essentially ahistorical.

5. Much of Sirach's instruction is taken up with the traditional wisdom concerns of family and social justice. The social teaching is quite conventional. Sirach has a keen sense of class distinctions: 'What peace is there between a hyena and a dog? And what peace between the rich and the poor? . . . Humility is an abomination to the proud; likewise the poor are an abomination to the rich' (13:18, 20). Observations of this sort are commonplace in Proverbs and in Egyptian wisdom literature. More distinctive is Sirach's negative characterization of merchants: 'A merchant can hardly keep from wrongdoing, nor is a tradesman innocent of sin. Many have committed sin for gain, and those who seek to get rich avert their eyes' (26:2927:1). Martin Hengel has argued that such passages reflect the conditions of the early Hellenistic period in Palestine, as exemplified in the story of the Tobiad family in Josephus (*Ant.* 12.154–236; Hengel 1974: 1. 138). But Sirach's admonitions lack historical specificity, and his remarks on merchants must also be read in the context of his general condescension to the trades in ch. 38.

6. The family ethic is also grounded in tradition, but here again Ben Sira strikes some

original notes, especially in his negative view of women (Trenchard 1982). He affirms the authority of mothers as well as fathers, and is aware of the benefits of a good wife. He discourses at greater length, however, on the bad wife. His most distinctive utterance is found in 25:24: 'From a woman sin had its beginning and because of her we all die.' There is no precedent in the biblical tradition for this interpretation of Genesis. He regards daughters as occasions of anxiety, lest they lose their virginity before marriage or having married, be divorced (42:9–10). In part, Ben Sira's worries reflect the reality of life in ancient Judea. Honour and shame loom large in the value system of the society, and the danger of shame through a daughter's indiscretion was all too obvious (Camp 1991). If a woman should be divorced, she would return to her father's house, and become, again, his responsibility. Yet Ben Sira is exceptional in so far as his worries are not relieved by any joy or delight in his daughters. In part this may be attributed to his anxious personality—compare his view of the human condition at 40:2: 'Perplexities and fear of heart are theirs, and anxious thought of the day of their death.' But for whatever reason he also shows a personal antipathy for women that goes beyond the prejudices of his society: 'Better is the wickedness of a man than a woman who does good; it is a woman who brings shame and disgrace' (42:14). Negative statements about women are more plentiful in Greek literature than in the Hebrew scriptures (see Lefkowitz and Fant 1982). Familiarity with Hellenistic views may have been a contributing factor of Ben Sira's view of women, but he was quite selective in his borrowings from Hellenistic culture, and so a deeper explanation must be sought in his personality.

H. Canonicity and Influence. Of all the pre-Mishnaic writings that were eventually excluded from the Hebrew canon, the book of Ben Sira was the most widely used. The fragments found at Qumran and Masada show that the book was widely used in antiquity. (Nothing about it was especially congenial either to the Essenes of Qumran or to the Zealots.) Although its use was reputedly banned by R. Akiba, it was venerated by many rabbis in the subsequent generations. Verses from the book are often cited as popular proverbs, and it is also often cited by name (Leiman 1976: 92–102). None the less, the Hebrew text was eventually lost. In Christian circles, the status of the book was

ambiguous, like that of the other Apocrypha. On the one hand it was widely cited, and included in some canonical lists; on the other hand some authorities, most notably St Jerome, limited the canonical scriptures to those found in the HB (see Box and Oesterly 1913: 298–303). Unlike the Hebrew text, however, the Greek and Latin versions of Sirach were transmitted continuously with the other scriptures.

COMMENTARY

The Prologue

The prologue was written by Ben Sira's grandson, who translated the book into Greek. It establishes approximate dates for both the original Hebrew book and the translation. The grandson arrived in Egypt in the thirty-eighth year of Ptolemy Euergetes, or 132 BCE. Assuming that the grandson was a young adult at this time, the grandfather would have been in his prime some fifty years earlier. It has been argued that the translation was made after the death of Euergetes in 117 BCE, since the grandson uses the aorist participle *synchronisas* to indicate that he lived through the remainder of that king's reign (Smend 1906: 4; Skehan and DiLella 1987: 134).

The prologue falls into two parts, the first addressing the grandfather's purpose in composing the book, the second dealing with the translation. The grandfather, we are told, was well versed in the law, the prophets, and the other writings, and wished to add to the tradition. His goal was to help people live according to the law. The translation is undertaken in the same spirit, presumably for the benefit of the Jewish community in Egypt. The prologue attempts to deflect possible criticism of the translation by asking the readers' indulgence. In fact, the corrupt state of the text probably has its root cause in the difficulties of the Hebrew, which often result in a Greek translation that is less than felicitous.

The most controversial point raised in the prologue concerns the formulaic reference to 'the Law, the Prophets and the other books of our ancestors'. By the time of Sirach, there can be little doubt that the Torah had taken its definitive shape. There was evidently also an authoritative collection of prophets, although we cannot be sure where the boundary line was drawn between the prophets and the writings. (David, the putative author of the Psalms, is often regarded as a prophet in the NT era.)

The collection of writings that eventually became canonical was certainly not current at this time. The book of Daniel had not yet been completed. Ben Sira does not refer to Ruth or Esther, and surprisingly fails to mention Ezra in the Praise of the Fathers. It is not apparent that Ben Sira's collection of Scriptures included any book that did not eventually become part of the HB. Early sections of 1 Enoch, which seem to have been authoritative for the Qumran sect, would not have been congenial to Sirach, but most of the books now classified as apocrypha and pseudepigrapha had simply not been composed when he wrote.

Part I. Chs. 1–24

(1:1–4:10)

(1:1–10) The Source of Wisdom The book begins with a short hymnic passage in praise of wisdom. Similar passages are found in 4:11–19; 6:18–37; 14:20–15:10, and at greater length in ch. 24 (Marböck 1971; Rickenbacher 1973). The opening affirmation is characteristic of Sirach: all wisdom is from the Lord. On the one hand, this sentence affirms the priority of Yahwistic revelation over all philosophy and wisdom. On the other hand it co-opts all philosophy and wisdom into divine revelation. Wherever wisdom is to be found, it is the work of the Lord.

Two biblical passages come directly to mind here. Prov 8 asserted that the Lord created wisdom as the beginning of his way. Temporal priority here bespeaks primacy of importance. The midrash on Genesis, *Genesis Rabbah*, ascribes this priority to the Torah, which was supposedly created 2,000 years before the creation of the world. In Proverbs, and also later in Sirach, wisdom then becomes God's implement in creation. The second biblical passage that comes to mind here is Job 28, which emphasizes that no one but God knows where wisdom can be found. Unlike Job, Sirach does not consider wisdom to be hidden: God has poured it out upon his works. Sirach does, however, pick up the conclusion of Job 28:28: 'the fear of the Lord, that is wisdom'. The fear of the Lord becomes the *leitmotif* of the following passage in Sirach. A few Greek MSS read 'he lavished her on those who fear him' in v. 10, instead of 'those who love him'.

(1:11–30) Fear of the Lord This passage begins and ends with reference to the fear of the Lord. The motif recurs over 60 times throughout the book. (For a tabulation, see Haspecker 1967:

48–50.) Fear of the Lord is constitutive of wisdom, and as such it pertains to the central theme of the book, which is laid out here in the opening chapter.

Fear of the Lord is primarily an attitude of reverence towards God and respect for received tradition. Some of its practical implications will become clear as the book unfolds. One fundamental requirement is noted here: 'if you desire wisdom, keep the commandments' (v. 26). Even though Ben Sira pays scant attention to the ritual commandments of Leviticus, their observance is probably taken for granted. We may compare the attitude of Philo of Alexandria, who was far more strongly inclined to emphasize a spiritual meaning than was Ben Sira. None the less, Philo faulted those who neglected the literal observance of the laws, and argued that Jews should be 'stewards without reproach . . . and let go nothing that is part of the customs fixed by divinely empowered men greater than those of our time' (*Migr.Abr.* 89–93). For Sirach, too, fear of the Lord entails diligence even in matters to which he does not otherwise accord importance.

Beyond observance of the commandments, fear of the Lord entails patience (v. 23), discipline, trust, humility (v. 27), and sincerity (vv. 28–9). These are age-old virtues of Near-Eastern wisdom. They offer a pointed contrast to the behaviour of profiteers such as the Tobiads in the Hellenistic period, but there is nothing peculiarly anti-Hellenistic about them. The fruits of wisdom and fear of the Lord are often described in rather vague terms, such as glory and exultation. vv. 12–13 are most specific. Wisdom leads to a long life and happiness even in the face of death. This is the traditional view found in the HB, especially in the Deuteronomic and sapiential books. By the time of Ben Sira, however, its inadequacy was widely perceived. Within the wisdom tradition, Job and Ecclesiastes had pointed out the all too obvious fact that wisdom does not guarantee a long life, and that those who ignore the counsels of the sages often prosper. The religious persecution of the Maccabean era would put a further strain on the traditional theology of retribution. Accordingly, notions of retribution after death were gaining credence in Judaism by the time of Ben Sira (cf. 1 Enoch, 1–36, which may date from the 3rd cent. BCE) and would become widespread in the apocalyptic writings of the Maccabean era (e.g. Dan 12).

At least one commentator has argued that Sir 1:11–13 implies a belief in retribution after death

(Peters 1913:13–14). He points to the parallel in the Wisdom of Solomon 3:1–11 ('The souls of the righteous are in the hand of God…'). Cf. also the eschatology of the *Rule of the Community* from Qumran. The children of Light, who walk in the way of humility, patience, and goodness, are rewarded with 'great peace in a long life, and fruitfulness, together with every everlasting blessing and eternal joy in life without end, in a crown of glory and a garment of majesty in unending light' (1QS 4). But Sirach lacks the specific references to eternal life that are explicit both in Wisdom (Wis 3:4: 'their hope is full of immortality') and in the *Rule of the Community* Since Sirach states unequivocally in ch. 41 that there is no retribution after death, there is no justification for importing ideas of an afterlife into ch. 1. However problematic Sirach's belief in this-wordly retribution may be, even for his time and place, he holds to it consistently.

(2:1–18) Trust in God In one MS this passage has the title 'On Patience'. The address to 'My child' suggests the paradigmatic setting of wisdom instruction, a father speaking to his son. The testing in view here consists of the normal trials and setbacks of life. It does not imply persecution with the threat of death, as it does in Dan 11:35 and in Wis 3. Sirach echoes the language of older Scripture to make his point. The questions in vv. 10 and 11 recall the arguments of Job's friends (e.g. Job 4:7; 8:8) and the assertion of the psalmist that he has never seen a righteous man go hungry (Ps 37:25). Since Job's friends are eventually rebuked by God, we might have expected more reticence on the part of Sirach here. He could, of course, point to the restoration of Job to support his point. The scriptural warrant for Sirach's confidence is found in Ex 34:6–7: the Lord is 'a God merciful and gracious'. This appeal to divine mercy is exceptional in the wisdom literature of the Hebrew tradition, where God does not normally interfere in the workings of the universe, but lets the chain of act and consequence take its course (Koch 1955; this view seems applicable to Proverbs and Ecclesiastes, though not to Job). Sirach's view of God is informed by the Torah and the prophets in a way that the earlier wisdom books were not. The result is a more personal view of God, which also opens up a space for prayer in the world-view of the sage.

vv. 12–14 are cast in the form of 'Woes', a form also found in prophecy (Isa 5), apocalyptic literature (1 *Enoch*, 98–9), and Luke (6:24–6).

The notion of the Lord's visitation (v. 14) is also exceptional in the Hebrew wisdom literature. In Wis 5, the visitation in question clearly takes the form of judgement after death. This is not the case in Sirach. (Sir 2:9c, which promises an everlasting reward, is an addition and belongs to the second Greek recension.) The Hebrew prophets often speak of a day of the Lord which does not involve a judgement of the dead, but brings about a dramatic upheaval on earth (e.g. Am 5:18; Joel 1:15; 2:1; Mal 3:2). Sirach seems to have something less dramatic in mind, but he insists that each individual must sooner or later face a reckoning with the Lord. The chapter concludes by recalling the words of David from 2 Sam 24:14, that it is better to be judged by God than by human beings.

(3:1–16) Honour of Parents The command to honour father and mother is found earlier, in the Decalogue. In Lev 19:2 this commandment follows immediately on the command to be holy, before the injunction to keep the sabbath. It occupies a similarly prominent place in the moral instructions of Hellenistic Judaism. Pseudo-Phocylides, 8, tells the reader to 'honour God first and foremost, and thereafter your parents'. Josephus, in his summary of the Jewish law in *Ag. Ap.* 2.206, likewise links honour of God and parents. (For further references see van der Horst 1978: 116.) The 'unwritten laws' of Greek tradition likewise demand honour first for the gods and then for parents, and this injunction is ubiquitous in Greek gnomic poetry (Bohlen 1991: 82–117). Ben Sira is the first Jewish writer to offer an extended discussion of the subject. In this, as in several other respects, he parallels the late-Egyptian wisdom book of *Phibis*, found in Papyrus Insinger (Bohlen 1991: 138–9; J. T. Sanders 1983: 81).

Sirach is in accordance with the Decalogue when he suggests that honouring parents leads to well-being (cf. Ex 20:12; Deut 5:16). The logic of this suggestion is shown by v. 5: one who honours his parents can expect to be honoured by his own children in turn. There is then a very practical reason for admonishing the son to be kind to the father who is old and senile (vv. 12–13). The son may find himself in the same position one day. Sirach does not rely entirely on the reciprocity of human behaviour, however. He also offers that one who honours his parents atones for sins (vv. 3, 14). This idea is in accordance with the tendency in Second-Temple Judaism to associate atonement for sin with good works (cf. Dan 4:24). Sirach attributes

potency to the blessing of a father (cf. the blessing of Isaac in Gen 27) but also to the curse of a
mother (v. 9; the parallelism of the verse implies
that both cursing and blessing are effective on
the part of both parents).

Throughout this passage, mothers are honoured equally with fathers, although the sage
mentions the father more often. This is also true
in the wisdom text 4QSapA. This Qumran work
also promises 'length of days' to one who honours his parents, and exhorts children to honour parents 'for the sake of their own honour'
(Harrington 1994: 148; cf. Sir 3:11). Here again the
honour of the parent is linked to the self-interest of the son, as his honour too is at stake. The
theme of honour and shame will recur frequently in Ben Sira.

(3:17–29) Humility and Docility Exhortations
to humility are common in Jewish writings of
the Hellenistic period. It is a recurring theme in
the *Rule of the Community* (e.g. 1QS 2:23–5; 3:8–9;
5:24–5), and a posture of humility is characteristic of the Thanksgiving Hymns or *hodayot*. Cf.
also the beatitudes in Mt 5. Sirach, however,
goes on to urge intellectual modesty and to
polemicize against speculation. We are reminded of the redactional postscript to Ecclesiastes, which discourages the pursuit of books
and study and recommends the fear of the Lord
instead (Eccles 12:12–13).

It is possible that Ben Sira is polemicizing
here against Greek philosophy, and the inquisitive pursuit of knowledge that it represented (so
Skehan and DiLella 1987: 160–1). It is equally
possible that he wished to discourage the kind
of speculation found in rival Jewish wisdom
circles, such as those represented in the apocalyptic writings of 1 Enoch, which frequently speculate about the matters beyond the range of
human experience. It is also possible, however,
that what we have here is simply the attempt of
a teacher to keep inquisitive pupils in line. This
passage must be read in conjunction with the
rebuke of stubbornness in vv. 25–9. Ben Sira
wants his pupils to accept what he says and
not question it. This is not good pedagogy by
modern standards (nor by those of a Socrates or
an Ecclesiastes) but it is typical of much wisdom
instruction in the ancient world.

(3:30–4:10) Charity to the Poor Sirach rounds
out this introductory section with exhortations
to almsgiving and social concern. For the
notion that almsgiving atones for sin, cf. Dan
4:24; Tob 4:10–11. Concern for the poor,

specifically for the orphan and the widow, is a
staple of ancient Near-Eastern wisdom literature. In Proverbs, God is the guardian of the
poor: cf. Prov 14:31, 'those who oppress the
poor insult their Maker'. The rights of the poor
rest in their status as creatures of God: 'The poor
and the oppressor have this in common: the
LORD gives light to the eyes of both' (Prov
29:13). Accordingly, Sirach argues that God
will hear their prayer (4:6). For the idea that
one who spurns the poor is cursed, cf. Prov
28:27. Sir 4:10 promises that one who is like a
father to the orphan will be like a son to God.
The phrase recalls the covenantal relationships
between God and Israel (Ex 4:22) and between
God and the Davidic king (2 Sam 7:14). In Sirach,
however, the relationship does not derive from
a covenant but from a style of behaviour. Cf. Ps
68:5, where God is called 'Father of orphans and
protector of widows'. Similarly, the righteous
man is called son of God in Wis 2:16, 18. For
God as father, see further Sir 23:1.

There is a significant textual variant in 4:10c–
d. The Hebrew reads: 'God will call you son, and
he will show favour to you and rescue you from
the pit.' The Greek reads: 'You will be like a son
of the Most High, and he will love you more
than does your mother.' The Hebrew reading is
more likely to be original (Smend 1906: 38). The
Greek attempts to improve the parallelism, possibly with an eye to Isa 49:15; 66:13 which compare God to a mother. The translation may also
be influenced by the reference to 'their mother'
in 10b.

(4:11–6:17)

(4:11–19) The Rewards and Trials of Wisdom
The second in the series of wisdom poems falls
into two parts. vv. 11–16 discuss the rewards of
wisdom. vv. 17–19 describe, in metaphorical
terms, the process by which wisdom is
acquired. The 'children' addressed by wisdom
are her pupils. Cf. Lk 7:35. Wisdom is associated
with the love of life (cf. Prov 3:16; 8:35). The
terminology suggests an absolute, unlimited
life, but the word 'life' is used in Proverbs and
Psalms in a sense that is qualitative rather than
quantitative (von Rad 1964). Cf. Ps 84:10: 'For a
day in your courts is better than a thousand
elsewhere.' For the term 'glory' in v. 13, cf. Ps
73:23–6. In v. 14, wisdom is a virtual surrogate
for God. The verb to serve, or minister, often
has a cultic connotation. The elusive relationship between wisdom and God is explored at
greater length in ch. 24. The notion that the
wise will judge the nations is found in an

eschatological context in Wis 3. It is not clear what form this judging will take in Sirach, except that it affirms the superiority of those who serve wisdom to the rest of humanity. vv. 16–19 make clear that wisdom is not acquired without a period of testing. Wisdom is not mere knowledge, but is a disciplined way of life that involves the formation of character.

(4:20–31) True and False Shame The notions of honour and shame were fundamental to the value system of the ancient Mediterranean world (Moxnes 1993. See further 10:19–25; 20:22–6; 41:16–42:8). Sirach seeks to modify commonly accepted notions of shame, by suggesting that one should not be ashamed to admit ignorance or confess sin. The notion of the proper time received its classic expression in Eccl 3:1–8, but is intrinsic to ancient wisdom. Ben Sira here uses the concept in a more restricted sense. He is concerned with the proper time for speech. It is typical of Ben Sira's cautious approach to life that bold exhortations to fight to the death for the truth are tempered by warnings not to be reckless in speech. v. 31 is cited in *Did.* 4.9 and *Barn.* 19.9.

(5:1–6:4) Cautionary Advice This ethic of caution is also in evidence in ch. 5. For the thought of 5:1–2, cf. Prov 16:1; 27:1. vv. 1, 3–4, 'say not . . .' make use of a literary form that can be traced back to old Egyptian wisdom (the *Instructions of Ani* and *Amen-em-ope*, ANET 420, 423) and is still found in the late-Egyptian *Instruction of Onchsheshonqy*. It is rare in the biblical wisdom books (but see Eccl 7: 10). In most cases, but not all, the form is used to forestall questions about divine justice. Sir 5:1 has a parallel in the *Instruction of Onchsheshonqy*: 'Do not say: I have this wealth. I will serve neither God nor man' (Crenshaw 1975: 48–9).

vv. 5–6 qualify the emphasis on divine mercy in 2:11. A similar warning is found in the Mishnah: 'If a man said, "I will sin and repent, and sin again and repent," he will be given no chance to repent. If he said, "I will sin and the Day of Atonement will effect atonement," then the Day of Atonement effects no atonement' (*m. Yoma*, 8:8–9; Snaith 1974: 32). For the 'day of wrath' (v. 8) cf. 2:14 above. The reference is not to an eschatological day of judgement, but to a day of reckoning for the individual, within this life. 5:9–6:1 deals with duplicitous speech, with emphasis on its shameful character. A good reputation is of fundamental importance for the sage. vv. 10–12 guard against even

inadvertent duplicity by deliberation. Cf. Jas 1:19: 'Let every one be quick to hear, slow to speak, slow to anger.' Cf. also Jas 3:1–12 on control of the tongue. The expression 'put your hand over your mouth' indicates restraint. It occurs in Prov 30:32*b* in the context of exalting oneself, and in Job as a gesture of respect in the presence of superiors (Job 29:9*b*; 40:4*b*; cf. Wis 8: 12). In Sirach, the restraint is for the sake of discretion.

This section concludes with a warning against desire. The text of 6:2 is uncertain. The Hebrew is corrupt, and the Greek is also problematic ('lest your strength be torn apart as a bull'). Skehan and DiLella 1987) restore 'lest like fire it consume your strength', which makes good sense but lacks textual support. The original text seems to have involved comparison with the raging of a bull. Sirach suggests that desire is selfdestructive. The expression 'a dry tree' is taken from Isa 56:3, where it refers to a eunuch. Control of the passions was a trademark of Stoicism but the ethic of restraint was typical of Near-Eastern wisdom. We may compare the various warnings against adultery and the 'loose woman' in Prov 1–9. Cf. also Prov 23 on control of the appetite, and see further Sir 18:30–19:3.

(6:5–17) On Friendship Friends should be chosen carefully and trusted slowly, but a true friend is invaluable (see further 22:1–26). The theme of true and false friendship is sounded briefly in Prov 18:24 (cf. Prov 19:4, 7). Job complains that his friends have failed him (7:14–23; 19:19–22). The closest parallels to Ben Sira, however, are found in the Greek gnomic poet Theognis and in the late-Egyptian *Instruction of Phibis* (J. T. Sanders 1983: 30–1; 70–1). *Phibis* is especially close to Sirach in warning against premature trust. On Sir 6:13 cf. Theognis 575: 'It is my friends that betray me, for I can shun my enemy.' Theognis also says that the trusty friend outweighs gold and silver (cf. Sir 6:15). Sirach strikes his own distinctive note, however, when he says that one who fears the Lord should seek a friend like himself.

(6:18–14:19)

(6:18–37) The Pursuit of Wisdom The third poem about wisdom resembles the second (4:11–19) in focusing on the process of acquiring wisdom, but does not speak in wisdom's name. Several analogies and metaphors are used to convey the need for discipline. The student is like a farmer who ploughs and sows, but who must be patient if he is to reap. (Cf. the NT parable of the sower in Mark 4 and par.) Wisdom is like a stone in the path, and the short-sighted fool casts it aside. Finally, wisdom is compared to various restraining devices—a net, a yoke, or bonds. Cf. the image of the yoke in the teaching of Jesus in Mt 11:28–30 and the yoke of the law in *m.'Abot*, 3:5. Cf. also Sir 51:26, a passage found independently at Qumran. Another set of images describes the delight of wisdom for one who perseveres: garments of gold or purple, and a crown. A crown is often a symbol of immortality, but here it represents the glory of wisdom.

vv. 32–7 give more straightforward advice to the pupil. He should frequent the company of the elders and attach himself to a teacher. Cf. the call in 51:23 to enrol in the house of instruction. He should also reflect on the law of the Most High. It appears then that the student has two sources to study, at least initially: the discourse of the elders and the book of the Torah. Neither is simply equated with wisdom here. Rather, they have the character of a pro-paideutic. Wisdom is a gift of God, over and above what one can acquire by study. It is a disposition of the mind and character, and as such it can not be equated with any collection of sayings or laws, although these are indispensable aids in the quest for wisdom.

(7:1–17) Humility and Piety This passage is noteworthy in two respects. First, the sage discourages the pursuit of public office. We find later that the role of the scribe was to serve high officials, not to hold office himself (Sir 39:4). This advice acquires added relevance in the time of Antiochus Epiphanes, when first Jason and then Menelaus sought the office of high priest by bribing the king (2 Macc 4). Both men subsequently came to grief. Hengel (1974: i. 133–4) has suggested that these verses fit Onias III, the high priest deposed by Jason, who had pleaded his case already before Seleucus IV, before Epiphanes came to power. It is more likely that Sirach is articulating his general approach to life, rather than responding to any specific occurrence. None of the high priests had sought to become judges. While we may admire the modesty of the sage this passage shows a serious limitation in his political commitment. While he holds strong views on such matters as social justice, he is unwilling to take the personal risks that might put him in a position to implement them.

The second noteworthy aspect of this passage is the attention given to the subject of prayer, which was scarcely noted in Proverbs. Ecclesiastes has a few comments that accord in substance with those of Sirach (cf. Eccl 5:2). Proper behaviour at prayer is essentially the same as in public speech. One should not be curt, but neither should one run on (v. 14; cf. Mt 6:7).

Respect for physical work (v. 15) is grounded in the divine command in Gen 3:17–19. According to the Mishnah: 'Study of Torah along with worldly occupation is seemly; for labour in the two of them makes sin forgotten. And all Torah without work ends in failure and occasions of sin' (*m.'Abot*, 2:2). The same Mishnah also parallels Ben Sira's reflection in v. 17 on death as the demolisher of human pride: 'Be exceedingly humble, for the hope of mortal man is the worm' (*m.'Abot*, 4:4). The Greek changes this verse in Sirach to read 'fire and worms,' thereby implying punishment for the wicked after death (cf. Isa 66:24).

(7:18–36) Social Relations Similar manuals on social relations can be found in *Pseudo-Phocylides*, 175–227, Jos. *Ag. Ap.* 2. 198–210. The household codes in the NT differ in so far as they often prescribe the duties of wives, children, and slaves as well as those of the master, husband, and father (e.g. Col 3:18–4:1; see Balch 1988). None of the relationships is discussed in detail here, but several are treated at greater length elsewhere (friends in 6:5–17 and 22:19–26, wives in 26:1–4, 13–18, slaves in 33:25–33, sons in 30:1–13, and daughters in 26:10–12 and 42:9–14). All the relationships here are viewed in the light of the interest of the patriarchal male, with the unfortunate consequence that wives, slaves, cattle, and children are all on the same level (cf. the tenth commandment, Ex 20:17; Deut 5:21, where wife and animals are grouped together as possessions).

The advice not to 'reject' (v. 19) or 'abhor' (v. 26) one's wife probably concerns divorce (but see the objections of Trenchard 1982: 26–8, who points out that this is not the usual divorce terminology). Divorce appears to have been widespread in Second-Temple Judaism. We have several divorce documents from Elephantine in Upper Egypt in the fifth century BCE and from Naḥal Ḥever near the Dead Sea from the early second century CE. Divorce was the prerogative of the husband. According to the Mishnah, 'A woman is divorced irrespective of her will; a man divorces of his own accord' (*m. Yebam.* 14:1). Notoriously, Hillel ruled that a man was entitled to divorce his wife even ifshe spoiled a dish for him and Akiba allowed it even if he found a fairer woman (*m. Git.* 9:10; Archer 1990: 218). The Jewish community at Elephantine was apparently exceptional in allowing women to initiate divorce. There has been much debate as to whether women could initiate divorce in the Roman era, but the evidence is at best ambiguous (Collins 1997). Ben Sira here cautions against gratuitous divorce, but he does not challenge the right to divorce as such. Such challenges first appear in the Dead Sea scrolls (CD 4:20–5:2) and then in the NT (Mk 10:2). Sir 7:26*b* is ambiguous. The Hebrew literally reads 'do not trust a woman who is hated'. Skehan and DiLella (1987) render 'where there is ill-feeling, trust her not'. The verb 'to hate', however, is often used in the sense of 'divorce' (e.g. at Elephantine). Ben Sira here is most probably advising against trusting a divorced woman, probably on the pragmatic grounds that 'Hell hath no fury like a woman scorned.' So the advice is: be slow to divorce, but do not trust a woman you have sent away.

On the subject of slaves, Ben Sira counsels kindness, but again he does not question the institution of slavery. His ethic is based on enlightened self-interest. Slaves and animals are more profitable when they are well treated. It has been suggested that 7:21*b* is an allusion to the biblical law that Hebrew slaves should be released after six years (Ex 21:2; Skehan and DiLella 1987: 205), but Sirach only recommends freedom for a wise slave (cf. Paul's plea for Onesimus in the letter to Philemon).

Ben Sira takes a somewhat stricter view of children than does Pseudo-Phocylides, who counsels 'be not harsh with your children but be gentle' (Ps.-Phoc. 207). But he shares with the Hellenistic Jewish author the concern for the chastity of unmarried daughters (cf. Ps.-Phoc. 215–16). See sir 42:914. The debt to one's parents, and especially to one's mother, is often noted in Egyptian wisdom literature (J. T. Sanders 1983: 65).

Sirach departs from the conventions of wisdom literature when he dwells on the honour due to priests (vv. 29–31). Sirach's admiration for the priesthood is clear especially in praise of the high priest Simon in ch. 50. Deut 14:28–9 associates the Levites with the aliens, orphans, and widows as people who need support. Sirach, however, does not view the offerings to the priests as charity, but as the fulfilment of a commandment.

It is not clear what kindness to the dead (v. 33) is supposed to entail. The simplest explanation is that it means a decent burial for the poor (cf. Tob 1:16–19; 2:4, 8). It is possible that it entails the placing of offerings at the graveside, a custom noted in Sir 30:18, but with apparent disapproval. Cf. also Tob 4:17. Sirach concludes this section by reminding people of their own latter days, when they too may be in need of kindness. The thought of death reminds us of our common humanity. Cf. *m.'Abot*, 3:1: 'Keep in mind three things and you will not come into the power of sin: whence you come, whither you go, and before whom you are to give strict account.'

(8:1–19) Prudential Advice Caution and prudence are fundamental virtues in the wisdom tradition. This passage warns against contention with the powerful, the rich (vv. 1–2), or a judge (v. 14), since in each case there is an imbalance of power. It also warns against becoming embroiled with people of a foolish or violent disposition (vv. 3–4), sinners (v. 10), the ruthless or the quick-tempered (vv. 15–16), because the situation can get out of control. The dangers of dealing with a 'heated' man figure prominently in the Egyptian *Instruction of Amen-em-ope* (ANET 421–4, esp. ch. 9). Cf. Prov 22:23. The image of fire in v. 10 captures both the way in which anger flares up and its destructive consequences. This image is more commonly used to describe sexual passion (cf. Job 31:9–12; Sir 9:8). The warning against giving surety beyond one's means is another time-honoured piece of sapiential advice, nicely captured in Prov 22:27: 'why should your bed be taken from under you?' In all of this the concern of the sage is not with principles of right and wrong but with practical consequences.

Two of the admonitions in this chapter are of a different kind. vv. 4–7 warn against making fun of others or treating them with disdain. Here as in 7:36 mindfulness of one's own mortality is the key to the sage's ethics. The Talmud also forbids reproaching the reformed sinner (*y. B. MeṢ.* 4:10). The warning not to slight the discourse of the sages (vv. 8–9) is also positive advice, of a line of action to be pursued rather than one to be avoided. Warnings against revealing one's thoughts (v. 19) can be traced back to old Egyptian wisdom (e.g. the Instruction of Ani, 4:1; 7:7; ANET 420). The Egyptian instruction warned not to reveal one's thoughts to a stranger. Sir 8:19 (lit. do not reveal your mind to all flesh) should probably be read in the same vein as a warning against indiscretion, rather than as against ever confiding in anyone at all.

(9:1–9) On Women Ben Sira now applies his ethic of caution to the subject of women. The meaning of 9:1 is disputed. It is usually taken to mean that the husband's jealousy might suggest the idea of infidelity to the wife (so Snaith 1974: 50: 'and so put into her head the idea of wronging you'). Trenchard (1982: 30) suggests that the wife might then become jealous of the husband and discover infidelity on his part. Camp (1991: 22) takes the verb *qn'* to refer to ardour rather than jealousy, so that 'the evil the wife learns from the husband is sexual ardor itself'. Against the latter suggestion, it must be said that the sense of 'jealousy' is far better attested. Cf. the notorious ritual for the woman suspected of adultery in Num 5, and the use of the word in Prov 6:34; 27:4. The word *qn'h* most probably means sexual passion in Song 8:6, however (although even there the nuance of jealousy may also be present). Ardour provides a better parallel than jealousy to 9:2 ('do not give yourself over to a woman'; the Hebrew text is corrupted by dittography of the word *qn*) and the theme of the following verses is the danger of yielding to sexual attractions. The notions of jealousy and excessive passion are not unrelated. In view of the usual usage of the word, the meaning 'jealousy' should probably be retained in 9:1. For the general sentiment of this passage cf. Ps.-Phoc. 194: 'For "eros" is not a god, but a passion destructive to all.'

Sirach follows Proverbs in his warnings against the 'strange woman' (cf. Prov 5:1–6; 7:1–27; note esp. the motif of wandering the city streets in Sir 9:7 and the decline to the pit or destruction in 9:9). The danger of losing one's inheritance (9:6) recalls Prov 5:10. Sirach's admonitions also bear the stamp of the Hellenistic age. The enticements of the singing girl (9:4) recall the story of Joseph the son of Tobias, who allegedly fell in love with a dancing girl during a visit to Alexandria (Jos. *Ant.* 12.186–9). The motif of gazing at a virgin recalls the elders in the story of Susanna, but cf. earlier Job 31:1 where Job protests his innocence in this respect. Descriptions of female beauty become somewhat more common in Hellenistic Jewish writings than in the HB—e.g. contrast the description of Sarah in the *Genesis Apocryphon* from Qumran (1QapGen 20) with the text of Genesis. Public banquets and symposia were a feature of Hellenistic life (cf. Sir 31:12–32:13), but

married women were normally excluded from them (Corley 1993: 24–79). The only women found at such gatherings were courtesans and dancing girls. Roman women enjoyed more liberty in this regard, but even they were often criticized for participating in public meals. Roman practice, however, can scarcely have made an impact on Ben Sira in the early second century BCE. It is all the more remarkable then that such socializing with married women appears as a problem in his historical setting. There was a precedent for married women who revelled in wine in ancient Israel (Am 4:1) but they are not said to have done so with men other than their husbands.

(9:10–16) Heterogeneous Advice On the subject of friendship, see SIR 6:5–17. On loyalty to old friends cf. Theognis, 1151–2: 'Never be persuaded by men of the baser sort to leave the friend you have and seek another.' Ben Sira often reassures himself that the wicked will yet be punished: cf. 3:26; 11:28. 'Those who have power to kill' (v. 13) are presumably rulers. Cf. the advice against seeking office in 7:4–7, but the advice here would seem to be in tension with the sage's desire to serve before the great and mighty (39:4). The tales of foreign courts in the books of Esther and Daniel typically portray the king as erratic and the courtiers in danger of sudden death (cf. the king's peremptory decision to put all the wise men of Babylon to death in Dan 2). The importance of making friends with the righteous was already noted in 6:16–17. Contrast Mt 5:43–8, where Jesus reminds his disciples that their Father in heaven makes his sun shine on the wicked and the righteous alike. The reference to the 'law of the Most High' in v. 15 is not found in the extant Hebrew text, which reads 'let all your counsel be among them' (i.e. the wise). For an example of dinner-table conversation that a Hellenistic Jewish writer considered edifying see the *Epistle of Aristeas*, 187–294.

(9:17–10:18) On Rulers and Pride 9:17 contrasts the skill of the tradesman with the wisdom of the ruler (cf. ch. 38). The Hebrew of 9:17b is corrupt. Read *bînâ* instead of the unintelligible *bîtâ*, so the ruler of the people is wise in understanding. Wisdom is associated with kingship in Prov 8:15–16. Cf. also Plato's ideal of the philosopher king. Skehan and DiLella (1987: 223) assume that Ben Sira is thinking of the high priest, the ruler of Jerusalem at that time, but this passage is more likely to be a traditional wisdom reflection on the nature of authority. Cf. the discussion in the *Epistle of Aristeas*, 187–294. (The need for discipline on the part of the king is emphasized in 205, 211, 223.) The motif of the loud-mouthed person, who is hated by all, is also found in Theognis, 295–7.

The discussion of kingship passes over into a discussion of arrogance. It is because of human hubris that sovereignty passes from nation to nation. The belief that God brings low the proud and exalts the lowly is widespread in both Testaments: cf. 1 Sam 2:1–10; Lk 1:46–55. For the notion that God disposes of kings and kingship, cf. Dan 2:20–3; Wis 6:1–8. The motif that God overthrows nations and raises up rulers at the proper time is common to wisdom and apocalyptic literature, and this led von Rad (1972: 281–2) to speculate that apocalypticism developed out of wisdom tradition and the activities of the sages. But the similarity between Sir 10 and Dan 2 is quite limited. Daniel envisages a historical progression, with a climactic conclusion. Sirach sees no such progression, but only a principle that is always at work. This principle, moreover, applies to individuals as well as to kingdoms. The fundamental critique of pride is that human beings are only dust and ashes, living under the shadow of death. Nations are like individuals writ large.

(10:19–11:6) Honour and Shame Cf. Sir 3:1–16 and 4:20–31. Honour should attach to the fear of the Lord, and there should be no shame in poverty. Appearances are often misleading. Yet Sirach does not entirely abandon conventional wisdom. He acknowledges that one who is honoured in poverty will be honoured much more in wealth, and vice versa (v. 30). In part this is simple realism, a recognition of the way honour is actually conferred in his society, but there is an undeniable tension between this realism, which tends to accept things as they are and adjust to them, and the more idealistic affirmation that the intelligence should be honoured even in poverty (cf. Camp 1991: 9–10). Hengel (1974: 1. 151–2) has argued that this passage constitutes a social commentary on Hellenistic Judea, where people such as the Tobiads won honour and glory by opportunistic disregard for law and traditional ethics. Ben Sira is not so specific, and he surely intended to formulate general principles that would apply to any situation. None the less, it is not unreasonable to assume that he was influenced to some degree by the events of his time.

The virtue of humility, extolled in 10:26–31, is quite alien to the Greek sense of honour. In part this is the mentality of the sage, who does not want to occupy centre stage but gains honour through the service of others. In part it is a strategy to guard against humiliation: cf. Prov 25:6–7; Lk 14:7–11; cf. further Sir 13:8–13. 11:1–6 refers back to 10:6–18 for the notion that God brings low the proud, even kings and rulers. It also barely mentions a theme that will be treated at length in chs. 39–44, the wonderful works of the Lord.

(11:7–28) Patience and Trust vv. 7–8 involve elementary courtesy as well as being a prerequisite for wisdom: cf. Prov 18:13; *m.'Abot*, 5:10. The advice in v. 9 is expressed more pungently in Prov 26:17: 'Like somebody who takes a passing dog by the ears is one who meddles in the quarrel of another.'

In much of this section Sirach expounds a theme that is surprisingly reminiscent of Ecclesiastes: the futility of toil and effort. Success is determined by the favour of the Lord (cf. Eccl 2:26). Even if someone thinks he has acquired wealth, the acquisition is not secure. God can change a person's fortune, and whatever has been accumulated must eventually pass to another when the person dies (cf. Eccl 2:18–22; 6:1–3 and the parable of the rich fool in Lk 12:16–21). These observations lead to an attitude of resignation. The principle enunciated in v. 14, that all things, good and bad, life and death, come from the Lord, will be developed in Sir 33:14–15 into a systematic theory that the world is constituted by pairs of opposites. A similar view leads to resignation in the face of death in ch. 41. While Sirach has no place for judgement after death, he accords great significance to the manner of death. The sentiment expressed in 11:28 is a commonplace of Greek tragedy (e.g. Aesch. *Ag.* l. 928; Soph. *Oed. Rex*, l. 1529; see further Skehan and DiLella 1987: 241).

vv. 15–16 were added in a secondary recension, apparently by way of theological correction. v. 14 ascribes both good and evil to the Lord. v. 15 ascribes various good things to the Lord, but v. 16 goes on to say that error and darkness were formed with sinners from their birth. Cf. Wis 1:13, 16, which denies that God made death, and claims that the wicked brought it about by the error of their ways.

(11:29–12:18) Care in Choosing Friends Sirach here picks up the theme of true and false friendship, already broached in 6:5–17, but here the tone is more directly imperatival. The Hebrew text of 11:29–34 is garbled: see Skehan and DiLella (1987: 244). Much of the advice is practical. One must exercise some caution in inviting people into one's home, and beware of the friendship of an old enemy. The notion that prosperity attracts false friends is nicely illustrated in the book of Job, where his friends suddenly reappear after he is restored (Job 42:11; cf. Prov 19:4, 6). Theognis, 35–6, also counsels against mingling with the bad. For the image of the snake charmer, cf Eccl 10:11.

What is most striking about this passage, however, is the vigorous insistence that one should only do good to the just, and give no comfort to the wicked (12:2–3) and even that God hates sinners (12:6). Cf. the Qumran *Rule of the Community*, where those who enter the covenant commit themselves to hate all the sons of darkness, with the implication that God detests them (1QS 1:4,10). A similar proverb is found in *Midr. Qoh. Rab.* 5. 8f. §5 (Soncino edn.): 'Do no good to an evil person and harm will not come to you; for if you do good to an evil person, you have done wrong.' The contrast with the teaching of Jesus in the NT is obvious (Mt 5:43–8; Lk 6:27–8, 32–6). But the idea that God hates sinners is also exceptional in Jewish literature. Contrast Wis 11:24: 'For you love all things that exist, and detest none of the things that you have made, for you would not have made anything if you had hated it.' This idea is illustrated in a colourful way in T *Abr.* 10:14, where God tells the archangel Michael: 'Abraham has not sinned and has no mercy on sinners. But I made the world, and I do not want to destroy any one of them.' Ben Sira presumably could not claim to be as innocent of sin as Abraham was.

(13:1–23) The Rich and the Poor v. 1 continues the theme of selective friendship. This saying became a popular proverb and is quoted by Shakespeare (*Much Ado About Nothing*, III. iii. 61, and 1 *Henry IV* II. iv. 460). The passage goes onto speak of the inequities of rich and poor. These inequities are often noted in wisdom literature—e.g. Prov 14:20; Eccl 9:16; *Sayings of Ahikar*, 55. The need for caution in dealing with the rich and powerful is also commonplace. The Egyptian *Instruction of Ani* warns against indulging oneself at the table of a rich man (*ANET* 412) and the warning is repeated in the *Instruction of Amen-em-ope*, ch. 23 (*ANET* 424) and in Prov 23:1–3. vv. 9–13 have a parallel in the late-Egyptian *Phibis* (J. T. Sanders 1983: 92–3).

Similar warnings are found in *m.'Abot*, 2:3: 'Be cautious with the authorities, for they do not make advances to a man except for their own need.' The subject of proper behaviour when invited by the mighty is taken up at length in Sir 31:12–18. The notion that a powerful person may test his guests by conversation is illustrated (somewhat artificially) in the *Epistle of Aristeas*, 187–294.

None of these parallels, however, express the antagonism of rich and poor as sharply as vv. 17–20. The wolf and the lamb may be reconciled in eschatological prophecy (Isa 11:6) but not in historical experience. Sirach uses vivid imagery to express the violence of the rich towards the poor. They are lions; the poor are their fodder. (Cf. Job 24:4–5 for the poor as wild asses.) It is reasonable to assume that this picture is coloured by the social context in which Sirach wrote, in which families such as the Tobiads grew rich at the expense of the common people (Tcherikover 1970: 146–8). The general picture is reminiscent of the Epistle of Enoch (1 *Enoch*, 94–105), which may have been written about the same time. The Epistle pronounces woes against the rich and tells them that they will not have peace (94:6–8). Sirach's tone, however, is detached. He observes the antagonism of the classes as if it were an unalterable fact of nature. The wise man will avoid the excesses of this situation, but he will not attempt to overthrow it.

v. 14 has the character of a pious gloss, and belongs to the secondary Greek recension.

(13:24–14:19) Miserliness and Generosity For Sirach, wealth is good in itself (13:24); the guilt which is often attached to it is not intrinsic to it. Conversely, while a good person may be poor, poverty is not good in itself. Even though Sirach qualifies his condemnation of poverty by attributing it to the proud, he does not contradict it. The value of wealth is undercut, however, if the person has a guilty conscience or is a miser. For the notion that the heart is reflected in the countenance (13:25–6), cf. Prov 15:13; Eccl 8:1. The implication of 14:2 is that a person with a guilty conscience has no hope, presumably because of Sirach's belief that retribution must strike sooner or later. Cf. Ps. 1.

Sirach's exhortation to generosity is, again, in the spirit of Ecclesiastes. Since there is no joy in the netherworld, one should treat oneself well in the present. Cf. Eccl 8:15: 'So I commend enjoyment, for there is nothing better for people under the sun than to eat and drink and enjoy themselves,' and, centuries earlier, the advice given to Gilgamesh by the ale-wife Si-duri: 'When the gods created mankind | Death for mankind they set aside | Life in their own hands retaining. Thou Gilgamesh, let full be thy belly, | Make thou merry by day and by night…' (*ANET* 90). Sirach's endorsement of enjoyment, however, is limited to the correct use of wealth. It is not a goal to be pursued in its own right.

None the less the inferences drawn from mortality here provide an interesting contrast with the reasoning of the Wisdom of Solomon. In Wis 2:1–11, it is the wicked who reason 'unsoundly' that life is short and sorrowful and that therefore we should 'crown ourselves with rosebuds before they wither'. They go on to argue that might is right in a world where there is no post-mortem retribution. Sirach, in contrast, insists that there is retribution in this life. The lack of judgement after death, then, gives no licence to sin. But neither is there any reason for asceticism. Life has its fulfilment in the present and should be enjoyed. Moreover, wealth and enjoyment should be shared, since there is no reason to hoard it.

The comparison of generations to leaves (14:18) is found in Homer, *Iliad*, 6:146–9: 'As is the generation of leaves, so is that of human-ity … So one generation of men will grow while another dies.'

(14:20–23:27)

(14:20–15:10) The Pursuit of Wisdom This wisdom poem resembles 6:18–37 in so far as it describes the quest for wisdom in poetic images, and adds a brief comment associating wisdom with the law of the Lord (cf. 6:37; 15:1). The poem falls into two halves: 14:20–7 de-scribes the quest of the student for wisdom, 15:2–10 describes wisdom's rewards. 15:1, which associates wisdom with the law, stands as an editorial comment by Ben Sira, repeating a recurring theme in the book.

14:20–7 has the form of a beatitude or makar-ism, a form found about a dozen times in Sirach and almost as frequently in Proverbs (Rickenbacher 1973: 83). The wisdom text 4Q525 declares blessed 'the man who attains wisdom and walks in the law of the Most High' (García Martínez 1994: 395). There is prob-ably an allusion in 14:20 to Ps 1, which pro-nounces blessed those who meditate on the law of the Lord, with the implication that wis-dom can be substituted for the law- Ps 154, previously known only in Syriac but now found in Hebrew at Qumran, commends those

whose meditation is on 'the law of the Most High' (García Martínez 1994: 305). The passage goes on to describe wisdom as bride and mother. The pursuit of wisdom has a mildly erotic connotation in Prov 4:6–9, while wisdom is cast as the nourishing mother in Prov 9:1–5. Erotic motifs will appear more prominently in 51:13–28. Here the imagery of peering in at the window recalls Song 2:9; cf. also Prov 8:34. The maternal side of wisdom is expressed through the images of tent and tree, both of which give shelter. For the image of the tent or canopy, cf. Isa 4:6,

The identification of wisdom with the Torah in 15:1 is a favourite theme of Ben Sira, but it has little impact on the way in which wisdom is described. Rather, the poem continues with the images of bride and mother, but shifts from the agency of the student/suitor to that of wisdom. The imagery of food and drink (15:3) will be developed in ch. 24. In the HB the sup-port of the righteous is usually the Lord (Ps 18:19; 22:5; 25:2). Here wisdom acts as the surro-gate of the Lord. This notion too will be devel-oped inch. 24. The crown (15:6) is often a symbol of a blessed afterlife (see sir 1:11). Sirach's hope, however, is for an everlasting name. This is *not* a standard expectation in the wisdom books of the HB. It does not appear at all in Job or Ecclesiastes. According to Prov 10:4, the memory of the righteous is a blessing but the name of the wicked will rot, but the motif is far more prominent in Sirach (Rickenbacher 1973: 95–8). This interest reflects Sirach's heightened sense of honour and shame and reflects his Hellenistic milieu. It appears prominently in the Praise of the Fathers in chs. 44–50.

It is not immediately clear to what the 'praise' of 15:9–10 refers. Smend (1906: 141) takes it as the praise of God. Peters (1913: 129) thinks the reference is to the preceding praise of wisdom. In either case, the point is that the sinner cannot secure prosperity by reciting hymns; they must arise from wisdom if they are to be efficacious.

(15:11–16:23) Freedom and Responsibility The discussion of freedom of choice in 15:11–20 is complemented by a long discourse on the punishment of sinners in ch. 16. The closing unit (16:17–23) harks back to 15:11–12 in its use of the formula 'Do not say'. (See the comments on the form at Sir 5:1–4.) The passage on worth-less children (16:1–4) appears abruptly after the discussion of free will, but leads into the theme of punishment, which rounds out this treatise on sin. Sirach returns to the theme in

17:1–24–15:11–12 testifies to a lively debate on the origin of sin and evil. One current explanation was provided by the Book of the Watchers in 1 *Enoch*, 1–36, which expanded the story of the sons of God in Gen 6 and attributed various kinds of evil (violence, fornication, astrology) to the intervention on earth of the fallen angels. Even within the Enoch literature, however, this explanation of evil was questioned. In the Epistle of Enoch, which may be roughly contemporary with Ben Sira, we read: 'I swear to you, you sinners, that as a mountain has not, and will not, become a slave, nor a hill a woman's maid, so sin was not sent on the earth, but man of himself created it' (1 *Enoch*, 98:4). In the next generation, the Qumran *Rule of the Community* would adopt a new proposal, with overtones of Persian dualism, according to which God created two spirits within humanity, and so was ultimately the source of evil as well as good (Collins 1995).

In this passage, Sirach comes down unambiguously on the side of free will, with echoes of Deuteronomy. Cf. Deut 11:268; 30:15–20; Sir 15:17 alludes directly to Deut 30:15. The entire wisdom tradition represented in Proverbs presupposes free will. The clear-cut assertion that the Lord hates evil (15:13) accords with what we have read in 12:6- But Sirach is not consistent- He also maintains that God has made both good and bad (11:8) and reckons the sinner among the works of the Lord (33:14–15). There is evidently some tension between the belief that all the works of the Lord are good (39:33) and the actuality of sinners, whom God allegedly hates.

The origin of human sin is addressed most directly in 15:14. Sirach echoes Genesis in saying that God created man in the beginning, but then adds, according to the Hebrew, 'and set him in the power of his plunderer *(hōtĕpô)* and placed him in the power of his inclination *(yēṣer)'*. There is evidently a doublet here. The plunderer is most probably Satan (Peters 1913: 130; cf. Sir 50:4, where the same word is parallel to *Ṣār*, enemy) and this phrase is probably inserted as a theological correction. It has no equivalent in the Greek. The word 'inclination', however, becomes a loaded term in rabbinic literature, according to which human nature was endowed with both a good and an evil inclination. The Talmud attributes to R. Jose the Galilean the view that 'the righteous are ruled by the good inclination...the wicked are ruled by the evil inclination...average people are ruled by both' (*b. Ber.* 61b; Urbach 1975: 475). The potency of the evil inclination (or 'evil heart') is recognized

in 4 Ezra, written at the end of the first century CE (2 Esd 3:20–1). 4 Ezra stops short of saying that God created the evil heart, but the Sages are explicit on the point (Urbach 1975: 472). The notion of an evil inclination is now attested close to the time of Sirach in a fragmentary wisdom text from Qumran (4QSapA), where we encounter such phrases as 'the inclination of the flesh' and 'the thoughts of evil inclination' (Elgvin 1994: 187). The reference to 'the inclination of the flesh' follows a statement 'so that the just man may distinguish between good and evil' (García Martínez 1994: 383). The *Damascus Document* attributes the recurrence of sinful behaviour throughout history to following 'the thoughts of a guilty inclination' *(yēṣer ăšāmâ)*, which seems to be equated with stubbornness of heart. The Greek text of Sirach also refers to the evil inclination in 37:3, but the Hebrew does not support this reading. In view of the history of the term 'inclination', the usual translation here as 'free choice' (NRSV) is inadequate. To be sure, Sirach emphasizes free choice in the following passage, but the exercise of that choice is conditioned by the inclinations with which human nature is fitted at creation. Sirach stops a long way short of the teaching of two spirits that we find in the Qumran *Rule of the Community*, but we can see that he is wrestling with the same problem, in attempting to explain the presence of evil while preserving the sovereignty of the creator God.

The worthlessness of impious children is also emphasized in Wis 4:1–6. In ancient Israel, children provided a kind of immortality. The Wisdom of Solomon could dispense with this, because it preached personal immortality. Sirach maintains that the wicked come to grief in this life. On 16:4, cf. Wis 6:24: the multitude of the wise is the salvation of the world, but cf. also Eccl 9:15.

For the examples of divine punishment in 16:3–14, cf. CD 2:15–3:12. The sinners in CD follow their guilty inclination. Sirach seems to imply a similar view, in the light of 15:14. Both Sirach and CD also note the role of stubbornness. A similar tendency to view history as a series of examples is found in Wis 10–19. Wisdom underlines the typological character of the events by suppressing all names; cf. the reference here to 'the doomed people' in 16:9.

On the impossibility of hiding from the Lord (16:17–23), cf. Wis 1:6–11, which explains that the spirit of the Lord, which is closely associated with wisdom, fills the whole world and hears whatever is said.

Two additions to the Greek text of this chapter have theological significance: 16:15 recalls that God hardened Pharaoh's heart, by way of illustrating that God's mercy is balanced by severity towards sinners. The point is of interest, however, because of the preceding discussion of free will. 16:22 adds that 'a scrutiny for all will come at death', which is one of several attempts by a Greek redactor to introduce a belief in judgement after death into the text of Sirach. Contrast Sir 4.1:4.

(16:24–18:14) **Wisdom and Creation** The direct call for attention in 16:24 marks the beginning of a new section. Such calls are rare in Sirach after chs. 2–4. In v. 25, Ben Sira appropriates words attributed to Wisdom in Prov 1:23 when he says that he will pour out his spirit. 16:26–30 develops the theme of creation which had been touched on briefly in the preceding section. Here the emphasis is on the order of nature. Cf. Ps 104, or, closer to the time of Sirach, 1 *Enoch*, 2–5, 73–82. There are several allusions to Gen 1–3: from the *beginning* (16:26); he filled it with *good* things (16:29); all living creatures must return to the earth (16:30; 17:1; cf. Gen 3:19). In 17:1–10 the focus shifts to the creation of humanity, following the order of the biblical text. (The same progression is found in a fragmentary paraphrase of Genesis and Exodus from Qumran, 4Q422.) Again, there are several echoes of Genesis. Human beings are granted authority and dominion over the other creatures. They are made in God's image, an idea which is explained by juxtaposition with the statement that they are given strength like that of God. (The Gk. redactor adds a reference to the senses at this point.) Perhaps the most noteworthy aspect of this meditation on Genesis is that it ignores the sin of Adam completely. (Sir 25:24 ascribes the original sin to Eve.) Death is not here considered a punishment for sin. God limited human life from the start (17:2). In contrast, the sin is highlighted in other second-century retellings of the Genesis story, notably *Jubilees*, 3. Cf. also the Words of the Heavenly Luminaries (4Q504 8; García Martínez 1994: 417). Sirach chooses instead to emphasize here that the first human beings were endowed with wisdom and understanding.

The 'law of life' in 17:11 is most probably the Mosaic law. Cf. 45:5, where 'the law of life and knowledge' is given to Moses on Sinai. The designation 'law of life' is derived from Deut 30:11–20. In the context, the 'eternal covenant'

of v. 12 must also refer to the Sinai covenant, although 44:18 uses this phrase for the covenant with Noah. Cf. Bar 4:1, where the Torah is 'the law that endures forever'. v. 13 refers to the revelation at Mt. Sinai; cf. Ex 19:16–19. In 17:17, the rulers of the nations are angels, or 'sons of God', cf. Deut 32:8.17:19–20 recapitulates the theme of 16:17–23. Nothing is hidden from God. On the value of almsgiving, cf. SIR 3:30.

The call to repentence in 17:25 is more characteristic of prophetic than of sapiential literature. Here again Sirach uses the ambivalence of death for his purpose. No one sings the praise of God in the netherworld (cf. Ps 30:9; 88:11–13; 117:17; Isa 38:18–19). For the Wisdom of Solomon, the lack of a significant afterlife would undermine the demand for a moral life. For Sirach, it rather adds urgency to the present and so supports the appeal for repentance. The concluding verses of ch. 17 and 18:1–14 constitute a hymn praising the mercy of God. Sirach emphasizes the surpassing power of God and the insignificance of humanity. 18:8 echoes Ps 8:5 (cf. Ps 144:3) but Sirach will not conclude that human beings have been crowned with glory and honour, only that God has mercy on them. The estimate of life expectancy is slightly higher than Ps 90:10, but the difference is inconsequential. (In contrast, Isa 65:20 promises that in the new creation death before the age of 100 years will be premature.) Just as Sirach regards the imminence of death as a reason that people should be moral, he also regards it as a reason for divine mercy. 18:13, which extends the divine compassion to every living thing, is in sharp contrast to 12:6, where God has no pity on the wicked, but is in accordance with Hos 11:8–9; Wis 11:23: 'you are merciful to all because you can do all things'. Sir 18:14, however, seems to restrict God's compassion to those who submit to his law. The latter notion is more typical of Sirach, and is likely to reflect his own view over against a more generous tradition.

(18:15–19:17) **Caution and Restraint** After the extensive theological reflections in 14:20–18:14, Sirach now reverts to practical advice and admonitions. The sage guards against impulse and anticipates what needs to be done. The first admonition in 18:15–18 is an exception to this theme, and indeed to the usual moralism of Ben Sira. Even he recognizes, however, that there are times when admonition is inappropriate. On the spirit of giving, cf. 2 Cor 9:7 (God loves a cheerful giver) and Jas 1:5 (God gives ungrudgingly). 18:1927 gives various examples of prudence and caution. The advice on vows in 18:22–3 recalls Eccl 5:4–5: it is better not to vow at all than to make a vow and not fulfil it. Characteristically, Ben Sira undergirds his advice with a reminder of the day of death, seen as the day of reckoning when God settles accounts.

Sirach goes on to admonish against self-indulgence and against gossip. The main argument put forward against licentiousness is that itleads to poverty. Cf. Prov 5:10; 21:17; 23:20–1. There is also the threat of disease and early death (19:3; cf. Prov 2:16–19; 5:3–6, 11–12; 7:27). The argument against gossip is likewise grounded in self-interest. It may cause someone to hate you (19:9). Cf. Hesiod, *Opera et Dies*, 721: 'If you say a bad thing, you may hear a worse thing said about you.' This subject evokes a rare flash of humour from Ben Sira, when he compares the gossip to a woman in labour. Cf. Jas 3:1–12 on the need to bridle the tongue.

Both the Qumran *Rule of the Community* and the Gospel of Matthew advocate pointing out faults to offenders rather than rejecting them out of hand. Cf. 1QS 5:24–6:1; Mt 18:15–17. This procedure has a biblical warrant in Lev 19:17–18. Cf. Prov 27:5; 28:23. Sirach differs from all those passages, however, in leaving open the question of the person's guilt, and allowing that there may be a mistake or a case of slander.

(19:18–30) Wisdom and Fear of the Lord Like some other passages on the fear of the Lord (e.g. 15:1), this passage stands out from its context and has the character of an editorial comment by Ben Sira. vv. 18–19 belong to the second Greek recension, and include a trademark reference to immortality. v. 20 is ambiguous in principle. It could mean that the person who acquires wisdom, from whatever source, thereby fulfils the law, or it could mean that the fulfilment of the law constitutes wisdom, even if one draws on no other source (cf. Bar 3:4: 'Happy are we, O Israel, for we know what is pleasing to God'). v. 24 makes clear that Ben Sira intends the latter interpretation. Better a person with little understanding who keeps the law than a learned and clever person who violates it. Ben Sira would probably contend that a truly wise person will keep the law in any case, so there is no necessary conflict between the two interpretations. But he recognizes that a person may have many of the attributes of wisdom without the fear of the Lord. Keen but dishonest shrewdness was always a problem in the wisdom tradition. Cf. the advice of Jonadab to

Amnon in 2 Sam 13, which leads to the rape of Tamar. Already in Gen 3:1 the serpent is recognized as crafty. The Hellenistic age offered several models of wisdom to the people of a city such as Jerusalem. The resourcefulness of v. 23 is illustrated in the tale of the Tobiads in Josephus, *Ant.* 12, and appears again in the enterprising ways in which Jason and Menelaus secured the high-priesthood shortly after the time of Ben Sira. Sirach evidently does not restrict wisdom to the observance of the Torah, but he regards the rejection of law and tradition as incompatible with wisdom. He thereby stakes out a conservative position in the spectrum of Jewish opinion in the period before the Maccabean revolt.

The discussion of duplicitous behaviour in vv. 25–8 is suggested by the topic of false wisdom in vv. 22–3. vv. 29–30, however, are at odds with this passage, as they seem to disregard the possibility of being duped by appearances. Proverbial wisdom does not lend itself easily to consistent, systematic thought. In the book of Proverbs, contradictory maxims are sometimes placed side by side (Prov 26:4–5). Similarly, Sirach here brings together traditional advice on a topic, even though it is somewhat inconsistent.

(20:1–32) Miscellaneous Advice Like much proverbial wisdom, the maxims in this chapter are only loosely connected. The general theme is true and false wisdom. vv. 1–3 reprise the topic of admonition. Timely silence (vv. 5–8) is a favourite theme of prudential literature. Cf. Prov 17:28; Eccl 3:7; Plutarch's *Moralia*, 5.2 (for further examples see Skehan and DiLella 1987: 300–1). vv. 9–11 reflect on the variability of fortune. vv. 13–17 comment on the fool's lack of perspective, and impatience. The fate of the fool is to be laughed to scorn. While the fool is not guilty or subject to divine punishment, he incurs shame.

v. 18 echoes a proverb attributed to Zeno of Citium, founder of Stoicism: 'Better to slip with the foot than with the tongue' (Diog. Laert. 7.26). v. 20 shows the crucial importance of timing in the wisdom tradition. The principles laid out in Eccl 3:1–8 are fundamental to the application of all proverbs. Cf. Prov 26:7, 9. vv. 21–3 point out ambiguities in some commonly accepted values. Poverty is not desirable, but if it keeps one from sinning it can be beneficial. Honour is a good to be sought, but it can also mislead a person and lead to downfall. These comments, however, do not put in question

Ben Sira's acceptance of conventional wisdom on these subjects; they merely allow for exceptions.

Condemnations of the liar (vv. 24–6) are ubiquitous in moral literature (cf. Prov 6:17, 19; Sir 7:13). The particular nuance that Sirach brings to it here is the shame that the liar incurs. For the comparison with the thief, cf. Prov 6:30: 'The thief is not despised who steals only to satisfy his appetite.' None the less, neither sin is excused. The most notable advice in vv. 27–31 is that the wise should please the great. This advice contrasts with that given in 9:13, which warns people to keep their distance from the powerful, but accords with Sirach's account of the sage in 39:4, and is likely to reflect his own opinion. The wise courtier was a stock character in ancient wisdom literature (cf. Ahikar, Joseph, Daniel, etc.). Most remarkable is the statement that those who please the great atone for injustice (v. 28). It is not clear for whose sin the wise person would atone. The question of atonement for sin comes up in Dan 4 in the context of a wise man serving the mighty. In that case, Daniel advises the king that he can atone for his (the king's) sin by almsgiving. Smend (1906: 188) assumes that the phrase 'who pleases the great' is copied carelessly from the previous verse, so that the text is corrupt.

(21:1–12) Sin and Forgiveness Ben Sira differs from Proverbs and Ecclesiastes in his concern for atonement and forgiveness for sin. The serpent in v. 2 is not the tempter of Gen 3 but is avoided because it bites; cf. Am 5:19. Mention of the serpent here maybe prompted by Prov 23:32 which compares a drunken hangover to the bite of a snake. 1 Pet 5:8 compares the devil to a roaring lion. The pit of Hades in v. 10 is not the hell of Christian tradition but Sheol, abode of all the dead. vv. 11–12 repeat the association of wisdom with the Torah, but here a new rationale is given. The law is an instrument for controlling impulses. This understanding of the law is developed at length in 4 Maccabees, which was written in Greek, probably in Antioch or Alexandria, more than two centuries after Sirach. Cf. 4 Macc 1:13–17, which sets out the enquiry of the book as to whether reason is sovereign over emotions, and then associates reason and wisdom with education in the law. Control of the passions was a matter of high priority in Greek philosophy, especially in Stoicism. As in 19:25, Sirach distinguishes wisdom from mere shrewdness, but he acknowledges that resourcefulness is a necessary component of wisdom.

(21:13–22:18) Wisdom and Folly The sayings in this section are not overtly theological, and may well be part of the traditional lore that Ben Sira passed on. 21:13–28 contrasts the wise person and the fool, a contrast that is ubiquitous in Proverbs. For the comparison of the wise to a spring, cf. *m.'Abot,* 6:1. The fool is like a broken vessel because he cannot retain instruction. On the chatter of fools, cf. Eccl 10:13–14. Sir 38:32 notes that artisans are not sought out for the assembly. Presumably, the prudent man who is sought out in 21:17 must also be educated in wisdom. Education in itself, however, does not suffice. It has quite a different effect on the fool and on the wise person (21:18–21). 21:22–6 describes the impetuosity of the fool, especially regarding lack of verbal restraint (cf. 19:8–12). In 21:27, the Greek 'Satan' reflects the Hebrew *sāṭān,* adversary. The reference is to an ordinary human adversary, not to a demonic figure, although the Hebrew term is used to designate a specific supernatural figure in Job 1–2 and in 1. Chr 21:1.

22:1–2 characterizes the sluggard, who is the target of barbed wit in Proverbs (6:6–11; 24:30–4; 26:13–16). Sirach's analogies are crude. The 'filthy stone' is one that has been used as toilet paper (Smend 1906: 196; Skehan and DiLella 1987: 312). Hence the parallelism with 'a lump of dung' in v. 2. The Syriac adds: 'and everyone flees from the stench of it'.

22:3–5 comments on sons and daughters. On the unruly son, cf. 16:1–5. 22:3 may be influenced by Prov 17:21, which says that the father of a fool has no joy. Sirach switches the reference from the apparently male fool to a daughter (Trenchard 1982: 135). He appears to regard the birth of any daughter as a loss; cf. his comments on daughters in ch. 42. Later, the Talmud says that a man should bless God for not having made him a woman or a slave (*b. Menaḥ* 43b), and blesses the man whose children are male rather than female (*B. Bat.* 16b). The misogyny of Sirach's statement is modified only slightly by the concession that a daughter maybe sensible and obtain a husband (v. 4). It is clear from 7:25 that the daughter does not get the husband on her own initiative. She is given in marriage. Ben Sira's great fear about daughters is that they will bring shame on their fathers (or husbands) by 'shameless' behaviour. He will urge precautionary measures in 26:10–12 and 42:11. The second Greek recension adds the interesting comment that children who are well brought up can hide the ignoble origins of their parents (22:7).

22:7–12 is a scathing dismissal of the fool, whose life is said to be worse than death. The seven-day mourning period is observed by Joseph for Jacob (Gen 50:10), by all Israel for Judith (Jdt 16:24), and by orthodox Jews today. 22:13–15 counsels against the company of a fool; cf. the advice to avoid the wicked in ch. 12. In 22:13b the Syriac reads 'and do not travel with a pig', and this reading is preferred by Smend (1906:199) and some others. The second Greek recension seems to presuppose this reading when it warns 'you may . . . be spattered when he shakes himself' (13d). 22:16–18 stresses the importance of steadfastness and resolve in contrast to the fool's lack of conviction.

(22:19–26) On Friendship This section on friendship continues the sequence of advice on assorted matters; cf. Sir 6:5–17. The concern in vv. 19–22 is with dangers to friendship. v. 23 is an attempt to overcome a common pitfall—friendship that is contingent on prosperity. Cf. Sir 6:8–12 and the parallels cited there. vv. 25–6 are cast in the first person in the Greek. Thus the author reassures himself that his friend's reputation is at stake in the friendship. Many scholars think, however, that the first person here is a corruption, influenced by the following section (22:27–23:6) and that the reader was warned that his or her reputation was at stake in friendship (Smend 1906: 202). Friendship for Sirach is grounded in mutual self-interest, and in this he is typical of the wisdom tradition. This cautious approach can legitimately be contrasted with the NT commandment to love one's enemies (Skehan and DiLella 1987: 317; Lk 6:27–38), but the same NT passage contains the maxim: 'Do to others as you would have them do to you' (Lk 6:31). This suggests that mutual selfinterest may none the less also have a part to play in Christian ethics.

(22:27–23:27) Verbal and Sexual Restraint It is rare indeed to find a prayer of petition in a wisdom book. The only other example in this book, the prayer for national restoration in ch. 36, is very different in spirit and is probably not the work of Ben Sira. The prayer here introduces the themes that follow in ch. 23: sins of speech and of lust. The section concludes with another affirmation of the fear of the Lord and obedience to the commandments.

For the opening of the prayer in 22:27 cf. Ps 141:3. The main concern of the prayer is

protection from sin but it is noteworthy that Sirach's concern for honour and shame intrudes in v. 3 (but cf. Ps 13:4; 38:16).

The most noteworthy feature of the prayer is undoubtedly that God is addressed as 'Father'. God is only rarely called father in the HB, and is never so addressed by an individual. (God is called father of the people of Israel in Isa 63:16; Mal 2:10, and possibly in 1 Chr 29:10, where 'our father' could refer to either God or Israel.) In the Apocrypha, God is addressed as father in 3 Macc 5:51 and 6:3 and in Wis 14:3, passages that were composed in Greek. The Hebrew text of the psalm in Sir 51:10 reads: 'Lord, you are my Father', although the Greek has a confused reading 'Lord, father of my Lord'. The Hebrew of ch. 23 is not extant. Joachim Jeremias argued that there was no evidence for the use of 'my father' as a form of direct address to God in Hebrew before the Christian era (Jeremias 1967: 29) and suggested that ch. 23 originally read 'God of my father'. The direct address, however, is now attested in the Prayer of Joseph (4Q372), which is dated tentatively about 200 BCE (Schuller 1990). The Prayer begins, 'My father and my God'. In view of this parallel there is no reason to question the authenticity of the Greek text of Sir 24:1, 4. The familial title 'father' balances the appellation 'Master', which emphasizes rather God's power (Strotmann 1991: 83). For Sirach's understanding of the fatherhood of God, cf. Sir 4:10.

The phrase 'instruction of the mouth' in 23:7 is lifted out and set as a heading for this section in several MSS. The subject of loose talk has been treated in 19:4–12 and 20: 18–20. The present passage, however, is not concerned with gossip but with swearing (vv. 9–11) and coarse talk (vv. 12–15), which are matters of Jewish piety rather than common Near-Eastern wisdom. Avoidance of swearing is a matter of respect for the divine name. Cf. Ex 20:7; Deut 5:11; Mt 5:34–7; 23:18–22; Jas 5:12. Sirach evidently believes that oaths have consequences, even if they are sworn inadvertently (v. 11). The reference of 23:12 is not clear. Some commentators take it to refer to blasphemy (Smend, Skehan and DiLella), for which the death penalty is prescribed in Lev 24:11–16 (cf. Mt 26:65–6; Jn 10:33). Others think the 'speech comparable to death' is that which is described in the following verses (so Peters 1913). It is more likely, however, that v. 12 refers to a separate offence, and that Ben Sira deliberately avoids mentioning it directly. On respect for parents, see Sir 3:2–16. To curse the day of one's birth is the depth of despair. Cf. Job 3:3–10; Jer 20:14. The point here is the acute embarrassment of the person who disgraces himself or herself in the presence of the mighty. Remembering one's parents is a way to keep on guard.

The treatise on adultery (23:16–26) is introduced by a numerical proverb. For a cluster of such proverbs see Prov 30:15–31. Other examples are found in Sir 25:1–2, 7–11; 26:5–6, 28; 50:25–6 (see Roth 1965). The form 'two kinds… and three' invariably introduces the latter number. So in this case there are three kinds of sinner: the person of unrestrained passion, the person guilty of incest, and the adulterer.

Sirach gives equal time to the adulterer and adulteress. The discussion of the adulterer can be viewed as an extrapolation from Prov 9:17, which refers to the sweetness of stolen water and bread eaten in secret. Sirach speaks of sweet bread and dwells at length on the issue of secrecy. On the futility of hiding from the Lord, cf. 16:17–23 above. Here Sirach adds that God knows everything even before it is created. Cf. 1QH 9:23 (formerly numbered 1:23): 'What can I say that is not known?' In the Qumran theology, however, God not only knows what will happen but determines it (1QS 3:15–16; 1QH 9: 19–20). Sirach is closer to the position attributed to Akiba in m.'Abot, 3:19: all is foreseen, but free will is given. Sirach does not specify how the adulterer will be punished. Proverbs implies that the adulterer will be beaten up by the wronged husband and publicly disgraced and that he will have to pay a heavy fine (Prov 6:31–5: 'sevenfold', 'all the goods of his house'). Sirach evidently envisages public disgrace. Neither Proverbs nor Sirach make any mention of the death penalty for the adulterer prescribed by biblical law (Lev 20:10; Deut 22:22).

The treatment of the adulteress differs from that of the adulterer in several respects. Her sin is said to be three- fold—the offence against God and her husband and the fact that she produced children by another man. Sirach implies that the adulterer sins against God (v. 18), although he does not say so directly. There is no implication, however, that the adulterer sins against his wife. The imbalance in this regard reflects the common ancient tendency to group the wife with the possessions of her husband (see Sir 7:22–6). The sin against the husband is that she has violated his rights and his honour. The production of children by adultery is considered a separate offence. Sir 23:23 does not imply that the woman's adultery was prompted by the desire to have a child (against Trenchard

1982: 99). Neither is there any reason to think that the woman acts out of economic necessity (so Camp 1991: 27–8). If an adulterous affair ended in pregnancy, the woman would have little choice but to try to pass the child off as her husband's offspring. One of the main reasons for prohibiting adultery was to guarantee the legitimacy of a man's children. At issue here is the right of inheritance, and so the adultery has economic consequences, which are deemed to constitute a separate, third, offence.

While the adulterer will be punished in the streets of the city, presumably by the cuckolded husband, the adulteress is led to the assembly. Sirach is not explicit as to what action the assembly may take. The story of Susanna, which may be roughly contemporary, comes to mind. Since Susanna is not married, she is accused of fornication rather than adultery, but she is sentenced to death. The death sentence is also proposed for the woman taken in adultery in Jn 8. It is very unlikely, however, that these stories reflect actual practice in the Hellenistic or Roman periods. In the Elephantine papyri (5th cent. BCE), the punishment for adultery is divorce, with loss of some property rights. The extension of punishment to the children recalls Ezra 10:44, where the foreign wives were sent away with their children. Ben Sira, however, seems to indicate a divine punishment rather than a human one. His contention is that the children of an adulteress will not prosper. Cf. Wis 3:16–19. Sirach does not provide any human mechanism to ensure that this punishment will be effected.

Sir 23:27 brings this section to a conclusion by making the disgrace of the adulteress into a moral lesson that it is better to keep the law. It is noteworthy that his discussion of the punishment of the adulteress does not call for literal fulfilment of the law. Sirach's concern is with conformity to the tradition in principle, with the attitude of reverence rather than with legal details. The second Greek redactor adds a gloss (v. 28), which promises great glory and length of days to one who follows after God. In accordance with the usual theology of this redaction, 'length of days' probably means eternal life (so Skehan and DiLella 1987: 326).

(24:1–33) The Praises of Wisdom The great hymn to wisdom in ch. 24 may be regarded as the centrepiece of the book. It is often regarded as the introduction to the second part of the book (e.g. Segal 1972; Roth 1980; Skehan and DiLella 1987), with a view to finding a symmetrical structure in the book as a whole. Since each of the wisdom poems in 1:1–10, 4:11–19, 6:18–37, and 14:20–15:10, introduces a section, so it is argued does ch. 24. Against this, however, the second half of the book is not punctuated by wisdom poems as the first had been. The only true wisdom poem in the remainder of the book is found in 51:13–30, which serves as a conclusion, and maybe added as an epilogue. That passage is cast as a personal declaration by Ben Sira; vv. 30–4 are also a personal declaration. It seems better then to see ch. 24 as the conclusion of the first part of the book (Marböck 1971: 41–3). It sums up the theme of wisdom that has been treated intermittently in chs. 1–23, and will be paralleled by the concluding poem on wisdom in ch. 51.

Ch. 24 differs from other wisdom poems in Sirach in so far as vv. 3–22 constitute a declaration by Wisdom in the first person. As such, it is most accurately designated as an aretalogy, and is properly compared to the aretalogies of the Egyptian goddess Isis (Marböck 1971: 47–54). There is an obvious biblical precedent in Prov 8, which may itself be influenced by Egyptian prototypes. The argument that Sirach drew directly on the aretalogies of Isis has been made especially by Conzelmann (1971: 230–43). In addition to the formal similarity, there are also thematic parallels. Both Wisdom and Isis are of primeval origin, exercise cosmological functions, and claim dominion over the whole earth. Isis claims to have established law for humanity. v. 23, which stands outside the firstperson aretalogy, equates wisdom with the law of the Lord. It is quite likely then that the concept of Wisdom singing her own praises, in both Sirach and Proverbs, is indebted to the Egyptian Isis hymns. Sirach, however, also draws heavily on biblical phraseology, and so adapts the aretalogy form for his own purpose (Sheppard 1980: 19–71).

vv. 1–2 provide the setting for Wisdom's speech. v. 2 clearly locates her in the heavenly council (cf. Ps 82:1), with the implication that she is imagined as a heavenly, angelic being. It is possible that 'her people' in v. 1 refers to this heavenly assembly (so Smend 1906: 216), but it is more likely to refer to Israel, among whom Wisdom settles in vv. 8–12. She speaks, then, on both earthly and heavenly levels simultaneously. vv. 3–7 describe the origin and nature of Wisdom. The firstperson pronoun (Gk. *egō*) is especially characteristic of the Isis aretalogies, but cf. also Prov 8:12; 17. Even though the Hebrew text is not extant, the original Hebrew is clearly reflected in the idiom of v. 1, lit. 'Wisdom praises her soul'. The divine origin of Wisdom is also stressed in Prov 8:21 and Sir 1:1. The idea that Wisdom proceeds from the mouth of God may be suggested by Prov 2:6 ('For the Lord gives wisdom; from his mouth come knowledge and understanding'). This motif lays the foundation for the identification of Wisdom with the *word* of God, which also proceeds from the mouth (cf. Isa 45:23; 48:3; 25:11). The identification is clear in Wis 9:1–2. The Greek word *logos*, however, had far-reaching connotations in Greek, especially Stoic, philosophy, where it referred to the rational spirit that pervades the universe. This concept was also developed by the Jewish philosopher Philo (Mack 1973). The fusion of the Jewish wisdom tradition and Greek philosophy on this point is essential background to the use of the Logos/Word in Jn 1:1. The notion that Wisdom proceeds from the mouth also invites association with the spirit/breath of God (Gk. *pneuma*) which had similar philosophic connotations in Stoic philosophy (cf. the use of *pneuma* in Wis 1:7). The association with the spirit is suggested here in the statement that Wisdom covered the earth like a mist, which recalls Gen 1:2, although the allusion is not precise.

The statement that Wisdom lived 'in the heights' is suggested by Prov 8:2, but here, unlike Proverbs, the heights should be understood as heavenly. What is most striking about the following verses is how language used of God in the HB is now applied to Wisdom. The pillar of cloud of the Exodus (Ex 13:21; 33:9–10) is also identified with the Logos by Philo (*Quis Heres*, 203–6) and Wisdom is given a key role in the Exodus in Wis 10. Here, however, it is removed from the Exodus context, and associated with the primordial enthronement of Wisdom. While Prov 8:27 says that Wisdom was there when God established the heavens, Sir 24:5 has Wisdom circle the vault of heaven *alone*. Cf. rather Job 9:8, where God alone stretched out the heavens. In Job 38:16 God challenges Job whether he 'has walked in the recesses of the deep'. Rule over the sea is a divine prerogative in the HB (Ps 65:8; 89:10; 93:3–4, etc.). Wisdom is never said to be divine, but it appears to be the instrument of God's presence and agency. The quest for a resting place has been compared to the wandering of Israel in the wilderness (Sheppard 1980: 39). Ben Sira however shows no interest in the historical process by which Israel settled in its land. Wisdom's quest for a resting place completes the process of creation. There is an enigmatic passage in 1 *Enoch*, 42:1–2, that dramatically reverses Sirach's account: Wisdom found no place to dwell and so withdrew to heaven.

vv. 8–12 describe how Wisdom settles in Israel. The command to settle in Israel may be compared to the command given to Israel to seek out the designated place of worship in Deut12 (Sheppard 1980: 42). But Sirach implies that Wisdom had settled in Israel before Israel settled in its land. So Wisdom ministered already in the tabernacle, the tent-shrine of the wilderness (Ex 25:8–9). v. 9 suggests that the association of Wisdom with Israel is primordial. The most apt parallel to this passage in Sirach is found in Deut 32:8–9, which says that when God divided the nations among the 'sons of God' he took Israel as his own portion. Sirach has God exercise the election of Israel through Wisdom. The passage is remarkable, however, for its cultic emphasis. Wisdom finds expression in the cult of the Jerusalem temple. This idea is exceptional in the wisdom tradition, but it accords with Sirach's high esteem for the priesthood (cf. 44:6–26; 50:1–21). The notion of Wisdom making its dwelling in Israel is picked up in Jn 1:14, where the Word comes to dwell with humankind.

vv. 13–17 compare Wisdom to the luxuriant growth of various trees and plants. Such imagery is not found in Prov 8, but is familiar from other parts of the HB. Cf. Ps 1, which compares the righteous man to a tree planted by water, and in general Num 24:6; Hos 14:5–7. The cedar of Lebanon is the most celebrated tree in the Bible (Ps 92:12; Song 5:15). v. 15 changes the imagery to perfumes, and again evokes the cult by mentioning the incense in the tabernacle. vv. 19–22 compare Wisdom to food and drink. Cf. John 6:35, where Jesus says that whoever eats of him will never hunger and whoever drinks of him will never thirst.

v. 23 introduces a short commentary on the words of Wisdom, drawn in part from Deut 33:4. The word 'inheritance' also picks up a motif from vv. 8,12. The fact that the verse has three cola is exceptional in Ben Sira, and has led to the suggestion that the first colon, which refers explicitly to the book and which is not paralleled in Deut 33:4, is a secondary addition, influenced by Bar 4:1 (Rickenbacher 1973: 125–7). Sirach was certainly familiar with the Torah in its written form (cf. 38:34), but this is the only passage that identifies wisdom specifically with the book. The identification of wisdom with the law is implied again in the hymn at the end of

Sirach, by the metaphor of the yoke in 51:26. The repeated association of wisdom with the Torah is one of the principal ways in which Ben Sira modifies the wisdom tradition he had received. It has its basis in Deut 4:6, but is never hinted at in Proverbs or Ecclesiastes. Yet for Sirach, in contrast to Deuteronomy, wisdom is the primary category which is the subject of hymnic praise. The Torah is mentioned secondarily, by way of clarification. Wisdom is older than Moses, having been created 'in the beginning'. Later, rabbinic authorities would claim that the Torah too was created before the world, and was even the instrument with which the world was created (Urbach 1975: i.287). On this understanding, the law revealed to Moses was implicit in creation from the beginning (Marböck 1971: 93–4; for a contrary interpretation see Schnabel 1985). Cf. Rom 1:20, although Paul evidently did not regard all details of the law as part of the law of creation. Sirach also ignores most of the levitical laws, and does not address the question whether the whole law was implied in Wisdom from the beginning.

Sirach proceeds to compare Wisdom/Torah to the four rivers associated with Eden in Gen 2, and also to the Nile and the Jordan. The comparison with foreign rivers may be significant. Wisdom was always an international phenomenon, and its character is not changed in that respect by the identification with the Jewish law. The reason that the first man did not know wisdom fully (v. 28) is not because it was not yet revealed (so Skehan and DiLella 1987: 337). Sir 17:7 claims that when God created humanity he filled them with knowledge and understanding and gave them knowledge of good and evil. Besides, the last man is no wiser (25:28). No human being can fully comprehend Wisdom (cf. Job 28, which has a decidedly more negative view of human wisdom).

The chapter closes with a stanza in which Sirach compares himself to an offshoot of the great river of Wisdom. For the metaphor of light, cf. Prov 6:3. He also compares his teaching to prophecy, without claiming to be a prophet. Sirach views prophecy as part of the textual lore to be studied by the sage (39:1). It is not apparent that he recognized any active prophets in his own time. The specific point of comparison with prophecy here is that it remains for future generations. Sirach concludes with a protestation of disinterestedness. He has not laboured for himself alone. Cf. 51:25, where he invites the uneducated to acquire learning without money.

Part II. Chs. 25–51

(25:1–33:19)

(25:1–12) Sources of Happiness The three poems in this section are only loosely connected. The first and third are numerical sayings. The first contrasts three kinds of people of whom Sirach approves with three of whom he does not. Harmony among friends finds its classic expression in Ps 133. v. 1*d*, on the harmony of husband and wife, is an important corrective to some of Ben Sira's more patriarchal pronouncements on marriage. The adulterous old man is universally despised. Cf. the elders in the story of Susanna. Mention of the adulterous old man leads to a briefencomium on the wisdom appropriate to old age. In the third poem, Sirach lists ten beatitudes; see SIR 14:20. The makarisms here concern very practical matters that are typical of the instruction of Sirach. The joy of a sensible wife is reiterated in 26:1, and contrasts with the bitter denunciations of an 'evil' wife in 25:16–26. All of these sayings on marriage are formulated from the point of view of the husband. Ploughing with an ox and ass together is explicitly forbidden in Deut 22:10. Here it appears to be a matter of wisdom rather than of law. In the context, it may be a metaphor for polygamy (cf. 26:6; 37:11). The blessing of one who finds wisdom (v. 10) is paralleled in 4Q525 2 ii 3–4. The affirmation of the superiority of the fear of the Lord resumes the theme of 23:27. Fear of the Lord was similarly emphasized at the beginning of Part I in 1:11–21, 28–30. The distinction implied here between wisdom and fear of the Lord recalls the contrast of true and false wisdom in 19:20–5, especially 19:24, which prefers the God-fearing who lack understanding to the clever who transgress the law.

(25:13–26:27) Wives, Bad and Good This passage is Sirach's most sustained treatment of marriage, or rather of the good and bad wife from the husband's point of view. The bad wife receives more than twice as many verses as the good. The first stanza (vv. 13–15) sets the tone by comparing a woman's anger to a snake's venom. Smend (1906: 229) suggested that 'those who hate' and 'enemies' in v. 14 are mistakes by the Greek translator. (The Heb. is not extant.) The original would have read feminine forms, 'hated' (i.e. repudiated, divorced) and 'rival', and so the woman's anger would arise from a situation of either polygamy or divorce. The subject of rivalry between women is explicit in 26:6 and 37:11.

The contentious or nagging wife is a common subject of complaint in folklore, and appears also in Proverbs (21:19; 25:24; 27: 15). Sirach's comparisons are more violent. Even if we make allowance for Semitic hyperbole, the statement that any iniquity is small compared to that of a woman (v. 19) is exceptional. This sentiment is developed further in 42:14, which says that the wickedness of a man is better than the goodness of a woman! There is an extreme quality to these sayings that cannot be dismissed as simply part of the culture of the time. (A character in Eur. *Phoen.* 805, refers to women as the wildest evil (Middendorp 1973: 21), but the playwright does not necessarily endorse the view.) The wish that a sinner's lot befall her may mean that a sinner should marry her; cf. Eccl 7:26. vv. 21–2 warn against marrying a woman for either her beauty or her wealth. The deceptiveness of beauty was noted in Prov 31:30. The wealth of a wife might prevent a man from seeking divorce, since the woman could take her own possessions with her. The same sentiment is found in Ps.-Phoc. 199–200; Eur. *Melannipus*, frag. 502 (Middendorp 1973: 21).

No verse in Ben Sira is more pregnant with implications or more controversial in a modern context than v. 24. The notion that the 'strange woman' can lead a man to sin and death is developed in Prov 7, and finds colourful development in 4Q184 (The Wiles of the Wicked Woman). The Qumran text has been adduced as a parallel to v. 24 because it says that 'she is the start of all the ways of wickedness' (4Q184:8; Levison 1985: 622). Ben Sira, however, is not concerned only with the strange or loose woman. (It is clear from the parallels with Prov 7 that this is the figure envisaged in the fragmentary 4Q184.) Sirach does not only speak of the death of the sinner, but why we *all* die. There can be no doubt that v. 24 represents an interpretation of Gen 3, and that it is the earliest extant witness to the view that Eve was responsible for the introduction of sin and death (Meyers 1988: 75, *pace* Levison 1985: 617–23, who argues that the woman in question is the bad wife). Even the view that Adam was the source of sin and death only emerges in literature of the first century CE (Rom 5: 12–21; 1 Cor 15:22; Wis 2:23–4; 4 Ezra 4:30; 7:11–21; 2 *Bar* 17:3; 48:45–6. 2 *Bar* 54:19, however, contends that Adam is only responsible for himself). Sir 17, which clearly reflects Gen 2–3, contains no mention of an original sin. In the apocalyptic literature roughly contemporary with Sirach the origin of evil was attributed to fallen angels (1 *Enoch*, 6–11) or to God's design at creation (1QS 3). Sirach elsewhere insists that death is simply the decree of the Lord, with no implication that it is a punishment (41:3–4). None the less, this verse is extant in Hebrew and there is no reason to doubt its authenticity. Sirach's inconsistency on this matter shows only that his argumentation was influenced by the immediate context in which an issue is raised.

There is no precedent in Hebrew tradition for the view that woman is the source of all evil, but there is a clear Greek precedent in the story of Pandora's box (Hes. *Op.* 42–105; Middendorp 1973: 21; Kieweler 1992: 115 insists on the differences in context, but the parallel is none the less significant). It would be too simple to ascribe the misogynist aspects of Ben Sira's thought to Hellenistic influence. Ps.-Phocylides represents a more heavily Hellenized form of Judaism but does not pick up these elements. There is undoubtedly Greek influence here, but Ben Sira's personality also played a part in his selective use of Greek culture.

Ch. 25 concludes with the rather brutal advice that a wife who is outspoken and not compliant should be cut off or divorced. Contrast the advice not to divorce a good wife in Sir 7:26. The Hebrew verb k-r-t, cut off, gives rise to the standard word for divorce, *krytwt* (Deut 24:1). Deuteronomy allowed that a man could divorce his wife if she did not please him because he found something objectionable (*'erwat dābār*) about her. This text was invoked in a famous debate between the houses of Shammai and Hillel in the first century BCE. The Shammaites tried to restrict its application to cases of adultery. Hillel ruled that a man was justified in divorcing 'even if she spoiled a dish for him' (*m. Git.* 9:10). Rabbi Akiba went further, saying that it sufficed if he found another woman who was fairer (Archer 1990: 219). The Mishnah also provides that a woman could be sent away without her *kĕtûbâ* (the *mōhār* or bride-price owed by the husband) if she transgressed the law of Moses or violated Jewish custom, even by going out with her hair unbound, spinning in the street, or speaking with a man (*m. Ketub.* 7:6). R. Tarfon also permitted this in the case of a scolding woman, who spoke inside her house so that a neighbour could hear. Ben Sira does not suggest that the dowry can be retained in this case. Smend (1906: 233) explains the expression 'from your flesh' by suggesting that the financial settlement involved would be as painful as cutting off a piece of flesh. It is more likely, however, that the phrase reflects Gen 2:24 (man and wife are 'one flesh' while

they are married). The woman had no corresponding right to divorce in Mishnaic law (*m. Yebam.* 14:1).

Sir 26:1–4 turns briefly to the joys of a good wife. She is considered solely in terms of her effect on her husband. The point of this stanza is the converse of 25:19. As the sinner deserves a bad wife, the one who fears the Lord deserves a good one. The good wife here seems to exist to reward the deserving man rather than having a value in her own right. The value of a good wife for a wise man is also noted in the late-Egyptian *Instruction of Phibis*, 8:5 (J. T. Sanders 1983: 86).

26:5–9 repeats the thought of 25:13–20. The jealousy of a wife for her rival raises the question of polygamy. While polygamy is never forbidden by biblical law and is still permitted by the Mishnah (*m. Ketub.* 10:5; *m. Ker.* 3:7), it has often been thought to have died out by the Hellenistic period, except for people in high places such as the sons of Herod. This common assumption has been put in doubt, however, by the Babatha archive from the early second century CE (Lewis 1989: 19–22). Babatha was an illiterate woman from the region of the Dead Sea, who, after her husband's death, was involved in a dispute with another woman who claimed to be his wife, and whose claim is not disputed. While Babatha was not a poor person, she was far removed from the social class of the Herodian family. Polygamy may not have been as exceptional in the Hellenistic and Roman periods as was previously thought.

The Egyptian *Instruction of Phibis* refers to an otherwise unknown book 'Faults of Women' (*Phibis*, 8:10; J. T. Sanders 1983: 86), so we should assume that passages such as this were a topos of Near-Eastern wisdom in the Hellenistic period. On the eyelashes of the adulterous woman cf. Prov 6:25, where they appear to be instruments of seduction. The point here is that a woman intent on adultery makes up her eyelids, while the faithful wife has no reason to do so. On the making up of the eyelids cf. 2 Kings 9:30 (Jezebel); Jer 4:30; Ezek 23:40. In *1 Enoch*, 8:1, the art of making up the eyes is taught to human beings by the fallen angel Azazel.

The warning about a headstrong daughter in 26:10 will be taken up at length in 42:9–14; cf. Ps.-Phoc. 215–16. Several Hellenistic Jewish texts indicate that virgin girls were confined to the home (Philo, *Spec. Leg.* 3.169; Flacc. 89; 2 Macc 3:19; 3 Macc 1:18; 4 Macc 18:7; see further Archer 1990: 113–15). Sir 26:12 recalls Ezek 16:23–5 in its obscene portrayal of the promiscuous woman, but Sirach attributes this behaviour not to an

exceptional individual but to a daughter who
is not held in check. The tent-peg and arrow
are phallic symbols (Smend 1906: 236; Peters
1913: 217).

Sir 26:13–18 is more explicit than earlier passages on the attributes of the good wife.
Although she puts flesh on her husband's
bones, this is not the capable wife of Prov 31,
who can buy a field and deal with merchants.
Sirach's ideal wife is a homebody, characterized
by silence, modesty, and chastity. In part, the
difference in perspective reflects the transition
from a rural to an urban culture. The wife of a
scribe in Jerusalem has no occasion to buy a
field, and her labour is not needed outside the
house. Instead she is portrayed as an ornament
in his home. This is the only passage where Ben
Sira shows an appreciation of physical beauty
(contrast 25:21). It is characteristic of ancient
Near-Eastern love poetry to single out parts of
the body for praise. Cf. Song 4:1–7; 1QapGen
20:2–7. The description of Sarah in the latter
passage comments on the perfection of her legs.
Ben Sira differs from the other passages however in drawing his analogies from the furnish-
ings of the temple, and thereby projecting a
sense of admiration rather than physical desire.

26:19–27 are found in the second Greek
recension and are not extant in Hebrew. They
are usually regarded as secondary, but Peters
(1913: 218) and Skehan and DiLella 1987: 351)
regard them as authentic. They add little to the
foregoing discussion. v. 26c, d repeats 26:1a, b.
The advice in vv. 19–22 is closely parallel to Prov
5:7–14. The concern in sexual activity is to prop-
agate a line of offspring. Relations with a prostitute are wasted. v. 23 recapitulates 25:19 and
26:3. Some of the analogies in this passage are
very crude: a prostitute is like spittle and a
headstrong wife is like a dog.

(26:28–27:29) Miscellaneous Maxims The
extended discourse on women is followed by a
string of short units on traditional wisdom
themes, punctuated by pronouncements on
the inevitability of retribution (26:28c; 27:3, 29).
26:28 is a numerical proverb, which ends with
the condemnation of the relapsed sinner. 28c
should read 'wealthy man' (Syriac) rather than
'warrior' (Gk.)—the Greek translator evidently
misunderstood the Hebrew' iš ḥayil, which can
mean either man of valour or man of wealth
(Smend1906: 240). For the wise man despised,
cf. Job 29:2–30:10. Ifwe allow that the wise man
was not always despised (cf. Job), then in each
case the person has lost something that he or

she had for a time. On the relapsed sinner, cf.
Ezek 18:24.

26:29–27:3 gives a remarkably sceptical view
of commerce. Traditional wisdom denounced
cheating and the use of false scales, which was
evidently widespread in the ancient world (Prov
11:1; 20:10), but Sirach goes further in suggesting
that dishonesty is inherent in the pursuit of
wealth. Cf. Mt 19:23–4 on the difficulty of a
rich person entering heaven. This saying is
probably a comment on the increase of commerce in Judea in the Hellenistic period. The
Tobiads come to mind as the paradigmatic
profiteers of the era. According to 2 Macc 3:4,
a dispute over the city market was the initial
cause of friction that initiated the chain of
events that led to the persecution of Antiochus
Epiphanes and the Maccabean revolt. 27:3 is
typical of Sirach's rather naïve view that sinners
suffer retribution in this life.

27:4–7 emphasizes the importance of speech
as the reflection of a person's character; cf. 20:5–
8. The 'refuse' in v. 4 refers to the dung of the
oxen mixed in with the straw. For the comparison with the fruit of a tree, cf. Mt 7:16–19; 12:33.
This theme is illustrated in vv. 11–15. The inter-
vening vv. 8–10 emphasize the inevitability of
the link of act and consequence, which is typical
of ancient Near-Eastern wisdom (Koch 1955), cf.
Am 3:3–8. This theme is further developed in vv.
22–9, and is the underpinning of Sirach's belief
in the inevitability of retribution. 27:16–21 on
the betrayal of secrets illustrates another aspect
of indiscreet speech, and is a traditional concern
of wisdom literature. Cf. Prov 20:19; 25:9.
Finally, the sage turns to hypocrisy and mis-
chief-making. Here again there is a parallel in
Prov 6:12–19. Cf. also Theognis, 93–6. 27:25 is a
variant of Prov 26:27b, while Prov 26:27a is
reproduced exactly in Sir 27:26a. The unit ends
with an affirmation of retribution in this life.

(27:30–28:11) Anger, Vengeance, and Strife
Mention of the Lord's vengeance recalls Deut
32:35–6. The Qumran *Rule of the Community* also
eschews vengeance for the present, but only
defers it until the day of wrath (1QS 10:17–20).
Sirach here is closer in spirit to the Gospels,
especially in linking forgiveness to prayer (Mt
6:12, 14–15; 18:32–5; Mk 11:25; Lk 11:4). Similar
sentiments are found in T. Gad, 6:3–7; T. Zebulon,
5:3, but these passages are of uncertain provenance. In a later Jewish context, cf. b. Roš Haš.
17a; h. Meg. 28a. Characteristic of Sirach is the
reminder of death as an argument for forgiveness: cf. 7:36; 8:7; 14:12; 18:24; 38:20. The point is

that everyone is subject to divine judgement in the end, on the basis of the commandments. We have no secure place from which to pass judgement on others (cf. Mt 7:1).

(28:12–26) On Slander The discourse on slander has no real parallel in the earlier wisdom tradition, but cf. the discussion of gossip in 19:7–12. On the ambivalence of speech (v. 12), cf. Jas 3:10. The expression translated as 'slander' in the NRSV is literally 'third tongue', so called because it comes between the subject of the slander and the hearer. So b. 'Arak. 15b: 'The third tongue kills three' (the subject, the speaker, and the hearer). In the case of virtuous women (v. 15), slander could lead to divorce and loss of the marriage settlement. v. 17b echoes Prov 25:15b, but the context in Proverbs concerns persuasion. This section ends by reiterating the need for caution in speech, which is typical of ancient wisdom; cf. 20:18–19; 23:7–8.

(29:1–20) Loans, Alms, and Surety This section combines three poems on related themes: loans (vv. 1–7), alms (vv. 8–13), and providing surety or collateral for another (vv. 14–20). There is some tension in Ben Sira's advice on loans. The Torah requires that one help an indigent neighbour, and not exact interest (Ex 22:24; Lev 25:36–7; Deut 15:7–11; 23:19–20). Sirach endorses the commandment. No mention is made of interest. He also urges rectitude in repaying loans, thereby implying that even a scribe or an educated person may need a loan on occasion. The need to repay promptly is also emphasized in 4QSapiential Work A (4Q417 1 i 21–3). But much of the passage dwells on the difficulty of recovering a loan. Cf. Ps 37:21: the wicked do not pay back, the righteous keep giving. So in v. 7 Sirach shows considerable sympathy for those who refuse to lend because of fear of being cheated. On this issue, he is at odds with the spirit of the Gospels. Contrast Lk 6:34–5: if you lend to those from whom you hope to receive, what credit is there for that? Sirach abides by the letter of the commandment, but his pragmatic wisdom favours a more cautious course of action.

In the case of almsgiving, there is no expectation of repayment. Sirach has already treated this subject in 3:30–1. The NRSV translation of 9:11 ('Lay up your treasure . . .') is unduly influenced by the Gospel parallel (Mt 6:10 || Luke 12:33–4: 'Lay up for yourselves treasure in heaven'). The point here is rather 'dispose of your treasure in accordance with the

commandments of the Most High' (cf. Skehan and DiLella 1987: 368). The parallel with the NT holds, however, as Sirach goes on to say 'store up almsgiving in your treasury'. Good deeds earn credit with the Lord. Cf. Tob 4:8–9: 'If you have many possessions make your gift from them in proportion; if few, do not be afraid to give according to the little you have. So you will be laying up a treasure for yourself against the day of necessity.' Pss. Sol. 9:5 speaks of laying up treasure with the Lord by doing righteousness. 2 Bar 24:1 speaks of treasuries where the merits of the righteous are stored until the day of judgement. The notion that hoarded wealth rusts (Sir 29:10) parallels the thought of Mt 6:20 on the perishability of wealth. Cf. also Jas 5:2–3.

Proverbs uniformly counsels against going surety for another (Prov 6:1–5; 11:15; 17:18; 20:16; 22:26–7; 27:13). Sirach appreciates the helpfulness implied, but he also dwells on the pitfalls. He also includes a warning for the sinner, who tries to take advantage of such a situation, that lawsuits will follow. Retribution is not left entirely in the hands of God! He concludes with a typical middle way: help your neighbour if you can, but be prudent. The theme of surety also appears in 4QSapiential Work A (4Q416 7) but the passage is obscure (Harrington 1994: 147).

(29:21–8) On Self-Sufficiency The theme of self-sufficiency is illustrated by the misery of one who depends on others for lodging. A longer list of the necessities of life is given in 39:26. Ben Sira's concern is with honour and the lack thereof, the indignity of depending on others; cf. the critique of begging in 40:28–30. Self-sufficiency was widely entertained as an ideal in Greek philosophy, especially by the Stoics (Middendorp 1973: 30), but Prov 12:9 appreciates the advantage of working for oneself (reading 'ōbēd lô rather than 'ebed lô). See further Sir 31:19. Sirach warns, however, against inappropriate selfsufficiency (11:22).

(30:1–13) On Sons The education of sons, which is treated in scattered proverbs in Proverbs, is expanded into a section of 13 verses here. Phibis also devotes a whole instruction (the tenth, Papyrus Insinger 8:21–9:20) to the subject. Both rely heavily on physical punishment, as also does Proverbs (13:24; 22:15; 23:13–14; 29:15). Cf. Also the Sayings of Ahiqar, Syriac version: 'My son, withhold not your son from stripes, for the beating of a child is like manure to the garden, or like rope to an ass, or like a tether on the foot of an ass' (Skehan and DiLella 1987: 377). The goal is to instil discipline, but also to produce a copy of the father (v. 4; cf. Tob 9:6). The emphasis is on conformity, with little or no place for creativity. A very different emphasis is found in Ps.-Phoc. 207–9: 'Be not harsh with your children but be gentle, and if a child sins against you, let the mother cut her son down to size, or else the elders of the family or the chiefs of the people.' (This passage is based on Deut 21:18–21, but transforms the biblical text into a plea for paternal leniency.) Cf. also Col. 3:21: 'Fathers, do not provoke your children'. Sirach seems to have belonged to the 'old school' in the matter of family discipline.

(30:14–25) **Food and Health** The value of good health is universally appreciated. The sentiment that death is preferable to life in some circumstances is also found in Tob 3:6, 10, 13 in the prayers of Tobit and Sarah. Cf. also 1 Kings 19:4 (Elijah), Jon 4:3; Job 3:11, 13, 17; Eccl 4:2. Sirach, however, does not speak out of personal misery, nor is he a sceptic like Ecclesiastes. His observation is all the more remarkable for its dispassionate objectivity; cf. Theog. 181–2. Death is characterized as 'endless sleep' in the Greek text. (The corresponding Heb. has 'to go down to Sheol'.) The repose of the dead is commonly called sleep in Jewish epitaphs of the Hellenistic and Roman periods (van der Horst 1991: 114–17) but so also Job 3:13.

Greek MSS variously insert the heading 'About Foods' before v. 16 or v. 18. In either case, the heading is inappropriate. Food is introduced in v. 18 only to illustrate the frustration of sickness. Offerings placed on a grave are viewed as futile here, and are disapproved in Deut 26:14, but appear to be approved in Tob 4:17. See also the comment on Sir 7:33 above. The futility of offering food to idols is the theme of the satirical story of Bel and the Dragon. An ominous note is struck in passing in v. 19c, which implies that a person in bad health is being punished by the Lord. Compare the theology of the friends of Job, and the assumption of the disciples in Jn 9:2. This line is not found in the Hebrew, which refers instead to 'one who has wealth'. The Greek verse may have resulted from an attempt to make sense of corrupt Hebrew (Smend 1906: 270). The theological position it reflects was widespread, but not explicitly endorsed by Ben Sira. v. 20 is also corrupt. The eunuch embracing a virgin, and the comparison with one who acts under

compulsion are imported here from Sir 20:4. (The reference to the eunuch was apt enough in the context of ch. 30.) The thought of v. 23 is more typical of Ecclesiastes than of Sirach. Cf. Eccl 9:7–10; 11:9, but cf. also Sir 14:11–19 and the comments above. Modern medicine has come to appreciate the wisdom of the sentiment in v. 24.

(31:1–11) **Attitude to Wealth** The order of chapters in Greek and Hebrew diverges at this point (Gk. ch. 31 = Heb. ch. 34). vv. 1–2 are hopelessly corrupt in the Hebrew, and 30:2 is also corrupt in Greek. The general idea is that a person devoted to the pursuit of wealth suffers insomnia. According to 40:1–11, troubled sleep is an affliction of humankind in general, but sinners are afflicted more than others. Insomnia in itself is not necessarily a moral indictment. The statements in vv. 2–3 are neutral, simple observations of fact. Cf. 13:21–3. Proverbs is similarly realistic on the question of wealth and poverty (Prov 10:15; 18:23; 19:4, 6).

vv. 4–11 move on to moral judgement. v. 5 echoes 27:1 in condemning the inordinate pursuit of wealth. Yet v. 8 suggests Sirach's ideal: a rich person who is found blameless. Such a person may be hard to find, but not impossible. Wealth was traditionally regarded as a reward of wisdom. Sirach was aware that this view was problematic, but he had not given up on it entirely. In defence of his admiration for the blameless rich person, he points out that he had the power to sin, but refrained. Sirach's confidence in the security of the wealth of the righteous person, however, might have been dispelled by a reading of the book of Job.

(31:12–32:13) **Eating and Drinking at Banquets** Behaviour at banquets is a theme of Egyptian literature from an early time and is treated in the *Instruction of Ptah-hotep*, the *Instruction of Kagemni*, and the *Instruction of Amen-em-ope* (J. T. Sanders 1983: 67). The latter work was probably the source for Prov 23:1–3. Sirach's instruction follows the same pattern. (Cf. also 13:8–13.) The advice is directed towards someone who is inexperienced in such matters, and is likely to be excited by the abundance of food. Sirach counsels moderation, and this is in accordance both with age-old Near-Eastern wisdom and with Hellenistic philosophy (cf. Ps.-Phoc. 69 and the Greek parallels cited by van der Horst 1978: 160–1). vv. 19–20 note the beneficial effects of moderation. The advice on vomiting in v. 21 does not imply the Roman custom of using an emetic so that one could then eat more, but is simply practical advice to relieve distress. The need for such advice, however, is not reflected in the older wisdom literature.

vv. 23–4 shift the focus away from the inexperienced diner to the host of the banquet. Dinner parties were much more common in the Hellenistic world than they had been in the ancient Near East (cf. the passing reference to banquets in 2 Macc 2:27, which assumes familiarity with the practice). They were also a source of prestige for the hosts. The NRSV rendering of v. 24, 'the city complains', reflects the idiom of the Greek translator. The Hebrew speaks of murmuring in the gate, the traditional place of congregation in the Near-Eastern city.

In the Hellenistic banquet, the main course was followed by wine-drinking and entertainment, but this was also the custom in the ancient Near East (cf. Esth 5:6; Dan 5:1–2, which are set in the Persian and Babylonian periods, but, at least in the case of Dan 5, date from the Hellenistic). The eighth-century prophet Amos castigates those who lounge on couches while eating lambs from the flock, and then sing idle songs while drinking wine from bowls (Am 6:4–6. On the Greek banquet see Smith and Taussig 1990: 21–35). Wine-drinking was a problem long before the Hellenistic period. Isaiah taunts those who are 'heroes in drinking wine and valiant in mixing drink' (Isa 5:22) and Amos complains of the drinking of the women of Samaria (Am 4:1). Proverbs paints an amusing picture of drunkenness (23:29–35), but is invariably negative on the subject (cf. also 20:1; 31:4–5). Sirach is more positive, and proclaims wine to be 'life' to humans. Cf. Ps. 104:15; 1 Tim 5:23. He is no less cautionary than Proverbs on the danger of excess, but he recognizes the inadvisability of reproaching a person who is inebriated. The dangers of intoxication at a banquet are vividly illustrated in 1 Macc 16:15–16 and Jdt 13:2–8.

In 32:1–13, Sirach addresses in turn the conduct appropriate to the banquet master, the elder guests, and the younger guests. The position of banquet master or symposiarch reflects the Hellenistic context of this discussion. This person had the responsibility of arranging seating and ensuring good service. Since this was an honorary position, there was danger of self-importance (32:1). The Hebrew of 32:2 is corrupt. Smend (1906: 286) argues that the Greek 'crown' renders Hebrew 'glory' (kābôd), adding a distinctively Hellenistic nuance. Sirach acknowledges that older guests have the right to

speak but he urges moderation. He discourages speech-making by the younger guests. His preference is that people simply enjoy the music. Cf. Am 6:5. In Plato's *Symposium*, 176E, the flute-girl is dismissed so that the company can concentrate on philosophical discussion. The Greek text of Sir 9:14–16 (but not the Heb.) seems to imply that the righteous should discuss the Torah on such occasions, but ch. 31 envisages a social situation where all the company is not necessarily righteous. The well-educated person should also know how to behave in an urbane manner in such a setting. A fictional account of after-dinner conversation in a Jewish work can be found in the *Epistle of Aristeas*, 187–294, but this is exceptional as it is a royal banquet and the king questions the guests. Cf. however Sir 13:11, where Sirach warns that a powerful person may test a guest by prolonged conversation. Sirach, characteristically, concludes the section with an exhortation to piety. It was also customary at Greek banquets to pour a libation and sing a chant to the gods (Plato, *Symp.* 176).

(32:14–33:6) Prudence and the Law The long section 25:133:19, which is mainly taken up with practical advice, concludes with two theological poems (32:14–33:6 and 33:7–19). The first of these emphasizes observance of the Torah and fear of the Lord, which appear to be interchangeable here. Seeking God here is equivalent to seeking wisdom in other passages (14:22–5; 51:15–22). Those who seek the law are those who genuinely want to conform to it. The sinner who shuns reproof bends it to his own liking. Ben Sira here seems to have in mind people who pick and choose among the stipulations of the law. In contrast, 1 *Enoch*, 99:2, speaks of people who 'alter the words of truth' and seem to undertake a more serious revision or reinterpretation of the Torah. vv. 19–22 dwell on the need for caution. This too leads to keeping the commandments. Sirach recommends conformity to the Torah as the surest means of self-preservation. The comparison with a divine oracle (33:3) only concerns dependability. Sirach is not suggesting that the Torah be treated as prophecy. vv. 4–6 are traditional sayings, only loosely related to the rest of the poem by their characterization of the fool.

(33:7–19) Variety in Creation The final poem in this section addresses the question of theodicy. Why do things turn out differently from one case to another? Sirach takes his cue from the variation between ordinary time and holy days, which he attributes to divine decree. The idea that God controls the times for all things occurs frequently in the apocalyptic literature of the time (Dan 2:21; 1 *Enoch,* 92:2; von Rad 1972: 266–9). So also with humanity. Nothing is said here of Adam's (or Eve's!) sin as a cause for distinctions between people. Rather, God appointed their different ways. The illustration of this principle in v. 12 contrasts the election of Israel with the dispossession of the Canaanites, but both are taken by way of example. The idea that God makes people walk in their different paths sounds remarkably close to the deterministic view of the Qumran *Rule of the Community* (1QS 3:15–16), and is at odds with Sirach's vigorous defence of human responsibility in 15:11–20; 17:1–20. Sirach's thought on the subject seems to be influenced by the focus of his question. In chs. 15 and 17 he was primarily concerned with human behaviour. In ch. 33 he considers the question from the viewpoint of the order of creation, and the problem of theodicy or the justice of God. His solution is to assert that all God's works are in pairs. This notion is very probably influenced by Stoic philosophy (Pautrel 1963; Middendorp 1973: 29). Chrysippus (late 3rd cent. BCE) taught that nothing could be more inept than the people who suppose that good could have existed without the existence of evil, because antithetical concepts must exist in opposition to each other (frag. 1169; the contrast of opposites is also found in Pythagoras and Heraclitus). This doctrine is different from the systematic dualism of the Qumran *Rule of the Community,* which is probably indebted to Zoroastrian dualism. Sirach is not claiming that all things are divided between good and bad, light and darkness, only that everything must have its opposite. He was not a rigorous enough philosopher, however, to try to reconcile this doctrine with his other theological beliefs.

This section ends with an autobiographical passage in which Ben Sira protests his selflessness and asserts his authority as a teacher of wisdom. The image of the gleaner emphasizes his dependence on tradition. This passage is a counterpart to Sir 24:30–4, which concluded Part I of the book. Sir 51:13–30, which concludes the entire book, strikes similar notes. The suspicion arises, therefore, that 24:30–4 and 33:16–19 may have marked the conclusion of the book in earlier stages of its composition.

(33:20–39:11)

(33:20–33) Property and Slaves vv. 20–4 warn against handing over one's property prematurely.

This advice accords with Ben Sira's general preference for self-sufficiency. It also protects the honour and dignity of the parent. Ben Sira does not seem to envisage the possibility of making a will in advance that would only come into effect at the time of death. The literary form of testament, as found in the *Testaments of the Twelve Patriarchs,* imagines the father on his deathbed.

The existence of slaves was taken for granted throughout the ancient Mediterranean world. Ben Sira's advice on their treatment vacillates. First, he advocates harsh treatment, comparing the slave to a beast of burden. A slave who is underworked will seek liberty, and idleness creates mischief. This advice is in line with Prov 29:19, 21 and is also paralleled in *Phibis* (Papyrus Insinger, 14:6–11; J. T. Sanders 1983: 95). This advice, however, is severely qualified, if not undercut, by 33:30c, d, which warns against overbearing behaviour towards anyone. Here Sirach is probably influenced by the Torah, which granted slaves limited but important rights (Ex 21:1–11, 20–1, 26–7; Lev 25:39–55; Deut 15:12–18; 23:16–17). Lev 25:39, 46, permits the acquisition of Gentiles as slaves but says that Israelites who are forced into debt slavery should be treated as hired servants. The Hellenistic Jewish Ps.-Phocylides, 223–6, advocates humane treatment for slaves, as does Sirach also in 7:20–1 and 33:31. Finally Ben Sira takes his characteristic line of self-interest. A slave who is ill-treated will run away. According to Deut 23:15–16, it was forbidden to return a runaway slave to the owner. The need to take good care of a slave is especially acute if there is only one. It seems then that Ben Sira is transmitting a traditional hard line on the treatment of slaves, but recognizes that gentler treatment is more practical.

(34:1–20) On Dreams Dreams were a respected means of revelation in the ancient world, and so also in Genesis (e.g. Jacob's dream in Gen 28; the Joseph story). Close to the time of Sirach, Daniel was honoured as interpreter of the dreams of a foreign king, and received his own revelation in a dream (Dan 7:1). Deuteronomy, however, views dreams with suspicion and groups them with portents and omens (Deut 13:1–5). Jeremiah is derisive towards prophets who rely on dreams (Jer 23:23–40). Proverbs pays no attention to dreams, but Eliphaz in Job reports 'visions of the night' (Job 4:13). Sirach stands in the tradition of Deuteronomy and Jeremiah on this issue. He does not rule out entirely the possibility of revelation through dreams (34:6) but he emphasizes their deceptiveness. His debt to Deuteronomy is evident in 34:8: dreams are not necessary for keeping the law (cf. Deut 30:11–14). This passage shows clearly the gulf that separates Ben Sira from the roughly contemporary apocalyptic writers of 1 Enoch and Daniel. In the apocalyptic writings, some form of additional revelation, over and above the law, is essential. In fact, Sirach's sweeping rejection of dreams is exceptional in ancient Judaism. Josephus often introduces references to dreams where there were none in the biblical text, and the efficacy of dreams is widely accepted in rabbinic literature (Box and Oesterley 1913˙ 433).

The dismissal of dreams is followed by two short affirmative poems. First, Sirach stresses the importance of experience and travel, a point reiterated in 39:4. It is unfortunate that he gives no details of his travels. Travel was dangerous in the ancient world. Cf. Paul's litany of dangers in 2 Cor 11:25–6. Second, Sirach balances his acknowledgement of experiential wisdom with an encomium of the fear of the Lord. For the image of God as shelter, cf. Isa 4:6; 25:4–5; Ps 121:5–6.

(34:21–35:26) On Sacrifices Ben Sira is exceptional among the wisdom books of the HB and the Apocrypha in devoting a lengthy treatise to cult and sacrifices (Perdue 1977). The first part of this treatise, 34:21–31, is a critique of the abuse of the cult, in the spirit of the prophets. Especially striking are vv. 24–7, which equate social injustice with murder. Cf. Isa 65:3, which can be read as equating sacrifice with murder, although the text is ambiguous. Sirach is quite clear that the problem is not with sacrifice as such but with the abuse of the poor, but sacrifice cannot compensate for social injustice. Sirach may be commenting on contemporary abuses here, or he may be simply reflecting the teaching of the prophets (cf. Am 5:21–7; 8:4–8). In 34:25, Skehan and DiLella (1987) read 'bread of charity' (reading ḥesed, with the Syriac; the Gk. presupposes ḥeser, 'want/need'). If this is correct, almsgiving is not optional. To withhold it in some cases would be tantamount to murder. vv. 28–31 build an argument against superficial repentance. vv. 28–9 are examples of mutually negating behaviour. The person who fasts and sins again is self- negating. For purification after touching a corpse, see Num 19:9–12.

In 35:1–5 Sirach addresses those things that are most pleasing to the Lord, and insists that the ethical demands of the law are more

important than sacrifices. The point of 35:1 is not that the law requires many sacrifices (a point that Sirach would also grant) but that observance is the equivalent of many sacrifices. Sirach displays his familiarity with the different kinds of sacrifice, but the point is that kindness and almsgiving are as effective as sacrifice in pleasing God. This kind of spirituality of the cult is found already in the HB, e.g. Ps 51:17, in the Qumran Rule of the Community (1QS 8:1–4) righteousness serves as a substitute for the cult. Hellenistic Jews such as Philo also placed their primary stress on the spiritual, symbolic meaning of sacrifice. Ben Sira, however, goes on to say that one should also observe the literal commandments in this respect. Cf. Sir 7:31. The language of the Torah (Ex 23:14; 34:20; Deut 16:16) is echoed by 35:6. This is in accordance with Ben Sira's general insistence on the fulfilment of the law, and also with his criticism of miserliness (14:3–19). Sirach does not, however, attach value to the sacrificial cult in itself, except in so far as it is required by the fulfilment of the law. (For an argument that Sirach attached greater importance to the sacrificial cult, see Stadelmann 1980: 40–138.)

35:14–26 is a poem on the justice of God, related to the preceding passages by the shared theme of prayer. God cannot be bribed by sacrifice to overlook the injustice of the worshipper. The Hebrew of 35:15b reads 'for he is a God of justice' echoing Isa 30:18. (The Gk. reads: 'for the Lord is the judge'.) Concern for the widow and the orphan is a commonplace of ancient Near-Eastern wisdom. Deut 10:18 says that the Lord executes justice for the orphan and the widow. According to Ps 68:5, he is their father; in Prov 23:10–11 he is their redeemer. Cf. also Ex 3:9, where God hears the cry of the oppressed Israelites. The imagery of God as Divine Warrior, coming to wreak vengeance on his enemies, is widespread in the HB; cf. especially Deut 32:35–6. Typically in the HB, the Lord comes to vindicate his people, Israel. This biblical language is borrowed in v. 25, but in the context 'his people' are the poor rather than ethnic Israel.

(36:1–22) A Prayer for Deliverance This is the main passage in Sirach whose authenticity is disputed. Nowhere else in the book does Sirach express antagonism towards foreign nations. If this prayer was composed by Ben Sira, the hostile rulers would have to be the Seleucids, who ruled Palestine from 198 BCE. But Josephus reports that Seleucid rule was initially welcomed by the Jews, and that Antiochus III (the Great) helped restore the city and supported the temple cult (*Ant.* 12.129–53). The high priest of the day was Simon II (the Just), who is eulogized in Sir 50:1–21. The restoration of temple and city are listed as his outstanding achievements. It is scarcely conceivable, then, that Sirach would have viewed Antiochus III as a hostile ruler, or asked God to crush his head. In fact, such sentiments only make sense in or after the time of Antiochus IV Epiphanes, and there is no other reflection of that reign in Sirach's book (Middendorp 1973: 125). (The possibility that the poem was composed before the Syrian take-over, and regards the Ptolemies as the enemy, is unsatisfactory because of the generic denunciation of foreign nations.) The likelihood that this prayer is a secondary addition to the book is overwhelming. It is true that 35:21–6 provides a lead into the prayer (Skehan and DiLella 1987: 420). This explains why the prayer was inserted at this particular point. But the passage in ch. 35 is concerned with the universal judgement of God on the unrighteous, whereby 'he repays mortals according to their deeds' (35:24). The prayer in ch. 36 calls for a highly particular judgement on the enemies of Israel.

In the canonical psalter, communal prayers for deliverance are usually embedded in psalms of complaint, which include some description of the abject state of the community (Ps 44; 74; 79–80; 83; Gerstenberger 1988: 14). Comparable prayers from the Second Temple period also typically include a confession of sin (Ezra 9:6–15; Neh 9:6–37; Dan 9:4–19; Song of Thr (Prayer of Azariah); Bar 2:11–26; 4QDibHam—Words of the Luminaries). There is no confession of sin in Sir 36, and the distress of Jerusalem is only hinted at. Instead it is a direct appeal for divine intervention.

The expression 'God of all' in v. 1 recurs in 45:23c (Heb. only) and 50:22a (Gk. only; Heb. reads 'God of Israel'). Sir 43:27 goes further, saying that he *is* the all. The fear of God among the nations recalls the original conquest of Canaan. Cf. Ex 15:15–16. The language of manifesting holiness is especially characteristic of Ezekiel. Cf. Ezek 20:41; 28:25; 39:27, where God manifests his holiness in gathering Israel from among the nations. (In Ezek 38:23, the reference is to the judgement on Gog.) Since Sirach goes on to pray for the gathering of the tribes in v. 13, the display of holiness to the nations probably lies in the punishment of Israel. Sirach asks in effect that the nations be brought low just as Israel was. The goal of the

knowledge of God is also characteristic of Ezekiel (cf. Ezek 6:7, 14; 7:28, etc.). Insistence on monotheism is characteristic of Hellenistic Judaism. Cf. *Sib. Or.* 3:11; Wis 13:10–19; *Ep. Arist.* 135–8; Philo, *Dec.* 76–80. The signs and wonders of v. 6 evoke the Exodus (Ex 7:3).

The notion that God determines the times has been encountered already in Sir 33:7–9. In v. 10, NRSV 'day' corresponds to Hebrew 'end' (*qēṣ*), which the Greek renders as *kairos*, time. There is some tension in 36:10 between the belief that God can hasten the day of vengeance and the belief that the time is appointed and God need only remember it. The linking of the terms 'end' and 'appointed time' derives from Hab 2:3, and is reflected several times in Daniel (10:14; 11:27, 35), where it invariably implies that the time is fixed. The idea that God can hasten the end arises from the urgency of prayer. v. 11 calls for complete destruction of the enemy leaving no survivors. For the crushing of the heads of the enemy, cf. Num 24:18; Ps 110:6. The boast of the enemy is taken from Isa 47:8. For Israel as God's firstborn, cf. Ex 4:22; for Jerusalem as the place of God's dwelling, Ps 132:13. Especially noteworthy is the emphasis on the fulfilment of prophecy in vv. 20–1. While Sirach's sage studies prophecies (39:1) we do not get the sense that he expects them to be fulfilled. The fulfilment of prophecy is of urgent concern in Daniel (cf. Dan 9) and in the Dead Sea scrolls (e.g. the pesher on Habakkuk). The *Apostrophe to Zion* from Qumran (11QPs 22:5–6, 13–14) also recalls the visions of the prophets for the restoration of Zion. The final appellation, God of the ages, harks back to the divine title El Olam in Genesis (Gen 21:33).

(36:23–37:15) Discrimination and Friendship
The theme of this section concerns the need for discrimination in choosing friends and companions. 36:23 sets the tone by distinguishing between what is tolerable and what is preferred. The pattern is repeated in 36:26, 37:1, and 37:7. In each case Sirach makes a statement about a class (food, men, friends, counsellors) and then says that some members of that class are preferable to others. 36:26 stands out as an exception. Instead of moving from 'any man' (will a woman accept) to 'some men are preferable', he says 'one girl is preferable to another'. It is likely that Sirach has modified a traditional statement, so as to impose a male instead of a female point of view (Trenchard 1982: 20). The woman's willingness to accept any man does not imply promiscuity. It simply reflects the social

practice whereby the woman had little choice. Girls were given in marriage by their fathers (cf. Tob 7:10–14; in Gen 24:57–8, Rebekah is consulted as a courtesy, but she has already been given, v. 51). The marriage contract was an agreement between the groom and the bride's father. Moreover, women had little security in life outside marriage (Archer 1990: 125–6).

36:27–8 notes some of the things that make a woman attractive: beauty, kindness, and humility. The following verses digress on the advisability of marriage. Sirach borrows the phrase of Gen 2:18, 20 to refer to the help a wife can give her husband. Moreover, she can give him a 'nest' and prevent him from wandering. Sirach implies that the unattached man cannot be trusted (cf. the language applied to Cain in Gen 4:12). A wife is necessary for social respectability. Most revealing of Sirach's attitude on marriage, however, is the statement that a wife is a man's best possession (v. 29); cf. sir 7:26. Even while Sirach expresses the high value he places on a wife, he still regards her as a possession of her husband. The patriarchal quality of this statement is not negated by the fact that the language recalls Prov 8:22, which says that the Lord acquired (or created qānā), wisdom as the beginning of his way.

The subject of friends has been treated at length in 6:5–17 and 12:8–13:23, and touched upon in several places. The reference to the evil inclination (cf. 15:14 above) seems to have arisen from a translator's mistake. The Hebrew reads 'alas for the friend who says "why were you fashioned so?"' (Skehan and DiLella 1987: 428).

37:7–15 reviews some of the pitfalls involved in seeking advice; v. 11 probably refers to a polygamous situation, cf. 26:6. Characteristically, Sirach concludes the discussion of friends and associates by recommending the company of those who keep the law. Cf. 6:16–17; 12:13–15; 13:1.

(37:16–31) True and False Friends The theme of true and false wisdom was treated in 19:20–30 in religious terms, emphasizing that the wicked are not truly wise. vv. 16–26 make the contrast in practical terms. A person who is intelligent and a good speaker, but derives no personal benefit from this wisdom, is deficient. Wisdom entails enlightened self-interest. vv. 23–6, however, put the individual in a communal context. The people, Israel, transcends the individuals, whose days are limited. v. 26 expresses one of Sirach's major goals in life:

honour among the people and immortality through reputation. This ideal is repeated in 39:9–11; 41:11–13, and 44:13–15. Contrast the pessimistic view of Ecclesiastes that there is no remembrance of wise or fool (Eccl 2:16).

The brief stanza on moderation recapitulates a theme treated at greater length in 31:12–31.

(38:1–23) Attitudes to Physicians and Death The two instructions in this section are related by the themes of sickness and death. vv. 1–15 recommend respect for physicians. In the HB, physicians are rarely mentioned, and regarded as unreliable. King Asa of Israel is condemned because he sought healing from physicians rather than from God (2 Chr 16:12). Job derides his friends as 'worthless physicians' (Job 13:4). Jeremiah points to the uselessness of medicine for certain problems (Jer 8:22–9:6; 46:11; 51:8) but he at least shows familiarity with the practice of seeking balm from Gilead. In view of the Chronicler's comment on Asa, it seems safe to infer that some people in ancient Judaism had a negative view of physicians for religious reasons, and that Sirach's advocacy of the profession is in some part directed against such people. In contrast, Greece had a flourishing medical tradition, associated with the fifth-century figure of Hippocrates, and there was also a venerable medical tradition in Egypt.

Sirach argues that the healing power of God is mediated indirectly by physicians working with balms and herbs. The statement that God created medicine (38:4) is paralleled in *Phibis* (Papyrus Insinger, 32:12; J. T. Sanders 1983: 75). Ex 15:23–5 is taken as an illustration of the use of a balm, since wood was thrown in the water to sweeten it. Contrast the negative view of 'roots', which are taken to be part of the revelation of the fallen angels in the roughly contemporary Book of the Watchers (1 *Enoch*, 8:3).

None the less, Sirach does not rely completely on the ways of medicine. He also advocates prayer and sacrifice. He implies that illness is due to sin (38:10; cf. Deut 28:21–9; Job 4:7; Jn 9:2), which must be cleansed before the physician can be effective. The physician too prays for divine assistance (v. 14). The Greek and one Hebrew reading of v. 15 say that the sinner will be delivered into the hand of the physician, and this reading is preferred by some authorities (Smend 1906: 343; Peters 1913: 311). Yet the negative implication about the physician goes against the thrust of the passage. The reading of NRSV is supported by another

Hebrew MS and makes better sense (Skehan and DiLella 1987: 443).

vv. 16–23 treat the subject of mourning for the dead and counsel moderation. On the one hand, custom should be properly observed. The importance of burial is amply illustrated in Tob 1:17–18; 4:3–4; 6:15; 12:12; 14:12–13. Mourning was often performed by wailing women (cf. Jer 9:16–19). Sirach's counsel of moderation is paralleled in Ps.-Phoc. 97–8, and in several Greek authors (e.g. Soph. El. 140–2. See van der Horst 1978: 179). Sirach uses the occasion to remind the reader of the inevitability of death, including one's own. The practical tone here is typical of biblical wisdom: what matters is not the intention but the result. In this case, mourning does not help the dead and may injure the living.

(38:24–39:11) The Scribal Profession The contrast between the scribe and various professional artisans bears an obvious analogy to an Egyptian composition called the 'Satire on the Trades', the Instruction of Kheti, Son of Duauf composed in the early second millennium, but copied repeatedly over several centuries (ANET 432–4). It is derisive towards all kinds of manual work: the building contractor is dirtier than pigs; the embalmer smells of corpses; the metal worker stinks more than fish. Writing some 1500 years later, Ben Sira is much more diplomatic. He acknowledges that every city needs craftsmen, and that they are worthy of respect. None the less, his tone is condescending and his goal is to proclaim the superiority of his own profession. This superiority is reflected in the positions of honour listed in vv. 32–3, which are beyond the capacity of an artisan, but for which a scribe is well qualified.

The Greek of 38:24a preserves the better reading, as is shown by the parallelism with 24b. The Hebrew ('the wisdom of the scribe increases wisdom') is obviously corrupt. Sirach makes no apology for belonging to a leisured class. How else could he pursue wisdom?

The positive characterization of the scribe begins in 38:34. Pride of place is given to the study of the Torah. Ezra might be considered the prototype here, since he is described as a scribe well-versed in the law of Moses (Ezra 7:6) but Ben Sira singularly fails to acknowledge Ezra in the Praise of the Fathers (chs. 24–50). Unlike Ezra, moreover, Sirach's sage is concerned with the wisdom of all the ancients. His concern for prophecy has been the source of some debate (Stadelmann 1980: 216–46). Despite occasional flourishes, such as his

critique of false worship in ch. 35, Sirach breathes little of the prophetic spirit. Apart from the prayer in ch. 36, whose authenticity we have questioned, he is not concerned with predictions of national restoration or doom. For him, the books of the prophets are a source of wisdom just as Proverbs is. His hermeneutic of prophecy appears most clearly in chs. 48–9. The aspiration of the sage to serve before rulers is corroborated by the stories of Joseph, Daniel, and Ahiqar. On foreign travel, cf. Sirach's own claim in 34:12. The sage evidently has other sources of wisdom besides the Law and the Prophets. Sirach concludes, however, by emphasizing his piety. For prayer of petition, he could point to the precedent of Solomon in 1 Kings 3, but Sirach puts the stress on prayer for forgiveness. For the spirit of understanding, cf. Isa 11:2. For the imagery of pouring forth words, cf. Sir 24:30–4. The reward of wisdom is enduring fame, but Sirach also expresses resignation in the face of death.

(39:12–43:33)

(39:12–35) Praise of the Creator The first-person invitation in vv. 12–15 marks the beginning of a new section. Specifically, these verses introduce the praise of God's works in 39:16–35. This is followed by various reflections on human wretchedness. The section is concluded by another, longer, hymn of praise (42:15–43:33). The Instruction of Phibis also includes a section on the works of God in creation (24th instruction; J. T. Sanders 1983: 78).

Sir 39:15 characterizes the following passage as a hymn of praise, and the imperative to praise is repeated in 39:35. The passage itself is made up of declarative sentences. The affirmation that the works of the Lord are all good has its biblical warrant in Gen 1:31, but Sirach is aware of the problem of evil. In this passage he offers two suggestions as to how the evil in the world can be reconciled with the goodness of creation (Crenshaw 1975: 47–64).

First, everything will be clarified at the appointed time (v. 17). This solution is not unlike what we find in apocalyptic literature, especially in 4 Ezra, where Ezra's persistent questioning about the justice of God's dealing with Israel is overcome by a series of eschatological visions that shift the focus from past and present to future. But unlike the apocalyptic visionaries Sirach projects no eschatological scenario to silence the critics. The notion of the appointed time, however, is common to sapiential and apocalyptic writings (von Rad 1972: 263–83).

So also is the notion of God's synoptic view of history as a unity (v. 20), but again Sirach differs from the apocalypses by not attempting to describe history from a revealed perspective. Sirach would probably agree with Eccl 3:11 that such comprehensive knowledge is not accessible to humanity, but he is content that God knows even if we do not.

Second, everything has been created for a purpose (v. 21). This idea reflects the influence of Stoic philosophy. So Chrysippus is said to have taught that bed-bugs are useful for waking us and that mice encourage us to be tidy (Plutarch, *On Stoic Self-Contradictions,* 1044D). Carneades (mid-2nd cent. BCE) taught that everything is benefited when it attains the end for which it was born. So the pig fulfils its purpose when it is slaughtered and eaten (Porphyry, *On Abstinence,* 3.20.1, 3). The Stoics also conceded that the usefulness of some plants and animals remains to be discovered (Lactantius, *On the Anger of God,* 13.9–10; for the debates about teleology in antiquity see Long and Sedley 1987: 58–65; 121–2; 323–33). Sirach's elaboration of this notion, however, is somewhat confusing. All God's works are good (vv. 16, 33) but for sinners good things and bad were created (v. 25), or the same things are good for the righteous but bad for sinners (v. 27). In part, the confusion lies in the ambiguity of the term 'bad'. What is bad for sinners is really good. This ambiguity is also in evidence in the doctrine of pairs (33:14–15; 42:24–5). But there is also a reluctance on the part of Ben Sira to admit that bad things can happen to good people. The idea that nature discriminates between the righteous and the wicked is also found in Wis 19:6.

The language of this hymn has occasional biblical overtones. v. 17 alludes to the Exodus; v. 23 to the Conquest; vv. 29–30 to the curses of the covenant (Lev 26:14–22; Deut 28:20–4). Sirach's concern, however, is with the universal working of nature, not with the history of a particular people.

(40:1–41:13) Life in the Shadow of Death This cluster of short poems is framed by two reflections on death. Consistently in Sirach (except for 25:24!), death is viewed as the end for which humanity was created rather than as punishment for sin. Cf. 17:1–2. The language recalls Gen 3:19–20, but here the 'mother of all the living' is the earth, not Eve. The grim picture of life also accords with Genesis. Cf. Job 7:1–2; 14:1–2. The anxiety of disturbed sleep is also noted in Eccl 2:22–3; Job 7:4. The prevalence

of anxiety is assumed in Mt 6:25–34; Lk 12:22–31. Sirach modifies the traditional theme, however, by claiming that afflictions befall the sinner 'seven times more' (40:8). The context suggests that the wicked also suffer more from anxiety (Crenshaw 1975: 57) but this is not explicitly stated. Sir 31:1–4 also suggests that anxiety is universal. Sirach is here reiterating the point of 39:28–31, that disasters serve the purpose of punishing the wicked. 40:12–17 expresses a confidence that lawbreakers will fail that seems naïve in the light of general human experience. Cf. the theology of the friends of Job (e.g. Job 8:11–15).

Sir 40:18–27 provides relief from contemplating the misery of life by listing ten things that are surpassingly good. There is a traditional proverbial form, which asserts that one thing is better than another (Ogden 1977: 489–505). Examples can be found in the Egyptian *Instructions of Kagemni* and *Amen-em- ope* as well as Proverbs and Ecclesiastes. Within Sirach cf. 10:27; 20:31; 41:15. The present passage modifies the form by listing two things that are good, and a third that is better. So a good wife is preferred to cattle and orchards (v. 19) and also to friends and companions (v. 23). In passing, Sirach shows appreciation for wine, music, and beauty (vv. 20–2). Characteristically, Sirach concludes with the superiority of the fear of the Lord. 40:28–30 contains a sharp critique of begging. The crucial point is the shame and loss of self-respect that it entails; cf. Sir 29:21–8. 41:1–4 is Sirach's most definitive statement on the finality of death, and leaves no room for resurrection or a blessed afterlife. Sirach's views on this subject are no different than those of Ecclesiastes, except that he holds them with resignation. The attractiveness of death in certain circumstances received classic expression in the Egyptian *Dispute of a Man with his Ba* about 2,000 BCE. Such sentiments are not common in the HB but cf. Sir 30:17 and the references cited at SIR ibid. Closer to the spirit of Sirach here is Epicurus (*Ep. Men.* 124–7; Long and Sedley 1987: 149): death is sometimes a release from the evils of life. Sirach adds that it is the common lot of humanity and it is the good pleasure of the Lord. The denial of judgement after death in this context is also reminiscent of Epicurus. There is no reason to fear death. Neither Sirach nor Epicurus inferred that one could live a life of licentiousness with impunity. Contrast Wis 2:1–20. The denunciation of the children of sinners (41:5–10) resembles Wis 3:13–19, but Sirach carries no implication that childlessness is virtuous in itself. Cf. Sir 23:25. This passage concludes with another consideration mitigating the fear of death. A good name can provide a measure of immortality; cf. Sir 37:26. The same hope is professed in the *Instruction of Phibis*, 20:1 (J. T. Sanders 1983: 84–5).

(41:14–42:8) On Shame Hebrew MS B gives this section the title 'Instruction about Shame'. Honour and shame were pivotal values in Greek society. Homer's epics are dominated by the warrior's search for honour. In the Hellenistic world people gained honour by their benefactions to their cities. Honour and shame were very much at issue in sexual relations. A male was shamed by the loss of chastity on the part of a woman under his control. The pursuit of honour was sometimes criticized by Hellenistic philosophers, especially Epicureans and Cynics. (For a concise summary of current scholarship on this issue see Moxnes 1993.) The categories of honour and shame are much more prominent in Sirach than in earlier books of the HB (Camp 199l: 4–6).

The subject of honour and shame has appeared several times in Ben Sira (3:1–16; 4:20–31; 10:19–25; 20:21–3). In general, he seeks to retain the category, but also to modify it in accordance with his religious criteria. There is no place for false modesty with respect to wisdom (41:14–15, repeated from 20:30–1; cf. Mk 4:21–5; Lk 8:16–19). The catalogue of things of which one should be ashamed gives considerable prominence to sexual offences, even when they only involve gazing (cf. 9:1–9). All forms of lawbreaking are disapproved, but shame also extends to bad manners at table and lack of graciousness (41:19). Not surprisingly, the Torah heads the list of things of which one should not be ashamed. But Sirach also recommends keeping accounts in dealings with a companion, strict discipline for children and slaves, and even locking up an unreliable wife. Sirach here inclines to the practical, hard-headed side of traditional wisdom that has little place for trust (cf. 6:7; 11:29–12:18). While Sirach diverges from Hellenistic mores in his insistence on the honour of the Torah, he retains a quite conventional code of patriarchal control.

(42:9–14) On Daughters Patriarchal control is very much in evidence in Sirach's treatise on daughters (cf. 7:24–5; 22:3–5; 26:10–12). In part, his worries have an economic base. The father has to provide a dowry for his daughter, and if she is divorced it is to his house that she returns.

The greater concern for Sirach, however, is the threat of disgrace. Indeed, Sirach's view of daughters is entirely clouded by the danger of incurring shame. Hence the extraordinary preference for the wickedness of a man over the goodness of a woman (42:14). Contrast the more affectionate picture of family life in Tobit. Despite the fact that Sarah's first seven husbands died on their wedding night, the concern of the parents is simply that God give her joy instead of sorrow (Tob 7:16).

The theme of anxiety in v. 9 must be seen in the context of Sirach's generally anxious view of life (40:1–11). The 'fear that she may be disliked' is really that she may be divorced. (The verb 'hate', *ś-n-*, clearly has the sense of 'repudiate' in the Elephantine papyri. Cf. Deut 24:3.) Concern for the virginity of unmarried girls is ubiquitous in the ancient world, but especially in Hellenistic Judaism. The draconian laws of the Pentateuch that required the death penalty for a woman who was found not to be a virgin at marriage (Deut 22:20–1; cf. Gen 38:24) were not enforced, but a woman who was not a virgin would be difficult to give in marriage. Ps. Phoc. 215–16 advises that virgins be locked up and not seen outside the house until their wedding day (see van der Horst 1978: 251; Archer 1990: 101–22 for other references to the confinement of Jewish virgins). A lattice (v. 11) offered an opportunity to look out on passers-by (cf. Prov 7:6) but Sirach's main concern is that the young woman not be seen. Most remarkable is the advice that a daughter should not associate with married women. (The Heb. 'in the house (*byt*) of the women' is probably a mistake for 'among' (*byn*), Smend 1906: 394.) From the context, it would seem that Sirach's fear is that the young woman may become aware of her sexuality (Trenchard 1982: 158).

(42:15–43:33) Hymn to the Creator This section of Sirach concludes with a long hymn to the creator. 42:15–20 praises the omniscience of God. 42:21 43:26 lists the works of creation. 43:27–33 concludes the hymn with a call to praise. The praises of nature in ch. 43 recalls Job 28, 38–41, but also Ps 104, 148, and the Song of the Three Jews in the Greek additions to Daniel. It has been argued that the Egyptian genre of onomasticon, which compiled lists of various phenomena as an aid to the scribes, lies behind such passages as Job 38 (von Rad 1966). A more immediate Egyptian parallel to Sirach is found in the 24th instruction in the wisdom book of *Phibis* (J. T. Sanders 1983: 78–9). Cf.

also the praise of God as creator in the hymns of Qumran (e.g. 1QH 9:10–14, formerly 1QH 1).

The praise of God's omniscience in 42:15–20 is replete with biblical echoes. On v. 15*a*, cf. Ps 77:11; on v. 15*b*, cf. Job 15:17. On creation by the word, cf. Ps 33:6; Wis 9:1. The NRSV reading of v. 15*d* relies on the Syriac version. On God's knowledge of past and future, cf. Isa 41:22–3; 44:7. God's ability to reveal hidden things is also emphasized in Dan 2:22. The introduction to God's works in 42:22–5, however, introduces some non-biblical concepts. v. 23*a* expresses the teleological, Stoic, view that all things are created to meet a need (cf. 39:21 and SIR ibid.). v. 24 articulates the idea of complementary opposites, which also has its roots in Stoic philosophy (cf. SIR 33:14–15).

The praise of nature in ch. 43 envisages the sun as a charioteer racing his steeds (Heb. 'ab-bîrîm, see Skehan and DiLella 1987: 488). The horses and chariots of the sun were familiar in ancient Israel, but were destroyed in Josiah's reform (2 Kings 23:11). The image of the solar charioteer was standard in Greece, and this may have led to its rehabilitation here. The Greek translator (followed by NRSV) missed the reference. In 1 Enoch 72:5, the wind blows the chariots on which the sun ascends. Sir 49:7 is often taken to indicate that Sirach observed a lunar calendar, presumably the one that later became standard in rabbinic Judaism. Calendars were very much in dispute in Hellenistic Judea. A solar calendar of 364 days was advocated by the Astronomical Book of Enoch (1 Enoch, 73–82), Jubilees (esp. 6:32–8), and the Qumran sect. It is possible that Sirach is referring only to the observance of specific lunar festivals such as the new moon (cf. 1 Sam 20:5; Am 8:5). The Hebrew MS B reads 'by them is the appointed time...' which implies that both sun and moon had a part in determining the festal calendar. The creator's control of the calendar is also noted by Phibis (J. T. Sanders 1983: 79). On the permanence of the astral world cf. 1 Enoch, 75:1, but 1 Enoch, 80, anticipates that the order will be disrupted in 'the days of the sinners'. The rainbow is praised for its beauty, but no reference is made to its role as a sign of the covenant of Noah (Gen 9:13–17). The description of lightning and thunder has overtones of the traditional language of theophany (cf. Ps 18:7–15). vv. 23–6 refer to God's mastery over the deep and its monsters (cf. Job 41:1–11). It is possible that the word rabbâ, great, in the Hebrew of vv. 23, 25, should be emended to Rahab, a traditional name for the sea-monster (Job 26:1; Isa 51:9).

The most remarkable statement in this hymn, however, comes in 43:27: 'He is the all.' This formulation evokes the pantheism of the Stoics, as we find, e.g. in Cleanthes, *Hymn to Zeus* (Hengel 1974: i. 148; Marböck 1971: 170). Ben Sira is no pantheist, however. His use of the phrase is hyperbolic, and should probably be understood as equivalent to 'God of all' (sir 36:1). It is likely, however, that his formulation here has been influenced by Stoic notions, even if they were imperfectly grasped. The hymn concludes by emphasizing its own inadequacy.

(44:1–50:29) The Praise of the Fathers

(44:1–15) Introduction The last major section of the book bears the title 'Praise of the Fathers of Old' in the Hebrew and 'Hymn of the Fathers' in the Greek. The long review singles out individuals as examples to be praised, but presents no continuous historical narrative. There is no real parallel to this kind of review of history in the HB. The closest parallels are found in other books of the Apocrypha, 1 Macc 2:51–60; 4 Macc 16:20–3; 18:11–19. Cf. also Heb 11. There are ample Hellenistic precedents, however, for the listing of examples. The genre of the Praise of the Fathers has also been related to the Greek encomium (Lee 1986; Mack 1985: 136 implausibly designates it an epic).

vv. 1–15 are an introductory section. Sirach lists the kind of people he is about to praise. These reflect major categories of the Hebrew scriptures: kings and rulers, prophets and sages. Those who composed musical tunes (v. 5) may be the psalmists. In v. 6, the Hebrew 'stalwart men' is rendered somewhat tendentiously as 'wealthy men' in the Greek and NRSV. One category, the priesthood, that figures prominently in the subsequent chapters, is noticeably absent here. These people have acquired a qualified immortality in either of two ways, either by leaving behind a name or by the continuity and loyalty of their descendants. In the end, their honour is ratified by the congregation.

(44:16–23e) Enoch to Abraham The initial mention of Enoch is textually suspect. It is not found in the Masada MS or in the Syriac, although it is in the Greek and Hebrew MS B. Here he walks with the Lord, rather than with 'elōhîm, God (or angels) as in Genesis. In the Hebrew he is a sign of knowledge, because of his knowledge of the heavenly world. The Greek makes him a symbol of repentance, probably under the influence of Philo, Abr. 17.

Sirach shows no awareness of the story of Enoch as amplified in 1 *Enoch*. Noah was probably the first name on the list because he was the recipient of the first covenant. In some apocalyptic texts the deliverance of Noah serves as a paradigm for the end-time (1 *Enoch*, 93:4). Abraham's covenant is also emphasized. Abraham is said to have kept the law of the Most High, even though it was not yet revealed to Moses. This may indicate that Sirach associated the law with creation (cf. 17:11; 24:1–7), or it may reflect a tendency that we find in *Jubilees* to reject the observance of the law back to the beginnings. v. 20d is a passing reference to the sacrifice of Isaac, seen purely as a test of Abraham. No mention is made of Jacob's trickery. Isaac and Jacob are significant as links in the transmission of the blessings.

(44:23f–45:26) Moses, Aaron, Phinehas Moses, predictably, is praised as the recipient of the Torah. In contrast to some Hellenistic Jewish writers, such as Philo, Sirach does not call Moses a lawgiver, and does not attribute any creativity to him. He makes him equal in glory to the angels (holy ones), whereas Philo, following Ex 7:1, makes him a god (*Vit. Mos.* 1.155–8). For 'the law of life and knowledge' cf. 17:11. For 45:5ef cf. Ps 147:19. The most striking thing about the praise of Moses, however, is that it is less than half as long as the praise of Aaron.

Sirach does not acknowledge the priesthood of Moses (contrast Ps 99:6). Rather he follows the Priestly source in emphasizing the eternal covenant of priesthood with Aaron, but he ignores Zadok, and does not refer to the sons of Zadok (Olyan 1987: 261–86). We can scarcely infer, however, that he was polemicizing against the restriction of the priesthood to the Zadokites. He may have regarded them as the only legitimate Aaronides. The only individual who receives treatment of comparable length is the Zadokite high priest Simon II in ch. 50. The covenant with Aaron, however, extends to all the priesthood, not just the high priest. On the high priest's robe, cf. Wis 18:24, which claims that the whole world and the glories of the ancestors were engraved on it. Sirach touches only briefly on Aaron's role in offering sacrifices, and gives equal time to his teaching authority (cf. Deut 33:10; the teaching role of the eschatological priest is illustrated in 4Q541). Sirach's interest in sacrifices does not match his interest in the priesthood. In the Hellenistic period, the high priest also wielded political power in Jerusalem, and could be a powerful patron for a scribe such as Sirach. Sirach notes how rebellion against Aaron was put down by God. The implications for his own day were obvious. On 45:22, cf. Num 18:20.

Phinehas is third in the priestly line, after Aaron and Eleazar (v. 23). In 1 Macc 2:26, Phinehas is cited as the model for the violent action of Mattathias. Sirach's interest is in the covenant he receives. It is clear from v. 25 that this is not conceived as a separate covenant but is part of the heritage of Aaron. v. 25d should read 'so the heritage of Aaron is for all his descendants' (so Heb.; Gk. reads 'also for his descendants'). The contrast with the Davidic covenant (read: 'the inheritance of a man for his son alone', Skehan and DiLella 1987: 510) also implies the superiority of the more inclusive priestly covenant. It does not, however, imply that the priesthood has inherited the promise to David (*pace* Stadelmann 1980: 157). This section ends with a benediction addressed to the priesthood; cf. 50:22–4.

(46:1–20) Joshua to Samuel The extensive praise of Joshua is initially surprising, since there is little militancy in Sirach apart from the disputed prayer in ch. 36. Even more surprising is the statement that he was an aide (Heb.; Gk.: successor) to Moses in the *prophetic* office (neither Moses nor Joshua is said to have delivered oracles). Of primary importance to Sirach is the glory enjoyed by Joshua. In this respect he resembles the high priest Simon (cf. 46:2 with 50:5). He also resembles the priesthood in his role as intercessor (v. 5) although this role might also be deemed prophetic (Josh 10:6; cf. Moses in Num 14:13–19). The decisive role of the hailstones in the battle is already noted in Josh 10:11. Finally, Joshua and Caleb are praised for loyalty, a virtue already commended by Sirach (6:14–17; 26:19–26).

The prayer 2 for the judges in 46:11–12, that their bones sprout from their place, is not found in the Hebrew, but appears apropos of the minor prophets in 49:10. The new life envisaged by Sirach is the immortality of their names in their children.

Samuel is characterized primarily as a prophet, by anointing rulers, judging in the light of the law, and being a trustworthy seer. He is also admired for offering sacrifice (without consideration of his priestly rank), and for his profession of innocence. His apparition to Saul (46:20; cf. 1 Sam 28:19) adds to his glory, with no hint of disapproval of the consultation. Rather it shows how the glory of Samuel transcended his death.

(47:1–25) Nathan to Jeroboam After a brief mention of Nathan, ch. 47 deals with the early kings. David is glorified for his early exploits, with some elaboration. Where 1 Sam 17:34–5 has David rescue animals from lions and bears, Sirach has him play with lions and bears as if they were lambs and kids. Cf. the idyllic scene in Isa 11:6–9, but contrast the more subdued portrayal of David's youth in Ps 151 (11Q5 xxviii); Sir 47:8 reflects David's reputation as author of the psalms. Cf. the list of David's compositions in 11QPsalms (11Q5 xxvii). vv. 9–10 reflect the portrayal of David in 1 Chr 15–26. The most controversial statement about David is found in 47:11, which says that God exalted his 'horn' or strength forever. Some scholars see here an expression of messianic hope (Smend 1906: 452; Skehan and DiLella 1987: 526; Olyan 1987: 282–3), while others disagree (Caquot 1966; Pomykala 1995: 145). Sirach does not cite Nathan's oracle, and expresses no hope or expectation for the restoration of the Davidic line. He does, however, acknowledge the biblical record that everlasting kingship was promised to David. While the word translated 'covenant' in 47:11c is *ḥōq* (statute) rather than the usual word for covenant (*bĕrît*), the latter word is used in 45:25, and so there can be no doubt that Sirach affirmed a Davidic covenant. The perpetuity of the line is also affirmed in 47:22. In short, Sirach acknowledged the promise, but it was far from the centre of his own devotion. He attached far greater importance to the high-priesthood, the actual seat of authority in his time. On the issue of messianic expectation, see further the psalm found between Sir 51:12 and 13 in the Hebrew text.

The Greek translation says that Solomon's security was because of David, but this connection is not made in the Hebrew. Solomon is praised as the one who built the temple and, inevitably, for his wisdom. For the image of overflowing like the Nile, cf. 24:27, 30. But Solomon also illustrates a favourite theme of Sirach, the danger of women. The Hebrew of 47:19b reads 'and you let them rule over your body'. Cf. Prov 31:3; Sir 9:2, and the fear that a woman can trample a man's strength. Sirach makes Solomon's sexual transgressions rather than idolatry responsible for the division of the kingship (cf. 1 Kings 11:11–13, 33). He none the less affirms the enduring validity of the promise to David. While Solomon's record is mixed,

Rehoboam and Jeroboam are the only figures in the review who are entirely negative. Sirach follows the standard Deuteronomic line in making the sin of Jeroboam responsible for the exile of northern Israel.

(48:1–15d) Elijah and Elisha The treatment of Elijah dwells on the miraculous and therefore glorious aspects of his career. Cf. the passage on Joshua in ch. 46. His ascent in a chariot of fire (v. 9) fits this theme and is already found in 2 Kings 3:11. Sir 48:10, however, is exceptional in Ben Sira in citing a prophecy as eschatological prediction. The prophecy in question is Mal 3:23–4, supplemented by Isa 49:10. Because there is so little eschatological interest in Sirach, some scholars argue that this verse must be secondary (Middendorp 1973: 134; Mack 1985: 200). But Sirach here is only affirming what he found in the older scripture. There is no implication of imminent expectation. Like the promise to David, Elijah's return was part of the tradition, even if it had little importance for Sirach's overall scheme. The idea of an appointed time is reminiscent of Dan 10:14; 11:29, 40, etc., but is quite compatible with the wisdom tradition (von Rad 1972: 263–83).

Sir 48:11 is much more difficult. The Greek reads: 'Blessed are those who saw you and have fallen asleep in love, for we also shall certainly live.' The Hebrew (MS B) is fragmentary at this point. The first half of the verse reads 'Blessed is he who sees you and dies' (i.e. sees you before he dies). The second half has been restored, plausibly, to read 'for you give life, and he will live' (Puech 1990: 81–90). While granting that Sirach did not believe in a general resurrection, Puech thinks he anticipated a limited resurrection at the return of Elijah. The prophet is often associated with the eschatological resurrection in later tradition (m. Soṭa, 9:15; Pesiqta de Rab Kahana, 76a). In view of Sirach's emphatic insistence on the finality of death elsewhere, however, it is easier to suppose that this verse is a later addition (cf. Sir 14:11–19; 38:21–2; 41:4). If the Hebrew text is original, it must have meant something less than eschatological resurrection.

The praise of Elisha is in a similar vein to that of Elijah. The reference in 48:13–14 is to 2 Kings 13:21. As in the case of Samuel, Sirach is interested in the continuing power of the prophet after death, but there is no implication of a lasting resurrection. This passage ends by attributing the fall of the northern kingdom to the lack of repentance.

(48:17–49:16) **Kings and Prophets** Sirach repeats the Deuteronomic judgement on the kings of Judah (49:4; cf. 2 Kings 18:3; 23:25), using observance of the Torah as his criterion. He emphasizes the miraculous in the accounts of Hezekiah and Isaiah (cf. 2 Kings 20:8–11; Isa 38:7–8). The Hebrew of 48:21 attributes the destruction of the Assyrians to a plague. The Greek substitutes the angel of the Lord, in conformity to the biblical text (2 Kings 19:35; Isa 37:36). It is clear from Sir 48:24–5 that Sirach attributed the whole book of Isaiah to the eighth-century prophet, who is credited with foretelling the future return from the Exile. Cf. the theme of consolation in Isa 40:1–2; for the revelation of hidden things cf. Isa 42:9. The notion that Isaiah had predicted what would happen 'forever' (48:25a) may reflect such passages as Isa 65:17–25, but without any note of imminent expectation.

Jeremiah is credited with foretelling the destruction. Ezekiel is remembered only for his vision, which was influential in apocalyptic circles (e.g. Dan 10) and was also elaborated in 4QPseudoEzekiel (4Q385). Job is mentioned between Ezekiel and the Minor Prophets. It is possible that Josephus also included Job among the prophets when he said that they wrote the history from Moses to Artaxerxes in thirteen books (*Ag. Ap.* 40). The order of the biblical books was not set in the time of Sirach. The Minor Prophets are treated as one book, and are understood to convey a message of hope rather than doom. There is no reference to Daniel, which was presumably not yet composed. There is no mention of Esther, which is also absent from the Qumran scrolls, and may not have been known in Jerusalem at this time. Sirach also ignores Ruth, and fails to single out a single woman for praise. Most striking, however, is the omission of Ezra, especially in view of the inclusion of Nehemiah. It would be rash to conclude that the book of Ezra was not yet written. There is no apparent ideological reason for the omission. The most plausible explanation offered to date is that Sirach preferred Nehemiah because his building activity offered a precedent to that of Simon II (Begg 1988). Cf. the emphasis on the building activities of Hezekiah, Zerubbabel, and Joshua the high priest.

49:14–16 concludes the review of the ancient past. Except for the questionable reference to Enoch in 44:16, none of those extolled here has been mentioned in Praise of the Fathers. Only Adam has figured in the rest of Sirach's book. All except Joseph are antediluvian. (Shem is son of Noah; Gen 6:10.) The authenticity of this passage has been questioned, as it does not fit any pattern of characterization in Sirach (Mack 1985: 201) but this is not necessarily a cogent objection to a concluding stanza. If the passage goes back to Sirach, it represents the earliest reference to the splendour of Adam. This motif was later elaborated (e.g. Philo, *Opif.* 136–41). Another early reference to the glory of Adam is found in CD 3:20.

(50:1–28) **The High Priest Simon** Even though 49:14–16 seems to conclude the praise of the ancestors, the passage on Simon is the culmination of all that has gone before. Simon II was high priest 219–196 BCE. He was presumably dead when Ben Sira wrote (cf. 50:1). Under his leadership, Jerusalem welcomed Antiochus III of Syria, and assisted him in besieging the garrison of the Egyptian general Scopas (Jos. *Ant.* 12.129–53). Antiochus, in return, assisted in the restoration of the temple. Sirach does not mention the support of the foreign king, but he takes evident pride in the renewed splendour of the temple. Sirach had already noted building projects under Solomon, Hezekiah, Zerubbabel and Joshua, and Nehemiah. vv. 5–21 describe the splendour of the high priest performing his functions. The curtain in v. 5 *pārōket* normally refers to the veil at the entrance to the Holy of Holies (e.g. Ex 36:31–5; the Greek *katapetasma* can also refer to the outer curtain, between the temple and the forecourt). It is likely, then, that the occasion is the Day of Atonement, the only day the high priest entered the Holy of Holies (but see O'Fearghail (1978), who argues that the reference is to the daily offering). Cf. the account of Aaron's splendour in 45:6–13. A comparable account of the splendour of the high priest is found in the *Epistle of Aristeas*, 96–9. All the sons of Aaron share in the splendour. The recollection of the blessing pronounced by Simon (vv. 20–1) leads into the benediction in vv. 22–4. The Hebrew (MS B) reads 'God of Israel' instead of 'God of all'. It also includes in v. 23 a prayer for Simon, that God fulfil for him the covenant with Phinehas forever. In fact, the line came to an end in the next generation, in the reign of Antiochus IV. Simon's son Onias III was murdered in 172 BCE (2 Macc 4:34) and his son Onias IV fled to Egypt and founded a temple at Leontopolis. We cannot know whether Ben Sira had an inkling of impending problems when he prayed for the preservation of the line. The Greek translator dropped the prayer for Simon and substituted a prayer that God redeem Israel 'in our days'.

It is quite possible that the benediction in 50:22–4 was the conclusion of Sirach's book, except for the subscription in vv. 27–8. The numerical proverb in vv. 25–6 has no relation to the context, and could easily have been added by a scribe. The Edomites of Seir and the Philistines were old enemies of Israel. The thrust of the proverb is to express dislike for the Samaritans. There was conflict between Samaritans and Jews in the time of Ezra (Ezra 4). The books of Maccabees imply that the Samaritans were sympathetic to Antiochus Epiphanes in his suppression of Judaism (1 Macc 3:10; 2 Macc 4:2). At the end of the second century BCE, Shechem was sacked and the temple on Mt. Gerizim razed by John Hyrcanus. We have no evidence for Jewish-Samaritan relations in Sirach's time.

For Sirach's self-characterization as one who poured forth wisdom, cf. 24:30–4; 39:12.

(51:1–30) Appended poems Ch. 51 contains three poetic compositions, of which the middle one is found only in Hebrew MS B. It is generally admitted that this Hebrew psalm was not composed by Sirach, but many scholars defend the authenticity of the other two poems, despite the apparent finality of 50:27–8 (Smend 1906: 495; Skehan and DiLella 1987: 563). The Greek MSS have the heading 'Prayer of Jesus Son of Sirach', but the attribution is none the less doubtful. We know that prayers were added secondarily to other books (Esther, Daniel). The wisdom poem in vv. 13–30, which is closest to the style of Sirach, is found independently at Qumran.

Sir 51:1–12 is a thanksgiving psalm, analogous to Ps 30 or Jonah 2:2–9 (Gerstenberger 1988: 15–16) and to the thanksgiving hymns from Qumran (e.g. 1QH 10 (formerly 2)). The psalmist begins by declaring thanks, and goes on to give his reasons. The Hebrew speaks of deliverance from death, the pit, and Sheol (v. 2). Cf. Ps 30:3; Jon 2:2, 6; 1QH 11:19). The slanderous tongue is an object of frequent complaint in the Psalms (e.g. Ps 69:4–5, 11–12) and in the Qumran thanksgiving hymns (1QH 10:10–17; 13:22–5). The most noteworthy feature of this hymn is the direct address to God as father in

v. 10, which echoes Ps 89:27. See SIR 23:1, and Strotmann (1991: 87). The Greek rendering 'lord, father of my lord' is confused. The Hebrew of Sir 51:1 refers either to 'God, my father', or more probably 'God of my father', but this reading is not supported by the Greek.

The Hebrew psalm inserted between vv. 12 and 13 is modelled on Ps 136 in so far as it has the refrain 'for his mercy endures forever'. Two features of the psalm are noteworthy. First, line 9 of the hymn must be understood as expressing hope for a Davidic messiah; cf. 1QSb 5:26. While Sir 47:11 affirmed the covenant with David, it showed no such messianic hope. Second, line 10 affirms the priesthood of the sons of Zadok. Since messianic expectation was conspicuously lacking even in the Maccabean period, it is unlikely that this combination of Davidic hope and Zadokite priesthood dates from pre-Hasmonean times. It is more likely that this psalm originated in the Qumran community, which was staunchly pro-Zadokite and had lively messianic expectations. DiLella suggests that the Hebrew MSB from the Cairo Geniza was one of the documents found by the Qaraites in a cave near Jericho about 800 CE, and had originated at Qumran (Skehan and DiLella 1987: 569).

The wisdom poem in vv. 13–28 is also found in 11QPs[a], between Ps 138 and the *Apostrophe to Zion*. (Only vv. 11–17 and the last two words of the poem are preserved.) Like Prov 31:10–31, it is in the form of an acrostic. vv. 13–22 use the language of love to describe the sage's pursuit of wisdom. Cf. Sir 14:20–7. J. A. Sanders, editor of 11QPss (1965: 79–85), has argued for a highly erotic interpretation of the poem, but even those critical of Sanders' interpretation recognize that love imagery is intrinsic to the poem (Muraoka 1979: 167–78). The second half of the poem is an exhortation to the student to submit to the yoke of wisdom; cf. Sir 6:23–37. The themes and language of the poem all have close affinities with other material in Sirach, but it is not certain whether this reflects common authorship or a common tradition of wisdom poetry (cf. in part 4Q525).

We have three recensions of this poem, in the Qumran text, the Geniza text, and the Greek translation. The reference to travel in v. 13 is reflected in the Qumran text ('before I wandered'; Skehan and DiLella take it as 'while I was innocent'); cf. Sir 34:9–13; 39:4. v. 14 of the 11Q text reads 'she came to me in her beauty'.

The Greek, and NRSV, eliminated the erotic overtones of this verse. This is also true of v. 19 where both Hebrew texts have readings that indicate desire, but the Greek has 'grappled'. Hebrew v. 19e, 'my hand opened her gate' may be an allusion to Song 5:4, and v. 21, which even in Greek reads 'insides' rather than 'heart' (NRSV), recalls the same verse ('my inmost being yearned for him'). The teacher in v. 17 is God.

The 'house of instruction' (v. 23) is usually taken to refer to an actual school, but the expression could be metaphorical (Wischmeyer 1995: 176; cf. Prov 9:1). There can be no doubt, however, that wisdom is construed as a medium of education, whatever the institutional setting. The Hebrew (MS B) has a reference to 'my yeshivah' in v. 29 (see Smend 1906: 494), which the Greek converts into a reference to God's mercy. For vv. 24–5 cf. Isa 55:1. For the image of the yoke, cf. Sir 6:30; Mt 11:28–30, and m.'Abot, 3:5. The idea that God will give one's reward in due time is not eschatological in the context of Sirach, who consistently affirms this-worldly retribution. The Hebrew MS B has a second subscription at the end of ch. 51. In both cases, the sage's name is given incorrectly as Simon, son of Jesus, son of Eleazar, son of Sira. Simon is presumably introduced by mistake from ch. 50.

REFERENCES

Archer, L. J. (1990), *Her Price is Beyond Rubies: The Jewish Woman in Graeco-Roman Palestine* (Sheffield: JSOT).

Baillet, M., Milik, J. T., and de Vaux, R. (1962), *Les 'Petites Grottes' de Qumrân*, DJD 3 (Oxford: Clarendon).

Balch, D. L. (1988), 'Household Codes', in D. E. Aune, *Greco-Roman Literature and the New Testament* (Atlanta: Scholars Press), 25–50.

Beentjes, P. (1997), *The Book of Ben Sira in Hebrew* (Leiden: Brill).

Begg, C. (1988), 'Ben Sirach's Non-mention of Ezra', *BN* 42: 14–18.

Bohlen, R. (1991), *Die Ehrung der Eltern bei Ben Sira* (Trier: Paulinus).

Box, G. H., and Oesterley, W. O. E. (1913), 'Sirach', in R. H. Charles (ed.), *The Apocrypha and Pseudepigrapha of the Old Testament* (Oxford: Clarendon), I. 268–517.

Camp, C. V. (1991), 'Understanding Patriarchy: Women in Second Century Jerusalem through the Eyes of Ben Sira', in A.-J. Levine (ed.), *Women Like Us: New Perspectives on Women in the Greco-Roman World* (Atlanta: Scholars Press), 1–39.

Caquot, A. (1966), 'Ben Sira et le Messianisme', *Semitica* 16: 43–68.

Collins, J. J. (1995), 'The Origin of Evil in Apocalyptic Literature and the Dead Sea Scrolls', in J. A. Emerton (ed.), *Congress Volume, Paris* (Leiden: Brill), 25–38.

—— (1997), 'Marriage, Divorce and Family in Second Temple Judaism', in L. Perdue, J. Blenkinsopp, J. J. Collins, and C. Meyers, *Families in Ancient Israel* (Louisville, Ky.: Westminster/John Knox), 104–62.

Conzelmann, H. (1971), 'The Mother of Wisdom', in J. Robinson (ed.), *The Future of Our Religious Past* (New York: Harper & Row), 230–43.

Corley, K. (1993), *Private Women: Public Meals* (Peabody, Mass.: Hendrickson).

Crenshaw, J. L. (1975), 'The Problem of Theodicy in Sirach: On Human Bondage', *JBL* 94: 47–64.

DiLella, A. A. (1966), *The Hebrew Text of Sirach: A Text-Critical and Historical Study* (The Hague: Mouton).

Elgvin, T. (1994), 'Admonition Texts from Qumran Cave 4', in M. O. Wise et al. (eds.), *Methods of Investigation of the Qumran Scrolls and the Khirbet Qumran Site* (New York: New York Academy of Sciences), 179–94.

García Martínez, F. (1994), *The Dead Sea Scrolls Translated* (Leiden: Brill).

Gerstenberger, E. S. (1988), *Psalms with an Introduction to Cultic Poetry*, Forms of Old Testament Literature, 14 (Grand Rapids, Mich.: Eerdmans).

Gilbert, M. (1984), 'Wisdom Literature', in M. E. Stone (ed.), *Jewish Writings of the Second Temple Period* (Philadelphia: Fortress), 283–324.

Harrington, D. J. (1994), 'Wisdom at Qumran', in E. Ulrich and J. C. VanderKam (eds.), *The Community of the Renewed Covenant* (Notre Dame, Ind.: University of Notre Dame), 137–52.

Haspecker, J. (1967), *Gottesfurcht bei Jesus Sirach* (Rome: Pontifical Biblical Institute).

Hengel, M. (1974), *Judaism and Hellenism* (2 vols.; Philadelphia: Fortress).

Horst, P. van der (1978), *The Sentences of Pseudo-Phocylides* (Leiden: Brill).

—— (1991), *Ancient Jewish Epitaphs* (Kampen: KokPharos).

Jeremias, J. (1967), *The Prayers of Jesus* (Philadelphia: Fortress).

Kieweler, H. V. (1992), *Ben Sira zwischen Judentum und Hellenismus* (Frankfurt am Main: Lang).

Koch, K. (1955), 'Gibt es ein Vergeltungsdogma im Alten Testament?', *ZTK* 52: 1–42. ET: 'Is There a Doctrine of Retribution in the Old Testament?', in J. L. Crenshaw (ed.), *Theodicy in the Old Testament* (Philadelphia: Fortress, 1983), 57–87.

Lefkowitz, M. R., and Fant, M. B. (1982), *Women's Life in Greece and Rome* (Baltimore, Md.: Johns Hopkins University Press).

Lee, T. R. (1986), *Studies in the Form of Sirach 44–50* (Atlanta: Scholars Press).

Leiman, S. Z. (1976), *The Canonization of Hebrew Scripture* (Hamden, Conn.: Archon).

Levison, J. (1985), 'Is Eve to Blame? A Contextual Analysis of Sirach 25:24', *CBQ* 47: 617–23.

Lewis, N. (1989), *The Documents from the Bar-Kokhba Period in the Cave of the Letters* (Jerusalem: Israel Exploration Society).

Long, A. A., and Sedley, D. N. (1987), *The Hellenistic Philosophers* (2 vols.; Cambridge: Cambridge University Press).

Mack, B. L. (1973), *Logos und Sophia* (Göttingen: Vandenhoeck & Ruprecht).

—— (1985), *Wisdom and the Hebrew Epic* (Chicago: University of Chicago Press).

Marböck, J. (1971), *Weisheit im Wandel* (Bonn: Hanstein).

Meyers, C. (1988), *Discovering Eve* (New York: Oxford University Press).

Middendorp, Th. (1973), *Die Stellung Jesu Ben Siras zwischen Judentum und Hellenismus* (Leiden: Brill).

Moxnes, H. (1993), 'Honor and Shame', *Biblical Theology Bulletin* 23: 167–76.

Muraoka, T. (1979), 'Sir 51:13–30: An Erotic Hymn to Wisdom?', *JSJ* 10: 166–78.

Ogden, G. S. (1977), 'The "Better"–Proverb (Tôb-Spruch), Rhetorical Criticism, and Qoheleth', *JBL* 96: 489–505.

O'Fearghail, F. (1978), 'Sir 50, 5–21: Yom Kippur or The Daily Whole Offering?', *Bib.* 59: 301–16.

Olyan, S. M. (1987), 'Ben Sira's Relationship to the Priesthood', *HTR* 80: 261–86.

Pautrel, R. (1963), 'Ben Sira et le stoicisme', *RSR* 51: 535–49.

Perdue, L. G. (1977), *Wisdom and Cult* (Missoula, Mont.: Scholars Press).

Peters, N. (1913), *Das Buch Jesus Sirach oder Ecclesiasticus* (Münster: Aschendorff).

Pomykala, K. E. (1995), *The Davidic Dynasty Tradition in Early Judaism: Its History and Significance for Messianism* (Atlanta: Scholars Press).

Puech, E. (1990), 'Ben Sira 8:11 et la Résurrection', in H. W. Attridge et al. (eds.), *Of Scribes and Scrolls: Studies on the Hebrew Bible, Intertestamental Judaism and Christian Origins* (Lanham, Md.: University Press of America), 81–90.

Rad, G. von (1964), 'Life and Death in the OT', *TDNT*, II. 843–9.

—— (1966), 'Job XXXVIII and Ancient Egyptian Wisdom', in idem, *The Problem of the Hexateuch and Other Essays* (New York: McGraw-Hill), 281–91.

—— (1972), *Wisdom in Israel* (Nashville, Tenn.: Abingdon).

Rickenbacher, O. (1973), *Weisheitsperikopen bei Ben Sira* (Göttingen: Vandenhoeck & Ruprecht).

Roth, W. M. (1965), *Numerical Sayings in the Old Testament* (Leiden: Brill).

—— (1980), 'The Gnomic-Discursive Wisdom of Jesus Ben Sirach', *Semeia*, 17: 35–79.

Sanders, J. A. (1965), *The Psalms Scroll of Qumran Cave 11* (11Qpsᵃ), DJD 4 (Oxford: Clarendon).

Sanders, J. T. (1983), *Ben Sira and Demotic Wisdom* (Chico, Calif.: Scholars Press).

Schechter, S. (1890–1), 'The Quotations from Ecclesiasticus in Rabbinic Literature', *JQR* 3: 682–706.

Schechter, S., and Taylor, C. (1899), *The Wisdom of Ben Sira: Portions of the Book Ecclesiasticus from Hebrew Manuscripts in the Cairo Genizah Collection Presented to the University of Cambridge by the Editors* (Cambridge: Cambridge University Press).

Schnabel, E. J. (1985), *Law and Wisdom from Ben Sira to Paul* (Tübingen: Mohr).

Schuller, E. M. (1990), '4Q372 1: A Text about Joseph', *Revue de Qumran* 14: 349–76.

Segal, M. H. (1972), *Sēper ben Sîrā haššalēm*, 2nd edn (Jerusalem: Bialik).

Sheppard, G. T. (1980), *Wisdom as a Hermeneutical Construct* (Berlin: de Gruyter).

Skehan, P. W., and DiLella, A. A. (1987), *The Wisdom of Ben Sira*, AB 39 (New York: Doubleday).

Smend, R. (1906), *Die Weisheit des Jesus Sirach erklärt* (Berlin: Reimer).

Smith, D. E., and Taussig, H. (1990), *Many Tables: The Eucharist in the New Testament and Liturgy Today* (Philadelphia: Trinity).

Snaith, J. G. (1974), *Ecclesiasticus or The Wisdom of Jesus Son of Sirach* (Cambridge: Cambridge University Press).

Stadelmann, H. (1980), *Ben Sira als Schriftgelehrter* (Tübingen: Mohr).

Strotmann, A. (1991), '*Mein Vater Bist Du!*' (Sir 51,10) (Frankfurt am Main: Knecht).

Tcherikover, V. (1970), *Hellenistic Civilization and the Jews* (New York: Atheneum).

Trenchard, W. C. (1982), *Ben Sira's View of Women: A Literary Analysis* (Chico, Calif.: Scholars Press).

Urbach, E. E. (1975), *The Sages: Their Concepts and Beliefs* (2 vols.; Jerusalem: Magnes).

Wischmeyer, O. (1995), *Die Kultur des Buches Jesu Sirachs* (Berlin: de Gruyter).

Yadin, Y. (1965), *The Ben Sira Scroll from Masada* (Jerusalem: Israel Exploration Society).

Ziegler, J. (1965), *Sapientia Jesu Filii Sirach* (Göttingen: Vandenhoeck & Ruprecht).

7. Baruch

ALISON SALVESEN

INTRODUCTION

A. Title. 1. The book is known in Greek tradition as Baruch or the Epistle of Baruch. The name means 'blessed' in Hebrew, and is a shortened form of Berechyahu, 'the Lord blesses'. According to the book of Jeremiah, Baruch was Jeremiah's secretary. He recorded the Lord's words at Jeremiah's dictation, read them out to the people in the temple, was taken to Tahpanes in Egypt along with Jeremiah, and was given a promise from the Lord that his life would be spared wherever he went (Jer 32:12–16; 36:4–32; 43:3–6; 45:1–5). Baruch himself was a historical figure, and a clay seal impression of the late seventh century bears his name, patronymic, and profession: 'Berechyahu, son of Neryahu, the scribe' (Avigad 1986: 28–9).

2. However, there are a number of circumstances that make it very unlikely that this Baruch was the author of the book of Baruch. Given that Baruch was a close associate of Jeremiah and may even have been responsible for parts of the Jeremiah tradition, it is odd that the first part of Baruch does not tie in more closely with statements in Jeremiah: e.g. Baruch's presence in Babylon in Bar 1:1, the return of the temple vessels in Bar 1:9, and the imprecise dating in Bar 1:2. Baruch is a compilation of three very different parts, only the first of which explicitly has to do with the figure of Baruch. There are many similarities of thought and expression between Baruch and works known to date from the Hellenistic period such as Daniel (c.164 BCE), Sirach (mid-2nd cent. BCE) and the *Psalms of Solomon* (probably mid-1st cent. BCE). While it is conceivable that these depend on Baruch, the nature of the book is fundamentally derivative, a 'mosaic of Biblical passages' (Tov 1976: 111). Baruch is more likely to be dependent on them or to have originated in a common milieu. Finally, Baruch was not accepted as canonical by the rabbis, and was never cited by them, as if the book's pedigree were suspect at an early stage.

3. So why was the name Baruch attached to the book? Baruch as a whole is concerned with problems of faith during the Diaspora, and the outlook of the first part is strongly influenced by the book of Jeremiah. As recorder of the prophet's words, Baruch was no doubt accorded quasi-prophetic status by Jews in the Second Temple period and, later, by Christians. Thus a book bearing his name would have enjoyed a certain prestige. One can compare the high position accorded to Ezra as a scribe of the law in the Second Temple period and the pseudepigraphical works consequently ascribed to him.

B. Text and Language. 1. No fragments of Baruch in any language were found at Qumran, nor does the NT cite it. The earliest preserved text of the book is in Greek: it exists in the Septuagint MSS Alexandrinus and Vaticanus: it may have been part of the missing portion of Sinaiticus. The Latin, Syriac, Coptic, Armenian, Arabic, Bohairic, and Ethiopic versions of Baruch are all translated from the Greek. As for the original language of the book, Origen knew of no Hebrew text of Baruch in the mid-third century CE. Although at Bar 1:17 and 2:3 the Syriac translation of Origen's *Hexapla* notes in the margin that a certain phrase is not found 'in the Hebrew', this must refer back to the biblical sources Baruch is quoting, not to a Hebrew version of Baruch itself. However, there are occasional phrases that must arise from a mistranslation of a Semitic original. For instance, at 3:4 the strange expression in the Greek text, 'hear then the prayer of the *dead* of Israel' must arise from a misreading of the Hebrew *mĕtê yiśrā'ēl* '(people of Israel) as *mētê yiśrā'ēl* '(dead of Israel) (vowels were not represented in ancient Heb. script). Such mistranslations occur mainly in the first part of the book (1:1–3:8). The second and third parts are more generally thought to have been written in Greek (but see Burke 1982).

2. 2 Baruch (Syriac) and 3 Baruch (Greek) are later compositions, also pseudonymous.

C. Subject Matter and Literary Genre. 1. Baruch is composed of three principal parts, one in prose (1:1–3:8) and two poetic (3:9–44, 4:5–5:9), reflecting the separate documents that were combined by a later editor. The first part describes Baruch's reading of a book to the exiles in Babylon, to which they respond by sending money, the looted temple vessels, and a communal confession and prayer to Jerusalem. The second part, which is not obviously connected with the first, is a eulogy of Wisdom and has affinities with sapiential literature in both Hebrew and Greek. The third part consists of Zion's consolation of the exiles and an exhortation to Jerusalem in the manner of Isa 40–66, and to some extent at least answers the concerns of the first part.

2. Thackeray (1923: 80–111) suggested that Baruch was a compilation that served a liturgical function in a diaspora Jewish community, and he linked it to the seven sabbaths around the ninth of Ab, the fast on which the destruction of the temple was commemorated. While few scholars have accepted his theory, it does at least attempt to explain the association of three such disparate documents. In addition, the first part explicitly provides a communal confession to be read in the temple on behalf of diaspora Jewry, a reversal of the situation in 2 Macc 2:16, where the Judean Jews instruct the Jews of Alexandria to keep the Feast of Dedication.

D. The Religious Teaching. The theology of the book varies according to the section. The first part is strongly influenced by Deuteronomistic thinking, that the Diaspora is caused by Israel's sin and is something to be borne until God brings it to an end. The second part identifies Torah with Wisdom. The third part is close to the mood of Deutero-Isaiah. Interestingly, there are no references to messianism, angelology, or the resurrection, which are themes of some other Jewish literature of the period and might have seemed appropriate in this text also.

E. Date and Place of Composition. 1. The question of the date of Baruch is unusually difficult, partly because it is a compilation of three quite different compositions. However, a time in the second century BCE seems likely for the earliest material, the latest possible date for the work in its present state being within a few years of the destruction of the Second Temple in 70 CE.

2. Tov (1976: 165) argues convincingly that the distinctive revision of the Septuagint of Jer 29–52 also covered Bar 1:1–3:8. Since Sirach's grandson knows the Prophets in Greek in 116 BCE (Sir, Prologue) and quotes from the revised Greek Jeremiah, the first part of Baruch in Greek must have been in existence by that date. The Hebrew original would of course be older.

3. Baruch's assumption that it was still possible to make offerings at the temple in Jerusalem (Bar 1:8–10) may also point to a period before 70 CE, though we cannot be certain to what degree the story reflects the actual historical circumstances of the writer. Another feature which may be consistent with a pre-70 date is the generally positive attitude of the first part

towards foreign rulers, especially Nebuchadnezzar, who in rabbinic literature became the archetypal enemy of the Jewish people and was also regarded as the forerunner of the Emperor Vespasian in his destruction of Jerusalem.

4. The book is not attested until the time of the Church Fathers, being cited first by Irenaeus (*Adv. haer.* 5. 35), then Athenagoras (*Apologia* 69), in the 170s CE.

5. The provenance of the book is as uncertain as its date (Tov 1976: 160). The first part is written very much from the perspective of the diaspora Jews looking towards Jerusalem, but it is possible that this is a deliberate fiction on the part of the writer in order to encourage exiled Jews to regard Jerusalem as their cultic centre. Certainly, if the original language of Baruch was Hebrew, Judea is the most obvious place of composition.

F. Canonicity. 1. If there was a Hebrew original of Baruch, there is no evidence that it ever formed part of the Hebrew canon of the Jews. The Greek and Latin versions of Baruch, along with the Letter of Jeremiah, were generally regarded as part of the book of Jeremiah, and were thus treated as canonical in the early Christian church. The attribution to Baruch, who plays an important role in Jeremiah, also contributed to the book's acceptance in the Christian community. Only Jerome rejected Baruch, since it was not included in the Jewish canon.

2. Today, Baruch is regarded as canonical by the Roman Catholic and Eastern Orthodox churches, as part of the Apocrypha by Protestants, and is disregarded by Jews.

G. Outline.
Narrative Introduction (1:1–14)
Confession and Prayer (1:15–3:8)
Eulogy of Wisdom (3:9–44)
Address to Israel (4:5–9a)

Zion's consolation of her children in the Diaspora (4:9b–29), and a corresponding exhortation of Jerusalem (4:30–5:9). There is no formal conclusion to the book.

COMMENTARY

Narrative Introduction (1:1–14)

The structure and mood of this introduction are strongly influenced by Jer 29:1–2 and Jer 36. There are many historical problems surrounding the events and circumstances as described here.

(1:1) 'these are the words of the book': there are four main theories as to what is meant. (1) It is generally thought that the book of Baruch itself is meant, and that Baruch is envisaged as reading aloud either the whole composition or the first part (1:15b–3:8). However, this would give the response of the hearers to the book (1:5) before the reader knows its contents, which are revealed when the exiles send back the scroll in 1:10 for recitation in the temple. Such a device is far from impossible, and is upheld by Steck (1993: 5–60), who sees 1.1–15a as the introduction which attributes the book as a whole to Baruch. (2) Whitehouse (1913) considered that 1:1, 3 prefaced 3:9–4:4, while 1:2, 3b–3:8 and 3:9–5:9 formed separate documents. (3) Another solution would be to suppose that the order of the biblical books was Jeremiah-Lamentations-Baruch. Thus, 'these are the words' would refer to the book of Lamentations, a response to the fall of Jerusalem written by Baruch in Babylon to be repeated in front of the Jews there. The order Jeremiah-Lamentations-Baruch is not generally found in the Septuagint MSS, though it may have existed in the original form of Codex Sinaiticus (now truncated), and Epiphanius is the only commentator on the canon of Scripture to list the books in this order. But it would explain the response of the exiles and their dispatching of a prayer to be said on their behalf by their fellow Jews in Jerusalem. We would then have a lament sent from Jerusalem to Babylon (Lamentations), and its counterpart of a confession and petition sent back to Jerusalem from Babylon (Bar 1:15b–3:8). The structure of the book according to this hypothesis would be:

a. Lamentations sent from Jerusalem to Babylon
b. Response of exiles: prayer and confession sent from Babylon to Jerusalem (Bar 1:1–3:8)
c. Hymn to Wisdom (3:9–4:4)
a'. Zion's exhortation of the exiles (4:5–29)
b'. Consolation of Jerusalem (4:30–5:5).

(4) An alternative explanation of the opening words is that they may somehow refer to the book of Jeremiah (the normal order in LXX MSS is Jeremiah-Baruch-Lamentations), or to Jeremiah's letter sent to the exiles after Jeconiah's deportation, as described in Jer 29:1–28 (LXX 36:1–28). Jer 29 does not mention Baruch as either the scribe or the messenger of the letter, but it does begin in Greek in exactly the same way as Baruch: 'these are the words' (LXX 36:1). It also counsels the exiles to settle down in Babylon and pray for its welfare. This is exactly the response we find in Bar 1:11–12. On this interpretation, the structure of the whole book would not be very different from that described above, in (3).

'Book' is the Greek *biblion*, here and in 1:3a, 10. The same word is used for the scroll dictated by Jeremiah to Baruch in Jer 36:8, 10, 11, 18 (LXX ch. 43). A slightly different word, *biblos*, is used in Bar 1:3b for what Baruch recites, and in Jer 29:1 for Jeremiah's letter to the exiles (LXX 36:1). The difference is not significant: Jer 29:29 (LXX 36:29) uses *biblion* for a letter. 'Baruch son of Neriah son of Mahseiah son of Zedekiah son of Hasadiah son of Hilkiah': the patronymic 'son of Neriah son of Mahseiah' is found in Jer 32:12, but the other names are unattested as ancestors of Baruch.

'Babylon' refers to the region, and not just the city. According to Jeremiah, Baruch was taken only to Egypt (43:7), but both the book of Baruch and rabbinic tradition say that Baruch went to Babylon. In fact, the Babylonian Talmud improbably states that Baruch taught Ezra there (b. Meg 16b)! It is possible that a combination of the Lord's promise to spare his life wherever he went (Jer 45:5), Jeremiah's letter to the Babylonian exiles in Jer 29, and the presence of Seraiah, Baruch's brother, in Babylon (Jer 51:59–64) suggest that Baruch journeyed there. Bar 1:8 may imply that Baruch returned to Jerusalem.

The Syriac version of Baruch says that Baruch *sent* the book to Babylon, but this may be a later change in order to avoid the problem of an unattested journey to Babylon. On the other hand, it may represent an attempt to harmonize Bar 1:1 with 2 *Apoc. Bar.* 77:19, where Baruch is said to send two letters to Babylon.

(1:2–9) 'In the fifth year, on the seventh day of the month', the chronology of v. 2 is unclear, particularly as the month is not specified. The original reading was perhaps 'the fifth year, on the seventh day of the *fifth* month', the second 'fifth' having dropped out in the copying process. The fifth month was Ab (August), and the date is that of the burning of Jerusalem by Nebuzaradan, according to 2 Kings 25:8–9. So Baruch is depicted as writing the book as Jerusalem is being destroyed (586 BCE). But then there remains the problem of which 'fifth year' is meant. It may be an echo of Jer 36:9, where Baruch reads out Jeremiah's words before the people in the temple. Or it may refer to the fifth year after the capture of Jerusalem, which would be 581 BCE. The 'Chaldeans' are the Babylonians. v. 3, for similar public readings, see 2 Kings 23:1–2 (= 2 Chr 34:30), and Neh 8:1–8.

'Jeconiah son of Jehoiakim' (v. 3) is also known as Jehoiachin and Coniah (see 2 Kings 24:8–17, 25:27–30; Jer 22:24–30). According to Jer 52:31, he was in prison for 37 years, rather than dwelling among the other exiles. He is certainly not mentioned in Ezek 8:1.

v. 4, 'the princes', the Greek 'sons of the king'. Jer 22:30 says that Jeconiah will be childless, but 1 Chr 3:17 and Babylonian cuneiform inscriptions (*ANET* 308) say that he had sons. 'The river Sud': there is a reference in the Dead Sea scrolls (4QpJer) to a river Sur in the context of the Exile. The Hebrew letters *r* and *d* are very similar in form, and the Greek translator may have misread Sud for Sur. v. 5, 'they wept. and fasted': For a similar response, see Neh 8:9; 9:1, similarly followed by a prayer of national confession (Neh 9:6–37). v. 6, '*the high priest Jehoiakim son of Hilkiah son of Shallum*' is constructed from several biblical genealogies: J(eh)oiakim is a priest in Jerusalem much later, in the days of Ezra and Nehemiah (Neh 12:10, 12, 26, cf. Jos. *Ant.* 11.5.1); the high priest Hilkiah discovered the book of the law in the temple (2 Kings 22:8), and Hilkiah son of Shallum is a progenitor of Ezra in Ezra 7:1. According to 2 Kings 25:18–21, the high priest at the time of the Exile was Seraiah, who was taken to Babylon and executed. It is possible that Jehoiakim is to be understood as a deputy who remained in Jerusalem.

v. 8, Sivan is the third month, corresponding to May–June, evidently in the year following Baruch's reading of the book: 'the vessels of the house of the Lord ... the silver vessels that Zedekiah son of Josiah ... had made': according to 2 Kings 24:13 and 25:14–15 all the temple vessels were removed by the Babylonians (in 597 and 586 BCE), and they were not brought back until the end of the Exile (Ezra 1:7–8): Jer 27:22 certainly does not envisage an early return. Zedekiah is not known to have made anything for the temple, so perhaps this is an invention on the part of the writer of Baruch, to explain how an offering could be made in Jerusalem while the vessels were still in Babylon. The 'Lord': throughout the first part of Baruch, the Deity is referred to as 'the Lord' (*kurios*) in contrast to the second and third parts of Baruch, where 'Lord' never appears. The second part uses *theos* (God), and the third part *ho aiōnios* (the Eternal). 1.9, some MSS and versions add 'and the craftsmen' after 'the prisoners'. The Hebrew word for 'prison' is identical to that for 'smith', *masgēr*. The same double translation is found in LXX Jer 24:1 and 36:2 (Eng. versions 29:2).

(**1:10–14**) v. 10, 'grain-offerings' is Greek *manna*, an error for *manaa*, the transliteration of Hebrew *minḥâ* (offering), a further indication of a Semitic original for the first part of Baruch. '[O]ffer them on the altar': in spite of the burning of the temple, it seems from Jer 41:5 and Lam 1:4 that the temple cult continued in some form. The instruction to 'pray for the life of King Nebuchadnezzar' is an unusual sentiment, particularly in later Judaism where Nebuchadnezzar was regarded as the archetype of the evil ruler, and forerunner of Vespasian and Titus who destroyed the second temple. But cf. Jer 29:7, where Jeremiah tells the Jews taken to Babylon in the first captivity to pray for the land in which they are exiles; cf. also 1 Tim 2:1–3. In fact Belshazzar is not Nebuchadnezzar's son, as Baruch supposes, but the son of Nabonidus (555–538 BCE) whom Cyrus overthrew. The same error occurs in Dan 5:2, 11, 13, 18, 22, which has led some to date Baruch after Daniel (167–164 BCE). However, the error may be due to dependence on a common source and have no bearing on the dating. Some scholars identify Baruch's Nebuchadnezzar and Belshazzar with Antiochus IV (*c.*175–164 BCE) and his son Antiochus V Eupator (164–162 BCE) after the desecration and rededication of the Temple, or with Vespasian and Titus in the years just prior to or immediately after the destruction of the Second Temple (70 CE), and date Baruch accordingly. There is no convincing evidence for either identification.

v. 14, 'and you shall read aloud' is cited by some in support of a liturgical origin for Baruch. Cf. 2 Macc 1:1–2:18. In 'to make your confession', 'your' is not in the Greek text, which has merely 'to make confession'. The 'days of the festivals': the oldest Greek MS has 'day of festival'. It is not at all clear which, if any, specific festival the writer had in mind. Some have suggested the eight-day Feast of Tabernacles, held in the early autumn (Lev 23:33–6), while Thackeray (1923: 93) prefers a period in the summer, leading up to the ninth of Ab, when the burning of the temple was commemorated.

Confession and Prayer (1:15–3:8)

This section is a pastiche of biblical citations. The main parallels are with Dan 9:4–19 and there are many references to Jeremiah. Tov (1975) gives a full list. From 1:13–15*a*, it seems that the Jews in Judah and Jerusalem are to pray the following words on behalf of those in the Diaspora. Nickelsburg (1984) suggests that the Jerusalem Jews make their own confession in 1:15b–2:5, and then pray on behalf of the Jews in the Diaspora in 2:6–10, but there is no real sign of a change in speaker, and it is easier to assume that 1:15b–3:8 is all part of the prayer sent by the exiles to be recited by the Jews of Jerusalem for the Jewish people as a whole.

(**1:20**) 'the curse that the Lord declared... through Moses: see Lev 26:14–39, Deut 28–31.

(**2:1–2**) 'against our judges... under the whole heaven'... is based on Dan 9:12–13.

(**2:3**) 'Some of us ate the flesh of their sons'... is a reference to Lev 26:29, Deut 28:53, and Jer 19:9, which with Bar 2:3 was the origin of the frequent anti-Jewish jibe in early Christian writers that the Jews had eaten their own children. Josephus (*J.W.* 6.3.4) describes one such incident during the Roman siege of Jerusalem in 70 CE.

(**2:17–18**) 'the dead who are in Hades... will not ascribe glory' is a common theme: cf. Ps 6:5; 30:9; 88:10–12; 115:17; Isa 38:18; Sir 17:27–8. For 'the person who is deeply grieved... with failing eyes' see Deut 28:65.

(**2:21–6**) 'as you declared by your servants the prophets': in fact, the references are all to Jeremiah: 26:5, 27:9; 7:34; 48:9; 36:30; 16:4; 32:36; 11:17.

(**2:29–35**) a reworking of several passages, principally from Jeremiah (42:2; 24:7; 25:5; 30:3; 29:6; 32:40; 31:33), along with Lev 26:39, 45; Deut 30:1–10. vv. 34–5, there is no explicit request for a return from exile, but the prayer repeats God's promise to end the Dispersion. The wording is based on Jer 30:3; 32:40; 31:33; 1 Kings 14:15.

(**3:1–8**) a heartfelt plea for mercy ends this first section of Baruch. Although the people of Judah have turned in repentance, they are still suffering the punishment incurred by their ancestors.

The Eulogy of Wisdom (3:9–4:4)

The second section of Baruch commences without preamble, and with no obvious connection with the preceding section. The poem shows indebtedness to the style and ideas of Deut 30:15–19; Prov 1–9; Job 28:12–28; Sir 24.

(**3:9**) 'Hear the commandments of life, O Israel', or, 'Hear, O Israel, the commandments of life', is

deliberate verbal echo of Deut 6:4, 'Hear, O Israel...', the *Shema*, the 'creed' of Judaism, a feature cited as part of the evidence of a liturgical origin for Baruch. The identification of Torah with Wisdom is common in the late-biblical and intertestamental periods, the central text being Prov 1:7, and the idea is developed in Sir 1 and 24.

(**3:10–14**) Cf. Jer 9:12–16, which says that the wise can discern the reason for the Exile: disobedience to God.

(**3:12**) The 'fountain of wisdom', i.e. its source, is God: see Jer 2:13; Ps 36:8–9; Sir 1:1–20.

(**3:15–16**) Cf. v. 15 with Job 28:12, 20. v. 16, 'who lorded it over the animals on earth', is possibly an allusion to Nebuchadnezzar. Cf. Jer 27:6; 28:14; Dan 2:38.

(**3:22–4**) the repetition of Teman in two different geographical contexts indicates that two locations were originally intended. The first must refer to Teman of Edom, which was proverbial for wisdom in the Bible, hence Jer 49:7, Ob 8–9. Job's friend Eliphaz was a Temanite (Job 2:11). The second Teman is Tema of Arabia (Job 6:19, Isa 21:14, Jer 25:23). Merran is more puzzling, but may be due to a misreading of Hebrew *Midian* or *Medan* (Gen 25:2) by the translator: *r* and *d* were often confused (see Bar 1:4). Those who travelled widely were thought to gain much wisdom (Sir 34:9–12; 39:4), hence the association of the desert traders of Midian/Medan, Tema, and the descendants of Hagar with wisdom. v. 24, cf. Isa 66:1.

(**3:26**) 'The giants', a reference to Gen 6:4. There was much speculation in the intertestamental period concerning these giants: see Wis 14:6; Sir 16:7; *Jub.* 7:22–3; and especially 1 *Enoch* 6–7.

(**3:33–5**) For similar concepts to vv. 33–4 see Job 38:7; Isa 40:26; Sir 43:9–10. v. 35, 'This is our God': comparable expressions can be found in Deut 4:35, 39; Isa 25:9; 43:10–11; 44:6; 45:18; Jer 10:6; Ps 48:14.

(**3:37**) 'she appeared on earth and lived with humankind', or, 'was seen on earth and moved among humankind'. The personal pronoun 'she' is not represented in Greek and the verb *ōftē* (appeared), is not gender-specific. Therefore some early Christian exegetes took the subject to be God, following vv. 35–6, and understood v. 37 to be a proof-text for the incarnation.

Some modern scholars have dismissed the whole of v. 37 as a Christian interpolation, but Bar 3:8–4:4 is not the most obvious place to insert a Christological text, and it is much easier to understand the verse as original to its setting, describing how the inaccessible divine Wisdom (3:15, 29–31) was given as Torah to Israel and came to dwell on earth (3:36–4:1).

(4:1–4) v. 1, the explicit identification of Wisdom with Torah is also found in Sir 24:23. v. 3, 'Do not give your glory to another', cf. Isa 48:11. v. 4, 'Happy are we', literally, 'blessed (*makarioi*), are we, Israel, for the things that are pleasing to God are known by us', in the form of a beatitude resembling those in Ps 1:1 and Mt 5:3–11.

Address to Israel (4:5–5:9)

This section consists of encouragement of Israel (4:5–9a), followed by Zion's exhortation of her children (4:9b–29), answered by prophetic words of comfort addressed to Jerusalem (4:30–5:9). The words 'take courage' in 4:5 are repeated in Zion's speech at 4:21, 27, and mark the start of the message of consolation at 4:30. A prominent feature of the third part of Baruch is the personification of Zion as a mother. This is an idea found in the source for much of this section, Deutero-Isaiah (e.g. Isa 49:20–1; 50:1; 54:1–8), and also explicitly in the peculiar LXX reading of Ps 87 (86):5, 'Mother Zion'. Zion is

depicted as calling to her female neighbours, *paroikoi*, in 4:9, 14, 24. These seem to be witnesses of the exile of the citizens and of Zion's grief, and perhaps refer to other Judean cities, since they are portrayed as passive, not hostile, on lookers.

(4:7–8) 'to demons and not to God,' see Deut 32:16–17; Ps 106:37; 96:5 (LXX), 1 Cor 10:20. v. 8, 'You forgot the everlasting God,' SEE Bar 1:8; 'who brought you up', literally, 'who nursed you' or 'suckled you', a very maternal image of God, cf. Hos 11:4.

(4:15) See Deut 28:49–50.

(4:23) 'I sent you out with sorrow and weeping, but . . .', cf. Isa 62:3.

(4:35–5:9) A prophetic message of consolation, largely based on Isa 40–66. The wording of Bar 4:37–5:8 is also very close to that of *Pss. Sol.* 11:3–7. 4:35, for Babylon's punishment, see Isa 13:21–2; Jer 51:37, 58. 4:36–7, cf. Isa 49:18; 60:4. For 5:1 see Isa 52:1. The idea in 5:4 of the renaming of Jerusalem in the eschatological future is also found in Isa 1:26; 60:14; 62:4; Jer 33:16; Ezek 48:35. For 5:5 see Isa 51:17; 60:1, 4. 5:7 is close to Isa 40:4. 5:9, cf. Isa 52:12; 58:8; Ex 13:21.

The book has no formal conclusion, but ends on a note of promise and hope.

The Letter of Jeremiah

INTRODUCTION

A. Title. The KJV and Vulgate treat the Letter of Jeremiah as ch. 6 of Baruch. The Septuagint places Lamentations between the two works. The work purports to be a letter sent by Jeremiah to the exiles in Babylon, on the precedent of Jer 29, but is quite different stylistically from the work of the prophet, and must be pseudepigraphical.

B. Text and Language. Although the letter exists only in Greek and in versions based on LXX (Syriac, Sahidic, and Latin), there is linguistic evidence to support a Hebrew or Aramaic original. Crudely put, the Greek may sometimes indicate an imperfectly understood Semitic base text. Some examples are given in the Commentary below.

C. Subject-Matter and Literary Genre. The Letter is a heavy-handed prose satire on idolatry, rather in the manner of Bel and the Dragon, but it is cruder and less entertaining.

D. Date and Place of Composition. 1. There are several indications of the date of the Letter in Greek (any Semitic original would of course be rather older than the Greek text). There is an allusion to it in 2 Macc 2:1–3, a work composed some time in the second century BCE. The language of the Letter is koine Greek, which again supports a date from the second century BCE onwards. Finally, a fragment covering vv. 43–4 was found at Qumran (7Q486: DJD 3:143 and pl. xxx), and dated to *c*.100 BCE on the basis of the writing.

2. The work is addressed to the Jewish exiles in Babylon, and this has led some scholars to suggest an eastern provenance such as Mesopotamia. But this is merely a literary device, and it could be aimed at any Jewish community in the Diaspora. Another argument for an origin in the east is the writer's apparent familiarity with Babylonian customs, though this need not have been acquired at first hand. However, if the original language was Hebrew, it would tend to support a Palestinian provenance, and an Aramaic *Vorlage* would indicate a Palestinian, Mesopotamian, or Babylonian origin.

E. Canonicity. 1. Like Baruch, the Letter of Jeremiah was associated by the church with the book of Jeremiah from the second century or earlier, and considered part of that prophetic work. However, with the exception of Aristides, Tertullian, and Cyprian, Christian writers rarely allude to it. This may be in part because the worship of idols became less and less of a threat to the church as time went on, and also because similar ideas are expressed more succinctly in Deut 4:28; Ps 115:4–7; 134:15–17; Isa 44:9–20; 46:5–7; Jer 10:1–16, the very passages from which the Letter drew its inspiration.

2. The Letter of Jeremiah once circulated among Jewish communities, witness its presence at Qumran and the allusion to it in 2 Maccabees, but it was not recognized later by the rabbis.

F. Outline. Although at first sight there is no obvious structure to the work, Brooke (2007) has convincingly argued for the recognition of a chiastic structure to the Letter, with five 'design elements' in a ten-stanza poem, refrains, and chiastic items of vocabulary. Certainly the Letter makes the best sense when considered as a poetic composition.

In terms of content, as opposed to structure, the Letter could be outlined as follows:

Introduction (6:1)
Address to the exiles in Babylon; prophecy of their long stay there and eventual return (6:2–3)
Warning to avoid idols in Babylon and to maintain faith with the Lord (6:4–7)
Satirical denunciation of idols, focusing on their utter impotence and the tainted service offered by their worshippers (6:8–72)
Conclusion, reiterating the warning to keep away from idolatry (6:73)

COMMENTARY

(6:1) Introduction 'A copy of a letter that Jeremiah sent', cf. Jer 29. The Greek word used here, however, is *epistolē* (see Bar 1:1).

(6:3–4) 'for a long time, up to seven generations', in conflict with Jer 25:12; 29:10, in which the Exile is prophesied as lasting seventy years. The implication is that the writer is addressing a Diaspora of long standing. Some commentators have taken the expression literally, and dated the work 7 × 40 years after the exiles of 597 and 586, to 317–306 BCE. But it is most likely that 'seven generations' is to be understood figuratively, as a long period of time. v. 4, 'which people carry on their shoulders', a possible reference to the Babylonian *akitu* festival at the New Year, which involved solemn processions, though it is more likely to have been influenced by Isa 46:1–2. See also LET JER 6:26.

(6:7) 'My angel is with you', for the concept and expression, see Gen 24:7; 48:16; Ex 23:20, 23; 32:34.

(6:11–12) 'the prostitutes on the terrace', literally, 'on the roof', Greek *stegos* or *tegos*. This is explained in a number of ways. It may refer, as NRSV suggests, to part of the pagan temple where the cult prostitutes operated (Hdt. 1.181). Alternatively, the Greek word is being used in the sense of 'brothel'. Another suggestion is that the Greek translator misread the unvowelled Aramaic *'al'agrā* (for payment, hire), as *'al'iggār ā* (on the roof), v. 12, 'from rust and corrosion', the NRSV has attempted to make sense of the Greek *apo iou kai brōmatōn* (lit. from rust and food), in the light of Mt 6:19, *sēs kai brōsis* ('moth and eating'), rendered as 'moth and rust' in NRSV. Otherwise, there may be a mistranslation behind the Greek: the Hebrew word for 'food' is *'ōkel* or *ma'ăkāl*, whereas the Hebrew for 'from a moth' is *mē'ōkēl* (lit. from a devourer).

(6:22) 'bats . . . alight . . . and so do cats', Strabo (*Geog.* 16.7) says that bats were a particular nuisance in temples. The verb rendered 'alight' by NRSV has the literal meaning in Greek, 'to fly over, flit', which is hardly appropriate to cats. This has led to many emendations in order to provide another type of bird at the end of the list, but none so far has proved convincing. See Lee (1971).

(6:29) 'touched by women in their periods or at childbirth', in Judaism women were regarded as ceremonially unclean at these times (Lev 12:4, 15:19–20).

(6:31–2) In contrast to the cults of the Babylonian gods, women played very little part in the cult of YHWH. Torn clothes, shaved and uncovered heads were regarded as signs of mourning and unfitting for a supposedly holy place. Israelite priests were forbidden to mourn in the customary way, in order to remain ceremonially clean for the service of God (Lev 21:1–5, 10). The pagan priests described here may be participating in the cult of dying and rising gods such as Tammuz.

(**6:36–8**) The impotence of the idols is implicitly compared with the compassion of Israel's God (cf. Ps 68:5–6, 146:8; Isa 35:5).

(**6:40**) The 'Chaldeans' here are not Babylonians; the word is used in the sense of 'astrologers, magicians'. 'Bel' means 'lord', an epithet for the patron deity of a city, in this case Marduk (Merodach), god of the Babylonians. Cf. the apocryphal book Bel and the Dragon.

(**6:42–3**) Herodotos (1.199) gives a similar account of this practice. He says that once in her life, every Babylonian woman has to sit in the precinct of Aphrodite (Ishtar), and have intercourse with the first stranger who throws a silver coin into her lap. The cords here may refer either to the string that Herodotos says the women wear on their heads, or to the roped-off areas in which they sit. The accounts here and in Herodotos appear to be independent. Burning bran for incense is a strange custom, but perhaps some sort of grain offering or aphrodisiac is meant.

(**6:55**) 'like crows', this is a strange simile, and it has been plausibly suggested that the Greek translator read the unvocalized Hebrew *'ābîm* (clouds) as *'ōrĕbîm* (crows).

(**6:60**) For the theme of the obedience of the heavenly bodies, see Bar 3:33–4.

(**6:67–70**) These verses mirror the thought of Jer 10:2–5, with some reordering. '[A] scarecrow in a cucumber bed' is a vivid image, probably influenced by the similar expressions in Isa 1:8 and especially Jer 10:5, which occurs in a passage on the futility of idols. Since the clause does not appear in LXX Jer 10:5, the writer must have had direct knowledge of the Hebrew. The Greek *probaskanion*, rendered 'scarecrow' here, generally means something that averts witchcraft.

(**6:71–3**) Gardens were cultivated for food, not for leisure or decorative purposes, so a thornbush in a garden, attracting birds that would feed on the produce, would be a metaphor for uselessness (cf. Judg 9:14, 15). '[a] corpse thrown out in the darkness': corpses were ceremonially unclean, and for a body to be thrown out unburied was a sign of enormous disrespect. For similar expressions, see Am 8:3, Jer 14:16, 22:19, Isa 34:3, Bar 2:25. v. 72, for 'linen' the Greek reads 'marble', apparently having mistaken the Hebrew *šēš* (fine linen) for its homonym. For the combination with purple, describing luxurious attire, see Ex 26:1, Prov 31:22, Lk 16:19. The letter concludes at v. 73 with a recommendation to keep away from idolatry.

REFERENCES

Avigad, N. (1986), *Hebrew Bullae from the Time of Jeremiah: Remnants of a Burnt Archive* (Jerusalem: Israel Exploration Society).

Brooke, George J. (2007), 'The Structure of the Poem against Idolatry in the Epistle of Jeremiah (1 Baruch 6)', in A. Frey and Rémi Gounelle (eds.), *Poussières de christianisme et de judaïsme antiques: Études réunies en l'honneur de Jean-Daniel Kaestli et Éric Junod*, Publications de l'Institut romand des sciences bibliques 5 (Lausanne: Éditions du Zèbre), 107–28.

Burke, D. G. (1982), *The Poetry of Baruch: A Reconstruction and Analysis of the Original Hebrew Text of Baruch 3:9–5:9*, Septuagint and Cognate Studies Series 10 (Chico, Calif.: Scholars Press).

Lee, G. M. (1971), 'Apocryphal Cats: Baruch 6:21', *VT* 21: 111–12.

Nickelsburg, G. W. D. (1984), 'Baruch and Epistle of Jeremiah', in M. E. Stone (ed.), *Jewish Writings of the Second Temple Period* (Assen: Van Gorcum), 140–8.

Steck, O. H. (1993), *Das apokryphe Baruchbuch: Studien zu Rezeption und Konzentration 'kanonischer' Überlieferung* (Göttingen: Vandenhoeck & Ruprecht).

Thackeray, H. St J. (1923), *The Septuagint and Jewish Worship*, Schweich Lectures, 1920 (2nd edn; London: Oxford University Press).

Tov, E. (1975), *The Book of Baruch, Also Called I Baruch (Greek and Hebrew)*, SBLTT 8 (Missoula, Mont.: Scholars Press).

—— (1976), *The Septuagint Translation of Jeremiah and Baruch: A Discussion of an Early Revision of the LXX of Jeremiah 29–52 and Baruch 1:1–3:8*, HSM 8 (Missoula, Mont.: Scholars Press).

Whitehouse, O. C. (1913), '1 Baruch', *APOT*, I. 569–95.

8. Additions to Daniel

GEORGE J. BROOKE

INTRODUCTION

A. Background. The book of Daniel in the HB is composite; not only is it written in two languages (Hebrew and Aramaic), but its contents fall into two parts, one containing stories about Daniel as the wise man in the court of the foreign king, the other his visions. The scrolls from Qumran have shown that there were other traditions in the Second Temple period which are most suitably associated with Daniel (4Q242–6; 4Q551–3); notably 4Q242 seems to be an alternative form of Dan 4. It is not altogether surprising that the Greek versions of Daniel contain additions. All three additions are set in Babylon and concern in some way the deliverance of the faithful. For further detail on matters of background see the survey by C. A. Moore (1992).

B. Text and Language. 1. The Greek versions of Daniel are usually divided into two groups. On the one hand the OG is attested in the late second-century CE Papyrus 967 (which places Bel and the Dragon before Susanna), in Origen's *Hexapla* (which survives in a very literal Syriac translation made in the early 7th cent. CE, known as Syh), and in the ninth-eleventh century MS 88 (Codex Chisianus). On the other hand there is the text linked with the name of Theodotion (2nd cent. CE) which very early became dominant in the churches. It is widely agreed that this text predates Theodotion himself (Schmitt 1966). Both Greek versions contain three passages not found in the Hebrew and Aramaic Daniel. Whether the Theodotion text of these additions is a revision of the OG, perhaps in the light of a Semitic text (Moore 1977), or a fresh translation from a Semitic original (Schmitt 1966) is still unclear. There is nothing in the two traditions that distinguishes the Greek of the additions from that of the rest of Daniel.

2. In both Greek traditions the Prayer of Azariah and the Song of the Three Jews occurs between Dan 3:23 and 3:24 (not extant in Papyrus 967). This addition has three parts: the Prayer of Azariah, a narrative link, and the Song of the Three Jews. In Theodotion (and Papyrus 967) Bel and the Dragon form Dan 13 and Susanna comes before Dan 1. In Papyrus 967 Susanna follows Bel and the Dragon but in

MS 88, Syh, and Vg Susanna is Dan 13, and Bel and the Dragon Dan 14. The NRSV gives a translation of Theodotion's version of the additions, but they are printed in the order of the OG. The standard edition of the Greek texts is that of Ziegler (1954) which must be supplemented by the work of Geissen (1968).

3. Most scholars suppose that the Prayer of Azariah and the Song of the Three Jews were originally composed in Hebrew (cf. Kuhl 1940: 111–59). If the narrative interlude was original to the text of Daniel it would have been in Aramaic, but if it was composed to introduce the Song of the Three, then it would have been originally in Hebrew. Nothing can be deduced from the Aramaic forms of these additions in the eleventh-century *Chronicles of Jerahmeel* (Gaster 1895; 1896), which are versions produced independently from the Greek versions, probably to make a Hebrew original fit its Aramaic context. The two Greek versions are in close agreement with one another.

4. The differences between the OG and Theodotion are most significant in Susanna. They can be seen in English in some parallel presentations (Kay 1913; Collins 1993) and have been discussed extensively (Moore 1977: 78–80; Steussy 1993). Most scholars suppose that Theodotion supplements the OG either on the basis of oral tradition (Delcor 1971: 260), through redactional activity (Engel 1985: 56–7), or through using a Semitic source (Moore 1977: 83). For the story as a whole a Hebrew original is likely (*kai egeneto* = *wayyĕhî*: vv. 7, 15, 19, 28, 64), though the extant medieval Hebrew forms of the story are probably secondary. Since Julius Africanus in the third century CE (*Letter to Origen*, PG 11.41–8) some have argued for a Greek original because of the puns in vv. 54–5 and 58–9, but the Syh represents the puns easily enough so a Semitic original remains quite possible. Milik (1981: 355–7) has tentatively proposed that a three-part Aramaic fragment from Qumran (4Q551) reflects the story of Susanna. It talks of the appointment of a judge but there are no clear overlaps and the proper names found in the Aramaic fragment nowhere occur in the story of Susanna.

5. For Bel and the Dragon OG and Theodotion are close, though some argue that Bel is told more effectively in the OG, whilst the Dragon is stylistically better in Theodotion

(Moore 1977: 119). The greater number of Hebra-isms in Theodotion suggests that the OG may have been based on an Aramaic original, which Theodotion reworked on the basis of a Hebrew text. The Theodotion version seems to be some-what assimilated to Dan 6 while its OG coun-terpart may be older than Dan 6 (Wills 1990). The story of the Dragon is known in Aramaic in the *Chronicles of Jerahmeel*, which possibly reflects an early version independent from both Greek and Syriac versions.

C. Subject Matter and Literary Genre. 1. The Prayer of Azariah, though in its present context said by an individual, is a communal confession of sin and plea for mercy similar to Dan 9:4–19 (cf. Ps 44; 74; 79; 106; Ezra 9:6–15; Neh 1:5–11; Bar 1:15–3:8; 4Q504). It is full of the theology of Deuteronomy. The Song of the Three Jews is a hymn of praise; there is no need to suppose that its two parts ever existed separately. It is closely related to Ps 148 and the 'list science of nature wisdom' (Koch 1987: 1.205; Collins 1993: 207; cf. Job 38–41; Sir 43). These additions shift the emphasis in Dan 3 away from the king towards the faithfulness of the martyrs, who thus acknowledge and bless God before Nebuchad-nezzar does (Hammer 1972: 213).

2. Susanna is the story of the eventual vindi-cation of an innocent woman who thwarted an attempted rape by two of the elders of her community. Since the refutation of its historic-ity, the story has been variously categorized: as a moral fable (see Baumgartner 1926: 259–67), as a midrash (on Jer 29:21–32) which either cri-tiques perverted Jewish authorities (OG: Engel 1985: 177–81) or is designed to be an attack on Sadducean court practice (Brull 1877), as a folk-tale (Baumgartner 1929; Schurer 1987; LaCoque 1990), as a wisdom instruction (Theodotion: Engel 1985: 181–3), as a parable on Jewish rela-tions with Hellenism (Hartman and Di Lella 1989: 420), as a court legend adapted for the Jewish community (Wills 1990), perhaps with a particular 'democratized' stress on the perse-cution and vindication of the righteous (Nickelsburg 1984: 38), as a novella (Collins 1993: 437). For all its folkloristic feel, the story is replete with religious terminology and themes. Because Susanna is a woman, there has been some recent interest in the tale from that perspective. Through the contrast of the virtuous woman with the lecherous elders Sus-anna is subversive of the Jewish establishment (LaCoque 1990); she is also the story's object whose feminine passivity allows God to be the

avenger (Pervo 1991). Motifs in the story suggest that Susanna is a new Eve, the one who knows the law and is obedient in the garden (cf. T *Levi* 18: 10–11; *Pss. Sol.* 14:1–5; Brooke 1992; Pearce 1996). The story is told from a male angle which encourages the (male) reader to be voy-euristic like the elders and Susanna's choice of death rather than rape makes her subscribe to the idea that her purity, the hallmark of her husband's esteem, is more important than her life (Glancy 1995; cf. Steussy 1993: 118). What happens to Susanna challenges through stereo-typed feminine instability the notions of righ-teousness and true ethnic identity (Levine 1995).

3. Bel and the Dragon are two interwoven court tales about the falsehood of idolatry. They are typologically very similar to the stories of Dan 1–6. Some have supposed them to be historicizations of part of the Babylonian crea-tion myth *Enuma Elish* or to be interpretations of scriptural passages: Jer 51:34–5,44 (Moore 1977:122); Isa 45–6 (Nickelsburg 1981: 27). But both tales are principally polemical parodies of idolatry. In both the friendship between the king and Daniel is challenged, in Bel by Daniel mocking his friend's worship of the clay and bronze, in the Dragon by indignant Babylonians casting aspersions on the king's nationalism. In both stories there is a subtle interweaving of themes concerning life, food, and deity. In the story of Bel Daniel shows that the idol does not and cannot eat, and therefore cannot be said to be alive; his God, by contrast, is the living God. In the test it is the priests and their families who take the food offered to Bel. In the story of the Dragon Daniel shows that eating is not a sufficient criterion of divinity; the Dragon eats and dies and as a result Daniel is given to the lions for food, is himself miracu-lously fed while the lions fast, and those who have been his detractors are in the end them-selves turned into the lion's dinner. Though provided with some characteristics of historical verisimilitude, the two tales are polemics not against the Gentile world as such but against idolatry and all the religious attitudes that go with it (Collins 1993: 419). Not only is idolatry attacked (cf. Isa 44:9–20; Jer 10:1–6; Hab 2:18–19; Ps 115), but also the actual destruction of the idols is depicted (cf. *Jub* 12:12–13). Its similarity to Dan 6 suggests that the den episode may have originated as an independent tradition.

D. Date and Place of Composition. 1. About 100 BCE, the *terminus ante quem*, all three addi-tions were incorporated into the Greek text of

Daniel; determining actual dates of composition is much more difficult. Most scholars suppose that the Prayer of Azariah and the Song of the Three Jews are so typical in form and content that they are virtually impossible to date (Eissfeldt 1965: 590), but internal clues show that these psalms are post-exilic (as is the very similar Dan 9). It should be noted, however, that while the Prayer of Azariah supposes the destruction of the temple (v. 15), the Song of the Three may presuppose its existence (v. 31). If the description of the king in Prayer of Azariah 9b refers to Antiochus Epiphanes, then the Prayer may have been written during his persecution (167–164 BCE), when effectively there was no temple (v. 15) but a real need to pray for the destruction of one's enemies (v. 21). If Tob 8:5 is dependent on the Song of the Three Jews (Moore 1977:47), then the Song cannot be later than the third century BCE; at least it was composed before being translated into Greek at the end of the second century BCE.

2. Scholars are divided about the date and origin of Susanna. Those who see it as a Judaized folk-tale suggest that its outline is of Gentile origin and undatable (Eissfeldt 1965: 590). Many of those who see it as a Jewish composition have followed Brull in locating the tale as a Pharisaic illustration of the dispute between Pharisees and Sadducees at the time of Alexander Jannaeus (103–76 BCE) concerning the application of Deut 19:16–19 (cf. *m. Mak* 1:6; e.g. Kay 1913: 644). More recently a majority of scholars, while acknowledging that the story was probably translated at about 100 BCE, see the original Hebrew as belonging to any time in the Second Temple period, probably in Palestine (Collins 1993: 438).

3. There is a historical notice at the start of Bel and the Dragon (see Bel 1–2) but it does not help in dating the story. According to Herodotus the temple of Bel was plundered by Xerxes 1 (485–465 BCE). The phrase 'become a Jew' (v. 28) reflects an attitude first prevalent in the second century BCE (Collins 1993: 415–16). The tales were part of an extensive Daniel literature.

E. Canonicity. All three additions are clearly secondary, in their earliest form surviving only in Greek. In the early church Justin (d. 165) is the earliest to refer to the additions to Dan 3, Irenaeus (140–c.200) the earliest to refer to Susanna and Bel and the Dragon (Schurer 1987: 726–9). Julius Africanus (d. c.240) was the first to question the canonicity of the additions, as did Jerome, but they remained part of the Greek

Bible and the Vg. They are unattested amongst the Jews of antiquity, first appearing fully in the medieval versions of Josippon and in the *Chronicles of Jerahmeel*. Perhaps Susanna was never accepted by Jews either because it appears to contravene certain legal practices concerning witnesses (cf. *m. Sanh.* 5:1) or because it undermines the authority of elders, or because it was seen as an inept introduction to Daniel.

F. Outline.
The Prayer of Azariah and the Song of the Three Jews
  The Prayer of Azariah
    Introduction (1–2)
    Azariah's Prayer (3–22)
    Narrative (23–7)
  The Song of the Three Jews
    Introduction (28)
    Blessings (29–68)
Susanna
  Introduction (1–4)
  The Plot (5–62)
    The opportune day: in the garden (5–27)
    The next day in the house (OG synagogue) (28–64)
  Epilogue (63–4)
Bel and the Dragon
  Introduction (1–2)
  Two Idol Tales (3–42)
    Bel (3–22)
    The Dragon (23–42)

COMMENTARY

The Prayer of Azariah and the Song of the Three Jews

The Prayer of Azariah (1–22; Gk 3:24–45)

(1–2) Introduction A narrative link explains that Hananiah, Mishael, and Azariah are in the fire, singing to God; this would seem to be the introduction to the Song of the Three Jews. Theodotion has Azariah pray alone; the OG has his two companions join him. The names are Hebrew; in Dan 3 only the Babylonian Aramaic forms of their names occur: Shadrach, Meshach, and Abednego.

(3–22) Azariah's Prayer Like many of the biblical psalms the prayer of Azariah is composite, containing the blessing of God, a confession, and an intercession. Since the three are in the furnace because of their obedience to God in refusing to worship the gold idol, they pray on behalf of fellow Israelites rather than for themselves. vv. 3–5, the blessing of God: the blessing extols God for his righteousness (cf. Deut 32:4), i.e. his justice in judging the people and letting Jerusalem be destroyed. The opening 'Blessed are you, Lord' is common in contemporary prayers (1QH 13:20; 18:14; cf. 4Q414 27H2; 4Q504 6 H 20; 3:11). The address to God as 'God of our ancestors' places the prayer in the tradition of Deut (1:11, 21; 4:1, etc.) and Tob 8:5. Mention of 'the name' links this opening with the chiastic intercession (11, 20). The entire blame for what has happened rests with the sinful people, a recognition which leads naturally into confession.

vv. 6–9, the confession neatly declares how those who have broken the law have been justly handed over to the lawless rebels and an unjust king for punishment: the administrators of the punishment fit the crime. v. 9b, the descriptions may have been thought to have suited Nebuchadnezzar well, even though the prayer was not originally composed for its present context; perhaps it originally referred to Antiochus Epiphanes ('a sinful root', 1 Macc 1:10; Hartman and Di Lella 1989: 412b). For this confession cf. Dan 9:5, Ezra 9:6, Neh 9:26.

vv. 10–22, the chiastic intercession has six elements to it. These are arranged chiastically so that the poetry of the prayer has a balance which itself expresses the calm self-realization of the person praying it, whether Azariah in the fire or any other dispersion Jew. (The chiasmus is here indicated as follows: 1, 2, 3, 3', 2', 1'.) (1) God's servants and God's name (10–11). The first element in the chiasm concerns the shame the servants who worship God have become; but the poet requests God, for his name's sake, not to annul his covenant. (2) Call for mercy (12–13). The second and fifth elements in the confession are pleas for mercy. v. 12, Abraham is described as God's friend (ēgapēmenon; cf. Isa 41:8; 2 Chr 20:7; 4Q252 2:8; Jas 2:23; Apoc. Abr. 9:6; 1:5; T. Abr. A 1:6; 2:3 etc.; Philo, de Sobr. 55–6). Isaac, rather than Jacob (Isa 44: 1–2; Jer 30:10), is described as the servant (cf. Gen 24:4). The epithet 'holy one' is usually reserved for supernatural creatures, though Israel is called holy (Deut 7:6). v. 13, the promise of descendants derives from Gen 13:16, though the phraseology here is closer to Gen 22: 17 (Delcor 1971: 101); the promise of the land is omitted here. (3) No leaders or temple (14–15). The third and fourth elements in the intercession deal with leadership and the temple. This may suggest a likely origin for the prayer: perhaps it was compiled in the post-exilic period by a priestly group in

the dispersion who felt the lack of a temple. The lack of prophets would also suggest post-exilic times. Some have suggested that these lines reflect the Maccabean situation (Bennett 1913: 629; Collins 1993: 201). v. 14, Israel is diminished as of old (cf. Deut 7:7), hardly the fulfilment of the promise to Abraham. Similar pleas are made in Jer 42:2, Bar 2: 13. (3') Substitute for the temple, and God as leader (16–17). v. 16, in the literary setting in which it now stands Azariah in effect prays that he and his friends may be acceptable to God as martyrs (Koch 1987: 2.54–5). This is a development of the tradition that a contrite heart is acceptable to God in place of sacrifices (cf. Ps 40:6 (cited in Heb 10:5–6); 51: 17; 141:2; 11QPsᵃ 18:7–10 (Syr Ps 154: 17–21)). In place of the institutional leaders, God himself will be followed directly. The Greek is difficult to understand here. Theodotion reads 'to complete after you', usually taken as a literal rendering of the Hebrew phrase 'to follow you completely' (ml' 'ḥrhk, Num 4:24; Deut K36; Josh 14:8; Bennett 1913: 634). OG has literally 'to atone after you', perhaps a rendering of the Hebrew 'to atone for you' (cf. kpr b'dw: Lev 16: 11). With reference to the Aramaic (lr'w' mn qdmk 'to please you'), the OG might be seen as an attempt to render this, and Theodotion as a further inner-Greek corruption (Koch 1987: 2.55–9; Collins 1993: 202). (2') Call for mercy (18–19). The fifth element concludes as the second had begun with a plea for mercy. (1') God's servants and God's name (20–2). The sixth element rounds out the confession. It is a request that God glorify his name by putting to shame all who harm his servants.

Narrative (23–7; OG 46–50)

The narrative link, perhaps part of a Semitic original, serves to heighten the drama in the incident. To avoid contradicting Dan 3:22, the OG distinguishes between those who stoked the fire and those who threw the three Jews in. Though some consider the angel to be present to preserve the transcendence of God, it is just as possible to argue that the angel represents the saving presence of God himself. The angel of Dan 3:25 is identified as Gabriel in later Jewish tradition (b. Pesah. 118a–b). The narrative is reflected in 3 Macc 6:6.

The Song of the Three Jews (28–68; OG 51–90)

(28) **Introduction** The three praise, glorify, and bless (OG: also exalt) God.

(29–68) Blessings The body of this lengthy and elaborate hymn is in two parts, which may have existed separately (Moore 1977: 75–6), the first (29–34) a blessing addressed to God himself, the second (35–68) a call to the whole of creation to bless the Lord. It is unsuitable to let neatness of strophic division control the understanding of the blessings (Christie 1928). The refrains may suggest that the hymn had an independent life as a responsorial psalm (cf. Ps 136; also each verse of Ps 145 in 11QPs[a] 16:7–17:22 is given the refrain 'Blessed is the Lord and blessed is his name for ever and ever').

vv. 29–34, God is addressed as 'God of our ancestors' as in v. 3 (cf. Tob 8:5). God's name is blessed; he is blessed in the temple; as he sits on his throne on the cherubim (cf. 1 Sam 4:4; 2 Sam 6:2; 2 Kings 19: 15 (Isa 37: 16); Ps 80: 1; 99: 1); as he sits on the throne of his kingdom; in the firmament (cf. Gen 1:6–8; Dan 12:3) of the heaven. Each of the six ascriptions of blessing has a refrain. These give structure to the blessing. The first and the fourth are the same: in these two blessings God is described in relation to things outside heaven: the ancestors and the depths. The second and fifth both conclude with the same verb (*huperupsoun*): God's holy name and his kingdom are linked (cf. Mt 6:9–10 || Lk 11:2). The third (*huperumnētos* and *huperendoxos*) and sixth (*humnētos* and *dedoxasmenos*) are similar: the temple on earth (Delcor 1971: 104; Collins 1993: 205; rather than the heavenly temple: Bennett 1913: 635; Moore 1977: 69) is a veritable microcosm. v. 33: cf. Ps. 29: 10; *1 Clem.* 59.3.

vv. 35–68, the call to blessing, commonly known as the Benedicite from the opening word of the Latin translation, is in two parts, the first addressed to the heavens, the second to the earth. Though encompassing the whole of creation, these two spheres often occur together as witnesses to divine activity (cf. Deut 4:26; 30:19). v. 35, all the works of the Lord are addressed as a whole (Hammer 1972: 221); cf. Ps 103:20–2. vv. 36–51, blessing of heavens: there are sixteen verses in this section. v. 36, it is likely that this is to be considered as the overall address in this section as also v. 52 in the next. vv. 37–51, fifteen verses remain; it is difficult to discern their structure, but five sets of three are possible: 37–9,40–2,43–5,46–8,49,51. If so, then the following patterns emerge. A half-verse involving water features four times; as the central element in the first and last trio, and chiastically as the last element of the second trio and the first element of the fourth; in the second and

fourth trios the sun and moon and stars are balanced by the nights and days and light and darkness (cf. the similar balance in Gen 1:5 and 1:14). The refrain is the same in every verse. v. 37, the angels are called to praise God (cf. 4Q400 111–2). v. 38, for the waters above the heaven cf. Gen 1:7; Ps 148:4. vv. 39–41, the powers may be the heavenly armies (Delcor 1971:105) (cf. Ps 103 (Gk. 102): 21; 148:2). The sun, moon, and stars also praise God in Ps 148:3. v. 43, the Vg understands the winds as the spirits of God (*omnes spiritus Dei*). v. 47, night may be mentioned before day because for the psalmist the day began at sunset (cf. Gen 1:5, 8, etc.). v. 50, for snow and frost cf. Ps 148:8. vv. 52–68: blessing of earth. v. 52, the earth is addressed as a whole. vv. 52–9, four verses cover the earth's habitats (mountains (cf. Ps 148:9) and plants; seas and rivers and springs) and three their inhabitants (whales and other swimmers (cf. Ps 148:7; Gen 1:21; Ps 104:26); birds (cf. Ps 148:10); wild animals and cattle (cf. Ps 148:10)). Though echoing Ps 148, the overall order reflects Gen 1:21–6 vv. 60–8: the people of the earth are called upon to bless the Lord. vv. 60–5, first there are three couplets: all people and Israel; priests and servants of the Lord (cf. Ps 134:1); the spirits and souls of the righteous, and the holy and humble in heart. The priestly character of the list is all the more striking when comparison is made with Ps 148 in which it is kings, princes, and rulers who are addressed; there no priests are mentioned. The refrain in all these verses as in the next is the same. v. 66, second comes a verse which Hananiah, Azariah, and Mishael address to themselves. This is extended with the reason why they should praise God: he has rescued them from Hades, saved them from death, and delivered them from the fiery furnace. This verse is commonly regarded as a later interpolation into the hymn. v. 67, this general exhortation is the same as Ps 106 (Gk. 105): 1; 107 (Gk. 106): 1; 136 (Gk. 135): 1; Sir 51:12. v. 68, all those who worship the Lord are called upon to bless the God of gods (cf. Ps 136:2).

Susanna

(1–4) Introduction v. 1, the scene is set in Babylon (as in OG 5) in the household of Joachim (meaning 'the Lord will establish'). His name is the same as that of the king mentioned in Jer 29:2 and Dan 1:1. In Jewish tradition the two are identified: when Nebuchadnezzar gives King Joachim's wife permission to visit him for intercourse, she says 'I have seen something like a red lily' (*šwšnh*; menstrual blood; *Lev. Rab.* 19:6) and so he does not sleep with her. This identification may account for the association of the story with Daniel, who does not appear until v. 44. v. 2, Susanna (meaning 'lily') is introduced after her husband. Nobody else in the HB is named Susanna but the name occurs in Lk 8:3 and in some Jewish inscriptions (*CII* I. 627, 637). She is described first as the daughter of Hilkiah (meaning 'the Lord is my portion'; cf. Jer 29:3), and is thus narratively protected between husband and father, secondly as very beautiful (like Jdt 8:7–8; cf. the tree of knowledge, the object of desire, in Gen 3:6), thirdly as fearing the Lord, the sapiential expression for religious piety (cf. Prov 1:7; 10:27). In one Jewish tradition she is the wife of King Joachim and the daughter not of Hilkiah but of Shealtiel (*Chronicles of Jerahmeel*). v. 3, Susanna's parents are righteous and have taught their daughter in the law of Moses; mention of the law (not in OG) raises the expectation that some commandment may be challenged in what follows. v. 4, like the leading figures of many other Jewish stories (Job, Tobit, Judith), Joachim is very wealthy; wealth is a sign of divine favour, but in itself is no protection from the execution of the law. Perhaps alluding to Jeremiah's letter to the exiles (Jer 29:5), Joachim has a fine garden (*paradeisos*); though often referring to an ordinary garden, the juxtaposition with the keeping of the law suggests that Paradise itself (Gen 2:9) is also at stake. Joachim is also the most esteemed of all Jews.

(5–62) The Plot The plot of Susanna is in two parts (Brooke 1992; Steussy 1993): the first (5–27) takes place in the garden, the second (28–64) in Joachim's house (OG: the synagogue) which acts as a courtroom. The close narrative proximity of garden and court strongly implies that motifs from Gen 3 are being replayed.

vv. 5–27, the opportune day. The scene in the garden has two elements, the prelude (5–14) and the attempted rape (15–27), v. 5, 'That year' may indicate the year of Joachim's marriage. The elders (*presbuteroi*) are introduced as recently appointed judges; the exilic communities seem to have had some considerable autonomy. The quotation is an unknown saying, perhaps based on Jer 29:21–3 (cf. *b. Sanh.* 93a) or Zech 5:5–11. The term used for 'Lord' is *despotes* (as in OG Dan 9:8,15, 16, 17, 19). v. 6, because Joachim's house acts as a court, these elders have reason to be hanging around his property (OG: even hearing cases from

other cities). v. 7, after court business, Susanna is accustomed to walk in the garden (OG: 'in the evening'; cf. God in Gen 3:8). vv. 8–12, the elders' covetous lust (in breach of Ex 20: 17) increases and they turn away their eyes from heaven, a surrogate for God (cf. Dan 4:3! 34). The OG notes that Susanna was unaware of their lewd passions, vv. 13–14, catching each other out, they conspire together to rape Susanna. vv. 15–27, the attempted rape. There are three moments in this scene; the bath, the dilemma, and the false accusation. vv. 15–18, the bath (cf. 2 Sam 11; *Jub.* 33:1–9; *T. Reub.* 3: 11); the opportune moment comes for the rape when Susanna sends her maids to fetch oil and ointments (cf. Esth 2:3, 9; Jdt 10:3) for when she has finished bathing. When they leave they unwittingly shut the elders in the garden with Susanna. This scene is not in the OG. vv. 19–23, the dilemma; the elders threaten Susanna, putting her in a dilemma, which she instantly recognizes: to give in is to be liable for capital punishment for infidelity (Lev 20: 10; Deut 22:22), not to give in is to be liable for the same punishment but on the basis of the elders' false witness. She determines not to sin before the Lord (cf. Gen 39:9; 2 Sam 24:14). This complex psychological (and for some, erotic) moment has often been depicted by artists, notably by Rembrandt in 1647 (Gemäldegalerie, Berlin), to suggest even that Susanna is the cause of the elders' lust. vv. 24–7, the false accusation (not in the OG); a shouting battle ensues. The young woman who is sexually assaulted must cry out to attest her unwillingness (Deut 22:24, 27); the elders also shout and are listened to. When they tell their false story, Susanna's servants are ashamed.

vv. 28–64, the next day: in the house. The second part of the overall plot consists of the trial scenes either side of a dramatic interlude. The postlude sees the judgement carried out. vv. 28–41, the first trial is a perversion of justice from which there seems no escape. v. 29, the elders call for Susanna; she is mentioned first, no longer narratively protected by father and husband. v. 30, in the OG Susanna's servants are numbered at 500, and she has four children. Susanna's husband is absent from the trial: her supposed disgrace is his shame (Levine 1995: 312). vv. 31–3, Susanna is made to unveil (cf. m. *Sota* 1:5: accused beautiful women should appear veiled) so that the elders can once again feast their eyes on her great beauty; OG may imply that she was stripped (cf. Ezek

16:37–9; Hos 2:3), the elders pre-empting the judgement. None present discern their self-condemnatory leering gazes. v. 34, as witnesses the elders lay their hands on her head (Lev 24:14), thus finally managing to touch her. v. 35, Susanna looks up to heaven, which the elders had cast aside (v. 9); her appeal to a higher court has already begun. vv. 36–41, the elders give their fabricated testimony, two witnesses being sufficient (Deut 17:6); in the OG the elders refer to a stadium, a symbol of Greek perversity (1 Macc 1:15). There is no cross-examination, nor is Susanna allowed to testify. v. 41, as witnesses the elders cannot themselves pass sentence; the assembly does (cf. Jer 26:9–10; 1QS 6:8–13; 1 Cor 5:4). Adultery was a capital offence (cf. Lev 20:10), stoning the likely means of execution (cf. Deut 22:21; Jn 8:5).

vv. 42–6, before the sentence can be carried out there are two exclamations. vv. 42–4, the first cry is Susanna's prayer (in the OG Susanna's prayer precedes her sentence). She does not intercede for divine intervention on her behalf; she simply declares out loud to the eternal God (cf. Gen 21:33), who knows what is secret (cf. Deut 29:29; Sir 1:30) and what will happen (cf. 1 Enoch 9:11), that she is innocent. The story's audience is put in the privileged position of being able to assess the situation like God himself. The Lord hears the cry of the innocent and righteous one. vv. 45–6, as a result the young man Daniel is stirred into action by God himself (OG: by an angel). Mention of Daniel's youthfulness is often thought to account for why the story is put before Dan 1 in Theodotion and the OL. Daniel makes the second outburst and shouts out his refusal to participate in the execution of the assembly's sentence (cf. Mt 27:24). m. Sanh. 6:1–2 permits people to appeal against a verdict before sentence is carried out (Delcor 1971: 270). Similar sudden interventions by a youth are a common folklore motif.

vv. 47–59, the second trial takes place. vv. 47–9, it is initiated by Daniel railing against the people and urging them to return to court to consider things clearly; cf. Simeon ben Shetach's advice on careful cross-examination (m.'Abot 1:9; Brull 1877: 64). v. 50, Daniel's authority is recognized and he is invited to join the elders. vv. 51–9, Daniel undertakes the separate cross-examination of the two witnesses. With little impartiality Daniel lays into the first elder as a 'relic of wicked days', accusing him through Ex 23:7. When asked under which tree he had seen Susanna and her supposed lover he answers 'a

mastic tree' (schinos). Daniel declares the sentence: he will be cut in two (schizo). The second elder is addressed equally brusquely, this time as an off spring of Canaan (cf. Gen 9:205; Ezek 16:3; 4Q252 2:6–8). A cheap jibe is levelled against the daughters of Israel (perhaps the Samaritans for the author; Engel 1985: 126) who have given in when a daughter of Judah would not; Susanna is also called a daughter of Israel in v. 48. The second elder declares that Susanna and her supposed lover were under an oak (prinos). Daniel declares the sentence: he will be split in two (prio). Two trees also feature in the Garden of Eden story (Gen 2:17; 3:22) as does the sword (Gen 3:24; cf. Num 22:31).

vv. 60–2, postlude. v. 60, the assembly (sunagoge) blesses God for saving those who hope in him. v. 61, the two elders receive the punishment they had intended for Susanna (cf. Deut 19:16–19). That this law was a matter of dispute between Pharisees and Sadducees in the first century BCE (m. Mak. 1:6; y. Sanh. 6:3:23e) has been used to suggest a likely setting for the story (Brull 1877) which agrees with the Pharisee position. v. 62, the law of Moses which Susanna had been taught (3) is thus upheld and innocent blood spared.

(63–4) Epilogue The conclusion is a neat inclusio. As at the opening so at the close of the story Susanna is listed between her two male protectors; this time Hilkiah is mentioned first. Though exposed when initially brought to trial (29), she is now protected and redomesticated. Though she has in fact threateningly exposed the weakness of the community's judiciary and shown the community's patriarchal institutions to be flawed, nothing shameful was found in her (cf. Deut 24:1) and she is now neatly put back in her place and the reader is reminded that there are some righteous, law-abiding men around. Whereas vv. 1–4 have described Joachim's reputation, the story closes with a description of Daniel's. In the OG none of the story's participants are mentioned in the conclusion; rather all pious young men are declared 'beloved of Jacob' because of their knowledge and understanding (cf. Isa 11:2–4).

Bel and the Dragon

(1–2) Introduction v. 1, only the OG carries the title: 'From the prophecy of Habakkuk, son of Joshua, of the tribe of Levi'. This identification seems to depend on 33–9. No mention is made in Habakkuk of his tribe; in Lives of the Prophets 12:1 he is of the tribe of Simeon. The historical scene is set by mentioning the death of As-tyarges, king of Media (585–550 BCE) and the succession of Cyrus the Persian (cf. Dan 6:28; 10:1), who conquered Babylon in 539 BCE; nei-ther king is named in the OG. v. 2, Daniel is the companion (*sumbiotēs*) of the king and the most honoured of all his friends (cf. Dan 2:48); in the OG he is also described as a priest and son of Abal (Sabaan was father of Daniel according to Epiphanius, *Adv. Haer.* 55.3). The full introduction of Daniel suggests that the reader has not met him before and therefore that Bel and the Dragon were originally independent Daniel tales.

(3–42) Two Idol Tales Both stories have a similar structure of three parts in which a friend-ship is put to the test but emerges strengthened. The two tales are interwoven in as much as the second test (Daniel in the lions' den) relates to both idols (28) and only at the end of the chapter does the king confess Daniel's God.

vv. 3–22, Bel. vv. 3–7, friendship challenged. v. 3, the Babylonian god is introduced as an idol. Bel ('Lord'; short form of Baal) is Bel-Marduk, head of the Babylonian pantheon (cf. Isa 46:1; Jer 50:2; Let Jer 41). Enormous quantities are offered to Bel: twelve bushels (65.5 litres) of flour, forty (OG: 4) sheep, six measures of wine (OG: oil). vv. 4–5, the king worships Bel, but Daniel does not worship handmade idols (cf. Isa 46:6; *Sib. Or.* 3:606, 618) because he worships the living God (cf. Josh 3:10; Dan 6:26; OG: Lord God), the creator and ruler (cf. Gen 1:26) of heaven and earth (cf. Gen 1:1; Jer 10:11). vv. 6–7, the king claims rhetorically that Bel is a living god because he eats and drinks, but Daniel laughs impertinently (also 19) and states simply that the idol is a mere moulded statue (cf. Isa 44:14–17; Let Jer 4; Wis 13:10). vv. 8–18, the test. vv. 8–9, the test is set up and the sentence on those in the wrong agreed. For phrasing similar to Daniel's agreement cf. Luke 1:38. vv. 10–11, the enormous amount of food is consumed by sev-enty priests and their families. vv. 12–13, OG does not mention the pact again nor the hidden entrance. vv. 14–15, the king alone witnesses the laying of ashes by Daniel's servants. The temple doors are closed and sealed. vv. 16–18, in the morning, the king is assured that the seals are unbroken. When the temple doors are open he sees the empty table and exclaims that Bel is great (cf. 41). vv. 19–22, the temporary outcome. vv. 19–20, Daniel dares to laugh at the king's credulity and points out the footprints in the ashes. vv. 21–2, enraged, the king arrests the priests and their families for eating the food

and executes them (OG: hands them over to Daniel). The king does not himself declare Bel a fraud or make a confession of the greatness of Daniel's God, but hands Bel over to Daniel who according to the story destroys the idol and its temple (OG: the king destroys Bel). Herodotus (1:183) has Xerxes I (486–465 BCE) destroy the temple and statue.

vv. 23–42, the dragon. The Greek *drakon* most probably refers to a serpent. The story of the dragon repeats the motifs of its previous com-panion tale. vv. 23–30, friendship challenged. vv. 23–4, the king challenges Daniel to recog-nize the dragon as a living god, for surely it is alive. No Babylonian cult of a live serpent is known from written sources, though there is some iconographic evidence; serpents play var-ious cultic roles elsewhere (cf. Num 21:9; 2 Kings 18:4; cf. Kneph in Egypt; Asclepius in Greece). vv. 25–6, Daniel responds with a con-fession that the Lord his God is the living God, and with a request that he may be permitted to kill the dragon. The king grants the request. v. 27, Daniel bakes a cake of pitch, fat, and hair to feed to the dragon and explodes the idea of the dragon's divinity. The similarity to the opening up of Tiamat by Marduk is often noted, but no other motifs of that myth have influenced the story (Collins 1993: 414). *Gen. Rab.* 68 has the cake made realistically lethal by lacing it full of nails which perforate the dragon's intestines. vv. 28–30, the Babylonians are enraged and taunt the king with becoming a Jew (cf. 2 Macc 9:17). They demand Daniel. The king weakly yields to their demands. vv. 31–9, the test. vv. 31–2, with mob rule Daniel is thrown into the lions' den. This is the second time such a fate has befallen him (cf. Dan 6:16–24), where seven lions, fed on a daily ration of two humans and two sheep, are now given nothing so that they might devour Daniel. The punishment, being destroyed by an animal, fits the crime (Koch 1987: 2.195). OG notes that this means that Daniel would not even have a burial place (cf. Tob 1:17). vv. 33–9, Habakkuk is transported by his hair (cf. Ezek 8:3) from Judea with a stew he had just made (cf. Gen 25:29). It has been suggested that Habakkuk is linked to the meal through the Akkadian *ham-bakuku*, a plant used in soups (Delcor 1971: 288). The *Lives of the Prophets* 12:5–8 knows of his story. The angel transports Habakkuk 'with the swiftness of the wind' which *Gen. Rab.* represents as 'power of his holy spirit' (cf. 1 Kings 18:12; 2 Kings 2:16). Daniel thanks God for remembering him and eats the meal. Habakkuk is returned to Judea.

The whole incident is possibly a narrative interpretation of Ps 91:11–13 (Nickelsburg 1984: 40). vv. 40–2, the final outcome. v. 40, on the seventh day the king comes to mourn Daniel but finds him alive. v. 41, the king confesses Daniel's God: 'You are great' (cf. Ps 86:10; Jdt 16:13; 4Q365 6 ii 3), 'there is no other besides you' (cf. Isa 45:18; 46:9). v. 42, those who had thought themselves far from mealy-mouthed are thrown into the den and instantly eaten by seven very hungry lions.

REFERENCES

Baumgartner, W. (1926), 'Susanna—Die Geschichte einer Legende', ARW 24: 259–80.

—— (1929), 'Der Wiese Knabe und die des Ehebruchs beschuldigte Frau', ARW 27: 187–8.

Bennett, W. H. (1913), 'The Prayer of Azariah and the Song of the Three Children', APOT, I. 625–46.

Brooke, G. J. (1992), 'Susanna and Paradise Regained', in G. J. Brooke (ed.), Women in the Biblical Tradition, Studies in Women and Religion, 31 (Lewiston, N.Y.: Edwin Mellen), 92–111.

Brüll, N. (1877), 'Das apokryphische Susanna Buch', JJGL 3: 1–69.

Christie, E. B. (1928), 'The Strophic Arrangement of the Benedicite', JBL 47: 188–93.

Collins, J. J. (1993), Daniel, Hermeneia (Minneapolis: Fortress).

Delcor, M. (1971), Le Livre de Daniel, SB (Paris: J. Gabalda).

Eissfeldt, O. (1965), The Old Testament: An Introduction (Oxford: Blackwell).

Engel, H. (1985), Die Susanna-Erzählung: Einleitung, Übersetzung und Kommentar zum Septuaginta-Text und zur Theodotion-Bearbeitung, OBO 61 (Güttingen: Vandenhoeck & Ruprecht).

Gaster, M. (1895; 1896), 'The Unknown Aramaic Original of Theodotion's Additions to the Book of Daniel', PSBA 16: 280–90, 312–17; 17: 75–94.

Geissen, A. (1968), Der Septuaginta-Text des Buches Daniel: Kap. 5–12, Zusammen mit Susanna, Bel et Draco, sowie Esther Kap. 1, 1a–2, 15, nach dem Kölner Teil des Papyrus 967, Papyrologische Texte und Abhandlungen, 5 (Bonn: Habelt).

Glancy, J. A. (1995), 'The Accused: Susanna and her Readers', in A. Brenner (ed.), A Feminist Companion to Esther, Judith and Susanna, FCB 7 (Sheffield: Sheffield Academic Press), 288–302.

Hammer, R. J. (1972), 'The Apocryphal Additions to Daniel', The Shorter Books of the Apocrypha, CBC (Cambridge: Cambridge University Press), 210–41.

Hartman, L. F., and Di Lella, A. A. (1989), 'Daniel', NJBC, 406–20.

Kay, D. M. (1913), 'Susanna', APOT, I. 647–51.

Koch, K. (1987), Deuterokanonische Zusätze zum Danielbuch: Entstehung und Textgeschichte, AOAT 38/1–2 (Neukirchen-Vluyn: Neukirchener Verlag).

Kuhl, C. (1940), Die drei Männer im Feuer, BZAW 55 (Giessen: Töpelmann).

LaCoque, A. (1990), The Feminine Unconventional: Four Subversive Figures in Israel's Tradition, OBT (Minneapolis: Fortress).

Levine, A.-J. (1995), '"Hemmed in on Every Side": Jews and Women in the Book of Susanna', in A. Brenner (ed.), A Feminist Companion to Esther, Judith and Susanna, FCB 7 (Sheffield: Sheffield Academic Press), 303–23.

Milik, J. T. (1981), 'Daniel et Susannea Qumrân', in J. Doré, P. Grelot, and M. Carrez (eds.), De la Tôrah au Messie: Mélanges Henri Cazelles (Paris: Desclée), 337–59.

Moore, C. A. (1977), Daniel, Esther and Jeremiah: The Additions, AB 44 (Garden City, N.Y.: Doubleday).

—— (1992), 'Daniel, Additions to', ABD, II. 18–28.

Nickelsburg, G. W. E. (1981), Jewish Literature Between the Bible and the Mishnah (Philadelphia: Fortress).

—— (1984), 'Stories of Biblical and Early Post-Biblical Times', and 'The Bible Rewritten and Expanded', in M. E. Stone (ed.), Jewish Writings of the Second Temple Period, CRINT 2/2 (Assen: van Gorcum), 33–87, 89–156.

Pearce, S. J. K. (1996), 'Echoes of Eden in the Old Greek of Susanna', Feminist Theology 11: 11–31.

Pervo, R. I. (1991), 'Aseneth and Her Sisters: Women in Jewish Narrative and in the Greek Novels', in A.-J. Levine (ed.), 'Women Like This': New Perspectives on Jewish Women in the Greco-Roman World, SBLEJL 1 (Atlanta: Scholars Press), 145–60.

Schmitt, A. (1966), Stammt der sogenannte '9'-Text bei Daniel wirklich von Theodotion?, MSU 9 (Göttingen: Vandenhoeck & Ruprecht).

Schürer, E. (1987), The History of the Jewish People in the Age of Jesus Christ, III. pt.2, rev. and ed. G. Vermes, F. Millar, and M. Goodman (Edinburgh: T. & T. Clark), 722–30.

Steussy, M. J. (1993), Gardens in Babylon: Narrative and Faith in the Greek Legends of Daniel, SBLDS 141 (Atlanta: Scholars Press).

Wills, L. M. (1990), The Jew in the Court of the Foreign King: Ancient Jewish Court Legends, HDR 26 (Minneapolis: Fortress).

Ziegler, J. (1954), Susanna, Daniel, Bel et Draco, Septuaginta Vetus Testamentum Graecum, 16/2 (Göttingen: Vandenhoeck & Ruprecht).

9. 1 Maccabees

U. RAPPAPORT

INTRODUCTION

A. Text and Language. The textual tradition of 1 Maccabees is in general similar to that of the other books included in the Septuagint. 1 Maccabees is also known in other versions of the Holy Scriptures, such as the Syriac and Latin, which derive from the Greek version, which itself is a translation of a lost Hebrew original. This is evident from its style, which reveals Hebrew idiom (cf. *ABD* iv. 439–40). The original was probably known up to the 3rd and 4th centuries CE, but has not survived even in fragmentary form.

B. Author, Date, and Title. 1. The author of 1 Maccabees is anonymous, and whatever may be surmised about him comes from the book itself. He seems to be attached to the Hasmonean dynasty, both ideologically and personally, and to have some connection with the ruling circles.

2. Most scholars date 1 Maccabees to around 100 BCE. The principal disagreement is whether it was written in the last years of John Hyrcanus or in the days of Alexander Jannaeus. According to Momigliano (1976) and S. Schwartz (1991), 1 Maccabees was written in the beginning of Hyrcanus' rule, before 129 BCE, but it seems to me that the evidence is somewhat too narrow and that the last years of Hyrcanus' rule fit better (and see 16:23–4).

3. 1 Maccabees is named thus according to the Septuagint's textual tradition; obviously it has nothing to do with the original title, which some scholars think can be reconstructed from a reference in Eusebius, *Hist. Eccl.* 6.25. 1–2, which goes back to Origen (first half of the 3rd cent. CE). There it is cited under the Hebrew name of the book as *Sarbethsabanaiel.* Among the acute proposals to decipher it we will cite the following: 'Book (*sēper*) of the house of the ruler (*śar*) of the sons of God'; 'Book of the dynasty (*bêt*) of God's resisters', where God's resisters should mean 'resisters on behalf of God's cause' (Goldstein, 1975; 1976: 15–17).

C. The Author's Views. 1. Jews and non-Jews: the author takes for granted a sharp dichotomy between Jew and Gentile. This may be rooted in a traditional view, similar to the ideology expressed in the books of Ezra and Nehemiah (5th cent. BCE), but strengthened by the religious persecution under Antiochus IV and the Maccabean revolt. However, though stressing repeatedly the hatred of the nations round about, he is proud of the success of the Jews in forging friendly relations and alliances and in being honoured by various nations and rulers. The incongruency in this attitude towards the non-Jewish world is typical of Hasmonean politics in general—a mixture of national separation (related to religious abhorrence of paganism) with a pragmatic approach to politics.

2. God and the Jews: as in biblical historiography, the author postulates that God directs history according to his will. Yet, though history is directed by God, he does not intervene directly in human affairs, in contrast to some instances in the Bible (cf. e.g. Josh 10:11–14; 2 Kings 19:35) and 2 Maccabees, where miracles abound.

3. God's intervention is through human beings, in whom he instils courage or cowardice, wisdom or arrogance and stupidity. Success and failure are manifestations of God's will and plan, but this does not efface the human values of courage, devotion, wisdom, cunning, etc. It is similar to some elements of the 'fourth philosophy' described by Josephus, which postulated that God helps those who take action themselves (*Ant.* 18 § 5). Some scholars see these and other views, such as the absence of reference to an afterlife (cf. 9:7–10), as Sadducean. The present writer refrains from such a label, on the grounds that our knowledge of Sadduceanism is extremely poor and because it is not necessary to assume that the expression of every idea should be defined on sectarian lines.

4. The role of Mattathias's family: the author's political views may justify his description as a court historian. His book serves Hasmonean propaganda well, especially for John Hyrcanus. He attributes to Mattathias's family a divine role to deliver Israel (5:62), thus giving legitimacy to the Hasmonean dynasty in face of the traditional right both of the house of David to kingship and of the house of Zadok to the high-priesthood. In addition to this general message in favour of the house of Mattathias, there is a clear preference for Simon, the father of Hyrcanus and founder of the dynasty, among the sons of Mattathias. To him the author allocates the first and major role in Mattathias's testament. (2:49–64), where it is said that 'he [Simeon] shall be your father' (v. 65).

D. Historiography. 1. Style and Composition: 1 Maccabees is composed in a style and with a vocabulary similar to biblical historiography. It has compositional biblical elements such as poetic passages (including some prayers) interwoven with the narrative, a testament (2:49–70), documents (more than are usually found in the Bible, but see the documents in Ezra and the unhistorical correspondence of Hiram and Solomon, in 1 Kings 5:17–23), and speeches. The Bible is behind many passages in 1 Maccabees, either as explicit citations (e.g. 7:16–17), or implicitly (e.g. 5:48), or as historical exemplary precedents (e.g. 2:49–64). See Dimant (1988). In addition 1 Maccabees adopts biblical geographic and ethnic vocabulary, though most of it is anachronistic. The adoption of names such as Moab, Ammon, Philistines, Canaan, or sentences reminiscent of Joshua's conquest of Canaan, are used not only as literary conventions, but also serve an ideology that compares or assimilates Judas's wars to those of yore. The attachment of 1 Maccabees to the biblical heritage is expressed also by the citation of biblical exempla and precedents, which abound (e.g. 2:51–60). The author's views about God's interventions with humans is also similar to that of biblical historiography (see 1 Macc C.2). Though rooted in this tradition, 1 Maccabees is also a creation of its author's time. His treatment of non-Jewish history is much more ample than in the Bible, although he is Judeocentric as well. In this respect he resembles more the apocalyptic attitude of Daniel than that of the rest of biblical historiography, though the two books belong to completely different genres.

2. The author of 1 Maccabees utilized various sources in his book.

(1) Documents: the documentation in 1 Maccabees begins with the treaty between Rome and Judea, and goes on well into Simon's days. The documents from an earlier period cited in 2 Macc 11 apparently came from another source, probably unknown to the author of 1 Maccabees. It is probable that 1 Maccabees' documentary source was a Hasmonean archive in which the earliest document was the Roman-Judean treaty. This archive may be identical to that of the temple, which from the time of Jonathan's appointment as high priest was under Hasmonean administration, and may have been kept in the temple's treasury (14:4–9).

(2) Oral information: living close to Hasmonean circles—probably a member of court—a generation or less after the most recent events reported in his book, the author of 1 Maccabees was able to collect information from participants or eyewitnesses of various events, and to integrate it into his composition. Some of the oral testimonies could be also hearsay about previous events kept by leading families.

(3) Written sources: from where the author got his knowledge, especially about Seleucid history, is hard to tell. Was it oral information from informants at home in Hellenistic history (such as the Hasmonean diplomats)? Or had he at his disposal a written survey, in either Hebrew or Greek? We cannot tell. Yet, like his contemporaries the author(s) of Dan 7–12, he was interested enough in non-Jewish history to obtain the information he shared with his readers. Some of it is almost common knowledge (1:1–9), and some more specific (Trypho's rise to power; Demetrius II's fall into captivity, etc.).

(4) Parallel sources: for most of the period this book covers, it is the sole extant source. Josephus (*Ant.* 12 § 241–13 § 214) depends almost solely on it, up to 1 Macc 13:42. The main source to corroborate that part of the narrative covering Judas's revolt from its beginning to his last victory over Nicanor (approx. 165 to Adar 162 BCE) is 2 Maccabees. Apart from this we have only a little information about Judea at this time from pagan sources (see Stern 1974–1984; Diodorus, no. 63 (34–35.1.3–4); Timagenes, no. 80; Pompeius Trogus, via Justinus, no. 137 (Justinus, 36. 3.8); Tacitus, no. 281 (*Historiae*, 5.8.2–3), and scanty Talmudic references (see 1 Macc 7:5).

(5) Chronology: the dates given in 1 Maccabees, mostly according to the Seleucid era, raise certain problems because of the difficulty of fitting them all into one system, since the Seleucid calendar did not begin on the same date throughout the Empire (Bickerman, 1968: 71). There is no consensus about the system(s) used in 1 Maccabees, or about the use of any system in a consistent way. For a review of the problem and earlier literature on it, see Grabbe (1991).

(6) Creative writing: current and earlier *Quellenforschung*, though vital for any historiographical enquiry, can divert attention from the writers and historians themselves. 1 Maccabees is a work by a talented historian who composed a historical narrative out of various ingredients, not all of which we can identify. His narrative is coherent, sometimes chronological, sometimes thematic (cf. ch. 5, on wars with the neighbouring peoples). It is supported by documents (most of them authentic) and highlighted by the author's interventions or passages woven into his narrative. Some of them are poetic

passages, either written by him or based on suitable sources. His history is human, in the sense that it is activated by human actions, virtues or vices, wise or unwise, and God's share in it is either a *post factum* conclusion of what has already happened, or is shown by the motivation of the actors on the scene.

The author's talents served a political cause, as explained above (1 Macc c.3). Needless to say it diminishes the veracity of his narrative, along with his other apologetic aims and his Judeo-centric attitude. Nevertheless he succeeded in producing a historical narrative of high quality, although because the original language was lost, it can only partially be appreciated by us.

E. Outline. 1 Maccabees opens with Alexander the Great (356–323 BCE) and concludes with the murder of Simon (134 BCE). The first *c.*150 years are dealt with in only nine verses (1:1–9), so that the major parts are:

Introduction: From Alexander to the Revolt (1:1–64)
   Acts of Antiochus IV (1:10–64)
The Revolt Under Mattathias (2:1–70)
The Exploits of Judas Maccabaeus (3:1–9:22)
   The First Battles of Judas Maccabaeus (3:1–4:35)
   The Rededication of the Temple (4:36–61)
   The Wars with the Surrounding Peoples (ch. 5)
   More Wars of Judas (ch. 6–7)
   Rome and the Treaty between Rome and the
      Jews (ch. 8)
   The Last Stand of Judas (9:1–22)
Jonathan's exploits (9:23–12:53)
   The First Years of Jonathan (9:23–10:17)
   Jonathan High Priest and Ruler of Judea
      (10:18–12:53)
Simon's Rule (13:1–16:24)
   On the various proposed divisions of 1 Macc
   see Martola (1984) and Williams (1999).

COMMENTARY

Introduction: From Alexander to the Revolt (1:1–64)

(1:1–10) 1 Maccabees opens with a short introductory passage about Alexander the Great, whose exploits are concisely and negatively described (vv. 1–4). The author's conception of history is very similar here to Dan 11:2–4. Both saw Alexander's conquest of the East as the inception of a new destructive era in the history of mankind, which culminates in the religious persecution of the Jewish cult. This approach depicts the Hellenistic regime in general as an ungodly phenomenon, and is in line with, and

probably influenced by, the general Eastern (Egyptian, Babylonian, Iranian, and Indian) anti-Hellenic world-view (Rappaport 1993). v. 1, 'Kittim,' a generic word for peoples who arrived from the west. It derived from the name of the city Kition in Cyprus. Here it designates Greece. 'Darius' is Darius III, the last Achaemenid king of Persia (336–331 BCE) who was defeated by Alexander. vv. 2–3, on Alexander's conquests there is ample literature (See *ABD* I. 146–50). In general terms Alexander is the prototype of Antiochus IV (Dan 11:36–7 and see on v. 10). vv. 5–6, generally speaking this description is correct, though Alexander's empire was neither divided by him nor according to his will. Alexander did reign for about twelve years (336–323 BCE). vv. 8–9, the author is mainly interested in Antiochus IV, and refers to the intermediate period (323–175 BCE) in an extremely concise way. Nevertheless he stresses that Alexander's successors 'caused many evils on the earth'. That is, the chain of wickedness is continuous from Alexander to Antiochus IV. v. 10, Antiochus IV is linked here directly with Alexander, though there was no blood relationship between them. This linkage is expressed also in Daniel's visions of the horns (esp. 7:7–8; but also 8:8–9). This conception of Hellenistic history is eastern and based on anti-Hellenic, moralistic, religious, social, and cultural views of the changes that occurred in the Near East with the fall of the Persian empire. 'Hostage in Rome', Antiochus IV was sent by his father Antiochus III as a hostage to Rome after the Roman victory in the battle of Magnesia (190 BCE). He was replaced in 176 BCE by his nephew, Demetrius, and gained the kingship in 175 after his brother, Seleucus IV, was murdered.

The year 137, according to the Seleucid era, is approximately 175 BCE.

(1:11–15) The author does not tell us how the Hellenistic party in Judea came into being. He condenses it all around a 'manifesto' and certain acts ascribed to them. He also avoids mentioning any of their leaders by name. Almost all we know about the Hellenizers and their leaders comes from 2 Macc 3–5. v. 11, 'renegades', Greek *paranomoi*, lit. 'those who do not abide by the law (Torah)', a common designation in 1 Maccabees for the Hellenizers. It may also reflect such nouns as *pārîzîm*, which Dan 11:14 uses to describe them. 'Many' (Heb. *rabbîm*) does not signify the majority but an undefined big number.

'Let us go ... upon us' sounds like their manifesto, strictly opposed to common Jewish self-perception. v. 13, 'went to the king', this was not a single act by the Hellenizers, but a repetitive one. We are told in 2 Macc 4:7 that Jason met with Antiochus IV soon after his accession and obtained from him the high priesthood and permission to establish a gymnasium and an ephebeion and to enrol the men of Jerusalem as Antiocheans (2 Macc 4:9). This permission is understood by many scholars as sanction for a Greek *polis*, called Antioch-in-Jerusalem (to distinguish it from other Antiochs). See Bickerman (1937), developed by Tcherikover (1959: 161), and accepted by others (Hengel 1974; le Rider 1965: 409–11). v. 13, the concise narrative does not define in clear terms the constitutional changes that took place in Judea, but observation of the ordinances of the Gentiles gives an indication. v. 14, 'gymnasium', there is no doubt that the foundation of the *polis* Antioch-in-Jerusalem caused a most shocking intrusion into the traditional Jewish lifestyle. Especially abhorrent to Jewish sensitivities the performance naked of sporting activities that took place there. v. 15, as a result of exercising in the nude there came about the phenomenon of uncircumcision, which necessitates surgical intervention. This was an extreme act of repudiation of allegiance to Judaism, circumcision being considered the primary sign of being a Jew (Gen 17:11).

(**1:16–19**) Antiochus IV's invasion of Egypt is a famous event in Hellenistic history. Here it is merely a hinge on which the author suspends Antiochus' invasion and plunder of the Jerusalem temple (vv. 20–8). For Antiochus' expeditions to Egypt see Rappaport (1980: 66–8 (Heb.)).

(**1:20–8**) It seems that Antiochus entered Jerusalem three times: the first time on an inspection tour, when he was received favourably by the populace and Jason (in 172 BCE, 2 Macc 4:22); the second time after his first invasion of Egypt (in 169 BCE); and the third time after his second invasion of Egypt, from where he was repulsed by a Roman delegation (in 168 BCE, see 2 Macc 5). The second visit to Jerusalem (169 BCE) after the first invasion of Egypt is the one described here; see Rappaport (1980). The absence of any mention of the Hellenized high priests Jason and Menelaus, who play a prominent role throughout the account in 2 Maccabees, should be noticed. This is intentional, as a kind of *damnatio memoriae*, to erase the names of the wicked from Jewish memory. v. 21, the entrance of Antiochus IV into the temple was a breach of Jewish law, since

Gentiles were not allowed inside. Cf. 3 Macc 1:10–2:24, and 2 Macc3. vv. 21–3, Antiochus stripped the temple of its more sacred and valuable objects, mainly those of gold and silver. It was known, as were many other temples, for its riches gathered from obligatory taxes, donations, official contributions, and private deposits. 'Hidden treasures', in addition to the various expensive vessels, there were in the temple other deposits kept in secret places for security. These were either discovered, or divulged by priestly treasurers co-operating with Menelaus' party. The author does not give any reason for this confiscation. It may have had the co-operation of the Hellenized high priest Menelaus, who was perhaps in arrears in paying his tributes, or it may have been caused by the avarice of the king. The common explanation that Antiochus was short of money because of the huge indemnities (12,000 talents) his kingdom still had to pay to Rome is not valid, since this debt was already paid. See le Rider (1993: 49–67). vv. 24–8 are the first poetic passage, but such passages abound in 1 Maccabees. This literary device is not rare in biblical historiography. Naturally it was intended to bear to the reader a certain message.

(**1:29–40**) This passage deals with measures taken by the Seleucid government to crush Jewish opposition to Menelaus' regime, prior to the religious persecutions. 2 Macc 5 supplies more details for the period of approximately two years that elapsed between Antiochus' second visit to Jerusalem (169 BCE) and the religious persecution (167 BCE). These include another visit of the king to Jerusalem (a third one, see above) and the appointment of Philip the Phrygian (2 Macc 5:22) as governor of Jerusalem. v. 29, 'collector of tribute' may reflect a Hebrew phrase in the original lost version of 1 Maccabees: *sar hammissîm*, may have been wrongly translated into Greek as *archōn phorologias* (officer for tribute collection) rather than 'officer of the Mysians', i.e. of soldiers or mercenaries from Mysia, a region in Asia Minor. The name of this officer is given in 2 Macc 5:24, Apollonius. For the rate of taxes in Judea see 1 Macc 10:29–30. v. 30: the fact that the Seleucid officer entered Jerusalem 'deceitfully' is one of the arguments for the supposition that the city was in the hands of a pre-Maccabean opposition to Menelaus. 2 Macc. 5:25 specifies that Apollonius took advantage of the sabbath to enter the city. See Tcherikover (1959: 188–9). vv. 31–2, Apollonius' behaviour in Jerusalem strengthens the impression that he took the city from the rebels' hands, not from Menelaus and his supporters. These rebels are not mentioned here probably because the pre-Maccabean period is in general abridged by the author, and he endeavours to concentrate on the Maccabean family, and avoid any distraction which might put them off-centre.

v. 33, 'citadel', two questions concern the building of the citadel (*akra*) in Jerusalem: what was its function, and where exactly was it located? In addition to its function in suppressing the Jewish opposition to the regime, it seems that it was (or became) a stronghold for the Hellenizers. Its location depends on the location of the 'city of David' (as understood in the Second Temple period) and on various archaeological-topographical considerations. See Bar-Kochva (1989: 445–65). v. 34, 'renegades' may signify the Hellenizers, in addition to the Seleucid military force. v. 35: see 1 Macc 9:52 about storage of food in fortresses for the purpose of subduing the population. vv. 36–40, in this poetic passage, we learn about the flight of residents from Jerusalem (v. 38), on which cf. 2 Macc 5:27 and 2:1.

(**1:41–53**) The religious persecution ordered by Antiochus IV is an unprecedented historical event. The main difficulty in explaining the king's policy is that polytheists were generally tolerant in religious matters, and we have no real analogy elsewhere to the events in Judea. Moreover, what we encounter in Judea is not only the prohibition of a certain cult, but a violent compulsion to transgress its religious laws. There is no consensus at present on an explanation of this problem, yet two suggestions which may contribute to our understanding of it have been proposed. One is that the initiative for the persecution came from Menelaus' circle, either as an ideological repressive act (Bickerman, 1937; 1979) or otherwise. The second is that a revolt in Judea, led presumably by religious leaders, preceded the persecution, which was aimed to subdue it (Tcherikover 1959: 197). For more expanded discussion and bibliography see *ABD* iv. 437–9. vv. 41–3, no such ordinance by Antiochus IV is preserved, and no evidence of interference in religious matters is known elsewhere in the Seleucid empire. 'All the Gentiles' is didactic, and in line with the message of the book, see 1 Macc 2: 19–22. According to Hellenistic royal procedures an order by Antiochus IV must have been issued, though it is not preserved. Otherwise Antiochus III's letter (*Ant.* 12 §§ 138–44), which confirmed the ancestral laws of Judea, would be

binding. To invalidate it, there must have been some enactment by Antiochus IV, the contents of which may be reflected in the following verses. vv. 44–50, the compulsion that the Jews must transgress their customs, not merely refrain from the observance of them, has no precedents. vv. 51–3, cf. Esth 1:22; 3:13; 8:11; 9:21, 31.

(**1:54–61**) The 'fifteenth day of Chislev', that is ten days before the profanation of the altar (v. 59). 'A desolating sacrilege' (Gk. *bdelygma hermōseōs*), evidently represents *siqqûs mĕšōmēm* in the lost Hebrew original version (cf. Dan 11:31) but what it was materially is unclear: a pagan altar placed on the temple's altar (cf. v. 59); an effigy of Zeus or of the king; or a sacred stone (*bêt-'ēl*; Phoenician, *bettilu*). See Bickerman (1979: ch. 4); Rowley (1953); Hengel (1974: 294–5); Millar (1993: 12–15) (who doubts Bickerman's supposition). vv. 56–7, books of the law, i.e. Torah scrolls. It seems to be the first known historical occurrence of the burning of books. It also shows the centrality of the Torah in Jewish religion, which was well understood by the persecutors. v. 59, 'twenty-fifth day', of the month of Chislev. Some commentators suggest that it was a special day (Abel 1949; Dancy 1954 suggest the birthday of Antiochus), but this view has no basis here or in 2 Macc 6:7, nor elsewhere. vv. 60–1, this horrible event was chosen by the author as an example of the cruelty of the persecutors. It is mentioned also in 2 Macc 6:10, where other events, probably not all of them historical, are told (cf. 2 Macc 6–7).

(**1:62–4**) v. 62, as many were misled by the Hellenizers (1 Macc 1:10), so many stood firm in Jewish tradition (cf. Dan 11:33–4). A decisive question in the confrontation within Jewish society was which side would be more persuasive and turn the many into a majority. v. 63, this is the first time that a case of martyrdom is mentioned in 1 Maccabees but see another at 2:29–38. Dan 11:33–4; 12:2–3 and 2 Macc (esp. ch. 7) are even more concerned with this theme. The Jewish martyrs, especially the 'Maccabean' martyrs of 2 Macc 7 became models of martyrdom for Christianity (Bickerman 1951: 63–84).

The Revolt under Mattathias (2:1–70)

(**2:1–14**) When the religious persecutions became extremely severe, Mattathias and his family appeared on the stage. The dynastic inclination of 1 Maccabees is clear. It wholeheartedly supports the Hasmoneans, and especially Simon's branch. Former rebels are not mentioned and martyrs are appreciated (1:63), but their example was not followed up (below). 'Joarib', the first priestly division among the twenty-four divisions of priests (see 1 Chr 24:7). 'Jerusalem', 'Modein', it seems that the opulent family of Mattathias was well-established both in Jerusalem and in Modein, where their landed property was. (For doubt about their relation to Jerusalem see Goldstein (1976).) Modein was a village in the region of Lydda, which belonged to the eparchy of Samaria (see 1 Macc 10:30). vv. 2–5, we do not have an explanation for the nicknames of Mattathias's sons. For Judas's nickname, Maccabeus, several proposals have been made, such as that its origin was the Hebrew word *makkebet* (hammer), but though attractive, this view is baseless. vv. 6–14, a lament in poetic form on the dreadful lot of the holy city.

(2:15–18) The decrees of Antiochus are about to be forced on the inhabitants of Modein, beyond the frontier of Judea, at the outskirts of the territories populated by Jews. The persecution is executed by the Seleucid government, through its military forces. Co-operation from the local population, either voluntary or compulsory, is expected. The government encountered the first active opposition to its policy in Modein from Mattathias and his sons. vv. 17–18, the speech of the king's officers is evidently a rhetorical piece which stresses the obedience of all others (Jews and Gentiles) to the king's decrees.

(2:19–28) vv. 19–22, Mattathias's speech is totally opposed to the king's men's speech. Its central point is unconditional faith in God. vv. 23–6, Mattathias's speech could have been terminated by a martyrological conclusion, but at this point the parting of the ways between martyrdom and zealotry comes out clearly. Mattathias prevents by force the breach of the Torah, being ready not only to die but to kill for it. At this moment the Maccabean revolt breaks out. v. 26, 'Phinehas', the priest who acted bravely and decisively when the people of Israel sinned in the plain of Moab (Num 25:8–13) was the model of zealotry. vv. 27–8, the first step of the rebels was to leave the populated area and find shelter in the wilderness. Commentators have assumed that it was in the Judean desert that Mattathias and his followers sought refuge (as with Jonathan and Simon after Judas's death (1 Macc 9:33). Recently it has been suggested

that at this stage of the revolt the Maccabees' base was in the desert of Samaria, not far from the thickly populated Jewish area of southern Samaria (see J. Schwartz and Spanier 1991).

(2:29–41) Mattathias's position was taken up against those who co-operated with the persecutors or acquiesced to them. Here the case of martyrdom is dealt with, and though the author's attitude is sympathetic to the martyrs, martyrdom is shown to be no alternative to Mattathias's zealotry. v. 29, the ideological affiliation of those who went to the desert is unknown. Proposals identifying them with the Hasideans, with the Essenes (proto-Essenes), or with the *maskîlîm* of Daniel, though possible, cannot be substantiated. 'Wilderness', see J. Schwartz and Spanier (1991). v. 32, 'sabbath', that Jews refrained from fighting on the sabbath was known to pagans and sometimes ridiculed by them (see Josephus, *Ant.* 12 § 6; *CA* I. 209–10), as well as used by them to their advantage (the above reference; 2 Macc 5:25). v. 37, 'heaven and earth testify for us', note that the meaning of the Greek for 'martyr' is 'witness'. No mention is made of after life, which is an important motif in 2 Maccabees. vv. 39–40, Mattathias and his supporters are sympathetic to those who died in the caves, but disagree with their ideology. They fear for their own lives and are not expecting an eschatological deliverance or resurrection of the dead (cf. Dan 12: 2–3). This signifies a major difference between the Hasmoneans and various contemporary nascent Jewish sects. v. 41, the decision by Mattathias's party, to take arms and fight even on the sabbath, raised voluminous discussion. On what authority was this decision based? What was the preceding situation? How could Jewish mercenaries (and there were many) serve in imperial armies if they did not fight on the sabbath? Was this an ad hoc decision or a permanent and valid legal one? How did it fit with Jewish law and especially with more recent *hǎlākâ*? See Bar-Kochva (1989: 474 93); Goodman and Holladay (1986: esp. 165–71); Johns (1963).

(2:42–8) The first military act on the part of Mattathias was in Modein (2:1). A second stage in the revolt was when it spread over Judaea (but outside Jerusalem). v. 42, we learn about a growth in the number of Mattathias's supporters. An organized group joined him—the Hasideans (lit. 'the pious'). Scholars differ about their identity. Are they related to those who died in the caves, having changed their attitude to the revolt as a consequence of this horrible event? Or do they belong to the *maskīlim* in Daniel, who decided to appeal to arms at the call of Mattathias? Or are they a sect of their own, and if so, when did they come into being? How are they related to the later sects—Pharisees, Sadducees, and Essenes/Qumranites? See Davies (1977). D. R. Schwartz (1994: 7–18) prefers a variant reading of this phrase, 'a company of Jews' instead of 'a company of Hasideans', which is the current reading. See also 1 Macc 7:12–18. 'Mighty warriors' fits both readings: if we take it with Hasideans, it fits the conception of 'sect' (not a very suitable term in any case) or 'order' with some military flavour (cf. some Dead Sea scrolls, esp. *War Scroll)*; if with Jews, it signifies the military prowess of those who joined Mattathias. v. 43, 'fugitives', those who lost their property and domicile, and were an important source of recruitment for the rebels. Cf. *J.W.* 2. 588. v. 46, 'circumcised all the uncircumcised', the intention, in line with the destruction of altars (v. 45) is to undo what was done by the persecutors; 'forcibly', might mean against the orders of the Seleucid government, or, in the case of Hellenized families, without their consent. The first explanation is preferable.

(**2:49–70**) The following testament of Mattathias in poetic rhyme brings to mind Jacob's blessing of his sons in Gen 49. It exposes the author's views and his attitude towards the ruling Hasmonean family, and the ideology and atmosphere at the royal court. vv. 51–60, this section is a series of illustrious examples from biblical history relevant to the actual situation and recommended by Mattathias to his sons. Phinehas, a model of zealotry, is given a special highlight ('our ancestor [father]'; and see v. 26 above); David's inheritance of kingship is interpreted by commentators as either an indication that the book was written before Hyrcanus I's sons put the crown on their heads (i.e. not after 103–104 BCE), or as a criticism of Hasmonean royalty. With Elijah the word 'zeal' (or its derivatives) is repeated again, and the last are the 'saved martyrs' whose acts are told in the contemporary book of Daniel. See Dimant (1988: 394–5). v. 65, 'Simeon ... he shall be your father', this is explicit propaganda for the Hasmonean dynasty, which indeed was founded by Simeon. To strengthen its legitimacy it is related here to the testament of Mattathias, the ancestor of all the family. v. 66, Judas's military talent and task

is stressed here, but in line with the message of v. 65. Though Judas was the leader of the revolt till he fell on the battlefield (165–160 BCE), he is ranked here as second to Simeon. His appointment as leader of the revolt was surely because of his military talent and/or experience, about which we know nothing. v. 70, 146 ES is 166 BCE; 'tomb of his ancestors at Modein' demonstrates clearly that the Hasmonean family had its roots in Modein, though it does not mean that they could not also have been involved in the political life in Jerusalem (see on v. 1).

The First Battles of Judas Maccabaeus (3:1–4:35)

(**3:1–9**) The acts of Judas begin with a poetic encomium (vv. 3–9) about Judas, the great hero of the revolt. v. 2, the author stresses here, and elsewhere, the unanimity of all the brothers. It may have been a message for his own time. vv. 3–9, the encomium precedes the acts of Judas. Cf. the encomium for Simon (14:4–15) which precedes his appointment by the 'great assembly'. Both serve as a poetic introduction to what follows.

(**3:10–12**) This is the first military encounter of Judas that we are told about. Formerly, under Mattathias's command, the rebels made surprise attacks on civilian settlements (2:45–8 above). And cf. 2 Macc 8:6–7. v. 10, 'Apollonius', unknown otherwise, but evidently a commander, probably the governor (*stratēgos* according to Josephus, *Ant.* 8 § 287) of Samaria, an important city in the centre of Mt. Ephraim, formerly the capital of Israel (the northern kingdom) and of the Assyrian and Persian province of Samaria. A military settlement was founded there in Alexander the Great's time, and the city served as a principal strategic base under the Ptolemies and the Seleucids (see Rappaport 1995a: 283–4). v. 11, 'killed him', killing the commander of the enemy obviously gave a great advantage to the opposing army. Judas endeavoured to achieve it, since it could compensate for his weaker army and demoralize the enemy (see also 1 Macc 7:43). v. 12, 'spoils', an important source of arms for the ill-equipped rebel army.

(**3:13–26**) The encounter with Seron is the second battle of Judas. The author of 2 Maccabees ignores the first two battles of Judas and relates his battles in detail only from the battle of Emmaus (below) onwards. This may indicate that the encounters with Apollonius and Seron were guerrilla clashes not full-fledged battles. v. 13, Seron is not known elsewhere. (See Bar-Kochva 1989: 133.) v. 14, 'I will make a name', a biblical idiom, which signifies Seron's arrogance and strengthens the effect of his defeat at the end. v. 16, 'Beth-horon', the slope of Beth-horon could have turned into a trap for armies invading Judea (the Romans suffered a severe defeat there in 66 CE. See Josephus, *J.W.* 2 §§ 546–50). vv. 17–22, according to 1 Maccabees the result of a battle is from God, and so the few can overcome the many. This idea is different from 2 Maccabees where God intervenes in human actions and changes the course of events. In 1 Maccabees it is only through the courage of the Jewish fighters that God instils in their hearts, that he may tip the scales of battle. See also 1 Macc C.2. Actually it does not seem that the rebels were numerically inferior to the Seleucid forces which were sent against them. They also had professional military officers and soldiers in their ranks, though they were inferior in arms, at least in the initial stages of the revolt. This view was recently put forth by Bar-Kochva (1989). v. 24, 'land of the Philistines', a biblical name for the southern coastal plain of the land of Israel.

(**3:27–31**) Here we have a typical Judeocentric view of Seleucid history. Antiochus IV's plan to reconquer the Eastern satrapies is explained as an offshoot of Judas's victories. Nevertheless some objectively correct points are made, such as the lavishness of Antiochus, emphasized perhaps by the advance payment of a year's salary to the army.

(**3:32–7**) v. 32, Lysias was regent for Antiochus V, son of Antiochus IV, both in the latter's lifetime (165–164 BCE) and after his death, until Demetrius I conquered the kingdom (162 BCE). v. 33, 'his son Antiochus' was about 7 years old, according to Appian (11.46), or ii according to Eusebius (*Chronica*, 1.253). Appian seems preferable on this point. See Houghton and le Rider (1985: 27 n. 30). v. 34, the division of the army into two halves is probable, as well as the giving of instructions to Lysias. v. 36, 'settle aliens' is reminiscent of Dan 11:39. The repressive measure of settling foreigners on land confiscated from the local population is well-known under Hellenistic rule. It is less clear whether it was implemented in Judea or mentioned only as a potential threat against the Jews. v. 37, 147 ES is 165 BCE; 'upper provinces' the Seleucid provinces east of the Euphrates.

(**3:38–41**) v. 38, the appointment of three commanders of the expedition against Judas is misleading. Ptolemy the son of Dorymenes was the governor of Coele-Syria and Phoenicia and supported an anti-Jewish policy (cf. 2 Macc 4:45; 6:8) but did not personally command the forces sent against Judas. According to 2 Macc 8:8–9, the one who called for military support was Philip, the governor of Jerusalem. Lysias is not mentioned there at all, and may be introduced by the author of 1 Maccabees to increase the importance of the battle. Nicanor was son of Patroclus, according to 2 Macc 8:9. Gorgias was the military expert of the two (see 2 Macc 8:9). v. 39, the numbers of military forces are in many cases exaggerated. The greater the difference between Seleucid and Jewish forces the greater was the victory of the Jews, or their defeat was better explained (see Bar-Kochva 1989: ch. 2). v. 40, Emmaus is a strategic location at one of the main entrances into the Judean mountains. v. 41, merchants accompanied armies, and naturally were eager to gain from slave trade. 'Forces from Syria', probably in the Hebrew original text it was Edom, which was read wrongly by the translator as Aram, the only difference in Hebrew being the letter *resh* instead of *daleth*, which are very similar in form. If so, we are informed here about additional local forces, presumably the militia of the Hellenistic towns of Idumea and the coastal plain.

(**3:42–60**) This relatively long passage deals with the preparations for battle on the Jewish side, in opposition to those in the Seleucid camp. It is probably in part historical, in part embellished. v. 46, 'Mizpah', for historical reminiscences cf. 1 Sam 7:5–7. Here we see the historical consciousness of the Jewish rebels (beside the historical-biblical awareness of the author), and the use of precedents for the moral preparation of the rebel army for battle. v. 47, the fasting in 1 Sam 7:6 is accompanied here by common mourning customs, mentioned often in the Bible and elsewhere (e.g. 1 Macc 2:14). v. 48, this consulting of the Torah replaces the older way of consulting God, either through a prophet, or a priest who possessed the Urim and Thummim. But at this time there were neither signs nor a prophet (cf. Ps 74:9). v. 49, these are acts which should have been performed in the temple had it not been desecrated, and may be understood as a performance in place of the usual ceremonies, in an attempt to convince the deity to respond to believers who manifest their inability to perform their religious duties properly. v. 54, 'trumpets' (hăsôsĕrôt), were used in warfare (see Num 10:9–10 and the *War Scroll* (1QM ii. 15–iii. 11). v. 55, that there would be organization of the rebel army at this stage is very probable, since Judas is turned from guerrilla to more regular warfare and has to manœuvre greater forces; cf. 2 Macc 8:21–2. The division of an army into units of tens, fifties, etc. is common in the Bible. v. 56, Judas is following Gideon (Judg 7:3, according to Deut 20:5–9). vv. 58–60, this short speech of Judas, hardly historical, sums up well the main targets of the revolt and the belief in heavenly succour.

(**4:1–5**) vv. 1–2, Gorgias adopted new tactics, to avoid the failures of his predecessors, Apollonius and Seron. From a base on the outskirts of the Judean hills, he went with a select column to surprise his opponents, thus taking from them the initiative in choosing the time and place of battle. His audacious step was accompanied by 'intelligence' service, rendered to him by men from the Akra, who knew the Judean terrain. v. 3, Gorgias's audacity was forestalled by Judas. He quickly left his camp, which Gorgias was going to attack by surprise, and moved towards the Syrian base at Emmaus. vv. 4–5, the deserted Jewish camp misled Gorgias into thinking that the rebels fled in panic, and he turned to chase them in the hills. Josephus adds that Judas left unextinguished fires to strengthen this impression (*Ant.* 12 § 306). This information is probably a conjecture of Josephus, based on military tactical textbooks, which he knew well.

(**4:6–11**) v. 6, 'At daybreak', the appearance of Judas's army was a surprise, as it was thought to be fleeing before Gorgias's storm troops; 'armour', the shortage of arms was endemic in the rebels' camp in the first stages of the revolt (see 3:12). The lack of arms also increases the impact of the ensuing victory. v. 7, the Seleucid army, like other Hellenistic armies, fortified their camps, even when in use for short periods. vv. 8–11, Judas's harangue before his men repeats the author's ideas about God's power in battle (see 1 Macc C.2).

(**4:12–18**) v. 13, 'trumpets', see 1 Macc 3:54. About Jamnia see 1 Macc 5:58. vv. 17–18, Judas disciplined his army, not an easy task with guerrilla fighters. Yet as only half of his military plan was achieved, it was necessary in order to achieve a final victory.

(**4:19–25**) Assuming the details are historical, we have here an illuminating case of the psychological defeat of the Syrian army. Arriving at their camp after a futile night chase after Judas and his men, they saw before them a burnt camp and the rebels drawn up for battle; thus they retreated, morale broken, v. 23, the details of the plunder are embellished, but, strangely, no arms are mentioned. v. 24, hymns, cf. Ps 106:1; 118:1; 136:1.

(**4:26–9**) The defeat at Emmaus finally brought home to the Syrian government the seriousness of the revolt in Judea. The royal army itself now became involved in the war. v. 28, the numbers here are obviously out of all proportion. At least half the royal Seleucid army went with Antiochus IV to the eastern front, and even from the rest Lysias was obliged to leave some behind. 'Next year', 164 BCE. v. 29, Beth-zur was a strategic point on the border between Judea and Idumea. It lost its importance when John Hyrcanus conquered Idumea.

(**4:30–3**) In this poetic passage, as elsewhere, the author invokes historical precedents in the prayer he puts in Judas's mouth. The examples cited here are David's victory over Goliath (1 Sam 1:17), and Jonathan's victory over the Philistines (1 Sam 14:1–16).

(**4:34–5**) The description of this battle is extremely schematic, untrustworthy, and hardly comprehensible. 2 Macc 11:1–16 is more detailed and embellished but also untrustworthy. The only conclusion that can be safely drawn is that Lysias's invasion of Judea was blocked. He probably did not persist in his efforts because of news of the death of Antiochus IV. According to 2 Macc 11:14, Lysias's withdrawal was accompanied by a truce.

The Rededication of the Temple (4:36–61)

(**4:36–41**) Soon after Lysias's retreat the rebels took over the temple (164 BCE). v. 37, Mount Zion is the Temple Mount. v. 38, 'desolate', this description refers mainly to the results of negligence. The profanation of the altar refers to what happened at the beginning of the religious persecution, not to any ongoing pagan performances at the altar; 'bushes sprung up', various scholars (esp. Bickerman 1979: 72) have interpreted this as a sign of some oriental syncretistic cult, to which a sacred grove was necessary. Yet it seems to indicate simply the negligence and deficient maintenance of the temple's court. v. 41, it is strange that military activity is mentioned only at this stage. It seems therefore that no fighting was involved when Judas took control of the temple.

(4:42–51) Here a detailed description is given about the replacement of the stuff of the temple and of the polluted objects in it. v. 44, 'altar of burnt-offering', the most sacred object in the temple. Dan 12:11 counts the duration of the persecution according to the number of days when there was no daily sacrifice. v. 46, 'until a prophet should come', cf. 1 Macc 3:48 and 14:41.

(4:52–9) A new festival was established which is not mentioned in the Bible (there was one other, Purim). It took some effort (see 2 Macc 1) before it was accepted by Jews everywhere. It was incorporated into the Jewish calendar by the rabbis, although in Talmudic sources it is related to divine miracles and the Hasmoneans are hardly mentioned. (On the attitude of the sages and Pharisees towards the Hasmoneans, see D. R. Schwartz 1992: 44–56.)

vv. 52–3, the renewal of the daily sacrifice at the end of 164 BCE (Chislev is December), three years after the desecration of the temple (v. 54), and half a year earlier than the 3½ years envisaged in Dan 9:27. v. 54, 'songs', music had an important place in the worship at the temple (cf. 2 Chr 7:4). v. 56, 'eight days', the dedication of Solomon's temple was prolonged also for eight days (1 Kings 8:65; 2 Chr 7:9), as was Hezekiah's sanctification of the temple (2 Chr 29:17). In 2 Macc 10:6 the dedication of the temple is compared to Sukkot (Booths), which lasts eight days.

(4:60–1) Judas did not neglect military preparations. He fortified the temple against, probably, the forces in the Akra, but it served him well also when Lysias invaded Judea again. Beth-zur was fortified in view of local skirmishes and possible invasion by Lysias, who has already traversed the same route.

The Wars with the Surrounding Peoples (ch. 5)

(5:1–8) The chronology of Judas's war against the Gentile neighbours of Judea is not clear, because they are arranged thematically. vv. 1–2, 'Gentiles all around', meaning those who lived in the land of Israel. The language and attitude of the author are influenced by the biblical account of the conquest of Canaan by Joshua ben Nun. See Schwartz (1991: 16–38). The Gentiles becoming angry against the Jews

because of their success cannot be a historical explanation, but it fits well with the author's idea that the Gentiles drew satisfaction from the desecration of the temple (see 4:45, 58). Now that the situation was reversed, they became frustrated and angry. As opposed to the other wars against the Gentiles, there is no mention here of Jews living among the Idumeans being attacked, and it seems that Judas was tackling marauders (see v. 4). v. 3, 'descendants of Esau', a biblical, anachronistic designation for the Idumeans. 'Akrabattene', despite textual difficulties, usually located in eastern Idumea, south-west of the Dead Sea. For a different location see Goldstein (1976: 294). v. 4, 'Baean', a nomadic tribe, probably located in Transjordan (cf. Num 32: 3), which took advantage of the insecurity of the region for marauding purposes. v. 6, 'crossed over', this shows that the events here are not arranged chronologically, as both the Baeans and the Ammonites were east of the river (i.e. Jordan). Timothy, probably a Seleucid official or commander, is mentioned also in v. 11. vv. 7–8, there is no mention of the Jews here either, though it is to be supposed that Judas came to their succour, both according to v. 2 and to the more detailed account below.

(5:9–13) Here the author returns to the theme of v. 1, the Jews being attacked by their neighbours. v. 9, Gilead is normally the area between the rivers Yarmuk and Arnon, in which Ammon is also included. The location of Dathema is unknown, but probably connected to the 'land of Tob' (see v. 13). It may be that this and other strongholds in which the Jews were seeking shelter were locations which they held as soldiers, or descendants of soldiers, who had served already under the Ptolemies. Cf. v. 13. vv. 10–13, the appeal for help of the Gileadite Jews is in the form of a letter. Though incomplete in its present form, there is nothing in the letter to render it unauthentic. It may be a fabrication, to dramatize the story, or an abridged letter (without the opening and concluding phrases), or a formulation of known events into epistolary form. Timothy is probably the same person who is mentioned above. If so it creates a link between the two passages vv. 1–8 and vv. 10–13. 'land of Tob', probably the land of Tobiah, where the palace of Hyrcanus the Tobiad was, in Arak el-Emir. Some scholars locate it in the north of Transjordan, but see Gera (1990: esp. 27–9). There was there a military colony (Gk. *katoikia*), headed by the Tobiad family, and composed, at least in considerable part, of Jewish soldiers. The Tobiad family, or dynasty, is known at least from the time of Nehemiah. See *ABD*, s.v., vi. 585.

(5:14–19) v. 14: note the dramatization of the story and see 1 Kings 1:42; Job 1:16–18. The attacks on the Jews in Gilead and Galilee seem to be simultaneous, as told here, otherwise there is no point in the division of the Jewish forces (v. 17). v. 15, 'Ptolemais and Tyre and Sidon', these three Phoenician cities were among the first oriental cities in the east to be Hellenized and to become *poleis*. They had territories (Gk. *chōra*) in Galilee, and may have been worried by the success of the Jewish revolt, and its possible repercussions on the local population in Galilee, mostly Semitic and partly Jewish. About Ptolemais see also 1 Macc 10:1, 39, 57, and 2 Macc 13:25–6. 'Galilee of the Gentiles', for this expression see Isa 8:23. In the present context it may simply be a repetition of the three cities mentioned before. See *ABD* ii. 879, 895. v. 17, as usual in 1 Maccabees, Simon, the founder of the dynasty, is described as second in command to Judas, and almost equal to him. Yet Jonathan succeeded Judas as leader of the revolt, and we may assume that he, not Simon, was second in command to Judas at that time. v. 18, 'Joseph . . . Azariah', this is one of the few places where 1 Maccabees raises the curtain and allow us a glimpse of other people who shared the leadership of the revolt. Nothing is known about these two men, except what is told below (vv. 55–62), which is not sympathetic. v. 19, leaving some reserve forces behind accords well with the evidence in the approximately contemporaneous Dead Sea *Temple Scroll* (col. 58).

(5:20–2) Though Simon had the smaller army (3,000 as against the 8,000 of Judas), his exploits are told first. The information about the fighting is very scanty, and the pursuit of the enemy 'to the gate of Ptolemais' may be more poetic than real. The number of the enemy's casualties equals that of Simon's soldiers (3,000) and may be fictitious. (For such equal numbers see v. 34.)

(5:23) There were Jews in Galilee at that time, but it is difficult to tell how many. There are unanswered questions: did Simon rescue all the Galilean Jews, or only those who were at greater risk? How many Jews were then left, and what was their position in Galilee until its conquest

by the Hasmoneans about forty years later? Arbatta is identified by many commentators as Arbel in Galilee, yet other proposals compete, and see 1 Macc 9:2.

(5:24–7) v. 24, here again Judas crosses the Jordan, as in v. 6. Maybe it is a double recounting of the expedition? v. 25, the Nabateans were a tribal organization, mentioned already in the time of Alexander of Macedon. They are thought to have been an Arab people, though the epigraphic evidence about them is mostly in Aramaic. (See *ABD* s.v., iv. 1053.) At this period they were friendly towards the Jews because of their common interest in weakening the Seleucid empire. Later they turned into bitter enemies of Judea.

(5:28–34) v. 29, 'of Dathema', a conjecture not found in the MSS, after v. 9. v. 30, the fact that the Jews found shelter in a stronghold outside the city of Bozrah may point to their military task in the region; if they were installed in a fortress which was guarded by them, this will have made it possible for them to hold out against their enemies even though they were outnumbered. v. 34, for the meaning of Maccabeus see 1 Macc 2:2–5. Here the author wishes to tell us that Judas's fame was such that his nickname alone could strike panic among his enemies. 'Eight thousand', here again the number of the enemy casualties equals that of Judas's soldiers.

(5:35–9) v. 37, mention of Raphon helps to place the battlefield in northern Gilead. Raphon became a *polis* in the Roman period, and belonged to the Decapolis. v. 39, 'Arabs', we are not told to which tribe those Arabs belonged. Arabic nomads of Transjordan should not be viewed as enemies of the Jews, but as opportunistically co-operative with whomever they can gain from.

(5:40–4) The description of the battle is influenced by 1 Sam 14:9. v. 43, the city, also known as Ashtaroth Carnaim, was famous because of its temple to Ashtaroth (Astarte). v. 44, the burning of the sacred precincts at Carnaim is the first act of destruction of pagan temples recorded in 1 Maccabees, but not the last (see 1 Macc 5:68; 10:83–4; *Ant.* 12 § 364). Had it been a lone event, it could have been explained as an act of retaliation, but because it was repeated it should be considered as a policy of purification of the holy land from idolatry.

(5:45–51) v. 45 poses the same problems as v. 23. It is unclear how it is to be interpreted: as a proof of Jewish population in Transjordan, or as an evacuation of its Jewish minority. v. 46, Ephron is east of the Jordan on the road to Beth-shan. Mentioned in Polybius (5.70), under the name Gephron (note the interchangeability of the Semitic 'ayin into G in the case of 'Aza = Gaza), it did not seem to exist very long, as was the case with some other contemporary settlements in Israel, such as Tel-anafa and Hargar-izim. v. 47, we are not told why the inhabitants of Ephron were inimical towards the Jews. It may be guessed that it was a strategic fortified place, maybe with a Seleucid garrison. Anyhow, this passage is modelled after Num 20:14–21. See Dimant (1988: 407). v. 51, the cruel treatment of the people of Ephron recalls the ruling of Deut 20:10–18.

(5:52–4) v. 52, 'the large plain', the valley of Jezreel, of which Beth-shan is in the eastern part. 'Beth-shan' is a transcription of the Semitic name of the city, which in Greek was called Scythopolis. In contrast, the city of Acco is called by its Greek name Ptolemais. Beth-shan received the passing Jews in a friendly manner according to 2 Macc 12:30 unlike Ephron, mentioned above. Probably 1 Maccabees intentionally refrained from recording an act of friendship by Gentiles. v. 53:2, Macc 12:31 tells that the refugees arrived at Jerusalem on the festival of Pentecost.

(5:55–64) This passage is a clear indication of the dynastic inclinations of 1 Maccabees. The disobedience to Judas's instructions is harshly criticized by the author, and he puts forth clearly his conviction that the deliverance of Israel was deposited with Mattathias's family (v. 62). v. 56, for the two commanders see 1 Macc 5:18. They may have had ambitions of their own which competed with those of Mattathias's sons. v. 57, the motive attributed to Joseph and Azariah is to 'make a name'. This motive of name or honour is repeated often in 1 Maccabees (see 1 Macc 10:10). Surely had they been successful they could have created competition for the Hasmoneans, but since they failed, they serve as a proof of the divine election of the Hasmoneans. v. 58, Jamnia (see also 1 Macc 4:15) was an important base for the Seleucid forces confronting rebellious Judea. A Seleucid inscription, dated to Antiochus V's reign, was found there. It mentions some co-operation of the Sidonians there with the king, presumably

in relation to the rebellion in Judea. See Isaac (1991). vv. 61–2, the dynastic propaganda sounds very loud here.

(5:65–8) The setting of this passage is bizarre. The chapter was nicely concluded with an encomium for Judas and his brothers (vv. 63–4), so the return to the battles against the Idumeans is odd, having been treated at the beginning of the chapter. v. 65, 'descendants of Esau', cf. v. 3 above. Hebron is about 30 km. south of Jerusalem, and in this period was in the heart of Idumea. v. 66, 'land of the Philistines', again a biblical phrase. Marisa was on the western edge of Idumea. It was a Hellenized town, with a Hellenized population of Idumeans and Phoenicians, and some immigrants from the Greek cultural sphere (see Peters and Thiersch 1905; Oren and Rappaport 1984; Kloner, Regev, and Rappaport 1992). The battles carried on by Judas are clearly no more than retaliatory border skirmishes. v. 67, the incident referred to here is enigmatic. It may have been a case of disobedience, which is criticized. v. 68, the idolatrous worship was destroyed in Azotus (the old Philistine city of Ashdod); cf. the case of Carnaim (v. 44).

More Wars of Judas (chs. 6–7)

(6:1–4) On Antiochus' expedition to the east ('the upper provinces') see 1 Macc 3:27–37. For his attempt on the Temple of Nanaia (Artemis) see Polybius, 31. 9; Appian, 11. 6. v. 1, the author is mistaken: Elymais was not a city but a country, bordering south-west Persia. 'Persia' is a common anachronism for Parthia, the rising power, which finally swallowed most of the Seleucid provinces east of the Euphrates. v. 2, Alexander is a famous figure also in Jewish legends, but no story about treasures he left in Elymais is mentioned elsewhere. v. 3, 'the city', other sources speak about a temple. v. 4, 'Babylon' seems to be wrong, because other sources tell that Antiochus went to Tabae (should probably be Gabae, modern Isfahan).

(6:5–7) This report was, needless to say, written by the author, and represents his view of the situation. A report to the king would not refer to the 'abomination'. v. 5, 'someone', probably Menelaus himself. For Menelaus' visit to the king see 2 Macc 11:29,32, and Habicht (1976:11,14). The author refrains from mentioning either Jason or Menelaus anywhere by name; cf. 1 Macc 1:11–15. v. 7, 'abomination', i.e. the 'desolating sacrilege' (šiqqûs mĕšômēm) of Dan 11:31, and see 1 Macc 1:54.

(6:8–13) The story of Antiochus IV's death follows a common pattern in Jewish literature. The wicked person becomes arrogant (afflicted by *hybris*, to use a Gk. term), is punished, repents, and then is either pardoned or condemned. To the first group belong the stories in Dan 1–6, and the story of Heliodorus in 2 Macc 3. This belongs to the second group, as does the much more elaborate story of Antiochus' death in 2 Macc 9.

(6:14–17) The appointment by Antiochus IV of Philip as regent, either while in full command of his decisions or not, caused turmoil in the Seleucid empire. To this year (148 ES is 165/4 BCE) are dated two royal letters, the first by Antiochus IV, the other by Lysias (cited in 2 Macc 11:27–33; 16–21 respectively). These events alleviated the Seleucid pressure on the rebels. v. 17, Eupator means 'of a good father', the good father being Antiochus IV.

(6:18–27) The siege of the Akra shows that the rebels became stronger in the course of the war. This first attempt was repeated under Jonathan. Capture was achieved finally by Simon (see 1 Macc 13:50–3). v. 20, 'siege-towers', the use of these and siege-engines shows a professional military knowledge among Judas's followers. It brings to mind the proposals of various scholars that some groups or individuals who had prior military training joined the rebellion. These could have been Jewish veterans of Hellenistic armies, soldiers of the Tobiad troops, or Jewish volunteers from Ptolemaic Egypt. v. 21, in the Akra lived Jewish Hellenizers, probably citizens of the *polis* Antioch-in-Jerusalem, and soldiers of the Seleucid garrison. vv. 22–7, the speech before the king, attributed to the delegation from the Akra, is clearly the work of the author of 1 Maccabees who had in mind both earlier and later events related to the Hasmonean dynasty. v. 24, 'our inheritances' may refer to the allotments (Heb. *naḥălôt*) which were confiscated from the rebels and given to the Hellenizers (see 1 Macc 7:6). v. 27, cf. EZRA 4:12–16.

(6:28–31) The decision to renew the war in Judea and the preparations for the expedition are attributed to the 7-year-old king (see 1 Macc 3:33), but were almost certainly made by Lysias. The numbers of the soldiers are incredible. v. 30, 'elephants', shortly after this war the elephants were destroyed by a Roman delegation (162 BCE), because their use was contrary to the treaty of Apameia concluded between the

Romans and Antiochus III, after his defeat at Magnesia in 190 BCE. v. 31, Beth-zur—this time Lysias invades Judea from the south also, probably because he had at his rear the friendly population of the coastal region. The siege of Beth-zur is a new phase in the war, when Judas tries to fight neither in the open field nor by surprise, but from a strategic fortress which he held.

(6:32–41) v. 32, the first achievement of Lysias seems to be that Judas was forced to lift the siege on the Akra. v. 33, Bethzechariah is on the way from Beth-zur to Jerusalem. v. 34, 'juice of grapes', wine was used to excite elephants before battle. Here we should accept the textual proposal 'saturated' instead of 'offered' (the elephants) (the two words are similar in Heb.). vv. 35–7, the exotic appearance of elephants on the battlefield caused the author to give them the central place in his description, which though dramatic is, generally speaking, plausible. vv. 39–42, the description is very embellished but may reflect an authentic impression made by the Seleucid troops. v. 39, 'shields of gold' is an obvious exaggeration; 'ablaze', since the disposition of the army took place in the morning (v. 33) the blazing of the arms may have been more striking because of the sun shining from the east, that is from in front of them. v. 42, 'the clanking of their arms' might have been an intentional noise meant to strike fear in the enemy. Gera (1996) thinks the description is not realistic but influenced by military scenes in Greek literature. Bar-Kochva (1998) opposes this opinion, and thinks that the battle's description is credible.

(6:42–7) The main theme of this passage is the heroic deed of Eleazar, Judas's brother. His self-sacrifice is in line with Maccabean tactics, trying to kill the enemy's commander (cf. 1 Macc 3:11–12 and 8:40). The failure of Eleazar to tip the scales of the battle is due not to a lack of courage, but to a wrong guess he made about the whereabouts of the king. Eleazar's death serves as an excuse for Judas's withdrawal. v. 44, 'everlasting name', a typical phrase in 1 Maccabees, similar to 'honour' (Gk. *timē* or *doxa*), to describe the reward for heroic death or deeds. Cf. 1 Macc 9:7–10.

(6:48–54) After his victory at Beth-zechariah Lysias turned to besiege Judas and his men in the Temple Mount. He also forced the Jewish garrison of Beth-zur to surrender, an act which the author explains as a result of shortage of food. Judas's position very quickly becomes desperate. Some scholars stress the fact that Judas's name is not mentioned explicitly in this passage, and doubt the adherence of the besieged to his supporters. This is one of the arguments for the opinion that there were other rebel groups at this stage of the revolt which are ignored by 1 Macc. v. 49, 'sabbatical year', every seventh year the cultivation of the fields was interrupted according to biblical law (Ex 23:11; Lev 25:3–7). This sabbatical year explains the weakness of Jewish opposition in Beth-zur and the great difficulties in defending Mt. Zion. It seems quite probable indeed that letting the fields lie fallow at the time of war, when many of the farmers were serving in the rebels' ranks, could cause a situation more severe than in a normal sabbatical year, yet it seems that it is also used by the author as an excuse to explain the dire situation of the rebels. v. 52, 'engines of war', their use by the Jews in the siege testifies again to professional elements in Judas's camp (cf. v. 20). v. 53, here an explanation is brought forth as to why the usual preparations for a sabbatical year, such as the storage of provisions in advance, did not help. Yet at the same time it shows the altruistic and brotherly attitude of Judas towards the refugees.

(6:55–63) On the verge of destruction Judas was saved by a turn in the political situation in Syria. Philip appeared in Antioch as the new regent, appointed by Antiochus IV on his deathbed (v. 15). This forced Lysias to return immediately to the capital. The author puts Lysias's decision into a speech attributed to him (vv. 57–9). Judas accepted Lysias's conditions, and Lysias left to attend to more urgent business which awaited him at home. v. 57, 'our food supply is scant', it is very probable that the sabbatical year also made difficult the supply of the besieging army, because it would usually live off the country in which it was camping. Yet at the same time the author tries to depict the Syrian army as being forced to evacuate Judea. v. 60, what were the conditions of this peace? If we follow Habicht's (1976) interpretation, that the letter of Antiochus V preceded the surrender of the rebels at this juncture, then it seems that the rebels' sole benefit was that they were let out with immunity from Mt. Zion. v. 61, according to the most simple reading, the Jews left the Temple Mount as a result of the peace conditions. This is strengthened by the fact that later on the temple was not in the rebels' hands. See 1

Macc 7:33. v. 62, it is hard to say if indeed the king broke his word, or if the author describes the destruction of the wall as a breach of the agreement with the rebels. It seems to me that, as in Beth-zur, the besieged got a free leave from the place and nothing else. By attributing to the king this act the author tries to save the prestige of Judas, who was forced into an almost unconditional surrender. Compare this to the similar blame laid on Antiochus VII when John Hyrcanus surrendered to him (Ant. 13 § 247). v. 63, although the king is the subject here, it was Lysias who got the upper hand against Philip—but not for long.

(7:1–5) Demetrius was the son of Seleucus IV (187–175 BCE). When his father was murdered he was young and was kept as a hostage in Rome, while his uncle Antiochus IV (175–164 BCE), took advantage of the situation and usurped the throne. After the death of Antiochus IV Demetrius tried to get permission from the Roman government to return to Syria to try to regain his ancestral throne. As the Romans were reluctant to let him go, he escaped from Rome. When he arrived in Syria he easily dismissed Lysias and his protégé the boy-king Antiochus V, and took over the government. In the first years of his rule, and despite Roman enmity, he succeeded in suppressing various rebellions in the empire, among them the one in Judea. v. 1, 151 ES is 162/1 BCE; 'a town by the sea' is Tripolis (cf. 2 Macc 14:1).

(7:5–7) 1 Maccabees does not differentiate any specific groups among the Hellenizers. Yet there were various groups within the Jewish nobility that differed not solely on religious questions, but also on political issues (such as Ptolemaic versus Seleucid orientation) and social issues (such as power struggles between the leading aristocratic families). In contrast to Jason and Menelaus, who were condemned to damnatio memoriae by 1 Maccabees, Alcimus is mentioned by name, though very little is told about him (but see below). We do not know his father's name, his priestly tribe, who his supporters were, or their attitude to Menelaus and his policy. Nevertheless it may be guessed that Alcimus did not represent the former Menelaus' party, led probably by the 'house' of Bilga and by what remained of the Tobiads; that he did not support the desecration of the Jewish cult (but see 1 Macc 9:54–7); that he had no pro-Ptolemaic inclination; and that he represented a certain segment of the nobility, who were trying to keep their property in Judea (see v. 6). v. 5, Alcimus maybe referred to in a Talmudic story (*Gen. Rab.*, Theodor-Albeck edn, pp. 742–3). There it is told that when Rabbi Yossi ben Yoezer was led to his execution, he was met on the road by his nephew Yakim, who is identified as Alcimus, about whom Josephus told that his Hebrew name was indeed Yakimos (*Ant.* 12 § 385; 20 § 235). v. 6, 'your Friends' is stressing the pro-Seleucid inclination of Alcimus' party. 'Our land' may stress the main grievance of this group, who felt that their property, acquired rightly or wrongly, is jeopardized (see 1 Macc 6:24). v. 7, Antiochus IV was looking for a strong pro-Seleucid government in Judea, but he got the opposite. He was forced militarily to support Menelaus, and if Lysias hoped that by replacing him he would have a supportive leadership in Judea, he was wrong again. The new high priest, Alcimus, also could not rule without the active military support of the government in Antioch. No wonder, as will be seen below, that the patience of the Seleucid government ran short, till power was transferred to the Hasmoneans, the only ones who were not in need of support, but could even supply troops to their Seleucid overlords.

(**7:8–11**) v. 8, Bacchides is known only from 1 & 2 Maccabees; a namesake officer is mentioned in 2 Macc 8:30, but this maybe a coincidence. At this juncture he is the governor of the western part of the Seleucid empire, anachronistically called Beyond the River (*'eber hannāhār*), as in the Persian period and in the Bible (see Ezra 4:11). v. 9, Alcimus was probably already appointed high priest by Antiochus V, to replace Menelaus (cf. 2 Macc 14:3), and confirmed by Demetrius I. vv. 7:10–11, it is not the only time that peaceful messages are repudiated by Judas (see Nicanor's message to Judas, v. 26). The author tries to present Judas as both a peace-lover and a clever leader who will not let himself fall into a trap.

(**7:12–18**) This is one of the most discussed passages in the book, the issues being whether the Hasideans deserted Judas, what their attitude was towards the revolt, and so on. The common understanding of this passage is that the cancellation of the religious persecution made the Hasideans reluctant to continue the revolt, which from now on was aimed at political, national, or personal achievements. So they were ready to recognize an Aaronide high priest and to end the war. Their fate is a *post factum*

proof for the author that Judas was right in disbelieving Bacchides' and Alcimus' peaceful overtures. Recently D. R. Schwartz (1994) proposed that 1 Macc 2:42 should be read differently (*ioudaiōn* (Jews) instead of *hasidaiōn* (Hasideans)), because of textual and other considerations. If Schwartz's suggestion is accepted, and it seems convincing, then there is no question of the Hasideans deserting the Maccabean camp, but only of their negotiations with Alcimus and Bacchides, which failed for some unknown reason. vv. 12–13, 'Scribes … Hasideans', there seems to be no satisfactory answer to the question of whether these two words are synonymous, or, if not, what the relation is of one group to the other. v. 16, no information is given here or elsewhere as to why these Hasideans were butchered. v. 17 is a citation of Ps 79:2–3 (see Dimant 1988: 390–1).

(**7:19–20**) It seems that Bacchides, on a grand scale, took punitive measures aimed at various groups of the population. v. 19, 'men who had deserted'—why would Bacchides kill deserters who joined him? Perhaps for 'crimes' which he did not forgive. Anyhow Bacchides' punitive expedition was intended to intimidate any potential opposition.

(**7:21–5**) The struggle between Alcimus and his supporters and Judas and his party seems to be now mainly in the countryside outside Jerusalem, where the interests of many of the Judean nobility were in danger. Probably part of the land had once belonged to their opponents, and had been confiscated by the Seleucid authorities and allocated anew to pro-Seleucid aristocrats, probably citizens of Antioch-in-Jerusalem. Being shut in Jerusalem they could not benefit from their fields, which the rebels tried to regain. v. 25, the opponents of the Maccabees were unable to overcome Judas with their own power, even with some small governmental support. Their constant need of Seleucid help was finally the cause of their desertion by the government in Antioch.

(**7:26–32**) When, after Bacchides' repressive activity, Judas resumed attacks on the supporters of Alcimus, again help was needed from the central government. For whatever reasons, the force under Nicanor seems to have been relatively small and insufficient. Nicanor's peaceful message is described as treacherous, either rightly so or as an excuse for Judas, for whom the appointment of Alcimus was unacceptable.

It is quite possible that the Seleucid government inclined to a peace agreement, as is clear from its policy since the cancellation of the religious persecution. But Judas's demands were unacceptable to it at this stage, though similar conditions were accepted later on, when Jonathan was appointed high priest (see 1 Macc 10:18–20). But to arrive at such a decision the Seleucids needed about ten years more. v. 26, 'Nicanor', the name is a common one, and various Nicanors are mentioned in 1 & 2 Maccabees (see Bar-Kochva 1989: 352–3). vv. 29–30, it is unclear why, if 'the enemy were preparing to kidnap Judas', they did nothing on this occasion, and gave Judas the chance to avoid further meetings with Nicanor. It makes the story about Nicanor's treacherous intentions more apologetic then historic. v. 31, Capharsalama was about 5 miles north-east of Jerusalem. v. 32, nowhere is the number of Nicanor's army given. The number of those who fell in the battle is relatively small, and it seems that Nicanor's force was not a big one. 'The city of David', where the Akra was located. This too shows the limited size of Nicanor's force.

(7:33–8) v. 33, 'priests…elders', these two groups seem to represent a kind of institution or representation of the people, probably the *gērousia*, which is mentioned in various documents of this period (see 1 Macc 12:6,35; 2 Macc 11:27; *Ant.* 12 § 138, and 'elders', as here, at 1 Macc 13:36). It also shows that the temple and its staff are not under Judas's authority, and it may even be supposed that Alcimus is the chief authority in the temple (a fact, that, even if true, 1 Maccabees is not expected to tell). Anyhow, we have here a component of Judean society which belongs neither to Judas's followers nor to the Hellenizers. 'Burnt-offering', offerings or prayers for the welfare of foreign rulers of Judea are known well before this period (Ezra 6:11), and after it (Josephus, *J.W.* 2 § 408–17). v. 34, the reason for the anger of Nicanor is told only after his outburst against the priests (v. 35); 'defiled', probably by spitting.

(7:39–50) v. 39, Beth-horon, see 1 Macc 3:16; 'the Syrian army', its arrival shows again that up to now Nicanor's army was small, and the size of this reinforcement was probably also limited, and composed of local recruitments. Even the name of their commander is not mentioned. v. 40, Adasa is located between Beth-horon and Jerusalem. vv. 41–2, as in other cases the author brings historical precedents to encourage the

people, i.e. his readers. Here he refers to Sennacherib, king of Assyria, as a very suitable antecedent. v. 43, 'first to fall in the battle', attacking the commander was an effective tactic pursued by Judas (cf. 1 Macc 3:11–12). 'On the thirteenth day', see v. 49. The year is 161 BCE. vv. 44–6, the victory of Judas was complete and Nicanor's army was routed. The description of their débâcle is vivid, and may be realistic. v. 47, for Nicanor's fate cf. 2 Macc 15:30–5. v. 49, 'the thirteenth day of Adar', see also 2 Macc 15:36. This day is included in *Megilla Taᶜanit* (a tannaitic work which preceded the Mishna, and which lists the days of joy, on which fasting (Heb. *taᶜanit*) is prohibited). In this work the story and its moral are the same as in 1 & 2 Macc, but Judas's name is not mentioned.

Rome and the Treaty between Rome and the Jews (ch. 8)

Chapter 8 deals with the relations between Rome and Judea in Judas's time. It has three parts: (1) what Judas heard about the Romans, which is probably what was common knowledge in Judea when 1 Maccabees was written down; (2) the delegation sent by Judas to Rome; (3) the treaty between Rome and the Jews. It raises many important questions: Is the document of the alliance authentic? What does this initiative mean from Judas's point of view? Is he striving now for political independence? How should this Roman intervention in the internal affairs of the Seleucid empire be understood? These and further questions have been profusely dealt with in the scholarly literature (for further bibliography see Gruen 1984: 748–51).

(8:1–16) This passage includes some mistakes and provides some clues for its own dating and for that of the whole book. The sources for the information are not known, but it may be guessed that it was brought by Jewish diplomats, who visited Rome quite often from the time of Judas Maccabeus until the end of the rule of John Hyrcanus I. Additional sources could have been Roman propaganda, which either influenced such reports, or found its way somehow to Judea. v. 1, 'Judas heard', Judas could not have received the following report because some details in it postdate his time. Nevertheless he was in no way ignorant about Rome. A Roman delegation which passed along the coast of Israel in about the spring of 164 BCE sent a friendly letter to the Jews (2 Macc 11:34–8), probably the rebels under Judas. Also Dan 11:18, 30, written about the same time, or even a little bit earlier, mentions the Romans. So Judas knew enough about Rome to be able to weigh up the situation. 'Pledged friendship', indeed the Romans made many treaties at that period, with both important and small states, and intervened in the internal affairs of independent ones. v. 2, 'Gauls' refers either to the Galatians of Asia Minor, beaten by the Romans in 189 BCE, or to the Gauls of Gallia Cisalpina (northern Italy). Galatians are also mentioned in 2 Macc 8:20. vv. 3–4, Spain was known for its rich silver mines; the Romans began to infiltrate there in the third century BCE and continued to subdue its various tribes after their victory over Carthage; 'kings', since the kings defeated by Rome are mentioned below, it seems here it must refer to Spanish chieftains, who fought against the Romans. v. 5, 'Philip, and king Perseus', Philip was defeated by the Romans in 197 BCE and Perseus, his son, in 168. v. 6, 'Antiochus the Great', Antiochus III (223–187 BCE) was beaten by the Romans in the battle of Magnesia, in Asia Minor, in 190 BCE. This defeat accelerated the disintegration of the Seleucid empire. vv. 7–8, the details here are wrong. Antiochus III was not taken captive, though the rest of v. 7 is correct. Antiochus was obliged to pay a huge amount of money as war indemnities, and to give hostages, and he lost all the territories held by the Seleucids in Asia Minor, west of the Taurus mountains. 'Eumenes', the closest ally of Rome in this war and a winner at the expense of the Seleucids, but India and Media had nothing to do with either the Romans or Eumenes. vv. 9–10, this war against the Greeks is probably the Achaean war, which terminated with the destruction of Corinth in 146 BCE. If this is so, then it postdates Judas. It is somewhat astonishing to note the positive attitude of the author towards Roman brutality, especially when contrasted to the critical and negative stance of the Dead Sea sectarians (*Pesher on Habakkuk* (1QpHab), e.g. 3:5–6; 6:6–8, 10–12, etc.). vv. 11–12, this sounds almost like a slogan of Roman propaganda, cf. Virgil, *Aeneid*, 6. 853: 'to be merciful to the conquered and beat the haughty down' (tr. J. W. Mackail). v. 13, there are various cases in which the Romans interfered in the inheritance of thrones in eastern kingdoms. vv. 14–16, some commentators suggest that the admiration for the non-royalist character of the Roman constitution is directed against royalist inclination, or actual kingship, in the Hasmonean court. I think that it is simply a factual description of the Roman constitution, with admiration and a focus on what was

extraordinary in it, in the eyes of one who was used to the Hellenistic monarchies of his day. 'Purple' was a sign of royalty, but could be worn by various dignitaries in the Hellenistic courts, as also by Simon (see 1 Macc 14:43–4). The number of senators at that time was 300. At v. 16 we find a surprising mistake by the author of 1 Maccabees, in his description of the Roman constitution; he does not know about the system of two consuls, and thinks that there is only one at a time.

(**8:17–22**) v. 17, 'Eupolemus . . . Jason', the envoys bear Greek names, as was fashionable among the Hellenizers (cf. to Jason, Lysimachus, Menelaus, mentioned in 2 Maccabees, and Alcimus). Their fathers' names, John (i.e. Yohanan) and Eleazar, are purely Hebrew, which shows that before their generation this custom was not yet fashionable, and that, unlike their fathers, their grandfathers gave Hebrew names to their children. Both were priests: Eupolemus was of the Accos family, a distinguished priestly clan. His father was active in foreign affairs at the time of Antiochus III (see 2 Macc 4:11). Jason was also, very probably, a priest, because his father's name Eleazar was common among priests in the Second Temple period. Their names show some Hellenistic colouring; their mission necessitated at least some knowledge of Greek, international politics, and worldly affairs. So through them we know that Judas had support not only among Judean farmers and shepherds, but also among the Jewish nobility, who may have been to some degree Hellenized, but were not of the Hellenizers' party. Some think that Eupolemus is the author of 'On the Kings of Judea', see Holladay (1983: 93–156; *ABD* s.v.).

'Friendship and alliance', a common Roman terminology; the allies of Rome are often called 'allies and friends' (Lat.: *socii et amici*). v. 18, the author of 1 Maccabees thought, and may have been right, that Judas was already aiming at full political independence at this stage of the rebellion. v. 20, 'alliance and peace', an awkward expression, because there was peace between Judea and Rome. 'Friendship' might have been more suitable here (see v. 17). v. 21, this is the first authentic document cited in 1 Maccabees, and see 1 Macc D.2(1). The original text, perhaps in Latin, was kept on bronze tablets in Rome.

(**8:23–30**) The majority of scholars today accept the authenticity of this document. Its oddities are explained by the various translations, from the Latin original into Greek, then to Hebrew (the original version of 1 Maccabees), then back to Greek (the surviving Gk. translation). v. 23, this opening formula is common in documents of this kind. v. 24, parallel and equal stipulations on both sides (cf. v. 27) were also a convention in this kind of treaty, though the difference in political and military importance between them was tremendous. This convention is best seen in the treaty between Rome and Astypalaea, a small city in the Aegean (see Sherk 1969: no.16, 94–9). v. 26, 'ships', a convention, as the Jews had neither a harbour nor any exit to the open sea. v. 28, 'without deceit', probably a translation of the Latin formula, *sine dolo malo*. v. 30, this permission to introduce changes to the terms is common in such treaties.

(8:31–2) These verses clearly do not form part of the treaty. They might be a part of an accompanying letter, or oral information brought by the envoys. In any case either Demetrius ignored the message, or it arrived too late to save Judas, or, indeed, it restrained Demetrius from taking extremely harsh measures after Judas's defeat (see 1 Macc 9:19–22).

The Last Stand of Judas (9:1–22)

(9:1–4) Again the Seleucid government is forced to send a considerable army to put down the revolt. Small reinforcements and local recruits do not suffice. v. 1, 'the right wing', inexplicable as it stands. For the proper meaning see at v. 12. Dancy (1954: 131) explains it as a gloss, to which explanation Bar-Kochva (1989: 382) also adheres. v. 2 poses great historiogeographical problems. The reading *arbēlois* is certain, and is usually taken to be Arbela in eastern Galilee, overlooking the Sea of Galilee, which argues that there was a Jewish population in Galilee before its conquest by the Hasmoneans. But then what is the connection of Arbela with the road to Gilgal (further south on the Jordan)? Bar-Kochva (1989: 383–4, 552–9), proposes that the translator wrongly transcribed *har* (mountain) *bêt-êl* in the Hebrew original into Arbelois, and he locates Har Beth-el west of Gilgal and north of Jerusalem. Mesaloth is probably not a place-name but a Hebrew word *mĕsālôt*, meaning 'trails'. v. 3, the date is about April/May 160. v. 4, various readings and locations have been proposed for Berea; Josephus thought it was Beer-zaith (*Ant.* 12 § 422). The numbers of Bacchides' soldiers are acceptable to many scholars.

(9:5–7) Judas's camp is small from the beginning (3,000) and dwindles to 800 soldiers, which are hardly sufficient to oppose Bacchides' powerful army. Some explain this as a reaction of many who, having fought with Judas from religious motives, now deserted him, feeling that the war was becoming more and more political and national in character. Bar-Kochva (1989: 388–9) suggests that the final small number given by the author is an excuse for Judas's defeat.

(9:7–10) Judas decided to go to battle to keep his 'honour' (Gk. *doxa*) intact. When the author makes him speak about dying bravely, there is no mention of afterlife or of any reward but honour. See 1 Macc C.3. Also rare in 1 Maccabees is the spirit of resignation on Judas's part, which reflects the author's attempt to cope with the death of his hero, a problem which the author, or epitomizer, of 2 Maccabees avoided by ending his book before the defeat of Judas, with his victory over Nicanor.

(9:11–18) The description of the last battle of Judas is detailed. Bar-Kochva (1989: 64), who assumes its authenticity, thinks that it shows that Judas must have had a larger army, because it would have been impossible for him to accomplish what is described here with only 800 men. Shatzman (1991: 19 n. 42) suggests that the description is more literary than actual. v. 14, it may be that Judas's attack on the right flank, where Bacchides himself had been, was in accordance with his tactics, aiming to hit at the commander of the enemy. v. 15, 'Mount Azotus', no mountain of this name is known and many commentators accept a textual correction, based on an assumed mistranslation of the lost Hebrew original ('*ašĕdôt-hāhār*), which should be translated 'the slopes of the mountain'.

(9:19–22) Taking Judas's body for burial could have been done either some time after the battle, when the enemy left the scene, or under truce. Some scholars think that a truce was indeed granted by the Syrians, because of the Jewish treaty with Rome. v. 19, Modein was where the family property was located, and where its mausoleum was later built by Simon (13:25–30). v. 21, this dirge is reminiscent of 2 Sam 1:19. v. 22, 'the rest of the acts of Judas... have not been recorded' is a phrase often repeated, in a positive form, in Kings (e.g. 1 Kings 11:41). It seems then that the author of 1

Maccabees did not have any written sources for Judas's acts.

The First Years of Jonathan (9:23–10:17)

(9:23–7) The extremely sombre situation is a suitable background for the difficult and slow reorganization of the revolt under Jonathan.

v. 23, 'renegades … wrongdoers', all opposition to the Hasmoneans is encompassed in one package, without differentiating the various groups which composed it. v. 24, 'famine' might be connected with the sabbatical year that preceded (see 6:49, 53) and with the continuous war. As Bacchides now ruled the country he could have control of the agricultural produce, and through it dominate the population outside Jerusalem. We assume that the fortresses built by him were also intended to achieve this aim (vv. 50–2). v. 25, 'the godless', cf. v. 23. The word might also reflect the effort of some groups of the nobility to regain or take over land which changed hands in the course of the revolt. v. 27, see 1 Macc 4:46,14:41; Ps 74:9.

(9:28–31) The election of Jonathan to lead the revolt raises some questions. He was the youngest among the five sons of Mattathias, and so we must assume that militarily he was the fittest for the task among them. The same consideration was valid for Judas's election after Mattathias's death, as he was also younger than John and Simon, but he may have been Mattathias's choice, and now an assembly of the rebels elected his successor. The election of Jonathan also demonstrates that the senior position given to Simon in Mattathias's testament (2:65–6) above does not reflect the actual situation at that time. As for the legal aspects of Jonathan's appointment, it seems to be irregular: the electing body consisted of the warriors who were present at this point in the camp, and they must have been few in number.

(9:32–4) The major achievement of Jonathan in an almost desperate situation was the mere survival of the Hasmonean party, v. 33, Tekoa and Asphar are in the wilderness of Judea, south-east of Bethlehem. v. 34, 'sabbath day … crossed the Jordan', probably there is here some conflation with v. 43.

(9:35–42) This passage gives a good idea of the situation of the rebels at this time. They were forced to fight for their lives at the outskirts of the inhabited land, being supported by the Nabateans, who were already on friendly terms with them (5:25), but were ambushed by another tribe, who took advantage of the unstable conditions in the area (cf. 54–5, 35). v. 36, 'family of Jambri', an Arab tribe, acting independently of the Nabateans, though living at Medaba, near the Nabatean territory. See Kasher (1988: 34–5). v. 37, 'Canaan', see 1 Macc D.1. The location of Nadabath is unknown but must be in the approximate area of biblical Moab.

(9:43–9) Jonathan's dire position is clear. His encampment near the Jordan was probably intended to enable him to escape to the other side of the river when in danger, as indeed came to pass. v. 43 is a repeat of v. 34, and resumes the story, interrupted by the sons of Jambri incident, which for some reason was inserted here. 'Sabbath', this detail points to Bacchides' ignorance of Mattathias's decision to fight on the sabbath (see 2:40), which is not very probable. In any case it casts him in a negative light, as one who despises the Jewish religious ordinances and tries to take advantage of them. v. 47, the battle itself is a kind of a skirmish. Jonathan tried to repeat Judas's tactics, and to kill the commander of the enemy, Bacchides— as Judas had done to Apollonius (3:11–12) and Nicanor (7:44–5, 47). Though he failed, it shows that, like Judas, Jonathan took part personally in battle, an activity which is not recorded about Simon, and which may explain the preference given to Judas and Jonathan as leaders of the revolt.

(9:50–3) Bacchides' decision to build fortresses in strategic locations in Judea is the most serious attempt to rule over the Judean countryside, and shows that Bacchides and Alcimus understood well that a basis of power in Jerusalem alone was not sufficient to rule Judea as a whole. The hard core of the revolt was in the land, the *chōra* of Antioch-in-Jerusalem and the presence of armed forces was necessary to dominate Judea. For the location of the various fortresses see Galil (1992). v. 52, 'stores of food', storing food, which in part at least came as taxes in kind, in royal fortresses helped the government to subdue the population, because it was dependent on those food reserves, especially in years of shortage, like the present time (see v. 24). And see Rappaport, Pastor, and Rimon (1994). Also cf. 1 Macc 13:33. v. 53, 'hostages', this may indicate that the local aristocracy outside Jerusalem was not trusted by the Seleucid government, and was suspected of supporting the Hasmoneans.

(9:54–7) The motivation of Alcimus to destroy the wall of the inner court is not clear. Was it an architectural enterprise described by 1 Maccabees as sacrilege, to blacken Alcimus, or was it a meaningful ideological step, intended to open to the view of all, including Gentiles, the cultic performances in the temple? For an ideological interpretation see Schmidt (1994: 98–9). v. 54,153 ES is 159 BCE, and the second month is about May. vv. 55–6, the illness (probably a stroke) and death of Alcimus are interpreted as a divine punishment, which put an end to his sacrilegious plan. v. 57, Bacchides' return to Syria after Alcimus' death shows that his arrangements were efficient, and kept the country quiet for two years (approximately from mid-159 BCE to mid-157 BCE). The author of 1 Maccabees does not inform us about the arrangements which took place after Alcimus' death. Was there an *intersacerdotium* period of about seven years (from 159 to the appointment of Jonathan in 152 BCE (see 10:20))? Or was there a high priest, whose name and very existence are concealed by 1 Maccabees for political reasons? And if there was no high priest for such a long period, how did the temple function?

Josephus, when he lists the high priests from beginning to end, mentions a vacancy of seven years between the death of Alcimus (Jacimus in the text there, *Ant.* 20 § 237) and Jonathan's appointment to the high-priesthood. Most commentators follow this statement of Josephus, which is in accordance with 1 Maccabees. In *Ant.* 12 §§ 414, 419, 434, Josephus gives contradictory information, probably wrong. This vacuum in our information has tempted some scholars to propose that the Teacher of Righteousness mentioned in the Dead Sea scrolls was the high priest in these years. Needless to say, no proof can be posited for this ingenious proposal. See Murphy O'Connor (1976).

(9:58–61) The enemies of the Hasmoneans initiated a new attempt to get rid of Jonathan. Their dependence on Seleucid help against the Hasmoneans finally brought about their abandonment by the government, because they became an unbearable burden to it. In spite of what is said about the large force Bacchides assembled, it looks like a limited military operation, the success of which depended mainly on secrecy. v. 61, 'men of the country', it seems that Bacchides was successful in installing (or reinstalling) the pro-Seleucid nobility to their lands in the country, and now Jonathan was trying to

undo it. The main struggle took place in the countryside, as in the beginning of the revolt.

(9:62–9) When his plan for a surprise attack failed, Bacchides tried to crush Jonathan in his base in the desert. Clearly he did not muster a big force, and probably the king could not spare great forces for a small war in Judea because of more serious preoccupations. v. 62, Bethbasi is between Jerusalem and Tekoa, not far from Bethlehem. Bacchides' co-operation with his local allies, which did not bring any valuable results, finally led to a reversal of Seleucid policy in Judea. v. 66, 'Odomera...Phasiron' are unknown Arabic tribes. Jonathan is again involved in skirmishes with the nomads, or seminomads ('in their tents' here), near the scene of battle. vv. 678, Bacchides is unable to face the attack on both sides, though performed by a small force (v. 65, Jonathan 'went with only a few men'). Despite the text ('he was crushed by them'), it is clear that he was forced only to give up the siege. v. 69, Bacchides' rage and frustration were turned now against the 'renegades', who called him but did not deliver any valuable goods for the Seleucid government. It is reminiscent in a way of Lysias's reaction towards Menelaus.

(9:70–3) The relations between the Seleucids, represented by Bacchides, and the Hasmoneans are now reversed. Whatever remained of the former Judean nobility, it was almost ignored by the Seleucid government. Jonathan gradually became the real representative of the Seleucids in Judea, and the agreement with Bacchides was the first step in this direction. v. 73, Michmash is eight miles north of Jerusalem; 'to judge the people', a biblical phrase, common in the book of Judges. It associates with the judges of old, and is in line with the style of 1 Maccabees in general. 'Destroyed the godless', the internal war goes on, though now, without Seleucid support, the liquidation of the aristocratic opposition to the Hasmoneans arrives at its almost final stage.

(Ch. 10) The agreement between Jonathan and Bacchides made Jonathan the one who could supply military reinforcements to contending Seleucid pretenders in their internecine wars. The opportunity to exploit Seleucid difficulties for his own aggrandizement came when Demetrius I was challenged by a certain Alexander, who pretended to be Antiochus IV's son. The threat to his rule incited Demetrius to look for support wherever he could get it. To prevent Jonathan from joining Alexander, Demetrius made friendly overtures to him.

(10:1–14) v 1, 160 ES is 152 BCE. 'Alexander Epiphanes', many ancient sources and most contemporary scholars reject an affiliation between Alexander and Antiochus IV. He was put forward as Antiochus IV's son by the enemies of Demetrius, who utilized for their aim a certain outward similarity between him and Antiochus V, who was a real son of Antiochus IV. Alexander is known by his nickname Balas, the meaning and origin of which is not clear. This nickname is never used in 1 Maccabees. Ptolemais was an important harbour west of Galilee, which became at this period a kind of secondary capital, and served as a base for the invasion of Alexander into Demetrius' realm. On Ptolemais see 1 Macc 5:15. v. 6, the permission to raise and to equip an army was intended to encourage Jonathan to render support to Demetrius in the war against Alexander. vv. 7–11, Jonathan took full advantage of Demetrius' gestures to strengthen his position. The release of the hostages increased his support by various families; he left Michmash and turned Jerusalem into his seat, fortifying the city and the Temple Mount. v. 12, 'fled', actually the withdrawal of most of the Seleucid garrisons from Judea was part of the preparations for the war with Alexander. Their withdrawal made Jonathan the uncontested master of the Judean countryside. v. 14, the remaining forces, in the Akra and Beth-zur, were composed of both Syrian soldiers and Jews, the remnants of the once powerful nobility.

(10:15–17) The great opportunity for Jonathan came when Alexander tried to draw him to his side. Jonathan accepted his proposal to appoint him high priest. It meant the achievement of the highest position in Judea, equal to princely or even royal status, though under Seleucid suzerainty. It surpassed by far Demetrius' proposals, of which Jonathan had already made use. Jonathan's support of Alexander had various goals: to achieve national aims through his own personal advancement; to obtain the high-priesthood; to co-operate with Rome and the Ptolemies (and perhaps also other states) for the weakening of the Seleucids. This last target was already adopted by Judas and was in line with Ptolemaic interests. It was a policy developed constantly by Jonathan, by Simon, and by John Hyrcanus,

until Alexander Janneus. For Janneus' change of policy see Rappaport (1968).

Jonathan, High Priest and Ruler of Judea (10:18–12:53)

(10:18–20) This is the first document, beside the treaty with Rome, that is cited in 1 Maccabees. On documents see 1 Macc D.2(1). The appointment of Jonathan as high priest was a new starting-point for the house of Mattathias, on his way to hegemony over Judea. Yet it aroused criticism from various quarters. It is similar, from a legal point of view, to the appointment of Jason and Menelaus by Antiochus IV, and of Alcimus by Antiochus V, and not in accordance with the laws of the Torah and the traditional inheritance of the high-priest-hood by the house of Zadok. It is also quite possible that there were still in Judea supporters of the Zadokite Oniad family, and there may have been others who doubted the moral quality of Jonathan to serve as high priest. It is no wonder then that some Qumranic scholars see Jonathan as the one who is called in the Dead Sea scrolls the Wicked Priest. Cf. 1 Macc 9:57. v. 20, 'king's Friend', Jonathan was the first Hasmonean to be a Friend (Gk. *philos*), a hierarchical rank in Hellenistic courts. 'He also sent him ... crown', this sentence is not part of the letter, because it is not in direct speech as is the rest; 'purple robe and a golden crown', both were symbols of royalty or high rank, and under various regimes their use was restricted to privileged persons. See Rheinold (1970).

(10:21–4) v. 21,160 ES is 152 BCE. Jonathan begins to perform as high priest on Sukkoth (the Feast of Tabernacles or Booths) of that year. vv. 22–4, the disappointment of Demetrius provides an explanation of his letter cited below.

(10:25–45) The authenticity of this long letter is doubtful according to various scholars. Those who accept it explain the difficulties as problems of textual transmission. v. 25, the opening of Demetrius' letter is more formal and less personal than Alexander's letter (v. 18). Jonathan is not mentioned by name, which is strange in a letter which tries to convince Jonathan to join Demetrius. vv. 26–8, the contents of these verses are blatantly untrue, but may serve Demetrius' effort to draw Jonathan to his side. v. 29, 'all the Jews', is this to be understood as an exemption of all the Jews in the Seleucid empire, as some commentators think? It seems unreasonable from a Seleucid point of view and irrelevant for Jonathan. It may refer to all those who are within Jonathan's jurisdiction, or at most to those in the land of Israel.

These three categories of tax are known in the Seleucid empire: tribute (Gk. pl. *phoroi*) was an annual payment by communities and may refer here to taxes in general; tax on salt, a vital product for conservation of food; and the crown (Gk. *stephanos*) tax, which from a voluntary donation on the crowning of a new king became a permanent tax. v. 30, 'third of the grain...half of the fruit', this is a very high rate, especially when we consider the relatively low fertility of the land of Judea. Some scholars suppose that it was not the usual rate of taxation, but a punitive measure imposed on Judea because of the revolt. See Mørkholm (1989: 285). The three districts—Aphairema, Lydda, and Ramathaim—are mentioned in 11:34. They were populated mainly by Jews. Modein itself was in the district of Lydda. It is evident that the administrative division of the land did not suit its ethnic division. It is not at all clear when and why these districts were transferred from Judea to Samaria, but be that as it may, they were annexed to Judea by Jonathan's days, and it seems that *de facto* they were already in Jewish hands and under Hasmonean influence. 'Samaria and Galilee', the three districts bordered on Samaria, and the mention of Galilee is either a mistake in the Hebrew original or a mistake by the translator (*galîl* in Heb. means 'district', and this may have caused confusion), vv. 31–2, the complete cancellation of taxation and the evacuation of the Akra were achieved only in Simon's days (see 13:39). The inclusion of these privileges already in a document from Demetrius I's time makes the authenticity of the document suspicious, though those who believe in its authenticity claim that his desperate situation could have brought him to such extreme concessions. v. 33, the release of captives is a common stipulation in post-war arrangements, cf. Josephus, *Ant.* 12 § 144. A tax on cattle is well-known, but mention here seems out of place, belonging better in vv. 29 or 30.

vv. 34–5, the exemption of the Jews from any disturbance on their holidays is quite understandable, but what are the three days before and after, and why is it declared for the whole kingdom? The three days are explained as the time necessary for a journey to Jerusalem (probably from other districts, because in Judea no more than one day was necessary for such a trip). But the exemption to all the Jews of Demetrius' kingdom is incomprehensible. See

Wise (1990). vv. 36–7, on the one hand this passage fits well with the need of Demetrius to muster whatever military support he can get, on the other hand the number of 30,000 seems to be far beyond the manpower potential of Judea. Generally speaking the conditions of service proposed to those who register are within the norms of Hellenistic military customs. The Jews often served as mercenaries in Persian and Hellenistic armies, see Shatzman (1991: 14, 17–18, with further lit.). v. 38, the three districts were mentioned in v. 30 in relation to the removal of taxation. Here the king allows them to be annexed to Judea. The high priest is mentioned here, but not his name. v. 39, the annexation of Ptolemais to Judea and its being granted to the temple is either an absurd or a cunning move by Demetrius to incite Jonathan to attack the city, which served as a temporary capital for his adversary, Alexander. On this city see 1 Macc 10:1. v. 40, royal contributions to temples were common, and we know of such donations given to the Jerusalem temple. See Ezra 6:5; 8:9–10; 7:20; *Ant.* 12 § 138; 2 Macc 3:2–3. vv. 41–2, the details of this account are not clear, yet it seems to be intended to regulate, and add important sums of money to, the temple treasury, which was probably in bad shape after the troubles of the last two decades or more. v. 43, this is reminiscent of the *asylia*, granted to temples and cities by Hellenistic kings. In this case it is limited to debts to the government. vv. 44–5, there are precedents for subsidies by the king to various building projects, as for example by Cyrus (Ezra 6:4) and Darius (Ezra 6:8), and by Antiochus III (*Ant.* 12 § 141).

(10:46–7) This explanation is right, but not full. For additional reasons see vv. 15–17.

(10:48–58) About the international political activity involved in these affairs see Gruen (1984: 11. 585–6, 666–8, 709–11). vv. 51–4, the support Alexander got from Ptolemy VI Philometor and other rulers, with Roman tacit encouragement, is omitted here. The message of Alexander's ambassadors is given in direct speech, as quite often in 1 Maccabees, but it cannot be taken as authentic. The same is true of Ptolemy's reply. v. 57, on the importance of Ptolemais see 1 Macc 5:15; 10:1,39.

(10:59–66) v. 60, Jonathan's meeting with the two kings cemented his participation in the pro-Roman coalition, which included Ptolemaic Egypt, the Attalids, and in this case also

Alexander. Yet the pomp and presents of Jonathan remind one of the Tobiads' relations with the Ptolemaic court in the third century BCE, and show Jonathan's urge to take part in political affairs. v. 61, 'malcontents . . . renegades', we do not know who these opponents of Jonathan were. Cf. 1 Macc 15:21. vv. 62–4, the description of the change in Jonathan's position is reminiscent of that of Mordecai in Esth 6:6–9. v. 65, 'chief Friends', the Greek *prōtoi philoi*, 'first friends', a rank above Friends. See 1 Macc 10:20. 'general and governor', Greek *stratēgos* and *meridarchēs*. The second office is known mainly as a Ptolemaic one, and may show a persistence of Ptolemaic terminology in Israel or the strong Ptolemaic influence on Alexander, who was, to some extent, a vassal of Ptolemy VI; or it may be a usage of a translator familiar with Ptolemaic terms (especially so if we suppose that the translation was made in Egypt). The area entrusted to Jonathan is not specified, so that it is reasonable to assume that it was Judea. Later on Jonathan and Simon were appointed as governors of some additional regions.

(**10:67–9**) In 147 BCE the war between the two branches of the Seleucid dynasty was resumed. The branch of Seleucus IV is represented now by his grandson Demetrius II. v. 69, Apollonius cannot be identified, because it is a very common name. He represents Demetrius against Jonathan, a supporter of Alexander, his adversary.

(**10:70–3**) The message of Apollonius is a literary invention by the author of 1 Maccabees or one of his sources. Yet it stresses some interesting points. v. 71, 'come down to the plain', the Jewish forces were well-adapted to fight in the mountainous area of Judea, but deficient in the plain, where the Seleucid forces could use their phalanx and cavalry. The readiness of Jonathan to descend to the plain is a turning-point in Hasmonean warfare, and shows the considerable development of the Jewish army (see Shatzman 1991: 12). The 'power of the cities', Apollonius' force included, or was mainly composed of, the *poleis*' militia. These Hellenistic cities were inimical to the Hasmoneans, and lent their support to Apollonius against Jonathan.

(**10:74–85**) For this important battle see Bar-Kochva (1975; 1989: 76–81); Shatzman (1991: 19, 23,311). v. 75, Joppa was an important harbour and the main sea-route out of Judea. v. 77,

Azotus was formerly one of the five Philistine cities, and now served as a base for Apollonius. v. 83, 'Beth-dagon' means the house of Dagon, a god whose identity is somewhat unclear. It was once thought to be derived from the Semitic root *d-g* (fish), but a derivation from root *d-g-n* (corn) seems preferable. vv. 84–5, the motivation for this cruel act is not clear. It may have been a savage revenge for the evildoings perpetrated on the Jews in earlier times, or, as sometimes understood, an attempt to clean the holy land from idolatry (cf. 1 Macc 5:44).

(**10:86–9**) v. 86, Askalon was the only city towards which the Hasmoneans were friendly, because of the strong Ptolemaic influence on it; this caused it to be immune to Hasmonean expansionist policy. vv. 88–9, the difficult situation of Alexander because of Demetrius II's success in gaining support from within and without his kingdom made Jonathan's alliance even more important to him, and he poured on him even greater benefits. A 'golden buckle' was a symbol of honour in the hierarchic Seleucid order. Ekron was formerly a Philistine city. Probably it was a royal domain (Gk. *gē basilikē*), which was given to Jonathan as a present (Gk. *gē en dōrea*). This is the first known territorial annexation to Judea, seemingly under personal title.

(**11:1–12**) This passage discusses mainly the relations between the Seleucids and the Ptolemies. In it Ptolemy VI is the bad guy and Alexander the good one. But we should be cautious regarding the author of 1 Maccabees, who manifests a great sympathy towards Alexander. v. 1, 'like the sand by the seashore', a biblical expression, cf. e. g. Gen 22:17; 'by trickery', 1 Maccabees attributes to Ptolemy sly intentions (see also v. 8), yet it is doubtful if Ptolemy thought it feasible to annex the Seleucid empire without incurring a collision with Rome, and more so at such an early stage of his intervention in Syria. v. 2, it seems that at this stage Alexander was friendly towards Ptolemy. v. 3, 'stationed forces as a garrison' may show that Ptolemy had in mind the reannexation of southern Syria to the Ptolemaic empire. vv. 4–7, Jonathan's position was strong enough to sustain the blame of the people of Azotus, and Ptolemy was not yet, at least openly, an enemy of Alexander. The Eleutherus was a river north of Tripolis, in what is now Lebanon. v. 8, Seleucia in Pieria was the harbour of Antioch, at the mouth of the river Orontes. vv. 9–12, Ptolemy transferred his support from

Alexander to Demetrius, perhaps because of the feeble and weak personality of Alexander, or, conversely, his refusal to give up southern Syria to Ptolemy. In any case, neither was very popular, and Ptolemy was acclaimed by the Antiochians. It should also be remembered that Ptolemy had Seleucid blood in his veins, through his mother, Cleopatra I, daughter of Antiochus III the Great.

(11:13–19) v. 13, it is not credible that Ptolemy made himself king of the Seleucid empire, as he never deposed Demetrius II. According to Josephus (*Ant.* 13 §§ 113–15) and Diodorus (32. 39c), the crown was offered to him, but refused. 'Asia' is a non official term for the Seleucid empire (cf. 1 Macc 8:6; 12:39; 13:32). v. 17, Zabdiel was an Arab chieftain in the Syrian desert, called Arabia in v. 16. With the decline of the Seleucid empire, Arab tribes became important all along the fertile crescent. Zabdiel had a Greek name too: Diocles (*ABD* s.v. no. 3,1031–2, and see 1 Macc 11:39; 12:31). v. 18, 'Ptolemy died', he was wounded in the battle against Alexander and died after three days. v. 19, the year 167 ES is 146/5 BCE.

(11:20–9) Jonathan appears as an assertive and astute politician, who used brinkmanship in his negotiations with Demetrius II (esp. v. 23). v. 20, 'engines of war' shows the professional and technological advancement of the Hasmonean army. See 1 Macc 6:20, 52. v. 21, 'renegades', despite its constant failure there remained a hard core of Jewish opposition to Jonathan. The motivation of his opponents is not known. v. 23, three acts of Jonathan are listed here: continuation of the siege of the Akra; choosing of elders and priests; risking his own life by going to Ptolemais. Many commentators follow Josephus (*Ant.* 13 § 124), and assume that the elders and priests went with Jonathan to Ptolemais. It seems to me more probable that they compose the *gērousia*, which Jonathan left in charge of the siege and the state's business, and which is mentioned in various documents, cited below.
v. 25, see v. 21. vv. 26–7, the reinstallation of Jonathan shows his strong position and the weak position of Demetrius at this time. v. 28, waiving of taxes in return for one sizeable instalment was agreed upon by Demetrius II in Simon's days. See 13:37; 'three districts', see v. 34 and 1 Macc 10:30.

(11:30–7) This letter from Demetrius II to Jonathan contains many characteristics of a genuine Seleucid royal letter. From this aspect it is different from the letter of Demetrius I to Jonathan (10:25–45), which is considered by some scholars to be a forgery, probably influenced by this genuine letter. v. 30, the opening formula is regular, and contains both the ruler and the people, as is true from now on in similar documents (e.g. 15:2). v. 31, 'copy', it was a regular chancellery rule to send copies of relevant orders to various functionaries, and to other interested parties (cf. *Ant.* 12 §§ 138–44). Lasthenes was from Crete, a leader of mercenaries who became prime minister to Demetrius II (Diodoros, 33.4.1). He is ranked as 'kinsman' and 'father' (v. 32), in line with the Seleucid hierarchic order (see *ABD* s.v.). v. 34, 'Aphairema and Lydda and Rathamin'—see 1 Macc 10:30. 'To all those who offer sacrifice in Jerusalem' differentiates between Jews and Samaritans, who offer sacrifice on Mt. Gerizim (see Rappaport (1995a). v. 37, putting important documents in public places was common, and the Temple Mount was such a place. Cf. 14:48.

(11:38–40) v. 38, Demetrius decided to release the regular Seleucid troops, who were recruited from among the military settlers in Seleucis, in northern Syria, either because of pecuniary considerations, or because their fidelity to him was questionable. This aroused the enmity of the core of the Seleucid army, and pushed it to support the rival Seleucid branch of Alexander (issued from Antiochus IV). 'Recruited from the islands of the nations', i.e. the Cretan mercenaries under Lasthenes. v. 39, 'Trypho', an appellation for Diodotus, an officer of Alexander, a native of the region of Apamea in north Syria. Trypho was influential among the soldiers of this region, whom Demetrius had estranged. He began as regent for Antiochus VI, Alexander's son, and later set himself up as a king, the only pretender who was not of the Seleucid dynasty. 'Imalkue the Arab', son of Zabdiel, who killed Alexander (v. 17) but brought up his son.

(11:41–51) vv. 41–4, Jonathan tried to benefit from the difficult situation of Demetrius II, and to achieve more independence. He requested the evacuation of the remaining forces in Judea, especially those in the Akra. Demetrius prudently agreed to Jonathan's demand, but on condition of military help against the rebels. Jonathan accepted, and sent Jewish troops to Antioch. vv. 45–51, the revolt of the Antiochians and its suppression is told also by other historians (Diodorus, 33. 4.2 and others). These do not mention the Jewish involvement, whereas 1 Maccabees does not mention the involvement of the mercenaries. Josephus (*Ant.* 13 § 137) combines 1 Maccabees' report with some Hellenistic source, and mentions both the Jewish soldiers and the mercenaries. We see here Jonathan's deep involvement in the internal affairs of the Seleucid state, but at the same time his intention to get advantages for Judea.

(**11:52–3**) The refusal of Demetrius to evacuate the fortresses in Judea pushed the frustrated Jonathan to support Demetrius' enemies.

(**11:54–9**) The most natural step for Jonathan was to renew his alliance with the son of Alexander, the child Antiochus VI, who was now under the tutelage of Trypho. This branch of the Seleucids was his reliable ally in Alexander's days. v. 54, despite Trypho's success Demetrius was able to keep some bases in the kingdom. For the chronology and division of the Seleucid empire at this time see Houghton (1992). vv. 57–8, Antiochus VI confirms to Jonathan what was given to him by his father, Alexander. There is no mention of the evacuation of the Akra here, which means that Trypho refused to give up the last vestiges of Seleucid sovereignty in Judea. v. 59, 'from the Ladder of Tyre to the borders of Egypt', the appointment of Simon as a governor of the *Paralia* (Gk. 'the coastal plain'), shows the relative great importance of the Hasmoneans in Seleucid politics, and their progress and involvement in it. Jonathan was already a *stratēgos* (10:65), though the area under his control is not defined. The *Paralia* was one of the subdivisions of southern Syria, and some other governors of it are known (see 15:38; 2 Macc 13:24). The idea behind this appointment was to encourage Simon and Jonathan to take control of this area from Demetrius II's supporters.

(**11:60–74**) Two fronts now confronted Jonathan and Simon. Jonathan was fighting against Demetrius' supporters in the north and on the southern coastal plain and Simon against Beth-zur in Judea. v. 60, 'beyond the river', see 1 Macc 7:8; 'the army of Syria', the Syrian army, which supported Antiochus VI, joined Jonathan against Demetrius. Askalon sided with Jonathan as before (cf. 10:86). vv. 61–2, Gaza participated in the eastern commerce of luxuries in co-operation with the Nabateans and in competition with the Ptolemies. On Askalon and Gaza see Rappaport (1970). Damascus was the most important city in southern Syria. Jonathan's

arrival there shows his involvement in matters and areas not related to Jewish interests. v. 63, Kadesh was a city in northern Galilee, in the territory of Tyre, which supported Demetrius II. v. 64, the two brothers are not fighting in their respective provinces, and it seems that their activity is functional. v. 65, Beth-zur was the second most important Seleucid base in Judea after the Akra. With its conquest the Akra remained the last Seleucid fortress in Judea. v. 67, 'waters of Gennesaret', the Sea of Galilee. Hazor was in upper Galilee, a city well-known in biblical times (Josh 11:1). v. 70, we do not know anything else about these two officers. The mention of Jewish individuals, other than the Maccabees, is relatively rare in this book. v. 71, here Jonathan's courage and piety are exemplified, as well as the importance of divine help. Yet divine help is not miraculous, but through human acts, that is, through Jonathan's bravery and the return of his men to the battlefield; cf. also 9:47.

Jonathan's Exploits (12:1–53)

(**12:1–4**) If the order of events here is chronological and not thematic, then Jonathan considered his rule stable enough to embark on diplomatic activity, and to renew and expand Judea's involvement in the political activity of the Mediterranean world. v. 1, since the Roman state and senate were stable and kings and rulers were transitory, they were expected to take the initiative and to renew former alliances with Rome. This was done by Jonathan. v. 2, 'Spartans', see 14:16–23;'other places', it was common to assign to an embassy more than one destination; cf. 15:22–4. v. 3, 'senate chamber', *bouleutērion* in the Greek, not an exact term, but a suitable one in the transmission of Roman institutions into Greek. We do not know the Hebrew word behind it. v. 4, giving letters of recommendation to envoys for the authorities in the places along their route was a common custom in Hellenistic diplomacy.

(**12:5–23**) The relations between the Jews and the Spartans have intrigued many scholars, and various explanations have been suggested for the problems raised by this passage, including the historicity of Jonathan's letter to the Spartans; the authenticity of the letter of Arius to Onias, cited in Jonathan's letter (vv. 19–23); and the supposed 'brotherhood' of the Jews and the Spartans. The last problem is the easiest to resolve. Assertion of relations between various peoples was popular in the ancient world (see

Gen 10), and was revived in the Hellenistic period, when new connections were invented to suit the new map of the world. It was utilized also to facilitate diplomatic relations, or to forge alliances and friendships between states. v. 6, the letter is addressed to the Spartans by the Jewish authorities of that time. The formula is a common one, including the *gērousia* (the senate) and the people, with a special mention of the priests. 'Brothers', in accordance with the genealogy specified at v. 21. vv. 7–8, for Arius and Onias see at v. 19. v. 8, 'the envoy', Josephus relates that the envoy's name was Demoteles (*Ant.* 12 § 227), but we do not know on what authority this information was based. v. 9, this passage is considered impolite by various scholars, and therefore not authentic. v. 13, 'the kings', this expression is rather strange, but may refer to various kings attacking the Jews not simultaneously, but successively (Antiochus IV, Antiochus V, and Demetrius I). v. 16, here we have the names of the envoys mentioned in v. 1. Numenius is a relatively rare name in Greek, and his father's name, Antiochus, is even more surprising. Yet it could have been given to him in honour of Antiochus III, a benevolent king in Jewish eyes. The name of the other envoy, Antipater son of Jason, may be connected to Judas's envoy to Rome, Jason son of Eleazar (1 Macc 8:17). We may conclude that diplomatic tasks were confided, in some cases at least, to members of families that had provided diplomats for more than one generation (cf. ibid.).

(**12:19–23**) The authenticity of this letter of Arius is based on even less firm foundations than the letter of Jonathan. Many ingenious proposals were made to support it, but nevertheless it remains bizarre that Sparta would appeal to a small people under Ptolemaic suzerainty. Some scholars have therefore repudiated the authenticity and historical value of this letter, and even of the whole correspondence between Sparta and Judea. If there is any good argument to support the authenticity of this letter, it is, to my mind, the lively interest shown in various quarters at that period in ethnic genealogies, which triggered here and there diplomatic activity as well. Even if the letter is a forgery, it shows an interest, in Jewish circles, in ethnic genealogies and in their potential help in forging relations between oriental peoples and the Greeks. For further bibliography see Schurer (1973–87: I. 184–5). v. 19, Arius is usually identified with the Spartan king Areius II (309–265 BCE); Onias is supposedly Onias II,

who began his office *c.*270 BCE. v. 21, around the figure of Abraham various stories were entwined, which relate him to different peoples. Cf. Josephus, *Ant.* 14 § 255, and further references in Stern (1974–84, nos. 46, 83, 335).

(**12:24–32**) Jonathan is again active in the service of his Syrian ally, this time Trypho, Antiochus VI's regent. The war is far north of Judea proper, but probably within the borders of southern Syria, of which Jonathan was *stratēgos*. v. 24, Demetrius II, the enemy of Trypho and now also of Jonathan. v. 25, Hamath was probably on the river Orontes, north of Israel; 'his own country', probably not the small Judea of that period, but the greater area encompassed by Jonathan's administration. v. 28, the kindling of fires is a well-known stratagem to cover withdrawal (cf. 1 Macc 4:5). vv. 30–1; the Zabadeans were one of the Arab tribes on the borders of the cultivated land of the fertile crescent. On other Arab tribes see 1 Macc 5:4, 25; 9:36–7; 11:17. v. 32, Damascus was probably included in Jonathan's *stratēgia*. See 1 Macc 11:62.

(**12:33–4**) Simon was occupied with defending his *strategia*, the *Paralia* (see 1 Macc 11:59) against Demetrius II's supporters, as his brother Jonathan was doing in his own area. v. 33, for Askalon, see 1 Macc 10:86. v. 34, the annexation of Joppa by the Jews was gradual. This time it was the installation of a garrison, but later on the pagan population was replaced by Jews (see 1 Macc 13:11).

(**12:35–8**) Jonathan and Simon tried at this stage to stabilize their achievements by occupying the Akra and by strengthening the strategic places on the borders of the Jewish territory. v. 35, 'the elders', Jonathan was co-operating with the senate (Gk. *gērousia;* Heb. *zĕqēnîm*), the assembly of elders usually translated 'elders' except in 12:6. The functioning of the *gerousia* gives a glimpse of the internal constitution of Judea at the time, and reflects a certain power base of the Hasmoneans in Judean society. No wonder the elders appear also when Simon is appointed by national decision as ruler and high priest (14:28). v. 36, the Jews could not storm the Akra, and so they resorted to a prolonged siege, which indicates the limits of their military power. v. 37, Chaphenatha was probably a quarter of Jerusalem, but its location is unknown. v. 38, Adida was a village north-east of Lydda (Heb. *hadid*), guarding one of the western entrances to Judea (see 13:13).

(12:39–53) That Trypho resorted to enticing Jonathan into a trap shows the limits of his power to impose his will on the Jews. vv. 39–40, indeed, Trypho did assassinate Antiochus and replace him on the Seleucid throne. Yet Jonathan was not an obstacle for him, and it seems to be a Judeocentric point of view that he had to get rid of Jonathan before murdering Antiochus. It is also interesting to note the persistence of the author of 1 Maccabees in his sympathy for the descendants of Alexander Balas. v. 41, 'forty thousand', the strength of Jonathan's army is considered by many commentators to be exaggerated. v. 47, 'three thousand…one thousand', the numbers may refer to various components of the Hasmonean army: 40,000 may represent the full conscription of Judea, including the reserve; 3,000 may be a unit in the standing army, which may have been composed of two or three similar units; the 1,000 soldiers who remained with Jonathan may have been his bodyguard. Cf. Shatzman (1991: 28–31). v. 48, for the hostility of Ptolemais towards the Jews see 1 Macc 5:15;Macc 6:8; 13:25. The capture of Jonathan may be reflected in the *Temple Scroll*, lvii 9–11, where very strict rules for the king's bodyguard are stated.

Simon's Rule (13:1–16:24)

(13:1–11) These verses are concerned with the transfer of leadership from Jonathan to Simon, which did not follow the usual hereditary pattern. It avoids the problem of the succession of Jonathan's sons, and ignores the fact that Jonathan was still alive at that time. Indeed Simon's position was consolidated about two years later (see ch. 14). Interestingly Simon initiated the proposal that he should take the leadership, and was not called upon by the people (cf. Jonathan's appointment in 9:28–31). To sum up, this seems to be a passage with an apologetic flavour, written by the author of 1 Maccabees under Hyrcanus (see 1 Macc B. 2). v. 6, 'all the nations', a common stereotype in 1 Maccabees (see 5:7 and 12:53). v 8, 'leader' (Gk. *hēgoumenos*), cf. 14:35, 41. Jonathan was still alive (see above). v. 11, 'Jonathan son of Absalom' was probably a brother of Mattathias son of Absalom, mentioned in 11:70. At this time Simon did not garrison Joppa, but replaced its Gentile population with a Jewish one (cf. 12:33–4, and 14:34).

(13:12–19) This is a very strange passage, which ascribes to Simon action taken against his better judgement. Since Simon inherited from his brother, under very difficult circumstances, it might have given place to various rumours and laying of blame, as well as rivalries and tensions within the ruling family. So we may see in this passage an apologetic or even polemical effort to vindicate Simon, the real founder of the dynasty, from culpability for the fate of Jonathan (and his two sons), murdered by Trypho (see v. 23). v. 13, 'Adida', see at 12:38.

(13:20–4) Trypho failed to invade Judea by surprise, and was unable to overcome Simon's defensive tactics. v. 20, Adora was a Hellenistic town in eastern Idumea, also called Adoraim. Trypho arrived there after encircling Judea, trying in vain to invade it. v. 22, 'heavy snow', indeed, very rare in Judea. 'Gilead', we do not know why Trypho chose this way. v. 23, Baskama was probably in the Golan, but identification is uncertain.

(13:25–30) This passage, like some other passages, stresses Simon's role as the head of the dynasty. v. 27, burial monuments are known all over the Mediterranean world. Similar to this one are the monuments from the Kidron valley in Jerusalem and the tomb of Jason, which are not much later than this period. v. 28, 'pyramids', as in the tomb of Jason, v. 29, 'columns', as in the tomb of Benei Hezir. The carvings, or basreliefs, are common in Hellenistic art, but less common on Jewish monuments of this period. Yet it does not seems out of place on a royal monument, and it bears neither anthropomorphic nor zoomorphic figures, as was customary in Jewish art of that period. 'Ships', though often signifying death and afterlife, in this case, and in the author's eyes, their message is related to Hasmonean maritime aspirations. Cf. the paintings in the tomb of Jason. v. 30, 'to this day', i.e. some time before Hyrcanus' death in 104/3 BCE (see 1 Macc B.2).

(13:31–40) v. 31, the sympathy of the author is clearly with the branch issued from Antiochus IV, through Alexander Balas; cf. at 12:39–40. v. 32: 'Asia', cf. at 11:13. v. 33, 'stored food in the strongholds', see at 9:52.

(13:36–40) Simon renewed the alliance with Demetrius II, who issued a royal letter announcing the complete release of Judea from taxation. This was considered to liberate Judea from Seleucid rule and to be the beginning of its independence. v. 36, the letter formally addresses the high priest, the *gērousia*, and the nation in general. v. 37, the release from tribute was not given gratuitously. A lump sum, in the form of a gold crown and palm branch, was paid for it. Cf. at 11:28. vv. 38–40, the sweeping measures of the king's decision included the evacuation of Judea, general amnesty, and an appeal to Jews to join the Seleucid army.

(13:41–2) Our author pauses here in his narrative to declare solemnly the beginning of the independence of Judea. v. 41, 170 ES is 142 BCE. v. 42, dating according to a local ruler is one of the symbols of sovereignty, as is, for example, the issuing of coins (cf. 15:6). Evidence for the use of dating according to Hasmonean regnal years is meagre, but see 14:27, and some coins of Janneus bearing dates (Naveh 1968).

(13:43–7) Simon's policy and military activity were generally directed inwards. Contrary to Jonathan he refrained from intermingling with Seleucid affairs. v. 43, Gazara was on the road between Jerusalem and Joppa. It served as a military base under the command of John Hyrcanus, who lived there (v. 53). 'siege-engine', the Greek has helepolis (lit. city taker—a movable tower). It shows the continuation of the military development of the Hasmonean army. See Shatzman (1991: 24).

(13:47–8) The cleaning of Gazara from impurity stresses the religious motivation behind the Hasmonean conquest. See 1 Macc 5:44. v. 48, Simon was severe in replacing the pagan population with a Jewish one (cf. 11:66; 13:11; 14:34). This policy combines military, national, and religious motivations. Later on, in Idumea and Galilee, it was replaced by the enforced conversion of the population.

(13:49–53) The Akra was not taken by storm, as Gazara partially was, but by prolonged siege and starvation (cf. 12:35–7). The procedure of its recovery was similar to that of Gazara, but it served as an occasion for festivity and commemoration, being the last vestige of foreign rule and part of the holy city. v. 51, the date is the 23rd of Iyyar (the second month in the Jewish year, which begins from Nisan), and the year is 141 BCE. This date is also mentioned in Megillath Taʿanith, as one of the days on which mourning and fasting are prohibited. v. 53, Simon took measures to assure an orderly succession to his rule, by preparing his successor in advance and giving him enough authority and power to take over the

government. His old age played a role in his decision, as shown at 16:3.

(14:1–3) This is a digression, correct in its major lines but its source unknown. v. 1, 172 ES is 140 BCE. The reason given for Demetrius' expedition is incorrect, as it was forced on him because of the Parthian advance westwards. v. 2, 'Arsaces' is a generic name of all Parthian kings. The king at this time was Mithridates I (171–138 BCE). 'Persia and Media', it is because of biblical influence that the Parthian empire is so-called. In Jewish sources it is often called Persia.

(14:4–15) This is one of the most important poetic passages in 1 Maccabees, because of the service it renders to the ruling dynasty. It was composed by the same hand as the rest of the book as can be seen from the common motifs (unlike the decision about Simon's appointment in ch. 14). It is written in a biblical style and includes factual statements. The principal topics mentioned here are: Simon's broadening of the borders of Judea; caring for peace; security and material prosperity; caring for the law and the temple. v. 5, Joppa, see 13:11. v. 10, the supply of food was one of the main concerns of Hellenistic rulers, and cf. 13:33.

(14:16–23) vv. 16–19, the author tries to make of Jonathan's death and Simon's installation as high priest a major international event. Yet this is not supported by his own report, because the Spartan letter is a response to Jonathan's letter, and does not mention, even out of politeness, Jonathan's murder, and the Romans are approached by Simon, not vice versa (see below). vv. 20–3, this letter is taken to be a forgery by various scholars, and as authentic by others. We think that in the light of the author's source for other documents he cites (see 1 Macc D.2(I)), we should consider the correspondence of Jonathan/Simon and Sparta as authentic, with the exception of Arius' letter (1 Macc 12:19–23). v. 22, for the envoys see 1 Macc 12:16. v. 24 is out of context here, and should be linked with the Roman document later. For its contents see 1 Macc 15:16–24. A 'gold shield weighing one thousand minas': sending a decorative shield made of precious metal, like a golden crown (see 13:37), was a common custom, and may have been a sign of submission. The weight of 1,000 minas, about 500–1,000 kg., depending to which mina it is equated, is excessive; see 1 Macc 15:18.

(14:25–49) The document cited here is a most important one for the history and constitution of Hasmonean Judea. It is the only document which tells about the internal procedure of an appointment of a Jewish ruler, his responsibilities, legal standing, titles, and authority. This is the starting-point of the new state, and dynasty, and its consequent history is to be viewed in the light of this document. Its authenticity is undisputed, because, among other reasons, it is not fully in accord with the point of view of 1 Maccabees. The structure of the document is similar to Hellenistic usage (most parallels are decisions of Hellenistic *poleis*). Its composition is the following: date (v. 27); place and circumstances (v. 28); motives for the decision (vv. 29–40); the decision (vv. 41–5); the people's and Simon's mutual agreement (vv. 46–7); details concerning its copying, publicizing, etc. (vv. 48–9).

vv. 25–7a, an introduction to the decision, which explains the motivation for it and the whereabouts of the document. v. 27b, there is here a double dating, Seleucid era and Simon's era, and the equation is correct, the date falling on 13 September, 140 BCE. v. 28, 'Asaramel', an incomprehensible combination of letters, thought to be a transcription derived from the Hebrew original. From among the various ingenious suggestions we prefer *Azara megale* (*azara*, Heb. 'a court', esp. in the temple, and *megalē*, Gk. 'big' which becomes Heb. *gĕdolâ*), as proposed by Schalit (1969: 781). 'Great assembly', some scholars think it refers to the great synagogue, mentioned in the Mishnah ('*Abot*, 1:1). It is indeed the Greek word *sunagōgē*, which appears here, but in the Greek of the Septuagint it translates various Hebrew words, so that it is not necessary to restore the Greek into *kĕneset haggĕdolâ* (great synagogue). This assembly is supposed to represent the nation (cf. Neh 10:1 for the assembly in his days). When the will of God could not be known, as there were neither true prophets (see v. 41), nor Urim and Thummim, the national assembly is called forth to legitimize the appointment of Simon.

vv. 29–40, the reasons that justify the appointment of Simon are listed here in the form of a review of Hasmonean history. v. 32, 'own money', this detail in the catalogue of Simon's virtues discloses one of his sources of power, which was a direct pecuniary connection with the army. v. 35, this appointment refers either to that by the people immediately after the kidnapping of Jonathan by Trypho (13:8–9), or when independence was declared after Demetrius II's letter (13:41–2). vv. 38–40: Simon's success and prestige abroad are highlighted. The mention of Demetrius II's confirmation of Simon as high priest shows that, in spite of the effort made by Simon to get national legitimation of his position, the royal appointment was not ignored, and even if it did not carry much weight legally it was considered to be prestigious. The alliance with Rome is mentioned for the same reason. v. 41 is the beginning of the decision of the assembly, which is the core of the document. Simon gets two appointments, as leader and high priest. We do not know what was the Hebrew title behind the *hēgoumenos* (Gk. leader) here (and in 13:8). On some Hasmonean coins of John Hyrcanus I the inscription reads: 'Head of the community of the Jews' (Heb. *Rō'sh heber hayyĕhudîm*), so *rō'š* may be proposed, but *nāśi'* and *mōšēl* have a good claim too. As high priest, Simon is not dependent any more on the appointment of a pagan king, yet his nomination by *vox populi* is not comparable to divine appointment. But this was out of the question at the time, so the national approval was the best he could get. 'For ever', usually understood to mean that Simon's post is hereditary, as indeed it was; 'until a trustworthy prophet should arise', considering the problematic nomination of Simon (at least from a religious point of view), this sentence seems to be a kind of a compromise, to achieve a wide agreement for his appointment. Criticism of his nomination could have come from various quarters, such as Pharisees, supporters of the Oniad dynasty, Essenes, or other sectarian or political groups. Some of them, and especially the Pharisees, could have been positively responsive to such a formula, which theoretically acknowledged the temporariness of Simon's nomination, but in practice did not affect his rule over Judea. vv. 42–3 give a list of Simon's tasks, which are part of his double office as both leader and high priest. His military tasks are part of his leadership, not a third role as a general. vv. 44–5, these stipulations made the decision irreversible, and also show the ephemeral place of the assembly in the Jewish constitution. 'Purple...gold', see 1 Macc 10:29. vv. 46–7, there is here a mutual agreement as to the contents of the decision, and some scholars point out its contractual character. 'Ethnarch' is again a Greek word, chosen by the translator perhaps for the same Hebrew word translated as *hēgoumenos* in v. 41. vv. 48–9, the arrangements to be taken with the decision are specified here.

They may have been a part of the decision, or an authorial expansion.

(15:1–9) v. 1 refers to Antiochus VII Sidetes (so-called because he was raised in Side, in Asia Minor), son of Demetrius I and younger brother of Demetrius II, who fell in Parthian captivity (see 14:1–3). vv 2–9, this document is considered to be genuine, and to reflect the situation of Antiochus VII at the beginning of his struggle to regain his hereditary kingdom. Trypho was still powerful, and Antiochus needed all the support he could get. His friendly attitude towards Simon changed when his position became more secure (see vv. 26–31). v. 3, 'scoundrels', obviously Trypho and his supporters. v. 5, probably for conciseness' sake, details about tax release are skipped, and the reference is made to former arrangements. v. 6, 'your own coinage', this privilege was one of the more conspicuous symbols of sovereignty in the Hellenistic-Roman world, especially in the case of silver coinage. Nevertheless Simon did not utilize it, and the earliest Hasmonean coinage known is from John Hyrcanus' time. See Rappaport (1976) and Meshorer (1990–1: 106).

(15:10–14) Dor was a Phoenician coastal city south of Acco/Ptolemais. Excavations there revealed some vestiges of the siege by Antiochus, e.g. lead missiles bearing the inscription: obv. 'For the victory of Trypho'; rev. 'Dor, year 5, of the city of the Dorians, Have the taste of sumac'. See Gera (1985). For an alternative reading see Fischer (1992). v. 10,174 ES is 138 BCE. Antiochus' landing in Syria brought him general support. Trypho, who was a usurper, was quickly driven away and was besieged in Dor.

(15:15–24) According to many commentators, this passage should have come after 14:24, to which it is related. The linkage is not only because it is the same envoy and delegation, with the same golden shield, but also because chronologically it was already mentioned in the document about Simon's rule, from September 140 BCE (14:40). It is reasonable to assume a misplacement of this passage somewhere in the chain of the transmission of 1 Maccabees. v. 15, 'Numenius', see 12:16; 14:22, 24. v. 16, Lucius Caecilius Metellius was consul in 142 BCE. 'Ptolemy' refers to Ptolemy VIII (VII) Euergetes II Physcon (145–116 BCE). The copy of the Roman letter, cited here, is the one sent to Ptolemy, though there were other recipients (vv. 22–4). v. 17, 'renew', see 14:24. v. 18, 'thousand minas',

here it is not said that the shield weighed 1,000 minas (despite the NRSV tr.). Various scholars understand it to mean 'of the value of a thousand minas', and correct it and 14:24 accordingly. v. 19, circular letters announcing Roman policy and decisions were an instrument of Roman diplomacy; see at vv. 22–4. v. 21, 'scoundrels', such an extradition clause is not common in our sources, yet some incomplete analogies can be found. See Rappaport (1995b). vv. 22–4, the list of *poleis*, kings, and states, recipients of a letter similar to the one sent to Ptolemy, cited above, has evoked many suggestions, aimed mainly at finding a common denominator for these incongruous political units. Some have suggested that all had Jewish communities; others that the itinerary of the envoys back to Judea passed through these places; others that those states were allied to Rome. But none of these criteria can be applied to all the states on this list. It has also been suggested that it is metaphorical: that such an impressive list is meant to express the whole sphere of Roman influence.

My opinion tends to the list being accurate, that the letter was indeed sent to those addressees, with intent to demonstrate the wide extent of Roman activity and influence, especially in the east (see Rappaport 1995b: 282). Most of the kings and cities mentioned in the list need no comment. Ariarathes V was king of Cappadocia, 162–130 BCE; for Arsaces see at 14:2. The name Sampsames is unknown and probably corrupt. Among the suggestions made to replace it are Lampsakos and Amisos (in western and northern Asia Minor respectively). The names in this list also include regions, which do not always represent a political entity. v. 24, the copy cited above is the one to Ptolemy, who is properly not mentioned in the list. It would have been superfluous to send copies of every letter, all of them being similar, to Simon. Probably each one of them had an appendix with all the other addressees except himself, like the copy of the letter to Ptolemy.

(15:25–31) Here our author resumes the story of the siege of Dor, cut off after v. 14. The siege is going on (v. 25), and the end of it is told in v. 37 after a digression about Simon. v. 26, Simon, like a faithful vassal, sent aid to Antiochus. v. 27, Simon's support became unnecessary in view of Antiochus' imminent victory over Trypho, and the king's interest was now to curtail his power. v. 28, Athenobius is known only from 1 Maccabees. vv. 28–31, it is important to notice that the king is not trying to restore Judea to its prior position, as a province under direct Seleucid rule, but to curtail its expansion, especially into the coastal region, and to restore it to its former borders. Simon could even have kept these places had he been ready to pay for them. So Antiochus' policy was not to return to the glorious days of his ancestors, but to restore obedience of the vassal princes and to replenish his treasury in preparation for a war against Parthia.

(15:32–6) vv. 33–4, Simon's response to the demands of the king is extremely important. It may not be a verbatim citation, but it reflects, at least, the current opinion in the Hasmonean court or the author's circle. This response is based on the idea of historical right, as an ideological and legal argument, to justify Hasmonean conquests in the land of Israel. It is in contrast to the legal basis of the rule of the Hellenistic dynasties, which was the conquest itself—their kingdoms were *doriktētoi*, conquered by the spear. So it is not a conquest, runs this argument, but a reacquisition of an inheritance. v. 35, typically of Simon, he is not rushing into an armed conflict, and proposes a small sum of money, 100 talents as against 1,000 demanded, to placate the king.

(15:37–41) v. 37, Orthosia was in what today is northern Lebanon. v. 38, Cendebeus was *stratēgos* of the *Paralia*, as was Simon before him. v. 39, for the use of Kedron to put pressure on Simon by harassing the population see vv. 40–1. 'The king pursued Trypho', Trypho fled further on to Apamea, where, with the support of the Seleucid military settlers, his revolt had originally begun, and was slain there.

(16:1–3) v. 1, for Gazara becoming John's seat see 13:53; now it was on the front line, against Cendebeus. v. 2, we know by name three sons of Simon: John, Judas, and Mattathias (v. 14). All three names are common in the Hasmonean family. John, the successor of Simon, is known also as Hyrcanus in the writings of Josephus Flavius, but not in 1 Maccabees, nor in Talmudic sources, nor on his coins. We do not know Simon's age, but since about thirty years have passed from the beginning of the Maccabean revolt, and at that time Simon was not a young person, he should by now be about 70 years old.

(16:4–10) v. 4, the number of soldiers is quite reasonable here. Cavalry in the Hasmonean army is explicitly mentioned here for first time (but cf. 2 Macc 12:35). Bar-Kochva (1989: 68–81) thinks that cavalry was already used by Judas and Jonathan. Shatzman (1991: 19, n. 42, 22) is more sceptical. v. 6, John, following the example of the Maccabees, took part in battle in person.

(16:11–17) v. 11, nothing is known about Ptolemy except what is told here. His patronymic may point to an Arabian origin (Hababus/Habib). Was he born Jewish or was he a proselyte? (It is unlikely that he was a non-Jew, as he was the son-in-law of the high priest, Simon, himself.) We may then consider the possibility that Ptolemy was a local chief who accepted Judaism and married into the Hasmonean family. He may have been a prototype of Antipas, Herod's grandfather, but there is no way to prove it.

'Governor' We may learn from this passage that Judea was divided into regions, Jericho and its surroundings among them, under governors (Gk. *stratēgoi*) who might have the power to build fortresses (v. 15), and that they could come from the local nobility (see above). v. 14, Simon attended to the administration of the country by means of inspection tours. The year 177 ES is 134 BCE. v. 15, Dok was a fortress above Jericho to the north-west. v. 16, according to Josephus, who is not relying on 1 Maccabees on this matter (see 1 Macc 0.2(4)), Ptolemy murdered only Simon, and took his two sons and wife prisoner (*Ant.* 13 §§ 228–9).

(16:18–22) Ptolemy's appeal to Antiochus VII after the murder raises the possibility that the conspiracy itself was coordinated with him. His motivation to murder the high priest, his father-in-law, may hint that he was not integrated into Jewish society, and was linked to the Hasmoneans very lightly (see v. 1). Ptolemy tried also to get rid of John, but the men whom he sent to murder him were forestalled. Josephus (ibid.) has some more details, which stress that the popularity of the Hasmoneans caused the failure of Ptolemy's conspiracy.

(16:23–4) This passage is very similar to the concluding verses in Kings, at the end of the acts of the various kings (e.g. 1 Kings 14:19, 29; 16:14, 27; 22:40; 2 Kings 1:18; 10:34, etc.). It raises the question of whether there was a book, named 'The Chronicles of the High-Priesthood of John', or whether this is merely an imitation of biblical style, adopted by the author of 1 Maccabees. Since the formula used here is not complete, and does not contain the number of the ruler's regnal years and the name of his successor, it leads to the conclusion that 1 Maccabees was written before Hyrcanus' death in 104 BCE.

REFERENCES

Abel, F.-M. (1949), *Les livres des Maccabées* (Paris: Gabalda).

Bar-Kochva, B. (1975), 'Hellenistic Warfare in Jonathan's Campaign Near Azotos', *Scripta Classica Israelica* 2: 83–96.

—— (1989), *Judas Maccabaeus* (Cambridge: Cambridge University Press).

—— (1998), 'The Description of the Battle of Beth-Zacharia: Literary Fiction or Historical Fact?', *Cathedra* 86: 7–22 (Heb.).

Bickerman, E. (1937), *Der Gott der Makkabäer* (Berlin: Schocken).

—— (1951), 'Les Maccabées de Malalas', *Byzantion* 21: 63–84.

—— (1968), *Chronology of the Ancient World* (London: Thames & Hudson).

—— (1979), *The God of the Maccabees* (Leiden: Brill).

Dancy, J. C. (1954), *Commentary on First Maccabees* (Oxford: Blackwell).

Davies, P. (1977), 'Hasidim in the Maccabean Period', *JJS* 28: 127–40.

Dimant, D. (1988), 'Use and Interpretation of Mikra in the Apocrypha and Pseudepigrapha', in J. Moulder (ed.), *Mikra* (Assen: Van Gorcum), 379–419.

Fischer, T. (1992), 'Tryphons verfehlter Sieg von Dor?', *ZPE* 93: 29–30.

Galil, G. (1992), 'Parathon, Timnatha and the Fortifications of Bacchides', *Cathedra* 63: 22–30 (Heb.).

Gera, D. (1985), 'Tryphon's Sling Bullet from Dor', *IEJ* 35: 153–63.

—— (1990), 'On the Credibility of the History of the Tobiads', in A. Kasher, U. Rappaport, and G. Fuks (eds.), *Greece and Rome in Eretz Israel* (Jerusalem: Yad Izhak Ben-Zwi), 21–38.

—— (1996), 'The Battle of Beth Zacharia and Greek Literature', in I. Gafni et al. (eds.), *Studies in Memory of Menahem Stern*, 25–53 (Heb.).

Goldstein, J. A. (1975), 'The Hasmoneans: The Dynasty of God's Resisters', *HTR* 68: 53–8.

—— (1976), *I Maccabees*, AB (New York: Doubleday).

Goodman, M. D., and Holladay, A. J. (1986), 'Religious Scruples in Ancient Warfare', *CQ* 36: 151–71.

Grabbe, L. J. (1991), 'Maccabean Chronology, 167–164 or 168–165 BCE', *JBL* 110: 59–74.

Gruen, E. S. (1984), *The Hellenistic World and the Coming of Rome* (2 vols.; Berkeley: University of California Press).

Habicht, C. (1976), 'Royal Documents in Maccabees II', *HSCP* 80: 1–18.

Hengel, M. (1974), *Judaism and Hellenism* (2 vols.; London: SCM).

Holladay, C. R. (1983), *Fragments from Hellenistic Jewish Authors* (Chico, Calif.: Scholars Press).

Houghton, A. (1992), 'The Revolt of Tryphon and the Accession of Antiochus VI at Apamea', *RSN* (= *SNR*) 71: 119–41.

—— and G. le Rider (1985), 'Le deuxième filo d'Antiochos IV à Ptolémaïs', *RSN* 64: 73–85.

Isaac, B. (1991) 'A Seleucid Inscription from Jamnia-on-the-Sea: Antiochus V Eupator and the Sidonians', *IEJ* 41: 132–44.

Johns, A. F. (1963), 'The Military Strategy of Sabbath Attacks on the Jews', *VT* 13: 482–6.

Kasher, A. (1988), *Jews, Idumeans and Ancient Arabs* (Tübingen: Mohr [Siebeck]).

Kloner, A., Regev, D., and Rappaport, U. (1992), 'A Hellenistic Burial Cave in the Judean shephela', *Atiqot* 21: 27*–50* (Heb. with Eng. summary, 175–7).

le Rider, G. (1965), *Suse sous les Séleucides et les Parthes* (Paris: P. Geuthner).

—— (1993), Les ressources financières de Séleucos IV et le paiement de l'indemnité aux Romains', in M. Price et al. (eds.), *Essays in Honour of R. Carson and K. Jenkins* (London: Spink), 49–67.

Martola, N. (1984), *Capture and Liberation* (Åbo: Åbo Akademi).

Meshorer, Y. (1990–1), 'Ancient Jewish Coinage: Addendum I', *INJ* 11: 104–33.

Millar, F. (1993), *The Roman Near East 31BC–AD337* (Cambridge, Mass.: Harvard University Press).

Momigliano, A. (1976), 'The Date of the First Book of Maccabees', in *L'Italie préromaine et la Rome républicaine, Mélanges offerts à J. Heurgon* (Rome: École française de Rome), 657–61.

Mørkholm, O. (1989), 'Antiochus IV', *The Cambridge History of Judaism*, II. 278–91.

Murphy O'Connor, J. (1976), 'Demetrius I and the Teacher of Righteousness, I Macc., X, 25–45', *RB* 93: 400–20.

Naveh, J. (1968), 'The Dated Coins of Alexander Janneus', *IEJ* 18: 20–6.

Oren, E. D., and Rappaport, U. (1984), 'The Necropolis of Maresha Beit Govrin', *IEJ* 34: 114–53.

Peters, J. P., and Thiersch, H. (1905), *Painted Tombs in the Necropolis of Marissa* (London: Palestine Exploration Fund).

Rappaport, U. (1968), 'La Judée et Rome pendant le règne d'Alexandre Jannée', *REJ* 127: 329–45.

——(1970), 'Gaza andAscalon in the Persian and Hellenistic Periods in Relation to their Coins', *IEJ* 20: 75–80.

——(1976), 'The Emergence of Hasmonean Coinage', *AJS Review* 1: 171–86.

——(1980), 'Notes on Antiochus' Persecutions as Reflected in the Book of Daniel', in B. Bar-Kochva (ed.), *The Seleucid Period in Eretz-Israel* (Tel-Aviv: Hakibbutz Hameuchad) (Heb.).

——(1993), 'The Hellenistic World as Seen by the Book of Daniel', *RASHI: Hommage à E. E. Urbach* (Paris: Éditions du Cerf), 71–9.

——(1995a), 'The Samaritans in the Hellenistic Period', in A. D. Crown and L. Davey (eds.), *New Samaritan Studies: Essays in Honour of G. D. Sixdenier* (Sydney: Mandelbaum Publishing), 281–8.

——(1995b), 'The Extradition Clause in 1 Maccabees 15:21', in K. van Lerberghe and A. Schoors (eds.), *Immigration and Emigration in the Ancient Near East: Festschrift für E. Lipinski* (Leuven: Peeters), 271–83.

——, Pastor, J., and Rimon, O. (1994), 'Land, Society and Culture in Judea', *Transeuphratène* 7: 73–82.

Rheinold, M. (1970), *History of Purple as a Status Symbol in Antiquity* (Brussels: Collection Latomus).

Rowley, H. H. (1953), 'Menelaus and the Abomination of Desolation', *Studia orientalia J. Pedersen dedicata* (Copenhagen: E. Munksgaard), 303–15.

Schalit, A. (1969), *König Herodes, der Mann und sein Werk* (Berlin: de Gruyter).

Schmidt, F. (1994), *La Pensée du Temple de Jérusalem à Qoumrân* (Paris: Éditions du Seuil).

Schürer, E. (1973–87), *The History of the Jewish People in the Age of Jesus Christ* (3 vols.; Edinburgh: T. & T. Clark).

Schwartz, D. R. (1992), 'On Pharisaic Opposition to the Hasmonean Monarchy', in *Studies on the Jewish Background of Christianity* (Tübingen: Mohr [Siebeck]).

——(1994), 'Hasidim in 1 Maccabees 2:42?', *SCI* 13: 7–18.

Schwartz, J., and Spanier, J. (1991), 'On Mattathias and the Desert of Samaria', *RB* 98: 252–71.

Schwartz, S. (1991), 'Israel and the Nations Roundabout: 1 Maccabees and the Hasmonean Expansion', *JJS* 42: 16–38.

Shatzman, I. (1991), *The Armies of the Hasmoneans and Herod* (Tübingen: Mohr[Siebeck]).

Sherk, A. K. (1969), *Roman Documents from the Greek East* (Baltimore, Md.: Johns Hopkins University Press).

Stern, M. (1974–84), *Greek and Latin Authors on Jews and Judaism* (3 vols.; Jerusalem: Israel Academy of Sciences and Humanities).

Stern, M. (1981), 'Judea and her Neighbors in the Days of Alexander Jannaeus', *Jerusalem Cathedra* 1: 22–46.

Tcherikover, V. (1959), *Hellenistic Civilization and the Jews* (Philadelphia: Jewish Publication Society), 189–222.

Williams, O. S. (1999), *The Structure of Maccabees* (Washington, D.C.: CBQ).

Wise, M. O. (1990), 'A Note on the "Three Days" of 1 Maccabees X. 34', *VT* 40: 116–22.

10. 2 Maccabees

R. DORAN

INTRODUCTION

A. Title. The title, the Second Book of Maccabees, is a convenient tag to distinguish this collection of documents from the other history of the Maccabean revolt known as the First Book of Maccabees, 1 and 2 Maccabees, therefore, are not the titles for a two-volume work on the Maccabean revolt, but are quite distinct.

B. Subject-Matter and Literary Genre. I. 2 Maccabees is composed of three documents, two letters prefixed to an epitome of a larger historical work. There is no explicit connection between the two prefixed letters and the epitome, although scholars have attempted to show interrelationships (Momigliano 1975; Doran 1981). The first letter (1:1–10a) is addressed to

Egyptian Jews and exhorts them to celebrate the Feast of Hanukkah. The second (1:10b–2:18) has a similar addressee and message, but also contains an account of the death of Antiochus IV, and attempts to show the continuity between the first and second temples. The first letter follows the conventions of letters written in Aramaic, while the second does not. The epitome (2:19–15:39) covers the history of the Maccabean revolt from the reign of Seleucus IV Philopator (187–175 BCE) to Judas's defeat of Nicanor in 161 BCE, The epitome therefore covers a different time-period from that of 1 Maccabees. 1 Maccabees in one verse (1:9) notes the time between Alexander the Great and Antiochus IV, and in five verses (1:11–15) the events of Antiochus IV's reign before the persecution of the Jews in Judaea; the epitome, on the other hand, devotes a whole chapter to events under Antiochus IV's predecessor (2 Macc 3) and another chapter to events prior to the persecution (2 Macc 4). The epitome ends with the defeat of the Seleucid general Nicanor in 161 BCE at the hands of Judas Maccabeus, while 1 Maccabees continues through the death of Judas and the successive leadership of his brothers Jonathan and Simon down to Simon's death in 134 BCE. The two works also differ in style: 1 Maccabees is the translation of an original Hebrew work and its style betrays its translation quality at times; the epitome follows the conventions of Hellenistic historiography, and is written in good Greek style. 1 Maccabees focuses primarily on the heroic exploits of the Hasmoneans: they are the family 'through whom deliverance was given to Israel' (1 Macc 5:62). 1 Maccabees in fact closes with a refrain which echoes those found about the kings of Judah and Israel in 1–2 Kings, e.g. at 1 Kings 11:41. Judas is certainly a warrior hero in the epitome, but victory comes from the epiphanies of the God of Israel and God's mercy is gained through the sufferings of the martyrs. The epitome in fact falls within the genre of epiphanic collections which narrate how a god defends his/her temple.

2. A totally different question is how faithfully the epitomist preserves both the content and the style of the author he is condensing, Jason of Cyrene. The rapid-fire telling of events as at 13:22–6 and 4:25 and the brief mention of characters' names, e.g. Callisthenes at 8:33, without further introduction suggest a fuller fund of narrative events which Jason would have supplied. Did Jason's five-volume work end where the epitome ends, with the victory over Nicanor? Some scholars suggest so, and even go so far as to identify Jason of Cyrene with Jason son of Eleazar who was sent by Judas Maccabeus on an embassy to Rome after the defeat of Nicanor (1 Macc 8:17): Jason therefore would have ended his story with the defeat of Nicanor because that was where his participation in the events ended. Others would argue that the rhetorical style and flourish of the epitome would not have been present in Jason's work. Behind both these suggestions lurks the desire to show that the epitome is based on 'real' history, on the word of an eyewitness who wrote in a sober style. Unfortunately, all we have is the epitome and we simply are not able to say anything about what Jason wrote. The epitome ends where it does because it provides a fitting literary and rhetorical flourish as the blaspheming attacker of the temple is appropriately destroyed.

C. The World-View of the Epitome. The author of the epitome confronts Judaism with Hellenism, particularly emphasizing traditional Jewish values as opposed to innovations such as Jews being educated at Greek gymnasia. Yet the author also stresses that Jews can be good citizens and can interact well with their Greek neighbours. Theologically the epitome is Deuteronomistic in tone: as long as the Jews obey the Torah, God will protect them. Punishment always fits the crime. One particularly important part of the world-view that God rewards the righteous is the author's strong belief in individual bodily resurrection for the pious (2 Macc 7). God will give back to the martyrs all their bodily parts in a new creative act.

D. Date and Place of Composition. In discussing date and place, one has to ask about both the date of Jason of Cyrene and the date of the epitome. The only secure date for Jason's work is that it was written before the epitome. If one assumes that Jason was an eyewitness to the events or that he drew on oral reports from contemporaries, he might have written not long after 161 BCE, the date of the battle against Nicanor. In attempting to date the epitome, one has to decide whether the prefixed letters, particularly the first, were originally joined to the epitome or not. If one does assume this, then one has to decide whether the epitome was written along with the letter or previously. Since the first letter is dated to 124 BCE, then the epitome would have been written on or before that date. If the epitome and the letters were written separately and then joined later, then one has to rely on other clues in the epitome itself. In a work which emphasizes God's defence of the temple, one might suggest that it was written before Pompey the Great entered Jerusalem and the temple in 63 BCE. The chronological differences between 1 and 2 Maccabees have also been used as a clue to argue that Jason/the epitomist wrote to refute 1 Maccabees with its pro-Hasmonean bias, and thus after 1 Maccabees (Goldstein 1976; 1983), but this is unlikely. So no one knows either when Jason of Cyrene wrote his five-volume work or when the epitomist did his shortening, with dates for the latter ranging from around 124 to 63 BCE. Nor can one be sure *where* the works were written. The epitomist has clearly learnt Greek well, and is aware of Greek historiographical conventions, so he could have written anywhere in the Greek-speaking world. The opposition he shows towards the gymnasium suggests a city where some Jews were beginning to attend the gymnasium, but that again could be anywhere.

E. Outline.

COMMENTARY

The Prefixed Letters (1:1–2:18)

(**1:1–100**) **The First Letter** The first letter follows the normal format of letters in the Hellenistic period as it first indicates who the recipients and senders of the letter are (v. 1), then follows this with good wishes for the recipients (vv. 2–6), the body of the letter (vv. 7–9), and closes with the date (v. 10a). The letter was written in 124 BCE, a year in which a bitter civil war in Egypt had ended. The letter makes no reference to these events, however, nor does it refer to any specific individuals. Rather, it emphasizes that both recipients and senders are all brothers. A somewhat similar greeting is found in the letter of 419 BCE found in the Elephantine papyri (Cowley 1923: 60–5). One wonders who were the senders—John Hyrcanus the high priest and his council?—and who were the recipients—the Jewish community in Alexandria, or the military colony at Leontopolis? The greeting combines a Jewish formula—'true peace'—and a Greek formula—'greetings'.

The initial greetings are followed by a long prayer of blessing which emphasizes the common covenant with the patriarchs, and the role the Torah should play in their lives. Particularly interesting is the stress on God's active role in the following of the Torah. The Greek verb for 'be reconciled' at v. 5 (*katallageiē*) is unusual in the rest of the LXX. It is found with this meaning at 2 Macc 7:33; 8:29, and this may constitute one piece of evidence for seeing a connection between the letter and the epitome. The same notion is found in the prayer of Solomon at the dedication of the first temple (2 Chr 6:19). Some scholars have found in v. 5 an allusion either to the civil war in Egypt or to the need for reconciliation because of the sin of Onias IV in

building a temple at Leontopolis (Jos. *Ant.* 13.62–73). The terms are those used for general good wishes, however, and so such specificity need not be present.

The body of the letter contains a quotation of a previous letter. Since there are no quotation marks in Greek, where does the quotation begin? Does the 'critical distress' of v. 7 refer to the time of Demetrius II in 169 of the Seleucid Era, i.e. spring 143 to spring 142 BCE, the time when Jonathan was captured (1 Macc 12:48)? If that were the case, why is Jonathan's capture not mentioned whereas an event over 20 years previously, the withdrawal of Jason, is? Would the body of the letter begin with a quotation of a letter with no indication of the fact? We should probably begin the letter at 'In the critical distress …' It is not exactly sure what event is being described as the time of distress. It is not Jason who is said to have burned the gates, but others (2 Macc 8:33; 1 Macc 1:31; 4:38). 1 suggest that the withdrawal, not revolt, of Jason is being referred to (2 Macc 5:1–9) and the subsequent destruction of the city by the Seleucids is described using the traditional figures of burnt gates and the shedding of innocent blood.

The end of the quotation is marked by the formula, 'And now'. Only here and at 2 Macc 1:18 and 10:6 is the festival of Chislev connected with the Feast of Booths. The date is given at the end of the letter, as is usual.

(**1:10b–2:18**) **The Second Letter** The second letter bristles with problems. The first section (1:10b–18) speaks of the death of Antiochus IV and seems about to stop at 1:18 with an invitation to celebrate the festival of the purification of the temple, but then the letter continues on with a digression on the holiness of the second temple until the exhortation to celebrate the festival of Chislev is repeated at 2:16. No date is given. While the first letter had as recipients and senders only the brothers in Judaea, Jerusalem, and Egypt, this letter provides a range of people with Judas and Aristobulus being specifically named. The reference would seem to be to Judas Maccabeus, the leader of the revolt in Judea, and possibly to the Aristobulus whose fragments are preserved by the later Christian bishop, Eusebius of Caesarea (*Praep. Evang.* 7.32. 16–18; 8.9.38–8.10.17; 13.12.1–16). Aristobulus is said to have presented a work to Ptolemy VI Philometor (180–145 BCE), whereas in this letter he is called the teacher of Ptolemy. Most scholars do not regard this letter as genuine. Rather it is creative historiography, wherein an author writes what should have been written. What is in evidence is the attempt to show a close connection between Jews in Egypt and in Judea.

The account of the death of Antiochus IV differs from that in Polybius, 31, and Appian, *Syriaca*, 66, and, more interestingly, from that in 1 Macc 6:16 and 2 Macc 9. All these other sources agree that Antiochus IV did not die at the temple of Nanea. One cannot reconcile the death accounts in this letter and in the epitome, and one must conclude that they were written by different people.

(1:19–36) The Miraculous Fire At 1:18, the text unexpectedly speaks of a festival of fire at the time of Nehemiah. The author has this Nehemiah commissioned by the Persian king (1:20), and seems to refer to the Nehemiah who is the central figure of the book of Nehemiah. However, he sets the scene at the end of the Babylonian exile, when another Nehemiah accompanied Zerubbabel back to Judea (Ezra 2:2; Neh 7:7; 1 Esd 5:8), and so has conflated the two figures. Here Nehemiah, not Jeshua and Zerubbabel (Ezra 3–6), is credited with the restoration of temple worship. Nehemiah is also important at 2 Macc 2:13–14; perhaps his role as governor and temple restorer provided a model for the activity of Judas. The fire on the altar was never to go out (Lev 6:12–13) and so its miraculous preservation emphasizes the continuity between the first and second temple, which some had questioned (Ezra 3:12; 1 *Enoch* 89:73; 2 *Apoc. Bar.* 68:5–6).

The prayer of the priests stresses God's election of Israel, and his role as the Divine Warrior who fights for his people and leads them to their home, as in the hymn in Ex 15. The miracle of the fire is verified and acknowledged by the Persian king, and Nehemiah is recognized as the discoverer of naphtha, a kind of petroleum well known to Hellenistic scientists and geographers (Dioscorides, *De materia medica*, 1.73; Strabo, *Geog.* 15–3.15; 16.1.15). He is thus ranked with other 'inventors' of benefits to mankind, as in Dionysos of wine and Demeter of grain. Among Jewish Hellenistic authors, Abraham was said to be the inventor of astrology and mathematics (Eus. *Praep. Evang.* 9.17.3) and Moses the discoverer of ships, weapons of war, and Egyptian religion (ibid. 9.27.4–6).

(2:1–15) The Temple and Earlier Traditions The narrative now answers the question of who had ordered the sacred fire to be taken to Babylonia, and the answer is Jeremiah. While that story shows the continuity between the first temple and the second, the hiding of the sacred vessels on Mt. Nebo shows the discontinuity. The sacred vessels are returned to God's mountain until the ingathering of the people when, as during the Exodus (Ex 40:34–8) and at the dedication of the first temple by Solomon (1 Kings 8:10), God's glory will appear again.

v. 4, many traditions clustered around the figure of Jeremiah. He will appear again as an intercessor for his people at 2 Macc 15:14–16. Eupolemus, perhaps the ambassador of Judas Maccabeus, stated that Jeremiah preserved the ark and the tablets from the Babylonians (Eus. *Praep. Evang.* 9.39.5) and the Letter of Jeremiah similarly exhorts the exiles to refrain from idolatry.

vv. 9–12, the reference to Moses and Solomon in v. 8 is further developed. There is no mention of Moses' praying at Lev 9:23–4 when fire consumes the burnt offering, although at Solomon's prayer fire came down (2 Chr 7:1). The saying of Moses in v. 11 is not found in the HB although the event referred to derives from Lev 10:16–20. The command to celebrate the Feast of Tabernacles for eight days given at Lev 23:33–6 seems to be missing before v. 12. These stories all testify to the lively narrative world of Second-Temple Judaism as the traditional stories were told and retold with creative nuances.

vv. 13–15, after discussing the divine fire at the time of Moses and Solomon, the author returns to Nehemiah and his fire exploits. Interesting is the reference to Nehemiah's founding a library and collecting books. After Ptolemy I founded the great library at Alexandria, others imitated him as did the Attalid kings of Pergamum in Asia Minor. Nehemiah is being put in good company! Scholars have puzzled over exactly what is referred to in the list of books. Rather than attempting to align this list neatly with specific books of the canonical HB, one should recognize that, as the finds at Qumran are showing us, Judean society was filled with many more stories, hymns, and retellings of traditional narratives than are extant today. 1 Macc 1:56–7 relates how the books of the law were ripped apart and burnt if found. Judas is said to act similarly to Nehemiah, and so another element of the comparison made at 2 Macc 1:18 is introduced. Does v. 15 suggest a superiority of the library at Jerusalem as regards Jewish books to the one in Alexandria?

(2:16–18) Conclusion The request of 1:18 is repeated here, and interwoven with the themes of God as Divine Warrior (1:25), of the people as God's inheritance (1:26–7), and of the ingathering of the people (1:27–9; 2:3). The reference in v. 18 to God's rescue of his people and his purification of the place provides the appropriate introduction to the epitome. As mentioned in the introduction, we do not know what exactly the relationship is between the two prefixed letters and the epitome. One can suggest corresponding themes, but there is no intrinsic connection.

The Epitome (2:19–15:39)

(2:19–32) Prologue The author writes an elegant preface to his work, outlining his source, the contents of the work, his aims, and his methods. He shows his control of the current historiographical methods and style, and his command of Greek. The source of his work is Jason of Cyrene, of whom we know nothing. Ptolemy I Lagus is said to have settled a group of Jews in Cyrenaica (Jos. *Ag. Ap.* 2.44) and Jewish inscriptions have been located there. At the time of Sulla (around 85 BCE), Strabo stated that the city of Cyrene was composed of four elements, citizens, farmers, resident aliens, and Jews (Jos. *Ant.* 14.115). Jason would therefore have been a Greek-speaking Jew from Cyrenaica which was under the control of the Ptolemies.

As for the content of the book, the author says nothing about the events under Seleucus IV which open the book (ch. 3) nor those under Demetrius I which close the book (chs. 14–15). The operative word for the author appears to be the term 'epiphany'/'appearance', a word which the author uses throughout the work, and which appears also in these chapters (3:24; 14:15; 15:27). In this prologue, the author, who loves to play on words, contrasts Antiochus IV Epiphanes and the 'epiphanies' which God gave his people. A further contrast is between Judaism and the barbarian hordes. This is the first known use of the term 'Judaism', seemingly coined to contrast with 'Hellenism' (2 Macc 4:13) and 'allophylism/foreign ways' (2 Macc 4:13; 6:25). The Greeks called those who did not speak their language 'barbarians'. Here the author is calling the Greek-speaking Seleucids the barbarians.

The aims and methods that the author espouses are those standard for Hellenistic historians, as is the motif of hard work undertaken willingly for the benefit of the reader. At v. 24, the author does not really claim to get rid of 'the flood of statistics'; the terms rather mean that the author is concerned to shorten the number of lines, of which there would have been quite a few in a five-volume work.

(3:1–39) The First Attack on the Temple The first attack and the first epiphany are set during the reign of Seleucus IV Philopator (187–175 BCE). The story is similar to other accounts written in praise of a deity who defends his/her temple: the attack, the plea for help, the response of the deity, the rout of the enemy, and the rejoicing of the defenders. One finds such a scheme, for example, in the repulse of Sennacherib from Jerusalem (2 Chr 32:1–22; 2 Kings 18:17–19:36), and in the defence of Delphi by Apollo against the Persians under Xerxes in 480 BCE (Hdt. 8.37–9) and against the Gauls in 179 BCE (Paus. 10.23.2).

(3:1–8) The Problem The city is described as idyllically at peace. The author stresses that peace depends on the piety of the leader, the high priest, a theme found in the books of Kings (1 Kings 9:1–9; 2 Kings 17:7–8; 21:11–15). The behaviour of Onias will stand in sharp opposition to that of his successors in the office. This utopian picture contrasts with the conflict and division described in the history of the Qumran Covenanters (CD 1) and in the narrative of 1 *Enoch* 1–11. The benign relationship of the ruling powers depicted here is similar to what is found elsewhere as the Persian kings had provided for the sacrificial cult (Ezra 6:9–10; 7:20–3), and Josephus states that the Ptolemies and Antiochus III had bestowed privileges on Jerusalem (*Ant.* 12.50, 58, 138–44; *Ag. Ap.* 2.48).

vv. 4–8, this utopian scene is disrupted. One should follow the Latin and Armenian translations which show that Simon belonged, not to the tribe of Benjamin, but to the priestly clan of Bilgah (Neh 12:5,18; 1 Chr 24:14). Simon's exact position is not known, as the term for 'captain' could cover civil and military as well as religious functions, nor do we know if he had been appointed by the high priest or by Seleucid authorities. Precisely what the conflict was over is not known either: was the disagreement over what the duties of the supervisor of the market were, or who would supervise all aspects of buying and selling? According to the Temple Scroll (11QT 47:7–18), only hides from clean animals sacrificed in Jerusalem could be brought into Jerusalem, whereas the decree of Antiochus III on the temple only forbade the hides of unclean animals and did not require that the hides be from animals sacrificed in Jerusalem (Jos. *Ant.* 12.146). This purity debate obviously has economic implications. Is this the basis for the conflict, or is it more likely a power-play between two factions in the small city-state of Judea? Such power-plays were earlier evident in Jerusalem in the historical romance of the Tobiads (*Ant.* 12.154–222). Simon was the brother of Menelaus, the future high priest, and one should see here a struggle between important families for control of the city. Simon makes his move by appealing to the governor, who, not willing to interfere in temple affairs, sends the question to the Seleucid ruler. The Peace of Apamea in 188 BCE had imposed a large indemnity on the Seleucids and so they were looking for funds. According to the Heliodorus inscription, Seleucus IV in 178 BCE appointed Olympiodorus to take responsibility for the sanctuaries in Coele-Syria and Phoenicia. This new administrative structure was intended to make the satrapy similar to the rest of the Seleucid empire. The authorities in the Jerusalem temple may have seen the reform as a threat, whereas others, like Simon, may have seen it as an opportunity for advancement. The author of the condensed narrative, to intensify the situation, substituted the chancellor of the realm, Heliodorus, for the middle-level manager, Olympiodorus.

(3:9–14a) The Attack on the Temple The author stresses the friendly reception of the Seleucid minister to underline the unexpectedness of the attack. The high priest cleverly responds, basing his argument on the idea that deposits in temples should not be violated, particularly those of widows and orphans who are particularly protected by God (Ps 146:9; Deut 27:19; Isa 1:23). The mention by the high priest of deposits in the temple by a Hyrcanus, son of Tobias, has led some scholars to suggest that Onias was pro-Ptolemaic and the leader of an anti-Seleucid faction. Within the Tobiad romance preserved in Josephus' *Antiquities* (12.154–222), the Tobiads and the youngest son Hyrcanus are depicted as closely allied with the Ptolemies. However, such a suggestion seems totally out of place in a context in which the high priest is trying to win over the Seleucid minister. Would he bring his anti-Seleucid leaning to the attention of Heliodorus? More likely, Hyrcanus is simply mentioned as an important personage.

(3:14b–21) The Plea for Divine Help The description of the distress of the citizens is highly emotional. The author stresses the involvement of the whole populace, as married women, usually excluded from public business, and unmarried women, normally hidden out of sight, are included.

(3:22–30) The Response of the Deity The author highlights the sovereignty of God through the title given to him at v. 24 and the reference to God's sovereign power at v. 28. This first epiphany has first a horseman and then two young men and so Bickerman (1979) suggested that there were two intertwined accounts, one with the horseman (vv. 24–5, 27–8, 30) and another with the two young men (vv. 26,29, 31–4). However, one could also argue that the author is displaying God's power through several agents. The description of the avenging figures as dressed in golden armour and extremely handsome is how divine interveners are usually portrayed in Hellenistic literature.

(3:31–9) The Effect of the Miracle Heliodorus later appeared in history in a plot to assassinate Seleucus IV, and so this story sees his recuperation. His recognition of the power of the God of Israel does not mean that Heliodorus converted, only that he acknowledges the power of the deity who resides there. A similar story is told of Ptolemy IV Philopator in 3 Macc 1–2, but Ptolemy does not repent on his recovery. Recognition of the power of the resident deity is a theme in the story of how the Persian commander Datis was forced to proclaim the power of the goddess Athene who sent a miraculous thirst on the Persian forces when they besieged the isle of Lindos (Faure 1941). The healing of Heliodorus through a sacrifice, possibly a reparation offering about deposits (Lev 6:1–7; Num 5:5–10), and the prayer of the high priest, highlight that Heliodorus was defeated by divine aid, not by some human ambush. Heliodorus in turn offered sacrifice, perhaps a sacrifice of well-being (Lev 7:11–18), as Alexander is reported by Josephus to have done (*Ant.* 11.336). Both sacrifices emphasize the power of the God of Israel and suggest that Jews and Gentiles can live on good terms, as long as the rights of the Jews are respected.

(3:39–10:8) The Second Attack on the Temple The second attack encompasses the time of Antiochus IV. The section has the same structure as in the earlier part of ch. 3: attack against the temple and the traditional way of life (4:1–6:17); the cry for help (6:18–7:42); God's answer (chs. 8–9); the reversal of the effects of the attack (10:1–8).

(3:39–6:17) The Attack on the Traditional Way of Life The traditional way of life is disturbed when the pious high priest Onias is removed from Jerusalem and replaced by an innovative high priest, Jason, and his usurper, Menelaus (4:1–5:10). This internal disruption is then followed by the attack of the outsider, Antiochus IV (5:11–6:10). The author has interspersed his narrative with reflections on the significance of events (4:16–17; 5:17–20; 6:12–17), which evidence the author's belief in the election of Israel by God and the requirement that Jews live according to the laws of the covenant.

(3:39–4:6) The Removal of Onias 3:39 sums up the events in the previous chapter, but 4:1 shows that the underlying problem, the rivalry between families of the ruling élite, still exists. The increase in violence is an index of the breakdown of the polity, but now the new Seleucid governor takes an active role in the political in-fighting by supporting Simon against Onias. We do not know why he would encourage such unrest. Onias' response is to go over his head to the king. The author insists that this is not Onias playing politics, but altruistic concern for the welfare of Jerusalem. This selflessness of Onias will contrast sharply with the self-seeking motives of his successors.

(4:7–22) The High-Priesthood of Jason The author omits the details of Seleucus IV's assassination, the installation of his young son, and the usurpation of the throne by Seleucus' brother, Antiochus IV Epiphanes, who returned from Rome where he had been a hostage (App. *Syr.* 45; cf. Dan 11:20–1). A new monarch would appoint or confirm rulers in their position, and Jason, Onias' brother, seized the opportunity to grasp for the position of high priest. The annual indemnity imposed by the Romans on the Seleucids at the Treaty of Apamea was 1,000 talents of silver, and so Jason's offer of 590 talents, quite a hefty sum for a small country like Judea, would have been welcomed towards paying the few last instalments.

Exactly what Jason wanted in exchange has long been debated. The gymnasium was the sign par excellence of Greek life. Originally designed for physical and military training, the gymnasium normally had a running-track and a wrestling area, and sometimes areas for jumping and javelin- and discus-throwing. There were buildings for changing and bathing, and for storing oil. Later, gymnasia became centres for intellectual training with halls for lectures on various topics, but exactly when this changeover took place is unclear. One does not know how much intellectual training would have been carried on in a city like Jerusalem in the early second century BCE. The group called 'ephebes', translated 'body of youth' in NRSV, were boys who had reached the age of puberty. At Athens for a short period of time in the late fourth century BCE, all young men aged 18–20, the ephebes, had to do compulsory military training for two years before being enrolled as citizens of Athens. In the late second century, ephebes were still doing such military exercises as archery and the use of siege-engines. Few families could afford not to let their sons work for two years, and this period of training, as with education in general, became primarily for the sons of rich families. The ephebate involved the young men in the public life of a city, and they would participate in its religious festivals and processions. It is important to note that education in the Hellenistic world was to fit a student to be a citizen of that particular city with its peculiar civic and religious responsibilities. The physical exercises would remain the same, as would the study of mathematics and the ability to read and write Greek, but such lessons would take place within the context of the city's traditional culture. Even the physical exercises, however, evidenced a desire to be part of the larger world, as athletes from different cities would compete against each other (4:18–20). Construction and maintenance of such a facility would have been costly and one gains a sense of the wealth of these aristocratic families. According to 4:12, the gymnasium lay right under the citadel. If one locates the citadel on the south-eastern hill of Jerusalem, the gymnasium would lie either between the city of David and the temple or in the broad ravine which separated the Lower from the Upper City (Jos. *JW* 5.140).

Jason's further request in 4:9b has been much disputed: should one translate 'to enrol the people of Jerusalem as Antiochenes, i.e. as citizens of Antioch', or 'to enrol the Antiochenes in Jerusalem'? Who were these Antiochenes? Four suggestions have been made: (1) the Hellenized Jews would be made citizens of Antioch of Syria; (2) that Antiochus IV had set up a new republic on the pattern of the Roman one and its citizens were to be called Antiochenes

(Goldstein 1983); (3) that a Hellenistic corporation was to be set up in Jerusalem whose members would be called Antiochenes (Bickerman 1979); (4) that Jerusalem itself would now become a Greek *polis*, called Antioch-in-Jerusalem, and its citizens called Antiochenes (Tcherikover 1961). The first three seem unlikely: even a king could not force a city to bestow *en bloc* citizenship on those of another city; Antiochus IV seems to have supported local traditions rather than instituted a new republic; the word for Antiochene always refers, not to members of a corporation, but to citizens. In light of the correspondence between Eumenes II and the Tyriaions wherein the king is asked to grant them a city constitution and the use of their own laws as well as a gymnasium, and where the language is remarkably similar to that in this passage, the last suggestion seems the best. It remains intriguing that the author of 2 Maccabees does not complain about a name change, and 1 Maccabees does not mention it. Many ancient cities received new Greek names, and this seems the best explanation for this verse. What did such a name change involve? Tcherikover (1961) argued that the change had constitutional implications: theoretically the Mosaic law could be overthrown as the law of the city, and Jason would control who became citizens of the city—only those who underwent ephebic training could become citizens of Antioch-in-Jerusalem. However, there is no evidence that a name change meant a change in constitution, nor that ephebic training was the only way to become a citizen. All we can say is that the name was changed, but even that implies that Jason wanted to connect Judea more closely with the Seleucid empire. Jason's position depended on royal favour, and Antiochus not only gained more money but a secure ally on his southern border.

The author of 2 Maccabees uses all his rhetorical skill to condemn what Jason did. As noted above, education was intimately tied to preparation for public life in a city. The author depicts Jason's educational reforms as a denial of traditional Jewish culture. Hellenization, which formerly meant the use of a pure style of the Greek language, is now labelled as foreign, and Jason is said to be a wicked priest. The author mocks concern for physical pursuits rather than spiritual. At v. 13, the Greek hat is the broad-brimmed hat worn by athletes to protect them against the sun, and said to be that of Hermes, the god of athletics. At v. 14, the signal was that given to start activity, not

specifically discus-throwing. The reflection of the author at vv. 16–17 shows the author's notion of just deserts, whereby the punishment meted is appropriate to the crime committed (4:26, 38; 5:9–10; 13:8; 15:32).

vv. 18–22 show further how Jason was concerned to integrate Judea into the Seleucid empire. Every four years games were held at Tyre in honour of the god Melqart/Heracles, perhaps in imitation of Alexander the Great's celebration of games to Heracles after capturing Tyre in 331 BCE (Arr. *Anab.* 3.6.1). Jason sends official representatives of Antioch-in-Jerusalem. The author contrasts the action of Jason with that of the envoys who use the 300 silver drachmas, the customary price for a sacrificial ox, to fit out triremes, Greek ships with three rows of oars. Such a fitting-out would seem to go against the stipulations of the Treaty of Apamea. Did Jason reason that such a sacrifice was not against the Torah, in line with the Greek translator of Ex 22:28 who translated 'You shall not revile the gods', a translation which seems to imply that the gods of other nations could be honoured as subordinate to the supreme God of Israel? The author clearly sees Jason as an apostate. Jason's welcome to Antiochus on his visit to Jerusalem is similar to the ceremonial reception of Hellenistic kings and again emphasizes the friendly relations between Jews and their Greek rulers.

(4:23–5:10) The Rule of Menelaus The Bilgah clan gained control of the city as Simon's brother, Menelaus, successfully outmanoeuvred Jason, who fled across the Jordan. The reader is now informed that there was a Seleucid garrison in the city, perhaps stationed in response to the Ptolemaic threat, and manned by mercenaries from Cyprus. Since Sostratus' duties involved collecting the revenue, there was probably a division of authority within Jerusalem, with a regular royal functionary operating within and above the city's political structure.

Menelaus' tenure is marked by murder and intrigue. Short of cash, he had sold temple treasure perhaps to pay his taxes, as had Hezekiah (2 Kings 18:13–16). Using temple vessels to pay taxes is one thing, using them to connive at murder is quite another matter. Clearly Onias III, as well as the epitomist, thought it wrong to sell temple vessels. Onias is depicted as upholding tradition, but yet appears to take sanctuary in the famous temple of Apollo and Artemis in Daphne. The murder of Onias by the utterly treacherous Andronicus, perhaps the same

Andronicus who is said by Hellenistic historians to have murdered the son of Seleucus IV (Diod. Sic. 30.7.2), has the author emphasize the motif of just deserts, and also the fact that non-Jews can have a sympathetic attitude towards Jews unjustly punished.

(4:39–50) Further Charges against Menelaus
Whereas Onias had protected the temple, Menelaus and Lysimachus despoil it, and launch an armed attack against the unarmed citizens who protest their actions. Divine help is intimated in the fact that unarmed citizens put to flight the armed followers of Lysimachus, who dies. Where Onias had been slandered by Simon (4:1), the true charges against Menelaus are dismissed and justice is perverted through bribery. Ptolemy son of Dorymenes may already have been governor of Coelesyria and Phoenicia as at 8:8. He certainly continues the favourable attitude to the Bilgah faction that Apollonius is said to have shown (4:4). He acts against the three members of the Jewish council, a body known from a letter of Antiochus III (Jos. *Ant.* 12.142), but whose exact function is unknown. As at the murder of Onias, non-Jews are shown as sympathetic to the unfairly condemned councillors.

(5:1–10) Jason's Uprising The author of 2 Maccabees locates the events after the second invasion of Antiochus IV in Egypt in 168 BCE, while 1 Maccabees places them after his first invasion (170/169 BCE). According to Dan 11:28–30, there were two invasions of Egypt and two attacks against the temple, but Daniel does not explicitly state that Antiochus IV came in person against Jerusalem the second time. The chronology of 1 Maccabees is to be preferred, and the epitomist has perhaps run the two attacks on the temple together. 1 Maccabees gives a precise date for the second attack by the captain of the Mysians (1 Macc i:29), whereas 2 Maccabees does not (5:24).

Portents are frequently described in non-Jewish literature as occurring before a momentous event (Tacitus, *Histories*, 2.50.2; 78.2). The closest parallel to this passage is found in the narrative of Josephus about events before the destruction of Jerusalem (*JW* 6.298–9). Such portents could be interpreted in different ways: Jason must have hoped that Antiochus' successor would accept the fait accompli of his defeat of Menelaus, but he failed. Tcherikover suggested that he did so because a third force of pious crowds as at 4:40 rose up to repel him, but it is more likely that the citadel, well- stocked and

defended by the Seleucid garrison, could hold out until reinforcements came. Jason's death is depicted in terms of just deserts. 1 Macc 12:6–18, 20–3 also speaks of a fictive relationship between the Jews and the Spartans. Many Hellenistic cities sought to connect themselves to famous events and cities, as the Romans traced their origins to Aeneas the Trojan.

(5:11–6:17) The Attack on the Temple This section contains Antiochus' own attack on Jerusalem (5:11–20); the repressive measures he imposed on Jerusalem (5:21–7); the new cult imposed (6:1–11). The author includes two reflections on what was happening (5:17–20; 6:12–17).

(5:11–20) Antiochus' Attack The parallel account is found at 1 Macc 1:20–4, but there no reason is given for Antiochus' assault after his first invasion of Egypt. At that time, Antiochus had not captured Alexandria, but had installed his nephew Ptolemy VI Philometor, with himself as Ptolemy's guardian. It is not known why Antiochus withdrew from Egypt, but perhaps he was satisfied with a weakened Ptolemaic empire. A Babylonian text records that Antiochus celebrated his victory with a great festival in August/September 169 BCE, and such a festival suggests that Antiochus was satisfied with his incursion. If Jason's coup attempt occurred after the second invasion, the author of 2 Maccabees makes no mention of the rebuff of Antiochus by the Romans and writes as if the only reason Antiochus left Egypt was to put down the revolt in Jerusalem. He dehumanizes Antiochus with animal-like descriptions—'inwardly raging' is literally 'wild-beast-like in soul'. The author is not concerned with exact chronology or exact numbers so much as with rhetorical polemic. At about the same time, Antiochus was forcibly extracting treasures from a temple in Babylon, so Jerusalem must not be seen as a special act of temple despoliation on the part of Antiochus. His liberal gifts to Greek cities, particularly to Athens where he wanted to complete the magnificent temple of Zeus, made him always on the lookout for more revenue. The contrast between Onias and Menelaus is shown as Onias had defended the deposits in the temple while Menelaus now guides Antiochus in his plunder of the temple.

At 5:17–20, the author reflects on the discrepancy between Antiochus' purpose and that of God: Antiochus is uplifted, thinking himself special, but God is simply using him as the instrument of his anger. This motif is found earlier at Isa 10:515 concerning the role of the king of Assyria. The theology is that of Deuteronomy where, if the people disobey God's laws, they will be punished (Deut 11:13–17; 28; cf. Jer 18–19). The hope of restoration expressed in v. 20 looks forward to the events of ch. 8, and reflects the prayer of Solomon at the dedication of the first temple (1 Kings 8:46–53).

(5:21–7) Antiochus' Measures in Jerusalem
The arrogance of Antiochus is described as was that of the Persian king Xerxes who dared to bridge the Hellespont and cut a canal through Mt. Athos (Hdt. 7:22–4, 34–7; Aesch. *Pers.* 69–72, 744–51). Philip appears again at 6:11; 8:8 and was perhaps the commander of the Seleucid garrison in Jerusalem. The enemy of the Jews is called a barbarian, as at 2:21. It is fascinating to note how the author of 2 Maccabees binds the Jews and the Samaritans as one people in v. 22 and 6:2, whereas Josephus reports a letter from same Samaritans which forcefully argues that the Samaritans are not like the Jews (*Ant.* 12.257–61).

The account parallels that of 1 Macc 1:29–40. There a purpose for the attack is given—to install and fortify a strong Seleucid garrison in the city. In 2 Maccabees, however, the attack seems unprovoked and senseless, duplicating the action of Antiochus at 5:13–14. The author also dates it to the sabbath, thereby heightening the offence (cf. Jos. *Ag. Ap.* 1.209–12). The author of 1 Maccabees dates the event two years after Antiochus' first invasion of Egypt, i.e. to 167 BCE, and so not long after Antiochus' humiliation by the Romans in Egypt. These further fortifications might be part of an attempt to strengthen Antiochus' southern border.

In the midst of this tragedy the author strikes a hopeful note with the mention of Judas Maccabeus. The author has Judas living in Jerusalem until this. He makes no mention of Mattathias, the father of Judas, who is such an important personage in 1 Maccabees. The author of 1 Maccabees, concerned to highlight the Hasmonean family (1 Macc 5:62), focuses on the reaction of Mattathias to the persecutions but gives little attention to the martyrdoms. The author of 2 Maccabees, on the other hand, views the martyrdoms as the appropriate reaction to persecution and God's mercy comes through the martyrdoms (7:38; 8:5). Judas's story is placed before the persecution to provide hope for the reader. The wilderness was the traditional place

of refuge (1 Sam 23:14; 1 Kings 19:19). Here Judas escapes from the pollution in the city into the natural world of the mountains (cf. Hos 2:14–15; Mk 1:12).

(6:1–11) The Imposed Cult Further measures are now taken by the king, measures directed against the Jews in Judea, not all Jews in the empire. We do not know why Antiochus took this extremely unusual step of outlawing Jewish religion in Judea. 1 Maccabees blames the megalomania of the emperor who is said to have wanted all nations to be the same and to give up their particular customs (1 Macc 1:41–2). Antiochus is thus portrayed as zealous in the spread of Hellenization. However, all the evidence we possess points in the direction of Antiochus encouraging local customs, rather than attempting to suppress them (Mørkholm 1966). Rather, Antiochus must have considered the cult in Judaea to be the focal point of resistance to his administration, even though the high priest Menelaus was his friend, and its suppression a final step in trying to stabilize conditions in this restless southern border region. The king's agent is Geron the Athenian (NRSV marg.). Jews are no longer to follow the civic institutions of their ancestors, not even privately, as the stories at 6:10–11 show. The first change is to the name. Olympios and Xenios ('the Friend-of-Strangers') are both common epithets for Zeus. The author gives a reason for the name Xenios, but the translation is uncertain. The NRSV accepts an emendation of the text to bring it into line with the petition, known from Josephus (*Ant.* 12.261), of some Samaritans to Antiochus IV requesting that their temple be renamed Zeus Hellenios. However, the author seems to hold no antipathy to the Samaritans but rather links the two together in undergoing oppression from Antiochus (5:22–3), and so one could maintain the present text and translate 'as those who live there are hospitable'.

What exactly was the cult imposed? In posing the question in this fashion, scholars have undertaken to find one particular cult substituted for the cult in Jerusalem. Noticing how the Hebrew expression for 'abomination of desolation', which is used in Dan 9:27; 11:31 and is reflected in the corresponding Greek terms at 1 Macc 1:54, is a play on the name Baal Shamem, i.e. Lord of heaven, scholars such as Bickerman (1979) argued that the cult imposed was a Syro-Canaanite cult. Tcherikover (1961) followed him in this, adding that the cult was that of the

Syrian garrison stationed in the citadel, while Goldstein (1983) suggested it was the cult of a heterodox Jewish garrison in the citadel. Bringmann (1983) noted that the sacrifice of pigs and the prohibition of circumcision would be against Syrian religion and so suggested that the cult was created by Menelaus. Rather than looking for one cult to substitute for another, however, perhaps simply the worship of many gods was introduced. 1 Macc 1:47 speaks of many altars, sacred precincts, and shrines for idols, and 2 Macc 10:2 mentions that altars had been built in the public square of Jerusalem and that there were sacred precincts. Besides Zeus Olympios and Dionysos, other gods would have been worshipped.

The description at 6:3–6 differs from the accounts in 1 Maccabees and Dan 7–12. Cult prostitution is prohibited at Deut 23:17; getting rid of cult prostitutes is praised (1 Kings 15:12; 22:46; 2 Kings 23:7), while their presence is a sign of evil (1 Kings 14:24). The author of 2 Maccabees seems to be using stereotypical accusations to point out the barbarism of the actions. Antiochus III had proclaimed that only the sacrificial animals known to their ancestors were to be introduced into Jerusalem (Jos. Ant. 12.145–6), and this is now done away with. It is noteworthy that the author does not mention the desolating sacrilege of Dan 11:31; 1 Macc 1:54. Also, one wonders what precisely is meant by 'confess themselves to be Jews'. Does Jew mean more than a geographical designation, i.e. someone who follows the Torah, or does the phrase mean that one had to call oneself an Antiochene? The author insists that the Jews were forced to take part in the pagan festivals, in contrast to 1 Macc 1:52 which states that many were eager to follow the new practices. The attempt to force Jews to follow Greek ways is extended to neighbouring cities, probably those which bordered on Judea so that the Judeans could not slip across the border to practise their religion. v. 8 is difficult: the verb can mean either the less forceful 'suggest' or the stronger 'enjoin'; and the MSS read either 'Ptolemais', i.e. the coastal city, or 'of Ptolemy', i.e. Ptolemy the governor of Coelesyria and Phoenicia (4:45). Ptolemais was later hostile to the Jews (1 Macc 5:14; 2 Macc 13:25), but so was Ptolemy.

Two examples of the persecution are then adduced (cf. 1 Macc 1:60–1; 2:31–8). Women with babies at their breasts, who would normally enjoy privacy at home are paraded publicly through the streets as opponents of Antiochus' ideals for the city. Men who meet outside the city and away from sight are still burnt, their rituals seen as a threat to the state. The ritual of initiation into Judaism, circumcision (Gen 17:9–14), and the sabbath, the sign of God's delivering his people from Egypt (Deut 5:12–15), are outlawed.

(6:12–17) Reflections of the Author The persecution is interpreted as God's discipline of his people, pre-empting a harsher judgement. As at Deut 8:5, God is seen as a parent who trains and educates his child. In some ways this differs from Wis 11:10–12:27 where God's forbearance towards other nations is to give them time to repent (cf. Sir 5:4–8).

(6:18–7:42) The Cry for Help After providing a reflection on the events, the author focuses on the martyrdoms of Eleazar and the mother and her seven sons. That the two narratives are tied together is shown by the concluding note at 7:42: 'the eating of sacrifices' is a term found in the story of Eleazar (6:18), the term for 'tortures' is found at 7:1,13,15. The author sees these events as the pivotal point in turning God's anger into mercy (7:38; 8:5).

(6:18–31) Eleazar The story of Eleazar is retold in greater detail in 4 Macc 5–7. There he is a priest (4 Macc 5:4), here he is a scribe. The exact social meaning of this term is not certain, but it means more than someone who copies or writes documents. He is a leading official, well known to those in charge of the sacrifices. We do not know if they are Jews or non-Jews. As all heroes, Eleazar is handsome, of noble birth, and dignified. Pork was prohibited by the Torah (Lev 11:7–8; Deut 14:8). The method of torture is unclear: *tympanon* is a drum, stick, or wagon-wheel and so the sense is of something turning around, perhaps a rack. The narrative is full of rhetorical flourishes and contrasts, as the last words are designed to arouse emotion in the reader. Eleazar refuses any contradiction between his private and public behaviour; consistency, not hypocrisy, is his watchword. He is a model of *arete* (Simonides, *Lyra Graeca*, LCL 11 359, no. 127), just as Achilles chose death with honour rather than long life without glory (Homer, *Iliad*, 9.410–16). Here a Jew rather than the Seleucid officials symbolizes this classical Greek virtue. What is interesting is that there is no mention of restoration to life in this story. Eleazar asks that he be sent down to the bleak world of Hades. Eleazar is not seeking a reward, only to live nobly.

(7:1–42) The Mother and her Seven Sons
After the martyrdom of an important male comes the story of the deaths of a mother and her sons. Stories of whole families perishing under attack are found in Jewish literature, for example in the story of Taxo and his seven sons (As. Mos. 9) and in that of the Galilean martyrs (Jos. JW 1.312–13; Ant. 14.429–30) and in Greek literature, as in the deaths of Theoxena and her sister's children (Polyb. 23.10–11). The particular story of a mother with her seven sons, so laden with emotion, was a favourite one in later rabbinic literature, either before a Roman emperor (b.Git. 57b; Midr. Lam. 1:16) or more generally in the days of persecution (Pesiq. R. 43). The folklore motif of the importance of the youngest son is also found in this traditional tale. The story is loosely connected with the preceding account, and scholars have wondered where it took place. Later tradition, both Jewish and Christian, located it at Antioch. However, there is no indication of a change of scene from the preceding account, and the folk-tale type where a ruler is bested by a wiser underling argues against any search for a specific locale. The wicked character of the emperor is stressed, as the martyrs respond calmly while the emperor loses control of himself!

vv. 3–5, the brothers are all dehumanized, as first the tongue, the instrument of human communication, is cut out and then, with legs and arms lopped off, the first brother is fried like an animal. vv. 6–7, the quotation from Deut 32:36 is apt, as the purpose of the song of Deut 32 is to confront the people as a witness. The quotation is from that section of the song where God, after chastising his faithless people, begins to take vengeance on his instruments of anger who think they have conquered God's people by their own power.

vv. 7–9, the boy uses his last breath to contrast Antiochus' limited power with that of the King of the universe. The mention of a renewal of life evidences the growing belief in a resurrection and judgement after death. As noted, the story of Eleazar only speaks of the traditional shade-like existence in Sheol/Hades. In the psalms, however, there are passages which speak of a longing for a continued enjoyment of God (Ps 73:23–6; 16:9–10; 84:10), and also passages which speak of resurrection in the context of national restoration (Ezek 37; Hos 6:2; the fascinating Isa 26:19). 1 Enoch speaks of an after-death judgement (1 Enoch 22–7; 91:10; 93:2; 104:1–16) and Dan 12:2–3 clearly expresses a belief in resurrection (cf. also 1 Enoch 90:33).

The Greek translators of passages such as Isa 26:19; Job 19:24–6; 14:14 seem to speak of individual renewal. The threefold repetition of the first person plural in v. 9 shows that the author of 2 Maccabees is speaking of individual resurrection. There probably was a rich tradition about the shades in Sheol (cf. Isa 14:9–22); they can be brought back, but do not like to be disturbed (1 Sam 28:18–19), and Job 14:722 asserts that the shades do not come back to this present existence. The boy about to be martyred, however, is made to proclaim that the dead will be given life again, presumably life on this earth as the description at 7:23 resonates with the description of the first human at Gen 2:7.

vv. 13–19, Antiochus is threatened with punishment. Since kings were granted divine honours, this is a radical statement. Hope for the people as a whole is now expressed: the suffering is attributed to their sins, not to the power of Antiochus. Antiochus is now listed among those who fight against God and therefore sure to lose (Isa 14; cf. Eur. Bacch.).

vv. 20–9, the mother's attachment to her ancestral customs is shown, as earlier by the second son (7:8), in her use of Hebrew. In a patriarchal culture, her nobility is shown by her possessing a man's courage. The origin of human life is unknown (Ps 139:13–16; Eccles 11:5), but the author uses language which resonates with the creation of humans at Gen 2:7 when God breathed life into the human's nostrils. Her wisdom is further shown as she tricks the emperor and tells her last son to recall God's creating power when he shaped the unformed world (Gen 1:2, particularly in the LXX). Later Christian writers, such as Origen (On First Principles, 2.1.5) and the Latin translator of 2 Maccabees, interpreted the phrase at v 28 to mean that God created out of nothing, but the text states that God did not make them from what already existed as properly formed. vv. 30–8, the last and most impressive speech is given to the youngest brother, as appropriate to traditional literature. Themes already met in 2 Maccabees are spoken again: the Hebrews suffer because of their sins as God disciplines them (5:17–20; 6:12–17); the king should not be arrogant (4:17, 21; 7:15) as God will punish him (7:14–19). The text of v. 36 is difficult to translate: 'endured a brief suffering in exchange for everlasting life and have fallen under God's covenant' or 'endured a brief suffering and have fallen to everlasting life under God's covenant'. The meaning reflects that of earlier statements that

God will renew their life for they have followed his laws (7:9, 23). vv. 37–8 foretell what the following narrative will show: the deaths of the martyrs have turned God's wrath to mercy, and Antiochus learns through sickness to confess the power of God. vv. 39–42, as at the beginning of the chapter, the king loses control of himself. 'In his integrity' is literally 'pure', suggesting not only the separation from unclean actions, but also the purification of the temple which will soon occur. We are not told how the mother died, a classic example of patriarchal neglect. Nothing is mentioned of her husband either, as the author focuses on the maternal role of the woman.

(Chs. 8–9) God's Response The response of God to the cry for help comes quickly as Judas wins the first victory (8), and afflicts Antiochus (9).

(8:1–36) The First Victory The parallel narrative in 1 Macc 3:10–4:25 describes a series of events and tactical manœuvres with various commanders, whereas the author of 2 Maccabees concentrates on one single battle against one commander. Such a focus heightens the dramatic effect. The main villain in 1 Maccabees is Gorgias, whereas in 2 Maccabees it is Nicanor, no doubt to balance the villain in the final battle in 2 Maccabees 14–15. Both are called thrice-wretched (8:34; 15:3).

(8:1–7) The Rise of Judas Last mentioned before the martyrdoms (5:27), Judas and his companions now gather a force of like-minded followers. They have persisted in following 'Judaism' (2:21; 14:38), not the 'Jewish faith' as NRSV translates. The number 6,000 is repeated at 8:16, although some are reported to have left at 8:13. The group prayer employs traditional language, with the motif of blood crying out from the ground recalling the blood of the innocent Abel (Gen 4:10; cf. Heb 12:24, and Deut 32:43). The mention of the levelling of the city looks forward to Antiochus' vow (9:13). God's aid renders Judas unbeatable, although he first used the tactic of surprise raids and ambushes.

(8:8–11) The Reaction of the Seleucids While the account in 1 Maccabees has the matter dealt with at the highest level (1 Macc 3:27), 2 Maccabees has the governor of Coelesyria and Phoenicia deal with the nuisance and is the more likely account. Many Nicanors are mentioned

at this time: one is a royal agent of the middle rank mentioned in the letter of the Sidonians in Shechem to Antiochus IV (Jos. Ant. 12.257–64); one is mentioned as being one of the closest friends of Demetrius, son of Seleucus IV (Polyb. 31.14.4; Jos. Ant. 12. 402); and there is Nicanor the Cypriarch (2 Macc 12:2). It is unlikely that all these references are to the same person. Gorgias was later governor of Idumea (2 Macc 10:14; 12:32), presumably someone with local experience. The author's estimate of a mixed army of 20,000 is half that of 1 Macc 3:38, but still high. Ninety slaves per talent was cheap, perhaps showing contempt for the Jews. At that rate, Nicanor would need to sell 180,000 slaves, many more than those already taken from Jerusalem (5:41). Nicanor is stated to be the author of the plan to enslave, thereby heightening his evil and preparing for the theme of appropriate retribution at the end of the story where Nicanor has to run away like a fleeing slave (8:35).

(8:12–20) Judas's Preparation While others fear, Judas is unafraid. The Gentiles act arrogantly, like Antiochus at 5:1721. The 'torture of the derided city' echoes the language used of the martyrs (tortures: 7:1,13,15, 42; derided: 7:7,10). Judas, as every good general would do, exhorts his troops. The unconquerable power of God is captured in the phrase 'with a single nod'. Two examples are adduced. The first is known from the HB, the defeat of Sennacherib in 701 BCE (2 Kings 19:35–6; Isa 37:36), the same as used at 1 Macc 7:41 and again at 2 Macc 15:22. The precise reference of the second example is unclear. The Galatians are the Celts who were forced to travel from western and central Europe towards the east and southeast. In 280/279 BCE some Celts invaded Greece, while others went towards Asia Minor in 278/277 BCE and overran many Greek cities. After a long process they were confined to an area north of Phrygia later called Galatia. Scholars have suggested three possibilities for the example Judas mentions: (1) a battle of Antiochus 1 against the Celts in the 270s BCE, although this took place in Asia Minor and the text would have to be emended from Babylonia to Bagadonia, near the Tauros mountains in Cilicia; (2) an incident during the rebellion of Molon, governor-general of the eastern satrapies, in 220 BCE; (3) an incident in the rebellion of Antiochus Hierax in 227/226 BCE in the east against his brother Seleucus III—Antiochus used Galatian mercenaries. The last-mentioned seems the best candidate. This passage shows that there were Jewish soldiers serving under the Seleucids, and supports Josephus who said that Antiochus III transferred Jewish soldiers from Babylonia to Phrygia and Lydia to maintain the loyalty of the local population (*Ant.* 12:147–53).

(8:21–9) The Battle The actual order of the Jewish army is not certain: some MSS read as if Judas appointed his four brothers, Simon, Joseph, Jonathan, and Eleazar, to be in charge of 1,500 men each while Judas read the Scriptures and led another division, the first, the word for which normally means a phalanx unit of 256 men; others suggest that Eleazar read aloud from the Scriptures. 2 Maccabees has one of the brothers named Joseph, while 1 Maccabees calls him John (1 Macc 2:3–5). Whatever the proper understanding, the author of 2 Maccabees wants to stress that the whole family is involved, and therefore divides the forces in a way that is not paralleled elsewhere. The focus is on the Jews following correct covenantal procedure, and so the Scriptures are read (Deut 20:2), and the sabbath observed. Note how the spoils are given not only to the fighters but to the widows and orphans (Deut 14:29; 26:12–15), and to the tortured, which brings back the role of the martyrs in obtaining God's mercy.

(8:30–3) The Defeat of Timothy and Bacchides The shortened character of the work is evident in this section as names and events are introduced without any preparation, and disrupt the flow of the Nicanor story. In 2 Maccabees, there seem to be two Timothys: one who appears at 9:3 and 10:24–38, where he is killed, and another at 12:10–25, where he escapes. In 1 Maccabees there is only one Timothy, who engages Judas's forces three times (1 Macc 5:6–8, 28–34, 37–44). 1 Maccabees appears to relate the events in the proper sequence, and so the author of 2 Maccabees has misplaced events. v. 31 has Judas in control of Jerusalem, which otherwise does not occur until 10:1–8. The author of 2 Maccabees tightly connects vv. 30–3 with the rest of the Nicanor story, however. The complex of widows, orphans, and tortured is used, the same word for collecting arms is found at vv. 27, 31, and the appropriate retribution motif appears in both. Perhaps the author wants to show how Judas's men behave after victory and also to heighten interest as to what happened to Nicanor. As for Bacchides, in 1 Maccabees he is a high-ranking Seleucid official (1 Macc 7:8–20) and it is unlikely that he

would be listed after such a low-level commander as Timothy. Perhaps another Bacchides is meant than the one in 1 Maccabees. The spoil taken to Jerusalem is probably God's portion as in Num 31:28. At v. 32, *patris* should probably not be translated with NRSV as 'city of their ancestors', but as 'fatherland'. Nothing else is known about Callisthenes except that he is appropriately punished. At 1 Macc 1:31, the city is said to have been burnt by the Mysarch commander.

(8:34–6) The Fate of Nicanor Nicanor's plan to enslave the Jews went awry and he himself had to flee like a runaway slave. The help of the Lord (v. 35) was the watchword of Judas's forces (v. 23); the word for defender at v. 36 (*hypermachōn*) resonates with the word for ally (*symmachōn*) at v. 24. The author returns to themes found in his opening chapter: the Jews are invincible when they follow God's law (3:1), and Nicanor, as Heliodorus before him (3:35–9), proclaims God's power.

(9:1–29) The Death of Antiochus Antiochus IV set out in mid to late 165 BCE to consolidate his rule in the eastern satrapies. Early in his reign, a local dynasty of priests and princes had risen to power around Persepolis and won their independence. This account appears confused as to the geography, as Persepolis, the old capital of the Persian empire, lay hundreds of miles south-east of Ecbatana in Media. This account of Antiochus' death is one of many versions (2 Macc 1:13–14; 1 Macc 6:1–16; Polyb. 31.9). According to Polybius, Antiochus died after attempting to rob the temple of Nanaia in Elymais, south of Ecbatana. Antiochus, a well-known plunderer of temples and someone always in need of ready cash, took the opportunity to help finance his eastern campaign.

According to a Babylonian chronicle, news of Antiochus' death reached Babylonia in the month Chislev of 148 according to the Babylonian calendar, i.e. between 20 November and 18 December 164 BCE (Sachs and Wiseman 1954). The order of 2 Maccabees, where Antiochus dies before the purification of the temple thus seems confirmed over against the order of 1 Maccabees, where Antiochus dies after the purification, although some scholars still dispute this point. However, the narrative of 2 Maccabees has significantly dramatized history. The author concentrates on the death of the arch-enemy of the Jews and places it as part of the victory of God over Israel's attackers, and ignores the more complex details. 1 Maccabees tells of an invasion by the regent Lysias (1 Macc 5:26–35) and there were negotiations to settle the rebellion as evidenced by the letters in 2 Macc 11 which have been put out of order. These negotiations may have included the replacement of the inimical Ptolemy son of Dorymenes by the more friendly Ptolemy Macron as governor of Coelesyria and Phoenicia (2 Macc 10:12–13). The death of Antiochus is told in gruesome detail to highlight God's power. The threat of 2 Macc 8:3 is repeated by Antiochus at 9:14, and 9:3 ties the narrative to the preceding one so that the two chapters work together to show God's vindication of his people.

(9:1–12) **The Punishment of Antiochus** The last time the king was mentioned he was in a rage (7:39), so now too he rages like a bully against those weaker than him. The seventh brother had prayed that Antiochus' arrogance be punished (7:36; cf. 5:21), and now it begins tobe. The punishment is said to fit the crime. The deeds impossible for a human reflect Isa 40:12 and 2 Macc 5:12, and v. 10 compares with the hymns of the prophets Isaiah (14:4–21) and Ezekiel (28:12–19) against proud kings. The cruel punishment of death by worms is found both in Greek (Hdt. 3.66; Diod. Sic. 21.16.4–5) and Jewish writers (Isa 66:24; Jdt 16:17). As Heliodorus came to confess the power of God when flogged (3:33–9), so Antiochus, 'under the scourge of God', came to understand that one must not fight against God.

(9:13–27) **The Repentance of Antiochus** Antiochus vows, but he will not be heard. One does not know exactly what freedom Antiochus was going to give to Jerusalem. Freedom in the meaning of autonomy was always a slogan that competing parties would use to gain allegiance as, for example, the counter claims of Antiochus Gonatas and Ptolemy 1 to set all Greek cities free, as well as the Roman Senate declaring in 196 BCE that all Greeks were to be free. Freedom here did not mean independence from the superior party. Each 'free' city would have been allowed to keep its own traditions and system of government, but the relationship between the monarch and each such city was a special one. Nor is one sure what is meant by making the Jews equal to the Athenians. Athens was relatively prosperous in the second century BCE; the Parthenon was restored and the Agora reconstructed. Antiochus IV promised in 174 BCE to complete the unfinished temple of

Olympian Zeus. He certainly promises to restore the status quo as at the time of Onias (3:1), but in what way will he become a Jew? Clearly the meaning here is not geographical, i.e. become a Judean, but religious. Would it mean more than the worship of Naaman (2 Kings 5:1–18), or Nebuchadnezzar's confession (Dan 4:34–6)? Does the author envisage Antiochus being circumcised and following the laws of Torah, or being a 'god-fearer'? Compare the debate in Josephus (*Ant.* 20.34–48) as to whether Izates, king of Adiabene, should be circumcised.

Even in such pain, the king pens a letter, a deathbed testament. The authenticity of the letter has been questioned: either an original letter has been added to, or this letter has been modelled on the form of a genuine letter, possibly a letter to the army for support in any change in leadership. The present letter, whether authentic or not, has been used by the author to further his own rhetorical plan. The addressees, the Jews, are placed before the king, and are said to be 'worthy', 'esteemed', and even 'citizens', although one does not know what the Jews are being said to be citizens of. The Jews as a whole were not usually given citizen rights in any community where they lived: note e.g. 2 Macc 12:3, where the citizens of Joppa are distinct from the Jews living among them. The phrasing, however, suits the author in his desire to show that the Jews are good citizens, i.e. not antisocial. The greeting formula is quite extravagant, and then the king is said to remember with affection the Jews' esteem and goodwill. After the description of Antiochus' condition in 9:5–12, to describe himself as suffering an annoying illness is a marvellous understatement to say the least, and it suggests that the letter does not belong in its current context. Antiochus trusts the Jews to help in the successful transfer of power, and Antiochus describes his policy towards the Jews as moderate and kind! The thrust of this letter is clearly to put the Jews in as good a light as possible and as good citizens of the empire, contrary to what was suggested by many anti-Jewish stories which circulated in the Hellenistic world.

(9:28) **The Death of Antiochus** Antiochus is said to die in a strange land, like Jason (5:9–10), although Antiochus died in his own empire. In 1 Macc 6:55–63, Philip was appointed guardian of Antiochus V but was forced out of Antioch by Lysias, who had been left in charge of Antiochus' son. A revolt led by a Philip is mentioned at 2 Macc 13:23, but the narrative in its extreme brevity seems to distinguish between this Philip and the guardian appointed by Antiochus IV. Ptolemy VI Philometor had been driven out of Alexandria in October 164, just before Antiochus' death, and did not return until mid-163, and so the conflict between Lysias and Philip must have occurred around that time. Lysias is said by Josephus (*Ant.* 12.386) to have had Philip murdered before he reached Egypt.

(**10:1–8**) **The Result of the Lord's Intervention** With the death of the contender against God, Antiochus, the people now regain control of the temple and purify it. As the author has emphasized how the temple was overthrown because of the sins of the people (5:17–20; 6:12–17), he stresses the sin of the people and the cleansing of the temple. In contrast, at 1 Macc 4:36–59 not only the purification is stressed but also the dedication of the temple as at 1 Kings 8:63; 2 Chr 7:5; Ezra 6:16–17. 1 Maccabees also underlines the need to defend the temple from those in the citadel (4:41, 60), whereas the epitomist does not mention it here. Setting altars around the agora reflects Greek custom. The restoration of temple worship shows Judas as following the Torah. 1 Macc 4:52 states it was an interval of three years, Dan 12:7 three and a half years. 1 Maccabees is the more likely: the providential care of God is shown by the renewal falling on the anniversary of the defilement. Judas's flight to the mountains is recalled (5:27) and the connection to the Feast of Tabernacles, as in the prefixed letters, is made. The carrying of branches was commanded at Lev 23:40, but the word used here—*thyrsoi*, ivy-wreathed wands—signified what was carried in processions to the god Dionysos and may have been chosen to show again the reversal of the persecution when Jews were forced to process in honour of Dionysos (6:7). The language at v. 81s repeated almost verbatim at 15:36 to bind the two festivals together.

(**10:9–15:36**) **Further Defence of the Temple** Further attacks against the temple by the successors of Antiochus IV are described in this third section. The first section shows marked signs of condensation, whereas the account of Nicanor's expedition is treated more extensively. The author dramatizes his account by focusing on the attacks of the two Nicanors.

(**10:9–13:26**) **The Attacks under Antiochus V** The events in this section seem to be structured

in such a way that attacks by local leaders (10:14–38; 12:3–45) alternate with major expeditions (chs. 11, 13). First, however, come changes brought about by the new dynasty. Antiochus V was 9 years old and under the guardianship of Lysias (1 Macc 3:33). Lysias kept the position given him by Antiochus IV (1 Macc 3:32), and appointed Protarchos as governor of Coelesyria and Phoenicia. The NRSV at v. 11 is wrong, as the offices of chief minister and governor of Coelesyria did not overlap. A new governor is appointed at 13:24. Ptolemy Macron, former governor of Cyprus, had been loyal to Ptolemy VI Philometor, but the intrigues at the Ptolemaic court and the victory of Antiochus IV in 170/169 BCE led him to go over to Antiochus IV's side, possibly when Antiochus' fleet besieged Cyprus in 168 BCE. Ptolemy's friendly attitude towards the Jews should not be seen as something personal, but as part of Seleucid policy. The previous governors of Coelesyria and Phoenicia, Apollonius (4:4) and Ptolemy son of Dorymenes (4:45; 8:8), had been hostile to the Jews, and they probably reflected court policy. The appointment of Ptolemy Macron and his friendly attitude would then reflect the changed Seleucid policy after peace negotiations had begun under Antiochus IV (11:27–33) and after the first expedition of Lysias in 164 BCE (1 Macc 4:28–9; 2 Macc 11:14,16–21). These events have been rearranged by the author of 2 Maccabees as he wished to portray Antiochus, not as someone who negotiated peace with the Jews, but as their arch-enemy till overthrown by God. The restoration of the temple called for a rethinking of this friendly policy before the second expedition of Lysias (1 Macc 6:21–8).

(**10:14–38**) **Attacks by Local Leaders** Campaigns in Idumea (10:14–23): the author provides sparse details, both as regards geographical location and exact naming of opponents. His main concern is to emphasize that it was not the Jews who initiated the attacks, but the Seleucid forces, and that the Jews pray to God as their ally (see 8:24). The figures in vv. 17,18, 23 for those killed are high. The parallel account is found in 1 Macc 5:3–5. The names of the three commanders in charge of the siege are most likely two brothers of Judas (8:22) and an otherwise unknown Zacchaeus. Scholars have suggested that this episode is a doublet of 1 Macc 5:18, 55–61 where two commanders, jealous of Judas, attempt to win glory for themselves and are defeated. Moreover, Simon is glorified in 1 Maccabees, but not here in 2 Maccabees (see also 14:17): is this subtle anti-Hasmonean polemic on the part of the epitomist? Rather, the epitomist alludes to many stories of compromise (12:24–5), backsliding (12:39–40), and deception (13:21), so this story here should be taken, not as anti-Hasmonean, but as evidencing as do the others the faithfulness and incorruptibility of Judas. The accusation 'lovers of money' was a regular accusation against opponents (see Lk 16:14). The story here should be compared to the story of Achan in Josh 7.

(10:24–38) The Defeat of Timothy This campaign is also told with sparse chronological and geographical detail. It is often compared with the campaign of Judas into Ammonite territory reported in 1 Macc 5:6–8, but there are considerable differences. Whereas Judas attacks the Ammonites in their territory (1 Macc 5:6), here Timothy invades Judea (10:24–5) and the battle seems to take place in Judea, if at a considerable distance from Jerusalem (10:27). Timothy is killed in this campaign in 2 Maccabees, but not in the one in 1 Maccabees, and the town of Gazara (Gezer) in the Shephelah just outside the border of Judea appears to be captured, whereas it is not so until much later by Simon at 1 Macc 13:43–8.

Given that the author has Timothy die here and another Timothy emerge at 12:17–25, he must suppose there were two Timothys. The author emphasizes the size of the threat by speaking of mercenaries, i.e. trained soldiers, and excellent cavalry. The Jewish forces are pictured around the altar in Jerusalem, supplicating God in the traditional signs of mourning as if buried and wearing sackcloth from which shrouds were made. They refer to Ex 23:22, where God promises to be an enemy to their enemies if they listen to his words. After so praying, the Jews await in calm confidence in contrast to the animal rage of their opponents. The epiphany has many Greek touches. In the *Iliad*, a hero is often protected by a god (e.g. 5.436–7). Gigantic figures pursued the fleeing Persians and later the Gauls who had dared to attack Delphi while thunderbolts crashed about them (Hdt. 8.36–9; Paus. 1.4.4; 10.23.1–6). Zeus was pre-eminently Zeus Keraunos who hurls thunderbolts at his enemies (Homer *Od.* 23.330; Hes. *Theog.* 854). There is no satisfactory explanation of why five figures are involved. The motif of taunting defenders occurs again at 12:14–16, and is reminiscent of what happened at David's siege of Jerusalem (2 Sam 5:6–9). Timothy found a perfect hiding-place

in a cistern, a large pit with plastered walls for storing water, but to no avail. The victory hymn, as the army marched back to Jerusalem, may be compared to the song of Miriam at the defeat of Pharaoh (Ex 15:20–1), or that after David's defeat of Goliath (1 Sam 18:6–7).

(11:1–38) The Campaign of Lysias As mentioned above, the author of 2 Maccabees, to intensify the dramatic quality of the narrative, recorded only one major battle before the death of the arch-enemy, Antiochus IV, and so places the campaign of Lysias after Antiochus' death. The events as recounted in 1 Maccabees show much more action as the first campaign of Lysias occurs during the time of Antiochus IV. The displacement of the campaign of Lysias by the epitomist has made him place all the correspondence of peace negotiations out of order as well.

(11:1–12) The Campaign Lysias is given his full title here, rather than at 10:10, which may suggest some misplacement. He is guardian and in charge of the government, positions to which Antiochus IV had appointed him (1 Macc 3:32–3). 'Kinsman' was a high title in the Seleucid hierarchy (cf. 1 Macc 10:89). The number of his forces exceeds that given in 1 Macc 4:28, and is exaggerated. The description of Lysias's intentions at vv. 2–3 is fascinating given what happened under the high priest Jason (4:7–15). v. 4 shows how the author enjoys contrasts, particularly those between the might of men and the power of God. By the Treaty of Apamea, the Seleucids had been forbidden to use elephants. Lysias approaches from the south, as in 1 Macc 4:29. At v. 5, Beth-zur is located five *schoinoi*, not stadia, from Jerusalem by the author. A *schoinos*, a Persian measure, could equal anywhere from 30 to 60 stadia (Strabo, 17.1.24, 41). Five *schoinoi* of 30 stadia would locate Beth-zur about 30 km south of Jerusalem, which is almost right. The prayer is for God to send an angel as he had before the Israelites in the Exodus from Egypt (Ex 23:20; 33:2). The commander of the Lord's army had appeared to Joshua before Jericho (Josh 5:13–15), and Sennacherib's army had been struck down by an angel (2 Kings 19:35). Within the Greek tradition, Theseus is said to have rushed before the Greeks against the Persians at Marathon (Plut. *Thes.* 35), Athena had helped the citizens of Cyzicus (Plut. *Luc.* 10.3), and the twin gods, the Dioscuri, had led the Roman force against the Latins (Dion. Hal. 6.13). The author has taken over Greek descriptions. Here Lysias makes a disgraceful flight, while in 1 Maccabees he makes an orderly retreat in order to collect an even larger force.

(11:13–38) Peace Negotiations Further, 2 Maccabees has Lysias recognize, as Heliodorus had done (3:38–9) that the Hebrews are invincible while God is their ally, and to start peace negotiations. At this point the author brings in four documents which talk of peace. These letters have been much debated. The same year is given for the first, third, and fourth letters although it seems inconsistent with their contents. The second letter has no date. The month in the first letter, Dioscorinthius (11:21), is not known in the Macedonian calendar. Scholars have set out to find what is the correct setting and date for each letter. Habicht (1976) suggested that the third letter reflects peace efforts by Menelaus before Antiochus IV began his eastern mission. When this fell through, Lysias set out on his invasion and then negotiated with the rebels (first letter). The second letter would come at the accession of Antiochus V and be an amnesty to the rebels on that occasion. Bar-Kochva (1988) suggested that negotiations began after Nicanor and Gorgias were defeated, and the first letter represents an interim report and the fourth a sign of Roman willingness to help. Antiochus IV refused to negotiate with the rebels, but acceded to Menelaus' request for a conditional amnesty (third letter). The second letter would be the official reprieve of the persecution by Antiochus V. 1 would concede a larger role to Menelaus, and place the third letter after the local initiatives had failed. The amnesty offer was rejected, Lysias invaded and then sought peace (first letter) and the fourth letter is the request of the Roman emissaries for a report on the progress of the negotiations. The second letter would be placed either at the accession of Antiochus V, or after Lysias' second expedition.

(11:16–21) First Letter Lysias uses a neutral term *plēthos*, multitude, mass, sometimes people, to refer to the addressees, not the formal *ethnos*, nation, or *gērousia*, senate (11:27), or *dēmos*, people (11:34). Such an address may be a hint that the letter is not written to a formally recognized group. The envoys, John and Absalom, are otherwise unknown but carry Hebrew, not Greek, names. Two sons of an Absalom, Mattathias (1 Macc 11:70) and Jonathan (1 Macc 13:11), fight with Judas's successors. v. 18 should not read with the NRSV 'agreed to what was possible', but rather 'what lies within my competence, 1

have agreed to'. The year 148 of the Macedonian Seleucid calendar is from October 165 BCE to September 164 BCE. Dioscorinthius has been interpreted as the first month in the Macedonian calendar, Dios, or the fifth, Dystros, or the eighth, Daisios.

(11:22–6) Second Letter v. 23 is phraseology usual at the death of a king, and suggests a time near the accession of Antiochus V. The change to Greek customs most probably refers to the decrees of Antiochus IV: the same verb *politeuesthai* is found at 6:1 and 11:25. The language of v. 25 is similar to that used by Antiochus III (Jos. *Ant.* 12.142) allowing the Jews to live by their ancestral religion. If this letter is dated to the beginning of Antiochus V's reign with Habicht (1976), the temple was already in Judas's hands and the letter simply recognizes the status quo. If with Bar-Kochva (1988) it is dated to the end of Lysias's second expedition (1 Macc 6:55–62), it contains a real concession as Lysias had retaken Jerusalem.

(11:27–33) Third Letter The *gērousia* is the official municipal body in Jerusalem (4:44). Is the letter addressed only to supporters of Menelaus, as some have suggested? The phrase, 'to the other Jews', seems to make it quite general. The fifteenth and thirtieth Xanthicus refer to the middle and end of March respectively. As Antiochus IV left on his eastern campaign in 165 BCE, the concession must have been granted while he was away from Antioch in March 164 BCE, but the allowance of only 15 days to accomplish the conditions seems to cut things a bit close. At v. 31, one should read 'customs' (*diaitēmata*) rather than 'food' (*dapanēmata*), as the kosher laws would be included in the reference to the Torah. The offer is conditional on the cessation of hostilities and the return home of the rebels; if these conditions are not met, hostilities will break out again. The reference to Menelaus is intriguing: elsewhere in 2 Maccabees he is portrayed as a traitor to Judaism, but here he seems to come across as an advocate for allowing the Jews to return to their ancestral customs.

(11:34–8) Fourth Letter After forcing Antiochus IV from Egypt in 168 BCE, the Romans had kept an eye on him. An embassy had been sent to Antioch in 166 BCE, and another would come in 163/162 BCE. This embassy probably took place in autumn 164. The date in the text should probably be disregarded and seen as copying the date on the third letter. The tacit recognition of the rebels as a *dēmos*, a 'people', is a sign of how Rome liked to cause discomfort to other sovereigns: in 164 BCE, the Roman commissioner C. Sulpicius Gallus publicly invited accusations against Eumenes II of Pergamum in his own city of Sardis.

(12:1–45) Further Local Hostilities The author insists that the Jews are peaceful (10:14–15; 14:25), only wanting to follow their own ancestral customs, but they would not be let alone. Various hostile leaders are mentioned, about whom we know nothing more. This author must see the Timothy here as distinct from the earlier Timothy; Nicanor is not, as NRSV translates, governor of Cyprus as Cyprus was at this time in Ptolemaic hands, but rather the commander of Cypriot mercenaries and of a lower rank that the Nicanor of ch. 8 and chs. 14–15.

(vv. 3–9) Deceit in Joppa and Jamnia This incident is not found in 1 Maccabees. Both these events take place at coastal areas, and are linked through the burning of ships in the respective harbours. As non-citizens, the Jews would not take part in a public assembly, but would they have no inkling of the matter? The author wishes to insist on the peaceful character of the Jews, and stress the hatred of the citizen body of these towns. They stand in marked contrast to the citizens of Scythopolis (12:30).

(vv. 12–16) The Campaign in Gilead The scene shifts quickly from the west coast in a march towards Transjordan. The campaign in Gilead is also told in 1 Macc 5:9–36. Arabs are mercenaries in Timothy's forces at 1 Macc 5:39, but the first encounter between Judas's forces and the Nabateans is a peaceful one at 1 Macc 5:24–5. Judas is shown in this incident in 2 Maccabees to be a pragmatist, not someone completely antagonistic to non-Jews. A town named Chaspo is simply mentioned at 1 Macc 5:36, but here it is given a more prominent role. Here the result is much different from that with the Arabs, as the author stresses the blasphemous insults of the enemy. The image of the blood-filled lake is starkly emotional, and reminiscent of the way enemies are put under the ban in the book of Joshua as, for example, at Jericho (Josh 6:21).

(vv. 17–26) The Pursuit of Timothy The author of 2 Maccabees now has Judas and his men travel south. 1 Macc 5:13 states that all male Jews in the land of the Toubiani had been killed,

whereas our author insists that Timothy accomplished nothing. At this point in the narrative of 1 Maccabees, the Jewish forces are divided into three, one for Gilead, one for Judaea, and one for Galilee (1 Macc 5:17–18), whereas Judas in 2 Maccabees keeps his forces together. Most likely this reflects the author's intentions to show that, now that God is on the side of the Jews, nothing untoward can happen to them, and that the Jews are unified. The size of Timothy's forces is exaggerated, but only emphasizes the more the epiphany that takes place. vv. 24–6 stress the deceit of Timothy rather than the gullibility of the Jewish commanders, who are shown as deeply concerned about Jewish lives. Carnaim was where Timothy had sent the women and children for refuge, and one wonders if the slaughter encompassed them as well, i.e. was all that lived put under the ban?

(12:26–31) The Road Back to Judea The parallel story is in 1 Macc 5:45–7. As told here, the narrative has a formulaic quality like that at Caspin (vv. 13–16). v. 27 suggests that Lysias, the chancellor of Syria, had a residence in this Transjordanian town. The incident at Scythopolis shows that the Jews do not hate Gentiles but only wish to live peaceably among them. The piety of the Jewish forces is shown in their desire to be at Jerusalem to celebrate a major feast.

(12:32–42) The Battle against Gorgias Judas now turns south of Jerusalem to Idumea. After stories which show the piety of the Jewish forces comes a story which tells what happens to those who are not pious. The few details provided by the author all dramatize the event: the courage and near success of Dositheus, the weariness of the troops, the rallying prayer and the shouts and hymns in Hebrew, the sudden unexpected success. In the encounter at 1 Macc 5:55–61, Gorgias is victorious against the foolhardy commanders Judas had left behind in Judaea, Joseph and Azariah. In the account of 2 Maccabees, a commander called Esdris is mentioned without any explanation of who he is. Some scholars wish to identify him with the Eleazar of 8:23, but more likely one should recognize that we are dealing with a shortened account. While 1 Maccabees explains the defeat at the hands of Gorgias by the jealous behaviour of the two leaders, Joseph and Azariah (1 Macc 5:55–62), the epitomist sees the deaths as caused by lack of Torah piety. Judas is shown as ever observant, as he and his soldiers purify themselves. So far from the temple, why did they need to become ritually clean so that they could participate in temple service? The purification seems to refer to purifying oneself after coming into contact with a dead body (Num 19:10–22; 31:24; 1QM 14:1–2). The sacred objects may have been taken on the raid on Jamnia (12:8–9). Greek inscriptions from Delos set up by the people of Jamnia honour two Phoenician deities, Herakles and Horon. Such idolatrous objects were forbidden at Deut 7:25–6, and the transgression of such a command was embodied in the story of Achan (Josh 7). Most likely the soldiers wore amulets which were thought would protect them.

vv. 42–5 are difficult textually and also to translate. The language of v. 45 is similar to that of Lev 4:26, 35 and suggests that the sacrifice is similar to the reparation offering described at Lev 4:13–35 to make atonement for the sin committed. Each man contributes to the sacrifice, and thus the whole community is involved in reparation. As seen in 2 Macc 7, the author believes in resurrection, whereby the martyred brothers hope to live in a new created world. vv. 44–5 offer alternatives: *either* Judas does not think that the dead rise, that it is foolish to pray for the dead, *or* he considers that a reward awaits those who die piously, 'a holy and a pious thought'. In the light of recent research on rituals for the dead in Israel, e.g. those underlying Isa 57, 'to pray for the dead' may reflect a custom of which only traces can be discerned. The dead clearly had an existence in Israel, albeit a shadowy one (1 Sam 28:14–19; Deut 18:11–12; Isa 65:4). What the author seems to suggest is that there is a community which stretches beyond death and that atonement can be made for those who have died so that they gain a more splendid reward. Many of the burial practices among the Greeks and Romans were to help the deceased be properly integrated into the realm of the dead, and suggest that the dead could benefit from actions performed on their behalf by the living. In speaking of a splendid reward, one is reminded of the different regions of the underworld signalling different rewards found in Book 6 of Virgil's *Aeneid*. A similarly obscure ritual is mentioned by Paul at 1 Cor 15:29, where some Christians are baptized on behalf of the dead.

(13:1–26) The Second Invasion of Lysias The author gives no reason for the breaking of the agreements reached in ch. 11, except that

the young king wished to do worse than his father (v. 9). Perhaps the author sees the successes of ch. 12 as sufficient reason for this attack. Except for the dates given in the letters in ch. 11, only here and at 14:4 are dates given. They appear to follow the Seleucid Macedonian calendar which would place this event between September 164 and October 163 BCE. 1 Macc 6:20 dates the second invasion to 150 of the Seleucid Babylonian calendar, i.e. to 162 BCE. The force assembled is enormous, and no doubt exaggerated. One wonders in particular what use scythed chariots would be in the hilly terrain of Judea. Instead of both Antiochus V and Lysias each having a separate force, as the NRSV translation suggests, Antiochus came with Lysias as well as a huge force.

(vv. 3–8) The Death of Menelaus Menelaus resumes his role in the narrative as the opposite of the good high priest Onias, as a plotter against his own people. Perhaps the failure of Menelaus' peace overtures or simply the fact that he was a left-over from Antiochus IV's regime caused his death. Josephus (*Ant.* K.383–5) states that Menelaus died after the expedition. Death by ashes was a Persian punishment (Ctesias, *Persia, FGrH* 688): cold ashes suffocated the criminal, hot burnt him to death. The holiness of the altar fire had caused the death of Aaron's two sons (Lev 10:1–5). Menelaus is appropriately punished.

(vv. 9–17) The Battle at Modein The Greek king is said to be barbarous (2:21; 4:25). The Jewish response to the invasion is for the whole community to pray, as at 3:14–22. The elders with whom Judas consults may be members of the council/senate as at 4:44; 11:27. Judas is portrayed as not acting arrogantly. In the Temple Scroll from Qumran, the king is supposed to have twelve princes of his people, twelve priests, and twelve Levites with him at all times and he should not do anything without consulting them; before going to war he should have the high priest consult the Urim and Thummim (11QTemple 57–8).

The account of this battle is the opposite of that of 1 Macc 6:32–47 where the Jewish forces are defeated at Beth-zechariah. The author of 2 Maccabees is adamant that the loyal Jews cannot be defeated, and so the defeat is turned into a victorious assault at Modein, the hometown of the Maccabees (1 Macc 2:1), an account filled with heroic tales as Judas with twenty men kills over 2,000, creates havoc in the enemy camp, and yet retires unharmed.

(vv. 18–26) Treaty of Antiochus V The contrast with 1 Maccabees is again striking: there the forces at Beth-zur fight courageously but eventually are forced to capitulate (6:31, 49–50). The forces at Jerusalem hold out but survive only because the king withdraws at the news of Philip's return (1 Macc 6:51–62). It looks as if the author of 2 Maccabees has transferred the events at Jerusalem to Beth-zur as he did not want any hint of danger to the temple. The only setback to the Jews comes through a traitor, but even he does not succeed. All in all, the invasion of Antiochus V and Lysias is shown to be completely unsuccessful and the Jews remain undefeated. Both 1 and 2 Maccabees mention the approach of a Philip: in 1 Maccabees, he is the same as the one given charge of affairs at Antiochus IV's death (1 Macc 6:55); in 2 Maccabees, it appears to be a different Philip from that of 9:29.

In 2 Maccabees, the king behaves honourably, and honours the temple (cf. 3:2–3). Antiochus and Judas seem to be on good terms—another sign that the author stresses that Jews and Gentiles can get along. The installation of a new governor perhaps signals the new friendly policy of the Seleucids as the removal of Ptolemy Macron at 10:12 had been a sign of increased hostility. Some scholars place the land of the Gerrenians south of Gaza and west of Beersheba, others as far south as near Lake Pelusium, then under Ptolemaic control, others that it be placed north of Ptolemais at Gerrha, which lies south-east of Beirut. If the area covered by the new governor lay south of Ptolemais, he would have been in charge of Joppa and Jamnia and possibly Idumea, overseeing Gorgias (12:32–7). If north of Ptolemais, he would have overseen Tyre and Sidon. The citizens of Ptolemais, previously shown to hate the Jews (6:8; 1 Macc 5:15), have to be appeased in order to secure the king's rear. In glaring contrast to this rosy account, the author of 1 Maccabees has the king break his oath and tear down the walls of Jerusalem (1 Macc 6:61–2).

(14:1–15:39) The Attacks under Demetrius 1 The transition to the new ruler, Demetrius I, is made quickly. Demetrius, son of Seleucus IV and nephew of Antiochus IV had replaced Antiochus as a hostage in Rome in 178 BCE. Demetrius had tried to leave Rome at the death of Antiochus IV but had been refused permission. After the murder of a Roman envoy in Laodicea in 162 BCE, Demetrius had

again asked permission to leave, was again refused, but then slipped out of Rome anyway. 2 Maccabees states that he landed in Tripolis with a large force, whereas Polybius (31.12.11–13; 31.14.8–13) and 1 Macc 7:1 state that he arrived with only a handful of supporters. He was quickly successful in overthrowing Antiochus V and Lysias. Given the date at 2 Macc 13:1, the three years at 14:1 must refer to the beginning of the year 151 of the Seleucid Macedonian calendar, i.e. September 162 to October 161 BCE. Demetrius would have landed in 162 BCE, and so the three years must be interpreted as within the third year.

(14:3–25) The Expedition of Nicanor Just as the peace gained at the end of 2 Macc 11 was broken, so now the peace at the end of 2 Macc 13. Josephus states that Alcimus, also called Yakim, had been appointed high priest after Menelaus (*Ant.* 12.3857). When the new king came to the throne, he had come with the requisite gifts for confirmation of his office (1 Macc 10:604; 11:23–7; cf. 1 Macc 13:36–7). 'Olive branches' might be translated by the more general 'gifts'. Scholars have puzzled over what Alcimus had done in the times of separation (v. 3: *amixia*). At 1 Macc 7:12–18, Alcimus is said to have been acceptable to the Hasideans, and so scholars have argued that this 'defilement' of Alcimus could not refer to participation in actions like those of Menelaus. Some have suggested that the defilement refers to the incident in 1 Macc 7:12–18 where sixty Hasideans are executed, others that it refers to the division between the Hasideans and Judas over receiving Alcimus or not (1 Macc 7:10–11). However, the incident in 1 Maccabees takes place after Alcimus has been reappointed high priest by Demetrius, and so this interpretation seems unlikely. Other scholars have accepted another MS reading and translate 'in times of peace (*epimixia*)'. However, the use of *amixia* in the same chapter of 2 Maccabees to describe the loyal Razis (4:38) argues for retaining its use here. The term translated 'defile' can have the general meaning of 'disgrace' as at Sir 21:28; Tob 3:15, and so may not refer to some particular incident. Rather, it contrasts Alcimus with Razis and with Judas who left Jerusalem so as not to share in the 'defilement' (5:27). Alcimus must have been forced out of Jerusalem (1 Macc 7:6). Alcimus acts shrewdly in waiting until the king has a meeting about Judaea, for it would be appropriate for the king to ask someone with local knowledge.

The author provides Alcimus with the right speech for the circumstances: he first answers the king by throwing the blame on others while maintaining that he has only the king's and the country's best interests at heart in requesting help. He describes Judas as leader of the Hasideans, a group clearly demarcated from Judas in 1 Macc 2:42; 7:13. Here Alcimus lumps them all together under the term *hasidim* (pious, faithful ones), using it in a derogatory fashion much as people today talk of 'fundamentalists'. These Hasideans are distinguished from the nation (v. 8). The accusation against Judas is the opposite of what the reader knows from the earlier narrative: it is always the non-Jews who start trouble (10:14–15; 12:2). The charge that the state will never know peace while they are around (14:10) parallels the charge made by Onias against Simon (4:6). It is an accusation found also in the Greek Esther (3:13) and in 3 Macc 3:26; 7:4; 6:28.

v. 7 is sometimes interpreted to mean that Alcimus has had the high-priesthood taken away from him, but in this context it probably means no more than that he has left behind his high-priestly duties to come to the king, as Onias did earlier (4:4–6). The glory here would then refer to the glorious robe of the high-priesthood (Sir 45:8; 50:5–11): the verb translated 'laid aside' can mean 'take off a garment' as at Esth 4:4; LXX Esth 4:17*k*. As at 10:13, the king's counsellors instigate action against the Jews.

No mention is made in 2 Maccabees of the expedition of Bacchides and Alcimus' tenure as high priest told in 1 Macc 7:8–25, as such a defeat would have spoiled his thesis of the invincibility of the Jews. The Jews' response is to pray to God, who is said to uphold his heritage 'with an epiphany' (v. 15). The slight setback at Dessau is not mentioned in 1 Maccabees. Some scholars have seen in this 'defeat' of Simon an anti-Hasmonean stance, but I see it as in line with the feints and probes that take place before a major engagement. At v. 16 the armies were drawn up in battle array, rather than engaged in battle as NRSV. As in the dealings with Antiochus V, a very different picture emerges in the dealings of Judas and Nicanor from that in 1 Maccabees. Here Nicanor acts honourably, although Judas acts with commendable caution after again consulting with the people. The ambassadors are otherwise unknown, and the scene of the meeting is vividly drawn. In 1 Macc 7:27, Nicanor is pictured as

planning treachery, a motif common in 1 Maccabees (1:30; 7:10–18). The author of 2 Maccabees insists on the warm attachment that Nicanor had for Judas, although one might suspect that the Seleucid commander kept Judas close to him for more strategic reasons. The genuineness of the peace is underscored with the image of the battle-hardened Judas married with children and taking part in normal community life.

(14:26–46) The Change in Nicanor Alcimus intervenes to ruin the peace. The account assumes that Alcimus is in Jerusalem, presumably functioning as high priest. Alcimus charges that Judas has been appointed Nicanor's deputy as the word is used at 4:29, not 'successor' as NRSV. If Alcimus is not lying, Judas had become part of the normal bureaucracy of Jerusalem. The slander works. The author notes the distress of Nicanor, an honourable man, at breaking the covenant, but he obeys orders. The scene of Judas carefully observing the change in Nicanor reads like a movie script. No mention is made in 2 Maccabees of the battle at Capharsalama in 1 Macc 7:31–2, the narrative moves straight to the confrontation of Nicanor with the temple. Why would the priests know where Judas was hiding? Does Nicanor think they will follow the principle that it is better for one man to die than for the nation to be destroyed (2 Sam 20:14–22; John 11:50)? In any event, Nicanor's character changes: from being honourable, he turns into someone who fights against God. The contrast between Nicanor stretching out his hand against the temple (v. 33) and the priests stretching out their hands to God (v. 34) underscores the point. Nicanor, in his threat to level the temple to the ground, is likened to Antiochus (9:13; 8:3). Nicanor threatens to build a splendid (*epiphanēs*) temple to Dionysos, foreshadowing God's manifestation (*epiphaneia*) in defeating Nicanor (15:27). The prayer of the priests at v. 36 refers back to the purification at 10:4 and is fulfilled in the blessing at 15:34. It is interesting that the term used in v. 35 for 'habitation' is literally 'tenting' (*skēnōsis*), a term which reflects God's tent of meeting in the wilderness (Ex 25:8–9; cf. 1 Kings 8:4).

(14:37–46) The Death of Razis The episode of Razis lies between the threat of Nicanor and his final defeat. Just as the martyrdom accounts in 6:17–7:42 were placed after the desecration of the temple and brought about God's mercy, so now the death of Razis precedes the removal of Nicanor.

vv. 37–40, Razis is an unusual name. He is a lover of his compatriots in contrast to Alcimus who claims to be one. No reason is given why Razis was denounced. Nicanor is now simply said to hate the Jews. Five hundred soldiers to arrest one man emphasizes the importance of Razis. vv. 41–6, the scene takes place in a private house with a tower overlooking a courtyard, in which Razis is surprised. With no escape he kills himself, preferring to die nobly like Eleazar (6:23) rather than be insulted. A code of honour and disgrace is clearly at play here. Plato in Book 9 of his *Laws* had said that suicide was allowable: (1) under judicial constraint; (2) under the constraint of unavoidable misfortune; (3) in order not to participate in a dishonourable deed. Razis chooses not to be humiliated. vv. 43–6, the suicide is drawn out to the last grisly detail. He throws his entrails on the troops so that his blood is literally upon them. His last prayer is similar to that of the martyrs at 7:11, 22–3.

(15:1–5) The Defeat of Nicanor The confrontation between Judas and Nicanor continues. Bordering Samaria lie the Gophna Hills, just north-east of Modein, a favourite hiding place of the Maccabeans (1 Macc 2:28). The treachery of Nicanor is further emphasized by his desire to attack on the sabbath (cf. 1 Macc 2:29–38). Non-Jews knew how the Jews kept the sabbath and characterized it as a superstition which allowed them to be taken unawares (Jos. *Ant.* 12.4–6; *Ag. Ap.* 1.209–12). The Hasmoneans in 1 Macc 2:40–1 resolved to defend themselves even if attacked on the sabbath. Here Nicanor's wish shows him to be barbarous (cf. 2:21; 4:25; 10:4; 11:9). Nicanor taunts God as Goliath taunted the army of the living God (1 Sam 17:2–10, 26). His foolishness is shown in the fact that the sabbath observance is grounded in God's creating heaven and earth (Ex 20:8–11).

(15:6–19) The Battle Preparations As usual, the author contrasts the arrogance of the Seleucids with the trust in God of Judas and his forces. Following the injunctions for a speech before battle at Deut 20:1–4, Judas cites victories from the law and the prophets, where prophets here would include the books of the HB from Joshua to 2 Kings (Jos. *Ag. Ap.* 1.39–40). The perfidy of the Gentiles refers to Nicanor's breaking of the covenant he had made (14:20–2, 28). Judas then relates a dream. Dreams in antiquity

were one means by which humans kept company with the gods. People were aware that not all dreams were heaven-sent, but they were one way by which the gods communicated with humans. The author of 2 Maccabees describes the dream as 'a certain waking reality', reading *hypar ti* instead of *hyper ti* at v. 11. The detail of the description suggests that the elements of the dream were so clear that Judas thought he was awake. The characters in the dream are significant. Onias takes us back to the beginning of the epitome; he is called a perfect Greek gentleman, one trained in *aretē*, excellence, as Eleazar (6:18.23) and Razis (14:37–8, 42) were. As the priests stretched out their hands (14:34), so does Onias. The continuity between the dead and the living is shown by the dead praying for the living, as the living had prayed for the dead at 12:42–5. The second person in the dream is the prophet Jeremiah. Often his message is one of doom, but he is also sent to build and to plant (Jer 1:10). Although before the destruction of the temple Jeremiah had been instructed not to pray for the people (Jer 7:16; 11:14; 14:11), after the destruction he is told to pray for the people (Jer 42). Jeremiah in the dream gives Judas a golden sword. Heavenly weapons are of gold (3:25; 5:2). The giving of special weapons to a hero is a motif found widely in traditional literature. In Egyptian accounts, a god often gives a sword to Pharaoh to defeat his enemy. The giving of the sword thus provides divine assurance of victory. Polybius relates how the Roman general Scipio cynically used the motif of a dream to urge his soldiers on (10.11.5–8). v. 19 suggests that those inside the city could almost see what was happening out in the open, impossible if the location of the battle given in 1 Macc 7:40, Adasa, is correct.

(15:20–7) The Battle The armies are again contrasted. The presence of war elephants is unlikely: the Roman envoy Octavius had had them hamstrung in 162 BCE, just before Demetrius became king. Judas refers, as he had at 8:19 in the battle against the first Nicanor, to the defeat of Sennacherib (2 Kings 18:13–19:35). He asks for an angel as he had at 11:6, as happened against Sennacherib and as promised at Ex 23:20. At v. 25, the battle songs are perhaps those often addressed by soldiers to Apollo, and contrast with the prayers of Judas's forces. The battle is portrayed as a fight between gods. The God of Israel manifests himself (cf. 2:21). The numbers are exaggerated.

(15:28–36) The Feast of Nicanor The use of the ancestral language, as by the martyrs (7:8, 12, 27), signals the victory of the God of the Jews. Judas is described in terms reminiscent of Onias (4:2, 5). Decapitation and cutting off the sword hand, the right hand, is found among the Persians (e.g. Xen. *An.* 1.10.1; 3.1.17; Plut. *Art.* 13.2); dismemberment is also found among the Greeks (e.g. *Cleom.* 38) and Romans (e.g. Plut. *Cic.* 48–9). David had Goliath's head brought into Jerusalem (1 Sam 17:54), the Philistines cut off Saul's head and fastened his body to the wall of Beth-shan (1 Sam 31:9–10), and Judith had the head of Holofernes displayed on the walls of Bethulia (Jdt 14:1, 11). The details of the narrative may have been influenced by such heroic tales as these. Certainly the punishment fits the crime: 15:32 responds to 14:33, 15:34 to 14:36. The author distinguishes those in the citadel from Judas's compatriots. However, the fact that all bless the Lord (v. 34) and that Judas can hang Nicanor's head from the citadel suggests that the citadel is in Judas's control. This is rhetorically powerful but probably incorrect. The citadel remained under the control of the enemies of the Hasmoneans (1 Macc 9:53; 10:9) and was not captured until 141 BCE under Simon (1 Macc 13:49–52). According to 1 Macc 7:47, Nicanor's head and right hand were displayed just outside Jerusalem. It seems unlikely that the dead corpse of an unclean Gentile could be brought into the view of the priests around the altar. The skins of unclean animals were forbidden in Jerusalem (Jos. *Ant.* 12:145–6; see also 11QTemple 48:11–14), and how much more so a dead Gentile? There is debate among scholars as to whether some later rabbinic texts would allow a corpse into the court of women, although *m. Kelim* 1.7 explicitly forbids burial within towns.

The wording of v. 36 is very close to that of 10:8, and shows how the book was structured. Interestingly, the author identifies the feast by reference to Mordecai's day known from the book of Esther (3:7; 9:20 3). Since the author knows about otherwise unknown events in Babylonia (8:20), he also must know about this popular celebration.

(15:37–9) The Epilogue Even though the author seems to know of later events—e.g. perhaps the embassy of Eupolemus to Rome (4:11; cf. 1 Macc 8:17), although 4:11 may refer to earlier

contacts with Rome—he closes at this point. His statement that the city was in the possession of the Hebrews from this time on hardly agrees with what happened: a year after Nicanor's defeat, Bacchides returned and conquered Judea, killing Judas and reinstalling Alcimus (1 Macc 9:1–57). Just as the epitomist suppressed any mention of Bacchides' first expedition, so he ends here with a great victory of the Jews to promote his programme of how the God of Israel defended his temple. 2 Maccabees is propaganda history, and should not be judged by other criteria.

The last verse recall the images the epitomist used in his prologue (2:29–31) as well as his posture of humility (2:26–7). Wines in the ancient world were so strong they were usually mixed with water.

REFERENCES

Bar-Kochva, B. (1988), *Judas Maccabeus* (Cambridge: Cambridge University Press).

Bickerman, E. (1979), ET *The God of the Maccabees: Studies on the Meaning and Origin of the Maccabean Revolt*, SJLA 32 (Leiden: Brill). German original, *Der Gott des Makkabäer* (Berlin: Schocken, 1937).

Bringmann, K. (1983), *Hellenistische Reform und Religionsverfolgung in Judäa: Eine Untersuchungzurjüdisch-hellenistischen Geschichte (175–163 v. Chr)* (Göttingen: Vandenhoeck & Ruprecht).

Cowley, A. (1923), *Aramaic Papyri of the Fifth Century B.C.* (Oxford, Clarendon).

Doran, R. (1981), *Temple Propaganda: The Purpose and Character of 2 Maccabees* (Washington: Catholic Biblical Association).

Faure, P. (1941), 'La Conduite des armées perses à Rhodes pendant la première guerre médique', *Revue historique* 192: 236–41.

Goldstein, J. A. (1976), *1 Maccabees*, AB 41 (Garden City, N.Y.: Doubleday).

—— (1983), *2 Maccabees*, AB 41A (Garden City, N.Y.: Doubleday).

Habicht, C. (1976), 'Royal Documents in Maccabees II', *HSCP* 80: 1–18.

Momigliano, A. (1975), 'The Second Book of Maccabees', *CP* 70: 81–8.

Mørkholm, O. (1966), *Antiochus IV of Syria* (Copenhagen: Gylden-dalske).

Sachs, A. J., and Wiseman, D. J. (1954), 'A Babylonian King List of the Hellenistic Period', *Iraq* 16: 202–12.

Tcherikover, V. (1961), *Hellenistic Civilization and the Jews* (Philadelphia: Jewish Publication Society).

11. 1 Esdras

SARA JAPHET

INTRODUCTION

A. Title and Place in Canon.

1. Biblical and apocryphal 'Ezra literature' consists of three works: the Hebrew Ezra-Nehemiah, regarded by early Jewish tradition as one book; the Greek apocryphal book of the Septuagint; and the Ezra Apocalypse, found first in Latin in the Vulgate. The book discussed here is the apocryphal book found in the LXX. There it is called Esdras A (or 1 Esdras). The Latin translation of the book, found in the Vulgate, is there designated 3 Ezra. 1 Esdras has a complex relation to the Hebrew Ezra-Nehemiah and its Greek translation (known in the LXX as Esdras B).

2. 1 Esdras holds a peculiar position in the canon. Common to other works of the Apocrypha, its existence is not attested to by early Jewish sources, but its extensive use by Josephus, next to Ezra-Nehemiah (*Ant.* 11.3), suggests that it was known and appreciated. 1 Esdras was quoted and referred to by early Greek and Latin Christian fathers (Myers 1974: 17–18). However, its position in the Western church was greatly affected by Jerome's harsh criticism (with the Ezra Apocalypse). Its canonicity was rejected by the Council of Trent (1546 CE), although it was printed, in small type, as an appendix to the Tridentine Vulgate (Cook 1913: 3). It thus remained in a unique marginal position within large parts of the Christian world.

B. Nature, Scope, and Relationship to Chronicles and Ezra-Nehemiah.

1. 1 Esdras is a description of the history of Israel from the eighteenth year of King Josiah to the time of Ezra, and forms a parallel history to sections of Chronicles and Ezra-Nehemiah. Broadly ch. 1 is parallel to the two concluding chs. of 2 Chronicles (35–6), and chs. 2 and 5:7–9:55 are parallel to Ezra 1–10 and Neh 7:72–8:13a (with some differences in order and detail). Only chs. 3:1–5:6 are unique to this book. When compared with Chronicles and Ezra-Nehemiah, 1 Esdras seems to open at a peculiar point, in the last stages of Josiah's reign, and end abruptly with the first word of Neh 8:13: 'They came together'. These facts determined the literary context in which the book's nature was discussed (cf. *inter alia* Bayer 1911; Pohlmann 1970; Williamson 1977; Torrey 1970; Eskenazi 1986; Schenker 1991): does the present scope of 1 Esdras represent

the original format of the work, or is it a fragment of a longer work? If a fragment, what were the boundaries of the original work? And, in any case, how is the book related to the canonical books of Chronicles and Ezra-Nehemiah?

2. It is beyond the scope of this introduction to survey the history of research, in which every conceivable possibility was suggested (see, among others, Pohlmann 1970: 14–31). I will restrict myself to major views and a proposition of my own. Regarding the book's original format, two extreme views have been offered: the prevalent view, that the book is a fragment of a much larger work which originally included the entire so- called 'Chronistic history', from the beginning of Chronicles to the end of Ezra-Nehemiah (e.g. Cook 1913; Pohlmann 1970; Torrey 1945; 1970; Myers 1974; Coggins and Knibb 1979); and the less common view that the work is complete as it is, both at the beginning and end (e.g. Bayer 1911; Rudolph 1949; Williamson 1977; Eskenazi 1986). Within each of these general lines many varieties of opinion were expressed. Most conspicuous is the hot debate, among those who hold that 1 Esdras is a fragment of the Chronistic work, regarding the question of originality: where is the supposed original Chronistic history represented in a superior way, in the canonical Chronicles and Ezra-Nehemiah, or in 1 Esdras? This question was examined mainly in regard to three issues: the story of the three guards, found in 1 Esdras but not in Ezra-Nehemiah; the story of Nehemiah, found in the canonical Ezra-Nehemiah but not in 1 Esdras; and the order of the events at the beginning of the Persian period, where 1 Esdras places Ezra 4:6–24 after Ezra 1. Here too, opinions differ greatly, but it is interesting that within this line of research, although the originality of every other aspect of 1 Esdras was questioned, the originality of the continuity between Chronicles and Ezra- Nehemiah was taken for granted.

3. The consequences of this debate exceed the bounds of literary composition and have great significance for the understanding an devaluation of 1 Esdras. For if it is a fragment, then 1 Esdras may have no identity of its own, no purpose or theology. Consequently, there should be no sense in studying it, except for those aspects judged to be 'more original', or as 'aversion' for matters of textual criticism or translation techniques. This attitude is reflected in the book's history of research.

4. In recent years, the existence of a 'Chronistic history', encompassing both Chronicles and Ezra-Nehemiah, has been questioned (Japhet 1968; Williamson 1977; Japhet 1991) and denied by a growing number of scholars. A closer study of both Chronicles and Ezra-Nehemiah has shown that while they certainly belong to what may be termed post-exilic historiography, they are two independent works, written in different periods, with different presuppositions, theology, and purpose. This conclusion, reached independently, also has a bearing on 1 Esdras, for if there is no Chronistic history, 1 Esdras cannot represent a fragment thereof. If this is correct, 1 Esdras may be recognized as a work in itself, with its own purpose, method, and ideology, composed as one more description of the restoration period, the author choosing to gather existing literary excerpts and stitch them together rather than use his own words. The excerpts were taken from three sources: the biblical books of Chronicles and Ezra-Nehemiah, and another, no longer extant, source. The nature of the final work may be compared to Chronicles and best defined as 'corrective history' (Japhet 1996: 140, 148–9): a reformulation of history from a new, 'modern' perspective, responsive to its time. Such a history would provide a new interpretation of the past, be valid for the present, and lay the foundations for the future. For the specific theological features of this formulation, see below.

5. The success of the 1 Esdras effort may be judged by two criteria: his work was translated into Greek and eventually included in the Septuagint, and it was extensively used by Josephus, who followed it faithfully and in great detail, as he did with other biblical works. There still remains the matter of the book's scope. We find no difficulty in its beginning; this is where the author chose to begin his story. As for the end, it is possible that a few words or a short paragraph had accidentally been dropped at this point (see Commentary).

C. Basic Structure and Contents. 1 Esdras can be rightly called 'The Book of Destruction and Restoration'. It describes the history of Israel from the last period of the monarchy, at the eve of its downfall, until the reading of the law and the celebration of the festivals in the time of Ezra, the ultimate expression of restoration. This long period encompasses three historical foci: the last kings of Judah and the fall of Judah

and Jerusalem (ch. 1); the material restoration of Jerusalem during the reigns of Cyrus and Darius (chs. 2–7); the spiritual restoration under the leadership of Ezra (chs. 8–9). The details of this structure are:

The Last Kings of Judah and the Destruction of Jerusalem (1:1–58)
  Josiah (1:1–33)
  The Last Kings of Judah (1:34–58)
The Material Restoration (chs. 2–7)
  First Beginnings (2:1–30)
  New Beginnings (3:1–4:63)
  The Return (5:1–46)
  Laying the Foundations (5:47–73)
  New Start and Final Realization (6:1–7:15)
Spiritual Restoration (chs. 8–9)
  Ezra's Return to Jerusalem (8:1–67)
  Dissolving the Mixed Marriages (8:68–9:36)
  Reading the Law (9:37–55)

D. Sources and Composition. 1. The material of 1 Esdras can also be outlined from the perspective of its sources, with the division of paragraphs intending to clarify the different structure and order of the parallel works.

Parallel:		Parallel:	
1:1–22	2 Chr 35:1–19	6:23–34	Ezra 6:1–12
1:25–33	2 Chr 35:20–7	7:1–15	Ezra 6:13–22
1:34–58	2 Chr 36:1–21	8:1–27	Ezra 7:1–28
2:1–15	Ezra 1:1–11	8:28–67	Ezra 8:1–36
2:16–30	Ezra 4:6–24	8:68–90	Ezra 9:1–15
5:7–46	Ezra 2:1–70	8:91–6	Ezra 10:1–5
5:47–66	Ezra 3:1–13	9:1–36	Ezra 10:6–44
5:67–73	Ezra 4:1–5	9:37–55	Neh 7:73–8:12
6:1–22	Ezra 5:1–17		

The remainder, peculiar to 1 Esdras (1:23–4; 3:1–5:6), is composed of two elements: material taken from other sources no longer extant, and editorial notes written by the author. In the absence of comparative material, and with the original language of the work having been disguised by the Greek translation, a precise division between the two elements cannot be made, but some observations may be offered.

2. The Story of the Three Guards (3:1–5:6) The general scholarly consensus that this story was drawn from some Hellenistic source is followed by disagreement on the details: the scope and form of the original story, its original language, and when it was included in the present context. I will refrain from presenting all the divergent views and propose my own conclusion. An analysis of the story reveals clear signs of literary development: (*a*) The core of the story is a conventional wisdom story, in the form of a riddle: 'Who, or what, is the strongest?' Three candidates compete for the status of 'the strongest': wine, king, and women, in this order or in a different one. In all the answers the concept 'strongest' is viewed from a human perspective: who (or what) in the mundane world has the greatest control over the life of the individual man? (*b*) This original wisdom-riddle was then put in the framework of another wisdom-riddle, revolving around the question: 'Who is the smartest?' and formulated as a court-story: a competition between three of the great king's courtiers for the title 'the smartest'. The long speeches, which are examples of the genre, probably belong to this stage. (*c*) This court-story, formulated around the conventional pattern of 2 + 1, was again reformulated by the introduction of a fourth element, illustrating the pattern 3 + 1. The decision is now to be made between wine, king, and women on the one hand, truth on the other. The three are indeed strong, but they are all limited, because they belong to the petty and evil world of human beings. The 'strongest' is what transcends this world, is spiritual and abstract rather than material and concrete, namely, truth.

3. This courtly wisdom story, which seems to be drawn from the universal wisdom lore in its specific Hellenistic garb, also underwent a development of historicization and nationalization. The 'great king' was identified with Darius; the third, winning, guard, with Zerubbabel; and his reward was conceived in national rather than personal terms. This is the final, Jewish form of the wisdom-story, which then continued to describe the historical consequences of the competition (4:49–5:3) and was integrated into the history of the restoration by a new introduction to the list of returnees. Three different literary activities are evident in this final stage: editing an existing wisdom story, composing its sequel, and integrating it into the present context. Although different solutions are possible, we prefer to refrain from speculation and ascribe them all to the author of 1 Esdras.

4. (1:23–4) As will become clear in the commentary, the author of 1 Esdras did not add much to what he took from Chronicles, and intervened in the text only at the level of details.

Only this short paragraph can be ascribed to his editorial efforts, in the attempt to express his own view on the changing fortunes in the history of Israel (see the Commentary).

5. Another aspect of the literary composition is the peculiar contents and structure of ch. 2. As illustrated by the comparative table of sources, 1 Esdras presents a different order from that of the canonical Ezra, with Ezra 4:6–24 following Ezra 1. What is the origin of this order? Is it the original order, later changed in Ezra-Nehemiah, or is it secondary? If the latter, who was responsible for it, the author of 1 Esdras or a later 'interpolator'? Although some scholars have argued that the order of 1 Esdras was original and superior (e.g. Schenker 1991; Dequeker 1993; Böhler 1997), a close scrutiny of the comparable texts makes it clear that the original order—although in itself problematical—is represented by Ezra-Nehemiah, and the general view in this regard should be upheld (e.g. Rudolph 1949: xii–xiii). The new order of 1 Esdras is not a result of misunderstanding, or a later mishandling of it, but an intentional act of structuring by the author himself. The inclusion of the story of the three guards and the identification of the winner with Zerubbabel, intended to anchor Darius's favourable measures in the cultural milieu of the time and glorify Zerubbabel, demanded a clear distinction between the time prior to 'the second year of Darius' and the time following it. The hostile intervention in the building, which is explicitly circumscribed in Ezra 4:6–23 to 'until the second year of the reign of King Darius' (Ezra 4:24), had to be put before the story of the competition, while the founding of the temple by Zerubbabel (Ezra 3) had to be placed after Zerubbabel's appearance in the time of Darius. The present structure is thus a logical result of these considerations and should be ascribed to the author of 1 Esdras himself. While the general perspective of these changes is easily demonstrated, their practical results for historical cohesion were negative. As will become clear in the commentary, the reorganization was applied only to the major blocks of material and neglected the adaptation of the details, thus demonstrating the secondary character of the work.

E. Language, Translation, and Transmission. 1. What was the original language of 1 Esdras? The prevailing answer, although by no means the only one, is that it was Greek. This view conformed with the other prevalent view that 1 Esdras was a fragment of the

Chronistic history, and probably its more original form. The fine Greek idiom in which the book is written led scholars to conclude that it was, from the outset, a Greek work. Another possibility, that it was a reworking of Ezra B, was soon disproved, and it was regarded as an independent and much better translation. Torrey's early observation, that the original language of the story of the three guards was Semitic, probably Aramaic (Torrey 1970), did not change his position that 1 Esdras was 'merely a piece of the oldest Greek version of the Chronicler's work' (Torrey 1945: 395), but led him to see in the story a later interpolation into 1 Esdras. This view determined to a great degree the development of research—the scholarly concentration on the study of 1 Esdras as a 'version', a textual evidence for Ezra-Nehemiah (see e.g. Walde 1913; Bewer 1922; Klein 1966; Talshir 2003).

2. This view can no longer be maintained. As demonstrated by Torrey (1970), followed by Zimmermann (1963–4) and further by Talshir and Talshir (1995), the peculiar linguistic character of the story of the three guards cannot be explained as a 'Judeo-Greek'. Although the Greek in which it was written seems free-flowing, it is nevertheless a translation Greek, the *Vorlage* of which was certainly Semitic. The scholars mentioned above suggest Aramaic, but it cannot be excluded that this pericope, like the books of Ezra and Daniel, was itself bilingual, containing both Hebrew and Aramaic sections.

3. Combined with the view that 1 Esdras is not a fragment but a literary work of its own, and that the integration of the story of the three guards and the reorganization of the material are the work of its author, the consequences of this observation are self-evident: the original languages of 1 Esdras as a whole were Semitic—Hebrew and Aramaic—and as was the practice at the time, the work was then translated into Greek. 1 Esdras cannot be considered merely a version, a textual witness for the MT of Chronicles and Ezra-Nehemiah, with no further qualification. Its position in this regard may be compared to that of Chronicles *vis-à-vis* the MT of Samuel and Kings. While in many cases the source-text was followed literally, and the Greek translation may bear witness to a divergent Hebrew or Aramaic *Vorlage*, in other cases the change was the work of the author and cannot be considered within the framework of scribal transmission, or translation technique.

4. In dealing with the text of 1 Esdras one should try to distinguish between the work of the author at the level of composition, the work of the Greek translator at the level of translation techniques, and the process of transmission, which affected both the MT and the Greek of 1 Esdras at all stages.

F. Provenance and Date. 1. A general consensus sets the provenance of 1 Esdras in Egypt in the second century BCE (e.g. Eissfeldt 1966: 576). The basis for this conclusion is the nature of the Greek idiom in which the book is written, which has clear affinities with the language of the Papyri of the second century and some of the Apocrypha, particularly the books of Maccabees (see Myers 1974: 12–13; Talshir 1984), and the assumed literary affinities of the book to the canonical books of Esther and Daniel.

2. Again, the two aspects of the work should be distinguished. It seems very plausible that the Greek translation was done in the second century BCE in Egypt; there is nothing to contradict this view and many reasons to support it. The original work should be dated earlier, but its date and provenance cannot be suggested with precision. The influence of the book of Esther on the story of the three guards (see 1 ESD 3:1–4:41) sets an upper date for its composition, whereas the affinity with the book of Daniel is of a general nature and rather doubtful. The historical reality and general cultural milieu of 1 Esdras seems to be that of the Hellenistic period, with no trace of the Hasmonean period. We would place the composition of 1 Esdras in the third century BCE, and its Greek translation in the second century, probably in Egypt.

G. Purpose and Theology. 1. The most important feature of 1 Esdras is the concept of historical continuity. 1 Esdras bridges the gap between the periods of the First Temple and the Second by the flow of the story, with destruction, exile, and restoration fully integrated into the historical sequence. As a result, the fall of Jerusalem loses the severe meaning it had in Kings, and Cyrus's decree becomes one in a series of events rather than a decisive turning-point. It no longer marks, as in Ezra-Nehemiah, the beginning of the new period nor, as in Chronicles, is it the springboard toward a new future. The realization of the concept of continuity can be seen as the motive for the book's structure. The author does not show any interest in the history of the interim period, as he does not 'fill in' the bridged gap with any additional data—not even ready materials that he may have found in 2 Kings 25 or Jer 39–45, 52. Nor are theological explanations given for the transition from destruction to restoration. A direct and uneventful path leads from the one to the other, through the decree of Cyrus and beyond it.

2. A different historical perspective is seen also in the understanding of the restoration itself. According to Ezra-Nehemiah the restoration was achieved in two distinct phases, the building of the temple during the reigns of Cyrus and Darius, in which Zerubbabel was the most prominent figure, and the building of the city, initiated and carried out by Nehemiah in the time of Artaxerxes. 1 Esdras 'condensed' this history so that the restoration applied from the outset to both the temple and the city of Jerusalem. Both were undertaken under the same orders of the Persian kings (see e.g. 2:18–20; 4:43–5), and completed together. Therefore, after having transferred Nehemiah's main undertaking, the building of Jerusalem, to the time of Zerubbabel, 1 Esdras had no need for the story of Nehemiah and omitted it—but not before he had moved Nehemiah himself to the time of Zerubbabel (e.g. 5:40), and borrowed motifs from his story for the history of Zerubbabel (e.g. 4:47–8). The result is a different periodization, which is also expressed in the view of the political order in Judah during the restoration period.

3. According to Ezra-Nehemiah, during the two generations of the restoration Judah was ruled by pairs, a secular and a clerical ruler working together (Zerubbabel and Joshua for the first period, Nehemiah and Ezra for the second). This is changed in 1 Esdras in three ways: For the first period of the restoration 1 Esdras augments the role of Zerubbabel without doing the same for the priest Joshua; Joshua is no longer Zerubbabel's equal but acts very much in his shadow. The omission of the story of Nehemiah leaves Ezra as the sole protagonist of his time, following immediately after Zerubbabel. Finally, by beginning the story with Josiah, the entire periodization of Ezra-Nehemiah has been changed.

4. Perhaps the best-known feature of 1 Esdras is his presentation of Zerubbabel, who becomes the major protagonist of the restoration. Although we find in Ezra-Nehemiah a tendency to extend the span of Zerubbabel's office from the time of Darius back to that of Cyrus, we do not find therein any form of glorification of his figure (Japhet 1982–3). This is modified in 1 Esdras in several ways. The Davidic descent of

Zerubbabel, which is totally absent in Ezra-Nehemiah, is reaffirmed in 1 Esdras by an explicit genealogy tracing his descent to the tribe of Judah and the house of David (5:5). He is also explicitly referred to as the governor of Judah, a fact that is suppressed in Ezra-Nehemiah, and he is connected with the completion of the temple (6:27). With the introduction of the story of the three guards, Zerubbabel is presented as full of wisdom and piety, devoted to the welfare of his people. He is unquestionably the central figure, 'the governor', perhaps the symbol, of the restoration.

5. On the other hand, while 1 Esdras follows Haggai in calling Zerubbabel 'my servant' (6:27; Hag 2:23), he does not adopt the eschatological perspectives of the restoration prophets. Zerubbabel is not the bearer of any eschatological expectations, not even the hope of political renewal and independence. In this respect, 1 Esdras follows Ezra-Nehemiah, seeing in the Persian rule the 'good hand' of the Lord towards his people. Thus, Zerubbabel's office is subordinate to the foreign rulers and there is no political independence. Nevertheless, he is presented as the legitimate heir of the earlier monarchy and in some way the continuation of the Davidic kings.

COMMENTARY

The Last Kings of Judah and the Destruction of Jerusalem (1:1–58)

1 Esdras begins his story with the last period of the kingdom of Judah, from the eighteenth year of the reign of Josiah (622 BCE) to the destruction of Jerusalem in the time of Zedekiah (586 BCE). Except for a short section in vv. 23–4, it faithfully follows 2 Chr 35–6.

(1:1–33) Josiah (2 Chr 35:1–27) The story of Josiah comprises two major parts, the celebration of Passover (vv. 1–22) and the story of Josiah's end (vv. 25–33), connected by the author's note in vv. 23–4.

(1:1–22) Celebrating Passover (2 Chr 35:1–19) After a brief introduction of the historic event in v. 1—a Passover held by Josiah in Jerusalem at the appropriate date (echoed and elaborated in the conclusion of the story, vv. 19–22), vv. 2–9 begin the detailed description of Josiah's preparations, referring to two matters: the summoning of the cultic personnel for the performance of the ritual (vv. 2–6), and the grant of sacrificial animals (vv. 7–9). Only one verse deals with the priests (v. 2), with special attention to their garments—the external representation of their special status and privileges (see also 7:9 in comparison to Ezra 6:18)—a matter which seems to have been of great import at the time. It is followed by Josiah's long address to the Levites (vv. 3–6), which seeks to legitimize their 'trespass' into the performance of the ritual: the change in circumstances, which freed the Levites from the task of carrying the ark, made them available for other roles, to 'worship the Lord' and 'serve his people'. They are now asked to take upon themselves the main burden of the festival: to prepare the Passover sacrifices for all the people of Israel, according to their organization into divisions.

vv. 7–9 enumerate the sacrificial animals: lambs and kids for the Passover sacrifice, and cattle for the peace-offerings of the festival (Japhet 1993: 1050). The four groups of donors in Chronicles (35:7–9)—the king, his officials, the priestly and levitical heads—here become three, with the omission of the king's officers (see also v. 54 versus 2 Chr 36:18). The levitical heads are unexpectedly changed (a textual corruption?) into 'captains over thousands'. The complex ritual, regarding both the Passover sacrifice and the peace-offering of the festival, is described in 2 Chr 35:10–16 in great detail, relating to the various stages of the sacrifice and the division of work between the Levites, priests, singers, and doorkeepers, from the perspective of the levitical service. This precision is not preserved in ch. 1 (vv. 10–18). With the omission of 2 Chr 35:11–12a and the rephrasing of v. 12b, the details concerning the slaughtering of the Passover sacrifice, the sprinkling of the blood, the flaying of the animals, the removal of the fat parts, and their delivery to the representatives of the people, are not recorded. Due to these changes, the description of the ritual begins with the roasting of the Passover sacrifice (v. 12), the cooking of the other sacrifices, and their distribution. In addition, a completely unknown feature is introduced, namely, the priests and Levites standing 'with the unleavened bread' (v. 10), most probably a result of a textual corruption (běmiswāt, 'according to the king's command', to bemiāsot 'with the unleavened bread'). Each sector of the clergy performed its task with great precision and dedication: the priests offered the fats 'until nightfall', the singers were 'in their place', the gatekeepers were at 'each gate', and the Levites made it all possible, for they prepared the Passover sacrifices for everyone: the people, the priests, the singers, the gatekeepers, and themselves. Even more than Chronicles, 1 Esdras emphasizes the brotherhood (NRSV: kindred) of the Levites, not only to the singers and gatekeepers (v. 16 || 2 Chr 35:15) but also to the priests (vv. 13, 14).

vv. 19–22 (2 Chr 35:17–19) are a detailed conclusion of the story, summing up the general facts and the significance of the event: the celebration of the Passover and the feast of unleavened bread for seven days, the uniqueness of the festival and, again, the precise date, the eighteenth year of king Josiah.

In all, 1 Esdras retains the emphases of 2 Chr 35: the innovative character of the Passover, its having been celebrated in Jerusalem as a national festival; the magnitude of the festival, demonstrated by the number of sacrifices; the conformity of the ritual with the prescribed rules, the emphasis on matters of authority: the command of the king, of the Lord, as prescribed, etc.; and the diligence and sense of responsibility displayed by all, particularly the Levites.

(1:23–4) The Author's Comment The author's only explicit theological reflection points to the purpose of the chapter: the transition—in the very glorious days of Josiah—from glory to doom. According to the author's view, the end of Josiah marks the turning-point in the history of Israel and demands an explanation. In 2 Chr 35, the story moves from the Passover to Necho's campaign, with a broadened conventional formula: 'after all this, when Josiah had prepared the house, Necho king of Egypt went up to fight' (v. 20). Although Pharaoh's war is not waged against Judah, its end with the death of Josiah poses a grave theological problem: rather than being rewarded for his zealous dedication to the Lord, Josiah is confronted with a test that he does not pass.

The book of Kings provides the necessary explanation in the form of a special paragraph; it juxtaposes Josiah's unprecedented merits with Israel's accumulated sins, and concludes that God did not repent his decision to destroy Judah (2 Kings 23:25–7). This theological explanation was rejected by the Chronicler, who omitted the passage altogether (for his own theological solution see Japhet 1997: 156–65), but its absence was felt by 1 Esdras, who supplemented it in the present passage in his own words. The juxtaposition of vv. 23 and 24 draws a contrast between Josiah, whose heart was 'full of godliness', and the 'former times' (NRSV: ancient times), when the people of Israel sinned against God and made him angry. The last statement, 'the words of the Lord fell against [NRSV: upon] Israel' are the necessary introduction to the next paragraph: Josiah's merits could not change the Lord's decision to destroy Israel, which now begins to be carried out with the untimely death of Josiah.

(1:25–33) Josiah's End (2 Chr 35:20–7) Several changes have been introduced in 1 Esdras to the passage that describes the defeat of Josiah, his death and burial, and the conclusion of his reign. In the phrasing of v. 25: 'After all these acts of Josiah' the reference to the preparation of the temple (2 Chr 35:20) has been omitted, an obvious adaptation to the new literary context, since the 'preparing of the house' has not been told in 1 Esdras and a reference to it became irrelevant. In the story itself, the proper name of the king of Egypt is omitted, and more significantly, the theological part of the story—the address of the king of Egypt and the explanation of Josiah's sin—is rephrased. In 2 Chr 35:21 Pharaoh speaks and threatens Josiah in the name of *his* god, '[g]od who is with me', and Josiah is blamed for not listening to the words of Neco from the mouth of [g]od'. In 1 Esdras, Pharaoh speaks in the name of 'the Lord God' (*kuriou tou theou*) or 'the Lord' alone (mentioned altogether four times), which may refer only to the God of Israel. Josiah is blamed outright for not listening to the 'words of the prophet Jeremiah from the mouth of the Lord' (v. 28). These changes overcome the pressing theological difficulty, implied in the Chronicler's phrasing, that Josiah was punished for not obeying Pharaoh's god, and express the belief that the foreign rulers serve as instruments of God's works in history. This universal biblical concept is reformulated here (also elsewhere, e.g. the decree of Cyrus in Ezra i:i) to say that it was not only the Jews who saw world history in this way but the foreign rulers themselves adopted this view and conceived their task in history similarly.

In Chronicles (in contrast to 2 Kings), the text followed by 1 Esdras, the devastating significance of Josiah's death was recognized by his own generation as well as by later ones, and was acknowledged in the unprecedented scope and depth of mourning: the people of Judah, the prophet Jeremiah, the princes and their wives (a misreading of *haśśārîm wĕhaśśārôt* for the original *haśśārîm wĕhaśśārôt* 'singing-men

and singing-women'), all mourn upon his death 'to this day'. In v. 33 the conclusion to Josiah's reign is recorded in great detail, as appropriate for the last great king of Judah. His fortunes and achievements were recorded in two books rather than one: the mourning over him was written in the 'book of the histories of the kings of Judea', while every one of his deeds and his great virtues were put down 'in the book of the kings of Israel and Judah'.

(1:34–58) The Last Kings of Judah (2 Chr 36:1–21) The story of the last kings of Judash faithfully follows the source in Chronicles and presents a similar historical picture. There are, however, several differences in the names of the kings and their relationship to each other, which do not seem to result from mere textual corruption (an attempt at harmonization is seen in the various MSS). A comparison of the three sources, with the order of reign in parentheses may clarify the picture.

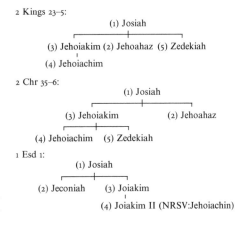

2 Kings 23–5:

(1) Josiah

(3) Jehoiakim (2) Jehoahaz (5) Zedekiah
(4) Jehoiachim

2 Chr 35–6:

(1) Josiah

(3) Jehoiakim   (2) Jehoahaz
(4) Jehoiachim   (5) Zedekiah

1 Esd 1:

(1) Josiah

(2) Jeconiah   (3) Joiakim
(4) Joiakim II (NRSV:Jehoiachin)

The relationship of (5) Zedekiah is not recorded.

In 1 Esdras, Joahaz/Jehoahaz disappears (as in 1 Chr 3:15); Jeconiah, who is elsewhere presented as another name for Jehoiachin (e.g. 1 Chr 3:16–17), the son of Jehoiakim and Josiah's grandson, is placed as Josiah's son and successor; Joiakim/Jehoiakim's son carries the same name as his father, and the relationship of Zedekiah—the son of Josiah in 2 Kings, of Jehoiakim in 2 Chronicles—is not given. Although no precedence should be given to the historical picture created by 1 Esdras, it reveals some independent traditions and an effort at reconciliatory interpretation.

(1:34–8) Jeconiah (2 Chr 36:1–4: Jehoahaz)
The clear historical picture drawn in 2 Kings
24:31–4, blurred somewhat in Chronicles by
the omission of the death of Jehoahaz, is further
obscured here. After having reigned for three
months, Jeconiah was removed by the king of
Egypt and replaced by his brother, Joiakim.
Beyond that, the details are impenetrable: why
did Joiakim 'put the nobles in prison'? Who was
'Zarius', whose brother was he, and how did he
get to Egypt? Why and how was he taken out of
Egypt? It is not clear what part of the picture is a
result of textual corruption, and what echoes
conflicting traditions, like those of 2 Kings,
which were not repeated in Chronicles. In any
event, the historical picture of 2 Kings should
clearly be preferred.

(1:39–42) Joiakim (2 Chr 36:5–8) 1 Esdras presents the abbreviated and reworked form of the
history of Jehoiakim, as drawn in 2 Chronicles.
Jehoiakim is the only king in 1 Esdras for whom
the standard Deuteronomistic framework is
preserved (vv. 39, 42). Recorded within the
framework are two matters: (1) Nebuchadnezzar
took Joiakim as prisoner to Babylon—a tradition which appears for the first time in 2 Chr
36:6, and then in Dan 1:1. The date given in
Daniel for Jehoiakim's exile (the third year of
his reign) explains well why 1 Esdras has
completely omitted to mention the length of
his reign. (2) Nebuchadnezzar took the holy
vessels from the temple in Jerusalem and put
them in his own temple (rather than his palace—2 Chr 36:7; cf. also Ezra 1:7) in Babylon.
Thus, following 2 Chronicles, 1 Esdras views the
spoiling of the temple's vessels as a multi-stage
process, during the reigns of Jehoiakim, Jehoiachin, and Zedekiah, parallel to the fate of those
kings who were all exiled to Babylon.

**(1:43–58) Joiakim II and Zedekiah (2 Chr
36:9–21)** The strict Deuteronomistic structure
of Kings, followed also in Chronicles, in which
the descriptions of the kings are clearly distinguished by standard formulas, is disrupted in 1
Esdras. The formulas are abandoned in favour
of a more continuous and fluent discourse,
which combines the stories of Joiakim II (vv.
43–5) and Zedekiah (vv. 46–58) into one sequel.
Contrary to 2 Kings and 2 Chronicles, in all MSS
of 1 Esdras the name of Joiakim's son is not
Jehoiachin but Joiakim, like his father. It probably reflects the reality of the author's times, in
which consequent kings would bear the same
name. Other than this change, the history of the
king is described along the lines of 2 Chronicles:

the king reigned just over three months and was
exiled to Babylon, together with the holy vessels. The history of Zedekiah is the story of the
destruction, following the Chronicler and
adopting his theological presuppositions. According to the Chronicler's philosophy of history, the destruction was God's reaction to the
transgressions of the generation in which it
happened—that of Zedekiah and his people.
Thus the measure of their sins has been augmented in the necessary proportion. Moreover, since God does not exert punishment
without first warning the sinner and trying
to make him repent his sin, God's warning
through the prophets is described in great
detail and the people's rejection of the prophets' rebuke is added to their sins. The destruction relates to Jerusalem and its people: many
were killed; all the great buildings were burnt
to ashes; the treasures were spoiled and
brought to Babylon; and those who survived
were exiled. All those who sinned received
their due, and the place of their transgression
became desolate.

The Chronicler's description assumes a
poetic character, while the actual fortunes of
the king (reported in detail in 2 Kings 25:4–7),
the details of the deported bronze vessels (2
Kings 25:13–17), the fate of the dignitaries
from Jerusalem who were deported and killed
(2 Kings 25:18–21), as well as some facts regarding the aftermath of the destruction (2 Kings
25:22–30), are all passed over in silence. Jerusalem became desolate, and was to stay in this
situation for seventy years, until it had repaid its
debt, until the land had enjoyed its sabbaths.

The Material Restoration (chs. 2–7)

(2:1–30) First Beginnings Following the hint of
the Chronicler, who concluded his work with
the decree of Cyrus, 1 Esdras moves directly
from the destruction in the days of Zedekiah,
to the new beginnings in the time of Cyrus. The
theme of prophecy and fulfilment, found in his
sources (esp. Ezra 1:1; 2 Chr 36:21), is further
emphasized by the augmented role of the
prophet Jeremiah in the time of the destruction
(1:28, 32, 47, 57). His prophecies of doom have all
come true, and now the time has arrived for the
fulfilment of this prophecy of hope, with the
first steps towards restoration undertaken by
Cyrus, king of Persia. Ch. 2 covers all the events
that preceded 'the second year of Darius', that
is, Cyrus's decree and the people's response
(vv. 1–9), the transfer of the holy vessels to
Sheshbazzar (vv. 10–15), the intervention of Judah's
enemies and the cessation of the work (vv. 16–30).

Following the literary method of Ezra (cf. Japhet 1996: 127–8; Williamson 1983: 1–26), the chapter's three paragraphs are composed in a similar way: a document, embedded in a narrative framework. The decree of Cyrus (vv. 3–7) is framed by an introduction (vv. 1–2) and a narrative conclusion (vv. 89); the list of holy vessels (vv. 13–14) has a narrative introduction (vv. 10–12) and conclusion (v. 15), and the official correspondence with Artaxerxes (vv. 17–24, 26–9) has the necessary introductions (vv. 16, 25) and narrative conclusion (v. 30).

(2:1–9) Cyrus's Decree (Ezra 1:1–6) Cyrus's declaration in his first year as king of Babylon (538 BCE) is addressed to the Jews in Babylon and grants them permission in three matters: to rebuild the house of the Lord in Jerusalem, to return from Babylon to Jerusalem for that purpose, and to take with them money and presents that were to be collected in the Diaspora. Immediately after the decree the people start to effectuate it. They organize the return (v. 8) and collect money and presents from those who remained (v. 9). Another version of Cyrus's decree, in a bureaucratic style and with some differences in content, is recorded in 6:24–6 (Ezra 6:1–3). The relationship between the two documents, and the question of their respective authenticity has drawn the constant attention of scholars (cf. the commentaries on Ezra and the specialized studies), but the existence of such a document seems to be generally accepted. A consistent difference between the text of 1 Esdras and his source is expressed in the representation of the divine names, mainly in two features: the avoidance of the common title in the Persian period, 'God of heaven' (Japhet 1997: 256), and its replacement by various other titles (cf. Ezra 5:11,12; 6:9,10; 7:12, 21, with 1 Esdras 6:13,15, 29, 31; 8:9,19, respectively), and the preference of 'the Lord' (kuriou, usually representing the tetragrammaton) over the more general 'God'. Here, in v. 3, 'the God of Heaven' is replaced by 'The Lord of Israel, the Lord Most high' (see Moulton 1899: 226–30).

(2:10–15) The Return of the Holy Vessels (Ezra 1:7–11) The theme of the holy vessels, pillaged by Nebuchadnezzar, kept in Babylon during the period of the captivity, and returned by Cyrus, is greatly emphasized in the book of Ezra and serves as a concrete symbol of restoration and continuity (cf. Ackroyd 1972). The holy vessels are also prominent in 1 Esdras, but their fortunes are differently conceived. Contrary to the picture given here (= Ezra 1:11) and repeated, although with some rephrasing, in 6:18–19 (= Ezra 5:14–15), according to 4:44 Cyrus took the vessels out of Babylon, but did not send them to Jerusalem. They were transferred to Jerusalem only in the time of Darius, by Zerubbabel.

The list of vessels includes only the small ritual utensils, such as cups, censers, and vials, which were not broken up or damaged during the destruction of Jerusalem. Unlike at Ezra 1 there is full correspondence in numbers between the details and total.

(2:16–30) Disruptions in the Time of Artaxerxes (Ezra 4:6–24) Outside interference with the building begins immediately, during the reign of Artaxerxes, who is conceived here as Cyrus's successor. This obvious divergence from the historical sequel of the kings of Persia is 'corrected' by Josephus, who identifies the king as Cambyses, heir to Cyrus (Ant. 11.2.1–2). However, the problem is not historical but literary, since the whole episode comes at this point as a surprise. According to 1 Esdras, the building has not yet begun and the description of the energetic construction in Jerusalem, as well as its cessation, are all premature. All these are the consequences of the literary reorganization of the material, which dealt with the larger blocks of the story but did not take care of the details. (See 1 ESD D. 1)

After the introduction to the correspondence (v. 16), the heading of the letter is recorded in v. 17, which is a fine example of the author's reworking method. In Ezra 4:6–10 three letters are mentioned: an 'accusation' sent to Ahasuerus (Xerxes), regarding 'the inhabitants of Judah and Jerusalem' (v. 6); a letter written to Artaxerxes by 'Bishlam and Mithredath and Tabeel and their associates' (v. 7), and another letter to Artaxerxes, sent by Rehum the royal deputy, Shimshai the scribe, and a long list of officials (v. 8). The last letter is actually quoted. These complex data have been condensed in 1 Esdras to form one single letter, sent to Artaxerxes. However, rather than writing the new narrative in his own words, the author made use of selected phrases gleaned from Ezra 4:6–11 thus:

In the time of king Artaxerxes of the Persians [= Ezra 4:7, 8], Bishlam, Mithridates, Tabeel [= Ezra 4:7], Rehum, Beltethmus, the scribe Shimshai [= Ezra 4:8], and the rest of their associates [= Ezra 4:8], living in Samaria and other places [= Ezra 4:10], wrote him [= Ezra 4:6, also 7, 8] the following letter [= Ezra 4:11] against those who were living in Judea and Jerusalem [= Ezra 4:6]: 'To king Artaxerxes [= Ezra 4:8, 11] our lord, your servants the recorder Rehum and the scribe Shimshai [= Ezra 4:9] and the other members of their council [= Ezra 4:9] and the judges [= Ezra 4:10, 11] in Coelesyria and Phoenicia [= Ezra 4:9: beyond the river] ... '

The letter itself (vv. 18–24) begins by presenting the situation: the Jews who came 'from you to us' are building the city of Jerusalem. It follows with the threat: if the city is built, the Jews will refrain from paying tribute and the income of the king will be damaged. Then comes the basis of this deduction: the city has a record of being rebellious, which was the cause of its initial destruction; and conclusion: if the city is rebuilt, the interests of the king will be greatly damaged. The accusational intent of the letter is revealed already at its beginning, where Jerusalem is described as 'that rebellious and wicked city' (v. 18), and is continued through various rhetorical means, such as the emphatic repetition of 'Judeans' (*ioudaioi*, NRSV: Jews), who were 'rebels and kept setting up blockades in it from of old' (v. 23; in addition to the parallel of Ezra 4:12 with v. 18).

In structure and contents, the version of 1 Esdras faithfully follows its source in Ezra 4:12–16, but there are some interesting changes in detail, most important of which is the scope of the construction. In Ezra 4 the complaint is directed exclusively against the building of the city and its walls (vv. 12, 13, 16), as is confirmed by the king's answer (v. 21). In 1 Esdras the accusation also refers to the building of the temple: they 'are building that ... city ... and laying the foundation for a temple' (v. 18). The change expresses the author's historical criticism of the original story and his own view that the temple and the city were built at once, and not—as in Ezra-Nehemiah—in two different stages at different periods. However, this change does not do away with the initial difficulty of the new structure, since according to 1 Esdras, the reference to the building of either the city or the temple is premature, from both the literary and historical points of view. Another difference, of less significance, is the accusers' attempt to justify their intervention by pointing to their loyalty and lack of self-interest: 'because we share the salt of the palace and it is not fitting for us to witness the king's dishonour, therefore we send and inform the king' (Ezra 4:14). This is rephrased in 1 Esdras in neutral language: 'Since the building of the temple is now going on, we think it best not to neglect such a matter, but to speak to our lord the king' (vv. 20–1a). Through slight rephrasing, the tone of the king's response (vv. 25–9 = Ezra

4:17–22) has become more strict and final. Rather than leaving the order in the hands of his deputies (Ezra 4:21: 'Therefore issue an order that these people be made to cease'), Artaxerxes issues the order himself, 'Therefore I have now issued orders to prevent these people from building the city' (v. 28). The possibility that this order may be revoked at some point (Ezra 4:21: 'until I make a decree') is omitted, and the general, rather ambiguous, warning (Ezra 4:22), becomes a straightforward reference to the circumstances at hand: 'take care that nothing more be done and that such wicked proceedings go no further to the annoyance of kings' (vv. 28b–29). v. 30 reports the conclusion of the event, its anticipated purpose: the accusers hasten to cause the work to stop 'until the second year of the reign of King Darius'.

(3:1–4:63) New Beginnings The pericope is composed of two units: the competition (3:1–4:41) and its consequences (4:42–63).

(3:1–4:41) The Competition The story of the competition is composed of two uneven units, representing two genres: the wisdom story, in itself comprising 'story' and 'speeches', and the historical narrative. The inclusion of a fully fledged wisdom story seems out of place in a historiographical work, but the literary inclination of the author leads him to retain the wisdom story in its entirety, including the speeches. (Somewhat similar is the inclusion of Esther in the records of Josephus; see *Ant.* 11.b. 1–13.) The structure of the story follows the lines of the plot: the circumstances, terms, and setting of the competition (3:1–17); the speech of each of the contestants (3:18–24; 4:1–12; 4:13–40), and the decision (v. 41).

(3:1–17) Proposition Since the introductory, narrative part of the wisdom story had been already adapted to fit the specific historical situation, it is difficult to say how much of it belongs to the original source and how much was reformulated for the present context. The circumstances as described are somewhat problematic. Following Esth 1:1–3, Darius is described as having held a grand feast for all his courtiers, officials, and subjects, from all the 127 provinces of his empire, after which he went to his chambers but could not sleep (vv. 1–3). Then his three bodyguards brought up the idea of a competition, decided between them on its terms, and took the first steps towards its execution by writing down their answers and putting the written note under Darius's pillow for his decision after he had arisen (vv. 4–12). When

Darius got up, he read the writing and accepted the idea, but turned the competition into a public event. The guards were asked to present their case before the assembly. The problematic nature of this exposition seems clear. The 'great feast' which opens the story plays no role in the development of the main theme. The motif of the king's sleeplessness stands in contrast to the sequence, in which the note is put under his pillow during his sleep. Even more difficult are the consequences for the image of Darius, who is presented as totally passive. Indeed, while the idea of the competition might have come from the guards, it is difficult to see how they could decide upon the winner's reward and make the king comply with their terms. All these seem to result from an elaboration of an original story with motifs borrowed from the book of Esther (the feast, the king's sleeplessness, the participants deciding upon the rewards to be extended by the king), but not fully integrated. Josephus's version is smoother in all these aspects (*Ant.* 11.3.2), but seems to be a secondary adaptation rather than a reflection of the original.

(3:18–4:40) The Speeches The speeches are set in a conventional pattern of openings and conclusions, retouched by small stylistic variations: 'Then the first who had spoken of the strength of wine began and said' (v. 17); 'When he had said this he stopped speaking' (v. 24, and see 4:1, 12; 4:13). Only the conclusion of the third speech deviates from that pattern, probably as a result of the new literary sequel.

3:18–24, the power of wine is presented from various perspectives, individual and social, positive and negative, with some ambivalence. Most important of all, wine is seen as depriving a human being of his greatest advantage, his mind and reason. Wine obliterates the social differences within society because it transfers people from the world of reality to a world of illusion. There, all are equal, all are masters, all are rich, all are happy. This blurring of distinction may lead a person to treat a friend as an enemy, but he cannot be asked to take responsibility for his deeds, for the world under the influence of wine is unreal: when the wine is gone nothing remains of the illusory world, not even memory.

Although this speech is independent of the other themes, it already refers to the next contestant, 'the king'—which might suggest a different original order. The king is mentioned from two different angles: the influence of wine on the king himself, whose wisdom then becomes similar to that of an orphan (v. 19), and

its influence on his subjects, who then forget their masters and rulers (v. 21). The king may be strong, but wine overcomes him.

4:1–12, the focus of this speech is the control of the king over his subjects: people may be strong because they dominate nature (v. 2), but the king is the strongest because he masters people (v. 3). The power of the king is then illustrated by several examples: he commands wars in which people kill and are killed, pillage and destroy (vv. 4–5); by means of his tax-system he is a partner of everyone's toil (v. 6); and he demands and receives absolute obedience (vv. 7–10a). The apparent illogical nature of the people's obedience is greatly emphasized: they fulfil the king's command although they themselves are strong, although the king is but one person and they are many, although he may deprive them of their property and even life, and command them to do things that they do not agree with. Thus, while wine controls man by affecting his body and mind, the king subordinates the human will!

Two textual notes: (1) v. 4 describes the army as overcoming 'mountains, walls and towers', 'mountains' being a misreading of the Hebrew 'cities' (*'ārîm/hārîm*); (2) the absolute obedience to the king's command is expressed in vv. 7–10a in a series of oppositions in a conditional structure. The list has seven items (kill/release; attack; lay waste/build; cut down/plant), and one wonders whether the list originally had four pairs, with one of the items having been lost (attack), or was built originally around the typological number seven.

4:13–33, the third guard takes advantage of his position as the last contestant, and utters two speeches rather than one, on women and on truth. The two speeches are already connected in the present context, together with the identification of the third guard as Zerubbabel (v. 13), but this sequel may still be broken down into its several components. The first speech, about women, is in itself structured in two parts: a general exaltation of the power of women (vv. 14–27,32), and a secondary concrete example, taken from the court-life of the present king and his mistress (vv. 28–31). The speech opens with a rhetorical question directed at the two earlier contestants: the king is great, people are great (Gk. 'many' is a mistranslation of the Heb. *rabbîm*) and wine is strong—but are they not ruled by a higher master, women (v. 14)? As mothers, women are the origin; they give birth to the king, to the people who master nature, and to the farmers who prepare wine (vv. 15–16).

They provide the physical and spiritual needs of men—clothes and honour (v. 17). A man may give away everything that he had amassed for a beloved woman (vv. 18–19); he may leave his parents and country to stay with his wife until his death (vv. 20–1). He may adopt all kinds of lifestyles—good or bad, on sea or land—to satisfy his wife (vv. 22–5). In sum, many men who loved women were led to insanity or slavery, or lost their way (vv. 26–7). Isn't this proof that women rule men and are the strongest (v. 32)?

Into this general praise of women, fully in line with the preceding two speeches, a short passage of the most surprising and dramatic nature was interpolated: a 'hot' story from the king's private chambers. It is an illustration of the general statement that women may lead men to madness and improper behaviour, as exemplified by the person who is supposed to be the measure of all things, the present king. This is in fact a penetrating criticism of the king, almost bringing him to trial, in which the guard betrays the king's trust by exposing his misconduct. This unexpected move is indeed followed by general embarrassment: 'the king and nobles looked at one another' (v. 33). Would the guard's words about the power of women be judged for their value, or would he be punished for his outright criticism of the king? At this point, the guard takes advantage of the general embarrassment and continues his argument, as if saying: 'I told what I did because this is the truth. I speak in the name of truth—the greatest value of all.' This bold and dramatic turn offers the king a way out of the embarrassing situation and brings the guard the longed-for victory.

4:34–40, this speech, too, begins with a comparison to the preceding argument: women are strong, but truth is stronger. Henceforth, the speech goes its own way and moves onto an elevated plane, in both content and style. The speaker refers to the foundations of the world—the earth, the heavens, and the sun (vv. 34–5), and these are but a path towards the highest of all: the Creator. Having made this cursory identification of truth and God, the speaker goes on to eulogize truth, through praise of the earth, the heavens, and everything else (v. 36). The essence of truth is that it has absolutely no injustice, a statement that highlights the concrete, moral concept of truth as 'justice'. With great rhetorical force, and with a fourfold repetition of the word 'injustice' in a parallel rhythm, the speech compares truth with all the other claimants to the throne of 'the strongest'. Wine, king, and women are unrighteous, indeed, all human beings are unrighteous. They are all transitory, having no lasting existence or value (v. 37). The speaker moves from the petty world of mankind to the eternal world of absolute values and ends in a hymnal eulogy, 'to it belong the strength, and the kingship, and the power, and the majesty, for ever and ever' (v. 40), which leads to what is now self-evident: 'Blessed be the God of truth!' The speech is a mixture of Jewish and Hellenistic elements, but its origin seems to be clearly in the Hebrew psalmodic style, with echoes from Isaiah, 1 Chr 29:11; Ps 148:13, etc., and the repetitious use of keywords: truth, injustice, great, strong.

(4:41) Decision The spirit in which the words were said overtakes the audience; they react to the rhetoric of the speech and are moved by its force. Their reaction, 'Great is truth and strongest of all' is a verbal echo of the keywords of the speech: truth, great, and strong! In its Latin translation, this sentence has become a universal slogan, whose force and validity have not waned.

(4:42–63) The Consequences of the Competition vv. 42–6, the beginning of the king's address continues in the vein of the wisdom story and accentuates the king's generosity toward the guard (v. 43). But the guard's response does not follow this lead, and rather than asking for additional personal favours, he moves boldly from the personal to the political sphere and addresses the king as the political sovereign. The scene seems to have its origins in the book of Nehemiah, where Nehemiah addresses the Persian king Artaxerxes with the request to build Jerusalem (Neh 2:3–9), but the differences are noteworthy. Zerubbabel's request is much longer than that of Nehemiah, and more important, it is presented as if he does not really ask anything new. He only reminds the king of his vow and provides him with an opportunity to be 'righteous'—in line with the spirit of the speech. Darius's vow is not known from any other source, and its historical basis seems doubtful. When did Darius make this vow? Why? How did Zerubbabel come to know about it? And if he made the vow—why did he not fulfil it? Darius's vow is not a historical datum but a literary device, which elevates his dedication to the building of Jerusalem on the one hand, and affords Zerubbabel the opportunity to achieve his goals with no need for explanations on the other. The king had already recognized, by his earlier vow, the need to build the city of Jerusalem, to return the holy vessels, and to build the temple.

The historical picture drawn by Zerubbabel has several peculiar points: (1) The burning of the temple is not ascribed to the Babylonians who conquered the city, but to the Edomites. The participation of the Edomites in the destruction of Jerusalem is attested in several places (e.g. Ps 137:7; Ob 11–14), but the main story in 2 Kings 25:8–10 ascribes its burning to Nebuzaradan, the king's general. Does the information given here reflect the more precise historical facts, or is it one more trick of the speaker, avoiding possible embarrassment on the part of Darius who, as 'the king of Babylon', might find it difficult to revoke an earlier 'Babylonian' deed? (2) The holy vessels were not sent to Jerusalem by Cyrus—who only took them out of Babylon and made a vow to send them to Jerusalem—but were still in the hands of the Persians. This twist of the story (see 1 ESD 2:15) is another aspect of shifting the credit for the restoration from Cyrus to Darius. Cyrus's decree is not mentioned; what remains is his unfulfilled vow regarding the holy vessels. (3) The story seems to imply that Cyrus actually destroyed Babylon, a fact which is not confirmed from any other source.

vv. 47–57, it seems that Darius was only waiting for the opportunity provided by the guard's request. He turns energetically to the project, issues a bill of rights, and begins to implement it by writing to all the officials who were to be involved. These measures provide for: (1) Permission for Zerubbabel and others to leave Persia and go up to build Jerusalem, to be supported by the officials' help in this matter (v. 47). (2) Permission to build the city, to be supported by the right to transport cedar wood from Lebanon (v. 48). (3) Exemption of the people going up to Jerusalem from taxes (v. 49). (4) Exemption from taxes on the territory under their control (v. 50). (5) Recovery of the land that had been taken over by the Edomites (v. 50). (6) Concrete allowances for the furtherance of the building: twenty talents a year for the construction of the temple (v. 51), and ten talents a year for the maintenance of the temple cult (v. 52). (7) Tax exemption of all those who came from Babylon and their descendants (v. 53). (8) Priestly exemption from taxes (v. 53). (9) Special allowance for the upkeep of the priests and provision of their vestments (v. 54). (10) Special allowance for the Levites, until the completion of the temple and the city (v. 55). (11) Provision of land and wages for the guards of the city (v. 56). (12) Return of the holy vessels

that Cyrus 'set apart' (v. 57). (13) A general confirmation of all the rights extended in the past by Cyrus (v. 57). This extensive bill of rights is taken from many sources and goes beyond the original request. For example, it opens with the securing of a safe journey for Zerubbabel and his caravan, although Zerubbabel did not mention that he wanted to go to Jerusalem. This feature, as well as the provision of wood, is certainly taken from the story of Nehemiah (Neh 2:7–8). Issues concerning the taking of land by the Edomites may reflect actual historical facts, but were not relevant to the building of Jerusalem, and are nowhere mentioned in Ezra–Nehemiah. The generous exemption from taxes also seems to reflect some reality of the Hellenistic, rather than the Persian period; in the latter period, only the letter of Artaxerxes refers to this matter and that only concerning the clergy (Ezra 7:24).

No mention is made in this context of the appointment of Zerubbabel as the governor of Judah, and the exact political order envisaged by Darius is not specified. The freedom from taxes and tributes seems to imply a broader concept of self government than is usually known in the Persian period. In any event, the political terminology of 1 Esdras is very similar to that of Maccabees.

vv. 58–63, the episode is concluded in accordance with the conventions of the time: a thanksgiving prayer of Zerubbabel (cf. Ezra's prayer after he had received the letter of Artaxerxes, Ezra 7:27–8), and the celebrations of the community. The conventional hymnal style of the prayer, as well as its parallel structure, are obvious.

Aware of the historical reality, the competition having taken place in Persia and the Jews living in Babylon, the author concludes by telling of Zerubbabel's journey to Babylon. The people react to the news with thanksgiving and rejoicing. The special emphasis of 1 Esdras that the city and the temple were built together is expressed here too: 'to go up and build Jerusalem and the temple'. With these celebrations, the story of the competition has completed its role as an opening for a new beginning, and comes to an end.

(5:1–46) The Return Due to the new arrangement of the material, the great return to Jerusalem, ascribed in Ezra 2 to the time of Cyrus, is here transferred to the time of Darius, and Ezra 2 is connected to the new sequel by a new narrative introduction (vv. 1–3) and a new preface to the list of returnees (vv. 4–6). The author then resumes his source, and follows it faithfully (with small divergences) from v. 7 onwards (Ezra 2:1–70).

vv. 1–3, the preparations for the return consist of one thing: the choice of returnees. The idea that only a fraction of the people returned from Babylonia to Jerusalem probably represents the historical reality, but the explanation of this fact as a result of 'choosing', namely, that permission was extended only to a minority that was to be chosen from the great multitude, seems to be the author's own. It was probably suggested to the author by the story of Nehemiah's repopulating of Jerusalem, in which he designated by lot one out often to live in the city (Neh 11:1–2). The end of the passage refers again to this issue but from a different perspective: the people who accompanied the returnees were so joyful that they too were allowed to go up!

The caravan described is similar to that of Nehemiah who went to Jerusalem with an escort (Neh 2:9: 'the king had sent officers of the army and cavalry with me'), rather than to the caravan of Ezra who 'was ashamed to ask the king for a band of soldiers and cavalry to protect us against the enemy on our way' (Ezra 8:22). 1 Esdras sees the return as a festive procession, a pilgrimage to Jerusalem accompanied by musicians and song (see Isa 30:29), rather than a long voyage through the desert.

(vv. 4–43) The List of Returnees vv. 4–8, the introduction is composed of two parts: the original heading of the list, taken from Ezra 2:1–2, which appears in vv. 7–8 following the author's presentation of the leaders (vv. 4–6). After establishing the fact of the return (v. 4), three leaders are mentioned (vv. 5–6): 'the priests...Jeshua the son of Jozadak...and Joakim his son, and Zerubbabel, the son of Salathiel'. (Due to a minor textual corruption in the Heb. bnw w to bn, the three leaders have become two, both of them priests: Jeshua the son of Jozadak, and Joakim the son of Zerubbabel. For various attempts to explain the text as it is, or to restore it differently, see Cook 1913: 34; Myers 1974: 66.) The leaders are provided with short genealogies which connect them to the constitutive periods of their respective authority. The priests are related to Phineas the son of Aaron on the one hand, and to Seraiah, the last high priest of the First Temple (2 Kings 25:18; following 1 Chr 5:40) on the other. Zerubbabel is connected to the house of David, the family of Perez, and the tribe of Judah, but nothing is said about his descent from Jehoiachin, the exiled king of Judah (cf. 1 Chr 3:17–19), perhaps

because of the divergent traditions in this regard, in 1 Esdras as well. Tracing the hero's genealogy to his ancient, tribal origin is a literary mark of the period—see Esth 2:5–6; Tob 1:1; and Jdt 8:1. This is the most elaborate genealogy of Zerubbabel at our disposal; it reflects in an unmistakable way one of the important features of 1 Esdras—the glorification of Zerubbabel and his Davidic lineage. The short note that Zerubbabel was the person who 'spoke wise words before Darius' highlights the sequence of the events. The date of the competition, here added to the story, seems to have been created under the influence of several sources: the date of Nehemiah's approach to Artaxerxes, 'In the month of Nisan in the twentieth year' (Neh 2:1), illustrating again that Nehemiah's memoirs were drawn upon for the story of Zerubbabel; Esth 3:7, 'In the first month which is the month of Nisan'; and perhaps also Ezra 7:9.

In vv. 7–8 the text returns to its source in Ezra 2 and produces the original introduction, with small changes. Most important is the replacement of the term: 'people of the province' with 'people of the land of Judah' (NRSV: the Judeans), which is the term generally used in this book. Also worth noting is the emphatic rendering of 'each to his own town', and the twelve names of the leaders (as in Neh 7:7) rather than the corrupt eleven in Ezra 2:2.

vv. 9–43 (see Ezra 2:2b–67; Neh 7:7b–72), while the literary structure and general contents of the list faithfully follow its source in Ezra 2, there are numerous differences in the details of names and numbers. Some names in Ezra 2 are not found in 1 Esdras, and some names in 1 Esdras are missing in Ezra 2. There are also changes in the order of names, and above all, their forms—as everywhere in the book—are sometimes unrecognizably reshaped. There are also several changes in the numbers, which could be easily explained as a result of corruption, but the original version cannot be determined. In what follows we will not deal with the variant details (see Cook 1913: 35–8), but present only the list's broader lines. It is structured in three main parts: vv. 9–35, register of the people according to their ancestry; vv. 36–40, register of those who lack a genealogical record or could not verify it; vv. 41–3, summary, including servants and property.

vv. 9–35, the register of the people is divided between the laymen (vv. 9–23) and the clergy (vv. 24–35). Among 'those of the nation' (v. 9), the people are registered in groups in two ways: by their ancestral genealogy or by their settlements. From a formal point of view, some are described as 'the descendants of' and others as 'those of', and while in general there is some correspondence between these criteria ('the descendants of Parosh', 'those of Netopha'), the correlation is only partial, and with the obscurity of some of the names, no precise division can be made. It is worth noting, however, that the groups registered according to their ancestry are usually larger than those of the settlements. Also, the settlements, as far as they can be identified, are mostly in Benjamin, with only a few place-names (Bethlehem, v. 17b; Netophah, v. 18a) in Judah. The list does not refer to Jerusalem, and it is hard to say how many of those enumerated were regarded as living in Jerusalem.

The clergy are divided into six groups, representing the temple orders in a declining hierarchy: priests (vv. 24–5), Levites (v. 26), singers (v. 27), gatekeepers (v. 28), temple servants (vv. 29–32), and the descendants of Solomon's servants (vv. 33–4). In matters of terminology, the singers are termed—as throughout 1 Esdras—'the holy singers' (NRSV: temple singers), probably to distinguish them from non-cultic singers, mentioned for instance in v. 42; and the Nethinim (Ezra 2:43 etc.) are consistently defined as 'temple servants' (*hierodouloi*). In all versions of the list, the priests outnumber all the other orders put together: 4,288 (4,289) priests against 713 (733, 752) for all the others.

vv. 36–40, two groups are mentioned in this supplement to the list of persons without proper record: three families who could not prove their Israelite ancestry (vv. 36–7), and three families of priests, who could not prove their priestly origin and were rejected from service until the restoration of the now lost priestly Urim and Thummim (Ex 28:30; Num 27:21, etc.), that is, indefinitely (vv. 38–40). In listing the Babylonian origins of those without record, 1 Esdras presents three of the place-names, Cherub, Addan, and Immer, as the names of the people's leaders—in harmony with his general tendency to emphasize the role and person of the leaders (cf. above, vv. 5–6, 9). An interesting rephrasing is found in v. 40, which cannot be fully explained on textual grounds. According to Ezra 2:63 the decision regarding the priests was made by the Tirshata, a Persian loanword probably meaning 'his highness', referring anonymously to the officiating governor. In Ezra-Nehemiah 'the Tirshata' is identified twice with Nehemiah (Neh 8:9; 10:2) and this identification is similarly assumed here, introducing Nehemiah at this period, alongside Zerubbabel. However, as a result of misunderstanding or a later corruption, the title 'Tirshata'

has been transformed to a proper name and presented in transliteration.

vv. 41–3: the summary provides the final numbers: the free people of Israel and, as against Ezra 2:64, 1 Esdras distinguishes explicitly between freemen and slaves, substituting for the original 'the whole assembly together', 'All those of Israel, twelve or more years of age, besides male and female servants' (v. 41). The age of 12 years as denoting maturity or a change of status, is not recorded anywhere in the Bible; the general age for full membership in the community being 20 (*inter alia* Num 1:3–46). The specification of age may either reflect a certain reality of the time which is not otherwise attested to (but cf. Lk 2:42), or another typological use of the number 12.

(vv. 44–6) Arrival and Settlement The arrival in Jerusalem is not stated explicitly, as in Ezra 8:32 or Neh 2:11: 'We/I came to Jerusalem'; rather, it is stated apropos the principal information: the vows of the returnees to build the temple. An interesting change of contents is introduced by the rendering of 'made freewill-offering' (*hitnadbû*) as 'vowed' (*nādrû*). This turn of phrase is evidenced throughout 1 Esdras and may have originated with the Greek translator. The derivations of the root *n-d-b* are almost consistently rendered with 'vow' (see 2:7, 9, as compared to Ezra 1:4, 6, and more). The actual donation of Ezra 2, made by the heads of the families 'according to their resources' (vv. 68–9, in itself a summary of Neh 7:69–71), is turned into a vow 'that to the best of their ability, they would erect the house…and…they would give'.

The settlement of the returnees is described somewhat differently in the various versions of the list (Ezra 2:70, Neh 7:72a), but according to 1 Esdras the higher ranks of clergy, the priests and Levites, and some of the people of Israel settled in Jerusalem and 'in the land', whereas the other clerical orders, the singers and the gatekeepers, together with all Israel, settled 'in their towns'. It seems that an original distinction between 'Jerusalem' and 'their towns' has been obscured by the addition of 'in the land' for the first group (NRSV: 'and its vicinity' is a nice way out of the difficulty). Why none of the lower orders of the clergy settled in Jerusalem is not made clear.

Concerning the reality behind the list, it seems self-evident, and indeed is generally accepted, that the list cannot be taken at face value; all these people could not have come up at once from Babylon to Jerusalem. The magnitude of the return would be impossible for the journey assumed here, and it may be compared to the return under Ezra, already of an outstanding size (Ezra 8:2–14, 18–19). On the other hand, there can be no doubt that a return to Judah did occur at that time as both Joshua and Zerubbabel were born in Babylon and their activity in Jerusalem is reflected in the prophecies of Haggai and Zechariah (Hag 1:1, 12, 14; 2:2–4, 21; Zech 3:1–9; 4:6–10). There are two main solutions suggested: that several, separate returns, throughout a longer period of time, hinted at by the twelve leaders at the heading of the list, have been condensed into one record, as if they represented a single event (Williamson 1985: 30–2); or, that a distinction should be made between the list proper and its narrative framework. While the introduction and the narrative section refer to a return, the list itself represents a census of all the inhabitants of the province, returned exiles and non-exiles alike. In this context, all these inhabitants are legitimized as 'returned exiles'. This second view is supported by the archeological data, which estimates the population of the province of Judah in the fifth century BCE to have been around 50,000 (Lipschits 1997: 331–6; for a much smaller estimate see Carter 1994: 133—7), and it is no longer possible to regard them all as returned exiles.

(5:47–73) **Laying the Foundations** Following his source faithfully, 1 Esdras records the first steps towards the restoration of Jerusalem as the religious centre of the Jews: constructing the altar and establishing the pattern of worship, making preparations for the building of the temple, and laying its foundations in joy and celebrations. This is followed by the intervention of Judah's enemies, which brought the effort to a halt.

(vv. 47–55) **Building the Altar and Establishing a Regular Cult** (Ezra 3:1–6) With the arrival of the seventh month, the date of the great pilgrimage, the people gather in Jerusalem to perform their duties. The place of the convocation, 'the square before the first gate towards the east', is not mentioned in Ezra 3:1, but is probably influenced by Neh 8:1 in the version of 1 Esd 9:38. Their first step, under the leadership of Joshua and Zerubbabel, is to build an altar on which sacrifices can be offered. As at Ezra 3, it is emphasized that everything was done properly: the altar was built 'in its place' (v. 50), the burnt offerings were 'in accordance

with the directions in the book of Moses the man of God' (v. 49); they offered sacrifices 'at the proper times' (v. 50), and kept 'the festival of booths, as it is commanded in the law' (v. 51). In fact, two sets of sacrifices are described here: the daily sacrifices and those of the festivals, as of that specific date (vv. 50b–51), and the regular sacrifices throughout the year from that point onwards (v. 52). The free-will offerings, here termed 'vows' (cf. vv. 44–6 above), were also resumed at that time.

In an interesting rephrasing of his source, the attitude of the 'other peoples' is differently conceived. According to Ezra 3:3 'they were in dread of the neighbouring peoples', alluding to the animosity that accompanied all their actions. According to 1 Esdras there were two groups among the 'other nations': those who 'joined them from the other peoples of the land' (v. 50a), and others, who were 'hostile to them and were stronger than they' (v. 50b). The stereotypical negative attitude to the 'other nations', characterizing Ezra-Nehemiah, is somewhat qualified.

At the same time, first steps are taken towards the building of the temple, with the provision of building materials: hewn stones, probably found in the immediate vicinity and mentioned cursorily, and cedar wood, brought from Lebanon with the special permission of Cyrus (vv. 54–5). The reference to this permission, as the whole chapter, follows the source of Ezra 3 (v. 7), and although there is no explicit reference to this item in Cyrus's decree (either in Ezra I or 6), one may assume that this was one aspect of his general support of the building. However, in the context of 1 Esdras, our chapter is explicitly placed at the time of Darius and follows his explicit order to this effect (4:48); the reference to Cyrus here is a glaring deviation from the new historical sequel.

(vv. 56–65) **Laying the Foundations of the Temple** (Ezra 3:7–15) Seven months later, at the beginning of the second month of the second year, the work on the temple, the main goal of the return and the symbol of restoration, is begun with a great ceremony under the leadership of Joshua and Zerubbabel. The ceremony is described as a grand liturgy—the priests in their holy vestments with trumpets, and the Levites with musical instruments, accompany the builders in music and song. In a touching scene, the reaction of the people is described: the old people, who had seen the previous temple and witnessed its destruction, react in 'outcries and loud weeping', while the majority of the assembly 'came with trumpets and joyful noise'. These voices mingle together in an indistinguishable loud voice, heard from afar. The inspiration for this story, based literally on Ezra 3:12–13 and somewhat rephrased, comes from Hag 2:3–4. While in Ezra 3 the event occurred in the time of Cyrus, in the present context it is transferred to the time of Darius, where Zerubbabel's return is placed.

(vv. 66–73) Intervention of Judah's Enemies (Ezra 4:1–5) This scene is connected to the previous one in a narrative chain: The noise of the celebrations raised the interest of the neighbouring foreigners and caused them to come to Jerusalem. These people are described in three different ways: the enemies of the tribes of Judah and Benjamin (v. 66); those who were brought to the land by 'king Esar-haddon of the Assyrians' (v. 69); and 'the peoples of the land' (v. 72). Although, even according to this text, they have obeyed and worshipped the Lord for many years, the threefold identification marks them as complete foreigners whose intentions are met with great suspicion. It is generally assumed that the people designated in this way are the inhabitants of the former northern kingdom, but no single ethnic term is used to identify them. This is an authentic reflection of the prehistory of the Samaritans and their early relations with the people of Judah. Their origin and loyalty are questioned and they are totally rejected, but their separate identity in religious and ethnic terms is not yet established.

The natural off shoot of rejection, aggression, does not take long to appear: the rejected people now take every possible measure to obstruct the building, which stopped 'as long as king Cyrus lived...for two years, until the reign of Darius' (v. 73). The insurmountable historical difficulties created by this statement are mainly two fold: (1) There is no direct sequel from Cyrus to Darius; Cambyses, Cyrus's heir, ruled for eight years between them, and so the time gap was longer than two years. (2) According to the context of 1 Esdras, the events described in ch. 5, including the laying of the temple's foundations, took place in the time of Darius, after the second year of his reign (2:30; 5:6). A reference to Cyrus at this point deviates from the historical sequence. These difficulties may be fully understood as a result of 1 Esdras's literary procedure. 1 Esdras has completely reorganized the story by transferring Ezra 4:6–24 to ch. 2 and relocating all the events of Ezra 3 to the time of Darius. However, these have not

influenced the phrasing of the original story, which is now continued in its original sequence.

(6:1–7:15) New Start and Final Realization Following Ezra 5–6 with small changes, the story now goes on to tell about the resumption of work on the temple 'in the second year of Darius' under the inspiration of the prophets, and its completion 'in the sixth year of King Darius' (7:5). In Ezra 5:1–2, the resumption of the building stands in outright contradiction to Artaxerxes' command that no work should be executed 'until I make a decree' (Ezra 4:21).With the removal of the correspondence with Artaxerxes (Ezra 4:6–24), the logic of the story in this regard has improved. Nevertheless, the broader historical context remains problematic, since it displays the short memory of everyone involved. According to the historical view of 1 Esdras, 'the second year of Darius', given here as the date of the governor's inspection (vv. 1, 3), is also the date of the competition of the three guards (5:6), which resulted in Darius's extended bill of rights and Zerubbabel's return. On that occasion Darius wrote letters to all the governors in Syria and Phoenicia and instructed them to help Zerubbabel on his way back and aid his projects (4:47–57). All this is completely ignored by the present story; neither the governor, nor the Jews, not even Darius himself, take cognizance of the events described in 4:47–57. This is another result of 1 Esdras's incomplete method of reworking.

(6:1–2) Resumption of Work (Ezra 5:1–2) The data about the role of Haggai and Zechariah in encouraging the people to build are probably dependent on their prophecies as preserved in their books (see Hag 1:1–11; 2:1–9; Zech 4:6–10; 8:9–13), although these prophecies speak about the construction and not its resumption.

(6:3–22) The Governor's Inspection (Ezra 5:3–17) Immediately after the successful resumption of the work, the builders are visited by the supreme authority of the satrapy, but contrary to other interventions, the inspection is described in neutral terms, as part of the governor's routine duties. Nevertheless, the high rank of the visiting officials may suggest an earlier unrecorded act of conspiracy. The circumstances of the inspection are recorded in two forms: briefly, in the introductory narrative passage (vv. 3–6), and more extensively, in the governor's letter to Darius (vv. 8–22). Its purpose is implied in the governor's questions:

to investigate doubts regarding the official authorization of the building. The point made at the beginning, that the inspection did not result in an immediate halt of the work, as would have been expected under such circumstances, is understood as an expression of special divine grace (vv. 5–6).

The letter of Sisinnes (Ezra 5:3: Tattenai) is an interesting example of official correspondence and local politics, structured carefully and phrased in official terminology. It begins with precise information regarding the governor's visit and observation (vv. 8–10), informs the king about the governor's investigation and his demand to be given the names of the responsible leaders (vv. 11–12), and continues with a lengthy recital of the answer he received, presented literally in the first person plural (vv. 13–20). The letter concludes with the governor's request: that the veracity of the elders' claim in the matter of authorization be checked, and that he be given further instructions (vv. 21–2). To the question of authorization, 'at whose command are you building this house.?', the elders of the Jews provide the formal answer by referring to Cyrus's edict in the first year of his reign. However, they set this answer within a long report of the history of the house, before and after Cyrus's command. Their central point is that they were not doing anything new! The house was built 'many years ago by a king of Israel', burned down by Nebuchadnezzar, began to be restored by the command of Cyrus, and had been being built since that time. Their words do not hint at any break in the process of building, nor at any previous intervention to stop it. The elders' answer is marked by strong religious tones, which are absent from the official language of the Persian visitors; they present themselves as 'the servants of the Lord who created the heaven and the earth' (v. 13), and explain the destruction of the temple as divine punishment (v. 15).

The version of the letter in 1 Esdras has undergone several changes from the version in Ezra in both content and style. The term 'God of heaven' has been replaced by other divine titles (vv. 13, 15, as against Ezra 5:11, 12; see 1 ESD 2:1–9); the city of Jerusalem is mentioned right at the beginning (vv. 8, 9, with no parallel in Ezra 5), and the house is glorified in several ways (vv. 9, 10). Also, the king is addressed more formally as 'our lord the king' (vv. 8,22) and the Jews are defined as those 'who had been in exile' (v. 8, absent in Ezra 5).

A matter of special interest is the addition of the name Zerubbabel to that of Sheshbazzar as

the one who received the holy vessels from king Cyrus (v. 18). While the theological goal of this insertion seems obvious—the wish to glorify Zerubbabel by connecting him from the very beginning with the fortunes of the vessels and the restoration of the temple—the historical result is embarrassing. Contrary to the picture drawn in this book, where Zerubbabel makes his first appearance as Darius's guard and receives the holy vessels from him, he is projected here back to the time of Cyrus and the vessels are seen as already delivered in Cyrus's time.

(6:23–34) Darius's Response (Ezra 6:1–12) Darius's response is a precise reaction to the governor's request: he conducts a search in order to find confirmation for the Judeans' claim of authorization (vv. 23–6) and issues his own instructions (vv. 27–34). The search throughout the empire produces an archival record of Cyrus's decree, found in Ecbatana, the king's summer residence in Media. The record confirms the main claim, that the permission to build the temple was granted by Cyrus, but differently from the decree in 2:3–7, it refers to the measurements of the house and the manner of its building, imposes the coverage of the expenses on the royal treasury, and contains an explicit order to return the holy vessels. It does not mention the people's return to Judah. All these create a coherent picture in which the issues that involve the imperial administration are set down, and the features of the house carefully detailed, because the expenses are to be covered by the treasury.

Darius's own instructions (vv. 27–34) are styled somewhat differently from Ezra 6:6–12. In both versions, the instructions are presented as an excerpt from Darius's letter, addressed to the governor in the first person, with the heading of the letter omitted. 1 Esdras turns the one long excerpt into four passages, phrased alternately as direct speech (vv. 28–31, 33–4) and indirect speech (vv. 27, 32). The instructions provide the governor with the answer to his query, but go far beyond that. Their main point is the recognition of the temple as a 'king's sanctuary', under the direct protection of the emperor. The royal treasury assumes responsibility for the provision of the ritual, and the priests are required to make sacrifices and pray for the welfare of the king and his off spring. The orders are upheld by severe penalties to transgressors—death by hanging and confiscation of property—and a general prayer to God to punish anyone who would act against the temple. However, unlike Ezra 6:8, the contribution of the king towards the building is absent in the present version.

Note that contrary to Ezra 6, which refers in a general fashion to 'the governor of the Jews' (v. 7), or ignores him altogether (v. 8), Zerubbabel is mentioned here twice as the governor (vv. 27, 29).

(7:1–9) Completion and Dedication of the Temple (Ezra 6:13–18) The completion of the temple and its dedication are told in a very concise style: the governor and his escort complied with the contents and spirit of Darius's orders and helped the Jews to complete the building. The house was finished on the 23rd (Ezra 6:15: the 3rd) day of the month of Adar, in the sixth year of Darius's reign, and dedicated. Compared with the extravagant dedication of the first temple (1 Kings 8:1–66), the elaborate ceremonies reported in Chronicles (e.g. 1 Chr 15–16; 28–9; 2 Chr 29:20–36), and even some of the events described in Ezra-Nehemiah (e.g. Neh 12:27–44), the conciseness of the description and the modesty of the ceremony and its puristic character are striking. The ritual includes only sacrifices, with no accompaniment of music or song, which had become a hallmark of Second Temple ceremonies. The number of sacrifices—although quite high in itself—is minimal in comparison to the extent of the other ceremonies, and no details at all are provided regarding the actual ritual practice. In Ezra 6, the ceremony is qualified succinctly in two ways: that it was conducted 'with joy' (v. 16), and 'as it is written in the book of Moses' (v. 18). 1 Esdras omits even the single reference to 'joy', and replaces it by another statement that the people did 'according to what was written in the book of Moses' (v. 6). On the other hand, 1 Esdras adds a few details of the ceremony: the priests and the Levites stood 'arrayed in their vestments' (v. 9), the gatekeepers were at their gates (v. 9, cf. 1:16), and the sin offerings were brought according to the number of the leaders of the tribes, rather than of the tribes themselves.

One more point should be made. According to Ezra 6:14, the complete success of the building was achieved 'by command of the God of Israel and by decree of Cyrus, Darius, and King Artaxerxes of Persia', expressing very loudly the book's view of the role of the Persian kings as the agents of God's will for his people (Japhet 1996: 132–6). Although 1 Esdras generally shares this view, it is softened here in his phrasing of the same verse: 'they completed it by the command of the Lord God of Israel. So with the consent of Cyrus and Darius and Artaxerxes, kings of the Persians, the holy house was finished' (vv 4–5).

(7:10–15) Passover (Ezra 6:19–22) The pericope is concluded with a short description of the Passover following the dedication. This sequel is clearly an imitation of earlier events, such as the dedication of Solomon's temple followed by the Feast of Booths (1 Kings 8:65), and Josiah's Passover following the restoration of the temple (2 Kings 23:1–20, 21–3). The description of the festival is again very concise, with brief mention of the date of the Passover and the celebration of the feast of unleavened bread after it; no details are provided concerning the sacrifices, the ritual, and the ceremony.

One matter stands out beyond the information of Ezra 6, that of purification, probably under the influence of 2 Chr 30. Ezra 6:20 refers to the general purification of the clergy, 'both the priests and the Levites', and says nothing about the people. 1 Esdras repeats this information, but extends it to relate to the status of the people 'Not all of the returned captives were purified', and repeats again that 'the Levites were all purified together' (v. 11). Another difference regards the composition of the celebrating community. According to Ezra 6:21 the celebrating crowd was composed of two groups: 'the people of Israel who had returned from exile, and also … all who had joined them and separated themselves from the pollutions of the nations of the land to worship the LORD the God of Israel'. While the identity of the latter group, mentioned in Ezra–Nehemiah only once more (Neh 10:29), may be debated, the note certainly refers to people outside the narrow circle of the returned exiles. This group disappears in the rephrasing of 1 Esd 7:13, where 'those who had separated themselves from the abominations of the peoples of the land' are the same as 'the people of Israel who had returned from exile'.

The peculiar view of the book of Ezra, emphasizing the role of the foreign rulers as the vehicle by which God's grace is extended to his people, is retained here too (v. 15).

Spiritual Restoration (chs. 8–9)

(8:1–67) Ezra's Return to Jerusalem By means of a conventional literary formula, 'After these things', the story now moves from the period of Zerubbabel to that of Ezra, from the physical restoration of Jerusalem and Judah to the spiritual plane. This kind of transition, already found in Ezra–Nehemiah, obscures the chronological gap of about seventy or 120 years (depending on whether Ezra should be placed in the time of King Artaxerxes I or II) between the events and creates the impression of direct continuation.

'The Story of Ezra', taken in full from Ezra–Nehemiah and followed faithfully, centres on religious issues and is composed of three parts: the story of Ezra's return (8:1–67), the issue of the foreign women (8:68–9:36), and the reading of the law (9:37–55). The story of Ezra's return is also composed of three parts: a general introduction (vv. 1–7), the letter of Artaxerxes (vv. 8–27), and the return (vv. 28–67).

(vv. 1–7) Introduction (Ezra 7:1–9) The introduction is to some extent a summary of the following story: It introduces Ezra by his genealogy and qualifications (vv. 1–3, 7), alludes to the letter of Artaxerxes (v. 4), and provides in a few words the bare facts of the return (vv. 5–6).

Ezra's genealogy is based on the common priestly genealogical scheme, which traces the descent of the high priests of Solomon's temple, from Zadok to Seraiah, back to Aaron through Eleazar and Phineas. The most elaborate form of this list is found in 1 Chr 5:27–41, and is abbreviated by the omission of a few generations in Ezra 7:1–5– It is further abbreviated in 1 Esdras, but in both versions (although the evidence of the MSS is not straightforward), Ezra is presented as 'the son of Seraiah', which means 'the descendant of Seraiah', since no matter what view one takes of his time, it is impossible—and nowhere claimed—that he was Seraiah's direct son.

Ezra's official Aramaic title is given in Artaxerxes' letter as 'the priest Ezra, the scribe of the law of the God of heaven' (Ezra 7:12, 21). The second part of the title was interpreted by some scholars as referring to an official position in the imperial court (following Schaeder 1930) In the Hebrew sections of Ezra, the official meaning of the title is less obvious and the connection of Ezra to the learning, teaching, and doing of the law is highlighted (Ezra 7:6,10, 11; also Neh 8:1, 4, 9, 13; 12:26, 28). This line of interpretation is developed further here, with Ezra described as one who 'possessed great knowledge, so that he omitted nothing from the law of the Lord or the commandments, but taught all Israel all the ordinances and judgements' (v. 7, cf. Ezra 7:10). In several places the title 'scribe' was rendered 'the reader of the law of the Lord' or simply 'the reader' (vv. 8, 9, 19; 9:39, 49), and rather than just 'priest', he is titled 'the high priest' (9:39, 40, 49) All these are meant to elevate his figure, in conformity with his reputation in later Jewish tradition, as illustrated for example by rabbinic sources.

The details of the return are summarized in vv. 5–6: the date of departure, the date of arrival, and the composition of the return, people representing all Israel.

(vv. 8–27) The Letter of Artaxerxes (Ezra 7:8–28) This unit is structured in the same literary manner that we observed before (cf. 1 ESD ch. 2), that is, as a document quoted literally (vv. 9–24) and embedded in a narrative framework, consisting of a short introduction (v. 8) and a conclusion (vv. 25–7). In an interesting manner, the style of the narrative moves from the third person of the introduction to the first person in the conclusion, and continues in this fashion until v. 90 (Ezra 9:15), where the narrative returns to a third-person record (vv. 91–9:36 = Ezra 10:1–5). The letter itself is written in a conventional official style and terminology, but some of the changes introduced clearly reflect the writer's provenance.

The official mission of Ezra, established by the king and his counsellors, is 'to make inquiries about Judah and Jerusalem, according to the law of your God' (Ezra 7:14), or, as it is phrased in 1 Esdras: 'to look into matters in Judea and Jerusalem' (v. 12). This seems to be a temporary nomination for a limited, distinct purpose, rather than a regular position in the Persian administration or the Jewish religious hierarchy. On the occasion of this mission, Artaxerxes grants Ezra authority in several matters, pertaining first to the return and then to his actions in Jerusalem. Regarding the return, Ezra is invested with authority in three matters: (1) to organize a return of Jews who wish to go with him to Jerusalem, in unlimited number and of all classes (vv. 10–11); (2) to transfer money and gifts from Babylonia to Jerusalem and use it according to his own judgement (vv. 13–16); and (3) to transfer to Jerusalem the vessels necessary for use in the temple (v. 17).

Regarding his activities in Judah, three matters are specified: (1) A special contribution of the imperial treasury for the maintenance of the cult, which should be provided by the local governors (vv. 18–21). However, the letter does not specify whether a regular yearly contribution or just a single donation is intended. (2) Exemption from taxes for all the clergy in whatever task (v. 22). (3) The authority to introduce the Jewish legal system, by the force of royal administrative measures, through the appointment of judges and the teaching of the law (vv. 23–4). Artaxerxes' letter is marked by a religious tone, culminating in the phrasing of v. 21: 'Let all things prescribed in the law of God be scrupulously fulfilled for the Most High God, so that wrath may not come upon the kingdom of the king and his sons.' This spirit, also found in the original version, is further intensified in 1 Esdras by his rendering of the divine titles, changing 'the God of Heaven' to 'the Most High God' and in some instances replacing the general title 'god' by the specific 'the Lord'.

A particular Hellenistic feature is introduced into the letter by the rendering of v. 10. While the original in Ezra 7:13 opens simply with 'I decree that' (lit. an order is issued by me), 1 Esdras precedes it with 'In according with my gracious decision I have given orders'– Officially this may mean that the king's special favour was outside and beyond the common procedure, but the use of the Greek term *philanthrōpia* certainly reflects the spirit of the author's time. With no transition of any kind and no introductory formula, the story now moves to Ezra's thanksgiving prayer after he had received the letter, phrased in the first person. In several MSS this elliptic transition is smoothed over by the interpolation of a preface: 'Then Ezra the scribe said', adopted also by the NRSV– The blessing is centred on one theme: blessed be the Lord who turned the heart of the Persian king and his counsellors towards Israel, the temple, and Ezra.

(vv. 28–49) Registration (Ezra 8:1–20) Ezra regards his caravan as a representative of the whole people, as 'Israel' in a nutshell, and he conducts the organization and registration of the returning people in two stages: the people who have gathered of their own initiative are registered according to their families (vv. 28–40), and then a special effort is made to express the idea of wholeness through the addition of the missing Levites (vv. 41–9). This symbolic aspect of the return also finds expression in the composition and hierarchy of the list. It begins with three individuals, representing the ruling families of Israel: the priesthood—represented by two priests, descendants of Aaron's two sons—and the kingship, represented by a descendant of the house of David. In principle, the same structure may also be found in the list

of returnees of Ezra 2, headed by the priest Joshua and the descendant of David's line, Zerubbabel. However, Ezra 2 does not spell out these genealogical lines (this intentional omission is 'corrected' in 1 Esd 5:4–8), whereas here these people are identified in terms of their distinguished origins. The laymen consist of twelve heads of families, listed in a formulaic manner: 'of the descendants of X, Y the son of Z, and with him N men'. This unified formula is modified slightly in two cases, the first (where the name of Zechariah's father is not given, and the word 'enrolled' is added; v. 30), and the next to last, where the descendants of Adonikam are qualified as 'the last ones' and three of them are mentioned by name only (v. 39). The basic structure and the main details of the list are the same as in Ezra 8, but there are some differences in names and numbers (1,690 here, 1,496 in Ezra 8). All the families also appear in the list of Ezra 2 (1 Esd 5:9–43), but their order is different and the numbers here are much smaller.

After having gathered the people at the 'river called Theras' (Ezra 8:15: 'the river that runs to Ahava'), Ezra found the composition of the caravan unsatisfactory. The absence 'of the descendants of the priests or of the Levites' (v. 42) meant an incomplete representation of 'all Israel', and Ezra makes special efforts to correct it. (In Ezra 8:15 the missing group are the Levites alone, whereas here it also includes the priests (cf. also v. 46), contrary to his own statement in v. 29 and the results of the search.) The descendants of two levitical families, eighteen and twenty men respectively, together with 220 temple servants, join the people preparing themselves to return.

An interesting misunderstanding is represented by the rendering of the place-name Casiphia as an adjective derived from the Hebrew word 'silver' (*kesep*), as: 'the place of the treasury' or 'the treasurers at that place' (vv. 45–6).

(vv. 50–67) The Journey (Ezra 8:21–36) A peculiarity of the story is seen in its unbalanced structure. The journey itself is described briefly in one verse: 'We left the river Theras . . . and we arrived in Jerusalem' (v. 61), including the date of the departure and a reference to the divine providence. All the rest of the story is dedicated to the preparations before the journey (vv. 50–60), and the people's whereabouts upon their arrival (vv. 62–7). Although the actual arrangements for the journey must have been extensive, as several thousand people were preparing themselves for a four-month journey in the desert, the details provided in this description relate to only two matters: a proclamation of fasting and prayer to the Lord before departure, and arrangements for the transfer of the money and gifts. It is interesting that the general fast of Ezra 8:21 is changed in 1 Esdras to 'a fast for the young men' (v. 50). Does this reflect the reality of the author's time and his presuppositions, or is it merely a result of textual corruption or misunderstanding (*hnhr*, 'the river', to *hn^{c}r* 'the young man')?

The description of the preparations is dedicated mainly to the transfer of the money and vessels from Babylonia to Jerusalem (vv. 54–60). Twelve priests and twelve Levites (Sherebiah, Hashabiah, and ten of their kinsmen) are nominated as trustees (v. 54),the gold and silver are weighed, the vessels are enumerated, and the transaction is concluded by an inspiring address of Ezra to the elected men: 'You are holy...and the vessels are holy...be watchful and on guard' (vv. 58–9). The conclusion of the journey focuses on the same subjects: the deposition of the money and vessels in the hands of the Jerusalem priesthood, including priests and Levites (vv. 6–24), and a religious ceremony revolving around sacrifices (v. 65). The numbers of the sacrifices are basically the same as in Ezra 8:35, and they are all of symbolic value: multiples of twelve, standing for 'whole Israel'. While the number of sacrifices is particular to this context, their composition—bulls, rams, and lambs for burnt offerings, and a male goat as a sin offering—represents the standard procedure for holy day sacrifices as, for example, in Num 28:11–15, 19–22, etc. In 1 Esdras the strict terminology of Ezra 8:35 is not preserved: the specific 'burnt-offerings' is replaced by the more general 'sacrifices', and the distinct 'sin-offering' is replaced by 'peace-offerings' (NRSV: thank-offering). The latter is completely irregular, since male goats were always brought as sin-offerings (e.g. Lev 4:23–4; 9:3, 15, etc.), and probably reflects the distance of the translator from the actual cult in the Jerusalem temple.

The end of the passage creates the frame for the larger unit, by returning to the beginning of the Ezra narrative, to the letter of Artaxerxes. Upon the arrival of the returning exiles, they transmitted the king's orders to the appropriate authorities, who acted upon it. It is interesting that the language here deviates from the first person singular of Ezra to a plural, '*they* delivered the king's orders', as if someone else and not Ezra himself was invested with this power.

One should also mention, perhaps, the constant dual presence of God on the one hand and the Persian king, on the other. Although the story is permeated with a religious spirit expressed in every way, the presence of the Persian king is also very strong, and his orders conclude the story.

(8:68–9:36) Dissolving the Mixed Marriages

The first thing that Ezra encounters upon arrival in Jerusalem is the problem of mixed marriage, presented to him by the leaders of the community. In Ezra-Nehemiah (chs. 9–10), attention to this problem seems to overshadow the other aspect of Ezra's activity in Jerusalem, namely the reading of the law (Neh 8). This is even more apparent in 1 Esdras, where the reading of the law is abbreviated (9:37–55), and the matter of intermarriage occupies the centre of the Ezra narrative. The story of the mixed marriages is presented in a detailed record:

8:68–9:2: The encounter with the problem (Ezra 9:1–10:6)
    8:68–70 (Ezra 9:1–2): The matter is brought to Ezra's attention
    8:71–90 (Ezra 9:3–15): Ezra's reaction and confession
    8:91–9:2 (Ezra 10:1–6): The decision
9:3–36: The solution (Ezra 10:7–44)
    9:3–14: The assembly in Jerusalem (Ezra 10:7–15)
    9:15–36: Investigation, recording and expulsion (Ezra 10:16–44)

(8:68–9:2) The Encounter with the Problem (Ezra 9:1–10:6)

The opening formula, 'After these things had been done', creates the impression of a direct sequel between the conclusion of the ceremonies and formalities involved with the return, and dealing with the matter of intermarriages. However, according to the chronological details of the narrative, Ezra arrived in Jerusalem 'on the new moon of the fifth month' (8:6), while the matter of intermarriages was dealt with four months later, in the ninth month (9:5). It is thus probable that the reading of the law in the seventh month (9:37; Neh 8) antedated the matter of intermarriages and was Ezra's first undertaking in Jerusalem. This original sequence was disrupted in Ezra-Nehemiah (see Rudolph 1949: xxiv); the new structure places the dissolving of the intermarriages—the wholesome purification of the people of Israel from the pollution of the foreign nations—as a necessary precondition for the sacred ceremony of the reading of the law.

(8:68–70), the leaders present Ezra with a grave problem; the people of Israel have mixed with the foreign population of the land by taking their daughters to be their wives, with the leaders of the community in the forefront. The list of foreign peoples is enlightening. Ezra 9:1 mentions two groups of peoples: five of the 'seven nations', the ancient inhabitants of the land of Canaan, about whom Deut 7:2–3 demands: 'you must utterly destroy them. Make no covenant with them ... Do not intermarry with them', and three peoples (Moabites, Ammonites, and Egyptians), about whom it is commanded that they 'shall [not] be admitted to the assembly of the Lord', either forever or for several generations (Deut 23:3, 7–8). It is obvious that the list is not historical but programmatic, identifying the contemporary foreigners with the forbidden nations. The list of 1 Esdras is different in two specifics: rather than Emorite it has Edomite— probably a better version—and the Ammonite people are omitted. This may be accidental, a result of some corruption, or a wish to keep the list to the number 'seven', the symbolic figure of the 'foreign nations'.

(8:71–90), Ezra's spontaneous reaction is that of the most profound grief and mourning: tearing garments including his priestly mantle, pulling out the hair of his head and beard, and fasting through the day. It culminates in his long confession of guilt, which represents the developing literary genre of prose-confessions typical of the late biblical period (see also Neh 9 and Dan 9). The confession opens with the first person singular (v. 74), but moves immediately to the first person plural, 'For our sins ... and our mistakes have mounted up ... and we are in great sin ...' (vv. 75–90). This style is retained to the end, as Ezra identifies himself completely with the iniquities of the people and becomes their spokesman.

The confession (vv. 74–90) is a piece of theodicy of the highest order. It juxtaposes the obstinate disobedience of the people throughout their history with God's unfailing mercy and compassion, and is permeated with the spirit of penitence: profound acknowledgement of the people's sins, and reminder of God's mercy. The argument develops as follows: (1) We are sinful and have always been so. Our sins have put us in a position of constant blame, from old 'to this day' (vv. 75, 6). (2)

We were duly punished, and suffered gravely for our sins (v. 77). (3) Then the Lord, because of his mercy, gave us some respite; he brought us into favour with the kings of Persia, and we now see the beginning of some consolation (vv. 78–81). (4) Now, we have sinned again, in the most grave historical sin of mixed marriages (vv. 82–5). (5) In view of our terrible ingratitude, what are our chances now? Would not the Lord's anger be justified? Are we not destined to the worst of all? (vv. 86–90). The confession does not end with a prayer. There is not even a request or a plea for forgiveness, only a confession of sin: you are faithful and we are sinful.

Each of the points made in the confession is expressed with great rhetorical force. The tone of self-accusation is achieved through a constant repetition of keywords denoting sin: 'Our sins have risen higher than our heads, and our mistakes have mounted up to heaven' (v. 75) ... 'and we are in great sin to this day' (v. 76). 'Because of our sins and the sins of our ancestors' (v. 77). 'We have transgressed your commandments ...' (v. 82), 'and all that has happened to us has come about because of our evil deeds and our great sins' (v. 86), 'but we turned back again to transgress your law' (v. 87), 'we are now before you in our iniquities' (v. 90). On the other side stands the merciful God: 'And now in some measure mercy has come to us from you, O Lord, to leave us a root and a name in your holy place, and to uncover a light for us in the house of the Lord our God, and to give us food ... Even in our bondage we were not forsaken by our Lord' (vv. 78–80), 'For you, O Lord, lifted the burden of our sins and gave us such a root as this' (vv. 86–7). 'O Lord of Israel, you are faithful' (v. 89).

This counterpoint of 'we, the sinners', 'you, the faithful' is further accentuated by the description of the extreme consequences of the people's sinful history. Although it may be implied that destruction and bondage were brought on Israel by the Lord, it is not spelled out explicitly. The disasters are described in an emphatic passive: 'Because of our sins ... we ... were given over to the kings of the earth, to the sword and exile and plundering, in shame until this day' (v. 77; also vv. 79, 80, 86).

The unique point of the confession lies in the definition of the national sin, the root of all the evil visited upon Israel. Unlike all other biblical sources, it is not the sin of idolatry, the worship of other gods, that evoked God's anger, but the sin of intermarriage. This was, according to the confession, the gist of God's warning before the conquest of the land, and the core of the prophets' rebuke. The conceptual context of this sin is impurity and pollution: 'The land... is... polluted with the pollution of the aliens of the land, and they have filled it with their uncleanness' (v. 83, also v. 87). The nature and source of this 'pollution' is not specified, but is ascribed to the very essence of these peoples and not to their conduct. The implication is self-evident: the only way for Israel to atone for this sin is to purify themselves, to detach themselves completely from the source of pollution, from 'the peoples of the land'.

Two details deserve attention: although the confession is transmitted faithfully from Ezra 9:3–15, even in the details, there is some rephrasing. The peculiar view of 1 Esdras that the restoration involved the city of Jerusalem from the very beginning, and not merely the house of God, is expressed clearly in the phrasing of v. 81, replacing 'to set up the house of our God, to repair its ruins' (Ezra 9:9) with: 'they... glorified the temple of our Lord, and raised Zion from desolation'. The repetitious reference to 'survivor' (Ezra 9:8,13,14,15—sometimes translated as 'a remnant'), is rephrased as 'a root' (vv. 78, 87, 88, 89). The basic formula of theodicy in Ezra 9:15: 'you are righteous' (NRSV: you are just) is rephrased in 1 Esdras to 'you are faithful' (v. 89).

(8:91–9:2), the extremity of Ezra's position and the rhetorical force of his confession set in motion a series of actions, leading to the desired goal: the dissolution of the mixed marriages, and the solution of the problem 'once and for all'. It should be noted that in all that follows, the motivating power is not Ezra but other people, probably laymen, whose position of leadership is not specified. Ezra is described as rather passive, reacting rather than acting. It is a popular movement, under Ezra's inspiration and authority. The first move, following the confession, is the proposition of necessary practical steps. One of the men who surrounded Ezra and witnessed his conduct, someone from Israel (Ezra 10:2: 'of the family of Elam'), takes upon himself to represent the people. In an eloquent address he admits the people's sins, accepts Ezra's authority, and suggests the solution: to expel the foreign women and their children. Ezra acts upon this immediately and makes the

people swear to follow this procedure. The scene ends with Ezra's withdrawal to the chamber of Jehohanan the son of Eliashib—probably the officiating high priest. If this identification is correct, it may serve as a chronological mark for the dating of the events—after Nehemiah, in whose time the high priest was Eliashib himself (Neh 3:1; 13:4).

(9:3–36) The Solution (Ezra 10:7–44) The decision made by the leaders of the community, to expel the foreign women and their children, now has to be implemented. This is done in two stages: a general assembly is called in Jerusalem, to have the proposed solution adopted by all those involved, and a procedure is suggested and carried out. The whole process takes about four months: the assembly was called in the ninth month (9:5); the procedure of recording the transgressors and dissolving the marriages began on the first day of the tenth month (9:16); and it was concluded on the first day of the first month (9:17).

(9:3–14), the initial decision is followed by a proclamation throughout the land to assemble all 'who had returned from exile' (lit. those who were of the exile) to Jerusalem. The authority behind the proclamation is that of 'the ruling elders', but the measures undertaken to have the people conform rest on both the imperial authority granted to Ezra to confiscate their property (thus Ezra 10:8; v. 4: their livestock would be seized for sacrifice), and the internal power of excommunication (v. 4). Whether because of their own free will or because of the threats, the people indeed gather in Jerusalem. The fine irony of Ezra 10:9, that the people sat 'trembling because of this matter and because of the rain' is lost in v. 6, where the people are described as 'shivering because of the bad weather'. This sets the tone for the assembly: everything is done directly and efficiently, even with some impatience and perhaps antagonism. In a straightforward statement, with no drama or elaboration, Ezra informs the people of their sin before the Lord, and demands that they confess their sin and separate themselves from their foreign wives (vv. 7–9). The people acquiesce, and since they wish to go home, ask Ezra to settle the matter in a more orderly and less public way, with the help of the judges of every locality (vv. 10–13). It should be pointed out that while administrative measures were taken in order to gather the people in Jerusalem, no authority is exerted to make them separate from their wives. This is left to their own discretion and decision, which indeed they make with full acceptance of Ezra's spiritual authority. The role of the five individuals mentioned in v. 14 (Ezra 10:15 has 'four'), remains unclear. In Ezra 10:15 it seems that these people formed an opposition to the general trend, while in 1 Esdras they are described as those who took upon themselves the execution of the people's decision. In either case, the actual procedure begins in the next verses, with Ezra appointing his own men for the task.

(9:15–36), the people comply with the proposals. A committee, headed by Ezra and some men of his choice, begins to investigate the matter systematically: to enquire in every settlement about the men who married foreign women, record their names, and dissolve the marriages. The result is a thorough list of people of all classes, from the highest ranking priests to the various families of laymen. The list is organized similarly to the other lists in Ezra-Nehemiah, beginning with the clergy. First mentioned are four individuals of the family of the high priest; they undertake to put away their wives and to offer sacrifices in expiation of their sin (vv. 19–20). This is the only reference to an individual pledge and sacrifice, and one may question whether it should be explained in literary or historical terms. Does the record imply that each of the transgressors was supposed to pledge himself and offer a sacrifice individually, or was a special procedure applied for the family of the high priest, the highest class on the hierarchal ladder?

In Ezra 10:18–43 the version of the list is apparently corrupt, as for example in the listing of the family of Bani (vv. 34–42), where twenty-seven individuals are traced to one family, while the average for the other families is between six and seven. In 1 Esdras the list has been corrupted further, and as in other cases, the names have been reformulated to a great degree. However, the general structure is clear: men of the four priestly families (Ezra 10:18–22; three families in 1 Esdras 9:21); of the Levites, singers, and gatekeepers (vv. 23–5), and of the laymen, the descendants often families (Ezra 10; eleven in 1 Esdras)—altogether above 100 individuals in either list. The end of the passage carries its final message: 'All these had married foreign women, and they put them away together with their children' (v. 36). This finality

is not clear in the obscure phrasing of Ezra 10:44, which leaves open the possibility that the women were not expelled but merely registered, but the doubt is removed in the straightforward phrasing of 1 Esdras.

As noted above, the matter of the mixed marriages occupies the centre of Ezra's activities in Jerusalem, the focus of his dedication. However, this does not prevent the reader from wondering about the phenomenon as a whole and its details. It seems that the motivation for this initiative was the fear of the returnees of losing their own distinct sense of identity, but was it dealt with in the best possible way? Who were these women who are described here as 'foreign'? How is it possible that what is regarded by Ezra and his followers as the worst possible sin, was practised by everybody in Judah, including the highest clergy? Were these women indeed 'foreign', or did they come from circles other than 'those of the exile' who were relegated to the status of 'foreigners'? Why were the measures suggested by the 'devotees' so strict and extreme? Why were the children expelled together with their mothers? Why was there no expedient, nor even a suggestion, for converting these 'foreign women'? And finally—was Ezra's undertaking really successful? As shown by such works as Ruth or Chronicles, Ezra's position was not the only stance in the Judean community; and, later, Judaism rejected his position altogether and provided a mode of conversion—for women of foreign origin as well as others. All these questions should be left for further reflection and study.

(9:37–55) **Reading the Law** In the book of Ezra-Nehemiah, the reading of the law and the celebration of the festivals form one event in the history of the restoration and one chapter in the course of the narrative. In 1 Esdras they stand at the end of the book, marking its conclusion. After solving the problem of the mixed marriages and the purification of the people, the time has come for Ezra to fulfil his mission: 'you shall teach those who do not know them' (i.e. 'the laws of your God' (Ezra 7:25)).

One of the matters that has attracted much scholarly attention is the scope of this passage. It opens with a reference to the people's settlement in 'Jerusalem and in the country' (v. 37)—a redundant and meaningless statement in the present context, but of great importance in illustrating the literary procedure of the author. Originally, this verse concluded the list of the returned exiles of Neh 7 (in itself a parallel to Ezra 2); 1 Esdras borrowed it from Neh 7:72 and rephrased it—a clear demonstration that 1 Esdras's *Vorlage* was the book of Ezra-Nehemiah as we know it, including the story of Nehemiah (cf. 1 Esd B).

The end of our passage concludes succinctly with 'and they came together', reflecting the beginning of Neh 8:13. This abrupt ending reflects a Greek rather than a Hebrew syntax for, in the Hebrew, the sentence opens with the time-phrase, 'and in the second day they came together', while in the Greek the subject + predicate came first. Although some scholars would see in this ending an intentional feature of the work (e.g. Eskenazi 1986: 56–9), we tend to accept the more prevalent view that some continuation of the story was lost. How far the story continued is impossible to say at this point. As the text now stands, the passage deals with two matters: the reading of the law (vv. 37–48), and the celebration of the holiday (vv. 49–55).

(vv. 37–49) Reading the Law (Neh 8:1–8) The reading of the law on the new moon of the seventh month is, again, the initiative of the people and not of Ezra: 'they told Ezra...to bring the law of Moses' (v. 39). It is described in two stages: a general description of the occasion (vv. 37b–41 = Neh 8:1–3), and a more detailed account of the ceremony (vv. 42–8 = Neh 8:5–8), all set forth in unique terms. Indeed, a public, ceremonial reading of the law has no precedent in the Bible and is inaugurated here for the first time (cf. also the cursory note of Neh 13:1). It is not clear from the story whether it remained a unique event, or became an organic part of the religious calendar. However, this is certainly the earliest evidence, in unusual circumstances, of the reading of the law, which became a regular part of later Jewish liturgy.

The details of the event are of interest: Ezra stood on an elevated wooden platform, made for the occasion (v. 42), with two groups of dignitaries, whose descent or status are not mentioned, to his right and left (six or seven on each side). He opened the reading with a blessing of the Lord (mentioned but not quoted), and the people responded in the conventional gestures of prayer: they 'answered

"Amen." They lifted up their hands and fell to the ground and worshipped the Lord' (v. 47). Ezra read aloud from the book for several hours, 'from the early morning until midday' (v. 41), and a group of thirteen Levites taught and explained the reading to the standing crowd (vv. 48–9).

Two matters should be noted: the event is described throughout as having a popular nature, encompassing the gathered crowd, both men and women. The people who attend are 'the whole multitude' (v. 38, also v. 40), both men and women (v. 41). The popular aspect of the ceremony is accentuated by the absence of any sacrificial aspect. One may sense a touch of ritualistic gesture in Ezra's bringing and opening the book (vv. 45–6) and in his prayer and the people's ceremonial response, but the event takes place outside the temple's precincts and with no participation of the clergy, except for the Levites acting as 'teachers'. Although Ezra is titled, as elsewhere in 1 Esdras, 'the chief priest and reader' (vv. 39, 40, 42, also 49), there is no expression of the priestly aspect of his mission; he is 'the reader of the law'.

(vv. 49–55) Celebrating the Holiday (Neh 8:9–12) The people's reaction of mourning, repeated three times (vv. 50, 52, 53), is matched by the statement of the leaders that 'this day is holy' (also repeated three times, vv. 50, 52, 53), and should be spent in joy. Unlike Neh 8:9, where the address to the people comes from Nehemiah the governor (the Tirshata), Ezra, and the teaching Levites, in 1 Esdras an unknown person, 'Attharathes', addresses Ezra, the Levites, and the people. It must be inferred that he was a person of the highest authority, although his title or position are not specified. In this way, and at the price of some unclarity, 1 Esdras omits the reference to Nehemiah in this chronological context (cf. also 1 Esd 5:36–40). Although the day is described emphatically as 'holy', it does not involve any cultic activity. It is described as a popular holiday, in which the expression of festivity is eating, drinking, sending portions to those who have none, and rejoicing. The date of the event, the new moon of the seventh month, is marked in the priestly holiday calendar as 'a day of complete rest, a holy convocation commemorated with trumpet blasts' (Lev. 23:24) and a set of special sacrifices (Num 29:1–6). All these are outside the purview of the present story, which focuses on the new, popular celebration of reading the law.

REFERENCES

Ackroyd, P. (1972), 'The Temple Vessels: A Continuity Theme', *Studies in the Religion of Ancient Israel*, VTSup 23: 166–81.

Bayer, E. (1911), *Das dritte Buch Esdras und sein Verhältnis zu den Büchern Esra–Nehemia* (Freiburg im Breisgau: Herder).

Bewer, J. A. (1922), *Der Text der Buche Ezra*, FRLANT 31 (Göttingen: Vandenhoeck & Ruprecht).

Böhler, D. (1997), *Die Heilige Stadt in Esdras α und Esra-Nehemia: Zwei Konzeptionen der Wiederherstellung Israels* (Göttingen: Vandenhoeck & Ruprecht).

Carter, C. E. (1994), 'The Province of Yehud in the Post-Exilic Period: Soundings in Site Distribution and Demography', in T. C. Eskenazi and K. H. Richards (eds.), *Second Temple Studies*, JSOTSup 175 (Sheffield: JSOT), II. 106–45.

Coggins, R. G., and Knibb, M. A. (1979), *The First and Second Books of Esdras*, CBC (Cambridge: Cambridge University Press).

Cook, S. A. (1913), 'I Esdras', *APOT*, I. 1–58.

Dequeker, L. (1993), 'Darius the Persian and the Reconstruction of the Jewish Temple in Jerusalem (Ezra 4:24)', *Orientalia Lovaniensia Analecta* 55: 67–92.

Eissfeldt, O. (1966), *The Old Testament: An Introduction*, tr. P. R. Ackroyd (Oxford: Blackwell).

Eskenazi, T. C. (1986), 'The Chronicler and the Composition of I Esdras', *CBQ* 48: 39–66.

Japhet, S. (1968), 'The Supposed Common Authorship of Chronicles and Ezra-Nehemiah Investigated Anew', *VT* 18: 330–71.

—— (1982–3), 'Sheshbazzar and Zerubbabel against the Background of the Historical and Religious Tendencies of Ezra-Nehemiah', *ZAW* 94: 66–98; 95: 218–29.

—— (1991), 'The Relationship of Chronicles and Ezra-Nehemiah', VTSup 43: 298–313.

—— (1993), *I&II Chronicles*, OTL (London: SCM).

—— (1996), 'L'Historiographie post-exilique: Comment et Pourquoi?', in A. de Pury, Th. Römer, and J.-D. Macchi (eds.), *Israel construit son histoire* (Geneva: Labor et Fides), 123–52. (Published in English as 'Post-exilic Historiography, How and Why', in A. De Pury, T. Römer, and J.-D. Macchi, *Israel Constructs its History: Deuteronomic Historiography in Recent Research*, JSOTS 306 (Sheffield: Sheffield Academic Press, 2000), 144–73.)

—— (1997), *The Ideology of the Book of Chronicles and its Place in Biblical Thought*, tr. Anne Barber, 2nd edn

(Frankfurt: Peter Long 1989). Hebrew original, 1977.

Klein, R. W. (1966), 'Studies in the Greek Texts of the Chronicler', Diss., Harvard.

Lipschits, O. (1997), *The Yehud Province under Babylonian Rule (586–539 BCE): Historic Reality and Historiographic Conceptions*, Ph.D. thesis, Tel-Aviv. (Published as *The Fall and Rise of Jerusalem: Judah under Babylonian Rule*, Winona Lake, Ind.: Eisenbrauns, 2005.)

Moulton, W. J. (1899; 1900), 'Über die Überlieferung und den text- kritischen Werth des dritten Esrabuchs', *ZAW* 19: 209–58; 20: 1–35.

Myers, J. M. (1974), *I and II Esdras*, AB 42 (New York: Doubleday).

Pohlmann, K. F. (1970), *Studien zum dritten Esra: Ein Beitrag zur Frage nach dem ursprünglichen Schluss des chronistischen Geschichtswerkes*, FRLANT 104 (Göttingen: Vandenhoeck & Ruprecht).

Rudolph, W. (1949), *Esra und Nehemia samt 3 Esra* (Tübingen: Mohr [Siebeck]).

Schaeder, H. H. (1930), *Esra der Schreiber* (Tübingen: Mohr [Siebeck]).

Schenker, A. (1991), 'La Relation d'Esdras A' au texte massorétique d'Esdras–Néhémie', in *Tradition of the Text, Festschrift D. Barthélemy* (Göttingen: Vandenhoeck & Ruprecht), 218–47.

Talshir, Z. (1984), 'The Milieu of 1 Esdras in the Light of its Vocabulary', in A. Pietersma and C. Cox (eds.), *De Septuaginta: Studies in Honour of John William Wevers* (Mississauga: Benben), 129–47.

—— (2003), 'Synchronic Approaches with Diachronic Consequences in the Study of Parallel Redactions: First Esdras, 2 Chronicles 35–36, Ezra 1–10, Nehemiah 8', in R. Albertz and B. Becking (eds.), *Yahwism after the Exile*, (Assen: Van Gorcum), 199–218.

—— and Talshir, D. (1995), 'The Story of the Three Youths (1 Esdras 3–4): Towards the Question of the Language of its *Vorlage*', *Textus* 18: 135–57.

Torrey, C. C. (1970), *Ezra Studies*, 2nd edn (New York: Ktav).

—— (1945), 'A Revised View of First Esdras', in *L. Ginzherg Jubilee Volume* (New York: American Academy for Jewish Research), 395–410.

Walde, B. (1913), *Die Esdrasbücher der Septuaginta* (Freiburg in Breisgau: Herder).

Williamson, H. G. M. (1977), *Israel in the Book of Chronicles* (Cambridge: Cambridge University Press).

—— (1983), 'The Composition of Ezra 1–6', *JTS* 34: 1–26.

—— (1985), *Ezra, Nehemiah* (Waco, Tex.: Word).

Zimmermann, F. (1963–4), 'The Story of the Three Guardsmen', *JQR* 54: 179–200.

12. Prayer of Manasseh

GEORGE W. E. NICKELSBURG

INTRODUCTION

A. Text and Language. 1. The Prayer of Manasseh claims to be the prayer that moved God to forgive the wicked king of Judah and restore him from his captivity in Babylon to his throne in Jerusalem (2 Chr 33:12–13). The text is preserved only in Christian sources, which are of two kinds. The first is the Odes, a collection of hymns and prayers that forms an appendix to the book of Psalms in three Greek biblical MSS (A, 5th cent.; T, 7th cent.; 55, 10th cent.) and in some daughter translations. A few Syriac MSS append the prayer to 2 Chronicles. Two church handbooks provide the second set of sources. The third-century *Didascalia Apostolorum* (*Teaching of the Apostles*) was written in Greek and has been preserved in a Syriac translation and some fragments of a Latin translation. Parts of the *Didascalia* have also been preserved in another church handbook, the 4th-century Greek *Apostolic Constitutions*. Both handbooks set the prayer in a narrative context that conflates and expands the accounts of Manasseh's reign in 2 Kings 21 and 2 Chr 33.
2. It is uncertain whether the Greek of the prayer is the language of its composition or a translation of a Semitic original (*APOT* I. 614–15; *OTP* II. 625–7). The Greek does have a strong Semitic flavour, but it also uses phrases paralleled in the LXX and has some linguistic constructions that suggest composition in Greek.

B. Literary Genre. This penitential prayer, or confession of sin, spoken in the first person singular, has relatively few counterparts among the individual laments of the canonical psalter. Its closest parallel is Psalm 51, whose language it appears to echo (*OTP* II. 630). Despite its prevalent concern with the covenant, it differs significantly from such penitential prayers as Ezra 9, Neh 9, Dan 9, Bar 1:15–3:8, Song of Three, the Qumran 'Words of the Heavenly Lights', and Tob 3:2–6. Its focus is consistently personal rather than national, and it lacks the language of the Deuteronomic tradition that permeates these prayers.

C. Narrative Context. Verbal allusions to details of the 2 Kings and 2 Chronicles narratives indicate that the prayer was composed in the voice of Manasseh. A question rarely discussed or even mentioned is whether the prayer was composed as an integral part of the conflated narrative context in which it stands in the *Didascalia* and the *Apostolic Constitutions* or whether it is an independent composition that was later placed in that narrative context (see, however, *APOT* I. 613–14). Two factors may support the former alternative. All but one of the other compositions in the Odes are drawn from biblical contexts (Ode 14 is, however, an expansion of Lk 2:14). The prayer and the narrative share at least one detail (v. 10) that is missing in both 2 Kings and 2 Chronicles. Claiming to recount the story in 2 Kings and 2 Chronicles, the narrative begins with a compressed revision of 2 Kings (with a few details from 2 Chr). Turning to 2 Chronicles, it mentions Manasseh's exile, elaborates the Chronicler's account by detailing the terrible conditions of Manasseh's imprisonment, picks up the report of his prayer and recounts the prayer, describes how a fire miraculously melted his chains, returns to the Chronicler's account of Manasseh's return to Jerusalem, adds that he worshipped God wholeheartedly and 'was reckoned righteous', and concludes with a summary of the Chronicler's report of Manasseh's restoration of the Jerusalem cult. As a whole, the rewritten narrative emphasizes the severity of God's judgement, the sincerity of Manasseh's repentance, God's direct intervention and restoration of the covenantal relationship, and Manasseh's transformation from sinner to righteous, attested by his deeds.

D. The Manasseh Traditions. According to both 2 Kings and 2 Chronicles, Manasseh's sins were mainly related to the cult, and 2 Kings states that these sins caused the destruction of the temple in 587 BCE. Scholars dispute whether the Chronicler's mention of Manasseh's prayer (which he ascribes to a source) and repentance are an attempt to explain his long reign, or whether the author of 2 Kings expurgated the incident from a form of the Deuteronomistic history that was subsequently used by the Chronicler (McKenzie 1984: 191–3). Some later Jewish texts depict Manasseh wholly in a bad light (*Mart. Isa.; 2 Apoc. Bar.* 64–5; *Apoc. Abr.* 25), while others emphasize his repentance (e.g. Josephus, *Ant.* 10.3.2 §§ 40–6; see Bogaert 1969: II. 296–304). One Qumran text (4Q381 33:8–11) preserves fragments of a prayer ascribed to Manasseh but it has no certain relationship to Prayer of Manasseh (Schuller 1986: 151–62).

E. Religious Teaching. According to Prayer of Manasseh, repentance is a divine gift that allows the worst of sinners to be accepted back into the covenant and have its curses turned to blessing. Even Manasseh, whose apostasy caused the destruction of the temple and the holy city, could be forgiven and, according to the narrative context, reckoned to be righteous, as was Abraham, the first recipient of the promise (*Ap. Con.* 2.22.16; Gen 15:6). This moralizing focus on the vices and virtues of a biblical figure, implicit in the prayer and explicit in the narrative, is typical of Jewish and Christian literature of the Graeco-Roman period (e.g. *Jub.*, *T. Job*, *T. 12 Patr.*).

F. Date and Provenance. The prayer's presence in the *Didascalia* indicates a date of composition before the third century CE, and the prayer's parallels to LXX Greek may indicate a date in or after the first century BCE. Whether the prayer is a Jewish or a Christian composition is disputed. Every concept and mode of expression in the prayer is paralleled in Jewish texts of the Graeco-Roman period, and nothing in it or its narrative context is demonstrably and exclusively Christian. At the same time, the prayer's attestation and documented usage are exclusively Christian, and it could have been composed by a Christian conversant in the LXX and other post-biblical Jewish traditions.

G. Function and Setting. In the *Didascalia* and the *Apostolic Constitutions*, the story and prayer of Manasseh are part of a long instruction to bishops and provide the basis for an appeal to accept penitent sinners back into the fold. Alongside this pastoral function, the prayer's inclusion among the Odes suggests a devotional or liturgical use for this text. A similar pair of alternatives can be imagined in a Jewish setting. The prayer and its narrative context should be studied together with an eye towards Jewish texts that recast Scripture (see e.g. 1QapGen20 and other texts discussed in Nickelsburg 1981: 231–68).

H. Canonicity. Although the prayer is regularly included in editions of the Apocrypha, only Eastern Orthodox churches consider it authoritative. This doubtless reflects its preservation in church manuals of Syrian provenance.

COMMENTARY

Invocation (vv. 1–7)

(v. 1) Address The title 'Almighty' (*pantokratōr*) anticipates vv. 2–3 and the prayer's first major theme, God's power in creation. It sets a tone for the prayer in its very first line, by expressing Manasseh's repentance from his polytheistic worship of rival gods. Taking up the Chronicler's reference to Manasseh's humility 'before the God of his ancestors' (lit. fathers, 2 Chr 33:12), the prayer strikes its second major theme, the covenant with Abraham, Isaac, and Jacob, and their righteous offspring. The appeal indicates Manasseh's repentance from his idolatrous apostasy from the covenant and is ironic, since Manasseh was anything but righteous, having 'shed innocent blood' (2 Kings 21:16).

(vv. 2–5a) God's Power in Creation God's creative power is a traditional topic in Jewish prayers (1 Enoch 9:5; Add Esth 13:10; Macc 2:9). The Greek noun *kosmos* (order) translates the Hebrew Ṣābā' (host) in Deut 4:19; 17:3; Isa 24:21; 40:26 with reference to the host of heaven (Osswald 1974: 23). Perhaps Manasseh is here acknowledging that the sovereign God created the host whose idolatrous worship he had instituted in Jerusalem (2 Kings 21:3, 5; 2 Chr 33:3, 5). The shackling of the sea and sealing of the abyss alludes to the mythic notion that the Creator brought order from chaos by taming the great sea monster (cf. Job 38:8–11; Ps 89:9–10; 104:5–9; Prov 8:29; Jer 5:22; 1 Enoch 101:6). Depicted here as capture and imprisonment, it may imply the king's concession that his own imprisonment is an act of divine power and judgement. Although vv. 4–5 assert that the *whole* creation fears and trembles in the presence of God's power and majestic glory, these characteristics of God recall descriptions of the divine throne room.

Employing language found in Jewish texts and orthodox and Gnostic Christianity, vv. 5–6 use the Greek alpha privative (a- = '*non-*' or '*un-*') to describe God in terms of what God is not: 'cannot be borne, unendurable, immeasurable, unsearchable'. This heaping up of adjectives reinforces Manasseh's repentance before the sovereign, almighty, and majestic God.

(vv. 5b–7) The Wrath and Mercy of the God of the Covenant The emphasis on God's majesty continues in a description of God's activity within the covenant, which juxtaposes the threat of wrath against the sinner and the promise of mercy to the repentant. In the idiom of the section, the one is unendurable, while the other is immeasurable and unsearchable. This first major section of the prayer closes with reference both to God's unique power ('Most High') and to God's covenantal activity. The latter is phrased in a quotation of Joel 2:13, which undergirds that prophet's appeal for repentance by allusion to the covenantal description of God in Ex 34:6–7. Thus the author comes to the major point of the prayer and sets the stage for Manasseh's repentant confession of his sins. Although the two earliest Greek MSS of the Odes (A, T) omit most of v. 7 ('O Lord, according to your great goodness … be saved') the originality of these lines is attested by their inclusion in a later Greek biblical text (55), in the Vg, and in the *Apostolic Constitutions* and the *Didascalia*. The passage interprets the promise of mercy in v. 6 as the mercy that God promises to those who accept the divinely initiated repentance. Although v. 7b, following Joel 2:13, could refer to the curses of the covenant that fall on sinners ('human suffering'), the present context seems to allude to human wickedness and Manasseh's sins in particular.

Manasseh's Confession of Sin (vv. 8–10)

(v. 8) Introduction The continuation of the description of God in v. 8 reprises themes in v. 1 and thus seems to conclude the prayer's invocation. However, Manasseh's personal reference to 'me, who am a sinner' in the last line links it to the confession that follows. Thus the verse serves as a transition between the first and second parts. Employing the traditional Jewish distinction between the righteous and the sinner, Manasseh contrasts Abraham, Isaac, and Jacob, who have not sinned against God, with himself, who epitomizes the category of 'sinner'. In normal Jewish usage, 'righteous' does not designate a person who never sins, but one who attends to his or her sins and does not let them accumulate; the 'sinner', by contrast, lives in effective rejection of God and the covenant (*Pss. Sol.* 3). The consequences of these two ways of life are the blessings and curses of the covenant. While the present verse is consonant with such usage, it emphasizes God's active role in establishing repentance as a means by which the sinner can become righteous (cf. v. 13).

(vv. 9–10) The Confession Manasseh's confession fits well with the emphasis of the biblical accounts on the quantity and quality of his sins. Although v. 9c recalls Ezra's confession (Ezra

9:6), the combined language of vv. 9a and 9c with reference to the multitude of Manasseh's sins may be an inverted allusion to the covenantal promises about the multitude of Abraham's descendants (Gen 22:17; 15:5). The verb 'they are multiplied' (*eplēthunan*) corresponds to the same verb in 2 Kings 21:6; 2 Chr 33:6, and the doubling of the verb 'I have sinned' (cf. v. 12) emphasizes the point. The vivid reference to the physical conditions of Manasseh's imprisonment ('I am unworthy to look up … I am weighted down', lit. bent down, v. 10) complements v. 9c, and his physical condition may be seen to symbolize the spiritual (cf. the variants of v. 10b in Gk. MSS T and 55 and the *Didascalia*). Manasseh's iron fetters are not mentioned in 2 Kings or 2 Chronicles, but the specification of 'iron' in the narrative section preceding the prayer in the *Apostolic Constitutions* (2.22.10) may indicate that the prayer was composed as an integral part of the narrative preserved in that text. Manasseh's lack of 'relief' from his torment also suggests an allusion to the specific conditions of his imprisonment described in that narrative. This particular complaint and its repetition in v. 13b recalls a similar repetition in the confession of the 'mighty kings' in 1 Enoch 63:1, 5, 6, 8). The language of the second half of v. 10 refers to details in 2 Kings 21:2, 6 and 2 Chr 33:2, 6.

Manasseh's Petition for Relief and Forgiveness (vv. 11–15)

(vv. 11–12) Introduction Like v. 8, these introductory verses provide a transition between what precedes (a double confession of sin; cf. 9b) and what follows (formal petition). The introductory 'And now' is formulaic in Jewish prayer (Add Esth 13:15; 14:6, 8; 3 Macc 6:9; 1QpGenAp 20:13; Tob 3:12; 1 Enoch 9:9–10). Again, external condition symbolizes the internal state. Physically bent down and, presumably, kneeling in prayer, he submits his will (heart) to the God against whom he has sinned. The sentiment again recalls Joel 2:13. The appeal for God's 'goodness' (*chrēstotēs*; cf. *agathosynē* in 14) is a request for the covenantal blessing (Deut 30:15, *tôb, agathon*), which God promises to those who repent (Deut 30:1–10). The second of the parallel lines in v. 12 is one of several resonances of Ps 51 (cf. Ps 51:3).

(vv. 13–14) Petition The language of v. 13ab with its participle, 'making petition' (*deomenos*), and its doubled verb reprise at vv. 11, 12a. Having twice confessed that he has sinned, he now twice begs for relief (Gk. *anes*) from the suffering (cf. 10c, *anesis*) that is a consequence of his sin. This implies God's forgiveness, although NRSV may overtranslate the verb as 'forgive'; cf. 'relief' in v. 10). The three parallel lines in 13cde expand on the notion in negative form, 'do not destroy, do not be angry, do not condemn me'. Most serious is the possibility of eternal destruction in the underworld. 'Evil things' (Gk. *kaka*), i.e. the covenantal curses (Deut 30:15), contrast with the 'goodness' he seeks in vv. 11, 14a. The rationale is expressed in the climax of a triad of divine appellations: 'Lord the God of our ancestors' (v. 1), 'Lord, God of the righteous' (v. 8), 'Lord, the God of those who repent' (v. 13f). v. 14a may allude to Ex 33:18–19, where Moses asks to see God's glory and is promised a vision of God's goodness, which is epitomized in a reference to the covenantal mercy that is now extended to the repentant Manasseh. On the king's unworthiness and need for 'much mercy', cf. v. 9cd and his unworthiness due to 'the multitude of my iniquities'. The wording of v. 14b recalls Ps 51:1.

(v. 15) The Praise of God The promise to praise God after relief from present distress is typical of the psalms. More importantly, it corresponds with the Chronicler's account of Manasseh's return to the worship of the true God (2 Chr 33:15–17), and it echoes specifically the wording of the narrative in *Ap. Con.* 2.22.16, 'He worshipped the Lord God alone with all his heart and all his soul all the days of his life.' Parallel to Manasseh's promise to praise God is the statement, 'For all the host of heaven sing your praises.' Coming from one who had instituted the worship of 'the host of heaven' (cf. v. 2), it is a fitting reinforcement of his repentance from polytheism and a suitable reprise of prayer's opening invocation of the 'LORD Almighty'. It remains only to assert the eternity of that God's glory(v. 15c).

REFERENCES

Bogaert, P. (1969), *Apocalypse de Baruch*, SC 144–5 (2 vols.; Paris: Cerf).

McKenzie, S. L. (1984), *The Chronicler's Use of the Deuteronomistic History*, HSM 33 (Atlanta: Scholars Press).

Nickelsburg, G. W. E. (1981), *Jewish Literature Between the Bible and the Mishnah* (Philadelphia: Fortress).

Osswald, E. (1974), 'Das Gebet Manasses', JSHRZ 4:1 (Gütersloh: Mohn), 17–27.

Schuller, E. M. (1986), *Non-Canonical Psalms from Qumran: A Pseudepigraphic Collection*, Harvard Semitic Studies 28 (Atlanta: Scholars Press).

13. Psalm 151

JOHN BARTON

Ps 151 occurs at the end of the book of Psalms in the Greek Bible, and can also be found in the ancient versions that depend on the Greek: Latin, Syriac—where it is one of a group of five non-canonical Psalms—and Ethiopic. The heading in the Greek indicates that it is 'outside the number' (and some texts add 'of the one hundred and fifty'), but it is regarded as canonical in the Greek and Russian Orthodox churches. As it stands it describes various aspects of the life of David and 'is ascribed to David as his own composition': his work as a shepherd, his musical ability, his choice by God even though his 'brothers were handsome and tall', and his victory over Goliath.

The Qumran *Psalms Scroll* 11QPs[a] preserves evidence of an earlier Hebrew version in which there were two separate psalms. The first corresponds to Ps 151:1–5; but the second was evidently a fuller version of Ps 151:6–7, though only two lines of it now remain. The first dealt with David's early career, the second (which originally had its own superscription) with his victory over Goliath. The superscription to the first psalm in Hebrew is 'A hallelujah for David the son of Jesse'. There is no scholarly consensus about the status of 11QPs[a]. It may reflect an early 'canon' of the Psalms differing from the later Hebrew one, or it may be a compendium of hymns for worship containing both canonical and non-canonical texts.

Verses 1–5 are based on 1 Sam 16. On David's musical abilities (vv. 2–3) the Hebrew adds, 'And I rendered glory to the Lord; I spoke in my soul. The mountains do not witness to him and the hills do not tell. The trees have cherished my words and the flock my deeds.' Verses 6–7 derive from 1 Sam 17.

14. 3 Maccabees

SARAH PEARCE

A. Text and Title. 1. Despite its title, the content of 3 Maccabees bears no obvious relation to events surrounding the Maccabean Revolt nor to its heroes. Nor does it pretend to do so, since it describes events affecting an earlier generation of Jews under Ptolemaic rule in Jerusalem and Egypt in 217–216 BCE. The title was no doubt attributed to this work on account of its position in the Greek canon where it lies between 2 and 4 Maccabees. However, its concerns with the defence of the sanctity of the Jerusalem Temple, resistance to idolatry, and belief in divine providence link it firmly with the ideology espoused in the other Maccabean stories.

2. 3 Maccabees survives in Greek, the language of its original composition, in the fifth-century uncial MS Alexandrinus and the eighth-century Codex Venetus as well as in minuscules of varying reliability, though the chief textual witnesses show few substantial variations. Otherwise, some sign of its popularity in the Christian east is reflected in fourth-century translations into Syriac and Armenian.

B. Provenance. Both the author and place of writing of 3 Maccabees are unknown. Any sense of the author's identity must, therefore, be surmised from the religious and political ideology and the intellectual influences apparent in this story. As to the author's background, the setting of 3 Maccabees in Egypt, and particularly in Alexandria, as well as clear signs of familiarity with Ptolemaic history and culture, point to Alexandria as home, but this is by no means certain.

C. Language and Genre. The Greek composition of 3 Maccabees is the work of a 'pseudo-classicist', combining both classical and koine forms of the language. Passages of purple prose and other rhetorical devices are employed both to entertain and to elicit strong sympathy for the heroes and villains of the story. In genre, 3 Maccabees is like a number of Hellenistic romances that embroider historical events or personalities with legendary developments characterized by their presentation in a historical framework and by narratives of the miraculous public rescue, by divine intervention, of the hero(es). In its function as an explanation for the origin of a festival, 3 Maccabees also bears some relation to Hellenistic antiquarian histories that seek to provide 'historical' explanations for ancient institutions.

D. Date. 1. A firm date of composition for 3 Maccabees remains elusive. It can be no earlier than the battle of Raphia in 217 BCE, with which the narrative begins. However, in spite of the narrator's efforts at verisimilitude, the overriding fantastic nature and improbabilities of the story, as well as the absence of any other evidence for a real persecution targeted at Jews in this period, cast serious doubt on its historical authenticity. A latest possible date is more difficult to fix, although the story's assumption that the Jerusalem Temple exists and stands at the heart of Judaism suggests (but does not prove) that it was written before the temple's destruction in 70 CE. In spite of the meagre evidence that serves to support any particular date within these boundaries, several specific settings have been proposed for the origins of 3 Maccabees.

2. Of the main proposals, the latest suggested setting for 3 Maccabees relates it to the persecution of the Jews of Alexandria in the time of the emperor Gaius Caligula. However, there is little proper correspondence between the situation described in 3 Maccabees and events in Roman Alexandria from 38 CE. If the story is a veiled criticism of that period of Roman rule, it is very cryptic indeed.

3. A dating to early Roman rule in Egypt under Augustus depends on the significance of the term *laographia*. In 3 Maccabees, this refers to a census imposed by Ptolemy IV for the registration of all Jews unwilling to commit apostasy and who are to be enslaved (2:28). This has been taken as a covert reference to the *laographia* introduced in 24 BCE that subjected the vast majority of inhabitants of Egypt to a poll tax. The Augustan measure was, however, by no means equivalent to enslavement, and certainly not directed exclusively at Jews. It carried no demands for religious observance, and certainly did not offer citizenship in the terms proposed in 3 Maccabees for Jewish apostates. It is quite possible that the term in 3 Maccabees, which also appears in the usage of Ptolemaic papyri, is meant simply to recall the strict taxation imposed under Ptolemy IV as a result of his expensive wars.

4. The author of 3 Maccabees seems to borrow from the Greek Daniel, which, in final form, must belong to a period after 165 BCE. However, the connection depends on just one word (6:6, cf. Dan 3:50), and the fluid nature of the composition of the Daniel corpus must make it impossible to prove our author's dependency on the Greek Daniel. An early first-century BCE date may be indicated by the formulae in the royal letters that appear in 3 Maccabees and reflect the style of late-Ptolemaic papyri. Caution, however, must be urged here too: the formulae might well be the work of a later writer, imitating the style of earlier chancery practice.

5. Finally, 3 Maccabees has been related to a persecution of the Jews of Alexandria under Ptolemy VIII Euergetes (Physcon) (145–116 BCE), which is recorded only in Josephus' *Against Apion*, 2.50–5. Josephus' narrative, though showing no clear dependence on 3 Maccabees, shares some similarities of detail with our story: a Ptolemy's attempt to destroy the Jews of Alexandria with a herd of drunken elephants; his repentance; and the commemoration of the Jews' deliverance by a special festival day. However, the two narratives, as their differences demonstrate, are best seen as different versions of a common folk-tale, adapted for different purposes. From a historical point of view it is not implausible that Physcon may have expressed hostility to Jews at the beginning of his reign, since Alexandrian Jews had sided with his opponent, subsequently his partner and queen, Cleopatra II. However, there is no other evidence for a persecution of Jews at this time. Indeed, Physcon is known from papyrological evidence to have favoured the Jews.

E. The Plot. 1. The story purports to record an otherwise unknown attempt to exterminate the Jews of Egypt under Ptolemy IV Philopator (221–205 BCE). Following his victory over the Seleucid Antiochus III at the battle of Raphia (217 BCE), Ptolemy made a tour of his subject territories, honouring their temples as he went. Responding to a warm invitation from Jerusalem, he also visited the temple there, but insisted on entering the Holy of Holies, to the horror of the Jews. However, following their prayers for deliverance from this violation, God's intervention struck the king unconscious. Full of rage at this rebuff, the king returned to Alexandria, determined on exacting revenge against the Jews. At the instigation of certain courtiers, he issued a decree removing all civil

rights from the Jews of Alexandria with the exception of Jewish apostates who, if they embraced the cult of Dionysus, would be treated like citizens of Alexandria. A further royal decree, fuelled by widespread resistance to the first plan and by rumours of Jews' disloyalty to the crown, planned for the extermination of all the Jews of Egypt. The king commanded that they be taken to Alexandria, registered, and executed.

2. As the burlesque dimension of the story unfolds, each attempt to destroy the Jews is foiled as God intervenes to rescue them in answer to their prayers. First, a complete registration fails because papyrus and calami (reed pens) run out after forty days of writing! Then all the king's attempts to kill the Jews in the hippodrome with 500 drunken elephants come to nothing. Thanks to the Jews' prayers and God's action, the king is prevented from carrying out the execution. First he oversleeps; then he forgets completely about his plan; and, finally, two angels appear to the Jews' enemies, paralysing them and forcing the elephants back to crush them and not the Jews.

3. The king is brought to acknowledge the Jews' loyalty and that 'the living God of heaven' protects the Jews (6:28). Ptolemy turns from annihilator to protector of the Jews, commanding their safe return home and decreeing a seven-day feast of deliverance for them which the Jews determine to celebrate as a festival forever. All ends happily except for Jewish apostates: with the king's permission, the Jews execute 300 who abandoned Judaism under the king's first decree, on the grounds that Jews disloyal to God will also be disloyal to the crown. On their return home, with further celebrations, the Jews can look forward to a secure future: 'They had even greater authority than before among their enemies and were regarded with high esteem and awe; no one at all extorted their property...The great God had accomplished great things for their salvation' (7:21–2; tr. Andersen 1985).

F. Purpose. 1. 3 Maccabees is often seen as a crisis document, hence the attempts to locate the story's origins in persecutions or perceived persecutions of the Jews under Ptolemaic or Roman rule. If so, there is little in the story itself to suggest that it represents the concerns of an alienated community unhappily struggling for survival in the Diaspora. The story does not oppose Alexandrian citizenship for Jews—only when such status is dependent on abandoning Judaism. Alexandrians themselves are depicted as close and loyal allies of the Jews in the time of persecution. Indeed, except when his mind is temporarily clouded by madness or the machinations of his evil counsellors, Ptolemy himself is seen as very positive towards the Jews. While the Jews of Alexandria are presented as the 'countrymen' of the people in Jerusalem who protested against the king's entry into the Holy of Holies, they do not yearn for refuge in Jerusalem. On the contrary, the story celebrates their return to their legitimate homes in Egypt, as does the festival that commemorates their freedom to do so. True, the festival is, we are told, to be held only for as long as the Jews' sojourn (*paroikia*) in Egypt continues, language that recalls the ancestors' toils in pre-Exodus Egypt (cf. Wis 19:10; Lev 26:44), and a hint that this is not their final home. There is, thus, a sense of looking forward to a 'return' to Judea, but this is not at all prominent in the story, and belongs to very common expectations for the future in Second Temple period Judaism.

2. The emphases of the story reveal several main concerns on the part of the author of 3 Maccabees. First, it is emphasized that Jews are loyal to the Ptolemaic monarchy, and that they are vital for the security of its empire. Above all, however, the author seeks to show, in the great tradition of the Exodus and the later history of the Jews, that the supreme king is the God whom the Jews serve and that only this king has power over the fate of the Jews and, indeed, of all things. The message is essentially a declaration of confidence in God's providence, manifested in response to the power of prayer. What is demanded of the story's Jewish readers is to be confident in that providence and to trust that, in all circumstances, loyalty to Judaism will be rewarded with life and security. In this, the author of 3 Maccabees adheres strongly to the Deuteronomic teaching that fidelity to the God of Israel will be rewarded with life, apostasy with death. Finally, the story serves, as does *Esther* for the feast of Purim, to explain and support an existing Jewish festival whose origins had perhaps been forgotten by the Jews of Egypt.

REFERENCE

Andersen, H. (1985), '3 Maccabees', *OTP*, II. 509–30.

15. 2 Esdras

PETER HAYMAN

INTRODUCTION

A. Background. 2 Esdras in the Apocrypha of the English Bible consists of three separate works which are found combined together only in manuscripts of the Latin Vulgate Bible dating from the ninth century CE onwards. It has become conventional amongst scholars to distinguish these three works by designating 2 Esd 1–2 as 5 Ezra, 2 Esd 3–14 as 4 Ezra, and 2 Esd 15–16 as 6 Ezra. The core work in the collection to which the others were subsequently added is 4 Ezra. This was written by a Jew not long after the Jewish War against the Romans in 66–73 CE and the destruction of the temple in 70 CE. The author was devastated by these events and felt that they severely threatened his inherited theological beliefs. His text was composed as a kind of catharsis in which he and the reader travel in the early chapters of the book through the dark night of doubt into the shining light of apocalyptic certainty which pervades the end of the book. But his book seems to have had little impact upon that mainstream of Jewish culture which eventually crystallized into Rabbinic Judaism. Its major impact was upon those groups on the periphery of Jewish life in the first century who eventually crystallized into the Christian church. They alone preserved it for posterity and included it in their collections of sacred and authoritative books.

B. Authorship. The author of 4 Ezra chose to write under the pseudonym of Ezra, apparently the person depicted in the biblical book of Ezra as the bringer of the law from Babylon. There is, however, a problem about identifying precisely whose persona the author is adopting and it emerges in the first verse of the book (3:1). This places Ezra in the middle of the Babylonian exile and identifies him with someone called Salathiel. Salathiel is the Latin form of the Hebrew name Shealtiel and it is taken from 1 Chr 3:17 where Shealtiel is identified as the son of King Jehoiachin who was taken into exile in

Babylon in 597; 1 Chr 3:19 makes Shealtiel the uncle of Zerubbabel who led the first return from Babylon in 537. Unfortunately, Ezra the scribe as depicted in the books of Ezra and Nehemiah lived 100 years later than this. Box (1912) regarded 2 Esd 3:1 as a clumsy attempt by the editor of our text to identify these two originally quite separate figures. He did so because in Box's opinion one of the main sources the author utilized for his work was an apocalypse ascribed to Salathiel. So, on his view, the verse is an editorial attempt to fuse together separate sources. Box's view here is part of a much more elaborate source-critical analysis of 4 Ezra which has since fallen out of favour with most scholars; see Hayman (1975), Stone (1990: 11–23). Most recent scholarly work takes for granted that the text is a unitary composition by a single author who yet had earlier sources available to him. The most probable explanation for the identification of Ezra and Salathiel/Shealtiel is that it arises from a misreading of the Hebrew text of 1 Chr 3:17 (Stone 1990: 55–6). Another seductive reason for the identification has often been pointed out. In Hebrew the name Shealtiel means 'I asked God'. Since in the book Ezra spends a good deal of time asking pointed questions of God, the name seems quite appropriate.

C. The Date of 4 Ezra. The book can be fairly securely dated by aligning the known facts of Roman history with the eagle vision of chs. 11–12, just as we can date the book of Daniel by running through its ch. 11 to the point where history ends and prediction begins. The point where the accurate history stops in 4 Ezra and the prediction begins seems to be near the end of Domitian's reign (81–96) towards the middle of the 90s CE. One other factor confirms a date for this apocalypse towards the end of the first century CE: in 3:1 and 3:29 the author sets these supposed visions of Ezra thirty years after the destruction of Jerusalem. In the pseudonymous structure of the book this refers to the destruction of Jerusalem by the Babylonians in 587 BCE. However, the real reference point of the book is to the destruction of Jerusalem by the Romans in 70 CE. The span of thirty years seems to come from Ezek 1:1, but is the author's choice of this date due to his own distance from the seminal event of his lifetime?

D. The Author's Audience and His Social Setting. 4 Ezra is probably to be related to other Jewish works (2 *Apoc. Bar., Apoc. Abr.,*

and Ps. Philo, *Bib. Ant.*) which may have been written in the aftermath of the destruction of Jerusalem and the temple in 70 CE. They have in common the urgent need to address the theological crisis occasioned by the recent events and to offer what reassurance they could to the Jewish people. But 4 Ezra clearly has two separate audiences in mind, as ch. 14 makes clear. There are the wise (represented by his five scribes in 4:24)—the ones really 'in the know', and the people (represented in 5:16 by Phaltiel, a chief of the people; see also 12:40–50). It is clear that 4 Ezra is designed for the inner circle of the wise; it is one of the seventy reserved books (14:46). But nevertheless the function of the book is to instruct the wise so that they will be in a position to 'reprove your people' (14:13). This social structure seems to be close to that which began to develop within the Jewish community of refugees from the disaster of 70. Rabbinic texts tell us that a small group of sages led by Yohanan ben Zakkai escaped from Jerusalem during the siege and obtained from the Romans permission to set up in Yabneh (near present-day Tel-Aviv) an academy for the study of the law. They formed a nucleus of order and authority around which at least parts of the Jewish community rallied and which eventually gave rise in the course of the next century to a new social and political order in Judaism based upon rabbinic authority to expound and administer the law. It is very tempting to set 4 Ezra within this nucleus of rabbinic sages at Yabneh. Recent students of 4 Ezra (Grabbe 1981, 1989; Longenecker 1995; Coggins and Knibb 1979; Essler 1994) seem to be succumbing to this temptation. But if this was the locus from which 4 Ezra originated we are left with the question: why, then, was this text preserved only by Christians and not by the rabbis? Could it have originated in a group whose long-term aim became to forge an enduring identity for Judaism that would preserve it from the Christian threat?

E. The Text of 2 Esdras. The original text of 4 Ezra, which was almost certainly written in Hebrew, disappeared at an early stage, as did the Greek translation of the Hebrew. Only a few traces of the Greek have been preserved in isolated quotations by Christian writers. We are dependent now for our knowledge of the text upon translations of this Greek version into Latin, Syriac, Ethiopic, Georgian, Armenian, and Arabic, plus a tiny Coptic fragment. Of these secondary versions the most important is the Latin which is preserved in a number of manuscripts dating from the seventh century onwards. In the Latin version the prevalent name given to 2 Esd 3–14 is 4 Esdras and hence the contemporary scholarly preference for calling this text 4 Ezra. 2 Esd 1–2,15–16 are found only in this Latin version and there they are always kept separate from chs. 3–14. They are two separate works, now called 5 and 6 Ezra, and consist of Christian material added to the original Ezra apocalypse in the course of the second to third centuries CE. None of the oriental versions contains these additions. The next most important version after the Latin is the Syriac. Apart from a few liturgical extracts this is preserved in only one manuscript, the Codex Ambrosianus, the most important and complete codex of the Syriac Bible, dating from the sixth to seventh century. Most translations of the text are based on the Latin and bring in readings from the other versions (principally the Syriac) only when the Latin does not make sense, is clearly corrupt, or has been altered tendentiously. The clearest example of Christian scribes at work 'improving' the text is 7:28 where the Latin has 'my son Jesus' but the Syriac 'my son the Messiah' and the Ethiopic has just 'the Messiah'. That the readings of none of the oriental versions can be passed over lightly is shown by one very interesting example inch. 8:23. At the end of this verse nearly all the versions attest to a text which read: 'and whose truth bears witness'. However, a quotation in the Apostolic Constitutions, a fourth-century collection of liturgical texts, and the second Arabic version read: 'and whose truth stands for ever'. The divergence is neatly explained by different readings of the same consonantal Hebrew text: l'd read as lā'ād(for ever) or lē'ēd (for/as a witness).

F. Structure of the Text. The text is carefully structured into seven episodes. These episodes are usually called visions although the vision genre only dominates the later parts of 4 Ezra. The divisions between the episodes or visions are clearly marked out by means of a chronological framework—usually, but not always, a seven-day period.

Macrostructure

Vision 1	3:1–5:20	⎫
Vision 2	5:21–6:34	⎬ Lament
Vision 3	6:35–9:25	⎭
Vision 4	9:26–10:59	Transformation/Fulcrum
Vision 5	11:1–12:51	⎫
Vision 6	13:1–58	⎬ Consolation
Vision 7	14:1–48	⎭

At the deepest level the text is structured by a movement from lament to consolation with the change of mood hinging on the fourth vision (Breech 1973). Visions 1–3 have similar internal structural patterns as (to a lesser extent) do visions 4–7. See the table in Stone (1990: 51). The primary literary genre used to structure the lament section is the dialogue between the prophet Ezra and the angel Uriel; in the consolation section the apocalyptic vision is the mould in which the author chooses to write.

G. Esdras 1–2 (= 5 Ezra). 1. As we have seen, these two chapters are not attested in any of the oriental versions which we have in abundance for 4 Ezra. They are found only in nine Latin manuscripts (eight of which also contain the text of 4 Ezra). These Latin manuscripts clearly divide into two main recensions which have been named the Spanish and French Recensions (Bensley 1895: xxi–xxii, xliv–lxxviii). It is unfortunate that the RSV and NRSV translations of 5 Ezra follow the manuscripts of the French recension since Bergren (1990) has confirmed James's view (Bensley 1895) that the readings of the Spanish recension (mostly confined to marginal notes in the NRSV) are almost always superior. See also Kraft (1986). Readers interested in a text closer to the original would be better to follow Bergren's Eng. translation (1990: 401–5).

2. The general scholarly consensus is that 5 Ezra dates from about the middle of the second century CE and is a Christian work (albeit from the hands of a Jewish Christian). Stanton (1977: 80) has argued that it represents a 'continuation into the second century of Matthean Christianity' and offers a Christian perspective on the recent cataclysmic outcome of the Bar Kochba revolt (132–135 CE). This view is strongly contested by O'Neill (1991) who argues that 5 Ezra is an originally Jewish work, probably of the first century CE, which has suffered interpolations and corruptions at the hand of Christian scribes. As for the original language of these chapters, Bergren (1990: 22), who has studied this at great length, is cautious in his conclusions: '5 Ezra could have been written either in Greek or Latin (with the former option being slightly preferable)' but 'a Semitic original (at least for parts of the book) also cannot be excluded.'

H. 2 Esdras 15–16 (= 6 Ezra). From internal evidence it would seem that these chapters were composed towards the end of the third century CE as a deliberate attempt to reapply 4 Ezra to a new situation facing, this time, not the Jews but the Christian church in the eastern Roman empire. Like 5 Ezra they are not found in the oriental versions of 4 Ezra. Except for a small Greek papyrus fragment (15:57–9) they are attested only in the Latin version. They were clearly written at a time of political upheaval and probably of persecution of the church (15:21; 16:68–70). Their aim is to encourage the persecuted righteous to stand firm, confident of their eventual vindication by God and the overthrow of their oppressors.

COMMENTARY

2 Esdras 1–2 (= 5 Ezra)

5 Ezra contains two principal blocks of material: (1) a prophetic indictment of Israel and the proclamation of the transfer of its status as 'people of God' to another people (1:4–2:9); and (2) a series of eschatological promises for the new people of God (2:10–48).

(1:1–3) Introduction A better and drastically shorter text of these verses (the Spanish Recension) can be found in n. *b* to the NRSV. The printed text (the French Recension) represents an attempt to bring the earlier version into line with biblical tradition (Ezra 7:1–5). The characterization of Ezra as a 'prophet' (only in the French Recension) contrasts with his biblical titles 'scribe' and 'priest' but agrees with 4 Ezra 12:42 and suits well his role in 5 Ezra.

(1:4–23) God's Actions on Behalf of Israel Like 4 Ezra, 5 Ezra begins with a recital of salvation history. However, the two recitals are used for very different purposes. Here the purpose is to point up the contrast between God's faithfulness to his people and their utter failure to respond as they ought. The text is closely modelled on Ps 78, see especially vv. 17–22, 59–62.

(1:24–40) The Rejection of Israel and the Election of A New People of God Whereas the purpose of Ps 78 is to demonstrate that God rejected the northern tribes (Joseph/Ephraim) in favour of the 'tribe of Judah' and 'David his servant' (Ps 78:67–72), the author of 5 Ezra uses his recital to demonstrate that Israel is entirely rejected in favour of the Christian church—the 'other nations' of v. 24 ('another people'—Spanish Recension) and the 'people that will come' (1:35, 37). The OT texts which he uses are part of a standard repertoire frequently found in Christian anti-Jewish polemic (Simon 1986: 135–78). Cf. v. 26 with Isa 1:15, 59:3, 7, Prov 1:28; v. 31 with

Isa 1:14 and Jer 7:22; and v. 32 with 2 Chr 36:15–16. In the OT denunciations such as these were meant to call the people to repentance; Christians used them to demonstrate the final rejection of Israel. This section of 5 Ezra is heavily dependent upon the Gospel of Matthew, especially the notorious ch. 23. Cf. v. 24 with Mt 21:43 (the conclusion added by Matthew to the parable of the vineyard), v. 30 a with Mt 23:37, v. 32 with Mt 23:34, and v. 33 with Mt 23:38. The purpose clause in v. 24—'that they may keep my statutes' (see also 2:40) suggests that the author of 5 Ezra may have been a Jewish Christian (Stanton 1977). For a full treatment of the text and history of the version of v. 32 quoted in n. *n* to the NRSV see Hayman (1973, CSCO 339: 11*–13*).

In vv. 38–9 Jewish hopes for the return of the Dispersion to Israel (particularly in Bar 4:36 and 5:5, but see also 4 Ezra 13:39–40) are reapplied to the new people who will replace them. Mt 8:11–12 is probably responsible both for the reference to the 'east' and to 'Abraham, Isaac, and Jacob'. This passage in Matthew's Gospel precisely summarizes the main theme of 5 Ezra. The reference to Ezra as 'father' is probably based on a misreading of the Greek text of Baruch (Bergren 1990: 290). n. *s* in the NRSV contains the more original Spanish Recension of v. 39; the French Recension in the main text eliminates the obscure elements in the earlier version and provides a correct list of the twelve minor prophets in the Septuagint order.

(2:1–9) Zion Denounces her Children vv. 2–5a draws closely on, and is scarcely comprehensible without reference to, Bar 4:8–23; cf. v. 3 with Bar 4:11. The 'mother who bore them' is Jerusalem/Zion as personified in Bar 4; cf. Isa 50:1; 54:1; 4 Ezra 10:7. In Baruch she consoles her children, but here in 5 Ezra she denounces them, a denunciation in which Ezra joins, vv. 5–7. In this latter section the MS tradition is hopelessly confused and the original text scarcely recoverable. However, we should read 'your covenant' at the end of v. 5 with the Spanish Recension. Ezra is the speaker and God the person addressed—'father'. Most commentators take the reference to Assyria in v. 8 as a cryptic allusion to Rome. (2:10–19) Israel's Blessings Transferred 'My people' (v. 10) refers to the new people of 1:24, 35, 37—presumably the Christian church. The old Israel is blotted out (2:7) and the old covenant promises transferred to the new legatees. Mother Zion now has a new set of children (vv. 15, 17); as the text progresses she seems to be transmuting into

Mother Church. The influence of the books of Revelation and 1 Enoch may be perceived in this section. Cf. vv. 12,16,18–19 with Rev 2:7; 14:1; 22:2,14; 1 Enoch 24–5. v. 18 probably refers to the role of Isaiah and Jeremiah as providing the prophecies which Christians applied to the events of Christ's life—a view confirmed by the addition of Daniel in the Spanish Recension. (2:20–32) Exhortations and Promises Israel's ethical and legal obligations are now incumbent upon the new people of God. These injunctions are found in many places in the OT but for the obligation to bury the dead (v. 23) see Tob 1:17–19. With v. 31 cf. 4 Ezra 7:32.

(2:33–41) Ezra, the Second Moses v. 33a is probably modelled on 4 Ezra 14:1ff. v. 33b probably alludes to the incident of the Golden Calf (Ex 32) which became a type of Israel's rejection of Christ in Christian anti-Jewish polemic. The pattern is as before: Israel rejects God, so he turns to a new audience (v. 34). The 'shepherd' (v. 34) could be God but more likely refers to Christ; see Jn 10:11; Heb 13:20; 1 Pet 2:25; 5:4. Like other parts of the 2 Esdras complex, 5 Ezra is marked by an intense expectation that the end of the age is at hand; see 4:26, 14: 18, 16:74. The end is at hand because the predetermined number of the saved has been reached. The theme may have been taken from 4 Ezra 4:36–7 but see also Rev 6:11; 7:4. The reference to the 'sealing' of the elect certainly seems dependent on Rev 7:4–8. 'The feast of the Lord' (v. 38) refers to the messianic banquet; see Isa 25:6; Rev 19:9; 2 Esd 6:52. For the white clothing (v. 40) see Rev 3:4; 6:11; 7:13–14.

(2:42–8) Ezra's Vision As frequently in 4 Ezra so here the prophet is granted a vision of the future, but the text breathes the atmosphere of the book of Revelation. See Rev 4:1; 7:9; 14:1, and cf. Heb 12:22–4. The tall young man (v. 43) is identified in v. 47 as 'the Son of God'. A similar figure appears in Herm. Sim. 9.6.1 and the Acts of John, 90, while in Gos. Pet. 40 Jesus is distinguished by his height ('overpassing the heavens') from the two angels who assist him at the resurrection. The description is also reminiscent of the appearance of the Son of Man in 1 Enoch 46:1–3. The vision seems to be describing the eschatological reward in heaven of the Christian martyrs.

2 Esdras 3–14 (= 4 Ezra): First Vision (3:1–5:20)

This vision consists of four major sections: (1) Ezra's prayer (3:1–36); (2) a dialogue between Ezra and the angel Uriel (4:143); (3) a vision

(4:44–9); (4) the interpretation of the vision (4:50–5:20). The same basic structuring of the material can also be seen in the second and third visions; in the fourth vision the dialogue element is missing, thus presaging the change of mood as we move into the consolation section of the text.

The principal problem that the author confronts in the first vision is God's apparent failure to carry out his promises to Israel viewed in the light of the distressing situation of the Jewish people after the end of the war against the Romans and the loss of the Temple in 70 CE. In the past Jews had always managed to cope with such crises by regarding the disasters they suffered as God's punishment for their sins, and then by looking forward to a restoration of their national fortunes. 4 Ezra's sister apocalypse 2 Apoc. Bar., which probably stems from the same Jewish circles, adopts this traditional response to the Jewish dilemma. But this traditional solution does not satisfy the character Ezra in the dialogue for two reasons: (1) He cannot understand why God deals more severely with his own people than with the Gentiles. After all, Israel has accepted God's law and tried to live up to it. Why then has God not dealt more severely with the Gentiles who now oppress Israel? Behind this complaint appears to lie the widespread Jewish belief that at Mount Sinai God offered the law to all the nations of the world but only Israel volunteered to take on its yoke (see 7:20–4). But all Israel has got for agreeing to fall in with God's plans is one disaster after another. The Gentiles seem to have been rewarded by God for not accepting his law!(2). But Ezra has a deeper reason for finding the traditional explanation for Israel's suffering unsatisfactory. Unlike the OT in general and in contrast to later rabbinic Judaism he seems to believe that humans beings are incapable of keeping God's law because the power of their 'evil heart' is too strong and overwhelms their desire to obey God (3:20–2). Christian doctrine as first formulated by Paul in Rom 5 holds that the power of sin took hold of humanity as a result of Adam's transgression. But the Jewish doctrine to which our author holds is that the 'evil inclination' (yēser hārā') was placed in humans at the time of creation and it is their task to strive to overcome it; see 4:30–1, 7:92, and Hayman (1976; 1984). The rabbis held, in line with the implied teaching of the OT, that God had created humanity with the ability to overcome the evil inclination by means of the law. But Ezra surveys the history of Israel and concludes that the facts warrant the opposite conclusion, namely, that the power of the evil inclination is irresistible. But if this is so, then God's justice is impugned because he is making demands which cannot be fulfilled (3:20, 8:35). How then can God with any justice blame Israel for transgressing the law, and why has he punished them so drastically?

(3:1–36) Ezra's Prayer This first speech by Ezra consists primarily of a review of the salvation history from the creation of Adam to the fall of Jerusalem to the Babylonians. The review ends at v. 27 and is then followed by a complaint and appeal to God based on the preceding review. The structure of this chapter is probably based upon the pattern of the communal lament psalms in the Psalter, e.g. Ps 44, 85, and 89. In these psalms we find a review of past history recited in order to motivate God's intervention in Israel's present distress. However, when we look more closely at Ezra's speech considerable differences between it and the communal lament psalms appear. The most striking difference is that in his review of past history there is already an element of complaint about God's actions. It is not only, as in the lament psalms, God's present actions or inactivity that are under attack; the salvation history itself is no longer a secure foundation for faith.

Each of the prayers of Ezra which begin the first three visions in the book has this same structure. 5:23–7 similarly gives us a review of God's past actions, in this case specifically his election of Israel, followed in 5:28–30 by a forthright lament. 6:38–54 offers a review of God's work in creation followed in 6:55–9 by a lament. But in neither of these two later visions is the review of God's past actions marred by any element of complaint. Hence ch. 3, placed at the beginning of the book, presents us with the strongest statement of Ezra's scepticism about the salvation history. This is one way in which the pattern of movement from fierce complaint to eventual acquiescence is built into the structure of the book.

(3:1–11) vv. 1–3 serve as an introduction both to the book and this specific prayer. For the problem of the identification of Ezra with Salathiel, the possible significance of the latter name, and the apparent setting of the book in Babylon see 2 Esd B. vv. 4–11 summarize the biblical story from Adam to Noah. The words 'and commanded the dust and it gave you Adam, a lifeless body' (vv. 4–5) rephrase Gen 2:7 in such a way as to give to the earth an active role in

Adam's creation. The author does this elsewhere: in 7:62, in 7:116, which has almost a dualistic tone, and in 10:14. But, as if to immediately counteract any dualistic implications, he goes on to emphasize God's direct involvement in the creation of Adam. This also he does elsewhere: 7:70, 8:7, 8–13,44. But why use this image of mother earth here? Probably it serves two purposes: first, it enables the author to avoid irreverence when addressing God by making the accusation indirect—God produced the earth but it, in its turn, produced this flawed creature, man; secondly, it enables the author to stress humanity's earthy origins as mitigating its guilt. The latter reiterates a common sentiment of the OT: Job 14:1–2, Eccl 3:19–20, Ps 90:3; cf. also Paul's use of the image in 1 Cor 15:47–9. v. 7 is obviously summarizing the story of Gen 2–3, though whether it is a correct exegesis is another matter. There is nothing in Gen 2 to suggest that Adam was created immortal and that death was his punishment for transgressing God's command. Gen 3:22–3 says that Adam and Eve were driven out of the Garden in order to *prevent* them from becoming immortal (Hayman 1984: 15). However, the author's exegesis of Gen 2–3 is in line with that first hinted at in Sir 25:24, and then more systematically in Wis 2:23–4, and, of course, Paul in Rom 5:12; see also 2 *Apoc. Bar.* 23:4. In this tradition of exegesis the way in which Adam's transgression brings death upon his descendants is not spelled out. The connection is stressed elsewhere in 4 Ezra (4:30, 7:11–12, 118) but never explained. 3:21 is the closest we get to an explanation and this is closely parallel to Rom 5:12. Both these texts are factual statements, not explanations. Explanations had to wait for St Augustine. The point made in vv. 9–11 is going to be echoed later in the chapter, for here God is behaving how Ezra thinks he should—punishing the wicked and saving the righteous.

(3:12–19) takes us from Noah to the Exodus. The Abraham presented in v. 14 belongs to the esoteric tradition which is read into Gen 15; see 2 Esd 14:1–18. This is the Abraham of the *T. Abr.* and *Apoc. Abr.*, texts approximately contemporaneous with 4 Ezra. See also 2 *Apoc. Bar.* 4:4–5. Emphasizing the miraculous and cosmic significance of God's theophany on Mt Sinai (vv. 18–19) serves the function of stressing the vital importance of the giving of the law. But our author does it not only for this purpose but also to heighten the contrast with the following verse.

(3:20–2) The Evil Heart With the Exodus we have reached the focal point of the salvation history as far as Judaism is concerned, and it is just here that Ezra raises his major objection. What was the point of giving the law if God did not first wipe out the 'evil heart' inherited from Adam which made it impossible for the people to keep the law? The author's terminology for the evil component within human beings is not consistent and there is a problem deciding exactly what he has in mind.

evil heart	3:20, 21, 26; 7:48
evil root	3:22; 8:53
grain of evil seed	4:30, 31
evil thought	7:92
mind	7:62–4

The problem is: do all these expressions refer to the same thing? Some scholars think they do, but others distinguish between the 'evil heart' and the other terms which it is admitted refer to what the rabbis called 'the evil inclination' (*yēser hā-ra'*). This was implanted in Adam at the time of creation (4:30–1; 7:92). But some scholars argue that in the author's thinking the 'evil inclination' developed into 'the evil heart' as a result of Adam's sin. The evidence for this differentiation is 7:48 and the Syriac/Ethiopic text of v 21 which Box (1912: 16) translates: 'the first Adam, clothing himself with the evil heart, transgressed', i.e. Adam 'clothed himself' with the evil heart by yielding to the suggestions of the evil impulse. Though none of its proponents clearly states it, the importance of this interpretation is that the irresistibility of the evil inclination dates from after the Fall; prior to that it was just a potential force. This exegesis aligns 4 Ezra somewhat closer to the specifically Augustinian Christian doctrine of original sin, and away from the general rabbinic view which regards humanity's free will as unimpaired by the Fall. However, there are strong reasons for resisting this line of interpretation: (1) To say that Adam clothed himself with the evil heart and then transgressed but (as 7:48 states) the result of his sin was the emergence or development of the evil heart does not make sense. (2) The Syriac text of 7:48 omits the word 'has grown up' and simply reads: 'for there is in us an evil heart...'. If Box and others wish to follow the Syriac in v. 21, why not in 7:48 also?

(3) Why does the author revert to the terminology 'evil root' at v. 22 and back to 'evil heart' in 3:26? The natural way is to take these as equivalent expressions for the same phenomenon.

These are weighty objections and it seems unlikely that the author of 4 Ezra had a more complicated and developed view of the effect of the Fall on humanity's constitution than that of the rabbis, or one more closely aligned to the later Christian position. It is undeniable, however, that he uses the metaphor of growth to describe the increasing influence of the evil inclination; see 4:30–1; 7:64; and the Latin text of 7:48. Possibly v. 22 carries this meaning also. The author clearly feels that sin has got a firmer and firmer grip on human beings and the influence of the evil inclination has become more and more irresistible. This fits in with the pessimism he expresses elsewhere in statements such as that in 5:55.

(3:24–7) Ezra now introduces the theme of Zion and its fate which is to play an important role in the book as a focus for his complaints. Again the point is made that each new initiative by God is neutralized by humanity's sin. v. 26 parallels v. 21. Ezra is saying that since God had not dealt with the root of the problem, then failure was inevitable. At v. 27 we reach the supposed author's own time, the Babylonian exile. The real, rather than the implied, readers can draw their own conclusions about the period from 587 BCE to 70 CE—the whole Second Temple period had ended as disastrously as the First.

(3:28–36) This section looks back over the salvation history which has just been recounted and highlights one contrast between the present and the past. At the time of the Flood God had acted as he ought to have done—punishing the wicked and saving the righteous. But now he seems to be doing the exact opposite (v. 30).

(4:1–43) Dialogue between Ezra and the Angel Uriel Having been exposed at some length to the complaints of Ezra we now get the response of the other partner in the dialogue, Uriel. The dialogue between them passes through two phases. In vv. 1–21 Uriel provides three illustrations of the limits of human understanding. The point made is very similar to the message Job gets when God appears to him out of the whirlwind (Job 38–41). In the second phase (vv. 22–43) Ezra asserts his right both to ask his questions and to have an answer. Uriel replies that all his problems will be solved, not in this age, but in the age to come. Ezra then asks how long it will be before the future age arrives, and receives a somewhat ambiguous answer, replete with characteristic apocalyptic determinism (vv. 36–7). As this dialogue proceeds Ezra's role gradually diminishes until he becomes no more than a stooge offering appropriate prompting questions to Uriel. Uriel, for his part, only picks up and answers the last of Ezra's questions in vv 23–5. He ignores the questions for which he has no answer—as often in the rest of the book.

(4:1–25) Uriel (v. 1) is listed as one of the four archangels in 1 Enoch 9:1 and occurs often in other lists. In 1 Enoch 20:2 he is said to be set 'over the world and over Tartarus'. vv. 5–8 contain a polemic against the exaggerated claims of part of the apocalyptic tradition. In texts like 1 Enoch the apocalyptic seer travels to the heavens precisely so that he can acquire the sort of knowledge which here both Ezra and Uriel accept is off limits to human beings. The scepticism of 4 Ezra towards these sorts of claims aligns it with the tradition marked out by Prov 30:1–4 and Sir 3:21–4 (much quoted by the rabbis for the same purpose). The author's reticence over revealing such matters probably accounts for the abrupt end of the fourth vision (10:55). Other apocalyptic works would have treated us here to a full tourist's guide to the heavenly city; we get not a word from Ezra.

(4:26–32) This paragraph presents us with the first systematic statement of 4 Ezra's view of history. In contrast to large parts of the OT (though not all of it) where history is seen as the sphere of God's saving actions, in 4 Ezra salvation is seen as a catastrophic intervention of God to wipe out this present world and to replace it with an entirely new heaven and earth. It is repeated time and again that this present age/world cannot possibly see the realization of Israel's hopes or the fulfilment of God's promises (4:27; 7:12–13). In the previous chapter Ezra looked back over the course of Israel's history and saw it as one long disaster leading nowhere and Uriel does not disagree with this analysis. The present age is evil, full of pain and sorrow, so must be eliminated before God's salvation can come, as must the 'evil heart'; the words 'place' and 'field' in v. 29 have this dual reference. The same general atmosphere pervades the NT and early Christianity; the temptation story presupposes that

the devil is in charge of this world, not God (Mt 5:8–9), and Paul goes so far as to describe the devil as 'the god of this world' (2 Cor 4:4). Christianity expresses this in a dualistic fashion alien to Judaism and to 4 Ezra but underlying both is despair of this present world and a concentration on the 'other world' as the real sphere of God's actions and the real goal of the saved.

(4:26) The phrase 'The age is hurrying swiftly to its end' in 4:26 reflects the tone of eschatological urgency which pervades 4 Ezra; see 6:20 and esp. 14:11–12, 18, where a timetable is laid down. However, just at this point the author's literary use of the device of pseudonymity is in real danger of unravelling. He, in the late first century CE, is writing as though he were living in the sixth century BCE. He believes that the tragic events of 66–70 through which presumably he has lived are the woes preceding the coming of the Messiah, an event which he expects to take place very soon. But in the fictional stance of the text the world had at least another 650 years to go! The writer has to suggest in a veiled way that the world will soon come to an end but not so overtly as to rupture his pseudepigraphic framework. This is a hard act to accomplish. Precisely at v. 26 and 14:18 we can feel him stepping out from behind his pseudonym; from the perspective of the implied rather than the real author the arrival of the Roman empire (whose demise was being predicted) was still several hundred years off.

(4:26–7) Throughout 4 Ezra a sharp distinction is made between this age/world and the next; see especially 6:7–10; 7:29–31, 50, 112–13; 8:1. It is probable that the term used for age/world in the original Hebrew text was ʿôlām. In biblical Hebrew this almost invariably has an adverbial use in the phrase lĕ ʿôlām (for ever); by the first century CE it had changed its meaning to 'world'. The rabbis used the phrases hā ôlām hazzeh (this world) and hā ôlām habbāʾ (the world to come) to distinguish the two time periods; possibly the original Hebrew text of 4 Ezra did likewise.

(4:33–42) 4:34 and similar verses (5:33; 8:47) hint at the 'experiential solution' to Ezra's agonizing that will come in the fourth vision—when he turns from his own, self-absorbed doubting to dealing with the concrete problems of his needy people, and so mirrors God's concern for 'the many'. v. 35, 'storehouse of souls' (NEB) rather than 'chambers' (NRSV) better reflects the Hebrew word' ôsār which probably underlies the Latin and Syriac here. The 'storehouse of souls' (located under the divine throne according to R. Eliezer b. Hyrcanus in b. Šabb. 152b) was the place where the rabbis believed the souls of the righteous were kept before they were reconnected with their bodies at the resurrection; see 7:32 and cf. 4:41; 7:80, 95. The archangel Jeremiel (v. 36) is mentioned in the Coptic Apoc. Zeph. as being in charge of the souls of dead. However, the Syriac here has Ramiel, who is the seventh archangel in 1 Enoch 20:8 (cf. 2 Apoc. Bar. 55:3—'the angel Ramiel who presides over true visions'). The idea that the end of the world has been predestined by God (4:36–7; cf. 7:74) is a common one in apocalyptic and other Jewish texts, as also is the idea that he has fixed beforehand the number of human beings that will be born. The two ideas are combined in 2 Apoc. Bar. 23:4–5 and strikingly in Gen. Rab. 24:4 ('The Son of David will not come until all those souls which are destined to be born will be born'). However, the author may intend to refer here to the completing of a fixed number of the righteous, as with the 144,000 in Rev 7:4; 14:1. Locating the chambers of the souls in Hades (4:41) hardly fits in with what the text later indicates is the fate of the righteous after death (7:88–99). It is better to follow the Syriac (supported by the Ethiopic) which reads: 'Sheol and the storehouses of the souls are like the womb'. The alternative is to think of the wicked being separately stored in Sheol away from the righteous (Box 1912: 37).

(4:43–5:25) A Vision and its Interpretation 4:44–6 leads into the actual parabolic vision in vv. 48–9; see 5:50 for a similar leading question. In 5:1–13 the vision is interpreted to show that most of human history has passed, and only a little while remains before the future age comes. All Jewish apocalyptists believed this. It is schematized in 14:10–11 but is a recurring refrain throughout the book. 5:1–13 contains a description of the hard times (conventionally referred to as 'the messianic woes') which will precede the end and by means of which the 'wise' may discern its approach. The list of signs is traditional material and may well have been drawn from a literary source. The beginning of 5:1 looks like a rubric to an already existing collection of material. Many parallels can be cited. See Mk 13 and parallels and the extensive list provided by Stone (1990: 110 n. 15). The signs catalogue the reversal of all order as the end

approaches—in nature and in human society. The theme of the reversal of the natural order reaches far back into the OT; see esp. Isa 24. In 5:3 the author alludes to a theme which will be vastly expanded in ch. 11 and 12, namely, the demise of the Roman empire as a sign of the end. In 5:6 he hints, and no more, at another standard theme of Jewish apocalyptic—the emergence of the Antichrist, a belief which is rooted in Jewish experiences at the hands of Antiochus Epiphanes in the Maccabean period. He does not develop this theme later in the book, which reinforces the impression that he is editing traditional material.

We have now had the two responses of Uriel to Ezra's complaints that will dominate the rest of the book: (1) who are puny you to challenge God?—mere mortals cannot understand God's ways; (2) the resolution of the problem can only be sought in the next world, not in this one.

(5:16–20) A transitional narrative that connects the first and second visions. Similar material is placed between the other visions. Phaltiel's rebuke is significant since it points forward to the resolution or assuaging of Ezra's problems by immersing himself in communal service. See 2 Esd 4:33–42. 12:40–5 expands the rebuke, this time on the lips of the people, but in 12:46–8 and esp. 14:27–36 Ezra responds and accepts the role required of him.

Second Vision (5:21–6:34)

This follows more or less the same pattern as the first vision: (1) Ezra's prayer (5:21–30); (2) a dialogue between Ezra and Uriel (5:31–6:10); (3) a vision (6:17–28); (4) conclusion of the vision (6:29–34).

(5:21–30) Ezra's Prayer This time Ezra's complaint has a much narrower focus than in ch. 3. What makes it less acute is the absence of the whole theme of the permanently diseased 'evil heart', though the language of v. 30 ('hates') pulls no punches. As here (v. 21) a period of seven days' prayer and fasting precedes each of the first three visions; see 5:13, 20; 6:31, 34. The pattern is broken at the end of the third vision where seven days of eating flowers replaces the period of fasting (9:23, 27)—a significant symbol of the change of mood in the fourth vision. The prayer is based on a series of seven images which illustrate God's unique choice of Israel, but in v. 28–9 the imagery of 'one out of the many' is neatly reversed by the complaint: the many oppress the one. Why? The series of images is based on traditional symbols for Israel in biblical and Jewish sources; cf. Ps 80:8–19; Hos 14:5; Ps 132:13; 74:1,19. The use of the language 'love' and 'hate' (v. 30) comes from the biblical comparison of the relationship between Israel and God with human marriage. The tone is reminiscent of Hos 1–3.

(5:31–6:10) Dialogue between Ezra and Uriel

This repeats in a different form the content of their previous dialogue. Cf. 5:36–40 with 4:5–11. Again Uriel states that the future age is imminent, that the time when it will come has been completely predetermined from the beginning of creation, and that history is moving inexorably towards this predestined goal.

(5:31–56) Since further dialogue is blocked on the issue of Ezra's competence to understand God's ways in creation, the text carefully creates an opening (v. 40, 'my judgement', 'the goal of [my] love') for the discussion to shift to the topic of eschatology, ground where the angel has answers to offer. We noticed the same technique in 4:23–5. Ezra's question in v. 41 refers back to the angel's future-orientated answer in the first vision to the problem of theodicy. Uriel does not know whether Ezra will be alive when the end comes (4:26, 52). Ezra wants to know if this means that he, and all the righteous born before him, will therefore miss out on part of this promised eschatological reward. If so, its power to soften the problem of theodicy is weakened. The issue raised by Ezra is very similar to that faced by Paul in 1 Thess 4:3–18. Note how in these verses the angel recedes into the background in the author's mind and God directly addresses Ezra. Uriel does not re-emerge until 6:30. This phenomenon occurs regularly in 4 Ezra just as in the OT the Angel of the Lord and the Lord constantly fuse together; cf. also Judg 6:12, 14. The image of the circle (v. 42) is not very clear and the text is uncertain. The point it makes has been aptly compared with 1 Thess 4:15. The general resurrection (7:32) will ensure that all will stand on an equal footing in the future age. v. 45 is a neat rejoinder by Ezra: if all who have ever lived will be resurrected and kept alive for the final judgement, then there is no reason why all who are destined to be born could not be alive now and so the end could come without any delay. With v. 46 cf. 4:40–3 where the deterministic potential of the image of human reproduction is similarly used. The pessimistic view of the world in vv. 50–5 (cf. 4:26–7; 14:10) is a deduction both from

the references to the giants in Gen 6:1–4 and the lengths of the lives of the prediluvian patriarchs in Gen 5. But the general sentiment was widespread in the ancient world; see Philo, *On the Creation*, 140–1, and 2 *Apoc. Bar.* 85:10.

(6:1–16) The text at the beginning of v. 1 is uncertain; see n. *l* to NRSV. Possibly Christian scribes in the Latin tradition removed the reference attested in the Syriac to the 'beginning' coming through 'man', feeling that it contradicted the divinity of Christ. If the phrase is original it could have referred either to the Messiah (see 7:28; 11:32–4; 13:37–8) or to the human agents of the messianic woes (5:1–13; 6:24). Here, and in the emphatic wording of v. 6*b*, there seems to be some polemical intention, perhaps against the heresy of 'the two powers'. On this see Segal (1977). The function of the list of elements in the cosmos in vv. 1*b*–6 is to reinforce the point made more prosaically in 7:70. The text of vv. 7–10 is much disturbed in the versions, especially in the Latin. Scribes found it difficult to understand and probably made matters worse by trying to 'improve' it. The section presupposes an eschatological interpretation of Gen 25:26 well-attested in later rabbinic texts: Esau = Rome, Jacob = the Jewish messianic kingdom which will seamlessly replace the Roman empire (5:3; 11:38–46; 12:31–4).

(6:17–28) Vision This is not really a vision but an audition. Ezra hears a voice proclaiming the arrival of the End. The messianic woes are again described and also the beginning of the messianic age (6:25–8). We get here in embryo the eschatological timetable that will be spelt out in much greater detail in the next vision. Cf., for example, 6:25 with 7:27–8, 12:34, 13:48–50; and 6:26*b* with 8:53. vv. 11–12 consciously hark back to 5:1–13, and some scholars have seen in what follows further material from the source the author may have used there. The foundations of the earth shake (vv. 14–16) because the prediction concerns their imminent end and transformation into a new heaven and earth (7:30–1). v. 17 alludes to Ezek 1:24. The heavenly books on which all human deeds are recorded (v. 20) are mentioned in many biblical and extra-biblical books; see Dan 7:10; Mal 3:16; Rev 20:12; 1 *Enoch* 47:3; 2 *Apoc. Bar.* 24:1. For the trumpet blast (v. 23) see Isa 27:13; Mt 24:31; 1 Thess 4:16 v. 26a refers to the OT saints who were assumed to heaven (Enoch, Gen 5:24; Elijah, 2 Kings 2:11, Mal 3:5–6) and who will appear with the

Messiah as his companions ('those who are with him', 7:28, 13:52). Ezra himself is elected to this select band—14:9,49 (Syriac). Other figures, such as Moses and Baruch, were similarly believed to have been assumed to heaven without dying.

(6:29–34) Conclusion of the Vision There is no interpretation of the vision because the message of the audition is fairly comprehensible on its own. Ezra is warned not to misinterpret what has happened in this present age; his attention is being firmly focused on the future, not the past. v. 34 refers back to the agonizing laments of ch. 3 and 5:22–30. The legitimacy of the laments is not denied, otherwise Ezra would not be praised in the terms of v. 32; see also 10:38, 57. This approval of Ezra performs the same psychological function as Job 42:7; it legitimizes the cathartic effect on readers who empathize with Job and Ezra in their railing against the incomprehensibility of God's ways.

Third Vision (6:35–9:25)
In this vision the pattern of the previous two is broken since we get only Ezra's prayer (6:35–59) and then a very long and involved dialogue between Ezra and Uriel (7:1–9:25). There is no vision and interpretation. These elements are replaced here by a series of apocalyptic predictions or monologues (7:26–44, 78–99; 9:1–13).

(6:35–59) Ezra's Prayer The structure of the prayer, like those which begin the first and second visions (3:4–36; 5:22–30), follows the pattern of the lament psalms. On the basis of God's deeds in the past, in this case his work in creation culminating in his election of Israel (6:54), a lament is raised over his inaction in the present (6:57–9). In the earlier prayers the emphasis was on God's acts in history. Here it centres on his work in creation (Gen 1) because the dialogue in this vision is going to confront the issue: if nearly all human beings are sinners and hence shut out of the future age, why did God bother to create them in the first place?

No exact parallel to the sevenfold division of the earth in v. 42. v. 49 expands on 'the great sea monster' (Gen 1:21). This is traditional material (possibly incorporated here by the author from another source) which is not utilized elsewhere in 4 Ezra; see 1 Enoch 60:7–10, and 2 Apoc. Bar., 29:4. Many OT passages allude to a mythical version of creation (with parallels in the Ugaritic and other ancient Near-Eastern texts) in which God is involved in conflict with a monster (Rahab/Leviathan) which is never really subdued and hence has to be definitively dealt with at the end of the world (Isa 27:1). See Ps 74:13–14; 89:10–11; Job 7:12; 26:12–13; Isa 51:9. Job 40:15–41:34 describes the two monsters and names them as Behemoth and Leviathan. v. 51 is based on Ps 50:10 where the word 'cattle' is in Hebrew *běhēmôt*. In a parallel passage in 2 Apoc. Bar., 29:4, and in rabbinic texts, Behemoth and Leviathan provide the menu at the messianic banquet (Isa 25:6). It is not explicitly said in the OT that the world was created for the sake of Israel (v. 55) but rabbinic and other Jewish texts took it for granted, as Ezra does here and the angel/God does in 7:11. Note the careful phrasing of vv. 55–7: 'you have said that ...', 'which are reputed to be ...' (referring mainly to Isa 40:15,17). Ezra attributes these views to God; in the subsequent dialogue they represent Uriel's position. In fact Ezra is going to dispute this attitude to the Gentiles on the basis of the doctrine of creation (8:14). The author is bringing to the surface the latent contradiction between the doctrines of creation and election in the OT. This contradiction is not resolved in 4 Ezra.

(7:1–25) First Dialogue The initial speech by Uriel (vv. 3–16) attempts to show that the harsh conditions under which human beings now live are the result of the Fall and that this world now serves as a testing ground, so that those who pass the test can enjoy eternal blessedness. Ezra retorts that this is a bit hard on those who have suffered the pains of humanity's mortal conditions yet will not receive any compensatory reward (v. 18). Behind Ezra's retort lies his concept of the evil inclination which he sees as mitigating the guilt of the unrighteous. Uriel will have none of this and reiterates in harsh terms the criteria by which human beings will be judged (vv. 19–24).

The parables in vv. 3–9 imply that 'the world' in 6:59 is the future world (contrary probably to what Ezra himself had in mind) and that Israel has first to negotiate this difficult world (the narrow entrance) before reaching the spacious future age: cf. Mt 7:13–14. The effects of Adam's sin spread out from human beings (3:7; 7:118) to encompass the whole of creation (9:19–20)—as in Rom 8:20–2. But there is a tension between this 'heavy' view of the Fall and the clear statement that God planned for it all in advance (7:70). What sense does it make to say that God made the world for Israel's sake when he knew that they would never inherit it and when he had planned another future world for at least the righteous Israelites? This tension accounts for the slippery meaning of 'world' in 6:59–7:11. Basically, our author here is up against the old problem of the contradiction between God's foreknowledge and human free will. He does not see the problem clearly, so some degree of muddle in his thinking is inevitable. v. 16 is a significantly placed harbinger of what is to come later in the text; turning his attention to the future is in the end what Ezra does because the issues raised in this vision are never (perhaps can never be) resolved. They are rather sidelined by the change of orientation in the last four visions. Note how in vv. 17–18 Ezra changes from being the spokesperson for Israel (6:57–9) to being 'spokesperson for humanity trapped in sin' (Longenecker 1995: 46). He persists in this role to the end of the vision (9:14–15). The dialogue fluctuates, sometimes confusingly, between having Israel in mind and broadening the scope to encompass the whole of the human race. In 8:15 the author alludes specifically to this double focus of attention.

(7:19–25) The angel states clearly the hard line to which he will stick right to the end of this vision: human beings know the score; they have only themselves to blame if they fail to observe the rules and end up with 'empty things'. Deut 30:15–20 lies behind the formulation of vv 20–1. But if the author's scope has widened to include all humanity—'those who come into the world'—then they can hardly be blamed for not observing the law of Moses. Something like the rabbinic notions of the Noachian commandments or the legend that all nations were offered the law at Sinai but only Israel accepted it must lie in the background if the angel's argument is to be coherent (Box 1912: 105). On the other hand, it is more likely that the focus is shifting back to the wicked within Israel, since vv. 22–4 retail the sort of accusations fired in the OT at wayward Israelites. Cf. v. 23 with Ps 14:1; 8:58 shows that the author has this psalm in mind.

(7:26–44) Apocalyptic Prediction This is the clearest and most systematic exposition of 4 Ezra's eschatological timetable. As has often been pointed out, the author combines here two different types of eschatological expectation (the this- worldly and the other-worldly) by placing them in chronological sequence. Here we can observe the fusion of ideas that gave rise,

both in Judaism and Christianity, to the concept of the millennium. In principle, these two types of eschatology are distinguishable. They line up with the different possible attitudes to history discussed in 2 Esd 4:26–32. They can be found in isolation in different Jewish texts or, as here in 4 Ezra, in combination. They are similarly combined in the book of Revelation, produced at almost the same time as 4 Ezra, and in 2 Apoc. Bar. In 4 Ezra the two types of eschatology neatly correlate to the two main problems raised by Ezra, namely, the current situation of his people Israel and the problem of the utter corruption of the world and human nature. The this-worldly eschatology responds to the first problem: it will be resolved by the Messiah's removal of the Roman empire and re-establishment of the kingdom of David and a totally renewed city of Jerusalem and land of Israel. The other-worldly eschatology explains how eventually this corrupt and worn-out world will be wiped out and replaced by a new heaven and a new earth. Thereafter the evil inclination will be extirpated from human nature (8:53).

Ezra gets a foretaste of the hidden city (v. 26) in 10:25–7, 55–6. See also 8:52; 13:36; Rev 21. On 'my son the Messiah' see Stone 1990: 208 for a table of the variant readings of the versions and a detailed treatment of the redeemer figure in 4 Ezra. For the most up-to-date survey of scholarship on the topic of the Messiah see Collins (1995). Christian scribal interference with the text of v. 28 is clearest in the Latin but has probably contaminated the other versions as well. The major critical issue is whether or not the term 'son' (if part of the original text) goes back to the Hebrew ben (son), or via the Greek pais (child, servant) to the Hebrew ʿebed (servant). The appearance of a Qumran text (4Q246 11 1, Martinez 1994: 138) which assigns the title 'son of God/of the Most High' to the redeemer figure swings the balance now in favour of the former option. Other references to the Messiah/son of God in 4 Ezra are 12:32–4; 13:25–39, 52; 14:9. The word 'revealed' suggests the pre-existence of the Messiah, a belief which is explicitly affirmed in 13:26, 52; 14:9. The idea that the Messiah is predestined to appear from the beginning of time is well- attested in rabbinic Judaism. However, the rabbis were more careful than our author in the way they phrased it; in their view it was the 'name of the Messiah' which had been fixed at the beginning of time (Moore 1927, ii: 348–9). Our author seems to believe that the Messiah is ready waiting in heaven. On the phrase 'those who are with him' see 2 Esd 6:26. There is no hint here of the militant role ascribed to the Messiah in chs. 11–13. The 400–year reign of the Messiah is an exegetical deduction from the collocation of Gen 15:13 and Ps 90:15. The same figure is found in some rabbinic texts with explicit reference to these biblical texts. The 1,000-year period (millennium) found in Rev 20 similarly arises out of biblical exegesis of Ps 90:4 (see 2 Pet 3:8) applied to the concept of the day of the Lord.

Cf. v. 27 with 6:25; 9:8; 12:34, and see 2 Esd 5:41. Mention of the death of the Messiah (v. 29) is unique to 4 Ezra in Jewish sources. In 2 Apoc. Bar. 30:1 the Messiah is assumed to heaven at the end of the messianic era. According to v. 30 the clock is wound back through the seven days of Gen 1 to the state of the earth in Gen 1:2. Compare 2 Apoc. Bar. 44:9 and Barn. 15:8. The Gen 1 paradigm shapes v. 43 as well. With v. 31 cf. 7:75 ('renew the creation') and see 2 Esd 6:14–16. v. 32 describes the general resurrection. Cf. Dan 12:2; Rev 20:5,12–13; and for the 'chambers' see 2 Esd 4:35. With the description of the final judgement (v. 29) cf. Dan 7:9 and 1 Enoch 47:3. That 'compassion will pass away' becomes a matter of fierce dispute later in this vision (7:102–15). Cf. the description of hell here with the parable of Dives and Lazarus (Lk 16:19–31) which also presupposes that hell and Paradise are within sight of each other, as does the setting of Wis 5. The earth as we know it will no longer exist so the promise of Gen 8:22 will no longer hold good (7:38–42). See also Zech 14:6–7 and Rev 21:23.

(7:45–74) Second Dialogue This expands out of the positions adopted by the two protagonists in 7:17–24. Again, as in the earlier dialogues, Ezra is not silenced by the account of the glory to come reserved for the righteous because he feels that there is no one, or at best only a few people, righteous enough to qualify for the future age (vv. 45–8). As ever the bugbear is the 'evil heart'. Uriel replies that God is only really interested in these few who are righteous; the rest can go to hell (vv. 49–61)! Ezra then, not unreasonably, asks why all the wicked (among whom he seems to include himself) have been created at all, if their ultimate fate is eternal damnation (vv. 62–9). The substance of v. 48 is dealt with at 2 Esd 3:20–7; for the textual problem in this verse see Hayman (1975: 54 n. 35). The view in v. 46 (see also v. 68; 8:35), that no human being is without sin, is widespread in the OT (2 Kings 8:42; Prov 20:9; Eccl 7:20) and outside it (Man and his God, ANET 590). But

Ezra's argument here seems to depend on such texts as Ps 90:3–8 and Isa 40:6–8, the grounds for his appeal being the frailty and weakness of human nature. The doctrine of the 'evil heart' gives this OT idea more precision. However, there is not necessarily a contradiction between this verse and the view with which both Ezra and the angel agree—that there will be at least a few righteous people saved for the future world. It is not sinlessness that qualifies people for the next world but the correct attitude to the law (7:72, and esp. 9:10–12). In vv. 49–61 the angel simply accepts what Ezra says about the righteous being few in number, explaining that that is why God has made not one but two worlds—so that they will get their just reward. For the address to the earth in vv. 62–4 see 2 Esd 3:4–5. What the author means here by the 'mind' is difficult to pin down. Myers (1974: 211) translates the Latin sensus as 'reason'. Stone (excursus on inspiration, 1990: 119–24) thinks it means something like 'consciousness'. In the role which he has adopted since 7:18 Ezra identifies himself with the wicked (v. 67; and see 8:31). The angel will have to try and stop him doing this (7:76–7; 8:47). v. 74 seems to be designed to forestall Ezra's subsequent attempts to plead for God's mercy on the wicked (7:132–40). The delay in the end is planned, not a sign that God is being or will be patient with sinners.

(7:75–101) The Fate of Souls after Death In this section the tension of the dialogue relaxes and, as in earlier visions (4:33, 44–6; 5:50; 6:11), Ezra lapses into the role of prompter. This allows the angel to launch into a long explanation of the fate of the soul after death, the purpose of which is to forestall Ezra's question whether there is any hope of repentance for the wicked after death, and whether the righteous will be able to intercede on their behalf (7:70–103). The souls are said to pass through three stages: (1) For a period of seven days after death each soul, whether good or bad, is given a foretaste of its fate after the Last Judgement (vv. 75–101). This state is described as 'separation from the body' (7:78, 88, 100). (2) After these seven days the souls depart to their resting-places to await the Last Judgement. Where the souls are located during this waiting period is difficult to discern. 4:35,41, and 7:32 suggest that they are all alike in Hades; v. 80 could be read to suggest that the wicked souls are left to wander about (ghosts?) while only the righteous go into their chambers. If it is the former, then the author's view of the intermediate state is similar to that found in 1 *Enoch* 22 where Sheol is the place where all the dead go to await the Last Judgement, but where moral distinctions are already made and the righteous enjoy bliss while the wicked suffer preliminary punishment. From elsewhere in the text we know that a privileged few of the saints are taken up immediately into heaven (6:26; 14:9, 48)—reflecting the OT stories of the ascensions of Enoch and Elijah and subsequent Jewish expansion of the number of ascenders. (3) At the Last Judgement all the dead are raised and a final separation is made between the righteous and the wicked. The righteous enjoy all the eternal delights described in vv. 88–99 and 8:52–4. It is not expressly stated, though it may be inferred, that the wicked suffer eternal punishment (7:36–7, 84; 9:10–13). 7:97, 125 reflect the belief that after death the risen righteous join the host of heaven/sons of God/stars (Job 38:7). Cf. Dan 12:3; Wis 3:7; 1 *Enoch* 104:3; 4 Macc 17:5; 2 *Apoc. Bar.* 51:10. This concept of astral immortality, widespread in the ancient world, also lies behind Lk 20:35–6. These views about the soul and its fate in 4 Ezra mark a considerable change from OT teaching. In the OT human beings are regarded basically as animated bodies; they are made from 'the dust of the earth' into which God infuses the life force/breath of life. But by the first century CE many Jews had come to accept both the ideas of the pre-existence of the soul and that souls could live on after death (at least for an interim period) without their bodies. See Wis 3:1; 8:19; 9:11; 2 *Enoch* 23:4–5; Josephus, *J.W.* 2:154–8.

(7:102–8:3) A Duel with Texts! In his efforts to avoid the conclusion that only a few will be saved if the test is full compliance with the law, Ezra seeks for alternative ways by which the vast numbers of the wicked might not be shut out of the future age. Could the righteous intercede for the wicked as they have certainly done in this age? Is it possible that God might not judge by strict justice but exercise mercy in line with the characterization of his nature found in Ex 34:6–7? The angel loads his pistol with Deut 30:19 (7:129) and fires off a firm negative to both suggestions (7:104; 8:3).

A dual numbering of the verses from 7:106 to the end of the chapter appears in the Eng. versions. The printed editions of the Vg, on whose numbering system the AV and later Eng. translations draw, all go back ultimately to one MS, the ninth-century Codex Sangermanensis, from which 7:36–105 had been cut out. Since Bensley published (1875; 1895: xii–xiii) what came to be known as 'The Missing Fragment' modern translations have preserved the old and the new numbering systems side by side.

For the intercessions of Abraham and Moses see Gen 18:22–33 and Ex 32:11–14. For the other biblical allusions in 7:107–10 see Josh 7:6–9; 1 Sam 7:9; 12:19–23; 2 Sam 24:17; 1 Kings 8:22–53; 18:42(?); 17:20–1; 2 Kings 19:15–19. It is difficult to reconstruct the text of v. 112 from the versions. The point seems to be that there is a decisive difference between this world and the next, marked primarily by the intermittent presence of God's glory in this world and his permanent presence in the next. His permanent presence dates from the Day of Judgement (7:33,113); from that point on everyone's fate is sealed. Only before that time is intercession possible. 7:113–15 spells out in detail how 'the day of judgement is decisive' (7:104).

As before in 6:62–9, when confronted with the angel's blank negatives, Ezra moves into lament mode (7:116–26). This preserves the basic psychological motivation of the lament psalms in the OT, namely, to evoke a merciful response from God by depicting one's miserable condition, often acted out by means of the symbol of sackcloth and ashes (cf. 938). It might have worked in OT times; it cuts no ice with Uriel! The substance of the lament harks back to the prayer with which this vision began: what is the point of all God's work in creation if nearly all human beings are fated to go to perdition? For 7:118 see 2 Esd 7:46 and 3:20–2. Ezra appears to be making the same move as before: we frail mortals cannot help sinning—it is all Adam's fault. The implication of the angel's words in 7:129 is that he rejects any notion that human freedom to obey the law was affected by the Fall.

7:132–40 is a midrash on Ex 34:6–7, a frequently used literary topos in both biblical and extra-biblical texts. Most of the elements of the biblical text are cited and expanded, but it is highly significant that everything after 'forgiving iniquity and transgression and sin' (Ex 34:7) is left out. The rest of the verse would not have helped Ezra's case in the present context! 8:2 harks back to 7:52–7 with the point of both sets of comparisons being bluntly stated in 8:3. With the angel summarizing the position he has taken throughout, these three verses mark the conclusion of the major dialogue cycle which began in 7:45.

(8:4–62) Two Prayers and a Subsequent Dialogue Yet again, as in 7:62–9 and 116–26, Ezra responds to the angel with a lament based on creation. The same point is made (v. 14) but this time emphasized by an elaborate description of the process of pregnancy and birth. Why such a marvellous process of birth if the end is only death? There follows the so-called Prayer of Ezra which was excerpted from the book and used in many early Christian liturgies (8:19–36). The wording of v. 19b is a result of this practice. In this prayer Ezra appeals to God to forgive those who have no store of good works to their credit. The grounds of the appeal in vv. 27–30 are that a few in Israel have been faithful to God. But this conflicts with what Ezra goes on to say in vv. 31–6, themselves not very internally consistent if we compare v. 33 with v. 35. This apparent inconsistency serves a literary purpose for it allows Uriel to pick up the first part of Ezra's prayer but ignore the second (8:37–40). 'Some things…rightly' (v. 37) presupposes 'some things incorrectly'. For the textual variant in 8:23 see 2 Esd E. On the issue of the criteria for salvation in vv. 32–3 see 2 Esd 9:7. The idea of a 'treasury of works' laid up for the righteous in heaven (7:77; 8:33, 36) was widespread in Judaism at the time and appears also in the NT (Mt 6:20). For v. 35 see 2 Esd 7:46.

The angel has no answer to the second part of Ezra's plea (8:31–6) and has to resort rather pathetically to claiming that despite appearances God loves his creation better than Ezra does (v. 47). Ezra is rebuked for identifying himself with the wicked. As always when the argument gets too tough for Uriel he resorts to recounting the eschatological bliss laid up for the righteous (vv. 51–4). This strategy comes explicitly to the surface in 9:13. For v. 47 see 2 Esd 4:33–42. vv. 52–4 give a fourteen-phrase summary of the rewards of the righteous—seven positive items (v. 52) and seven deleted negatives (vv. 53–4). Not only is the 'evil root' removed (cf. Ps.-Philo, *Bib. Ant.* 33.3; 1QS 4:20), hence neutralizing one of Ezra's more agonizing complaints, but all the consequences, material and spiritual, of Adam's sin will disappear. v. 62 hints at a theme to be developed at greater length in 12:36–8 and throughout ch. 14. As for the fate of the wicked, Uriel appeals to the concept of free will to justify their damnation (8:56, 59–60).

(8:63–9:25) Concluding Prediction and Dialogue As with the first and second visions (5:1–13; 6:11–28), so this vision draws to an end

with Uriel again describing the messianic woes and the Day of Judgement, and claiming that God is just (9:10–12). Ezra remains dissatisfied (9:14–16), and the discussion ends with yet another justification by Uriel of God's actions.

Commentators vary in their understanding of 9:5–6 which is made difficult by differences between the Latin and Syriac texts. The point seems to be that since observably everything has a beginning and an end, so has the world: it begins with the wonders of creation (referring back to 6:1–6, 38–54) and ends with the signs mentioned in 9:1–3. Note in v. 9:7 the criteria for being one of the saved. Stone (1990: 296) comments on this verse that 'while not asserting that these two concepts, faith and works, are identical, we may say they were not very clearly differentiated and are used interchangeably'. This would seem to be justified by 13:23 where 9:7's 'either works *or* faith' becomes 'both works *and* faith'. Nor does there seem to be much difference between 'treasures of faith' (6:5) and 'treasure of works' (7:77; 8:33). Contrast this with Paul's position in the NT (e.g. Rom 3:20, 27–8; Gal 3:10–11). The Pauline view on the issue of justification fails to take account of one vital ingredient in Jewish theology which our text mentions in v. 11, namely, repentance. In Judaism what matters is one's attitude to the law, not keeping it perfectly. Fully in line with this Uriel states in vv. 10–11 that it is the refusal to acknowledge God and 'scorning' his law which disqualifies human beings from salvation. For a detailed comparison of 4 Ezra and Paul on these issues see Longenecker (1991). 9:8 refers to the messianic age; see 6:25; 7:28; 12:34; 13:48–9.

Ezra's position, like the angel's, remains unchanged throughout this vision (9:15; cf. 7:45–8). He never explicitly accepts the validity of the angel's views, thus legitimizing the feelings of those who sympathize with his problems. See 2 Esd 6:32 and Hayman (1975: 53). Uriel's words in 9:20–2 seem to hint at a scheme at variance with 7:70, namely, that the second world/age to come and the salvation of only a few righteous people was a rescue plan by God, not something determined in advance.

Fourth Vision (9:26–10:59)

This vision serves as a transition from the tense dialogues of the first three visions to the apocalyptic revelations of the last three visions where the author has turned his attention away from the doubts and complaints occasioned by the current situation of his people in order to reaffirm his eschatological hopes. As was nicely observed by Breech, the change of mood in the fourth vision is comparable with that which we find in the lament psalms (Breech 1973: 271). It is possible that the change of mood in these psalms was occasioned by a cultic oracle (see esp. Ps 60:6–8 and Eissfeldt 1966: 113–20). If so, the vision in 10:25–7 performs the same role in 4 Ezra.

(9:26–37) Ezra's Prayer The introduction in vv. 26–8 contains most of the same elements as in those to the previous visions (3:1–3; 5:21–2; 6:35–7), but the change of venue and location are a hint that this vision will not end like the others. In 10:514 we discover the reason for the change of location. The main burden of the prayer is a contrast between the law, in all its glory and immutability, and the perishable human vessels who must keep it (9:36–7). Note that, as elsewhere in the book, there is no criticism of the law itself, only of people's inability to keep it. Although the prayer harks back to issues raised earlier in the book, its tone of complaint is considerably muted in comparison to the prayers which begin the first three visions (Longenecker 1995: 63).

(9:38–10:28) Vision of the Mourning Woman The vision does not respond directly to the issues raised by Ezra's prayer, reflecting the fact that the author has come to see that they are irresolvable in this world. In the vision Ezra sees a woman weeping and, when he asks her what her trouble is, she tells him that her only son, conceived after thirty years of barrenness, has just died on his wedding day. At the end of the vision the woman metamorphoses into the vision of a great city. Ezra's speech to the woman in 10:6–17 plays a crucial role in the transition from complaint to hope in 4 Ezra. The complaint is clearly restated in vv. 6–14 ('almost all go to perdition', v. 10), but in vv. 15–16 Ezra turns to give the woman some stern advice. v. 16 foreshadows what is to follow in the fourth to seventh visions. In effect, Ezra's advice to the woman is self-exhortation by the author to himself: what are your mental agonies worth in the context of the total disaster faced after 70 CE by the whole Jewish people? The author draws back from the chasm opened in the first to third visions. If he denies God's justice, if this fundamental tenet of the OT and Judaism can no longer be affirmed, then all is lost and there is nothing more to hope for. Despite all his doubts he wills to affirm God's justice because he must. His solution to the

problem of evil is experiential, not rational (Hayman 1975: 56). The God whom he knows simply cannot be unjust whatever the evidence to the contrary.

Ezra is transformed by the need to do what religious leaders have to do—hold the community together in times of crisis. Cf. the role of Rabbi Ephraim Oshry in the ghetto of Kovno during the Holocaust (Rosenbaum 1976). Ezra's changed role is expressed symbolically by his move from lamenter to comforter. Only then is he, himself, granted the vision which lifts him in the rest of the book into the realm of eschatological affirmation. Note how in 14:13 Ezra is commanded to do what here he did voluntarily and spontaneously—'comfort the lowly among them'. Ezra has also done what previously Uriel advised (8:55; 9:13). 9:39–40 and 10:5 show him taking this advice, but he only does so when faced by the grieving woman. We have already been prepared for this assumption of a leadership role by Ezra (5:16–18). Ezra is now doing his job as Phaltiel had requested. Progressively hereafter he accepts the 'Mosaic role' (12:40–8; 14:27–36).

The woman's 'thirty years' period of barrenness corresponds to the thirty years Israel has spent in exile in Babylon (3:1). The reference to 'Zion, mother of us all' in 10:7 is a literary hint of what is to follow later in the story. For the image cf. Gal 4:26. On the phase in 10:10 'almost all go to perdition' see 7:48 and Hayman (1975: 54 n. 35); also Thompson (1977: 303–10). 'You will receive your son back in due time' (10:16) refers, on the individual level, to the resurrection of the dead; on the symbolic level this represents the descent of the restored Zion from heaven. The events lamented in 10:21–3 fit in well with Josephus' description of the destruction of Jerusalem in 70 CE, in *J.W.* b. However, most of the items are conventional elements belonging to the lament genre; see Lamentations *passim* and 1 Macc 1:36–40; 2:7–13. The intensity of the lament fits in with the observation that part of the answer to Ezra's troubles is to recognize the legitimacy of lamenting (Humphrey 1995: 74). The graphic account of Ezra's experience in 10:25–8 probably relates in some way to the author's own experience of moving from doubt to faith, but cf. Dan 10:7–9 and 1 *Enoch* 71:11. In 10:27, 42, 44 the RSV's 'an established city' (following the oriental versions) is preferable to the NRSV's 'a city was being built' (following the Latin). The heavenly city/Jerusalem exists already and needs only to be revealed (7:26; 8:53; 10:54; 13:36). Cf. 1 *Enoch*

90:29, 2 *Apoc. Bar.* 4:2–7, and the Description of the New Jerusalem texts from Qumran (Martinez 1994: 129–35).

(10:29–59) Interpretation of the Vision and Dialogue with Uriel Uriel interprets the vision so that the grieving woman represents the real Zion, the heavenly Jerusalem which for 30,000 years had no earthly counterpart (vv. 44–5). Her son is the earthly Jerusalem built by Solomon (v. 45). The son's death represents the destruction of Jerusalem in 587 BCE (v. 48). In his vision (10:25–8) Ezra saw the real Zion which exists in heaven and will be revealed in the last times. This reflects the view of the apocalyptists that the events and personnel of the end-time (city, Messiah, immortality, Paradise, etc.) are preexistent realities which are only finally revealed to human beings in the future age. In the ancient Near East it was generally believed that earthly realities were but pale copies of heavenly originals (see Ex 25:40 and Ps 11:4; Heb 8:5). In apocalyptic a radical change takes place in that it is believed that at the end of time these heavenly originals will come down to earth. Ezra's consolation consists in the evidence of his own eyes that the heavenly Zion exists now.

There is no parallel known to the dating scheme behind the 'three thousand years' of 10:46, nor are any of the dating schemes hinted at in the book (14:11–12, 48 Syriac) consistent with each other (Stone 1990: 337). For 10:56–9 see 2 Esd 4:58. Contrast the Description of the New Jerusalem texts from Qumran and Rev 21–2. The theme of restricted apocalyptic secrets will be developed in ch. 14. Ezra is now placed on the same level as Abraham (3:14) and Moses (14:5–6).

Fifth Vision (11:1–12:51)

The eagle vision of chs. 11–12 is cast in the form of an elaborate allegorical prediction of the history of the Roman empire especially as it impacted on the Jewish people (2 Esd c). Such surveys of history are a common genre within the apocalyptic literature; two good examples are Dan 11 and 1 *Enoch* 85–90. For their authors they served two purposes: to enable them to demonstrate to their audiences that they were indeed living in the 'end of the times', and also to enhance their claims to speak with veracity and authority. If the presumed authors had been able to predict history so accurately before it happened, surely they must be right about the end of history!

The eagle vision is a reapplication for later times of Dan 7, as the author makes clear in 12:11. The beginning of the dream consciously alludes to Dan 7:1–3. The eagle is identified with the fourth kingdom seen by Daniel in his visions (11:39; 12:11). The eagle symbol was used on the standards of the Roman army and Jewish and Christian exegesis had by the first century CE updated Daniel and shifted the interpretation of this kingdom from Greece to Rome. Our author (unlike many later reinterpreters of Daniel) is aware of the fact that his view is not that of Daniel himself (12:12). His language implies that he knows better than Daniel—a claim to inspiration and authority worked out in detail in the Ezra legend of ch. 14. A similar claim is made by the author of the Habakkuk commentary at Qumran (1QpHab 7:1–8—Martinez 1994: 200). The eagle has twelve wings and three heads, and also eight little wings. All commentators are agreed that the eagle symbolizes the Roman empire but the identification of these wings and heads has been much disputed. There seem to be too many wings for the known Roman emperors and usurpers before the author's time. The problem of identifying them is not helped by some divergences between the vision and its interpretation. However, all contemporary commentators agree on the following identifications: the second wing which reigned for a long time (11:13–17; 12:15) is Caesar Augustus, and the three heads are the Flavian emperors Vespasian, Titus, and Domitian. 11:32 and 12:23–4 clearly reflect a Jewish perspective on the Roman rulers (Vespasian and Titus) who destroyed Jerusalem and enslaved the Jews. All the other wings must be, then, the Roman emperors and the pretenders to the throne who lived between Julius Caesar (the first wing) and Domitian (who reigned from 81–96 CE).

The author predicts the appearance of the Messiah (the lion) and the subsequent destruction of the Roman empire in the reign of the third head, Domitian (11:36–46; 12:31–4). There is a bit of a loose end in 12:2, 29–30 with a reference to two little wings, on the explanation of which scholars do not agree. They do not really fit Domitian's two successors Nerva and Trajan. The latter's reign from 98–117 could hardly be said to be 'brief and full of tumult'. So the point where the accurate history stops and the prediction begins seems to be near the end of Domitian's reign, presumably near the middle of the 90s CE.

The chapters can be divided into four sections: (1) The Dream (11:1–12:3a); (2) Ezra's Prayer for Enlightenment (12:3b–9); (3) The Interpretation of the Dream (12:10–39); and (4) A Dialogue between Ezra and the People (12:40–51).

(11:1–12:30) For the phrase 'rising from the sea' in 11:1 see 2 ESD 13:1–3 and cf. Dan 7:1–3 and Rev 13:1. What is most noticeable about the role of the lion in 11:36–46 is the absence of the use of military force or violence. His function is judicial and his speech to the eagle reads like a legal indictment, a characterization of his role that is continued in the interpretation in 12:31–4. As we shall see, this makes it all the more likely that the militant 'man from the sea' in 13:9–11 has roots in an earlier mythical tradition of cosmic conflict. 11:39 shows that, despite his gloomy view of this world, the author still conceives of God as in charge of human history. 'Laid low the walls' in 11:42 is probably a reference to the Roman destruction of Jerusalem in 70 CE. 11:46 hints at the messianic kingdom; its interpretation in 12:34 alludes to the eschatological timetable in 7:26–44.

(12:3b–9) Ezra's prayer in 12:3b–9 is parallel in structure and function to 13:13b–20; cf. 10:29–37 and Dan 7:15. The seer's reaction to the dream is a conventional element in the genre of the apocalyptic vision. For 12:9 see above on 10:59 (Ezra being placed on the same level as Abraham and Moses).

(12:10–39) For the implied pre-existence of the Messiah in 12:32 see 2 Esd 7:26–44. It is unfortunate here that the reference to the Davidic descent of the Messiah is missing in the Latin version where there seems to be a lacuna in the text; see the translation in the NEB. The textual basis for this belief is actually rather sparse in earlier Jewish texts outside the NT Knibb claims it is widespread but cites only *Pss. Sol.* 17:23 in support (Coggins and Knibb 1979: 252). However, the image of the lion here does seem to connect the Messiah with David and the tribe of Judah; see Gen 49:9–10 (interpreted messianically in the Targums and rabbinic texts) and Rev 5:5. 12:37–8 adumbrates a theme that will be developed at length in ch. 14. The purpose of the injunction is to explain how a revelation received during the Babylonian Exile remained secret until the end of the first century CE. The authors of other apocalyptic books had to use the same device; see Dan 12:4, 9; 1 *Enoch* 82:1,104:11–13; *As. Mos.* 1: 16, 10:11–12.

(12:40–51) For Ezra's changed role in 12:40–51 see on 9:38–10:28. 12:47 reveals the purpose for which 4 Ezra was written: to provide consolation and hope for the author's people, to assure them that, in the aftermath of 70, God had not forgotten them. Note that Ezra gives no indication to the people of what has really been going on while he has been out in the field, thus observing the injunction of v. 38.

Sixth Vision (13:1–58)

This chapter divides into three sections: (1) The dream of the Man from the Sea (Dan 13: 1–13a); (2) Ezra's response to the dream (Dan 13: 13b–20); and (3) the interpretation of the dream (13:21–58). The dream can likewise be divided into three sections:

(13:1–4) The Origin of the Man v. 1 immediately calls to mind Dan 7: 1, and we know from 12: 11 that our author consciously intended to update and rewrite Dan 7. By v. 2 we know that this is precisely what is happening here; cf. Dan 7:2. In Daniel the 'great sea' is an allusion to the old creation myth, probably in its Babylonian form (the *Enuma Elish*), in which the god Marduk, armed with the four winds of heaven, attacks Tiamat, the chaos monster and personification of the primeval ocean. So, given this background, we would expect the sea here to be the source of evil as it is in 11:1; Dan 7:3; and Rev 13:1 (also rewriting Daniel). That is why v. 3 comes as such a surprise for, instead of the chaos monster, it is the eschatological hero, the Man, who rises out of the sea. The continuation of the verse makes it quite clear that this figure is being equated with the figure of the Son of Man in Dan 7: 13–14; cf. also 1 *Enoch* 37–7E. But what can it mean that he rises 'out of the heart of the sea'? The best explanation is that it symbolizes the victory of the Man over the sea, the image of chaos in the OT. This would parallel YHWH's defeat of Leviathan (Ps 74: 12–17; 89:9–10). The subsequent 'flying with the clouds of heaven' also aligns this figure with YHWH, the 'rider on the clouds' (Ps 68:4; 104:3; 18:6–11; Isa 19: 1). v. 4 is likewise drawn from the standard imagery used to depict the theophany of YHWH in the OT (Ps 68:2; 97:5; 104:32; Mic 1:4). But the imagery here has deeper roots in ancient Canaanite mythology. 'Rider on the clouds' is Baal's title in the Ugaritic texts, and one of the important roles of Baal is to defeat and trample on Yam (Sea). 4 Ezra 13: 1–4 represents the resurgence of myth at the heart of apocalyptic. But here the Man's victory lies before him, not behind him. The great battle against the forces of evil has still to take place. This is precisely the shift discernible as we move from Ps 74 to Isa 27:! Jews such as the author of our text believed that the forces of chaos had not been defeated at the time of creation; they had come back and ruined God's world. The battle would have to be fought once again but this time with a definitive result.

(13:5–11) Armageddon/The Last Battle The final battle of the forces of evil against the Divine Warrior is an idea as old as the Gog and Magog narrative in Ezek 38–9; cf. Ps 2: 1–2; Joel 2: 1–11; and Zech 14. vv. 8–11 are full of allusions to the OT traditions of the Holy War and of YHWH's theophany. The effortlessness with which the Man defeats his enemies, the stream of fire he emits, the great storm, etc. are all conventional elements of this tradition; see Ps 97:3; 2 Sam 22:9 || Ps 18:9; Is 11:4. The cosmic mountain (vv. 6–7) is, on one level, an allusion to Dan 2:34, 45. But although the author intended it as a reference to Mt. Zion (13:35–6), behind it lies the ancient Near-Eastern idea of the cosmic mountain, the centre of the earth, the home of the gods. In the Ugaritic texts it is called Zaphon as Zion is in Ps 48:2. Baal has a house built for him on Zaphon after his victory over Yam. In ancient Israel the king sits on this mountain (Ps 2:6), but in Isa 31:4b the Man's eschatological role here is assigned to the Lord of Hosts.

(13:12–13a) Salvation for the People of God This is the final act in the eschatological drama and it corresponds to Dan 7:22, 27; Rev 20:4. v. 13 picks up some elements of Isaiah which were taken into the apocalyptic tradition; cf. Isa 11:10–12; 49:22–3; 66:18–20, and also Hos 11:10–11. There in v. 13a the original vision ends. It is a crucial text for confirming the correctness of the view that the Son of Man figure in Dan 7 and the NT represents the continuation in another form of a very old Israelite way of picturing YHWH, the Divine Warrior (Emerton 1958; Hayman 1991; 1998).

(13:13b–58) Ezra's Response and the Interpretation of the Dream After a paragraph recording Ezra's response to the dream (for vv. 18–20 see 2 Esd 5:41) there follows a lengthy interpretation extending to the end of the chapter. But the interpretation greatly expands on the dream; it both ignores parts of it and reads into it elements such as the return of the lost ten tribes

which have only a very tenuous basis in the original vision. Moreover it is clear that the author does not understand parts of the dream. He has three unsatisfactory attempts to explain why the Man arises from the sea (vv. 25–6, 32, 51–2). All the cosmic phenomena which accompany the Man are reduced to not much more than symbols of the law (v. 38). Hence it looks as though he has incorporated in his work a much older text closer to the world of Daniel and then provided a kind of midrash or expansionary exegesis of it, both updating it and infusing it with his own concerns (Stone 1990: 396–400, and *contra* Casey 1979: 124–9). In the interpretation the supernatural and mythological overtones of the Man are downplayed and he looks more like the Messiah pictured in chs. 7, 11, and 12. However, he is never called the Messiah in this chapter; rather he has the title son/servant of God like the Israelite king (vv. 32, 37, 52: cf. Ps 2:7; 89:26–7; and see 2 Esd 7:28).

v. 24 refers, like vv. 48–9, to the 400-year messianic era; see 2 Esd 7:28. vv. 37–8 refer to the denunciation of the Messiah's enemies already mentioned in 12:32–3, not the Last Judgement which God conducts (7:33). The purpose of spinning out the long tale of the lost ten tribes (vv. 39–47), which has such a tenuous base in the dream (13:12–13), is to set them up as a model for the author's contemporaries (vv. 41–2). Josephus, writing at about the same time as 4 Ezra, also knows of this legend (Ant. 11J133). The figure of nine and a half tribes in the oriental versions of v. 40 is found also in 2 *Apoc. Bar.* The variant readings derive from disagreements as to how much of, or whether, the tribe of Levi went into exile with the other northern tribes. 'Arzereth' (v. 45) is derived from the Hebrew for 'another land'; see end of v. 40. vv. 57–8 show how the revelation of the visions in chs. 11–13 has transformed the anguished Ezra of the first three visions in the way that, presumably, the author hoped his work would impact on his contemporaries.

Seventh Vision (14:1–48)

This chapter is based upon the Jewish legend, well-known to the early Christian fathers, that Ezra, like a kind of second Moses, restored the law to Israel after it had been destroyed along with Jerusalem by the Babylonians. The author has adapted this legend to further his own purposes of stressing the equal antiquity, inspiration, and authority of the secret apocalyptic writings alongside the publicly known and accepted books of the Old Testament. The chapter divides into three main sections: (1) A theophany of God to Ezra out of a bush which is deliberately modelled on the experience of Moses (14:1–26); (2) Ezra's last address to the people (14:2736); and (3) the climax of the book recording Ezra's supernatural inspiration which enables him to dictate, to five scribes over a period of forty days, ninety-four books, of which twenty-four are the canonical books of the Old Testament and seventy the corpus of apocalyptic writings (14:27–48).

The theophany in 14:1–26 divides into an introduction setting the scene (vv. 1–2), the address to Ezra (vv. 3–18), Ezra's response (vv. 19–22), and God's instructions to Ezra (vv. 23–6).

(14:1–18) The parallel with Moses is sustained by describing what happens here as a waking experience in which God deals directly with Ezra; Uriel has disappeared from the scene (vv. 1–2). In vv. 3–6 the author rewrites Ex 3 and locates Moses within the esoteric tradition to which he clearly feels that he himself belongs. This picture of Moses as a secret apocalyptist appears elsewhere in such earlier works as *Jubilees* and the *Assumption of Moses*. The author of 4 Ezra traces the tradition as far back as Abraham (v. 14);other authors took it back to Enoch or even as far as Adam (*Adam and Eve*, 50:1–2; 51:3–9). Other references in 4 Ezra to this esoteric tradition are 9:4; 12:37–8; and 14:26. Ch. 14 of 4 Ezra is the clearest statement we have of how the 'wise men' who wrote and preserved the apocalyptic texts saw their undertaking in relation to the overt biblical tradition. vv. 8 and 13 show our author aligning his book with this esoteric tradition. For the reference to the pre-existent Messiah in v. 9 see 2 Esd 7:28.

vv. 10–12 set out a kind of eschatological timetable. It is not certain that they were originally part of the text since the Syriac and Armenian versions leave out vv. 11–12 entirely. Even if they were there originally, the text has suffered badly from scribal attempts to revise the timetable. Violet (1924: 192) has argued convincingly that the Ethiopic has preserved the original division of the times into ten parts with nine and a half already passed. For the veiled hint here and especially in v. 18b that the world will soon come to an end see 2 Esd 4:26. vv. 14–15 provide reinforcement from the mouth of God himself for the injunctions of the angel in 6:34 and 7:16. Through them the reader is addressed: ignore the inglorious past and the dismal present; look to the future for hope!

(14:19–26) develop the claim for Ezra's authority based on the parallel with Moses. Like Moses he has to separate himself from the people for forty days (Ex 24:18) while the command in v. 26 parallels that to Moses in v. 6. The forty-day period is crucial for understanding what is going on in this chapter. If we add up all the indications of time for the events recorded from the beginning of the book to this point it comes to forty days (Stone 1990: 373–4). The reader thereby receives a hint that 4 Ezra itself is part of the secret revelation. Jesus' forty-day sojourn in the wilderness represents the same sort of claim to an authority like that of Moses (Mk 1:13 and par.). Ezra's claim to authority is also bolstered by the reference to inspiration by the holy spirit in v. 22. Two images are used to illustrate the experience of inspiration: 'lighting the lamp of understanding' in Ezra's heart (v. 25) and the cup of fiery liquid (14:3840). See the excursus on inspiration in Stone (1990: 119–24).

(4:27–36) For the function of this speech in the book as a whole see above on 9:38–10:28; cf. 12:40–51. The contrast with the way Ezra depicts the salvation history in ch. 3 could not be more clear.

(14:37–48) Here we come to the climax of the book. The commands given in 14:23–6 are carried out. The five scribes, like Ezra inspired by God, copy out all the ninety-four books (12:42). The phrase 'using characters that they did not know' refers to the square Aramaic script which replaced the old Hebrew (Phoenician) script after the Exile (*b. Sanh.* 21b). At the end of the forty days Ezra is told to make public the twenty-four books but to keep back the seventy to be read only by the wise. The scale of the author's claims for the authority of the esoteric books is noteworthy—'for in them is the spring of understanding, the fountain of wisdom, and the river of knowledge' (v. 47). Only the wise understand these books and only they really explain what the overt biblical tradition is about and what God is doing and will do in the world. By implication their authority exceeds that of the publicly known and acknowledged biblical books. Beneath the cover of his pseudonym our author is claiming greater authority for what he says than for any other biblical figure. We have already seen in 12:12 a striking example of his assumed superiority over biblical figures when he blithely tells us that Daniel misunderstood his vision of the four world empires.

The chapter concludes with an account of
Ezra's assumption to heaven which was cut
out of the Latin version when chs. 15 and 16
were added, but preserved in the oriental versions. 14:9 shows that something like the Syriac
text in the margin of the NRSV originally concluded the book. But this too is an overt claim
to inspired authority. The Bible states that
Enoch and Elijah were assumed into heaven
and by the first century this was claimed also
for Moses. A far more important figure such as
our author makes of Ezra must also have been
assumed into heaven. So we are assured that he
was.

2 Esdras 15–16 (= 6 Ezra)

These chapters are composed of two main types
of material: (1) apocalyptic predictions of political, social, and natural upheavals and disasters
(15:1–16:34); and (2) exhortation of the righteous
to remain faithful in the face of persecution
(16:35–78).

(15:1–63) The text begins with the commission
of the prophet who, being unnamed, must be
presumed to be Ezra (vv. 1–4). Behind the long
denunciation that follows scholars have seen
allusions in vv. 12–13 to a great famine in Alexandria at the time of the Emperor Gallienus
(260–8 CE), and in vv. 28–34 to the political
upheavals of the period 259–67 in Asia. In the
latter section the 'dragons of Arabia' have been
identified as the Palmyrenes under Odenathus
who prevented the Sassanian King Shapur 1 (the
Carmonians of v. 30) from detaching Asia from
the Roman empire. The name Carmonians
comes from Carmania (Kirman), the southern
province of the Parthian empire. v. 33 could be
an allusion to the death of Odenathus in 267. vv.
46–63 are seen by Myers (1974: 351–2) as a
denunciation of Odenathus's wife Zenobia
who for a brief while took advantage of
Roman weakness to establish Palmyrene hegemony over the eastern empire. These allusions
are the strongest evidence we have for dating 6
Ezra sometime after 268 CE.

(16:1–78) Like most of the material in ch. 15, the
apocalyptic woes in vv. 1–34 consist mainly of a
mosaic of material taken from the OT prophets.
Similar material can be found in the 'messianic
woes' sections in 4 Ezra (5:1–13; 6:18–34) and in
the NT (Mk 13 and par.). The exhortation section
in vv. 35–78 has a marked tone of apocalyptic
urgency (v. 52). Not much compassion is expressed for those who fail to meet the test (vv.

77–8), just as in the earlier section the rule of 'an
eye for an eye' prevails (15:21).

REFERENCES

Bensley, R. L. (1875), *The Missing Fragment of the Latin Translation of the Fourth Book of Ezra* (Cambridge: Cambridge University Press).

—— (1895), *The Fourth Book of Ezra*, with an introduction by M. R. James, Texts and Studies, 3/2 (Cambridge: Cambridge University Press).

Bergren, T. A. (1990), *Fifth Ezra: The Text, Origin and Early History*, Septuagint and Cognate Studies 25 (Atlanta: Scholars Press).

Box, G. H. (1912), *The Ezra Apocalypse* (London: Isaac Pitman & Sons).

Breech, E. (1973), 'These Fragments I Have Shored Against My Ruins: The Form and Function of 4 Ezra', *JBL* 92: 267–74.

Casey, M. (1979), *Son of Man: The Interpretation and Influence of Daniel 7* (London: SPCK).

Coggins, R. J., and Knibb, M. A. (1979), *The First and Second Books of Esdras*, Cambridge Bible Commentary on the NEB (Cambridge: Cambridge University Press).

Collins, J. J. (1995), *The Scepter and the Star: The Messiahs of the Dead Sea Scrolls and other Ancient Literature*, B. Reference Library (New York: Doubleday).

Eissfeldt, O. (1966), *The Old Testament: An Introduction* (Oxford: Basil Blackwell).

Emerton, J. A. (1958), 'The Origin of the Son of Man Imagery', *JTS* 9: 225–42.

Essler, P. F. (1994), 'The Social Function of 4 Ezra', *JSNT* 53: 99–123.

Grabbe, L. L. (1981), 'Chronography in 4 Ezra and 2 Baruch', *SBL Seminar Papers*, ed. K. H. Richards (Missoula, Mont.: Scholars Press), 49–63.

—— (1989), 'The Social Setting of Early Jewish Apocalypticism', *JSP* 4: 27–47.

Hayman, A. P. (1973), *The Disputation of Sergius the Stylite Against a Jew*, CSCO 338–9 (Leuven: Secretariat du Corpus SCO).

—— (1975), 'The Problem of Pseudonymity in the Ezra Apocalypse', *JSJ* 6: 47–56.

—— (1976), 'Rabbinic Judaism and the Problem of Evil', *SJT* 29: 461–76.

—— (1984), 'The Fall, Freewill and Human Responsibility in Rabbinic Judaism', *SJT* 37: 13–22.

—— (1991), 'Monotheism—A Misused Word in Jewish Studies', *JJS* 42: 1–15.

—— (1998), 'The Man from the Sea in 4 Ezra 13', *JJS* 49: 1–17.

Humphrey, E. M. (1995), *The Ladies and the Cities: Transformation and Apocalyptic Identity in Joseph and Asenath, 4 Ezra, the Apocalypse and the Shepherd of*

Hermas, JSP Suppl. Ser. 17 (Sheffield: Sheffield Academic Press).

Kraft, R. A. (1986), 'Towards Assessing the Latin Text of "5 Ezra": The "Christian" Connection', HTR 79: 158–69.

Longenecker, B. W. (1991), Eschatology and the Covenant: A Comparison of 4 Ezra and Romans 1–11, JSNTSup 57 (Sheffield: Sheffield Academic Press).

—— (1995), 2 Esdras (Sheffield: Sheffield Academic Press).

Martinez, F. G. (1994), The Dead Sea Scrolls Translated: The Qumran Texts in English (Leiden: Brill).

Moore, G. F. (1927), Judaism (2 vols.; Cambridge, Mass.: Harvard University Press).

Myers, J. M. (1974), I and II Esdras, AB 42 (New York: Doubleday).

O'Neill, J. C. (1991), 'The Desolate House and the New Kingdom of Israel: Jewish Oracles of Ezra in 2 Esdras 1–2', in Templum Amicitae: Essays on the Second Temple presented to Ernst Bammel, ed. W.

Horbury, JSOTSup 48 (Sheffield: Sheffield Academic Press), 226–36.

Rosenbaum, I. J. (1976), The Holocaust and Halakah (New York: Ktav).

Segal, A. F. (1977), Two Powers in Heaven: Early Rabbinic Reports About Christianity and Gnosticism, SJLA (Leiden: Brill).

Simon, M. (1986), Verus Israel, trans. H. McKeating, Littman Library (Oxford: Oxford University Press; original edn, Paris: 1964).

Stanton, G. N. (1977), '5 Ezra and Matthean Christianity in the Second Century', JTS 28: 67–83.

Stone, M. E. (1990), Fourth Ezra, Hermeneia: A Critical and Historical Commentary on the Bible (Minneapolis: Fortress).

Thompson, A. L. (1977), Responsibility for Evil in the Theodicy of IV Ezra, SBLDS 29 (Missoula, Mont.: Scholars Press).

Violet, B. (1924), Die Apokalypsen des Esra und des Baruch in deutscher Gestalt, GCS 32 (Leipzig: Hinrichs).

16. 4 Maccabees

DAVID J. ELLIOTT

A. Introduction. 4 Maccabees is a Jewish book vehemently opposed to the oppression and suppression of Jews in the Graeco-Roman world whilst simultaneously exhibiting some of the latter's most distinctive features. The work was well established in Christian circles some time before Eusebius wrote his *Church History*, where he refers to it under the title 'On the Supremacy of Reason' (*Hist. eccl.* 3.10.6). It can be divided into three main sections: a prologue (1:1–3:19), a narrative of the martyrdoms of the priest Eleazar and the seven brothers and their mother, and finally a third section from 17:2 that is a eulogy for the martyrs. This last section ends at 17:22, and the remainder of the book appears to be an addition to the original.

B. Outline.
Introduction and the Purpose for Writing (1:1–3:19)
Outline of the Author's Intentions (1:1–12)
Discourse on Reason (1:13–35)
Reason and the Law (2:1–24)
The Ability of Reason to Conquer Emotions (3:1–19) *Narrative of the Martyrdoms* (3:20–17:1)
Punishment and Deliverance of Apollonius (3:20–4:14) Antiochus' Treatment of the Jews (4:15–26)

Antiochus' Conversation with the Priest Eleazar (5:1–38) Eleazar's Steadfastness under Torture (6:1–35)
Panegyric on Eleazar (7:1–23)
Antiochus' Conversation with the Seven Brothers (8:1–9:9) The Torture of the Seven Brothers (9:10–12:19)
Panegyric on the Seven Brothers (13:1–14:10)
The Mother Unwaveringly Sacrifices Herself (14:11–17:1) *The Martyrs as Examples* (17:2–22)
Panegyric on the Mother (17:2–6)
The Importance of the Martyrs' Sacrifice (17:6–22)
The Martyrs' Faith is at One with the Faith of their Forefathers (17:23–18:23)

C. Sources. 1. Two major sources can be cited for the book of 4 Maccabees. The narrative part is clearly an embellishment on Maccabees. 4 Macc 5–7 is an expanded version of 2 Macc 6:18–31; the same can be said of 4 Macc 8–12 in relation to 2 Macc 7, while the historical preamble in 2 Macc 3:6–11 has been expanded in 4 Macc 3:20–4:26. These transformations have been achieved in two main ways: as Breitenstein (1976) has noticed, by means of characterization via the construction of speeches; secondly by didactic insertions to link the main illustrative narrative to the introduction. Without these two devices the narrative in 4 Maccabees would even more closely resemble that of 2 Maccabees.

2. The second major source is Plato's *Gorgias*. When 4 Maccabees embroidered the martyrdom of Eleazar he equated it to the death of Socrates. Eleazar, like Socrates, is controlled by his allegiance to his previous career and refuses to be swayed by an ultimate weakness. As in the case of Socrates, there are no supernatural interventions at the end. Both are old men revered as teachers by their followers, and for that reason mistrusted by the authorities who regard their teachings as suspect. They cling to their systems of thought and treat with disdain the option of extending their lives by denying their prior teachings.

D. Authorship, Provenance, Date, and Occasion. 1. Authorship 4 Maccabees is clearly a Jewish book written by a Jew for Jews. There are not only several references to figures from the OT (e.g. 2:2, 17, 19; 14:20; 16:3, 20–1), but in 4:20 there is an explicit reference to the citadel in Jerusalem, 'of our native land'. Whether the book was read orally, or by individuals in private, the book assumes the reader will have previous knowledge of its author's work. The author implies the existence of such works when he says in 1:12b 'as my custom is, I shall begin by stating my main principle, and then I shall turn to their story, giving glory to the all-wise God'. This appears to indicate that the recipients can be assured the book is authentic because it exhibits the same style as his previous works.

2. Provenance The reference in 4:20 to 'our native land' rules out Palestine as a place of composition. Other centres such as Alexandria and Athens are possible, but the strongest candidate is Antioch. The most immediate indicator is the person of the arch-villain Antiochus IV Epiphanes, who naturally had a close connection with his capital city of Antioch. John Chrysostom testifies that the Christians believed the tomb of the Maccabean martyrs to be situated at Antioch, in the quarter of the Kerateion, near the synagogue (*Fourth Homily on the Maccabean Martyrs*).

3. Ignatius of Antioch sent seven epistles from Antioch en route to Rome where he was martyred in 107 CE. He thought in the same sacrificial terms as the Jew responsible for 4 Maccabees. Perhaps the most striking example is his use of the Greek word *antipsychon*. Ignatius uses the word (*Smyrn.* 1.2; *Eph.* 21.1) to express

the idea of ransom, which is mirrored in its use in 4 Maccabees. The word is exceptionally rare, and appears in neither the LXX nor the NT, though it does appear twice in 4 Maccabees (6:29; 7:21). It is not unlikely that the Ignatian letters and 4 Maccabees are related. Both are concerned with the idea of martyrdom, use the rare word *anti-psychon*, and display a direct and vivid style. Due to the rifts in Antioch between Jews and Christians, and the fact that none of Ignatius' letters remained in Antioch, a common source may be the best solution. This may also explain the abundance of sea imagery found in 7:1; 13:6–7; and 15:31.

4. Date For Christians to have appropriated the work from Judaism, the book must have been extant in Jewish circles at a time when the two groups had cordial relations. The most desirable date would be a time when the majority of Christians still formed a Jewish sect. Incidentally, nowhere in the ancient world would the Christians be in a better position to appropriate the work than in Antioch. Acts 11:19–20 states that the church in Antioch was second only to Jerusalem. The main evidence for dating the book is the title assigned to Apollonius in 4:2: 'governor of Syria, Phoenicia, and Cilicia' (Bickerman 1945). There was only a single short period in early imperial Rome when Cilicia was associated with Syria for administrative purposes: 18–54 CE. There is no convincing reason why this title should be given to Apollonius rather than the one given in 2 Macc 4:4: 'governor of Coelesyria and Phoenicia', unless it was written in these years. Within this period there are two particular moments when the book may have been written. Three sources tell of angry Jewish reaction to Caligula's reign (38–41 CE), especially concerning the proposed erection of his statue in the Jerusalem Temple. Malalas chronicled in 39–40 that the animosity between Jews and Greeks in Antioch was at flashpoint (see also Philo, *Leg. ad Gaium*, and Jos. *Ant.* 18.8). The initial impetus for protests was probably at the seat of the governor himself: Antioch. The narrative of 4 Maccabees would have been quite pertinent at this juncture. The Jews are here exhorted not to compromise their faith, but to imitate their forefathers in defying the oppressive power.

5. Another contemporary allusion may be found in 4:15: 'When King Seleucus died, his son Antiochus Epiphanes succeeded to the throne, an arrogant and terrible man'. The author's source, 2 Maccabees, states correctly that Antiochus was Seleucus' brother. This is usually dismissed as an authorial error, but it is more likely that an author who is not afraid to use allusions is employing the same device again, perhaps with reference to the Roman emperor of his own time. In the period 18–54 CE, there were four emperors. Neither Caligula nor Claudius was the son of his predecessor, but Tiberius and Nero were. Both their predecessors had adopted them, and were their stepfathers. In Nero's case he came to the throne late in 54 CE, the year in which the governor's title reverted. Besides this, the case for Tiberius' reign is very strong. His predecessor Augustus was tolerant towards the Jews, as is demonstrated by the edict he promulgated, recorded by Josephus (Ant. 16.6.2). Tacitus and Suetonius similarly maintain his benevolence towards Jews (see e.g. Suetonius' *Augustus*, 2.93). In a striking contrast the same three authors describe how Tiberius disliked the Jews. The first persecution of Jews began when the Jews in Rome were expelled in 19 CE: four thousand were shipped to Sardinia where they were 'employed in suppressing brigandage' (Tac. *Ann.* 2.85). In addition Josephus reports Tiberius' incitement of Jewish feelings in Jerusalem itself, when through Pilate he introduced effigies of the Caesar (*J.W.* 2.9.2). It is clear that Tiberius had an axe to grind against the Jews and other so-called mystery cults. The reign of Tiberius therefore may provide the most congenial backdrop to the writing of 4 Maccabees.

6. Occasion The majority opinion prefers the idea that 4 Maccabees was written for oral delivery at an annual festival in memory of the deaths of the Maccabean martyrs, probably at the site of their tombs. However the book is of such a philosophical nature that it makes more sense if it were read in private where the terms could be inwardly digested rather than speedily passed over in speech. Commentators have pointed to 3:19 and 1:10 as the best proof that it was prepared for oral delivery on a day of commemoration. The Greek text of 3:19 reads: *ede de kai ho kairos hemas epi ten apodeixin tés historias tou sophronos logismou.* Hadas (1954) translated this passage: 'But the season now summons us to the demonstration of the theme of temperate reason.' Hadas claimed that 'the season' refers to a specific time of the year, but a better rendering of *kairos* may be 'time', referring to contemporary events. Whichever view is accepted will dictate the importance attributed to difficult parts of the book's narrative. The natural corollary of the commemoration theory is that the arguments

put forward in 1:1–3:19 and 17:2–22 are subordinate to the narrative describing the martyrdoms. However, the author claims the narrative is an illustration of his ideas, and is subsidiary to the rest of the book: 'I could prove to you from many and various examples that reason is dominant over the emotions, but I can demonstrate it best from the noble bravery of those who died for the sake of virtue, Eleazar and the seven brothers and their mother' (1:7–8). By the author's own admission the narrative supplements the argument and not vice versa. If the argument is the main focus, it is unwise to assume that the book was written for an annual commemoration of the martyrs.

E. Theological Points of Interest. 1. The author of 4 Maccabees uses philosophy to further his arguments. If philosophical Jewish texts of this period were graded on a line of philosophical sophistication with Philo Judaeus at one end and the Wisdom of Solomon at the other, 4 Maccabees would sit half-way along. Whilst much of the theology of 4 Maccabees is inextricably bound up with its philosophy, certain areas remain untouched. These are the classical theological areas of eschatology, salvation, and atonement, the latter being the linchpin for the whole narrative. Atonement in ancient Jewish and Christian literature is occasionally dominated by the debate between propitiation and expiation, and 4 Maccabees has much to offer in this area. Three short texts in 4 Maccabees provide the best way to understand the theology of the author as a whole.

2. (4:10–14) A Case of Gentile Propitiation This passage is essentially derived from 2 Macc 3:22–34. The starkest change is that the account in 4 Maccabees is considerably shorter and concerns Apollonius, not Heliodorus. Despite this, the eschatological element is still present and this is essential to the episode as a whole for it ushers in the manifestation of God's power to earth in order to confront Israel's enemy. Apollonius is all but dead at the hands of the heavenly host when he begs 'the Hebrews to pray for him and propitiate the wrath of the heavenly army' (v. 11). The idea of propitiation expressed here is important for the theology of 4 Maccabees. Of primary significance is the Greek word used to describe this form of atonement: *exeumenisontai*, from the verb *eumenizo* (cf. the Eumenides, Latin Furies). This form of the verb is in the third person plural (to agree with the plural Hebrews) aorist subjunctive. With *hopos*, it is clearly a purpose clause, but the voice used is middle. It is apparent from the narrative that in the process of propitiation, Apollonius can play no part but must ask the Hebrews to propitiate the wrath of their God on his behalf. In the author's view, the Gentiles have no means of contact with the Jewish God, but rather any petition must come from the Jews. By using *exeumenisontai* the author is diverging from the mother passage in 2 Macc 3:33 where the common word *hilasmos* is used. 4 Macc reserves the concept of *hilasterion* for 17:22 (see 4 Macc E.4). Here is a distinct dichotomy between Jew and Gentile in the mind of the author; these two groups are respectively represented by expiation and propitiation. It is clear that in Jewish thought the word *hilastorion* was not synonymous with *exeumenisontai*. The author of 4 Maccabees is making a distinction between propitiation that pertains to Gentiles, and expiation that is reserved for Jews. Another observation on this passage reveals that in comparison to 2 Macc 3:32, Onias does not sacrifice but prays for the life of the Greek. This points towards practice in the Diaspora rather than the homeland.

3. (6:27–9) Eleazar's Atonement for the Nation In this death-scene of Eleazar, attention is drawn to the salvific nature of the shedding of blood. This is reminiscent of the sacrificial language found throughout the HB where blood played such an important part (Isa 52:13–53:12; Lev 23:27–8). The portrayal of the martyrdom of Eleazar was intended as a vicarious sacrifice along the lines of the Day of Atonement ritual. Eleazar says, 'make my blood their purification, and take my life in exchange for theirs' (v. 29). It is the shedding of blood that seems to be the guarantee of the Jews' purification and expiation.

4. (17:20–2) Martyrdom and Expiation As in 6:29 *antipsychon* is used in v. 21 to express the idea of 'ransom'. The blood motif reappears here in connection with 'their death as an atoning (*hilasterion*) sacrifice' (v. 22). Through their deaths the martyrs were able to pardon the sins of all Israel as well as themselves. They achieved this by not compromising their faith, but instead living their lives according to the law and by reasoning through divine wisdom. Encapsulated in these three verses is the kernel of the author's earlier assertion: 'reason is sovereign over the emotions' (1:1b). These verses, with 6:27–9, also express the three essential tenets of Judaism: the Jewish belief in God, their election, and their partaking of the covenant. While they are elect, Apollonius must ask the Jews to intercede for him. Even when they do intervene he does not receive the full pardon of God, but merely a temporary reprieve. The Jews propitiated the wrath of God for Apollonius, but they themselves were able to effect expiation through these acts of vicarious suffering.

REFERENCES

Bickerman, E. (1945), 'The Date of Fourth Maccabees', in *Louis Ginzberg: Jubilee Volume on the Occasion of his Seventieth Birthday* (New York: American Academy for Jewish Research), 105–12.

Breitenstein, U. (1976), *Beobachtungen zu Sprache: Stil und Gedankengut des Vierten Makkabäerbuchs* (Basle: Schwabe).

Hadas, M. (1954), *The Third and Fourth Books of Maccabees* (New York: Harper).

Bibliographical Guide to Biblical Studies: the Apocrypha

1. Introduction to the Apocrypha

Charles, R. H. (ed.) (1912), *Apocrypha and Pseudepigrapha of The Old Testament* (2 vols.; Oxford: Clarendon).

Collins, J. J. (2000), *Between Athens and Jerusalem: Jewish Identity in the Hellenistic Diaspora*, 2nd edn (Grand Rapids, Mich.: Eerdmans).

De Lange, N. R. M. (1978), *Apocrypha: Jewish Literature of the Hellenistic Age* (New York: Viking).

Fritsch, C. T. (1962), 'Apocrypha', in *The Dictionary of the Bible* (Nashville, Tenn.: Abingdon).

Goodspeed, E. J. (1939), *The Story of the Apocrypha* (Chicago, Ill.: University of Chicago Press).

Harrington, S. J. (1999), *Invitation to the Apocrypha* (Grand Rapids, Mich.: Eerdmans).

Metzger, B. M. (1957), *An Introduction to the Apocrypha* (New York: Oxford University Press).

Nickelsburg, G. W. (2005), *Jewish Literature between the Bible and the Mishnah: A Historical and Literary Introduction*, 2nd edn (Minneapolis: Fortress Press).

Oesterley, W. O. E. (1935), *An Introduction to the Books of the Apocrypha* (London: SPCK).

Pfeiffer, R. H. (1949), *History of NT Times with an Introduction to the Apocrypha* (London: A. & C. Black).

Rost, L. (1976), *Judaism outside the Hebrew Canon: An Introduction to the Documents* (Nashville, Tenn.: Parthenon).

Schürer, E. (1987), *The History of the Jewish People in the Age of Jesus Christ*, rev. & ed. G. Vermes, F. Millar, and M. Goodman (Edinburgh: T. & T. Clark), III.1, 537–42.

Stone, M. E. (ed.) (1984), *Jewish Writings of the Second Temple Period* (Assen Van Gorcum; Philadelphia: Fortress).

2. Tobit

Brooke, A. E., McLean, N., and Thackeray, H. St J. (1940), *The Old Testament in Greek* (3 vols.; Cambridge: Cambridge University Press, 1906–40), III. 123–44 (VL of P. Sabatier).

Flusser, D. (1984), 'Prayers in the Book of Tobit', in M. Stone (ed.), *Jewish Writings of the Second Temple Period*, CRINT 2/2 (Philadelphia: Fortress; Assen: Van Gorcum), 555–56.

Gerould, G. H. (1908), *The Grateful Dead: The History of a Folk Story*, Publications of the Folklore Society, 60 (London: D. Nutt; repr. Folcroft, Pa.: Folcroft Library Editions, 1973), 45–7.

Moore, C. A. (1989), 'Scholarly Issues in the Book of Tobit before Qumran and After: An Assessment', *JSP* 5: 65–81.

Nowell, I. (1983), *The Book of Tobit: Narrative Technique and Theology*, Dissertation (Washington, D.C.: Catholic University of America).

—— (1989), 'Tobit', *NJBC*, 568–71.

Porten, B., and Yardeni, A. (1933), *Textbook of Aramaic Documents from Ancient Egypt Newly Copied, Edited and Translated into Hebrew and English*, III: *Literature, Accounts, Lists* (Jerusalem: Hebrew University; distrib., Winona Lake, Ind.: Eisenbrauns), 23–57 (Story of Ahiqar).

Soll, W. (1989), 'Misfortune and Exile in Tobit: The Juncture of a Fairy Tale Source and Deuteronomic Theology', *CBQ* 51: 209–31.

Zimmermann, F. (1958), *The Book of Tobit: An English Translation with Introduction and Commentary*, Dropsie College Edition, Jewish Apocryphal Literature (New York: Harper & Bros.).

3. Judith

Craven, T. (1983), *Artistry and Faith in the Book of Judith*, SBLDS 70 (Chico, Calif.: Scholars Press).

Moore, C. A. (1985), *Judith. A New Translation with Introduction and Commentary*, AB 40 (Garden City, N.Y.: Doubleday).

Wills, L. (1995), *The Jewish Novel in the Ancient World* (Ithaca, N.Y. and London: Cornell University Press).

4. Esther (Greek)

Clines, D. J. A. (1984), *The Esther Scroll: The Story of the Story* (Sheffield: JSOT).

Day, L. (1995), *Three Faces of a Queen: Characterization in the Books of Esther*, JSOTSup 186 (Sheffield: Sheffield Academic Press).

Fox, M. V. (1991), *The Redaction of the Books of Esther: On Reading Composite Texts*, SBLMS 40 (Atlanta: Scholars Press).

Moore, C. A. (1977), *Daniel, Esther and Jeremiah: The Additions*, AB 44 (New York: Doubleday).

—— (1982) (ed.), *Studies in the Book of Esther* (New York: Ktav).

Wills, L. (1995), *The Jewish Novel in the Ancient World* (Ithaca, N.Y.: Cornell University Press).

5. The Wisdom of Solomon

Barclay, J. M. G. (1996), *Jews in the Mediterranean Diaspora* (Edinburgh: T. & T. Clark).

Chester, A. (1988), 'Citing the Old Testament', in D. A. Carson and H. G. M. Williamson (eds.), *It is Written: Scripture Citing Scripture: Essays in Honour of Barnabas Lindars, SSF* (Cambridge: Cambridge University Press), 141–69.

Clarke, E. G. (1973), *The Wisdom of Solomon* (Cambridge: Cambridge University Press).

Emerton, J. A. (1965), 'Commentaries on the Wisdom of Solomon', *Theology* 68: 376–80.

Gilbert, M. (1984), 'Wisdom Literature', in M. E. Stone (ed.), *Jewish Writings of the Second Temple Period* (Philadelphia: Fortress; Assen: van Gorcum), 283–324.

Grabbe, L. L. (1997), *Wisdom of Solomon*, Guides to Apocrypha and Pseudepigrapha (Sheffield: Sheffield Academic Press).

Kloppenborg, J. S. (1982), 'Isis and Sophia in the Book of Wisdom', *HTR* 75: 57–84.

Salvesen, A. (1991), *Symmachus in the Pentateuch*, JSS Monograph, 15 (Manchester: University of Manchester).

Smalley, B. (1986), *Medieval Exegesis of Wisdom Literature*, ed. R. E. Murphy (Atlanta: SBL).

Sweet, J. P. M. (1965), 'The Theory of Miracles in the Wisdom of Solomon', in C.F.D. Moule (ed.), *Miracles* (London: Mowbray), 115–26.

Walbank, F. W. (1984), 'Monarchies and Monarchic Ideas', in F. W. Walbank, A. E. Astin, M. W. Frederiksen, and R. M. Ogilvie (eds.), *The Cambridge Ancient History* VII.1: *The Hellenistic World* (Cambridge: Cambridge University Press), 62–100.

Williams, M. H. (1998), *The Jews among the Greeks and Romans: A Diasporan Sourcebook* (London: Duckworth).

Winston, D. (1979), *The Wisdom of Solomon* (Garden City, N.Y.: Doubleday).

—— (1992), 'Solomon, Wisdom of', *ABD*, VI. 120–7.

Ziegler, J. (1962), *Sapientia Salomonis, Septuaginta. Vetus Testamentum Graecum Auctoritate Academia Scientiarum Gottingensis Editum*, XII.1 (Göttingen: Vandenhoeck & Ruprecht; reprinted 1980).

Collins, John J. (1997), *Jewish Wisdom in the Hellenistic Age* (Louisville, Ky.: Westminster/John Knox), 23–111.

Corley, Jeremy (2002), *Ben Sira's Teaching on Friendship* (Providence, R. I.: Brown Judaic Studies).

Crenshaw, J. L. (1975), 'The Problem of Theodicy in Sirach: On Human Bondage', *JBL* 94: 47–64.

—— (1981), *Old Testament Wisdom: An Introduction* (Atlanta: Knox), 149–73.

DiLella, A. A. (1966), *The Hebrew Text of Sirach: A Text-Critical and Historical Study* (The Hague: Mouton).

Elitzur, Shulamit (2010), 'Two New Leaves of the Hebrew Version of Ben Sira', *Dead Sea Discoveries* 17: 13–29.

Goering, G. Schmidt (2009), *Wisdom's Root Revealed: Ben Sira and the Election of Israel* (Leiden: Brill).

Goff, M. J. (2002), *The Worldly and Heavenly Wisdom of 4QInstruction* (Leiden: Brill).

—— (2006), *Discerning Wisdom: The Sapiential Literature of the Dead Sea Scrolls* (Leiden: Brill).

Hengel, M. (1974), *Judaism and Hellenism* (2 vols.; Philadelphia: Fortress), I. 131–52.

Mattila, S. L. (2000), 'Ben Sira and the Stoics: A Reexamination of the Evidence', *JBL* 119: 473–501.

Rad, G. von (1972), *Wisdom in Israel* (Nashville, Tenn.: Abingdon), 240–62.

Reiterer, F. V. (2007), '*Alle Weisheit stammt vom Herrn –': gesammelte Studien zu Ben Sira* (Berlin: de Gruyter).

—— (2010), 'Risks and Opportunities of Wealth and Poverty in Ben Sira's Wisdom', *Biblische Notizen* 146: 55–79.

—— (2011), '*Die Vollendung der Gottesfurcht ist Weisheit': Studien zum Buch Ben Sira* (Stuttgart: Katholisches Bibelwerk).

Rey, Jean-Sébastien and Jan Joosten (2011), *The Texts and Versions of the Book of Ben Sira: Transmission and Interpretation* (Leiden: Brill).

Sanders, J. T. (1983), *Ben Sira and Demotic Wisdom* (Chico: Scholars Press).

Sheppard, G. T. (1980), *Wisdom as a Hermeneutical Construct* (Berlin: de Gruyter).

Skehan, P. W. (1971), 'The Acrostic Poem in Sirach 51:13–30', *HTR* 64: 387–400.

Skehan, P. W., and DiLella, A. A. (1987), *The Wisdom of Ben Sira*, AB 39 (New York: Doubleday).

Trenchard, W. C. (1982), *Ben Sira's View of Women: A Literary Analysis* (Chico, Calif.: Scholars Press).

Wright, B. G. (2008), *Praise Israel for Wisdom and Instruction: Essays on Ben Sira and Wisdom, the Letter of Aristeas and the Septuagint* (Leiden: Brill).

Xeravits, G. G. and J. Zsengellér (2008), *Studies in the Book of Ben Sira* (Leiden: Brill).

Yadin, Y. (1965), *The Ben Sira Scroll from Masada* (Jerusalem: Israel Exploration Society).

6. Ecclesiasticus, or The Wisdom of Jesus Son of Sirach

Adams, S. L. (2008), *Wisdom in Transition: Act and Consequence in Second Temple Instructions* (Leiden: Brill).

Beentjes, P. C. (2006), '*Happy the One who Meditates on Wisdom' (SIR. 14,20): Collected Essays on the Book of Ben Sira* (Leuven: Peeters).

Box, G. H., and Oesterley, W. O. E. (1913), 'Sirach', in R. H. Charles (ed.), *The Apocrypha and Pseudepigrapha of the Old Testament*, Vol. I (Oxford: Clarendon), 268–517.

7. Baruch with the Letter of Jeremiah

Assan-Dhôte, I. and Moatti-Fine, J. (2005), *Baruch, Lamentations, Lettre de Jérémie: Traduction du texte grec de la Septante, introduction et notes*, La Bible d'Alexandrie 25.2 (Paris: Éditions du Cerf).

Baillet, M., Milik, J. T., Vaux, R. de (1962), *Les Petites Grottes de Qumrân*, DJD 3 (Oxford: Clarendon).

Bohak, G. (1997), 'Baruch, Books of', in R. J. Zwi Werblowsky and G. Wigoder (eds.), *Oxford Dictionary of the Jewish Religion* (New York: Oxford University Press), 101–2.

Coogan, M. D. (1993), 'Baruch', in B. M. Metzger and M. D. Coogan (eds.), *Oxford Companion to the Bible* (NewYork: Oxford University Press), 75.

Dentan, R. C. (1993), 'Baruch, book of', in B. M. Metzger and M. D. Coogan (eds.), *OCB* (New York: Oxford University Press), 75–6.

Mendels, D. (1992), 'Baruch, Book of', *ABD*, I. 618–20.

Moore, C. A. (1977), *Daniel, Esther, and Jeremiah: the Additions*, AB 44 (Garden City, N.Y.: Doubleday), 215–316.

Muilenberg, J. (1970), 'Baruch the scribe', in J. I. Durham and J. R. Porter (eds.), *Proclamation and Presence: Old Testament Essays in Honour of Gwynne Henton Davies* (London: SCM), 215–38.

Rost, L. (1976), *Judaism outside the Hebrew Canon: An Introduction to the Documents* (Nashville, Tenn.: Parthenon), 69–75.

8. Additions to Daniel

Collins, J. J. (1993), *Daniel*, Hermeneia (Minneapolis: Fortress).

Glancy, J. A. (1995), 'The Accused: Susanna and her Readers', in A. Brenner (ed.), *A Feminist Companion to Esther, Judith and Susanna*, FCB 7 (Sheffield: Sheffield Academic Press), 288–302.

Moore, C. A. (1977), *Daniel, Esther, and Jeremiah: The Additions*, AB 44 (Garden City, N.Y.: Doubleday).

Steussy, M. J. (1993), *Gardens in Babylon: Narrative and Faith in the Greek Legends of Daniel*, SBLDS 141 (Atlanta: Scholars Press).

9. 1 Maccabees

Dąbrowa, Edward (2010), *The Hasmoneans and their State: A Study of History, Ideology, and their Institutions*, Kraków: Jagiellonian University Press.

Osterley, W. O. E. (1913), '1 Maccabees', in R. H. Charles (ed.), *The Apocrypha and Pseudepigrapha of the OT* (Oxford: Clarendon), 59–124.

Rappaport, U. (2007), 'Lysias—An Outstanding Seleucid Politician', in S. J. D. Cohen and J. J. Schwartz (eds.), *Studies in Josephus and the*

Varieties of Ancient Judaism, L. H. Feldman Jubilee Volume (Leiden: Brill), 169–75.

Tedesche, S., and Zeitlin, S. (1950), *The First Book of Maccabees* (New York: Harper).

Xeravits, G. G. and J. Zsengellér (eds.) (2007), *The Books of the Maccabees: History, Theology, Ideology* (Leiden/Boston: Brill).

10. 2 Maccabees

Bar-Kochva, B. (1988), *Judas Maccabeus* (Cambridge: Cambridge University Press).

Bickerman, E. (1979), *The God of the Maccabees: Studies on the Meaning and Origin of the Maccabean Revolt*, SJLA 32 (Leiden: Brill).

Cotton, Hannah and Wörrle, M. (2007), 'Seleukos IV to Heliodorus. A New Dossier of Royal Correspondence from Israel', *ZPE* 159: 191–205.

Doran, R. (1981), *Temple Propaganda: The Purpose and Character of 2 Maccabees* (Washington, DC: Catholic Biblical Association).

—— (forthcoming), *2 Maccabees*, Hermeneia Series (Minneapolis: Fortress).

Geller, M. J. (1991), 'New Information on Antiochus IV from Babylonian Astronomical Diaries', *Bulletin of the School of Oriental and African Studies* 54: 1–4.

Gera, Dov (2009), 'Olympiodoros, Heliodoros, and the Temples of Koilê Syria and Phoinikê', *ZPE* 169: 125–55.

Goldstein, J. A. (1983), *2 Maccabees*, Anchor Bible 41a (Garden City, N.Y.: Doubleday).

Grabbe, L. L. (1992), *Judaism from Cyrus to Hadrian* (2 vols.; Minneapolis: Fortress).

Gruen, E. S. (1984), *The Hellenistic World and the Coming of Rome* (Berkeley: University of California Press).

Habicht, C. (1976), 'Royal Documents in Maccaabees II', *HSCP* 80: 1–18.

Habicht, C. (1976), *2 Makkabäerbuch*, JSHRZ 1.3 (Gütersloh: G. John).

Harrington, D. J. (1988), *The Maccabean Revolt: Anatomy of a Biblical Revolution* (Wilmington, Del.: Michael Glazier).

Jones, Christopher P. (2009), 'The Inscription from Tel Maresha for Olympiodoros', *ZPE* 171: 100–4.

Jonnes, Lloyd and Rici, Marijana (1997), 'A New Royal Inscription from Phrygia Paroreios: Eumenes II Grants Tyriaion the Status of a *Polis*', *Epigraphica Anatolica* 29: 3–4.

Kennell, Nigel M. (2005), 'New Light on 2 Maccabees 4:7–15', *JJS* 56: 10–24.

Mittag, Peter Franz (2006), *Antiochos IV Epiphanes: Eine politische Biographie* (Berlin: Akademie Verlag).

Momigliano, A. (1975), 'The Second Book of Maccabees', *CP* 70: 81–8.

Schürer, E. (1973–87), *The History of the Jewish People in the Age of Jesus Christ (175 B.C.–A.D. 135)*, rev. & ed.

G. Vermes, F. Millar, and M. Goodman (3 vols.; Edinburgh: T. & T. Clark).

Schwartz, Daniel R. (2008), *2 Maccabees* (Berlin/New York: de Gruyter).

Sievers, J. (1991), *The Hasmoneans and their Supporters: From Mattathias to the Death of John Hyrcanus* (Atlanta: Scholars Press).

Tcherikover, V. (1961), *Hellenistic Civilization and the Jews* (Philadelphia: Jewish Publication Society).

11. 1 Esdras

Böhler, D. (1997), *Die Heilige Stadt in Esdras und Esra-Nehemia: Zwei Konzeptionen der Wiederherstellung Israels* (Göttingen: Vandenhoeck & Ruprecht).

Brooke, A. E., and McLean, N. (eds.) (1935), *The Old Testament in Greek* (Cambridge: Cambridge University Press), II.4.

Cook, S. A. (1913), 'I Esdras', in R. H. Charles (ed.), *The Apocrypha and Pseudepigrapha of the Old Testament* (Oxford: Clarendon), I. 1–58

De Troyer, K. (2002), 'Zerubbabel and Ezra: A Revived and Revised Solomon and Josiah? A Survey of Current 1 Esdras Research', *Currents in Biblical Research* 1: 30–60.

Eskenazi, T. C. (1986), 'The Chronicler and the Composition of I Esdras', CBQ48: 39–66.

Fried, L. S. (ed.) (2011), *Was 1 Esdras First? An Investigation into the Priority and Nature of 1 Esdras* (Atlanta: Society of Biblical Literature).

Hanhart, R. (1974), *Text und Textgeschichte des I Esrabuches* (Göttingen: Vandenhoeck & Ruprecht).

—— (1974) (ed.), *Esdrae Liber I, Septuaginta Vetus Testamentum Graecum*, 8/1 (Göttingen: Vandenhoeck & Ruprecht).

Japhet, S. (1982), 'Sheshbazzar and Zerubbabel against the background of the Historical and Religious Tendencies of Ezra Nehemiah', *ZAW* 94: 66–98; (1983) 95: 218–29.

—— (1994), 'Composition and Chronology in the Book of Ezra-Nehemiah', in T. C. Eskenazi and K. H. Richards (eds.), *Second Temple Studies* 2, JSOTSup 175 (Sheffield: JSOT), 189–216.

—— (2006), *From the Rivers of Babylon to the Highlands of Judah: Collected Studies on the Restoration Period*, (Winona Lake, Ind.: Eisenbrauns), 307–30.

—— (2011), '1 Esdras: Its Genre, Literary Form and Purpose', in L. S. Fried (ed.), *Was 1 Esdras First?* 209–23.

Kooij, A. van der (1991), 'On the Ending of the Book of 1 Esdras', in C. Cox (ed.), *VII Congress of IOSCS, Leuven 1989* (Atlanta: Scholars Press), 31–49.

—— (1991), 'Zur Frage des Anfangs des 1 Esrabuches', *ZAW* 103: 239–52.

Myers, J. M. (1974), *I and II Esdras*, AB (New York: Doubleday).

Talshir, Z. (1999), *I Esdras: From Origin to Translation* (Atlanta: Society of Biblical Literature).

—— (2001), *I Esdras. A Text Critical Commentary* (Atlanta: Society of Biblical Literature).

—— (2003), 'Synchronic Approaches with Diachronic Consequences in the Study of Parallel Redactions: First Esdras, 2 Chronicles 35–36, Ezra 1–10, Nehemia 8', in R. Albertz and B. Becking (eds.), *Yahwism after the Exile* (Assen: Van Gorcum), 199–218.

Williamson, H. G. M. (1996), 'The Problem with First Esdras', in J. Barton and J. Reimer (eds.), *After the Exile: Essays in Honour of Rex Mason* (Macon, Ga.: Mercer University Press), 201–16.

12. Prayer of Manasseh

Charlesworth, J. H. (1983–5), 'Prayer of Manasseh', in J. H. Charlesworth (ed.), *The Old Testament Pseudepigrapha* (2 vols.; Garden City: Doubleday), II. 625–33.

Ryle, H. E. (1912), 'Prayer of Manasses,' in R. H. Charles (ed.), *The Apocrypha and Pseudepigrapha of the Old Testament* (2 vols.; Oxford: Clarendon), i. 612–24.

Schuller, E. M. (1986), *Non-Canonical Psalms from Qumran: A Pseudepigraphic Collection*, HSS 28 (Atlanta: Scholars Press).

13. Psalm 151

Charlesworth, J. H., and Sanders, J. A. (1985), 'Psalm 151', in J. H. Charlesworth (ed.), *The Old Testament Pseudepigrapha* II (Garden City, N.Y.: Doubleday), 612–15.

Harrington, D. J. (1988), 'Psalm 151', in J. L. Mays (ed.), *Harper's Bible Commentary* (San Francisco: Harper & Row), 935–6.

Sanders, J. A. (1965), *The Psalms Scroll of Qumran Cave 11*, 11QPss (Oxford: Clarendon Press).

—— (1967), *The Dead Sea Psalms Scroll* (Ithaca, N.Y.: Cornell University Press).

14. 3 Maccabees

Alexander, P. and Alexander, L. (2007), 'The Image of the Oriental Monarch in the Third Book of Maccabees', in T. Rajak et al. (eds.), *Jewish Perspectives on Hellenistic Rulers* (Berkeley: University of California Press), 92–109.

Anderson, H. (1985), '3 Maccabees', in J. Charlesworth (ed.), *The Old Testament Pseudepigrapha* (Garden City, N.Y.: Doubleday), II. 509–29.

Barclay, J. M. G. (1996), *Jews in the Mediterranean Diaspora* (Edinburgh: T. & T. Clark), 192–203.

Collins, J. J. (2000), *Between Athens and Jerusalem: Jewish Identity in the Hellenistic Diaspora* (New York: Crossroad), 122–31.

Croy, N. C. (2006), *3 Maccabees* (Leiden: Brill).

Gruen, E. S. (1998), *Heritage and Hellenism: The Reinvention of Jewish Tradition* (Berkeley: University of California Press), 222–36.

Hadas, M. (1953), *The Third and Fourth Books of Maccabees* (New York: Harper).

Johnson, S. R. (2004), *Historical Fictions and Hellenistic Jewish Identity* (Berkeley: University of California Press), 121–216.

Kasher, A. (1995), *The Jews in Hellenistic and Roman Egypt* (Tübingen: Mohr), 211–32.

Meleze-Modrzejewski, J. (1995), *The Jews of Egypt: From Rameses II to Emperor Hadrian* (Princeton, N.J.: Princeton University Press), 141–53.

Parente, F. (1988), 'The Third Book of Maccabees as Ideological Document and Historical Source', *Henoch* 10: 143–82.

Schürer, E. (1987), *The History of the Jewish People in the Age of Jesus Christ*, rev. & ed. G. Vermes, F. Millar, and M. Goodman (Edinburgh: T. & T. Clark), III.1, 537–42.

Tcherikover, V. (1961), 'The Third Book of Maccabees as a Historical Source of Augustus' Time', in *Scripta Hierosolymitana* (Jerusalem: Magnes), VII. 1–26.

15. 2 Esdras

Bergren, T. A. (1990), *Fifth Ezra: The Text, Origin and Early History*, Septuagint and Cognate Studies 25 (Atlanta: Scholars Press).

Box, G. H. (1912), *The Ezra Apocalypse* (London: Isaac Pitman & Sons).

Coggins, R. J., and Knibb, M. A. (1979), *The First and Second Books of Esdras*, The Cambridge Bible Commentary on the NEB (Cambridge: Cambridge University Press).

Grabbe, L. L. (1989), 'The Social Setting of Early Jewish Apocalypticism', *JSP* 4: 27–47.

Longenecker, B. W. (1995), *2 Esdras* (Sheffield: Sheffield Academic Press).

Myers, J. M. (1974), *I and II Esdras*, AB 42 (New York: Doubleday).

Stanton, G. N. (1977), '5 Ezra and Matthean Christianity in the Second Century', *JTS* 28: 67–83.

Stone, M. E. (1976), 'List of Revealed Things in the Apocalyptic Literature', in F. M. Cross et al. (eds.), *Magnalia Dei (G. E. Wright Memorial)* (New York: Doubleday), 414–54. Also in Stone (1991), 370–418.

—— (1983), 'Coherence and Inconsistency in the Apocalypses: The Case of "The End" in 4 Ezra', *JBL* 102: 229–43. Also in Stone (1991), 333–47.

—— (1990), *Fourth Ezra*, Hermeneia: A Critical and Historical Commentary on the Bible (Minneapolis: Fortress).

—— (1991), *Selected Studies in Pseudepigrapha and Apocrypha*, SVTP (Leiden: Brill).

Thompson, A. L. (1977), *Responsibility for Evil in the Theodicy of IV Ezra*, SBLDS 29 (Missoula, Mont.: Scholars Press).

16. 4 Maccabees

DeSilva, D. A. (1998), *4 Maccabees* (Sheffield: Sheffield Academic Press).

Hadas, M. (1954), *The Third and Fourth Books of Maccabees* (New York: Harper).

Renehan, R. (1972), 'The Greek Philosophic Background of Fourth Maccabees', *Rheinisches Museum* 115: 223–38.

Seeley, D. S. (1990), *The Noble Death* (Sheffield: Sheffield University Press)

Index

www.ingramcontent.com/pod-product-compliance
Ingram Content Group UK Ltd.
Pitfield, Milton Keynes, MK11 3LW, UK
UKHW020649040125
453040UK00013B/101